ACKNOWLEDGEMENTS

I wish to thank, first, the Carnegie Bosch Institute, Carnegie Mellon University and the Rutgers Center for International Business Education and Research (CIBER) for providing me with a grant to commission contributions for this volume; and also for helping to sponsor a workshop at Rutgers University, Newark in October 1998, at which the early drafts of the chapters were discussed. I am especially indebted to Professor Michael Trick, Director of the Carnegie Bosch Institute, for his support and encouragement.

In helping me to organize the workshop and in preparing this volume for publication, I was fortunate to have the guidance of the CIBER's administrative Director, Dr Hugo Kijne and the assistance of several of the Ph.D. students at Rutgers—and particularly that of Sangeeta Bansal and JhyDer Lin, who were my research assistants at the time. I also wish to express my deep appreciation to Mrs Phyllis Miller, who helped organize the travel arrangements of the participants and the preparation of the final manuscript for the publishers. I am most grateful to all these individuals—and, of course, to the authors of the chapters of this volume, who have contributed to the successful completion of this project.

Rutgers and Reading Universities
June 1999

Regions, Globalization, and the Knowledge-Based Economy

Edited by
JOHN H. DUNNING

OXFORD
UNIVERSITY PRESS

*This book has been printed digitally and produced in a standard specification
in order to ensure its continuing availability*

OXFORD
UNIVERSITY PRESS

Great Clarendon Street, Oxford OX2 6DP

Oxford University Press is a department of the University of Oxford.
It furthers the University's objective of excellence in research, scholarship,
and education by publishing worldwide in

Oxford New York

Auckland Cape Town Dar es Salaam Hong Kong Karachi
Kuala Lumpur Madrid Melbourne Mexico City Nairobi
New Delhi Shanghai Taipei Toronto
With offices in
Argentina Austria Brazil Chile Czech Republic France Greece
Guatemala Hungary Italy Japan South Korea Poland Portugal
Singapore Switzerland Thailand Turkey Ukraine Vietnam

Oxford is a registered trade mark of Oxford University Press
in the UK and in certain other countries

Published in the United States
by Oxford University Press Inc., New York

ISBN 978-0-19-925001-1

CONTENTS

LIST OF FIGURES

LIST OF TABLES

ABBREVIATIONS

ABS	Australian Bureau of Statistics
ADM	Asean Dollar Market
APEC	Asia-Pacific Economic Cooperation
ASEAN	Association of South-East Asian Nations
BEA	Bureau of Economic Analysis
BOT	build-operate-transfer
CDS	cadence design systems
CEC	Commission of the European Communities
CUSFTA	Canada–USA Free Trade Agreement
DEG	Deutsche Investitions—und Entwicklung sgesellschaft mbH
DIST	Department of Industry, Science, and Tourism
DTI	Department of Trade and Industry
EC	European Community
ECM	European Common Market
EDB	Economic Development Board
EPZ	Export Processing Zone
EU	European Union
FDI	foreign direct investment
FTA	Free Trade Area
GDP	gross domestic product
GFCF	gross fixed capital formation
GfW	Gesseilschaft für Wirtschafts förderung Nordhrhein-Westfalen mbH
GNP	gross national product
GRP	gross regional product
HKCSD	Hong Kong Census and Statistics Departments
HKTDC	Hong Kong Trade Development Council
H-O	Heckscher-Ohlin
IBB	Invest in Britain Bureau
IC	Industry Commission
IMD	Institute of Management Development
IMF	International Monetary Fund
IMP	Internal Market Programme
IMS-GT	Indonesia–Malaysia–Singapore Growth Triangle
IFDI	inward foreign direct investment
IPO	International Purchasing Office
ITA	International Trade Association
ITC	International Trade Commission
LIPS	large investment projects
LIS	Locate in Scotland
LQ	location quotient
MERCOSUR	Southern Core Common Market
M&A	mergers and acquisitions
MIAC	Microelectronics Imaging and Analyses Centre

MNC	multinational corporation
MNE	multinational enterprise
NAFTA	North American Free Trade Agreement/Area
NASSCOM	National Association of Software and Service Companies
NDC	Northern Development Company
NIE	Newly Industrialized Economy
NJ	New Jersey
NMI	National Microelectronics Institute
NSW	New South Wales
NPD	new product development
OECD	Organization for Economic Cooperation and Development
OEM	original equipment manufacturer
OFDI	outward foreign direct investment
OLI	ownership, location, internalization
PCB	printed circuit board
PPP	purchasing power parity
R&D	research and development
RCA	revealed comparative advantage
REA	revealed employment advantage
RHQ	regional headquarters
RIA	regional integration agreement
RLA	revealed location advantage
RSA	regional selection assistance
SBIDB	Small Business Administration's Innovation Data Base
SCDI	Scottish Council (Development and Industry)
SDA	Scottish Development Agency
SE	Scottish Enterprise
SEC	Scottish Economic Committee
SEP	strategic economic plan
SIC	Standard Industrial Classification
SLC	systems level integration
SME	small and medium-sized enterprise
SOC	system on chip
SSBF	Scottish Supplier-Based Forum
SSF	Scottish Software Federation
STP	Software Technology Park
TQM	total-quality management
TRIMs	trade-related investment measures
UBO	ultimate beneficial owner
UN	United Nations
UNCTAD	UN Conference on Trade and Development
UNCTC	UN Centre on Transnational Corporations
UNDP	UN Development Programme
UK	United Kingdom
USA	United States of America
WDA	Welsh Development Agency
WPM	world product mandate

LIST OF CONTRIBUTORS

DAVID B. AUDRETSCH, Ameritech Chair of Economic Development, Director, Institute for Development Strategies, Indiana University, USA.

V. N. and A. BALASUBRAMANYAM, Department of Economics, the Management School, Lancaster University, UK.

MICHAEL BEST, University Professor, University of Massachusetts, Lowell, USA, and Senior Research Associate, Judge Institute of Management-Studies, Cambridge University, UK.

JULIAN BIRKINSHAW, Associate Professor of International Business, Stockholm School of Economics, Sweden.

MAGNUS BLOMSTRÖM, Professor of Economics, Stockholm School of Economics and NBER, Sweden.

ROSS BROWN, Senior Research Executive, Scottish Enterprise, Glasgow, Scotland.

JOHN H. DUNNING, State of New Jersey Professor of International Business, Rutgers University, USA and Emeritus Professor of International Business, University of Reading, UK.

LORRAINE EDEN, Professor of International Business, Texas A&M University, USA.

MICHAEL J. ENRIGHT, Sun Hung Kai Professor, School of Business, University of Hong Kong, Hong Kong.

STEVEN GLOBERMAN, Professor of International Business, Western Washington University, USA.

H. PETER GRAY, Emeritus Professor of Economics, Rutgers University, USA.

BHAJAN GREWAL, Victoria University, Melbourne, Australia.

GARY HERRIGEL, Associate Professor of Political Science, University of Chicago, USA.

NEIL HOOD, Professor of International Business, University of Strathclyde, Glasgow, Scotland.

ARI KOKKO, Associate Professor of International Business, Stockholm School of Economics, Sweden.

ANTOINE MONTEILS, Texas A&M University, USA.

SAM OCK PARK, Professor, Department of Geography, Seoul National University, Korea, also Chairman of IGU Commission on the organization of Industrial Space and president-elect of Pacific Regional Science Organization.

EWEN PETERS, University of Strathclyde, Glasgow, Scotland.

PHILIP RAINES, European Policies Research Centre, University of Strathclyde, Glasgow, Scotland.

PETER SHEEHAN, Director, Centre for Strategic Economic Studies, Victoria University, Melbourne, Australia.

ÖRJAN SÖLVELL, Professor of International Business, Stockholm School of Economics, Sweden.

MICHAEL STORPER, Professor, School of Public Policy & Social Research, UCLA, Los Angeles, USA, and Ecole des Ponts et Chaussées & Université de Marne-la-Vallée, France.

LORNA H. WALLACE, Director of Global Market Analysis for Telcordia Technologies, Piscataway, NJ., USA.

STEPHEN YOUNG, Professor of International Business, University of Strathclyde, Glasgow, Scotland.

CHIA SIOW YUE, Director, Institute of South-East Asia Studies, Singapore.

Introduction

The underlying theme of this volume is the impact of the increasing globalization of economic activity, and the advent of the knowledge-based economy, on the spatial distribution of economic activity, both between countries and within countries. More especially, it seeks to reconcile the paradox of 'slippery space', as demonstrated by the growing transnationalization of the production of goods and services (UN 1998); and that of 'sticky places' as shown by the increasing tendency for certain kinds of economic activity—and particularly knowledge-intensive activities—to be concentrated, or clustered, in limited spatial areas (Markusen 1996).

These twin forces, both of which have been separately identified and extensively analysed in the literature[1] may be considered as opposite sides of the same spatial coin. Not only this, in this volume, they are viewed from the lens of several scholarly disciplines, each of which is advancing our understanding of one of the most significant trends of our day and age.

The volume is divided into main parts. Part one, which comprises Chapters 1–4, first identifies the key analytical issues later to be examined in some depth by several authors in the volume. It then goes on to present an industrial geographer's, an economist's, and two business school scholars' perspectives on how contemporary economic events are requiring us to rethink the size, shape, and contents of the optimal spatial area for analysing the range of wealth-creating activities of enterprises, but also for the tasks of governments.[2] Several scholars, for example, have suggested that the role of national governments is declining, while that of supranational and subnational authorities is becoming more significant.[3] Others—notably Michael Porter—have asserted that the locational decisions of enterprises, particularly multinational enterprises (MNEs), are becoming an increasingly important aspect of their global competitiveness.[4] What truth is there in these suggestions and assertions?

The second part of the volume looks at the role of *macro*regions as units of spatial analysis. After discussing the trend towards regional economic integration, and how this affects, and is affected by, foreign direct investment, Chapters 6 and 7 present two case studies—one on how recent events in Europe have affected the activities of both intra- and extra-European Union MNEs; and the other on the impact of NAFTA on the structure of US industry. Each of these chapters suggests that regional groupings are likely to play a more important role in the locational decisions of corporations in the twenty-first century, and on the attitudes of both regional and national governments to upgrading the competitiveness of the resources and capabilities within their jurisdiction. The important question as to whether regionalization is best thought of as an integral part of globalization, or as a substitute for it, is also touched upon in this part of the book, as, indeed, it is elsewhere in the volume. Here several authors express the view that the establishment of regional trading blocs might lead to more intraregional trade and efficient foreign direct investment (FDI), but less interregional trade and more defensive, e.g. non-tariff jumping, foreign direct investment.

Part Three perhaps contains the most original research material in the volume. Each author was given the brief of examining how contemporary events in the global economy are affecting the intranational distribution of economic activity, and especially the role of clusters, or agglomerative economies, in attracting knowledge-intensive activities, including research and development. To avoid unnecessary duplication, each author was asked to focus on one or two particular aspects of the interface between national and subnational economic issues.

The result is that the reader is treated to an examination of a wide range of contextual specific issues. Some chapters, e.g. Chapter 8, give special attention to the impact of inbound FDI on the intranational distribution of value-added activities. Others, e.g. Chapters 13 and 15, focus on the role of clusters in promoting the development of new industries and the upgrading of others; while Chapters 9, 11, 12, and 14, describe the actions taken by national and subnational governments to provide the kind of economic environment and institutional infrastructure deemed necessary both to attract foreign investment and to encourage indigenous firms to be more competitive in the global market place.

Part Four then turns to examine in more detail some of the policy implications of the subject matter dealt with in earlier chapters. Chapter 16 offers a theory of regional policy—or more accurately, a theory of policy, at various levels of governance, to deal with the allocation of resources and capabilities between and within subnational spatial areas (which, themselves, may vary considerably in size and function). Chapter 17 focuses on the role of promotional policies, and especially the provision of information and the 'right' kind of immobile assets as incentives to attracting and retaining inbound FDI. Chapter 18 is, I think, especially interesting and relevant to the main theme of the volume, as the author seeks to link the changing needs of innovating firms with that of the institutional (and especially the educational) infrastructure of the region in which their firms, including the affiliates of foreign MNEs, are located, or are likely to locate.

As a whole, the chapters in the volume clearly demonstrate that the advent of the knowledge-based economy, and the growing importance of innovation—including organizational innovation—as a competitive-enhancing attribute—is having very significant spatial implications. The volume also shows that the role of locational choice is becoming a more important component of the strategies of firms; and that governments, too, should give more attention to how best to organize and locate the spatially bound assets within their jurisdiction in order to attract and retain the mobile assets necessary to upgrade the productivity of, and better promote the (dynamic) competitive advantage of, their indigenous resources and capabilities.

NOTES

1. See Ch. 1 of this volume for further details.
2. The concept of the optimal spatial area, viewed from the perspective of the multinational enterprise, was first introduced by Charles Kindleberger (1974).
3. Notably Kenichi Ohmae (1995).
4. For a summary of these views, see Dunning (1998).

REFERENCES

Dunning, J. H. (1998), 'Locating and the Multinational Enterprise: A Neglected Factor'. *Journal of International Business Studies* 29(1): 45–66.

Kindleberger, C. (1974), 'Size of Firm and Size of Nation'. in J. H. Dunning (ed.), *Economic Analysis and the Multinational Enterprise* (London: Allen & Unwin).

Markusen, A. (1996), 'Sticky Places in Slippery Space: A Typology of Industrial Districts', *Economic Geography* 72(3): 293–313.

Ohmae, K. (1995), *The End of the Nation State: The Rise of Regional Economies* (London: HarperCollins).

UN (1998), *World Investment Report 1998: Trends and Determinants* (New York and Geneva: UN).

PART ONE
ANALYTICAL FOUNDATIONS

1

Regions, Globalization, and the Knowledge Economy:
The Issues Stated

John H. Dunning

1. Introduction

The purpose of this introductory chapter is to offer an analytical framework for evaluating the implications of recent economic events on the spatial distribution of economic activities; and of the role played by multinational enterprises (MNEs)[1] and cross-border interfirm coalitions[2] of firms on the international and intranational division of labour. In particular, we shall be concerned with the parallel, yet apparently antithetical, forces towards the geographical dispersion of asset-augmenting and asset-exploiting activities,[3] and the concentration of such activities in limited spatial areas; or what Ann Markusen (1996) has referred to as the paradox of 'sticky places within slippery space'.

The theme of this volume is of increasing interest to businesses practitioners and to policy-makers alike; and to the academic community. To business practitioners, research is revealing that, as the core competencies of firms become more knowledge-intensive, yet more mobile across space, so the choice of location in the production, organization and use of those assets is becoming a more critical competitive advantage.[4] To the national or regional policy-makers the challenge is to offer, both to indigenous and foreign-owned firms, the spatially anchored resources and capabilities within their jurisdiction, which are perceived by these firms to be at least as attractive complements to their own ownership-specific advantages as those offered by other countries or regions. To the academic scholar, locationally related studies are at the cutting edge of interdisciplinary research, and of the intersection of research being undertaken by trade, FDI, and evolutionary economists, by economic geographers, by industrial sociologists, and by business strategists.

This chapter proceeds in the following way. First, it identifies and describes the main features of four of the critical events of the past two decades which have affected the global locational options available to firms, and their choice between these options. Second, it examines and explains the trend towards the closer and deeper economic interdependence between, and among, countries, which is the critical characteristic of both (macro-)regionalization[5] and globalization.

The third section looks more closely at the nature of clustering and agglomeration of related value-added activities; and whether it is possible to offer a paradigm of why particular kinds of asset-augmenting and asset-exploiting foreign direct investment are attracted to certain countries and microregions. Fourth, the chapter examines the ways in which the growth of MNE-related activity has affected, and is affecting, both the international and intranational location of production; and of our thinking about its determinants and effects. Fifth, we analyse some of the consequences of our findings and our theorizing both for national and regional policy-makers, and for business practitioners. Finally, a concluding section will discuss some of their implications for scholarly research—and particularly that which draws together the different approaches to the issues under discussion.

2. The Changing World Economic Scenario: The mid-1970s to the late 1990s

In this section, we identify four main events of the last two decades which we believe have had a profound impact on both the nature and composition of global of economic activity, on its ownership and location, and on its organizational modes. These are:

1. The increasing importance of all forms of intellectual capital in both the asset-creating and asset-exploiting activities of firms.
2. The growth of cooperative ventures and alliances between, and within, the main wealth-creating institutions.
3. The liberalization of both internal and cross-border markets.
4. The emergence of several new major economic players in the world economy.

We deal with each of these in turn.

2.1. The Knowledge Economy

Over the last three centuries, the main source of wealth[6] in market economies has switched from natural assets (notably land and relatively unskilled labour),[7] through tangible created assets (notably buildings, machinery and equipment, and finance), to intangible created assets (notably knowledge and information of all kinds) which may be embodied in human beings, in organizations, or in physical assets. It has, for example, been estimated that, whereas in the 1950s, 80 per cent of the value added in US manufacturing industry represented primary or processed foodstuffs, materials, or mineral products, and 20 per cent knowledge, by 1995, these proportions had changed to 30 and 70 per cent respectively (Stewart 1997). No less significant, the book value of the tangible assets of corporations is becoming a decreasing component of their market value. One estimate (Handy 1990) put this at between 25 and 33 per cent in the mid-1980s, while Leif Edvinson (1997) has more recently calculated that, for most organizations, the ratio of their intellectual capital[8] to that of their physical and financial capital is between five-to-one and sixteen-to-one.

Between 1975 and 1995, expenditure on all kinds of research and development in the OECD economies rose three times the rate of output in manufacturing industry (OECD 1997*b*). Over the same period, while the number of patents registered in the USA increased from 76,800 to 113,600, i.e. by 48 per cent, those in the more knowledge-intensive sectors,[9] rose from 16,827 to 47,533, i.e. by 182 per cent (US Patent and Trademark Office 1997). The proportion of the age group 15–24 engaged in higher education increased from 35 per cent in 1980 to 56 per cent in 1993 (World Bank 1997). Finally, capital spending on information technology, which, in 1965, was only one-third of that on production technology, now exceeds it. Throughout economic activity, created intangible assets are replacing natural or created tangible assets as the main source of wealth augmentation in industrial societies. *Inter alia*, this is demonstrated by the rising contribution of services, relative to goods, in the gross national output (GNP) of most countries.[10]

These data all tell a consistent story, viz. the trend towards the cross-border augmentation of assets as an important instrument for increasing economic well-being. They also suggest that in evaluating the economic prosperity of societies, scholars need to give more attention to the dynamics of asset-seeking FDI. Most theories of the firm, of industrial organization, and of location are still caught in a static web, and are mainly interested in how existing assets may be deployed—and located—in the most efficient way. The advent of the knowledge-based economy demands that scholars should give at least as much attention to a scenario in which assets, far from being largely fixed and immobile as in bygone days, are now eminently increasable and mobile. This may require a fundamental rethink of the relevance of the leading paradigms and theories of the 1970s and early 1980s in explaining the contemporary spatial distribution of economic activity.

Intellectual capital is different from other forms of capital in its deployment in another way. While, to be effective, one piece of land, or a particular machine, or even 'x' dollars of financial assets, is (or are) largely independent of another piece of land, machine, or 'x' dollars of financial assets, this is not the case with a unit of knowledge and other forms of intellectual capital. Not only is knowledge a heterogeneous commodity and can be put to multiple uses; often, one kind of knowledge needs to be combined with several other kinds to produce a particular good or service. With the development of two of the key 'engines' of the knowledge economy, viz. the microchip and the computer, the distinction between 'high'- and 'low'-technology industries, as proxied by the final output they produce, is becoming less and less meaningful. In their use of knowledge, parts of the textile, food-processing, retail construction, and healthcare industries are

just as technologically advanced as the electronics, pharmaceutical, financial services, and management consultancy sectors.

The intellectual capital needed both to augment and to exploit assets is then
complex; and it is rarely the property of only one firm. For a firm to increase or
deploy its own knowledge effectively, it may have to complement this knowledge with that of other firms; and more often than not, by way of some kind of
collaborative agreement.[11]

There are, of course, several reasons for the growth of interfirm collaboration
which will be further discussed in the next section. Here we would offer just
three observations about the nature of contemporary knowledge. First, it can be
highly expensive; the cost of the next generation of microchips or a new generic
drug frequently runs into billions of dollars. Second, the outcome of much investment in augmenting knowledge, e.g. by research and development (R&D), is highly
uncertain. Third, many kinds of knowledge (and particularly those which can be
imitated) become obsolete quite speedily. Together, with its increasing complexity,
these features of intellectual capital—coupled with its competitive-protecting or
enhancing imperatives—have very considerable implications for both the location and the organization of firms; and, indeed, for the character and composition of microregions.

2.2. Alliance Capitalism

One of the particularly interesting features of the leading market economies of
recent years has been the extent to which the hierarchical form of governance
of both private and public organizations has been complemented with, and in
some cases replaced by, a variety of interorganizational cooperative agreements.
This has caused scholars to suggest that the present stage of capitalism may best
be described as alliance capitalism.[12] These alliances may, and do, take a variety of forms, and involve a large number of institutional entities. They may
be between the different stakeholders of the firm and/or between the various
operational or functional units, making up a firm's value chain (viz. *intra*firm
alliances). They may be between one firm and another—for example, between
a firm and its competitors, suppliers, or customers (viz. *inter*firm alliances).[13] They
may be between a private firm and a public institution; between public institutions, notably between regional and national governments. They may also be
between various interest groups, e.g. consumers, environmentalists, and labour
unions and so on.

Intercorporate alliances may be formed to promote asset-augmenting or asset-
exploiting activities. In the former case, partners are normally sought to access
synergistic or complementary knowledge-intensive assets, learning and organizational capabilities, and markets. Technology-advancing alliances may also be concluded to share the cost of R&D and to speed up the innovatory process. In the
latter case, alliances are usually formed to increase the efficiency of existing asset

deployment, by, for example, facilitating economies of scope and scale, and by making better use of existing managerial and marketing capabilities. In such cases, firms may engage in coalitions to protect or strengthen their competitive positions versus other firms; while, unless precluded from doing so by antitrust legislation, one firm may acquire another to increase its market power and gain additional economic rents.

The growth of knowledge capitalism has led to an explosion of interfirm alliances. Data on mergers and acquisitions (M&As) and collaborative non-equity coalitions suggest that, whether by FDI or by cross-border licensing, franchising and other agreements, alliances have been most pronounced, and increased the most, in knowledge-intensive sectors (UNCTAD 1998), and have been predominantly concluded between MNEs and other corporations in advanced industrial countries.[14]

2.3. Liberalization of Markets

Perhaps the most dramatic and most transparent economic event of the last two decades has been the growing liberalization of both national and international markets. Though most vividly demonstrated by the removal of the Berlin Wall in 1989, and the opening up of the People's Republic of China to inbound FDI, the reconfiguration of national economic policies of most Latin American countries, India, and some African economies, and the move towards closer macroregional integration in various parts of the world, have all contributed to the renewed vitality of the market system as the main instrument for the harnessing and deployment of scarce resources and capabilities throughout the world.

Since the early 1980s, artificial barriers to trade have tumbled—particularly at the macroregional level. At the same time, both transport and communication costs have dramatically fallen,[15] as have the intrafirm costs of doing business within and across national boundaries. As a result, the share of trade and FDI, as a proportion of the gross national product of the great majority of countries, has sharply risen.[16]

Several other indices of the growing openness of countries to the rest of the world point to the same conclusion. Most dramatic of these has been the spectacular expansion of cross-border financial flows, and of the extent and depth of international financial integration. For example, foreign portfolio investment flows rose from $56.2 billion in 1984 to $412.5 billion in 1995 (IMF v.d.), while the increase in international bank loans has consistently outpaced that of both world exports and FDI for most of the thirty years prior to 1994 (Perraton *et al.* 1994). Relatedly, the average daily trade in the foreign exchange market rose from $15 billion in 1973 to $880 billion in 1992 and $1,300 billion in 1995, while cross-border sales and purchases of financial assets rose from less than 10 per cent of gross domestic product (GDP) in 1980 in the USA, Germany, and Japan to 135, 170 and 85 per cent respectively in 1993 (Kozul-Wright 1997).

Scarcely less impressive is the increase in the use of cross-border communications media. In 1980, the minutes per capita spent on international telephone calls for all countries in the world was 3.6; by 1994 it was 9.4. In 1980, the internet was hardly in use; by 1995, together with e-mail it was the fastest-growing form of cross-border communication and doubling every three years (UNDP 1997).

Finally, we might mention the great increase in cross-border people traffic over the last two decades. Though part of this, e.g. the trebling of tourist expenditure, and the quadrupling of the number of passengers on international airlines[17] cannot be put solely at the door of the liberalization or deregulation of markets, these and other people movements (e.g. migration, employment of foreigners, cross-border travel to work, etc.) have most certainly been aided, directly or indirectly, by the reduction in obstacles to the movement of goods, assets, and services.

2.4. Emerging Markets

The last and most gradual—but by no means the least important—event (or trend is, perhaps, the better word) is the take-off of several developing economies as major players on the world economic scene. Most of these are in Asia and Latin America; and most are commonly referred to as 'newly industrializing' economies. Three, e.g. Hong Kong, Singapore, and Korea, were among the wealthiest thirty countries in the world in 1997 (World Bank 1998).

The clearest expression of the significance of the emerging economies, both as locations of production and as markets is their share of the world's GNP. In 1980, Latin American, South-East Asian, and East Asian developing countries accounted for 24.1 per cent of the world's GNP; the corresponding figure for 1995 was 26.8 per cent (World Bank 1997, 1998). Comparable figures for the share of world exports were 18.4 and 28.9 per cent; for the share of the world's inward foreign direct investment *stock*, 16.7 and 23.5 per cent (UNCTAD 1998); for the share of the world's inward foreign portfolio investment flows, 1.7 and 12.6 per cent (IMF v.d.);[18] for the share of commercial energy use 19.2 and 29.7 per cent; for the share of the world's patents registered in the USA 0.4 and 3.5 per cent (US Patent and Trademark Office 1999); and for the share of the world's telephone lines 17.8 and 43.8 per cent (UN v.d.).

Coupled with the economic events earlier described—all of which are intensifying the competitive pressures between corporations, and are leading to a reconfiguration of their product and innovation strategies—the emergence of new economies is helping to fashion a new North–South and South–South division of labour. Although, as they move along their investment development paths (Narula 1995; Dunning and Narula 1996), the economic structure of industrializing countries tends to move closer to that of their more advanced industrialized counterparts. The more knowledge-intensive asset-augmenting activities tend to still remain very heavily concentrated in the latter countries;[19] and, indeed, in microregions within these countries.[20] We shall take up this point further in Section 4 of this chapter.

3. Globalization: Extending and Deepening the Economic Interdependence between Nations

What then is the impact of the events described on the location of economic activity? Location theory has long since asserted that a profit-maximizing firm will site its value-added activities where it perceives this particular goal is best advanced.[21] Such profits represent the differences between revenue (a demand-related variable) and costs (a supply-related variable), plus taxes and duties, less allowances and subsidies. Costs are of four main kinds, viz. design and development, production, transportation, and transaction. Taxes, duties, allowances, and subsidiaries may be direct or indirect, general or specific. In imperfect—and particularly oligopolistic—markets, firms will also take account of the locational strategies of their competitors.

Each of these broad locational determinants, are to some extent, product-, activity-, and country- (or region-) specific. Besides the availability and costs of factor and intermediate inputs, the main supply-related variables influencing whether a firm concentrates or disperses its asset-augmenting or asset-exploiting activities over space are, on the one hand, the extent to which such activities can benefit from scale economies, and, on the other, the spatially related transaction costs involved. As George Stigler (1951) pointed out many years ago—and Adam Smith before him—division of labour, i.e. the specialization of economic activity, is limited by the size and geography of the market. Today, we might add to this variable the *character* of the market (and in particular the extent to which it is customized), and the transaction costs of exchanging goods and services between different political and cultural regimes.

We make these fairly obvious introductory points, as it is worth emphasizing that the extent, form, and pace of globalization is not uniformly spread across the planet, nor across different value-added activities. Some goods and services, for example, are non-tradable, i.e. they are immobile across space. Some are produced in their entirety in only one or a few countries and are exported across the globe. Some are replicated in their entirety in several countries, but only sold in their country of production. Some parts of the global activities of firms (e.g. research and development) tend to be concentrated in a few countries and regions, while others are spread more widely.

What then is economic globalization? We will not dwell on this well-researched topic, save to give (what we believe to be) an excellent interpretation by a political scientist—Anthony McGrew (1992: 23).

Globalization refers to the multiplicity of linkages and interconnections between the states and societies which make up the present world system. It describes the process by which events, decisions, and activities in one part of the world come to have significant consequences for individuals and communities in quite distant parts of the globe. Globalization has two distinct phenomena: scope (or stretching) and intensity (or deepening). On the one hand, it defines a set of processes which embrace most of the globe or which operate worldwide: the concept therefore has a spatial connotation. On the other hand it also implies an intensification on the levels of interaction, interconnectedness or interdependence between the states and societies which constitute the world community. Accordingly, alongside the stretching goes a deepening of global processes.

In short, globalization is a process leading to the structural transformation of firms and nations. It represents a discontinuity in the process of internationalization in the sense that it creates new and deeper cross-border relationships and dependencies. Sometimes, the transformation takes place at a regional level: much of the integrated production networks of MNEs is so focused. Sometimes, it occurs at a global level. For example, the advent of electronic commerce is dramatically truncating distance in financial and foreign exchange markets (Stopford and Strange 1991). One scholar has gone as far as to aver that the emergence of the internet and global financial integration is heralding 'the end of geography' O'Brien (1992). Sometimes, however, globalization, while facilitating the cross-border movement of intermediate products, notably technology, is also leading to the widespread replication of end products.

We have already identified some of the forces 'pushing' or 'pulling' in the direction of regionalization and globalization. We now set out a few additional facts, particularly as they relate to the growth of MNE-related activity

1. Over the last decades the growth of world trade has consistently outpaced that of world output—usually by a ratio of 2 to 1; while in 1997 the sales of the foreign affiliates of MNEs exceeded that of world trade by 48 per cent (UNCTAD 1998).
2. The majority of the global sales of MNEs are in knowledge or information sectors, or in sectors supportive of these activities.
3. Between one-third of cross-border trade in non-agricultural goods and services, and between one-half and three-fifths of all capital and technology flows is now internalized within MNEs.
4. There have been two important trends in MNE-related activity (FDI and alliance formation) over the past two decades. The first is the spectacular growth of asset-seeking mergers and acquisitions (M&As) and strategic alliances within the Triad countries, or within regions of USA, Japan, and Western Europe.[22] The second has been the no less dramatic growth of asset-exploiting FDI in some emerging markets, notably China,[23] an increasing part of which has been supplied from other Asian developing countries.[24]
5. A rising proportion of FDI in both developed and developing countries is in services—particularly information-intensive services.[25]
6. An increasing proportion of the total R&D expenditures is accounted for by their foreign subsidiaries.[26] Moreover, it is growing faster than that of other forms of MNE-related production,[27] and also than that of the indigenous

firms of the countries in which MNE subsidiaries are located.[28] Furthermore, an increasing proportion of the foreign R&D activities of MNEs is directed to augmenting their home-based intellectual capital—often by tapping into foreign R&D facilities—rather than to more effectively deploying their existing R&D capabilities (Kuemmerle 1996).

4. Localization, Clusters, and the Concept of 'Sticky' Places

We have already suggested that globalization does not necessarily mean that all wealth-creating activities are dispersed uniformly throughout the world. Far from it. If, indeed, the specialization of economic activity is limited by the size of the market, then it would be proper to hypothesize that globalization will be accompanied by more, rather than less, specialization; and hence, by implication, will lead to further spatial concentration of such activity. Much, of course, will depend on how the production, transportation, and transaction costs imposed by artificial barriers to trade, vary with size of output produced. The 'where' of concentration will depend on the national and micro regional-specific characteristics influencing such costs, and also on the spatial proximity of related activities (clusters), which generate both static and dynamic external economies.

In examining the proposition that some types of wealth-creating activities are becoming more concentrated in subnational clusters, it may be useful to distinguish between traditional and contemporary trade and location models. Traditional, i.e. Heckscher–Ohlin, type trade models were primarily designed to explain the optimum (i.e. the most efficient) patterns of trade between countries, based on the distribution of immobile factor endowments. Location theories were similarly concerned with the optimum siting of asset-exploiting activities, i.e. those designed to maximize the static efficiency of the investing firms; but, unlike trade theories, they explicitly acknowledged the role the transaction costs (and benefits) of spatially proximate activities.[29]

Contemporary trade and location theories are more contextual than their predecessors.[30] While those just described are still a robust explanation of some kinds of cross-border division of labour—particularly of natural resource intensive activities between developed and developing countries—they are less comfortable in explaining the distribution of knowledge-intensive activities, and particularly those between and within advanced countries and under the governance of MNEs. Such activities are not only likely to incur substantial overhead costs, and thus need non-decreasing returns to scale and the necessary volume to cover these; but, as already indicated, they frequently involve multiple and interrelated technological inputs.[31] To minimize distance-related transaction costs, and to maximize the benefits of dynamic learning economies, it frequently pays firms to concentrate their activities within a limited spatial area. Hence, the concept of the learning region (Florida 1995), and with it, the significance of dynamic agglomerative economies as a locational pull to firms—and particularly those seeking to augment their resources and capabilities.

Globalization may then lead to a dispersion of knowledge-intensive production between and within countries; and to a convergence in cross-border economic structures. It may equally lead to a concentration of such production in particular countries, and in microregions within those countries, in which case economic structures of the countries and microregions will tend to diverge from, rather than converge with, each other.

In fact, both trends are discernible, but it is the contention of this chapter—and, indeed, by several authors in this volume—that (i) the greater the degree of knowledge intensity of a particular activity, (ii) the easier it is for labour to migrate across regions or countries, (iii) the lower the distance related costs, and (iv) the more firms engage in FDI and alliance-related activities to augment, rather than exploit, their existing assets, then the more likely is it that national and microregional economies will develop specialized centres of excellence.[32] At the same time, it is quite evident that the main competitors to some microregions in attracting and retaining mobile investment are not other microregions in the same country, but microregions in other countries.[33]

This observation is consistent with the growing sophistication of both intraindustry trade and intraindustry FDI between countries and/or microregions. Such sophistication is not confined to the types of products produced. Rather, it extends to the innovatory milieu of the competing locations, and, in particular to the opportunities of firms within that milieu to tap into and learn from the resources, capabilities, and entrepreneurship of each other, i.e. augment their core competencies.[34]

These opportunities, and the benefits of spatial clustering, clearly vary between industries and firms; and they may be exploited through a variety of organizational routes, e.g. arm's-length markets, non-equity alliances, and FDI. Which modality is chosen will depend on the extent and character of the relevant *dynamic* spatially specific transaction costs, e.g. those associated with innovatory activities. In general, one might predict that (i) the less complex and/or independent the knowledge required for the production of a particular good or service, (ii) the more codifiable (i.e. less tacit) or idiosyncratic that knowledge is, (iii) the less the information symmetry there is between the related firms, (iv) the fewer the opportunities there are for opportunistic behaviour, (v) the less uncertain the outcome of any relationship is, and (vi) the more widely located the customers are, then the lower the spatial transaction costs, and the less the economies of agglomeration are likely to be.[35]

Clustering is, therefore, likely to be strongly activity-specific; and to be most marked where the critical decision takers in firms need to be in close physical proximity to exchange, or share, tacit knowledge. The City of London is a classic example of an agglomeration of interdependent firms each producing part of a final product.[36] Globalization and technological change have combined to strengthen such clustering, and also to upgrade the knowledge intensity of the constituent firms. At the same time, the increasing mobility of firm-specific assets and the growing complementarity between different kinds of technology has fostered more diversity of economic activity, often with beneficial consequences for innovatory output (Feldman and Audretsch 1999).

So far, we have tended to concentrate on supply-related reasons why firms cluster. We have argued that while the original Marshallian reasons for clustering[37] still hold good, those to do with a variety of 'soft' locational factors and access to knowledge and learning capabilities have become more important[38] (Florida 1995; Giersch 1996). At the same time, clusters may be fashioned by the needs of consumers, and some of these also possess all, or indeed most, of the characteristics so far identified. Such clusters are particularly noticeable in the consumer services sector; they tend to be city-oriented and include airline offices, car rental agencies, film distributors, medical services, and fast-food chains.

5. The Role of MNEs in Affecting the Location of Economic Activity

So far in our analysis, we have not considered the unique role of MNEs in affecting the location of economic activity. To this we now turn. What is distinctive about this particular organizational form? As defined earlier, an MNE is an institution which owns or controls value activities in at least two countries. Many of the larger MNEs own or control value-added activities in a large number of countries, and do so via both FDI and cross-border alliances. To what extent is the locational pattern of such activities different from what it would be if each of them had been separately and independently owned? Does the common ownership of production in two or more countries affect our theorizing about the geography of asset-augmenting or asset-exploiting investment, and its tendency to be concentrated or dispersed?

5.1. The Multidomestic MNE

To answer this question, let us consider two types of governance structures of MNEs.[39] The first is the *multidomestic* or 'stand-alone' structure, which most MNEs, outside the natural-resource-based sectors, adopted until the 1960s. The main feature of the multidomestic MNE is that it treats its foreign subsidiaries as autonomous wealth-creating units. Each subsidiary tends to replicate—albeit often on a truncated scale—the asset-exploiting activities of its mother company, and to supply its products to local and/or closely adjacent markets. Though the parent organization may export intangible assets (e.g. technology, managerial and marketing expertise) and other intermediate products (e.g. materials, components, and parts) to its affiliates, for the most part, there is likely to be little trade in finished products between the parent company and its affiliates, or among its affiliates. In short, the multidomestic MNE engages in little integrated production and little cross-border product or process specialization.

Frequently, in the past, the multidomestic or 'stand-alone' MNE has been prompted to engage in FDI to overcome tariff barriers and other restrictions to trade, or to be near to critical supply facilities and/or to the special needs of foreign consumers. *De facto*, this kind of defensive market-seeking FDI often replaces trade, and does little to promote a more efficient regional or global division of labour. However, there are also some kinds of *aggressive* market-seeking MNE activity which, while not replacing trade, do little to promote it. Examples include FDIs in some service sectors, e.g. in fast-food chains, building and construction, railroads, public utilities, and the regional offices of MNEs.

Yet, though globally dispersed, multidomestic MNEs may still favour particular locations *within* a country. Moreover, these are not always the same as those chosen by domestic firms. Several studies on the intranational distribution of inbound investment from 1958 onwards[40] have shown that foreign affiliates of MNEs tend to be located in or near large conurbations, and/or be adjacent to leading ports. They also tend to favour subnational clusters of related activities, and to be more sensitive to the regional policies of governments[41] (Yannopoulos and Dunning 1976).

One other frequently voiced need of first-time foreign investors is to reduce the costs of producing in an unfamiliar environment as much as possible. Several country-based studies[42] have shown that in various countries, either the presence of indigenous firms has attracted FDI into the same microregion, or the establishment and growth of one investor has had a positive signalling affect on other foreign investors (Liu 1998).[43] On the other hand, there is also some evidence that foreign-owned firms prefer to establish *de novo* clusters of related activities. Examples include the surge of biotechnology investments in California in the 1980s, and major new investments by the Japanese auto companies—Nissan in North-East England, Toyota in Derby—in the 1990s (UNCTAD 1995).

5.2. The Globally (or Regionally) Integrated MNE

The main feature of this kind of MNE is that it adopts a systemic and holistic approach towards its global operations, and treats its foreign affiliates as part of a network of interrelated activities, designed to promote the interest of the MNE *in toto*. Where possible, the integrated MNE will take full advantage of the geographical distribution of natural and created assets, of spatially related agglomerative economies, and of liberalized markets. This means it is likely to engage in more rationalized and efficiency-seeking FDI than is its multidomestic counterpart, and to source its inputs and augment its resources and capabilities from across the globe. It is also likely to engage in a good deal of intermediate and final product trade between its parent company and its affiliates, and among its affiliates—especially within regionally integrated areas. The activities of the globally integrated MNE are then likely to promote both trade and FDI.

The globally integrated MNE is very much a creature of the late twentieth century; and each of the events described in Section 2 have helped to foster such integration. Broadly speaking, the integrated MNE promotes three kinds of cross-border specialization. The first is *horizontal* specialization in which each of the products supplied by the same firm is produced in different regions or countries. The primary rationale of this specialization is to take advantage of the economies of scale and differentiated consumer needs, although where the products require a different mix of natural resources and capabilities, it may be of the H-O type. The second is *vertical* specialization where different stages of the value-added chain of a particular product are undertaken in different locations. The main object of this type of specialization—which predominantly (though not exclusively) occurs between developed and developing countries—is to take advantage of differences in factor costs and consumer tastes, although the opportunity to gain scale economies may also be relevant.

The third kind of specialization—asset augmenting-specialization—is an amalgam of the first two; but it is different in that it is designed less to advance the static efficiency of the MNE, and more to enhance its future wealth-creating capabilities in a cost-learning effective way. The geography of this kind of labour is mainly confined to the advanced industrial countries, and geared to either promoting the efficiency of the MNEs global R&D capabilities,[44] or gaining access to foreign-created assets which will best protect or enhance its competitive advantages.[45] It is this kind of specialization which is being increasingly fashioned by the imperatives of the knowledge-based global economy, and by the need of firms located in one country to complement their core competencies with those of firms located in another country.[46]

To what extent is the globally integrated MNE likely to prefer to locate the three kinds of cross-border specialization in particular microregions of host countries? The evidence is mixed. The primary issue with respect to horizontal and vertical FDI is the extent to which 'static' spatial transaction costs favour its proximity to a cluster of related firms, so it can exploit the benefits of 'untraded interdependencies' (Storper 1995). However, over time, most of these clusters have evolved their own nexus of innovating and learning capabilities; in other words, they also generate dynamic externalities to the participating firms.

Examples of both horizontal and vertical clusters abound.[47] The former include the watch industry of Geneva, the cork industry of Northern Portugal, the woollen textile industry of Prato and Biellia in Northern Italy, the film industry of Hollywood, the diamond industry of Amsterdam, the tomato-canning industry of Campania, Southern Italy, the cutlery industry of Solignen, and the financial services industry of the City of London and Wall Street (New York). Examples of the latter include the large number of export zones set up in developing countries—especially in Asia—to house relatively labour-intensive stages of the value chain by MNEs, in such manufacturing sectors as textiles, leather goods, and consumer electronics, and, more recently, in services such as insurance, shipping, shared support centres, and computer software.[48] In more advanced

countries, the Boeing agglomeration of related firms in the Seattle region and
the Toyota complex of firms in the Tokyo region are examples of vertically
integrated clusters, in which a flagship firm producing an end product, which
comprises a large number of components and parts, is surrounded by a satellite
of its suppliers.

It is our view that the dynamic externalities associated with these horizontal
and vertical clusters are becoming more important as intellectual capital becomes more sophisticated, idiosyncratic, tacit, complex, and context-dependent.
Furthermore, as the main repositories of such knowledge, and certainly the principal organizing unit for accessing and leveraging geographically dispersed units
(Doz *et al.* 1998), MNEs are not only drawn to regional clusters, but, by their
presence and impact, influence their character and growth.[49] Historical examples
include the chemical and cotton-thread industries of New Jersey (Wallace 1998)
and the office machinery industry of mid-Scotland (Dunning 1958, 2000). More
recent cases include clusters of the Japanese consumer electronics affiliates in
South Wales (Strange 1993), and a bevy of MNEs in the Bangalore software
sector (Balasubramanyam and Balasubramanyam, in this volume).[50]

It is, however, the third type of industrial specialization and clustering which
is increasingly engaging the attention of scholars; and it is one, too, in which
both national and microregional authorities are watching carefully. The spectacular development of business, industrial and science parks, and specialized
service sectors, are all testimony to the belief that the asset-augmenting activities
of firms benefit from being part of a knowledge-creating milieu—in which private firms, universities, technical colleges, and government research institutions
are all involved. Many of these clusters were initially initiated by microregional
authorities to help upgrade the resources and capabilities under their jurisdiction;
and, sometimes, they were targeted specifically at mobile investors.[51] For the most
part, such clusters tend to be concentrated in the Triad regions or nations; and
as intellectual capital becomes more geographically diffused and cross-border innovatory competition becomes more intense, firms from one part of the Triad are
finding it increasingly desirable to establish an R&D presence, and/or conclude
technology-enhancing alliances with firms in another part.[52]

But more than this: as firms increasingly scan the globe for knowledge capital, they are engaging in FDI specifically to tap into, and harness, country- and
firm-specific resources, capabilities, and learning experiences.[53] Such assets may
be synergistic with their core assets, or complementary to them. They can be
harnessed by the acquisition of, or merger with, foreign firms and/or by the conclusion of non-equity coalitions with them. MNEs may also use their foreign
affiliates or partners as vehicles for seeking out and monitoring new knowledge
and learning experiences; and as a means of tapping into national innovatory or
investment systems more conducive to their dynamic competitive advantages
(Doremus *et al.* 1998). In such cases, a presence in the innovating heartland
of the sectors will help to lower the transaction costs involved in such a task.
Thus, firms are likely to be attracted to pockets of intellectual capital in a foreign

economy, and, insofar as they are allowed to do so, to participate in joint research and development and collective learning experiences (Florida 1995).

There is some casual evidence that the R&D activities of firms tend to be more spatially concentrated in a country than other activities,[54] and are more likely to be drawn to centres of academic excellence and to industrial and science parks. There is also evidence that the major metropolitan areas and their surrounding hinterlands are becoming the loci of agglomerative knowledge-enhancing activities. Indeed, according to Allen Scott (1998), as sources of new employment, they are not only growing faster than the national average,[55] but are becoming the leading regional motors of technological change.

In summary, then, the changing geography of MNE-related activity is a microcosm of that of the world economy. On the one hand, MNEs are conducting a rising proportion of their value-added activities outside their home countries,[56] and also in more countries.[57] For the most part, too, their affiliates are becoming more embedded in their local environments; and are helping to foster the dispersion of at least some kinds of intellectual capital. MNEs from developing countries also tend to locate their activities away from the large industrial concentrations originally favoured by their developed countries' counterparts. For example, FDI in Europe by Korean auto and electronics MNEs has been more concentrated in Central and Eastern Europe and in the less prosperous areas of the UK and other EC countries than has FDI by US and Japanese MNEs (UNCTAD 1995, 1997, 1998). The number of cross-border M&As and strategic alliances has also risen faster than that of their domestic counterparts (Booz, Allen, and Hamilton 1997).

On the other hand, MNEs and their affiliates are being increasingly drawn to a network of 'sticky' places for their wealth-creating activities; and there is a strong suggestion that the events of the last two decades, and particularly the deepening of the knowledge-based economy and the growing interdependence between cutting-edge technologies, have increased the spatial costs of related economic transactions. This has prompted MNEs to locate their R&D and production units in a geographical area large enough to accommodate a concentrated nexus of competitors, suppliers, customers, and/or of firms using common support services, but small enough to maximize the benefits of 'untradable interdependencies' (Storper and Scott 1995).

We may infer then that there is no real paradox of geographical space; and that globalization and localization are opposite sides of the same coin.[58] This section of the chapter has further suggested that, because of their unique characteristics, MNEs are likely to display a different geography of economic activity than that of their uninational counterparts. In part, this is a reflection of the products they produce; but mostly it arises from their capabilities to harness and utilize resources, capabilities, and markets from throughout the world, and to do so within their own governance structures. Such advantages, we believe, make for more globalization and more spatial clustering than would occur if all the cross-border value-added activities, owned and controlled by MNEs, were undertaken by independent firms, and if all trade was conducted at arm's-length prices. But, much more research is needed if this suggestion is to be more than just a suggestion!

We would briefly make one further point. There is some evidence (see, for example, OECD 1996) to suppose that industrial clusters, particularly of small and medium-size (SME) firms, tend to generate the kind of external economies, which assist at least some of the clustering firms to internationalize their markets and/or production. In particular, several of the country studies in OECD (1996) reveal a close correlation between the export success of firms, their participation in cross-border alliances, and their involvement in domestic networks.

6. A Regional Perspective

We now turn to consider some of the implications of recent economic events for the role of microregions as spatial entities, and for the governance of those regions. Is it the case, as some writers (e.g. Ohmae 1995) have suggested, that microregions are replacing the nation state as the principal spatial mode of governance? Or is the more temperate view of geographers such as Allen Scott, and business strategists such as Michael Porter, that such regions will become increasingly important milieux for competitive-enhancing activities of mobile investors, and as engines of national economic growth, a more plausible one?

Much research has been conducted over the past thirty years on the role of FDI- and MNE-related activity in advancing the economic well-being of nation states,[59] but relatively little on how it has affected that of microregions.[60] In principal, one would expect the results to be very similar, and particularly so when the microregions are the size of small countries (c.f. the impact of FDI on the economy of Baden-Württemberg with that of Belgium, or that of Northern Ireland with that of Denmark). While, traditionally, scholars have always distinguished between intra- and inter-national economic activity, and have generally assumed that the sovereignty of subnational governments is more constrained than that of national governments, contemporary economic events are demanding a reappraisal of these views. This is particularly so in the case of countries which have become part of macroregional integration schemes.

Nevertheless, *de facto*, the economic governance of most microregions is shared and executed by a range of authorities—microregional, national, and supranational. The exact role of each will vary from macroregion to microregion, country to country, and over time. In many respects, the relation of microregional to national governance may be likened to that of a subsidiary of an MNE to its parent company. The subsidiary has its own goals and agenda for achieving these goals; so does the parent company. The amount of decision-taking responsibility devolved to the subsidiary is likely to depend on such variables as the functions performed by it, its size, age and experience, the respective capabilities of the managers of the parent organization and those of the subsidiary, and the extend to which the managers of the latter, while promoting their own goals, are perceived to advance those of the MNE of which they are a part.

The same principle of 'subsidiarity' may be applied to understanding how much sovereignty is decentralized from national to microregional governments.[61] But, from the perspective of the regional government, its economic tasks are clearcut. These are, first, to promote the full and most efficient usage of the resources and capabilities within its jurisdiction; and second—insofar as is within its power—to provide the supportive infrastructure for its existing resources and capabilities to be upgraded, and for its indigenous firm to be competitive in world markets.

The contribution of inbound mobile investment is normally judged by these criteria. However, the questions of particular interest to the contributors to this volume are: first, whether in the contemporary globalizing, knowledge-based economy, such investment is likely to make a more, or less, significant contribution to regional economic welfare; second, what should be the policies of regional governments to ensure that such a contribution is an optimum one; and third, how far are these policies supported by, or reconcilable with, those pursued by national, and/or supranational governments, which seek to promote a broader canvass of interests.

The governments of microregions are like the management of firms in another respect. They compete with each other for resources, capabilities, and markets. An increasing role of many subnational authorities, in recent years, has been directed to providing as many cost-effective incentives and as few obstacles as possible to the kind of mobile investment the region perceives it needs to promote its dynamic comparative advantage. Many of these incentives have taken the form of investment grants, tax holidays, free or subsidized land, and customized public utilities, the aggressive pursuance of which by some microregions, e.g. some states in the USA, has led some scholars to refer to them as locational tournaments (Mytelka 1996).

But, no less significant have been the concentrated efforts of some microregional governments to provide, or ensure that the private sector provides, the kind of location-bound assets which investors—be they from the region or elsewhere—perceive they need if they are to best exploit their more mobile core competencies. However, it is becoming clear that regional authorities need to do more than this, simply because many of these assets (e.g. cost-efficient utilities, educational facilities, transport and communication infrastructure) are either provided, or can be fairly easily replicated, by their competitors.[62] This suggests that they need to offer mobile investors a unique set of spatially fixed competitive advantage, which are either customized to their individual needs (Peck 1996), or are not easily imitated by other regional governments. There is also need for strategic collaboration between the different levels of subnational governance to minimize both private and public transaction costs.[63] Finally, local administrations, in conjunction with local cooperative, trade associations, educational and innovatory institutions need to create an environment, which not only helps to promote the agglomeration of related activities, but one in which mobile investors can accumulate resources and capabilities, yet from which they may find it difficult to exit (Harrison 1992).[64] This, more often than not, is an extremely difficult thing to do, although some microregions, e.g. Silicon Valley in California and some small countries, e.g. Singapore and Hong Kong, have done so very successfully.[65]

What also is becoming increasingly clear is that, to advance their economic objectives, microregional governments need to give as much attention to providing the right milieu for asset-augmentation activities of their resident firms— be they domestic or foreign—as for asset-exploiting activities. Once again, the idea of the dynamic learning region comes to the fore; and, with it, the need for local administrations to adapt their intrastructural systems to best meet the demands of the global economy,[66] and to work together with the private sector to minimize any structural distortions and transaction costs which might impede both the redeployment and upgrading of local resources and capabilities.

It is within this context that the role of microregional clusters needs to be evaluated. To what extent is regional prosperity advanced if the agglomeration of vertically or horizontally related activities is encouraged—or, at least, not inhibited—by regional governments?[67] If such spatial networks are to be facilitated, how best might this be accomplished and what form should the clusters take?

It is possible to identify several kinds of spatial clusters.[68] These are likely to vary according to their scope, density, pattern of activities, growth potential, innovatory capacity, and governance structures (Enright 2000). In this introductory chapter, we confine our discussion to six types of clusters. The first of these are 'hub-and-spoke' clusters, in which a hub or nucleus of flagship firms generate a circle of satellite (or spoke) firms. In this case (the Boeing complex around Seattle, the Toyota complex around Tokyo, the Pohang Steel complex around Pohang in Korea, and the newly emerging Jenoptak electronics complex at Jean in Eastern Germany are good examples) the success of the cluster is likely to rest on the capability of the flagship firm to leverage and develop a network of suppliers and customers which are able to gain external economies not only from the hub firm but from each other.[69]

The second kind of cluster is that exemplified by the northern Italian textile industry, the Portuguese cork industry, the Cambridge (New Zealand) horse-breeding industry, and the Geneva watch industry, and was first identified by Alfred Marshall (1920).[70] It comprises a concentration of enterprises engaged in similar economic activities, so that each can draw from such external economies as the availability of a common pool of natural resources and transportation facilities.

The third type of cluster, like the second, consists of a complex of firms producing similar goods and services. The difference is that while, in the former case, the main cluster-specific benefits arise from a reduction of static distance-related transaction costs, and from internalizing static external economies, in the latter they primarily take the form of institution-building learning economies and the sharing of collective knowledge. The R&D laboratory is, in fact, a major component in the success of the latter, but not the former cluster, as is the interchange of tacit knowledge and ideas between the constituent firms and local universities and technical colleges.

The fourth type of industrial district is that which arises from an agglomeration of government publicly sponsored institutions. Examples include a congregation of aerospace, military, and other research establishments which are concentrated around Farnborough and Aldershot in south-east England,[71] around Colorado Springs in the USA, and around San José dos Campos in Brazil;[72] and which generate a satellite of subcontractors in the adjacent regions. The willingness and capacity to create and develop such spatial networks is obviously strongly dependent on national, rather than on regional, priorities and policies. In general, the most regional governments can do is to provide the human and physical infrastructure required to make them a success. State governments in several countries, notably the USA, however, have played an important role in encouraging tertiary education. For example, state-funded universities explain much of the growth of cities such as Durham, Chapel Hill, Ann Arbor, Austin, and Madison in the USA, which rank among the fastest-growing US cities (Markusen and Gray 1999).

The fifth type of cluster is that typified by export-processing zones in developing countries. Here, often tempted by tax and other incentives offered by national and/or regional governments, foreign MNEs have set up primarily export-oriented labour-intensive activities, and, via the signalling affect, have encouraged the agglomeration of like firms. However, if such clusters are to be anything but enclaves, and fully benefit the local economy, a national or regional policy which promotes the continuous upgrading of indigenous resources, and the establishment of backward or forward linkages with local firms, is essential (McIntyre, Narula, and Trevino 1996).

The sixth type of cluster is specifically directed at encouraging all forms of asset-augmenting activities.[73] Science and technology parks are primary examples of such clusters. To be successful, they need an up-to-date and sophisticated institutional infrastructure, and an innovative milieu which helps to generate the fluidity of knowledge, learning externalities, and social capital, demanded by the participating firms (Putman 1993). As we have already indicated, such clusters are usually, though not exclusively, located in the major metropolitan areas or in university towns and cities in advanced industrial countries.

We have suggested that foreign MNEs may, and frequently do, play a major role in the formation, structure, and development of the third, fifth, and sixth types of cluster; in some cases, too, they may initiate the first type of cluster. In the second and fifth types of cluster, foreign MNEs would normally be expected to engage in resource-seeking, market-seeking, or efficiency-seeking investment; in the first, third, and sixth kinds, in addition to asset-exploiting activities, foreign investors may also be aiming to augment their existing competitive advantages. Some recent research by Birkinshaw and Hood (1997) on Canadian, Scottish, and Swedish MNEs suggests that, while, historically, the role and influence of foreign affiliates has been more pronounced in 'branch plant' clusters, in the future they are likely to make a contribution to the character and content of 'leading-edge' (i.e. innovating) clusters.

While, as we have already indicated, scholarly research has generally concluded that, in the absence of structural market distortions, the economic welfare of recipient countries has been advanced by asset-exploiting FDI, there have been few studies on the effects of asset-augmenting FDI on either national or regional economic welfare. Back in the 1960s, there was a good deal of concern in Europe about the possible 'poaching' of intellectual capital by US inbound investors in some knowledge-intensive sectors, notably the pharmaceutical industry. This concern was especially marked as and when US firms acquired European companies and transferred some of their innovatory activities back to the USA (Dunning 1970). Strangely enough, the huge wave of intra-Triad M&As, which have occurred over the last decade do not seem to have sparked off the same kind of worries. It is possible, although we think improbable, that this is because it is perceived that the price paid for such resources and capabilities is a socially acceptable one.[74] A more likely explanation is the fact that the recent spate of cross-border M&As and strategic alliances has been a two-way phenomenon; certainly European and US purchases of foreign firms have been fairly evenly matched by the foreign acquisitions of European and US firms[75] (DeLong, Smith, and Walter 1996; UNCTAD 1998).

At the same time, there has been some reluctance by national administrations to allow foreign-owned firms to participate in domestic R&D consortia—and particularly those publicly funded. Examples include the outlawing or limited participation of foreign-owned firms in SEMATECH—a US consortium of semiconductor firms; and, indeed, the somewhat ethnocentric attitude of successive US governments to the ownership of innovatory activities undertaken in the US.[76] By contrast, the European authorities take a more relaxed attitude to the foreign membership of such consortia, as, indeed, does the Japanese government.

The social benefits of inbound asset-augmenting investment deserve further study; and particularly, at a regional level, of the distribution of its benefits between the parent companies (and countries) of the foreign affiliates and the microregions in which the latter are located. Case studies of the consequences of such FDI, which is deliberately designed to acquire intellectual capital from the host locations, are sorely needed. In particular, is the price paid by the foreign investor for such capital, compared with that which might have been paid by a domestic firm, sufficient to compensate for any 'leakages' of proprietary knowledge to the investing country? Do the foreign firms bring other benefits to the microregion; or, should one not be concerned with the issue at all—particularly where host regions to FDI are also home regions to outbound MNEs—and let the market make the appropriate decisions?

7. Some Managerial Implications

The final section of this chapter will identify some of the possible implications of recent economic events for managers of MNEs apropos of their location decisions. The first point we would emphasize is that making the right location choice for a particular FDI, and attaining the right portfolio of locations for all FDIs by a particular firm can, itself, be an important competitive advantage. Moreover, as firms become more multinational, as firm-specific assets become more mobile, and as the options for locating most kinds of FDI widen, so, achieving the optimum mix of locations for the harnessing and deployment of geographically dispersed resources and capabilities, for the procurement of inputs, and for the supplying of their products to end markets, is becoming more critical.

At the same time, this issue has been largely ignored in the managerial literature. My guess is that for every fifty treatises, monographs, and papers published on the strategic management of resources and capabilities, and the appropriate entry mode into foreign markets, there has been only one on the impact of locational choice on firm-specific competitiveness. Maybe business scholars consider this outside their domain, and that locational decisions are taken only on purely economic grounds.[77] Yet even in the 1920s, it was being postulated that, in oligopolistic industries at least, one firm's locational choice was likely to be influenced not only by the existing location of other firms, but by how the latter might react to its own choice (Hotelling 1929). And certainly one of the central themes of the Multinational Enterprise Project led by Ray Vernon of Harvard in the 1960s[78] was 'why' and 'where' US, European, and Japanese businesses preferred to site their manufacturing business outside their home countries. In 1974, Vernon wrote a classic paper on the 'Location of Economic Activity' (Vernon 1974), in which he differentiated between the locational strategies of large asset-exploiting MNEs at different stages of their product cycles.[79] Though Vernon did not specifically couch his analysis in terms of the locational competitiveness of the investing firms, this, in fact, was his main interest.

For much of the last thirty years, academic interest in the geography of economic activity has been mainly confined to economists and economic geographers. While some of the earlier oligopolistic type models have been extended and refined,[80] they still do not address head-on the locational issues of critical concern to scholars of business strategy. In the last decade or so, however, three new research thrusts have emerged. The first is the influential work of Paul Krugman (1991, 1993, 1995) on the determinants of the geographical concentration of economic activity. The second is the extension of Michael Porter's earlier studies (Porter 1985, 1990) on the competitive advantage of firms to embrace a spatial dimension (Porter 1994, 1996, 2000). The third is the growing attention being given by MNEs to the dynamic interaction between the competitive (or ownership-specific) advantages of firms and the competitive (or locational) advantages of countries, particularly in respect of asset-augmenting FDI (Gray 1996; UNCTAD 1996; Dunning 1997a, 2000); and also the acknowledgement by some scholars (e.g. Oliver 1997) that the resource-based theory of the firm might be usefully widened to incorporate variables external to firms, and, in particular, the local institutional environment in which they operate.

We have already suggested that one of the unique competitive advantages of the large MNE in a knowledge-based, globalizing economy is its ability to identify, access, harness, and effectively coordinate and deploy resources and capabilities from throughout the world. This must surely include an explicit and appropriate locational strategy. Such a strategy should embrace not only all the activities of the MNE, but also those of its competitors, suppliers, and customers, over which it has some influence and/or control. On the one hand, decisions about the acquisition and use of technology, those about the cross-border sourcing of inputs, the siting of R&D and production, and the servicing of global markets, are becoming increasingly complex. On the other, as the product and production strategies of MNEs in any particular industrial sector are tending to converge,[81] their locational choices could become more critical to their overall competitive advantages. And this applies no less to their search for the right microregion(s) in which to site their investments as to their search for the right country (ies).

8. Conclusions

In this introductory chapter, we have sought to describe and analyse the impact which recent economic events have had on the location of value-added activities, and particularly on those of MNEs. More specifically, we have focused attention on the centrifugal forces making for the macroregionalization and globalization of FDI and interfirm alliances, and on the centripetal forces making for a more concentrated geographical pattern. We have also distinguished between those value-added activities embodying largely location-bound resources and capabilities and those embodying mobile resources and capabilities.

The chapter has also identified the differences between the kind of international division of labour fostered by multidomestic MNEs and globally (or regionally) integrated MNEs; and how each, and the growing significance of microspecific agglomerative economies, is affecting the intranational, as well as the cross-border, allocation of innovatory and productive activities.

In our analysis of these issues, we distinguished between the asset-augmenting and asset-exploiting motives for MNE-related activities, and their different locational needs. In particular, we discussed the notion of distance-related transaction costs; and argued that, in the contemporary knowledge-based economy, dynamic transaction costs, e.g. those to do with learning and the coordination of innovation-related tasks, were at least as, if not more, important in influencing locational decisions as were their static counterparts. This led on to an examination of the drawing power of clusters of related firms in microregions, and how MNEs have both responded to, and influenced, the form of these clusters. Empirical evidence suggests that, whereas in the case of asset-exploiting FDI, MNEs are most active in clusters involving below average knowledge-intensive activities, in the case of asset-augmenting FDI they are increasingly gravitating to above average knowledge-intensive activities.[82]

One of the key conclusions of this chapter is that a carefully planned and executed locational strategy of MNEs is becoming an increasingly important factor influencing their global competitiveness. Such a strategy essentially comprises the siting of firm-specific, but mobile intangible assets, in countries and/or microregions which offer the most congenial complementary immobile assets. This conclusion applies equally to asset-seeking and to asset-exploiting FDI. Since, too, the distance costs of the more idiosyncratic knowledge-intensive transactions are probably increasing—as are the number and complexity of these transactions—the advantages of the spatial clustering of related activity increase—and this is in spite of the huge advances in telecommunications and distance-learning facilities.

A second critical conclusion of the chapter is that the growing mobility of firm-specific core competencies is placing increasing responsibility on microregional authorities to ensure the availability and quality of location-bound complementary assets to attract the right kind of mobile investment. Moreover, as we have said, such a competitive advantage depends not only on the regional provision of general supportive assets (e.g. basic infrastructure), but on the identification and promotion of a set of the specific and unique advantages which cannot be easily imitated by other regions. These latter advantages—and the policies of microregional authorities necessary to secure and augment them—may well include the promotion of distinctive clusters of related activities which, as Section 5 has shown, may be of very varied forms.

This chapter has also identified various lacunae in our scholarly knowledge about the ways in which MNEs might affect the economic prosperity of host microregions—particularly where the objective of the former is to protect or add to their asset base. The changing relationship between microregional, national, and supranational governmental regimes, as each affects both the competitiveness of microregions and the behaviour of MNEs investing, or likely to invest, in those regions, is also an under-researched area. More attention, too, needs to be given by students of business strategy to the significance of locational choice as a competitive advantage of firms, and how it may impact on their resource base, learning capabilities, values, and entrepreneurial behaviour.

Finally, if it is true that microregions are increasingly becoming one of the leading motors of economic development (Scott 1998), and the gateways of countries to the global market place (Ohmae 1995), does it not make sense to view the MNE, not only as one of the critical channels for organizing cross-border asset-seeking and asset-exploiting activities not only between different nation states, but also between microregions within different nation states? Is it, indeed, not the case that the economic linkages between Silicon Valley in California and Silicon Glen in mid-Scotland, or between the New York and London financial districts, are at least as significant as those between the UK and the USA as factors determining the international location of economic activity, and patterns of cross-border trade?

NOTES

The author is grateful to H. Peter Gray for his comments on an earlier draft of this chapter.

1. Defined as enterprises which own or control foreign-owned value-added activities, and which internalize cross-border intermediate product markets.
2. Such as a variety of non-equity cooperative agreements, e.g. strategic alliances, licensing, franchising, subcontracting, turnkey agreements, and so on.
3. By asset-augmenting activities we mean those directed to increasing the existing stock of resources and capabilities within the domain of firms or countries; by asset-exploiting activities we mean those directed to utilizing existing assets in order to produce added value from them.
4. See e.g. some recent papers by Michael Porter (1994, 1996, 2000) on this subject.
5. Throughout this volume, we will define macroregions as a grouping of nation states located in geographically bounded but proximate space. A classification of a macroregion may vary according to the purposes of that classification. Examples of macroregions include the European Union (EU), the North American Free Trade Agreement (NAFTA), MERCOSUR, APEC, and ASEAN. By contrast, we shall use the term microregions to embrace subnational spatial units. These units may be large, e.g. states within the USA; or very small, e.g. cities, industrial estates, and science parks.
6. We use this expression to embrace all activities, both asset augmenting and asset exploiting, which create a future income stream.
7. A clear exception must be made of craftsmanship, which dates back to the Middle Ages and beyond.
8. This is a generic expression embracing all kinds of knowledge and competition embodied in both human, physical, and organizational capital. For further details, see Edvinson (1997).
9. Chemicals and pharmaceuticals, machinery and electrical equipment, computers and office equipment, industrial and scientific instruments.
10. In 1995, on average, services (excluding those part of primary or secondary production) accounted for 63 per cent of the world's GNP compared with 53 per cent in 1980 and 45 per cent in 1965). For further details see World Bank (1997), tables 11 and 12.
11. The knowledge content of a firm may be likened to a completed jigsaw puzzle. The central pieces represent its core competencies, which are usually created by itself. However, to obtain the complete picture, these pieces need to be locked into others. These, while representing the resources and capabilities of other firms, have to be shaped so as to fit into the central pieces.
12. Sometimes referred to as 'relational', 'collective', 'collaborative and associational', and 'stakeholder' capitalism. For a review of these and similar concepts, see Dunning (1997a) and Cooke and Morgan (1998).

13. Cooke and Morgan (1998), for example, distinguish between the principal–agent and trustee models of corporate governance; between hierarchical (M form) and heterarchical (N form) modes of organization; between stand-alone, or linear, and integrated approaches to innovation; between coercive and participatory forms of work organization; and between adversarial and collaborative supply chain relationships.

14. Estimates of alliances vary considerably. A recent study by Booz, Allen, and Hamilton has put the number of all cross-border alliances and M&As in 1995 and 1996 as high as 15,000 (Booz, Allen, and Hamilton 1997). Another estimate by Hagedoorn (1996) is that between 1980 and 1994 the number of newly established cross-border technology alliances (which are mainly directed at asset-augmenting activities) rose by over three times. Finally, the value of international M&As between 1991 and 1997 has increased by four times, and accounted for around three-fifths of all FDI flows over the same period (UNCTAD 1998).

15. Between 1920 and 1970 average ocean freight and port charges (per short ton of cargo) fell from $25 to $5; the average air transport costs per passenger mile fell from $0.68 to $0.11; while the cost of a three-minute telephone call from New York to London fell from $244.7 to $3.3 (Hufbauer 1991).

16. E.g. between 1980 and 1996 the combined exports and imports as a percentage of GNP × 2 of the USA rose from 9.1 to 12.0 per cent. Corresponding figures for the UK were 22.5 and 29.6 per cent; for Germany 23.2 and 22.2 per cent; for Korea 34.2 and 34.4 per cent; and for Venezuela 25.5 and 29.0 per cent. The relevant figures for FDI stock as a percent of GNP were 5.8 and 9.4 per cent for the USA, 13.6 and 25.6 per cent for the UK, 5.5 and 9.2 per cent for Germany, 1.0 and 2.7 per cent for Korea, and for Venezuela 1.3 and 9.1 per cent (IMD 1998).

17. For further details, see United Nations (1998).

18. Averaged over the years 1979 and 1994–6.

19. To give just one example, in 1996, of the worldwide research and development expenditure of around $580 billion, 91 per cent was concentrated in the advanced industrial countries. (Author's estimate, calculated from data contained in IMD 1998: table 7.01.)

20. Some evidence for this assertion in respect of changes in the location of economic activity in the European Community consequential upon the completion of the internal market is given in Dunning (1997b). In a more recent paper, Cantwell and Iammarino (1998) have shown that between 1969 and 1995 some 60.8 per cent of the R&D activities by foreign-owned firms in the UK was concentrated in the south-east of England, compared with 41.7 per cent for all large firms.

21. NB usually, but not always, those of its individual value-adding units.

22. Overall, between 1985 and 1997 the value of cross-border M&As, as a proportion to FDI flows, averaged 55 per cent, while between the early 1980s and 1996 the number of interfirm technology agreements increased by 2 to 3 times (UNCTAD 1998: 19 and 23).

23. The share of new FDI directed to developing countries rose from 19.6 per cent in 1983–8 to 29.6 per cent in 1989–94 (UNCTAD 1995).

24. Thus, in 1995 it was estimated that 75 per cent of the foreign direct investment stock in China was from other Asian countries.

25. In 1993, 11.7 per cent of the sales of US foreign affiliates was in services (other than trade) and 7.9 per cent in finance and business services. The corresponding figures for 1982 were 8.1 and 4.4 per cent (US Dept of Commerce 1985, 1995).

26. US Department of Commerce data reveal that, in 1994, some R&D performed by US foreign affiliates amounted to 13.0 per cent of that of their parent companies. This figure corresponds to the percentage in 1982 which was 7 per cent and in 1989 9 per cent (US Department of Commerce 1985, 1998; Dunning 1993).
27. Further details are set out in various articles and books. See esp. Granstrand. Hakanson, and Sjolander (1992), OECD (1997*a* and *b*), Archibugi and Iammarino (1998), and Cantwell and Harding (1998).
28. E.g. the share of patents registered in the home countries of OECD member states accounted for by non-resident firms doubled between 1984 and 1994, as did the share of patents registered abroad by firms from those countries.
29. Initially by Adam Smith (1776) and Alfred Marshall (1920) and then by most economic geographers and spatial economists.
30. For a review of some of these see Audretsch (1998) and other papers contained in a special issue of the *Oxford Review of Economic Policy* 14(2), Summer 1998.
31. As acknowledged and explored by James Markusen in his various writings. See esp. Markusen (1995).
32. For a summary of the main factors which facilitate intranational and intraregional agglomeration see Ottavinano and Puga 1997). For an analysis of why spatial clustering is more likely to occur *within* countries rather than *between* countries see Davis and Weinstein (1997).
33. Thus e.g. Silicon Valley in California, as well as competing with some other (but not all) regions in the USA for mobile knowledge-intensive investment, may also compete with, e.g. Silicon glen in Scotland and similar microregional complexes in Japan, Germany, and Italy. The main competitor to the Sheffield cutlery industry is not another UK region, but Solingen in Germany. For other examples see Enright (2000).
34. Such research as has been conducted (see e.g. Baptista and Swann (1994) suggests that firms which are located in strong clusters in the UK are more likely to innovate than those in other regions.
35. However, a recent study on interfirm alliances in the US semiconductor industry suggests that the 'optimum' spatial area associated with such economies may be larger than is commonly supposed (Arita and McCann 1998).
36. As documented in some detail by Dunning and Morgan (1971).
37. Notably, the access to a pool of flexible skilled labour, common support services and availability of non-tradable specialized inputs, the capturing of information spillovers, a more competitive and/or entrepreneurial environment, and a common set of shared values and ideologies.
38. According to Giersch, as the economic variables affecting production costs in different countries converge, so the non-economic variables affecting transaction costs become a more significant determinant of locational competition. Such variables include the ethics of property and contracts, attitudes to technical progress, modes of corporate and individual behaviour, economic and civic morality, and cultural assets.
39. As described by Michael Porter (1986). In practice, however, most large modern MNEs exhibit aspects of each of these structures.
40. See e.g. Dunning (1958) (repr. with a statistical update 1998), Hill and Munday (1992), Mariotti and Piscitello (1995), and Cantwell and Iammarino (1998). See also the chapter by Wallace in this volume and references cited at the end of that chapter.

41. Thus in the UK e.g. the proportion of post-World War II FDI located in areas of above average unemployment or below average rates of growth has been considerably higher than that of indigenous firms (Dunning 1958 (1998)).
42. Notably those of Srinivasan and Mody (1996), and Braunerhjelm and Svensson (1995).
43. A recent example is the 'follow-my-leader' strategy of Japanese MNEs in the consumer electronics industry in South Wales. Since Sony first invested in a Newport factory, several other Japanese companies have located in the same area.
44. An example in the pharmaceutical industry to undertake R&D on tropical medicines in the tropical countries and advanced biotechnology in the Triad countries.
45. As in the case of much of Japanese FDI in the European pharmaceutical sector, an internationally oriented sector in which currently Japanese firms have a competitive *dis*advantage.
46. This is not to deny there may be restrictions placed on foreign-owned firms from accessing some kinds of capital. This point is taken up further in Sect. 6.
47. For a recent catalogue of some of these see Enright (2000).
48. Note that not all of these clusters are based on semi-skilled labour; e.g. the comparative advantage of Bangalore computer software complex is based on the created availability of highly skilled and professional labour.
49. E.g. by encouraging 'follow my leader' tactics by other firms (Knickerbocker 1973). In his study of the interstate distribution of FDI in the USA, Miles Shaver (1996) showed that this was positively correlated to their separate agglomeration measures.
50. However, there are other clusters which have developed without the presence of MNEs. The City of London financial district, the North Italian woollen textile industry, and even (initially at least) the electronics industry, Silicon Valley are all cases in point.
51. In a recent paper, Enright (2000) gives several examples of foreign firms being drawn into spatial clusters by the presence of knowledge-enhancing facilities. Nissan, he observes, does a substantial part of its new design work in Southern California, a leading centre of auto design. Several European chemical and pharmaceutical companies do the bulk of their biotechnology research in biotechnology clusters in the USA. The established financial centres of London, New York, and Tokyo, far from losing their competitive advantage in high-value activities, seem to be consolidating this advantage. At the same time, banking and financial MNEs are being increasingly drawn to new financial clusters in Hong Kong and Singapore.
52. For some evidence of the increasing role played by the subsidiaries of MNEs in innovatory activities see Pearce (1995) and Pearce and Papanastassiou (1995). In this latter paper, the authors also point to the role played by supportive institutions in the UK, e.g. universities, scientific institutions, etc., in influencing the amount and character of R&D undertaken by foreign affiliates in that country.
53. There is widespread support for this statement. For a summary of the literature see Dunning (1996, 2000) and Makino (1998). Both papers also offer an interpretation of the theory of asset-seeking investment.
54. e.g. where in 1993, 68.4 per cent of the Japanese-owned R&D laboratories were concentrated in four US states, viz. California, Michigan, New Jersey, and Massachusetts, only 32.8 per cent of Japanese-owned manufacturing establishments were so located (Florida and Kenney 1994). In the UK, between 1969 and 1995 60.8 per cent of patents registered by the subsidiaries of foreign firms, were attributable to research undertaken in London and south-east England (Cantwell and Iammarino 1998). In Italy,

over the same period, 67.2 per cent of patents registered by such firms were attributable to research undertaken in two districts—Piedmonte and Lombardia (Cantwell and Iammarino 1998).

55. In his paper, Scott shows that the growth of the value added in manufacturing in the 40 metropolitan areas in the USA with more than one million people was 30.6 per cent between 1972 and 1992 (after discounting for inflation)—well above the national average of 20.3 per cent. However, he also shows that the fastest rate of growth (81.5 per cent) occurred in the 'sunbelt' group of metropolitan areas, which not only did not have the industrial heritage of the other, e.g. areas in the North-East, but made a focused effort to build their economies on knowledge- and information-intensive manufacturing and service activities.

56. Clearly this varies between countries and according to the respective investment opportunities offered by home and foreign countries. Over the last decade or so e.g. the proportion of the sales of the foreign affiliates of US corporations has remained around 30 per cent; but in the case of several European countries, e.g. UK and Germany and most Asian countries (especially Japan) it has markedly increased (UNCTAD 1997, 1998).

57. The spread of MNEs into more countries is particularly noticeable in the service sectors.

58. For a more detailed examination of this theme see Enright (2000).

59. See especially Caves (1996) and Dunning (1997a).

60. One recent exception is that of Wallace (1998), who has recently completed a Ph.D. dissertation on FDI in New Jersey.

61. We recognize, of course, there are many layers of microregional governance, e.g. from states, to countries, to districts, to cities, to business *et al.* parks.

62. This is not to deny there may be some 'X' inefficiencies in the actions of regional governments in providing these services, or in promoting a 'hassle free' business environment; or, indeed, of publicizing the benefits of the resources and capabilities within their jurisdiction to foreign investors as well, or aggressively, as they might. For a discussion of such policies pursued by US state governments see Donahue (1998).

63. For an examination of the importance of this kind of collaboration, and of the need for a reconstruction of some local institutions in the light of the increasing importance of mobile investment, see an interesting case study of the Korean MNE LG in South Wales (Phelps and Tewdwr-Jones 1998; Phelps, Lovering, and Morgan 1998).

64. Enright (2000) e.g. gives details of the specific needs of different kinds of clusters for complementary assets, some of which are under the governance of regional authorities. These include 'effluent treatment facilities for specific industries (Catalan leather), dedicated water (Malaysian electronics) or electricity lines (Venezuelan Metals) and specialized port (Hong Kong trading) or airfreight facilities (Dutch flowers), specific training programmes in software (Bangalore), motion pictures (Los Angeles), materials science (Sassuolo), wine-making (Napa Valley), and electronics (Singapore) among others'.

65. See e.g. a very interesting paper entitled 'Singapore Incorporated' by Haley, Low, and Toh (1996) and chs. 14 and 15 of this volume.

66. For a careful analysis of the role of institutional systems in minimizing the transaction costs of economic activity and maximizing the benefits of specialization and the agglomeration of related firms see Kasper and Streit (1998). Although the authors do not address the specific problems and challenges of microregional governments, much of what they write is directly relevant to them.

67. Michael Porter, in his 1990 book, argued that the main role of national governments was to do nothing which would prevent, retard, or distort cluster formation. In his latest thinking, Porter (1996, 2000) assigns a more positive role for microregional governments; and particularly that of promoting 'specialization, upgrading and trade among regions' (Porter 1996: 88). Porter goes on to assert that cluster formation can be encouraged by *specialized* infrastructure and institution in areas where factor endowments, past industrial activities, or even historical accidents have resulted in concentration of economic activity.

68. See Park (1996), Markusen (1996), and Markusen and Gray (1999).

69. For a detailed analysis of the Seattle hub-and-spoke district see Gray, Golob, and Markusen (1996). In his review of clusters, Park (1996) distinguishes between supplier and customer, and advanced supplier and advanced customer hub and spoke clusters.

70. And, indeed, before that by Adam Smith (1776) as recently highlighted by Ozawa (2000).

71. And documented by Hall *et al.* (1987).

72. As documented by Diniz and Razavi (1997).

73. As viewed from the perception of the microregion.

74. See Dunning (1970) for a discussion of the social and private price of domestic assets acquired by foreign firms.

75. Between 1990 and 1997 the combined foreign acquisitions by European and US firms amounted to $1,134 billion, while the foreign purchases of European and US firms totalled $957 billion (UNCTAD 1998).

76. The relationship between US technology policy and the competitiveness of US firms and inbound foreign direct investment is explored by Ham and Mowery (1997).

77. Sometimes as modified by the personal preferences or prejudices of the main decision taker(s)!

78. Most particular as explored by Knickerbocker (1973) in his 'follow my leader' hypothesis and Graham (1978) in his exchange of threats hypothesis.

79. Most noticeably from the innovatory through the mature to the senescent stage.

80. See e.g. Graham (1990) and Cantwell and Sanna Randaccio (1992).

81. Although we accept that firms might continue to differentiate their products from those supplied by their competitors—and, indeed, to do so even more intensively than in the past.

82. See an interesting paper by Birkinshaw and Hood (1997) which distinguishes between two kinds of clusters, viz. 'leading edge' cluster, e.g. Silicon Valley, and a 'branch plant' cluster, e.g. Scotland's electronics industry. They conclude that, historically, FDI has tended to be concentrated and has had the most influence on structure and development of the latter kind of cluster. They accept, however, that the advent of the globalizing economy may lead to more FDI in the leading edge clusters.

REFERENCES

Archibugi, D., and Iammarino, S. (1998), *Innovation and Globalization, Evidence and Implications*, Discussion Papers in International Investment and Business, March (Reading: University of Reading).

Arita, T., and McCann, P. (1998), *Industrial Alliances and Firm Location Behavior: Some Evidence From the US Semiconductor Industry*, Discussion Papers in Urban and Regional Economies, 130, March (Reading: University of Reading).

Audretsch, D. B. (1998), 'Agglomeration and the Location of Economic Activity', *Oxford Review of Economic Policy* 14(2): 18–29.

Baptista, R., and Swann, D. (1994), *Do Firms in Clusters Innovate More? An Exploratory Study* (London: London Business School), mimeo.

Birkinshaw, J., and Hood, N. (1997), *Foreign Investment and Industry Cluster Development: The Characteristics of Subsidiary Companies in Different Types of National Industry Clusters* (Stockholm School of Economics and Strathclyde University), mimeo.

Booz, Allen, and Hamilton (1997), *Cross Border Alliances in the Age of Collaboration* (Los Angeles: Booz Allen and Hamilton).

Braunerhjelm, P., and Svensson, R. (1995), *Host Country Characteristics and Agglomeration in Foreign Direct Investment* (Stockholm: Industrial Institute for Economic and Social Research), mimeo.

Cantwell, J. A., and Harding, R. (1998), 'The Internationalization of German Companies R&D', *National Institute Economic Review* 16(3): 99–115.

—— and Iammarino, S. (1998), *Multinational Corporations and the Location of Technological Innovation in the UK Regions*, Discussion Papers in International Investment and Management, 262 (Reading: University of Reading).

—— and Sanna Randaccio, F. (1992), 'Intra-Industry Direct Investment in the European Community', in J. C. Cantwell (ed.), *Multinational Investment in Modern Europe: Strategic Interaction in the Integrated Community* (Aldershot (Hants) and Brookfield (Vermont): Edward Elgar).

Caves, R. (1996), *Multinational Firms and Economic Analysis*, 2nd edn. (Cambridge: Cambridge University Press).

Cooke, P., and Morgan, K. (1998), *The Associational Economy* (Oxford: Oxford University Press).

Davis, D. R., and Weinstein, E. (1997), *Economic Geography and Regional Production Structure: An Empirical Investigation* (Cambridge, Mass.: NBER Working Paper, 6093).

DeLong, G., Smith, R. C., and Walter, I. (1996), *Global Merger and Acquisition Tables 1995* (New York: Salomon Center), mimeo.

Diniz, C. C., and Razavi, M. (1997), 'State Anchored Dynamos: São José Dos Campos and Campinos, Brazil', in A. Markusen and Yong Sook Lee, *Second Tier Cities: Explaining Rapid Growth in Brazil, Korea, Japan and the United States*.

Donahue, J. D. (1998), *Disunited States* (New York: Basic Books).

Doremus, P., Keller, W. W., Pauly, L. W., and Reich, S. (1998), *The Myth of the Global Corporation* (Princeton: Princeton University Press).

Doz, Y. L., Asakawa, K., Santos, J. F. P., and Williamson, P. J. (1998), *The Metanational Corporation* (Fontainebleau, France: INSEAD Working Paper 97/60/SM).

Dunning, J. H. (1958, 1998), *American Investment in British Manufacturing Industry* (London: Allen & Unwin; 1998 edn. published by Routledge, London and New York).

—— (1970), *Studies in International Investment* (London: Allen & Unwin).

—— (1993), *Multinational Enterprises and the Global Economy* (Wokingham, England and Reading, Mass.: Addison-Wesley).

—— (1996), 'The Geographical Sources of Competitiveness of Firms: The Results of a New Survey', *Transnational Corporations* 5(3): 1–30.

—— (1997*a*), *Alliance Capitalism and Global Business* (London and New York: Routledge).

—— (1997*b*), 'The European Internal Market Program and Inbound Foreign Direct Investment', *Journal of Common Market Studies*, 35 (1 and 2): 1–30 and 189–223.

—— (1998), 'The Changing Geography of Foreign Direct Investment', in K. Kumar (ed.), *Internationalization, Foreign Direct Investment and Technology Transfer: Impact and Prospects for Developing Countries* (London and New York: Routledge).

—— (2000), 'Globalization and the Theory of MNE Activity', in N. Hood and S. Young (eds.), *The Globalization of Multinational Enterprise Activity and Economic Development* (Basingstoke: Macmillan).

—— and Morgan, E. V. (eds.) (1971), *An Economic Study of the City of London* (London: Allen & Unwin).

—— and Narula, R. (eds.) (1996), *Foreign Direct Investment and Governments* (London and New York: Routledge).

Edvinson, L. (1997), *Intellectual Capital Development* (Stockholm: Skandia).

Enright, M. J. (2000), 'The Globalization of Competition and the Localization of Competitive Advantage: Policies toward Regional Clustering', in N. Hood and S. Young (eds.), *The Globalization of Multinational Enterprise Activity and Economic Development* (Basingstoke: Macmillan), 303–31.

Feldman, M. P., and Audretsch, D. (1999), 'Innovation in Cities: Science-Based Diversity, Specialization and Localized Competition', *European Economic Review* (forthcoming).

Florida, R. (1995), 'Towards the Learning Region', *Futures* 27(5): 527–36.

—— and Kenney, M. (1994), 'The Globalization of Japanese R&D: The Economic Geography of Japanese R&D Investment in the United States', *Economic Geography* 70: 343–69.

Giersch, H. (1996), 'Economic Morality as a Competitive Asset', in A. Hamlin, H. Giersch, and A. Norton, *Markets, Morals and Community* (St Leonards, Australia: Center for Independent Studies Occasional Paper 59).

Graham, E. M. (1978), 'Transatlantic Investment by Multinational Firms: A Rivalistic Phenomenon', *Journal of Post Keynesian Economics* 1: 82–99.

—— (1990), 'Exchange of Threats between Multinational Firms as an Infinitely Repeated Non-cooperative Game', *International Trade Journal* 4(3): 259–77.

Granstrand, O., Hakanson, L., and Sjolander, S. (eds.) (1992), *Technology, Management and International Business: Internationalization of R&D and Technology* (Chichester: Wiley).

Gray, H. P. (1996), 'The Eclectic Paradigm: The Next Generation', *Transnational Corporations* 5(2): 51–66.

Gray, M., Golob, E., and Markusen, A. (1996), 'Big Firms, Long Arms, a Portrait of a "Hub and Spoke" industrial district in the Seattle region', *Regional Studies* 30(7): 651–66.

Hagedoorn, J. (1996), 'Trends and Patterns in Strategic Technology Partnering Since the Early Seventies', *Review of Industrial Organization* 11: 601–16.

Haley, U. C. V., Low, L., and Toh, Mun-Heng (1996), 'Singapore Incorporated: Reinterpreting Singapore's Business Environments through a Corporate Metaphor', *Management Decision* 34(9): 17–28.

Hall, P., Breheny, M., McQuaid, R., and Hart, D. (1987), *Western Sunrise* (London and Boston: Allen & Unwin).

Ham, R., and Mowery, D. (1997), 'The United States', in J. H. Dunning (ed.), *Governments, Globalization and International Business* (Oxford: Oxford University Press): 283–321.

Handy, C. (1990), *The Age of Unreason* (London: Hutchinson).

Harrison, B. (1992), 'Industrial Districts: Old Wine in New Bottles', *Regional Studies* 26(5): 469–83.

Hill, S., and Munday, M. (1992), 'The UK Regional Distribution of Foreign Direct Investment: Analysis and Determinants', *Regional Studies* 26: 534–44.

Hotelling, H. (1929), 'Stability in Competition', *Economic Journal* 29: 41–57.

Hufbauer, G. (1991), 'World Economic Integration: The Long View', *Economic Insights* 30: 26–7.

IMD (1998), *The World Competitive Yearbook 1998* (Lausanne: IMD).

IMF (v.d.), *Balance of Payments Statistical Yearbook* (annual publication) (Washington: IMF).

Kasper, W., and Streit, M. (1998), *Institutional Economics, Social Order and Public Policy* (Cheltenham: Edward Elgar).

Knickerbocker, F. T. (1973), *Oligopolistic Reaction and the Multinational Enterprise* (Cambridge, Mass., Harvard University Press).

Kozul-Wright, R. (1997), 'The Size of Nations: Small Economies in a Globalizing World', *Development and International Cooperation* 13 (24 and 15): 105–38.

Krugman, P. R. (1991), *Geography and Trade* (Cambridge, Mass.: MIT Press).

—— (1993), 'On the Relationship between Trade Theory and Location Theory', *Review of International Economics* 1(2): 110–22.

—— (1995), *Development, Geography and Economic Theory* (Cambridge Mass.: MIT Press).

Kuemmerle, W. (1996), *The Drivers of Foreign Direct Investment into Research and Development: An Empirical Investigation* (Boston: Harvard Business School Working Paper 96: 062).

Liu, S. X. (1998), *Foreign Direct Investment and the Multinational Enterprise. A Reexamination Using Signaling Theory* (Westport, Conn.: Greenwood Publishing).

McGrew, A. G. (1992), 'Conceptualizing Global Politics', in A. G. McGrew and P. G. Lewis (eds.), *Global Politics: Globalization and the Nation State* (Cambridge: The Polity Press).

McIntyre, J. R., Narula, R., and Trevino, L. J. (1996), 'The Role of Export-Processing Zones for Host Countries and Multinationals: A Mutually Beneficial Relationship?', *International Trade Journal* 10, 435–66.

Makino, S. (1998), *Toward a Theory of Asset Seeking Foreign Direct Investment* (Hong Kong: Chinese University), mimeo.

Mariotti, S., and Piscitello, L. (1995), 'Information Costs and Location of FDIs within the Host Country: Empirical Evidence from Italy', *Journal of International Business Studies* 26(4): 815–41.

Markusen, A. (1996), 'Sticky Places in Slippery Space: A Typology of Industrial Districts', *Economic Geography* 72(3): 293–313.

—— and Gray, M. (1999), 'Clusters and Regional Development in New Jersey', in J. H. Dunning (ed.), *New Jersey in a Globalizing Economy* (Newark: Rutgers University, CIBER).

Markusen, J. R. (1995), 'The Boundaries of Multinational Enterprises and the Theory of International Trade', *Journal of Economic Perspectives* 9(2): 169–89.

Marshall, A. (1920), *Principles of Economics*, 8th edn. (London: Macmillan).

Mytelka, L. K. (1996), *Locational Tournaments, Strategic Partnerships and the State* (Ottawa: Carleton University), mimeo.

Narula, R. (1995), *Multinational Investment and Economic Structure* (London and Boston: Routledge).

National Science Foundation (1997), *Patenting Activity in the US* (Washington: National Science Foundation).

O'Brien, R. (1992), *Global Financial Integration: The End of Geography* (London: Pinter Publishers).

OECD (1996), *Networking Enterprises, Local Development* (Paris: OECD).

—— (1997*a*), *Science and Technology Indicators* (Paris: OECD).

—— (1997*b*), *Internationalization of Industrial R&D: Patterns and Trends* (Paris: Group of National Experts on Science and Technology Indicators, OECD).

Ohmae, K. (1995), *The End of the Nation State: The Rise of Regional Economies* (London: HarperCollins).

Oliver, C. (1997), 'Sustainable Competitive Advantage: Combining Institutional and Resource-Based Views', *Strategic Management Journal* 18(9): 697–713.

Ottavinano, G., and Puga, D. (1997), *Agglomeration in the Global Economy: A Survey of the New Economic Geography* (London Centre for Economic Performance, Discussion Paper 356).

Ozawa, T. (2000). 'Small- and Medium-Sized MNCs, Industrial Clusters and Globalization: The Japanese Experience', in N. Hood and S. Young (eds.), *The Globalization of Multinational Enterprise Activity and Economic Development* (Basingstoke: Macmillan), 225–50.

Park, S. O. (1996), 'Networks and Embeddedness in the Dynamic Types of Industrial Districts', *Progress in Human Geography* 20(4): 476–93.

Pearce, R. D. (1995), *Creative Subsidiaries and the Evolution of Technology in Multinational Enterprises*, Discussion Papers in International Investment and Business Studies 194 (Reading: University of Reading).

—— and Papanastassiou, M. (1995), *R&D Networks and Innovation: Decentralized Product Development in Multinational Enterprises*, Discussion Papers in International Investment and Business Studies 204 (Reading: University of Reading).

Peck, F. W. (1996), 'Regional Development and the Production of Space: The Role of Infrastructure in the Attraction of New Inward Investment', *Environment and Planning* 28: 327–39.

Perraton, J., Goldblatt, D., Held, D., and McGrew, A. (1997), 'The Globalization of Economic Activity', *New Political Economy* 2(2): 257–77.

Phelps, N. A., Lovering, J., and Morgan, K. (1998), 'Tying the Firm to the Region or Tying the Region to the Firm?', *European Urban and Regional Studies* 5(2): 119–37.

—— and Tewdwr-Jones, M. (1998), 'Institutional Capacity Building in a Strategic Vacuum: The Case of the Korean Company LG in South Wales', *Environment and Planning C: Government and Policy* 16: 735–55.

Porter, M. E. (1985), *Competitive Advantage* (New York: Free Press).

—— (ed.) (1986), *Competition in Global Industries* (Boston: Harvard Business School Press).

—— (1990), *The Competitive Advantage of Nations* (New York: Free Press).

—— (1994), 'The Role of Location in Competition', *Journal of Economics of Business* I(1): 35–9.

—— (1996), 'Competitive Advantage, Agglomerative Economics and Regional Policy', *International Regional Science Review* 19(1 and 2): 85–94.

Porter, M. E. (2000), 'Location, Clusters and Company Strategy', in G. L. Clark, M. S. Gertler, and M. P. Feldman (eds.), *The Oxford Handbook of Economic Geography* (Oxford: Oxford University Press), 253–74.

Putman, R. D. (1993), *Making Democracy Work: Civic Traditions in Modern Italy* (Princeton: Princeton University Press).

Schoenberger, E. (1988), 'Multinational Corporations and the New International Division of Labor: A Critical Appraisal', *International Regional Science Review* 11(2): 105–19.

Scott, A. (1998), *Regional Motors of the Global Economy*, CIBER Distinguished Lecture Series 1 (Newark: Rutgers University).

Shaver, J. M. (1996), *Industry Agglomeration an Foreign Greenfield Investment Survival in the United States* (New York: Stern School of Business), mimeo.

Smith, A. (1776), *An Inquiry into the Nature and Causes of the Wealth of Nations* (London, repr. in E. Cannon (ed.), New York, 1937).

Solvell, O., and Bengtsson, M. (1997), *The Role of Industry Structure Climate of Competition and Cluster Strength* (Stockholm Institute of International Business, Stockholm School of Economics), mimeo.

Srinivasan, K., and Mody, A. (1998), 'Japanese and US Firms as Foreign Investors. Do They March to the Same Tune?', *Canadian Journal of Economics* 31(4): 778–99.

Stewart, T. A. (1997), *Intellectual Capital* (London: Nicholas Bradley).

Stigler, G. (1951), 'The Division of Labor is Limited by the Extent of the Market', *Journal of Political Economy* 59: 185–93.

Stopford, J., and Strange, S. (1991), *Rival States, Rival Firms: Competition for World Market Shares* (Cambridge: Cambridge University Press).

Storper, M. (1995), 'The Resurgence of Region Economies: Ten Years Later: The Region as a Nexus of Untraded Interdependencies', *European Urban and Regional Studies* 2(3): 191–221.

—— (1997), *The Regional World* (London: Guilford Press).

—— and Scott, A. J. (1995), 'The Wealth of Regions', *Futures* 27(5): 505–26.

Strange, R. (1993), *Japanese Manufacturing Investment in Europe* (London and New York: Routledge).

UN. (v.d.), *Annual Statistical Yearbook* (New York: UN).

UNCTAD (1993), *World Investment Report 1993, Transnational Corporations and Integrated International Production* (New York and Geneva: UN).

—— (1995), *World Investment Report 1995 Transnational Corporations and Competitiveness* (New York and Geneva: UN).

—— (1996), *Investment Incentives* (New York and Geneva: UN).

—— (1997), *World Investment Report 1997: Transnational Corporations, Market Structure and Competition Policy* (New York and Geneva: UN).

—— (1998), *World Investment Report 1998: Trends and Determinants* (New York and Geneva: UN).

UNDP (1997), *Human Development Report* (Oxford: Oxford University Press).

US Dept. of Commerce (1985), *US Direct Investment Abroad 1982 Benchmark Survey Data* (Washington: Government Printing Office).

—— (1998), *US Direct Investment Abroad 1994 Benchmark Survey Data* (Washington: Government Printing Office).

—— (1995), *US Direct Investment Abroad. Provisional Results 1993* (Washington: Government Printing Office).

US Patent and Trademark Office (1997), *Patenting Trends 1997* (Washington: US Patent and Trademark Office).

—— (1999), *Patent Counts by Country/State and Year* (Washington, DC: US Patent and Trademark Office).

Vernon, R. (1974), 'The Location of Economic Activity', in J. H. Dunning (ed.), *Economic Analysis and the Multinational Enterprise* (London: Allen & Unwin), 89–114.

Wallace, L. (1998), *Foreign Direct Investment and the New Jersey Economy*, Newark, NJ: Ph.D. thesis, Rutgers University, Faculty of Management.

World Bank (1997), *World Development Report* (Oxford: Oxford University Press).

—— (1998), *World Development Report* (Oxford: Oxford University Press).

Yannopoulos, G. N., and Dunning, J. H. (1976), 'MNEs and Regional Development: An Exploratory Paper', *Regional Studies* 10(5): 389–401.

2

Globalization and Knowledge Flows:
An Industrial Geographer's Perspective

Michael Storper

1. Location, Trade, and Knowledge

Geographers and economists view globalization through the 'mirror images' of location and trade. The analysis of trade asks to what extent the trade flows of goods or money are becoming more international than they are national or regional, and it assumes that such changes are due to changing location patterns of production or investment. We often try to derive changes in the patterns of location of economic activities from the analysis of trade and investment flows, and then to ask what this might mean about the degree of specialization of national or regional economies. In concert with information about ownership or foreign direct investment patterns, others try to determine whether the locus of control over competition or investment is changing.

This focus on 'direct' exchanges (in the sense of hard flows of goods and money) may miss the most important aspects of the process, however. The geographical origins, destinations, and mastery of economically useful knowledge have more profound impacts on the changing shape of development than do standard issues of location and specialization. Moreover, with an analysis of such knowledge flows, some of the predictions of location and trade theories about physical location, specialization, and the economic performance of regions and nations, can be called into question.

2. Standard Approaches to the Question of Globalization and Territory

Analyses of trade and their impacts on location can be viewed through a number of different location theories, and each tends to lead to different interpretations of similar sets of trade data by asking rather different questions of the data.

The first is standard comparative advantage theory, which holds that patterns of location, specialization, and trade will be driven by the geographical distribution of factors of production. Since Ricardo, this theory has been recognized, at one and the same time, for its utility and its limits. It helps us to understand the rough match between labour-intensive low-wage activities and labour-rich developing areas, especially in activities with low barriers to entry and few necessary relations of proximity with other activities. As an account of the geography of economic development, however, it falls quite short, especially when it comes to the most complex and most advanced economic areas. It ignores spatial interdependence or proximity relations between activities (i.e. forces for localization and clustering) or even straightforward economies of scale; and, it has no way to account for the build-up of humanly created factors in particular places (e.g. knowledge, skill, institutions), treating all such factors as exogenous.

A second theory of location is the modified neoclassical theory of the 'new geographical economics', or—as it is also known—the New Trade Theory, whose main exponents are Helpman and Krugman (1987). In place of the assumptions of constant returns to scale, divisibility, and hence perfect competition process of the standard theory, they introduce scale economies and imperfect competition over space. In the context of the current globalization process, where traditional locational constraints are declining (transportation and communications improvements; institutional barriers to trade falling; diffusion of capitalist economic practices and norms), the theory predicts a world of greater territorial economic specialization, as market territories for particular goods and services are defined increasingly by the optimal scale of production. These activities, in effect, create territorial 'shadows' or oligopoly effects around them; thus, a world of highly imperfect competition, but one which is also efficient, and where market contestability, though territorially uneven, is still strongly present.

The third line of attack on globalization might be defined better as a framework than a theory: it consists of a large body of work concentrating on the development of firms and production systems. It explores the general theme that the strategic, financial, and technological capacities of large firms have developed to the point that what goes on inside these firms or, alternatively, in networks of key firms and their principal partners and dependent contractors, has become at least as important as the classical relations between firms and territories (Harrison 1997; Dicken 1998).

Because this is a more empirical and hence more complex body of work, we need to spend a bit more time examining it here. We may begin with its opposite, which can be called 'localization' or, better, 'territorialization'. Territorialized economic development is something quite different from mere location or localization of economic activity. It consists, for our purposes, in economic activity that is dependent on territorially specific resources. These resources can range from asset specificities available only from a certain locale or, more importantly, assets that are available only in the context of certain interorganizational or firm-to-market relationships that necessarily require geographical proximity, or where relations of proximity are markedly more efficient than other ways of generating these asset specificities. An activity is fully territorialized when its economic viability is rooted in assets (including human practices and relations) that are not available in many other places and cannot easily or rapidly be created or imitated in places that lack them. Locational substitutability is not possible, and feasible locations are small in number, making locational 'markets' highly imperfect.

In contrast to this we might imagine a pure 'flow-substitution economy'. Resources would flow between parts of a firm, between places, without having any particular dependence on any particular place. Such assets—whether goods or information—would be producible in so many different places as to constitute a true (almost) perfect 'market' in locations for their production. It matters little whether they are actually produced at many locations; one could imagine the extreme case of global supply from a single place (due to scale economies, for example) but where that place has no specificities that render it immune to substitution by another place.

This sort of economy could be the result of two possible developmental processes. On one hand, activities that are well developed in a wide variety of places make certain kinds of resources which are necessary to production available in near ubiquity, but have historically been separated by transport barriers or differentiated tastes. Improvements in transportation, standardization of tastes, or increases in the optimal scale of production open up these locations to global business organizations, who then enjoy huge potential locational choice and ubiquitous markets, but are not bound by locational specificities or local interdependencies. On the other hand, such organizations may develop production processes that eliminate the need for locationally scarce specific assets: technological change via product standardization and routinization of production processes does the job. In both cases, a pure flow form of direct globalization becomes possible.

2.1. The Limited Extent of Direct Globalization: The Shape of Emerging Specializations

The three theories referred to above, notwithstanding their differences, have a shared vision of the essence of globalization. It consists of the direct, physical denationalization of input–output relations, through progressively more international location of production relative to markets. Each theory has a somewhat different prediction about the ultimate spatial shape of the economy and its trade and specialization patterns, but all predict greater overall territorial specialization. All three see this process of increasing direct globalization as driven by the loosening of technological and institutional constraints referred to earlier. The logical extension of all three theories is to hold that the current globalization process has no natural ending point. They extend the notion (hyperbolic, it must be said)[1] that in the past, regional economies ceded to national territories as loci of input–output relations, to claim that now this process is shifting from the national to the global scale. National economies as physical units will become progressively less and less relevant to economic life. The process of globalization which was evident at the beginning of this century will now continue its inevitable upward sweep.

These claims of the three dominant theories can be questioned, however. There are reasons to doubt that certain input–output relations will inevitably come to be carried out at global scale; hence, there are also reasons to doubt the degree to which national economies will disappear as important physical components of the world economy. But, as we shall see, this story about direct (input–output) globalization may not be the most important one to tell nowadays. Instead, the globalization of knowledge and of certain forms of accompanying competition are likely to figure as the most important ways globalization is transforming the economy. We can get a first approximation of these claims by reviewing some common empirical categories found in discussions of globalization.

Developing areas and global commodity chains. The absolute magnitudes of increases in foreign economic presence in certain zones of the developing world in recent years, and in the peripheral and cheaper regions of developed countries, are very impressive. Overall growth rates in many of these places have generally been greater than in densely developed core areas of wealthy countries. There are now global commodity chains, especially in consumer non-durables and electronics, sometimes taking the form of direct global relocation of certain phases of the production process (Gereffi and Korzeniewicz 1994). But this is only a small part of the story of development in these places.

The vast majority of increases in output in the major developing areas of the world, especially the Asian 'tigers', have to do with local ownership of production. That is, even though a good proportion of their exports are caught up in global commodity chains (orders coming from major multinational firms abroad), local entrepreneurship plays an important role in the spatial distribution of such activity and in its organization and local economic consequences (Amsden 1992; Evans 1995; Wade 1992). It thus becomes difficult to claim that global network systems (in the sense of deterritorialized commodity chains) are the principal animus of the developmental experiences of these places. This is equally true whether we consider small-firm economies such as Taiwan or Hong Kong, or big-firm economies such as Korea. It is widely admitted that, underlying the Asian successes in export-oriented production, are specific forms of local economic coordination, relationships between local economic agents which permit them to meet global market needs and ultimately to profit from these interactions.[2]

The global firm. Another image we are given is that of the 'global firm', an organization that supposedly works on a planetary scale with ease. But most of the world's biggest firms are not very globalized. Of the 500 biggest firms, only a handful—virtually all originating in small, highly export-oriented countries with small internal markets, such as the Netherlands or Sweden—have more than a quarter of their sales, workers, or production volumes outside their country of origin (van Tulder and Junne 1988).[3] For Japanese firms, these rates are generally under 10 per cent.

Multinational enterprises (MNEs) are, however, the key agents in global trade, where the largest of these firms account for over a third of the total. They are also key agents of global finance. Most critically, as we shall see, they are the key agents in globalization of soft and intangible knowledge resources in many of the large-scale mass production industries.

Commodity trade. Trade in goods as a percentage of total world output has risen rapidly since the mid-1960s, and is now just about at the peak it previously reached in 1914, about a quarter of the total. This includes all inputs and outputs, manufacturing and services, capital goods and consumer goods. It is lower for certain countries such as the USA (about 13 per cent) and highest for small countries with dense neighbour-to-neighbour relationships, such as Belgium, the Netherlands, Austria, or Switzerland. The big countries in the European union, such as France and Germany, trade about 35 per cent of their total inputs and outputs. In general, outside of the neighbour countries in the EU and North America (intracontinental, neighbour trade), most industries import and export only a small percentage of their inputs and outputs from elsewhere in the world, i.e. regions that are not neighbours. The highest percentages of such intercontinental trade relationships are found in consumer non-durable industries such as clothing and footwear, where Third World–First World trading relationships around a division of labour are common (Gereffi and Korzeniewicz 1994). Even relationships between neighbour countries with many reasons to trade, however, remain a fraction of those between regions of the same country: this is the case even for the USA and Canada (McCallum 1995).

From this, we need to consider the meaning of this trade. Overall trade patterns show that the advanced countries are becoming slightly more specialized in what they trade (Amendola, Guerrieri, and Padoan 1991; Balassa, 1992). They are coming more and more to concentrate in particular capital goods or final products.[4] This may be due to the existence of scale economies. However, many analysts believe that the explanation lies in the knowledge specializations of these countries, embedded in complex institutional and interfirm relationships (Nelson 1993; Lundvall 1996; Romer 1986). For certain kinds of goods, particular places develop superior innovation or know-how capacities, and are able to keep learning and updating their knowledge faster than competitors, enabling them to take important shares of world markets in those goods. Frequently, this superior knowledge and know-how are externalities attached to a cluster of firms within a particular region of the country. Such clusters may have a few big leader firms or they may be comprised of firms of equal size. Usually, they have very complex local labour market processes which also serve to transfer knowledge between firms and enhance the knowledge development capacities of the whole cluster. Such clustered, knowledge-based industries are highly localized as production systems, but globalized on the output side; that is why they show up as export specializations. Some draw a high proportion of their inputs from the national economy or even the region, as in the mechanical engineering industries of Germany or the craft industries of Italy; some draw a moderate percentage from abroad, as in the aircraft or electronics industries of the USA. But their degree of import-openness on the input side is usually a lot lower than their degree of export penetration on the output side. They are cases of local economies which are motors of world trade.[5]

This is a form of globalization stimulated in part by the increasing openness of world markets which heightens the value of local resources. It is completely distinct from globalization via the construction of deterritorialized network production systems, even though both may involve the production networks of multinational enterprises.

Technology. The production of technologies (i.e. knowledge) and know-how are not becoming placeless. Countries are very specialized in terms of what kinds of technologies their firms patent (Patel and Pavitt 1991). The big firms of the world, moreover, generate a high percentage of their worldwide patents in their home countries, and these are quite consistent with the overall profiles of export specialization of the home country's economy. This is because even large firms partake of wider institutional contexts and systems of externalities which enable them to generate new, commercializable knowledge (systems of innovation), and these are highly specific to particular countries and regions.

In contrast, for their routine activities, large firms have technology-*use* profiles which are much broader than the profiles of the technologies they *invent* and *export* (Patel and Pavitt 1991). A given firm is therefore mostly using technologies which it does not invent or export. We will argue that it does so through increasingly international technology and technique borrowing;[6] it will only produce, patent, and export a subset of its technologies, those which underlie its specializations (Ben-David and Loewy 1997).

Non-tradables. At least two-thirds of employment and output of developed economies today are in services. Most of these services have to be 'fabricated' through delivery at the point of consumption. While some of their component elements can be produced at long distances and imported (their manufactured components, for example, or logistical services which the final service worker draws on to help the final consumer), substantial parts of the service industries are essentially non-tradable at the present time and will remain so. They are another case where input–output globalization is not very important. By the same token, many services seem to involve high levels of internationalized intangibles, especially knowledge, symbols (trademarks), and notions about product quality on the part of consumers (recognition, expectations, conventions). In a more restricted, but nonetheless important set of cases, they involve presence of MNEs and considerable foreign direct investment.

This rapid tour of a complex subject suggests that neither firms nor national economies are close to the image of a placeless network economy, where all factors of production are highly mobile and all locations can substitute for one another, and it is unlikely that they will be so anytime in the near future. This gives us the ability to reject the simplest and incorrect version of *globalization as a simple transformation of the geography of material or knowledge linkages, on the input or on the output side, leading to economies consisting of deterritorialized international networks.* We have also suggested that in every category of analysis used here, globalization of knowledge and its role in competition is important, but would tend to slip between the cracks of the standard location and trade categories.

3. The Four Levels of Globalization

Since the standard categories reviewed above do not give us a coherent perspective on the globalization (and territorialization) of economic activity, in their place the economy can be decomposed into different degrees and types of globalization; this is a starting point for constructing a more sensible picture of what is going on. There seem to be four essential tiers in the major developed economies today: these categories consist of activities (sectors), or parts of sectors, each of which has a distinctive economic dynamic and different overall degree and type of globalization or its opposite forms of territorialization.

The first tier can be labelled *world-serving local industrial specializations, and specific skill-based activities*. It describes some of the most advanced activities in our economies, and all are highly territorialized. This tier takes two major forms.

Winner-take-all products and services. In industries such as financial services, media, sports, higher-level corporate management, business consulting, science, and medicine, there are functions which are assured by individuals who either take part in an international labour market (in the sense that there is international competition for them, especially as consultants), or where the products or services they render are identifiable, scarce, and consumed over an increasingly wide market area. The legal services assured by the high-powered corporate attorney, the cinema which has internationally known stars in it, doctors with a global reputation, are examples of this internationalization of labour services. Internationalization enables them to earn very high returns with very low marginal costs of expansion to international markets. This is an example of specific skills 'taking the market' over a wide territory, through increases in information (e.g. about doctors or lawyers) or through generalization of consumption patterns (e.g. cinema, television). It is driven, on the one hand, by supplies that are produced in highly localized networks, and on the other, by increasingly, internationalized consumer action and appropriation of information.[7] Thus, it represents an interesting case of globalization driven by two very different geographies of knowledge.

Export-oriented, specialized industrial clusters. The second part of the first tier of the economy in the major developed countries has to do with their export specialization products. These specializations, as noted, have increased over the last twenty-five years (the coefficient of difference has risen, when it is measured at the four-digit or more levels) (Amendola, Guerrieri, and Padoan 1991).

These are the sectors or parts of sectors that each economy is particularly good at. Such advantages have many potential causes, among which are scale, resource-based comparative advantage, or skill and institutionally embedded know-how.

There is much reason to believe that the importance of the latter has generally increased, and that knowledge-based, export-oriented industries are major components of the emerging, knowledge-driven system of world capitalism. This is because such clusters are capable of continuous technological learning, and the resulting ongoing product differentiation continuously renews their competitive advantages, outrunning their imitators. They are capable of technological learning for many reasons, ranging from benefits conferred by the formal institutions of the national system of innovation to various kinds of informal advantages—including conventions, rules, and practices—which coordinate the production system's agents such that they learn.[8] It has frequently been observed, as well, that such export specialization industries function as networks of firms (ranging from small to big in size), often tightly clustered in a few subnational regions, variously known as 'industrial districts' or 'technology districts'.[9] We recognize here such famous cases as Silicon Valley, Hollywood, Emilia-Romagna, Baden-Württemburg, or the City of London. This *local, path-dependent, and highly embedded technological change* is a strong and positive driver of globalization on the output side, precisely because it supplies scarce resources to the global economy in the form of temporarily unique knowledge embedded in products or services. Technological learning makes immediate imitation and diffusion rather difficult, generating processes of imperfect competition, involving significant technological or knowledge rents in the prices of these outputs.

In both these cases, internationalization is reflected principally through exports of the output. There is a strong role for international demand, presupposing the international diffusion of information to consumers. But such demand meets up with a supply structure defined by strong barriers to imitation or diffusion of skills and knowledge from place to place. Hence, it leads to specialization and trade. It shows up as 'hard' globalization (trade), but it is largely driven by the soft factors of embedded knowledge and skills.

Globalization through deterritorialization (global commodity chains). The second tier consists largely of routine manufacturing and services which are amenable to offshoring to low-wage countries because of low levels of place-specific assets in the production process. In terms of our theoretical categories, they have a low level of territorialization and a high level of international flows. By place-specific assets, we mean physical or intangible assets that are rooted in the environments of particular places, blocking transfer of production elsewhere. Certain firm-specific assets, however, could be transferred through FDI or licensing. In general, this situation allows low-wage product competition to develop. These are the spectacular cases of offshoring which are so prominent in the media. Direct globalization—in the sense of production which is carried out through deterritorialized networks—is present here.

What is the overall importance of such deterritorialization? When measured in terms of its impact on labour markets in the developed countries, virtually all studies conclude that it creates low-wage competition for about 5 per cent of the workforce in the developed countries and accounts for about 12 per cent of the increase in wage inequality in these countries in recent years, through its effects on their labour markets (*Quarterly Journal of Economics* 1992; Levy 1999; Mishel, Bernstein, and Schmitt 1998).

This process also involves complex international flows of knowledge. For example, it is not uncommon for local partners of multinational firms in developing countries to speak the language of international product standards (ISO 9000), confirming that they are part of an international knowledge community. It may well be, in the long-run, that such knowledge flows (and accompanying experience effects) have important impacts on which activities can be deterritorialized.

Locally serving partially tradable or non-tradables. Large parts of the economy consist of partially tradable or non-tradable products and services. These industries must do point-of-purchase delivery, limiting their direct input–output globalization. Some such activities are purely and simply local, consisting of production for specialized local tastes; as a result, it is difficult for foreign firms to gain entry. Many, however, are carried out by firms with global brand names (whether through FDI or franchising); thus a long-distance commodity chain can supply point-of-consumption service delivery. The upstream producers deploy their firm-specific assets in many local markets. This globalization is a complex mix of the global and the local, motivated by changes in consumer behaviour, in the sense that consumers in different countries are imitating each other more and more, in the presence of more transparent and more abundant consumer information. This leads to a replication in many places of very similar locationally immobile services. It generates a certain statistical similarity in the economic bases of different places. The physical (input–output) system involves significant interpenetration of the global and the local.

More important is the knowledge and competitive forces which animate these locational processes. Insofar as services are standardized by a multinational corporation—its product lines, brand names, personnel practices, and so on—there is globalization through deployment of intangible assets, essentially the global circulation of information and ideas belonging to the MNE (Dunning 1988).

To place this in wider perspective, recall that in the case of the first tier, we suggested that in the presence of strongly asymmetric and place-bound producer skills/knowledge, but with increasingly internationalized consumer information, globalization takes the form of enhancing export specialization; this is a sort of 'comparative advantage' effect (but recast in terms of the notion of a knowledge economy). In the present case, where there is locational immobility of production (point-of-service delivery), such consumer convergence leads to locational diffusion of the activity as it locates near its markets. International flows of information about consumption are critical to both. We know very little about why and how consumerism develops over formerly separated territories, but certainly it needs to be analysed as a complex historical and geographical process, involving the creation of institutionalized networks which bring not just neutral bits of information to widely separated people, but also bring about the complex social practice of consumer demand and choice.

Contestable markets in manufacturing and services. The fourth tier is routine manufacturing and services, generally of the capital-intensive type, whether in consumer durables or in capital goods and other intermediates.[10] At the level of these *activities*, theory suggests that globalization should be very high. Routinized activities generally use codified information, so there are not problems of information impactedness or specificity which impede geographical transfer of this information, whether inside firms, or via interfirm imitation. As a result, their markets are inherently highly *contestable* (Baumol, Panzar, and Willig 1988).

Such contestability should also transform the geography of production. Routinization dramatically lowers transactions costs of all kinds (Scott 1988). In the presence of these conditions, theory then goes on to predict that—even when classical comparative advantage differentials do not exist (because information and inputs can be easily produced in many different places)—scale effects should lead to a pronounced pattern of locational concentration and hence specialization of regional economies and dramatic increases in international trade (Helpman and Krugman 1987). This trade could take many specific forms, whether intrasectoral or intrafirm trade around a division of labour (capital goods, components, final assembly), or exchange of final outputs.

4. Internationalization of Productivity and Price Norms in Routine Contestable Production

These routine, mass-oriented sectors are highly contestable, but less directly globalized than theory predicts they 'should' be. For the OECD, even though trade levels have risen rapidly in comparison to output, most of these sectors have not had significant changes in the degree of unevenness of their spatial dispersion.[11] In response to this, we would expect New Trade Theory to claim that intermediate (mostly intra-industry) trade would increase; as a result, a powerful specialization effect might go statistically undetected, to the extent that intermediate goods representing different parts of the commodity chain are classified as being in a given industry. This is an extremely important issue, and one which is also unfortunately very tricky to measure. We do know, however, that at the level of particular products in most of the big consumer-oriented sectors, both intermediate and final goods are subject to competition from quite similar products through international trade. For example, there is enormous international trade in automobiles of a *given* size and horsepower. This trade in similar products, measured at a very fine level, averages about 30 per cent of the trade of the Triad and goes beyond 50 per cent the trade of certain sectors (Fontagné *et al.* 1996). There is thus an increase in the number of very similar products in many markets of the Triad countries (more so in the USA and Western Europe than Japan, of course). In other words, it appears that a good amount of the increase in intra-industry trade does *not* represent the locational concentration and upstream specialization effect to which it is assigned by the New Trade Theory; instead, it represents interterritorial market contestation by firms doing similar things—precisely the opposite of specialization. So the rise in trade in these sectors has to be driven by something quite different.

A further consequence of this reasoning is that—insofar as multiple competitors from different countries remain in the same product markets—there is considerable *within-sector international quality, price and hence productivity convergence* (Baumol, Nelson, and Wolff 1995). This brings us back to standard theories, which would tend to argue that such price convergence is the result of converging productivity and techniques in the countries under consideration, in turn stimulated by their nearly identical factor prices. But there are significant problems with this explanation. Total factor productivity and techniques have probably converged more significantly than real factor prices. Factor prices in the Triad certainly converged from the mid-1950s to the mid-1970s, as did aggregate productivity. But labour and capital prices have remained far apart, whether in nominal unit terms or because of the institutions that regulate their usage. Labour market regulation, and banking, credit, and investment institutions, as well as custom are said to affect labour and capital prices and quantities. If then, in fact, there is price, quality, and productivity-technique convergence, it needs a different explanation from the standard one. So this leaves us with a process of international convergence in prices and qualities, and, it is hypothesized, productivity and techniques, without the factor price convergence predicted by standard theory and without the degree of locational concentration predicted by the New Trade Theory.

Thus, there appear to be two basic kinds of technological change occurring in advanced capitalism today, which correspond to the different parts of the four-tiered economy. On the one hand are the local, embedded, technological pathways of the (tiers 1 and 3) global-motor activities, their regions, and the occupants of winner-take-all positions within them; on the other hand is the appearance, *in many countries at roughly the same time*, of techniques of flexibilized mass or diversified quality production in manufacturing or mass services in the tier-2 and tier-4 industries. A plausible hypothesis concerning the latter, drawn from the management, organization, and technological change literatures, is that in spite of significant factor price differences and investment conditions in the developed countries, an indirect internationalization process exists, consisting of more and more thorough and rapid large-scale technology and technique diffusion in these tier-4 sectors. In other words, a major element of the knowledge economy is this large-scale diffusion of technique in certain sectors.

It is to this problem that we now turn in greater detail in order to build an alternative possible explanation.[12]

4.1. Technological Diffusion and Market Contestation through Exchange of Ideas

Let us imagine the scenario for diffusion of a set of norms for product quality, productivity, and prices of goods of the type we are considering here (routine manufacturing, with codifiable knowledge and reproducible assets), using the common example of the world car industry, and starting with the case of Japan and the USA. In the latter, car companies experienced a productivity slowdown and profitability crunch in the early 1970s, just like many mass production firms in a number of industries, in both North America and Western Europe. They experimented with their own 'indigenous' solutions to these problems. Following this, they were also strongly shaken by Japanese imports, where the new production techniques were implemented earlier and more powerfully than elsewhere. So, in a sense, the American story is one of import competition, not from a cheap or unregulated labour country, but from one where new productivity techniques and resulting prices and product qualities outcompeted the domestic producers and forced them, unwillingly, to take on restructuring towards what were to become global norms. The élites in the USA initially did not understand the import threat in manufacturing and simply let their markets be flooded with better products, especially from Japan, in the late 1970s and early 1980s. Later on, they did try to stem the tide with voluntary import restrictions and various stillborn attempts to restructure the firm, but did so when the damage was already done. These managerial élites were themselves quite divided over the appropriateness of any intervention in markets. Consumers in the USA voted massively for imports from Japan. The American producers finally responded to the new techniques in the late 1980s and early 1990s. There was no longer any possibility for staying with the old strategies for the 'American' two-thirds of the market, because consumer loyalties were being tendentially tested. The norms of price and quality for cars, for about a third of the American car market, were completely revised in a ten-year period. In essence, this amounted to a new set of *conventions of product quality, responsiveness to market trends, and relationship to price and long-term performance*.

This resembles a standard account, at first glance. Japanese firms invent a better method, invade markets, are copied, a new configuration of market shares and productivity, price and quality norms restabilizes the situation. The extent to which domestic goods are exposed to foreign trade affects the extent of knowledge spillovers across countries, insofar as this knowledge is codifiable.

Behind this sequence of events, however, there is a very interesting geographical process that the standard account assumes to exist, but does not take any pains to explain: the large-scale, long-distance diffusion and mastery of a set of post-Fordist production techniques—knowledge, essentially—which align American quality, productivity, and price norms with those of their Japanese competitors. This may not be the most typical case, however, since it is not often that a major industrial nation has a major and sudden spurt of integration into world markets, is strongly export-oriented, and encounters a major consumer market which is exceptionally open.

The more typical case may be that of Western Europe and here we must construct a richer account of how trade, technology, and national institutions interact in the contemporary knowledge economy. In most of the Western European car markets, Japanese competition has not had a strong direct influence. Today in France for example, Japanese car imports are less than 30 per cent of the total; and virtually the entire market is comprised of cars from other Western European countries with similar labour laws and wage levels often higher than those of France. In Europe, the response of producers to the severe slowdown of the late 1970s and early 1980s was to resist the new techniques. In the high-quality car market, this was not initially an issue, as there were no substitute products. In the mass market, producers were also quite sheltered from non-European (non-'labourist') imports. Some, such as Peugeot in France, turned to protectionism as a way of slowing down the process.

Even so, virtually all of the producers began to inch forward to the new world standard techniques. One presumes that this was either because they saw the inevitability of competition arriving one day (an expectations effect), or because they wanted to realize all the labour savings and quality advantages of the new techniques, even though this would involve a long and difficult process of political and social dialogue and conflict. We could say that, up to this point, relatively modest trade is a means of international exchange of productivity, price, and quality information, practices, and routines in the sense that moderate trade combined with intense mutual scrutiny of products is the spur to adapting one's techniques to those of one's competitors.

An extension of this reasoning takes us far away from the predictions of New Trade Theory. It appears that in the kinds of contestable markets under consideration here, once international diffusion of these ideas reaches a certain point, domestic producers effectively use those ideas to restructure and rebuff further import penetration. In this way, internationalization of knowledge switches from being a complement to direct internationalization to a *substitute* for it. If this hypothesis is correct, it follows that the current phase of globalization in these kinds of industries ultimately will reach a certain maximum point and level off, and that therefore the national economy will not become irrelevant as a territorial scale at which input–output systems operate. The current statistical evidence for the European car industry supports this view of things. Existing companies are surviving through restructuring to achieve quality and variety within rather narrow product ranges, rather than coming to specialize or to disappear (Fontagné *et al.* 1996). As noted, this appears to be generally consistent with the statistical evidence on location in the OECD.

In this view, moreover, the nature of current globalization process can be thought of as being quite different from that which occurred earlier in the twentieth century: instead of primarily concerning direct (physical input–output) internationalization, it has a stronger component of indirect globalization by ideas and knowledge. A major issue for the future of national economies, and in particular the major firms of any nation, is the appropriation and application of global ideas, and the degree to which this can substitute for input–output globalization.

4.2. The Politics of Globalization by Ideas

Of course, in most industries and countries, the techniques referred to are associated with a powerful labour-saving bias.[13] Since they are heavily labour-saving, workers have resisted them, and some national governments have resisted them because of the unemployment costs to both. But in the end, they did not succeed. In Europe, why haven't the firms and workers been able to shelter themselves from these techniques, and thereby preserve labour demand, maintain wage shares, and keep them growing with productivity? In other words, why do national institutions for national production not keep staffing, wage, and skill levels in a different configuration from that associated with the new technological, productivity, and price norms in this part of the economy?[14]

I would argue that in the late 1980s, the benefits of this process to *consumers* began to be apparent to the latter. In France, for example, both Peugeot and Renault dramatically increased the quality of their cars, their design, their reliability, the range of models; they adapted models more quickly to market changes by the late 1980s; and real prices declined when adjusted for quality. The evidence is quite clear that the real prices for many goods and services—sometimes in absolute terms, sometimes in quality-adjusted terms—have dropped over the past fifteen years in the USA and Western Europe (Gordon 1990; Maddison 1990). This, as in the USA, was the real point of no return, when *conventions of product quality between producers and consumers were irretrievably altered.*

In other words, in certain industries the knowledge exchanges from trade are not only between producers, but are embedded in consumer behaviour, while in sectors with little trade, the diffusion of consumer knowledge and practices probably comes about through media, travel, and other such means. Consumer expectations with respect to prices and qualities, a new set of conventions that links consumers and producers, have made it much more difficult, if not impossible, for a given country to use its local institutional structure (especially its labour market structure) to enforce local technical norms, especially those that would involve greater labour-intensity, less product differentiation, lower quality, or higher prices.[15]

This provides a starting point for understanding the diffusion of such techniques, in that producers in countries with strong labour laws and institutions may not have initially intended to go head-to-head with those strong social forces. There are at least three major elements of the way the story unfolded in different places: the commitment of producers to the new techniques in relationship to the labour market rules and institutions (referred to above); the degree to which they supported open markets; and the role of consumer society in the form of consumption norms and conventions. The first two are the almost-exclusive terrain of the literature; the latter, I want to argue, is a hugely important missing element of the story and has enormous implications for contemporary economic change.

Notice that this story of a globalized process of path-dependent technological change is different from those stories frequently told about 'globalized best practice' through competition and selection. It is not just about import competition, because it is reflected just as much in non-traded and non-tradable goods and services as in trade, and it concerns the way that convergence of techniques through idea diffusion acts as a substitute for locational concentration at world continental scales. The account here is about strategies and politics which take place against a large-scale collective action problem, the conventional interaction between producers and consumers. On the producer side, there is *an endogenization of learning as a way to head off potential loss of market share*; on the consumer side, there is *a diffusion of calculating, internationally informed and consciously comparative consumer behaviour*; and the two interact in a mutually supportive way. This space- and time-sensitive interaction between production norms and consumption norms has not been well studied, to my knowledge. I believe the geography of knowledge holds the key to many dimensions of industrial 'hypermodernity'—the ever more frantic race for product quality, variety, rapidity of adjustment, and cheapness—at the end of the twentieth century.

5. Analysing Ideas and Knowledge

We have chosen deliberately to eschew the standard economist's focus on 'information' in referring to the global exchange of ideas, even though there will be some areas in which the economics of information is useful to the present inquiry. This is because though information transfer is always necessary to knowledge exchange, the reverse is not always true. The category 'information' is too general to get at the transfer of *economically useful practices, routines, and conventions*, which are complex and coherent assemblages of different kinds of information.

How are these institutions transferred? They appear to be transferred by imitation. In social science, a unit of reproduction-through-imitation, a pattern of behaviour or idea stored in the human mind and then transmitted through culture (practices, language) is known as a *meme*. In theories of cultural evolution, memes have observable phenotypic effects, in the sense that the behaviours based on them encourage their own reproduction and discourage those at variance with them. Memes can be thought of as units by which patterns of coordination between actors are transmitted, such that those actors who do not observe the coordination pattern will be penalized. That is how the systemic effect comes about.

Memes, and their constituent practices, routines, and conventions, do not have a deterministic effect on behaviour. They interact with the environment and only insofar as they are pragmatically effective can they work. They do constrain and direct behaviour which, depending on other conditions in the environment and other memes, will make it likely that certain types of behaviour will be adopted over others. Moreover, in the social evolution we refer to here, there is nothing that ensures that the memes which are selected are in any way optimal, ideal, or even good in the long run.[16]

6. Conclusion

Location and trade appear to be underpinned by, and heavily influenced by, exchanges of knowledge. Knowledge, in this context, has to be understood not as 'information', but as institutionalized, embedded social practices, conventions, and rules, or memes, which are essential elements of economic coordination in the sectors of the economy. By understanding the geography of knowledge in different sectors, it becomes possible to interpret the outward tangible aspects of globalization—location and trade—differently, and in this light, their significance and probable evolution are viewed differently from most in standard analyses. Knowledge exchanges take many different geographical forms. In some cases, they are sourced from highly localized knowledge, which initially generates specialization effects in location. In other cases, there is internationalization of knowledge, and its tendency to make possible certain forms of deterritorialization, on the one hand, and to substitute for relocation and specialization, on the other. The development of better categories for analysing these intangible forces in the globalization process would be better adapted to contemporary knowledge-based, institutionally reflexive capitalism, than are the standard ways of thinking, with their limited images of an economy as either physical input–output relations or prices and quantities. Knowledge flows may be just as important.

NOTES

1. A substantial proportion of production, even in a highly integrated country like the USA, is still regionally sourced. It is difficult to get precise figures on this, because input–output data are not gathered regionally in the USA. But in France, where such data are available, the regional sourcing proportion is often as high as 50 per cent. National proportions are much higher (e.g. 87 per cent for the USA, 65 per cent for France).
2. On the other hand, it probably *is* true that the case of the garment industry in Central America is a deterritorialized commodity chain, and there are undoubtedly many other such examples.

58 *Michael Storper*

3. See also the well-known debate between Laura Tyson and Robert Reich on the 'nationality' of firms.
4. Thus it often shows up as intraindustry or intrafirm trade.
5. I have made this argument in a bit more detail in 'The Limits to Globalization' in Storper (1992).
6. This does not exclude the possibility of subsequent 'local' adaptation, including significant modifications (Antonelli 1995).
7. There are important misallocation effects that can occur when the best push out the satisfactory (Frank and Cook 1996).
8. On the role of conventions in learning, and different ensembles of conventions and products, see Storper and Salais (1997).
9. The literature on this subject is vast, of course. Since it's now so familiar to most students of the subject, we will not cite it here in detail.
10. These are no longer easily distinguished from tier 2 activities via their structural characteristics, such as capital intensity, durability, and so on, as used to be done. The distinction is better related to the nature of the production process. On average they are more durable goods, often involving a complex multi-phase production process, dense supplier networks, and with certain skill-intensive phases upstream. For services, there is an adaptation to customer and a skill-intensive phase or content.
11. This observation comes from my own as yet unpublished research, in which we calculated Herfindahl equivalent indexes by sector, for the OECD countries, from 1971 to 1995.
12. First we need to consider the possibility that such diffusion occurs through 'indirect globalization', which is a major theme of another branch of the existing literature. The main arguments centre on the roles of financial globalization and of management strategies to threaten workers.

The volume of foreign direct investment (FDI) is much higher than it used to be, suggesting an increase in globalization. In the domain of finance. there are enormous flows of capital in the world economy. and financial globalization appears to be greater than productive globalization. We can immediately dismiss the hypothesis that the globalization of finance is primarily about clubbing developed economies into lowering their costs to Third World levels. More than 85 per cent of foreign direct investment, the supposed vector of locational hypermobility, is between the rich, developed countries of Western Europe, North America, and Japan. This proportion is *much higher* than in the 1970s, when a much greater share of total world FDI went to developing countries. Because it is among countries with similar costs, the search for lower factor costs is largely irrelevant to it.

There are no reliable overall estimates of the magnitude of financial globalization and even less is known about how the financial economy relates to the real economy. Many analysts claim that globalization of finance causes firms to restructure production systems leading to plant closings, deindustrialization, reindustrialization with less labour and a more unequal income distribution, and (in Europe) higher levels of unemployment.

The argument is that firms have to show performance which corresponds to global financial performance norms. or they will not be able to attract money. The structure of the now highly globalized global capital market is now the club which allows firms to introduce international productivity and best-practice norms into even their nationally oriented production activities. Newspapers are full of stories about how stock prices rise when firms announce lay-offs of workers and this relationship is probably true for some set of cases. However, there is essentially no evidence which shows this cost-cutting logic to be the result of direct, institutionalized pressure by something called 'international financial markets', or even indirectly via competition for capital. Firms borrow on international markets for a variety of reasons, some of which are simply speculative (recent Asian financial crisis). In sectors with something approaching perfect competition with interchangeable products, in the short run, firms do have to try and align their production costs with sectoral standards. What does financial globalization have to do with this? Most accounts suggest that both domestic and foreign stock buyers and institutional investors (and their counsellors) seem to have subscribed, in some industries, to a logic which holds that cost-cutting will lead to greater profits and stock price increases. The question is why, if this account is true, such an idea has come to be central to investor behaviour? Does this idea reflect an efficient market-driven process of diffusing best practice, or a path-dependent behaviour-driven diffusion of an idea?

Firms' stock values rise and fall essentially on their profitability data, which are, in turn, the indirect result of their financial and productive performances. Research by Webber and Rigby (1996) confirms the existence of enduring differences in profit levels between regions and firms. In highly differentiated markets, usually characterized by market imperfections, the role of finance capital becomes more complex. There are numerous cases where investors do not demand any particular strategy on the part of the companies they invest in: they want the profits, and however they can be found is fine with the investor. Highly differentiated markets should leave a wide margin of manœuvre from firm to firm and hence from region to region.

Moreover, financial institutions, risk perception and evaluation, the degree of financial market capitalization, and financial incentives and pressures vary enormously from one country to another. That is, there is *not* one, big centralized world system of capitalizing firms, but a considerable diversity of practices (but we do lack definitive research measuring the relationship between local standards and global standards).

In addition, *even if*, as certain literature claims, there were one perfect global market with transparent information for financing companies, i.e. a single set of profit, asset value, and returns criteria for receiving investments, it would not follow that this would translate directly into precisely converging production techniques. This is true for a disarmingly simple reason: companies—especially big, multi-product and multinational ones—have financial results which are aggregates of many different lines of activity. The markets would merely dictate that they come up with a given *aggregate* result. But there would be no necessary relationship between these aggregate criteria and what firms actually do. Even in a given line of business, the result would be a loose one, rather than a tight one.

These remarks suggest that finance—as a globalized market or institution—does not have the independent motor force which some analysts have assigned to it. There is indeed a striking gap in the literature on globalization and international economic convergence: reasoning on exactly *how*, in terms of investor behaviour and the process of finance, the results attributed to financial globalization are concretely brought about by the agents of finance on the one hand and corporate decision-making on the other. Is there a financial 'market for control of production'? Probably not; there is a market for the aggregates ('bottom line') referred to above. As is, the literature which claims existence of such a market for control uses simple functionalism to get from postulated cause to result.

Another argument claims that there is a 'threat effect' at work, where the threat is direct, not passing through financial markets. With more open markets, firms tell workers that if they do not adopt something equivalent to the best obtainable productivity and price norms, then their products would be pushed out by cheaper or better imports. Cases of companies obtaining big concessions from workforces, and acquiescence to lay-offs, via this threat, are frequently aired in the literature and in the newspapers. Thus, there might be effects of globalization that do not show up as measurable flows of capital, labour, or products. Two problems crop up here. One is that the proportion of total restructuring which is carried out through such threat-based concession bargaining is probably fairly low. The other is that the provenance of production techniques to which managers aspire still would need to be explained.

13. For the historian of such techniques, the fact that they are labour-saving would say nothing about whether labour-saving is a principal reason for their adoption. Indeed, while some accounts suggest that labour-saving is the principal motivation of employers who adopted in the early days, many other accounts focus on the need to change practices of labour utilization (including staffing level, of course) in order to get the other benefits of the new techniques; labour-saving is something like a secondary and opportunistic benefit of adoption, not its only or primary purpose as is often assumed. Some analyses do claim that managers are aware of, and are explicitly promoting, a declining technology-skill complementarity. See Lazonick and O'Sullivan (1997).

14. Of course, to some extent they have, as in the differences in the low-wage service sector between continental Europe, the USA and Great Britain. But these differences are quite limited in manufacturing and they are being reduced in services.

15. The advent of consumer society predates the contemporary technological revolution. It has been a long-standing sociological phenomenon in the USA. But there were seeds of it already in the early 1960s in Europe. With the end of the post-war reconstruction in Europe, the consumer revolution got into full swing there. The advent of ICTs and the strong spur of the 1970s' 'crisis of mass production' did not put an end to it, but seemed to coincide with a great deepening and widening of consumer society in countries, such as those of Western Europe, where producer identities had up to then occupied at least a strong a place as consumerist ideologies.

16. Among some of the many relevant references are: Boulding (1981); Boyd and Richerson (1985); Cavalli-Sforza and Feldman (1981); Dawkins (1976); Mayr (1982); Mokyr (1990); Waldrop (1992). On the firm, see Douglas (1986); Douglas and Isherwood (1996); and Appadurai (1988).

REFERENCES

Amendola, M., Guerrieri, P., and Padoan, P. C. (1991), 'International Patterns of Technological Accumulation and Trade', Paper presented at the European Association for Research in Industrial Economics, Ferrara, 1–3 September.

Amsden, A. (1992), *Asia's Next Giant: South Korea and Late Industrialization* (Oxford: Oxford University Press).

Antonelli, C. (1995), *The Economics of Localized Technological Change and Industrial Dynamics* (Dordrecht: Kluwer).

Appadurai, A. (1988), *The Social Life of Things: Commodities in Cultural Perspective*, Cambridge: Cambridge University Press.

Balassa, Bela (1992), *Changing Patterns in Foreign Trade and Payments* (New York: W. W. Norton).

Baumol, W., Nelson, R., and Wolff, E. (eds.) (1995), *Convergence of Productivity: Cross-National Studies and Historical Evidence* (Oxford: Oxford University Press).

Baumol, W., Panzar, J., and Willig, R. (1988), *Contestable Markets and the Theory of Industry Structure* (Cambridge Mass.: Harvard Business School Press).

Ben-David, D., and Loewy, M. (1997), 'Free Trade, Growth, and Convergence' (Cambridge, Mass.: NBER Working Paper 6095).

Boulding, K. (1981), *Evolutionary Economics* (Beverly Hills: Sage).

Boyd, R., and Richerson, P. J. (1985), *Culture and the Evolutionary Process* (Chicago: University of Chicago Press).

Cavalli-Sforza, L. L., and Feldman, M. W. (1981), *Cultural Transmission and Evolution* (Princeton: Princeton University Press).

Dawkins, R. (1976), *The Selfish Gene* (Oxford: Oxford University Press).

Dicken, P. (1998), *Global Shift: Transforming the World Economy* (New York: Guilford Press, 3rd edn).

Douglas, M. (1986), *How Institutions Think* (Syracuse: Syracuse University Press).

Douglas, M., and Isherwood, B. (1996), *The World of Goods: Toward an Anthropology of Consumption* (London: Routledge).

Dunning, J. H. (1988), *Multinationals, Technology and Competitiveness* (London: Unwin Hyman).

Evans, P. (1995), *Embedded Autonomy: States and Industrial Transformation* (Princeton: Princeton University Press).

Fontagné, L., Friedenberg, M., and Keserci, D. U. (1996), 'Les échanges de biens inter-médiaires de la Triade', *Economie Internationale* 85: 143–66.

Frank, R. H., and Cook, P. (1996), *The Winner-Take-All Society: Why the Few at the Top Get So Much More than the Rest of Us* (New York: Penguin).

Gereffi, G., and Korzeniewicz, M. (eds.) (1994), *Commodity Chains and Global Capitalism* (Westport, Conn.: Praeger).

Gordon, R. J. (1990), *The Measurement of Durable Goods Prices* (Chicago: University of Chicago Press).

Harrison, B. (1997), *Lean and Mean: The Changing Landscape of Corporate Power in an Age of Flexibility* (New York: Guilford Press).

Helpman, E., and Krugman, P. (1987), *Market Structure and Foreign Trade: Increasing Returns, Imperfect Competition, and the International Economy* (Cambridge, Mass.: MIT Press).

Lazonick, W., and O'Sullivan, M. (1997), 'Organizational Learning and International Competition: The Skill-Base Hypothesis' (Annondale-on-Hudson, NY: Jerome Levy Economics Institute).

Levy, F. (1999), *The New Dollars and Dreams: American Incomes and Economic Change* (New York: Russell Sage Foundation).

Lundvall, B-A. (ed.) (1996), *National Systems of Innovation: Toward a Theory of Innovation and Interactive Learning* (London: Pinter).

McCallum, John (1995), 'National Borders Matter: Canada–US Regional Trade Patterns', *American Economic Review*. 85 (3): 615–23.

Maddison, A. (1990), *Dynamic Forces in Capitalist Development* (Oxford: Oxford University Press).

Mayr, E. (1982), *The Growth of Biological Thought* (Cambridge, Mass.: Belknap).

Mishel, L., Bernstein, J., Schmitt, J. (eds.) (1998), *The State of Working America, 1998–99* (Ithaca: Cornell University Press).

Mokyr, J. (1990), *The Lever of Riches* (New York: Oxford University Press).

Nelson, R. (ed.) (1993), *National Innovation Systems: A Comparative Analysis* (New York: Oxford University Press).

Patel, P., and Pavitt, K. (1991), 'Large Firms in the Production of the World's Technology: An Important Case of Non-Globalization', *Journal of International Business Studies*, 1st quarter: 1–21.

Quarterly Journal of Economics, Feb. 1992.

Romer, P. (1986), *Increasing Returns and Economic Growth, Journal of Political Economy* 94: 1002–37.

Scott, A. J. (1988), *Metropolis: From the Division of Labor to Urban Form* (Berkeley and Los Angeles: University of California Press).

Storper, M. (1992), 'The Limits to Globalization', *Economic Geography* 68: 60–93.

—— and Salais, R. (1997), *Worlds of Production: The Action Frameworks of the Economy* (Cambridge, Mass.: Harvard University Press).

Van Tulder, R., and Junne, G. (1988), *European Multinationals in Core Technologies* (London: Wiley).

Wade, R. (1992), *Governing the Market: Economic Theory and the Role of Government in Asian Industrialization* (Princeton: Princeton University Press).

Waldrop, M. M. (1992), *Complexity: The Emerging Science at the Edge of Order and Chaos* (New York: Simon & Schuster).

Webber, M., and Rigby, D. (1996), *The Golden Age Illusion: Rethinking Postwar Capitalism* (New York: Guilford Press).

3

Knowledge, Globalization, and Regions:
An Economist's Perspective

David B. Audretsch

1. Introduction

In the introductory chapter to this volume John H. Dunning raises five important issues involving the links between the geography of economic activity and the emergence of the knowledge-based economy.[i] The first issue involves the extent to which the spatial unit for examining the international allocation of economic activity is shifting. An important conclusion of this chapter is that along with an increased importance of global markets has also come an increased importance of the local component of economic activity. This is because globalization has shifted the comparative advantage of the leading industrialized countries to knowledge-based economic activity, which is a local phenomenon.

The second issue raised by Dunning involves how both the macro- and microregions have been impacted by globalization. This chapter shows that the welfare of the macroregion has benefited from innovative activities at the microlevel. This relates to the third issue, where spatial clusters are observed to be crucial for innovative activity. A key finding of this chapter is that innovation is primarily a local activity.

This leads to a number of insights about Dunning's third issue, which links FDI flows to globalization in a knowledge-based economy. In the knowledge-based economy outward FDI clearly is becoming a key instrument of the type of strategic asset-seeking described by Dunning (2000). Corporations open establishments in knowledge clusters in foreign countries in an effort to access that knowledge and transfer it back to the home country, or at least to the parent firm.

Finally, the last issue raised by Dunning involves implications for government policy. An important implication of this shift in this comparative advantage is that much of the production and commercialization of new economic knowledge is less associated with footloose multinational corporations and more associated with high-tech innovative regional clusters, such as Silicon Valley, Research Triangle, and Route 122. Only a few years ago the conventional wisdom predicted that globalization would render the demise of the region as a meaningful unit of economic analysis. Yet the obsession of policy-makers around the globe to 'create the next Silicon Valley' reveals the increased importance of geographic proximity and regional agglomerations. This chapter closes by identifying a number of government policies that are being implemented to generate such knowledge clusters. These policies, however, are associated with local governments and involve a new set of policy instruments that are oriented towards the creation and commercialization of new economic knowledge. In particular, the increased importance of innovation has triggered a fundamental shift in public policy towards business away from policies constraining the freedom of firms to contract and towards a new set of enabling policies implemented at the regional and local levels.

2. Innovation and Comparative Advantage

When the Berlin Wall fell in 1989 many people expected even greater levels of economic well-being resulting from the dramatic reduction of the economic burden in the West that had been imposed by four decades of Cold War. Thus, the substantial unemployment and general economic stagnation during the subsequent eight years has come as a shock. Unemployment and stagnant growth are the twin economic problems confronting Europe. Over 11 per cent of the workforce in the European Union was unemployed in 1997, ranging from 6.1 per cent in the UK and 6.2 per cent in the Netherlands, to 13 per cent in Germany, 12.6 per cent in France, and over 20 per cent in Spain.[2]

The traditional comparative advantage in mature, technologically moderate industries such as metalworking, machine tools, and automobile production had provided an engine for growth, high employment, and economic stability throughout Western Europe for most of the post-war economic period. This traditional comparative advantage has been lost in the high-cost countries of Europe and North America in the last decade for two reasons. The first has to do with globalization, or the advent of competition from not just the emerging economies in South-East Asia but also from the transforming economies of Central and Eastern Europe. The second factor has been the computer and telecommunications revolution. The new communications technologies have triggered a virtual spatial revolution in terms of the geography of production. According to *The Economist*, 'The death of distance as a determinant of the cost of communications will probably be the single most economic force shaping society in the first half of the next century.'

Globalization has triggered a virtual spatial revolution in terms of the geography of production.[3] The (marginal) cost of transforming information across geographic space has been rendered to virtually nothing. Confronted with lower-cost competition in foreign locations, producers in the high-cost countries have three options apart from doing nothing and losing global market share: (i) reduce wages and other production costs sufficiently to compete with the low-cost foreign producers, (ii) substitute equipment and technology for labour to increase productivity, and (iii) shift production out of the high-cost location and into the low-cost location.

Many of the European and American firms that have successfully restructured resorted to the last two alternatives. Substituting capital and technology for labour, along with shifting production to lower-cost locations has resulted in waves of *corporate downsizing* throughout Europe and North America. At the same time, it has generally preserved the viability of many of the large corporations. As record levels of both European and American stock indexes indicate, the companies have not generally suffered. For example, between 1979 and 1995 more than 43 million jobs were lost in the USA as a result of corporate downsizing.[4] This includes 24.8 million blue-collar jobs and 18.7 million white-collar jobs. Similarly, the 500 largest US manufacturing corporations cut 4.7 million jobs between 1980 and 1993, or one-quarter of their workforce.[5] Perhaps most disconcerting, the rate of corporate downsizing has apparently increased over time in the USA, even as the unemployment rate has fallen. During most of the 1980s, about one in twenty-five workers lost a job. In the 1990s this has risen to one in twenty workers.

This wave of corporate downsizing has triggered cries of betrayal and lack of social conscience on the part of the large corporations.[6] But it is a mistake to blame the corporations for this wave of downsizing that has triggered massive job losses and rising unemployment in so many countries. These corporations are simply trying to survive in an economy of global competitors who have access to lower-cost inputs.

Much of the policy debate responding to the twin forces of the telecommunications revolution and increased globalization has revolved around a trade-off between maintaining higher wages but suffering greater unemployment versus higher levels of employment but at the cost of lower wage rates. There is, however, an alternative. It does not require sacrificing wages to create new jobs, nor does it require fewer jobs to maintain wage levels and the social safety net. This alternative involves shifting economic activity out of the traditional industries where the high-cost countries of Europe and North America have lost the comparative advantage and into those industries where the comparative advantage is compatible with both high wages and high levels of employment—knowledge-based economic activity.

Globalization has rendered the comparative advantage in traditional moderate technology industries incompatible with high wage levels. At the same time, the emerging comparative advantage that is compatible with high wage levels is based on innovative activity. For example, employment increased by 15 per cent in Silicon Valley between 1992 and 1996, even though the mean income is 50 per cent greater than in the rest of the country.[7]

The global demand for innovative products in knowledge-based industries is high and growing rapidly; yet the number of workers who can contribute to producing and commercializing new knowledge is limited to just a few areas in the world. Economic activity based on new knowledge generates higher wages and greater employment opportunities reflecting the exploding demand for new and improved products and services. There are many indicators reflecting the shift in the comparative advantage of the high-wage countries towards an increased importance of innovative activity. For example, Kortum and Lerner (1997: 1) document an unprecedented jump in patenting in the USA, as evidenced by the explosion in applications for US patents by American inventors since 1985. Throughout this century, patent applications fluctuated within a band between 40,000 and 80,000 per year. By contrast, in 1995 there were over 120,000 patent applications. Similarly, Berman, Bound, and Machin (1997) have shown that the demand for less skilled workers has decreased dramatically throughout the OECD, while at the same time the demand for skilled workers has exploded.

3. The Knowledge Production Function

The starting point for most theories of innovation is the firm. In such theories the firms are exogenous and their performance in generating technological change is endogenous (Arrow 1962). For example, in the most prevalent model found in the literature of technological change, the model of the knowledge production function, formalized by Zvi Griliches (1979), firms exist exogenously and then engage in the pursuit of new economic knowledge as an input into the process of generating innovative activity. The most decisive input in the knowledge production function is new economic knowledge. Knowledge as an input in a production function is inherently different from the more traditional inputs of labour, capital, and land. While the economic value of the traditional inputs is relatively certain, knowledge is intrinsically uncertain and its potential value is asymmetric across economic agents.[8] The most important, although not the only source of new knowledge, is considered to be research and development (R&D). Other key factors generating new economic knowledge include a high degree of human capital, a skilled labour force, and a high presence of scientists and engineers.

There is considerable empirical evidence supporting the model of the knowledge production function. This empirical link between knowledge inputs and innovative output apparently becomes stronger as the unit of observation becomes increasingly aggregated. For example, at the unit of observation of countries, the relationship between R&D and patents is very strong. The most innovative countries, such as the USA, Japan, and Germany, also tend to undertake high investments in R&D. By contrast, little patent activity is associated with developing countries, which have very low R&D expenditures. Similarly, the link between R&D and innovative output, measured in terms of either patents or new product innovations is also very strong when the unit of observation is the industry. The most innovative industries, such as computers, instruments, and pharmaceuticals also tend to be the most R&D intensive. Audretsch (1995) finds a simple correlation coefficient of 0.74 between R&D inputs and innovative output at the level of four-digit standard industrial classification (SIC) industries. However, when the knowledge production function is tested for the unit of observation of the firm, the link between knowledge inputs and innovative output becomes either tenuous and weakly positive in some studies and even non-existent or negative in others. The model of the knowledge production function becomes particularly weak when small firms are included in the sample. This is not surprising, since formal R&D is concentrated among the largest corporations, but a series of studies (Acs and Audretsch 1990) has clearly documented that small firms account for a disproportionate share of new product innovations given their low R&D expenditures.

4. Knowledge Spillovers

The breakdown of the knowledge production function at the level of the firm raises the question, *Where do innovative firms with little or no R&D get the knowledge inputs?* This question becomes particularly relevant for small and new firms that undertake little R&D themselves, yet contribute considerable innovative activity in newly emerging industries such as biotechnology and computer software (Audretsch 1995). One answer that has recently emerged in the economics literature is from other, third-party firms or research institutions, such as universities. Economic knowledge may spill over from the firm conducting the R&D or the research laboratory of a university (Baptista 1997).

Why should knowledge spill over from the source of origin? At least two major channels or mechanisms for knowledge spillovers have been identified in the literature. Both of these spillover mechanisms revolve around the issue of appropriability of new knowledge. Cohen and Levinthal (1989) suggest that firms develop the capacity to adapt new technology and ideas developed in other firms and are therefore able to appropriate some of the returns accruing to investments in new knowledge made externally.

By contrast, Audretsch (1995) proposes shifting the unit of observation away from exogenously assumed firms to individuals, such as scientists, engineers, or other knowledge workers—agents with endowments of new economic knowledge. When the lens is shifted away from the firm to the individual as the relevant unit of observation, the appropriability issue remains, but the question becomes, *How can economic agents with a given endowment of new knowledge best appropriate the returns from that knowledge?* If the scientist or engineer can pursue the new idea within the organizational structure of the firm developing the knowledge and appropriate roughly the expected value of that knowledge, he was no reason to leave the firm. On the other hand, if he places a greater value on his ideas than do the decision-making bureaucracy of the incumbent firm, he may choose to start a new firm to appropriate the value of his knowledge. In the metaphor provided by Albert O. Hirschman (1970), if voice proves to be ineffective within incumbent organizations, and loyalty is sufficiently weak, a knowledge worker may resort to exit the firm or university where the knowledge was created in

order to form a new company. In this spillover channel the knowledge production function is actually reversed. The knowledge is exogenous and embodied in a worker. The firm is created endogenously in the worker's effort to appropriate the value of his knowledge through innovative activity.

5. The Importance of Location

That knowledge spills over is barely disputed (Audretsch 1998). In disputing the importance of knowledge externalities in explaining the geographic concentration of economic activity, Krugman (1991) and others do not question the existence or importance of such knowledge spillovers. In fact, they argue that such knowledge externalities are so important and forceful that there is no compelling reason for a geographic boundary to limit the spatial extent of the spillover. According to this line of thinking, the concern is not that knowledge does not spill over but that it should stop spilling over just because it hits a geographic border, such as a city limit, state line, or national boundary. As illustrated by the title page of *The Economist* proclaiming 'The Death of Distance',[9] the claim that geographic location is important to the process linking knowledge spillovers to innovative activity in a world of e-mail, fax machines, and cyberspace may seem surprising and even paradoxical. The resolution to the paradox posed by the localization of knowledge spillovers in an era where the telecommunications revolution has drastically reduced the cost of communication lies in a distinction between knowledge and information. *Information*, such as the price of gold on the New York Stock Exchange, or the value of the yen in London, can be easily codified and has a singular meaning and interpretation. By contrast, *knowledge* is vague, difficult to codify, and often only serendipitously recognized. While the marginal cost of transmitting information across geographic space has been rendered invariant by the telecommunications revolution, the marginal cost of transmitting knowledge, and especially tacit knowledge, rises with distance.

Von Hipple (1994) demonstrates that high-context, uncertain knowledge, or what he terms as sticky knowledge, is best transmitted via face-to-face interaction and through frequent and repeated contact. Geographic proximity matters in transmitting knowledge, because as Kenneth Arrow (1962) pointed out some three decades ago, such tacit knowledge is inherently non-rival in nature, and knowledge developed for any particular application can easily spill over and have economic value in very different applications. As Glaeser. *et al.* (1992: 1126) have observed, 'intellectual breakthroughs must cross hallways and streets more easily than oceans and continents.'

The importance of local proximity for the transmission of knowledge spillovers has been observed in many different contexts. It has been pointed out that, 'business is a social activity, and you have to be where important work is taking place.'[10] A survey of nearly one thousand executives located in America's sixty largest metropolitan areas ranked Raleigh and Durham as the best cities for knowledge workers and for innovative activity.[11] The reason is that

A lot of brainy types who made their way to Raleigh/Durham were drawn by three top research universities. US businesses, especially those whose success depends on staying at the top of new technologies and processes, increasingly want to be where hot new ideas are percolating. A presence in brain-power centers like Raleigh/Durham pays off in new products and new ways of doing business. Dozens of small biotechnology and software operations are starting up each year and growing like *kudzu* in the fertile climate.[12]

Not only did Krugman (1991: 53) doubt that knowledge spillovers are not geographically constrained but he also argued that they were impossible to measure because 'knowledge flows are invisible, they leave no paper trail by which they may be measured and tracked.' However, an emerging literature (Jaffe, Trajtenberg, and Henderson 1993) has overcome data constraints to measure the extent of knowledge spillovers and link them to the geography of innovative activity. Jaffe (1989), Feldman (1994), and Audretsch and Feldman (1996) modified the model of the knowledge production function to include an explicit specification for both the spatial and product dimensions:

$$I_{si} = IRD_1^{\beta}*(UR_{si})_2^{\beta}*[UR_{si}*(GC_{si})_3^{\beta}]*\varepsilon_{si}, \tag{1}$$

where I is innovative output, IRD is private corporate expenditures on R&D, UR is the research expenditures undertaken at universities, and GC measures the geographic coincidence between university and corporate research. The unit of observation for estimation is at the spatial level, s, a state, and industry level, i. Jaffe (1989) used the number of inventions registered with the US patent office as a measure of innovative activity. By contrast, Audretsch and Feldman (1996) and Acs, Audretsch, and Feldman (1992) developed a direct measure of innovative output consisting of new product introductions.

Estimation of equation (1) essentially shifts the model of the knowledge production function from the unit of observation of a firm to that of a geographic unit. The consistent empirical evidence that $\beta_1 \geq 0$, $\beta_2 \geq 0$, $\beta_3 \geq 0$ supports the notion that knowledge spills over for third-party use from university research laboratories as well as industry R&D laboratories. This empirical evidence suggests that location and proximity clearly matter in exploiting knowledge spillovers. Not only have Jaffe, Trajtenberg, and Henderson (1993) found that patent citations tend to occur more frequently within the state in which they were patented than outside of that state, but Audretsch and Feldman (1996) found that the propensity of innovative activity to cluster geographically tends to be greater in industries where new economic knowledge plays a more important role. Prevenzer (1997) and Zucker, Darby, and Armstrong (1994) show that in biotechnology, which is an industry based almost exclusively on new knowledge, the firms tend to cluster together in just a handful of locations. This finding is supported by Audretsch and Stephan (1996) who examine the geographic relationships of scientists working with biotechnology firms. The importance of geographic proximity is clearly shaped by the role played by the scientist. The scientist is more

TABLE 3.1. Counts of innovation normalized by population

Consolidated Metropolitan statistical area	Innovations	Population (thousands)	Innovations per 100,000 population
San Francisco-Oakland	477	5,368	8.886
Boston-Lawrence	345	3,972	8.686
New York-Northern New Jersey	735	17.539	4.191
Philadelphia-Wilmington	205	5,681	3.609
Dallas-Fort Worth	88	2,931	3.002
Hartford	30	1,014	2.959
Los Angeles-Anaheim	333	11.498	2.896
Buffalo-Niagara	35	1,243	2.816
Cleveland-Akron	77	2,834	2.717
Chicago-Gary	203	7.937	2.558
Providence-Pawtucket	25	1.083	2.308
Portland-Vancouver	25	1.298	1.926
Cincinnati-Hamilton	30	1.660	1.807
Seattle-Tacoma	37	2.093	1.768
Pittsburgh	42	2.423	1.733
Denver-Boulder	28	1,618	1.731
Detroit-Ann Arbor	68	4.753	1.431
Houston-Galveston	39	3,101	1.258
Miami-Fort Lauderdale	13	2,644	0.492

Source: Feldman and Audretsch (1999).

likely to be located in the same region as the firm when the relationship involves the transfer of new economic knowledge. However, when the scientist is providing a service to the company that does not involve knowledge transfer, local proximity becomes much less important.

Since Krugman (1991: 57) has emphasized, 'States aren't really the right geographical units', the relevant geographic unit of observation is at the city level (Table 3.1). In this chapter I rely upon a direct measure of innovative output, rather than on a measure of intermediate output, such as patented inventions. This US Small Business Administration's Innovation Data Base (SBIDB) is the primary source of data for this chapter. The database consists of new product introductions compiled from the new product announcement sections of over 100 technology, engineering, and trade journals spanning every industry in manufacturing. From the sections in each trade journal listing new products, a database consisting of the innovations by four-digit standard industrial classification (SIC) industries was formed. These innovation data have been implemented by Audretsch (1995) to analyse the relationship between industry dynamics and technological change, and by Audretsch and Feldman (1996) to examine the spatial distribution of innovation.[13]

The most innovative city in the USA was New York. Seven hundred and thirty-five, or 18.5 per cent, of the total number of innovations in the country were attributed to firms in the greater New York City area. Four hundred and seventy-seven (12.0 per cent) were attributed to San Francisco, 345 (8.7 per cent) to the Boston area, and 333 (8.4 per cent) to the Los Angeles area. In total, 1,890, or 45 per cent of the innovations, took place in these four consolidated metropolitan areas. In fact, all but 150 of the innovations included in the database are attributed to metropolitan areas. That is, less than 4 per cent of the innovations occurred outside of metropolitan areas. This contrasts with the 70 per cent of the population, which resided in these areas.

Of course, simply comparing the absolute amount of innovative activity across cities ignores the fact that some cities are simply larger than others. Cities vary considerably in terms of measures of city size, and we expect that city scale will have an impact on innovative output. Table 3.1 presents the number of innovations normalized by the size of the geographic unit. Population provides a crude but useful measure of the size of the geographic unit. Cities in Table 3.1 are ranked in descending order by innovation rate or the number of innovations per 100,000 population. While New York has the highest count of innovation, it has the third highest innovation rate. The most innovative city in the USA, on a per capita measure of city size, was San Francisco, with an innovation rate of 8.90, followed by Boston, with an innovation rate of 8.69. By contrast, the mean innovation rate for the entire country is 1.75 innovations per 100,000 population. The distribution of innovation rates is considerably skewed. Only fourteen cities are more innovative than the national average. Clearly, innovation appears to be a local phenomenon.

There is reason to believe that knowledge spillovers are not homogeneous across firms. In estimating equation (1) for large and small enterprises separately, Acs, Audretsch, and Feldman (1994) provide some insight into the puzzle posed by the recent wave of studies identifying vigorous innovative activity emanating from small firms in certain industries. How are these small, and frequently new, firms able to generate innovative output while undertaking generally negligible amounts of investment into knowledge-generating inputs, such as R&D? The answer appears to be through exploiting knowledge created by expenditures on research in universities and on R&D in large corporations. Their findings suggest that the innovative output of all firms rises along with an increase in the amount of R&D inputs, both in private corporations as well as in university laboratories. However, R&D expenditures made by private companies play a particularly important role in providing knowledge inputs to the innovative activity of large firms, while expenditures on research made by universities serve as an especially key input for generating innovative activity in small enterprises. Apparently large firms are more adept at exploiting knowledge created in their own laboratories, while their smaller counterparts have a comparative advantage at exploiting spillovers from university laboratories.

A conceptual problem arises with economies accruing to the knowledge transmission associated with agglomeration. Once a city, region, or state develops a viable cluster of production and innovative activity why should it ever lose the first-mover advantage? One answer, provided by Audretsch and Feldman (1996), is that the relative importance of local proximity and therefore agglomeration effects is shaped by the stage of the industry life cycle. A growing literature suggests that who innovates and how much innovative activity is undertaken is closely linked to the phase of the industry life cycle (Klepper 1996). Audretsch and Feldman (1996) argue that an additional key aspect to the evolution of innovative activity over the industry life cycle is *where* that innovative activity takes place. The theory of knowledge spillovers, derived from the knowledge production function, suggests that the propensity for innovative activity to cluster spatially will be the greatest in industries where tacit knowledge pays an important role. As argued above, it is *tacit knowledge*, as opposed to *information* which can only be transmitted informally, and typically demands direct and repeated contact. The role of tacit knowledge in generating innovative activity is presumably the greatest during the early stages of the industry life cycle, before product standards have been established and a dominant design has emerged. Audretsch and Feldman (1996) classify 210 industries into four different stages of the life cycle. The results provide considerable evidence suggesting that the propensity for innovative activity to spatially cluster is shaped by the stage of the industry life cycle. On the one hand, new economic knowledge embodied in skilled workers tends to raise the propensity for innovative activity to spatially cluster throughout all phases of the industry life cycle. On the other hand, certain other sources of new economic knowledge, such as university research tend to elevate the propensity for innovative activity to cluster during the introduction stage of the life cycle, but not during the growth stage, and then again during the stage of decline.

Perhaps most striking is the finding that greater geographic concentration of production actually leads to more, and not less, dispersion of innovative activity. Apparently innovative activity is promoted by knowledge spillovers that occur within a distinct geographic region, particularly in the early stages of the industry life cycle, but as the industry evolves towards maturity and decline may be dispersed by additional increases in concentration of production that have been built up within that same region. The evidence suggests that what may serve as an agglomerating influence in triggering innovative activity to spatially cluster during the introduction and growth stages of the industry life cycle, may later result in a congestion effect, leading to greater dispersion in innovative activity. While the literature on economic geography has traditionally focused on factors such as rents, commuting time, and pollution as constituting congestion and dissipating agglomeration economies (Henderson 1986), this type of congestion refers to lock-in with respect to new ideas. While there may have been agglomeration economies in automobiles in Detroit in the 1970 and computers in the North-East Corridor in the 1980s, a type of intellectual lock-in made it difficult for Detroit to shift out of large-car production and for IBM and DEC to shift out of mainframe computers and into minicomputers. Perhaps it was this type of intellectual congestion that led to the emergence of the personal computer in California, about as far away from the geographic agglomeration of the mainframe computer as is feasible on the mainland of the USA. Even when IBM developed its own personal computer, the company located its fledgling PC facility in Boca Raton, Florida, way outside of the mainframe agglomeration, in the North-East Corridor. Thus, there is at least some evidence suggesting that spatial agglomerations, just as other organizational units of economic activity are vulnerable to technological lock-in, with the result being in certain circumstances that new ideas need new space. Thus, while there is considerable evidence supporting economies of agglomeration, at least under certain conditions, diseconomies set in. Once technological lock-in becomes sufficiently rigid, the evidence suggests that new ideas need new space.

6. Penetrating the Black Box of Geographic Space

While a new literature has emerged identifying the importance that knowledge spillovers within a given geographic location play in stimulating innovative activity, there is little consensus as to how and why this occurs (Ellsion and Glaeser 1997; Henderson 1994). The contribution of the new wave of studies described in the previous section was simply to shift the unit of observation away from firms to a geographic region (Henderson, Kuncoro, and Turner 1995). But does it make a difference how economic activity is organized within the black box of geographic space? Political scientists and sociologists have long argued that the differences in the culture of a region may contribute to differences in innovative performance across regions, even holding knowledge inputs such as R&D and human capital constant. For example, Saxenian (1990) argues that a culture of greater interdependence and exchange among individuals in the Silicon Valley region has contributed to a superior innovative performance than is found around Boston's Route 128, where firms and individuals tend to be more isolated and less interdependent.

In studying the networks located in California's Silicon Valley, Saxenian (1990: 96–7) emphasizes that it is the communication between individuals that facilitates the transmission of knowledge across agents, firms, and even industries, and not just a high endowment of human capital and knowledge in the region:

It is not simply the concentration of skilled labour, suppliers and information that distinguish the region. A variety of regional institutions—including Stanford University, several trade associations and local business organisations, and a myriad of specialised consulting, market research, public relations and venture capital firms—provide technical, financial, and networking services which the region's enterprises often cannot afford individually. These networks defy sectoral barriers: individuals move easily from semiconductor to disk drive firms or from computer to network makers. They move from established firms to startups (or vice versa) and even to market research or consulting firms, and from consulting firms back into startups. And they continue to meet at trade shows, industry conferences, and the scores of seminars, talks, and social activities organised by local business organisations and trade associations. In these forums, relationships are easily formed and maintained, technical and market information is exchanged, business contacts are established, and new enterprises are conceived. This decentralised and fluid environment also promotes the diffusion of intangible technological capabilities and understandings.[14]

Such observations suggest a limitation inherent to the general knowledge production function approach described in the previous section. While economists tend to avoid attributing differences in economic performance to cultural differences, there has been a series of theoretical arguments suggesting that differences in the underlying structure between regions may account for differences in rates of growth and technological change. In fact, a heated debate has emerged in the literature about the manner in which the underlying economic structure within a geographic unit of observation might shape economic performance. This debate revolves around two key structural elements—the degree of diversity versus specialization and the degree of monopoly versus local competition.

One view, which Glaeser *et al.* (1992) attribute to the Marshall–Arrow–Romer externality, suggests that an increased concentration of a particular industry within a specific geographic region facilitates knowledge spillovers across firms. This model formalizes the insight that the concentration of an industry within a city promotes knowledge spillovers among firms and therefore facilitates innovative activity. To the degree that individuals in the population are identical and engaged in identical types of activities, the costs of communication and transactions are minimized. Lower costs of transaction in communication result in a higher probability of knowledge spilling over across individuals within the population. An important assumption of the model is that knowledge externalities with respect to firms exist, but only for firms within the same industry. Thus, the relevant unit of observation is extended from the firm to the region in the tradition of the Marshall–Arrow–Romer model, but the spillovers are limited to occur solely within the relevant industry.

By contrast, restricting knowledge externalities to occur only within the same industry may ignore an important source of new economic knowledge— interindustry knowledge spillovers. After all, Griliches (1992: 29) has defined knowledge spillovers as, 'working on similar things and hence benefiting much from each other's research'. Jacobs (1969) argues that the most important source of knowledge spillovers are external to the industry in which the firm operates and that cities are the source of considerable innovation because the diversity of these knowledge sources is greatest in cities. According to Jacobs, it is the exchange of complementary knowledge across diverse firms and economic agents which yields a greater return on new economic knowledge. She develops a theory that emphasizes that the variety of industries within a geographic region promotes knowledge externalities and ultimately innovative activity and economic growth.

The extent of regional specialization versus regional diversity in promoting knowledge spillovers is not the only dimension over which there has been a theoretical debate. A second controversy involves the degree of competition prevalent in the region, or the extent of local monopoly. The Marshall–Arrow–Romer model predicts that local monopoly is superior to local competition because it maximizes the ability of firms to appropriate the economic value accruing from their investments in new knowledge. By contrast, Jacobs (1969) and Porter (1990) argue the opposite—that competition is more conducive to knowledge externalities than is local monopoly.[15] It should be emphasized that by local competition Jacobs does not mean competition within product markets as has traditionally been claimed within the industrial organization literature. Rather, Jacobs is referring to the competition for the new ideas embodied in economic agents. Not only does an increased number of firms provide greater competition for new ideas, but in addition, greater competition across firms facilitates the entry of a new firm specializing in some particular new product niche. This is because the necessary complementary inputs and services are likely to be available from small specialist niche firms but not necessarily from large, vertically integrated producers.

The first important test of the specialization versus diversity debate measured economic performance in terms of employment growth. Glaeser *et al.* (1992) employ a data set on the growth of large industries in 170 cities between 1956 and 1987 in order to identify the relative importance of the degree of regional specialization, diversity, and local competition in influencing industry growth rates. The authors find evidence that contradicts the Marshall–Arrow–Romer model but is consistent with the theories of Jacobs. However, their study provided no direct evidence as to whether diversity is more important than specialization in generating innovative activity.

Feldman and Audretsch (1999) identify the extent to which the organization of economic activity is either concentrated or alternatively consists of diverse but complementary economic activities, and how the underlying structure of economic activity influences innovative output. They link the innovative output of product categories within a specific city to the extent to which the economic activity of that city is concentrated in that industry, or, conversely, diversified in terms of complementary industries sharing a common science base. Their results indicate that diversity across complementary economic activities sharing a common science base is more conducive to innovation than is specialization. In addition, their results indicate that the degree of local competition for new ideas within a city is more conducive to innovative activity than is local monopoly. Perhaps the most important conclusions from these two studies, however, is that more than simply an endowment of knowledge inputs is required to generate innovative activity. The underlying economic and institutional structure matters, as do the microeconomic linkages across agents and firms.

7. Implications for Foreign Direct Investment

With the publication of Stephen Hymer's (1976) Ph.D. thesis, *The International Operations of National Firms: A Study of Direct Foreign Investment*, scholars began to notice that the phenomenon of ownership concentration across geographic space using a strategy of multiplant operations also applied across national borders (Kindleberger and Audretsch 1983). The fundamental challenge of this growing literature was to address the question, 'Why do firms engage in ownership control of assets located beyond national borders rather than resorting to trade relationships or licensing agreements?' Most of the explanations have built on Hymer's seminal study by focusing on firm-specific advantages. Such firm-specific advantages enable rents to be created, which compensate for the various costs arising in foreign direct investment.

John Dunning (1993) points out that the literature on the multinational corporation has identified four major strategies motivating outward foreign direct investment: (i) market seeking, (ii) resource seeking, (iii) efficiency seeking, and (iv) strategic asset seeking.

According to the theories focusing on the geographic extension of firm-specific attributes, production by a corporation begins locally. After production has become established, the firm then expands geographically via shipping the product across geographic space. Thus, the product gains geographic exposure, while production and ownership remain local. In order to reduce costs and exploit the types of (multiplant) economies of scale described above, firms then substitute multiplant production for single establishment production and shipping the product across geographic space. Pursuing a strategy of foreign direct investment simply involves further scale economies to be gained across geographic space that supersedes national boundaries. As Kozul-Wright and Rowthorn (1998: 76) observe,

The two decisive elements in this process are firm size and market penetration. When sufficient sales have been achieved in the new market, it becomes feasible to set up local production facilities on a scale large enough to exploit economies of scale. Since large firms tend to have large exports and more capital at their disposal, they will normally do most investing and this investment will generally be attracted to large and expanding markets.

John Dunning has argued that no single theory of foreign direct investment can adequately and comprehensively explain transnational economic activity, and in particular, multinational corporations. Instead, Dunning proposes combining several of the most widely accepted theories in to an *eclectic paradigm*. In particular, this eclectic paradigm embraces both the neotechnology theories of trade and the theories of imperfect competition.

An emerging literature suggests that in order to access the source of that knowledge, that is to engage in the type of strategic asset-seeking of the type described by Dunning, corporations deploy transnational geographic strategies (Eden, Levitas, and Martinez 1997). For example, Cantwell and Piscitello (1997) find evidence suggesting that multinational corporations are increasingly engaging in foreign direct investment to obtain access to particular knowledge sources at specific locations. According to Cantwell (1998: p. iv), 'Multinational firms have increasingly been able to utilize this locational differentiation between alternative but complementary streams of technological innovation, by constructing a cross-border network as a means of furthering their own recent corporate diversification.'

An earlier line of literature (Buckley and Casson 1976; Teece 1981) focused on the non-codifiability of knowledge as a motivation for outward foreign direct investment, rather than licensing. As a result of the transfer of technological and other types of know-how from the host country via outward foreign direct investment, Cantwell (1995), Buckley (1997), and Cantwell and Iammarino (1998) have identified the existence of spillovers from the home country to firms in the host country, suggesting that there are externalities associated with inward foreign direct investment.

However, knowledge spillovers from the host country to the home country via outward foreign direct investment are less substantiated. According to Blomstrom and Kokko (1998: 251):

Although the existing literature on FDI has not discussed the home country effects of foreign investments in terms of productivity spillovers, it is still clear that some of the potential benefits from FDI to the home economy can be interpreted along these lines. In particular, outward FDI focusing on foreign industry clusters with leading technologies may be a way to get access to valuable foreign technology. However, in the home country context, it is often more difficult to identify productivity spillovers.

Analysing foreign direct investment as a strategy to access localized knowledge spillovers for transfer back to the home country is clearly an important topic that will see considerable attention in the coming years.

8. Conclusions

Globalization has drastically reduced the cost of transporting not just material goods but also information across geographic space. High wages are increasingly incompatible with information-based economic activity, which can be easily transferred to a lower-cost location. By contrast, the creation of new ideas based on tacit knowledge cannot easily be transferred across distance. Thus, the comparative advantage of the high-cost countries of North American and Western Europe is increasingly based on knowledge-driven innovative activity. The spillover of knowledge from the firm or university creating that knowledge to a third-party firm is essential to innovative activity. Such knowledge spillovers tend to be spatially restricted. Thus, an irony of globalization is that even as the relevant geographic market for most goods and services becomes increasingly global, the increased importance of innovative activity in the leading developed countries has triggered a resurgence in the importance of local regions as a key source of comparative advantage.

As the comparative advantage in Western Europe and North America has become increasingly based on new knowledge, public policy towards business has responded in two fundamental ways. The first has been to shift the policy focus away from the traditional triad of policy instruments essentially constraining the freedom of firms to contract—regulation, competition policy or antitrust in the USA, and public ownership of business. The policy approach of constraint was sensible as long as the major issue was how to restrain footloose multinational corporations in possession of considerable market power. This is reflected by the waves of deregulation and privatization along with the decreased emphasis of competition policy throughout the OECD. Instead, a new policy approach is emerging which focuses on enabling the creation and commercialization of knowledge. Examples of such policies include encouraging R&D, venture capital, and new firm start-ups.

The second fundamental shift involves the locus of such enabling policies, which are increasingly at the state, regional, or even local level. The downsizing of federal agencies charged with the regulation of business in the USA and Great Britain has been interpreted by many scholars as the eclipse of government intervention. But to interpret deregulation, privatization, and the increased irrelevance of competition policies as the end of government intervention in business ignores an important shift in the locus and target of public policy. The last decade has seen the emergence of a broad spectrum of enabling policy initiatives that fall outside of the jurisdiction of the traditional regulatory agencies. Sternberg (1996) documents how the success of a number of different high-technology clusters spanning a number of developed countries is the direct result of enabling policies, such as the provision of venture capital or research support. For example, the Advanced Research Program in Texas has provided support for basic research and the strengthening of the infrastructure of the University of Texas, which has played a central role in developing a high-technology cluster around Austin (Feller 1997). The Thomas Edison Centers in Ohio, the Advanced Technology Centers in New Jersey, and the Centers for Advanced Technology at Case Western Reserve University, Rutgers University, and the University of Rochester have supported generic, precompetitive research. This support has generally provided diversified technology development involving a mix of activities encompassing a broad spectrum of industrial collaborators.

Such enabling policies that are typically implemented at the local or regional level are part of a silent policy revolution currently underway. The increased importance of innovative regional clusters as an engine of economic growth has led policy-makers to abandon the policy cry frequently heard two decades ago, 'Should we break up, regulate, or simply take over General Motors, IBM and US Steel?' for a very different contemporary version, 'How can we grow the next Silicon Valley?'

NOTES

1. See also Dunning (1996, 1998).
2. OECD, *Employment Outlook*, 1997.

3. According to *The Economist*, 'The death of distance as a determinant of the cost of the communications will probably be the single most important economic force shaping society in the first half of the next century.' 'The Death of Distance', *The Economist*, 30 Sept. 1995.
4. 'The Downsizing of America', *New York Times*, 3 Mar. 1996, p. 1.
5. See Audretsch (1995).
6. As the German newspaper, *Die Zeit* (2 Feb. 1996, p. 1) pointed out in a front-page article, 'When Profits Lead to Ruin—More Profits and More Unemployment: Where is the Social Responsibility of the Firms?' the German public has responded to the recent waves of corporate downsizing with accusations that corporate Germany is no longer fulfilling its share of the social contract.
7. 'The Valley of Money's Delights', *The Economist*, 29 Mar. 1997, special section, p. 1.
8. Arrow (1962) pointed out this is one of the reasons for inherent market failure.
9. 'The Death of Distance', *The Economist*, 30 Sept. 1995.
10. 'The Best Cities for Knowledge Workers', *Fortune*, 15 Nov. 1993, p. 44.
11. The survey was carried out in 1993 by the management consulting firm of Moran, Stahl, and Boyer of New York City.
12. 'The Best Cities for Knowledge Workers', *Fortune*, 15 Nov. 1993, p. 44.
13. See also Almeida and Kogut (1997).
14. Saxenian (1990: 97–8) claims that even the language and vocabulary used by technical specialists can be specific to a region: 'a distinct language has evolved in the region and certain technical terms used by semiconductor production engineers in Silicon Valley would not even be understood by their counterparts in Boston's Route 128.'
15. Porter (1990) provides examples of Italian ceramics and gold jewellery as industries in which numerous firms are located within a bounded geographic region and compete intensively for new ideas.

REFERENCES

Acs, Z., and Audretsch, D. (1990), *Innovation and Small Firms* (Cambridge, Mass.: MIT Press).

—— —— and Feldman, M. (1992), 'Real Effects of Academic Research', *American Economic Review* 82(1): 363–70.

—— —— (1994), 'R&D Spillovers and Recipient Firm Size', *Review of Economics and Statistics* 100(2): 336–40.

Almeida, P., and Kogut, B. (1997), 'The Exploration of Technological Diversity and the Geographic Localization of Innovation', *Small Business Economics* 9(1): 21–31.

Arrow, K. (1962), 'Economic Welfare and the Allocation of Resources for Invention', in R. Nelson (ed.), *The Rate and Direction of the Inventive Activity* (Princeton: Princeton University Press).

Audretsch, D. (1995), *Innovation and Industry Evolution* (Cambridge, Mass.: MIT Press).

—— (1998), 'Agglomeration and the Location of Innovative Activity', *Oxford Review of Economic Policy* 14(2): 18–29.

Audretsch, D., and Feldman, M. (1996), 'R&D Spillovers and the Geography of Innovation and Production', *American Economic Review* 86(4): 253–73.

—— and Stephan, P. (1996), 'Company-Scientist Locational Links: The Case of Biotechnology', *American Economic Review* 86(4): 641–52.

Baptista, R. (1997), 'An Empirical Study of Innovation, Entry and Diffusion in Industrial Clusters', Ph.D. diss., University of London (London Business School).

Berman, Eli, Bound, John, and Machin, Stephen (1997), 'Implications of Skill-Based Technological Change: International Evidence', NBER Working Paper 6166 (Cambridge, Mass.: National Bureau of Economic Research).

Blomstrom, M., and Kokko, A. (1998), 'Multinational Corporations and Spillovers', *Journal of Economic Surveys* 12(3): 247–77.

Buckley, Peter J. (1997), 'International Technology Transfer by Small and Medium-Sized Enterprises', *Small Business Economics* 9(1): 67–78.

—— and Casson, M. (1976), *The Future of the Multinational Enterprise* (London: Macmillan).

Cantwell, J. (1995), 'The Globalization of Technology: What Remains of the Product Cycle Model?' *Cambridge Journal of Economics* 19: 155–74.

—— (1998), 'Technology and the Firm: Introduction', *Research Policy*, 27: iii–v.

—— and Iammarino, S. (1998), 'MNCs, Technological Innovation and Regional Systems in the EU: Some Evidence in the Italian Case', *International Journal of the Economics of Business* 5(3): 383–408.

—— and Piscitello, L. (1997), 'Accumulating Technological Competence—Its Changing Impact on Corporate Diversification and Internationalisation', Discussion Papers in International Investment and Management, 232, University of Reading.

Cohen, W., and Levinthal, D. (1989), 'Innovation and Learning: The Two Faces of R&D', *Economic Journal* 99(3): 569–96.

Dunning, J. H. (1993), *Multinational Enterprises and the Global Economy* (Boston: Addison-Wesley).

—— (1996), 'The Geographical Sources of Competitiveness of Firms: The Results of a New Survey', *Transnational Corporations* 5(3): 1–30.

—— (1998), 'The Changing Geography of Foreign Direct Investment', in K. Kumar (ed.), *Internationalization, Foreign Direct Investment and Technology Transfer: Impact and Prospects for Developing Countries* (London: Routledge).

—— (2000), 'Introduction', in John H. Dunning (ed.), *Regions, Globalization and the Knowledge-Based Economy* (Oxford: Oxford University Press).

Eden, L., Levitas, E., and Martinez, R. J. (1997), 'The Production, Transfer and Spillover of Technology: Comparing Large and Small Multinationals as Technology Producers', *Small Business Economics* 9(1): 53–66.

Ellsion, G., and Glaeser, E. (1997), 'Geographic Concentration in U.S. Manufacturing Industries: A Dartboard Approach', *Journal of Political Economy* 105(4): 889–927.

Feldman, M. (1994), 'Knowledge Complementarity and Innovation', *Small Business Economics* 6(3): 363–72.

—— and Audretsch, D. (1999), 'Innovation in Cities: Science-Based Diversity, Specialization, and Localized Competition', *European Economic Review* 43: 409–29.

Feller, I. (1997), 'Federal and State Government Roles in Science and Technology', *Economic Development Quarterly* 11(4): 283–96.

Glaeser, E., Kallal, H., Scheinkman, J., and Shleifer, A. (1992), 'Growth of Cities', *Journal of Political Economy* 100: 1126–52.

Griliches, Z. (1979), 'Issues in Assessing the Contribution of R&D to Productivity Growth', *Bell Journal of Economics* 10: 92–116.

—— (1992), 'The Search for R&D Spill-Overs', *Scandinavian Journal of Economics* 94: 29–47.

Henderson, V. (1986), 'Efficiency of Resource Usage and City Size', *Journal of Urban Economics* 19(1): 47–70.

—— (1994), 'Externalities and Industrial Development', NBER Working Paper 4730 (Cambridge, Mass.: National Bureau of Economic Research).

—— Kuncoro, A., and Turner, Matt (1995), 'Industrial Development in Cities', *Journal of Political Economy* 103(5): 1067–90.

Hirschman, A. O. (1970), *Exit, Voice, and Loyalty* (Cambridge, Mass.: Harvard University Press).

Hymer, S. (1976), *The International Operations of National Firms: A Study of Direct Foreign Investment* (Cambridge, Mass.: MIT Press).

Jacobs, J. (1969), *The Economy of Cities* (New York: Random House).

Jaffe, A. (1989), 'Real Effects of Academic Research', *American Economic Review* 79: 957–70.

—— Trajtenberg, M., and Henderson, R. (1993), 'Geographic Localization of Knowledge Spillovers as Evidenced by Patent Citations', *Quarterly Journal of Economics* 63: 577–98.

Kindleberger, C. P., and Audretsch, D. B. (1983), *The Multinational Corporation in the 1980s* (Cambridge, Mass.: MIT Press).

Klepper, S. (1996), 'Entry, Exit, Growth, and Innovation over the Product Life Cycle', *American Economic Review* 86(4): 562–83.

Kortum, S., and Lerner, J. (1997), 'Stronger Protection or Technological Revolution: What is behind the Recent Surge in Patenting?' NBER Working Paper 6204. (Cambridge, Mass.: National Bureau of Economic Research).

Kozul-Wright, R., and Rowthorn, R. (1998), 'Spoilt for Choice? Multinational Corporations and the Geography of International Production', *Oxford Review of Economic Policy* 14(2): 74–92.

Krugman, P. (1991), *Geography and Trade* (Cambridge, Mass.: MIT Press).

Porter, M. (1990), *The Comparative Advantage of Nations* (New York: Free Press).

Prevenzer, M. (1997), 'The Dynamics of Industrial Clustering in Biotechnology', *Small Business Economics* 9(3): 255–71.

Saxenian, A. (1990), 'Regional Networks and the Resurgence of Silicon Valley', *California Management Review* 33: 89–111.

Sternberg, R. (1996), 'Technology Policies and the Growth of Regions', *Small Business Economics* 8(2): 75–86.

Teece, D. J. (1981), 'The Market for Know-How and the Efficient International transfer of Technology', *Annals of the American Academy of Political and Social Science* 458: 81–96.

Von Hipple, E. (1994), 'Sticky Information and the Locus of Problem Solving: Implications for Innovation', *Management Science* 40: 429–39.

Zucker, L., Darby, M., and Armstrong, J. (1994), 'Intellectual Capital and the Firm: The Technology of Geographically Localized Knowledge Spillovers', NBER Working Paper 9496 (Cambridge, Mass.: National Bureau of Economic Research).

4

Multinational Enterprises and the Knowledge Economy:
Leveraging Global Practices

Örjan Sölvell and Julian Birkinshaw

1. Introduction

Multinational enterprises (MNE) today are facing major changes in their business environment. The theme of this book points towards three underlying and interacting forces behind these changes: (i) the globalization of economic activity, (ii) the increasing importance of regional/local processes as the source of innovation, new business ideas, and practices, and (iii) the advent of the knowledge-based economy. All three have a profound impact on the way in which MNEs are organized and run. Some of the well-established MNEs, in spite of their enormous resources, seem to be disadvantaged, whereas many new actors with a 'fresh start' build innovative capacity and leverage it on a global scale. To understand these changes in competitive dynamics we must bring together and link the processes of globalization, localization, and knowledge creation to the evolution of the MNE.

This chapter is in six sections. Sections 2 and 3 provide a brief review of the existing literature on the knowledge economy, and on the forces for globalization and localization, with the purpose of explaining why the nature of the competitive challenge facing MNEs is changing. Section 4 introduces the concept of *global practices* as a key driver of firm competitiveness in a knowledge economy. Sections 5 and 6 consider the implications of global practices, first in terms of the evolution of the MNE, and then in terms of the theory of the MNE. The chapter finishes with some concluding remarks in Section 7.

The argument can be summarized as follows. First, we suggest that the increased globalization of many markets goes hand in hand with the increased localization/regionalization of innovative capacity. In a world of global markets and global communication, certain regions within nations take on a leading innovative role within a certain business segment. Within such regions, a multitude of actors, involving rival firms, related and supporting industries, buying industries, various research and education bodies, and other industry-specific organizations, cluster within a limited geographical space (Porter 1990; Sölvell, Zander, and Porter 1991; Enright 1994). Examples such as Silicon Valley in IT,

Hollywood in film, and London in finance are often used, but these tendencies of an international division of labour, or rather international division of innovative strength, play a role *across* industries as well as *within* them (Porter 1990; Krugman 1991).

Second, we argue that in a knowledge economy the 'Hollywood' phenomenon (i.e. the clustering of core activities of key global competitors in a single region) has important implications for the development of leading-edge skills and practices in MNEs. If we model the MNE as a set of geographically dispersed activities and practices, then increasingly it is their practices—not their activities—that are the source of competitiveness. Such practices, we argue, usually emerge in 'Hollywood' settings, and it is then up to the MNE to identify, interpret, and make use of them on a worldwide basis.

2. The Knowledge Economy

The term 'knowledge economy' refers essentially to the increasing importance of knowledge as the source of wealth creation in society. Richness was once built on ownership of land and raw materials. Later capital became the scarce resource or the 'mine' from which firms could dig gold. With the advent of the Industrial Revolution the value of skills and technology became the new well. Gradually, the proximity to research bodies (universities and free-standing research organizations) in society became more important as did the development of in-house corporate R&D capacity. With emerging global markets offering a new potential to optimize the production function for all firms, irrespective of home base, the value of knowledge and unique practices as a basis for competitive advantage has become even more pronounced. Efficiencies based on scale and scope had to leave room for innovation and new knowledge creation.

The value of knowledge is obvious in today's economy when small start-up firms with limited resources (plants, people, accumulated capital, land, etc.), but with unique knowledge or practices, fetch very high prices on the stock market. For example, on 28 May 1998, Lucent Technologies of the USA paid roughly $US 1 billion for a tiny company in Maryland called Yurie, specializing in ATM and IP telephony technologies. Yurie had sales of $US 51 million in 1997. In Sweden, a small company named Netcom Systems with only some 1,200 employees, active in fixed telephony (starting 1991) and mobile telephony (starting 1981) in the Nordic countries, is valued at around 30 billion SEK. The Swedish state-owned Telecom operator Telia, active in telephone services (and up until the 1990s in telecommunication equipment) since the late nineteenth century, and with some 23,000 employees, is valued at only around twice the value of Netcom Systems.

In more and more industries we see firms with a 'fresh start': they build activities for a relatively open global market, they invest in new technologies and new people without enormous sunk costs, they face deregulated markets, they can outsource standardized activities on a global scale—utilizing the most efficient suppliers of services, production, design, and so forth. Established MNEs have a 'rucksack' of people with the wrong skills, plants, and other resources that constitute severe competitive disadvantages.

3. Forces for Globalization and Localization

3.1. **Globalization of Markets for Goods and Services**

Globalization is fundamentally changing the way business is done as it involves more and more markets, and offers new potential for competitive advantage. First, we will highlight five different areas where globalization is the most prevalent: financial capital, internal markets created within MNEs (both vertical flows involving headquarters and horizontal flows linking subsidiaries), transportation and communication, information and services, and sourcing and outsourcing of semi-finished as well as finished products.

The 'death of distance' (Cairncross 1997) is probably the most true for financial markets (bonds, stocks, currencies, futures, etc.). Local markets are connected through global, 24-hour, systems where trading is done at negligible cost. Also, most physical capital can be traded at low cost. Even raw materials and basic products such as iron ore, cement, and stone travel the world on specialized ships and other means of transportation. An example of global trade of extremely bulky materials is Swedish iron-ore pellets produced by LKAB in northern Sweden being shipped to distant markets in Asia. Japanese steel manufacturers bring home ore from Australia. Swedish-made cement made by Scancem is landed in Florida. For high-value-added products transportation costs are negligible. Localized geographical clusters or national boundaries mean almost nothing in these globalized markets. In the automotive industry, for example, up to 80 per cent of the content in a car is internationally traded.

Trade *within* the MNE is also increasingly global in nature. The underlying rationale for global intra-MNE trade is the same as for other global markets —increasing specialization of subsidiary units made possible through reduced tariffs facilitated by more efficient communication and reduced costs of transporting goods around the world. But the internalization of such transactions makes it possible to put together more ambitious and more global business systems than would be possible in the open market. As one example, Volvo Trucks' Pennsylvania assembly plant finds it efficient to buy much of its sheet metal from a stamping plant in southern Sweden.

If we move to information stored in databases, patents, or formulae, digitalization has added a new dimension where search costs have almost been obliterated and the 'death of distance' is finally coming true. The same goes for communication technologies (satellites, fixed telephony system, Internet) allowing for global transfer of voice, data, pictures, and video at rapidly diminishing costs. New global markets are created every day on the Internet, and the growth of e-commerce in expanding from air tickets, books and music to cars, tobacco, and drugs. Microsoft is now becoming one of the largest retailers of cars in the USA through its 'carpoint.msn.com' site.

Activities traditionally carried out inside firms are outsourced, utilizing the most efficient specialized firms in world markets. Early efforts involved production of low-skill products in Asia. Today, outsourced functions include the telephone switch (call centres), customer service over the phone, bookkeeping, advertising, internal administrative computer services (e.g. salary systems, storage control), computer programming and systems development. Industrial design firms in Italy offer service to manufacturers throughout the world. When a Korean manufacturer recently introduced a new line of trucks, the design had been carried out by British design engineers.

There is a vast literature on the potential hidden in these globalized markets and global infrastructure. Now we turn to the other side of the coin—localization—which is much less emphasized in the literature. What seems to stay highly local, or what might become even more local as we move into globalized markets?

3.2. Localization Forces

The more prevalent local aspects of economic life today involve labour markets, certain markets for goods and services with multidomestic or national competition (many household services, certain segments of food industries, and personal products), and business practices and the broader 'social capital' (Putnam 1993) involving history-bound routines and institutions. The local economics of certain markets can probably be overcome with digitalization and globalization of surrounding markets. But, people, in spite of increasing potential for migration, are as 'culturally programmed' as ever before, and local institutions, networks, and trust involve a different quality of localization from most other markets.

The phenomenon of centripetal forces, or agglomeration, is well covered in the economic geography literature. The economics of agglomeration is driven by the search for lowered transportation costs, economies of scale, flexibility and lower search costs, and labour pool efficiencies. The other side of the prosperity coin involves innovation and creation of new knowledge. The theme of innovation as an agglomerated phenomenon has re-emerged in the literature, very much helped by the works of Krugman (1991) and Porter (1990). Antecedents include Marshall's industrial districts (1890/1916), Weber (1909/1929), and Hoover (1948). More recent models of innovation and new skill formation as a process taking place within limited geographical clusters of competing and cooperating actors, include Lloyd and Dicken's localization economies (1977), new industrial districts (Piore and Sabel 1984), Scott's regional industrial systems (1983, 1988), innovative milieux (Aydalot 1986; Maillat 1994), industry clusters (Porter 1990), and learning regions (Saxenian 1994). Another set of models are built around the notion of national innovation systems (NIS), where national R&D policies and national institutions provide the framework for innovation and creation of new knowledge (Nelson 1993).

One central theme in these models is the new method of production in the post-Fordist era, involving a variety of networked firms, both small and large (Amin and Malmberg 1992; Storper 1995). Furthermore, emphasis is put on the intense exchange of business information and technological expertise, both in traded and untraded form (Scott 1995). If we now turn to the literature dealing with innovation and innovative networks, we find that it is reasonable to argue that proximity within clusters is in fact critical to the process by which new skills and new technology is formed (Malmberg, Sölvell, and Zander 1996; Porter and Sölvell 1998).

3.3. The Innovation Process in a Local Context

In the innovation and network literature we find several factors pointing to localization advantages. As Pavitt (1984) and others have shown, ideas behind an innovation frequently originate outside the firm that carries out the actual development or manufacturing work. Only a small proportion of all innovations has been found to be directed towards use within the innovating organization (Scherer 1984). The importance of customers as sources of innovation has been testified in several studies (Håkansson 1989; Laage-Hellman 1989), while others have added evidence that the development of functionally useful innovations is sometimes dominated by the suppliers (von Hippel 1988). In yet other cases, several firms might be involved in joint development work, by which each of the participants supplies a limited component of the resulting innovation. This makes the innovation process highly interactive—between firms and the basic science infrastructure, between suppliers and users at the interfirm level, and between firms and their wider institutional setting (Lundvall 1988). This exchange frequently involves sensitive information, which might cause damage if used opportunistically by the firms involved, and therefore requires a high level of trust between the parties. Similar linkages between the scientific community and firms engaged in technological improvements have also been illustrated (Freeman 1982).

Tight interaction and trustful relationships can of course be built on a global scale. However, in spite of increasingly sophisticated means of travel and communication, the need for personal, face-to-face contacts in the exchange of information has not disappeared (Fredriksson and Lindmark 1979; Cantwell 1989; Nohria and Eccles 1992). Personal contacts have been identified as important sources of technological information and improvements in the innovation process (Leonard-Barton 1982; De Meyer 1991, 1992; Lindqvist, Sölvell, and Zander 1998). And analysis of patent 'citations' shows that the frequency of citation is strongly correlated with the proximity of the cited patent (Almeida 1996; Frost 1996). Moreover, well-established geographical models suggest that there is 'friction of distance', implying that the probability of interpersonal communication through face-to-face contacts declines with increasing distance between individuals (Hägerstrand 1967: Pred 1977).

While agglomeration theory has picked up on the notion of knowledge accumulation in explaining the emergence and sustainability of spatial clusters of related firms and industries, the innovation literature provides a complementary illustration of the very same process. In the local cluster, the fluidity of knowledge will be improved by the development of common codes of communication and interaction, particularly when knowledge is difficult or costly to codify, and the build-up of trust between interacting parties. The local cluster thus offers an environment for the evolution of a common language, social bonds, norms, values, and institutions, or a social capital (Putnam 1993), which adds to the process of innovation and new practice creation. Within the local cluster, these institutional arrangements become increasingly specialized and unique, adding non-imitable competitive advantage to incumbent firms.

This discussion leads to the important conclusion that local processes of innovation and interaction represent an increasingly important source of competitiveness for firms operating in a global economic system. If capital, physical goods, and information are now able to flow relatively efficiently around the world, then the ability to manage them well represents a diminishing source of competitive advantage. Instead, *it is applied resources, i.e. capabilities or practices, that represent the real competitive edge for MNEs.* Given that such practices typically emerge in a local setting, and that they are therefore 'sticky' (Kogut 1993) our belief is that the ability to apply, adapt, or transfer practices on a worldwide basis is what separates the successful MNEs from the less successful. In the remainder of the paper we will examine this contention in more detail.

4. What are Practices?

We should be clear about what we mean by practices before taking the argument any further. A simple distinction is the following: activities are what the firm does, practices are how the firm does it. Thus, manufacturing is an activity, while lean manufacturing is a practice; marketing is an activity, key account management is a practice; and so on. Every activity has one or more practices associated with it that represent a way of adding value to that activity. Some practices also span several different activities, for example a company-wide quality programme. The activity–practice distinction can be usefully compared to the distinction between resources and capabilities. According to Amit and Schoemaker (1993: 35):

Resources are stocks of available factors that are owned or controlled by the firm . . . resources consist *inter alia* of knowledge that can be traded, financial or physical assets, human capital etc. Capabilities, in contrast, refer to a firm's capacity to deploy resources, usually in combination, using organizational processes, to effect a desired end. They are information based, tangible or intangible processes that are firm-specific and are developed over time through complex interactions among the firm's resource.

It should be clear that this distinction parallels the one we are proposing quite well. The firm's activities can be seen as a bundle of resources—a manufacturing plant, for example, consists of physical assets, human capital, some tradable technology, and so on. The firm's practices are the equivalent of Amit and Schoemaker's (1993) capabilities, in that they represent the way the firm deploys its resources. According to the so-called resource-based view of the firm (Barney 1991) resources and capabilities together form the basis for a firm's sustainable competitive advantage, and thus its strategy.

It should be noted that while no consensus exists on the definitions of these terms, Amit and Schoemaker's approach has been widely accepted in the field of strategic management. The reason we retain the terminology 'activities and practices' is simply that it has more inherent meaning in the context of the large firm. Managers talk in terms of their value-adding activities and their best practices, and others know what they mean. Resources and capabilities, by contrast, are such overused terms that their meaning is seldom clear.

Consider Figure 4.1 as a way of illustrating the distinction between activities and practices. Because of the tight interdependency between an activity and its associated practices one often finds that excellence in one goes hand in hand with excellence in the other. But this is not necessarily the case. For example, the emergence of lean production in Japan did not rely on the latest technology or large factory investments. On the contrary, much of the equipment used in Japanese factories in the 1960s and 1970s was old and past its best—Schonberger (1987: 95) referred to it as 'frugal manufacturing'. World-class practices, in other words, emerged on top of second-rate activities. In contrast, there are many cases

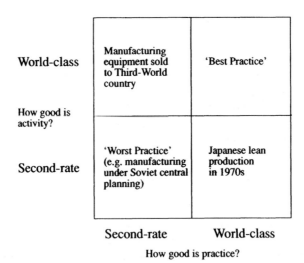

FIG. 4.1. Quality of activities vs. quality of practices

of firms selling their latest machinery to Third World countries without the relevant infrastructure or personnel training, and yielding weak results. Second-rate practices, in this case, can coexist with world-class activities.

These examples suggest some interesting implications. First, practices seem to be more tightly associated with competitiveness, in that world-class activities with second-rate practices are clearly outperformed by the opposite configuration. Second, practices are locally embedded—they are built on the social and institutional context of the immediate surroundings—while activities are relatively free-standing. Third and related to the second point, practices are inherently less tradable than activities. For example, when Ericsson sold its Karlskrona manufacturing plant in southern Sweden to Flextronics, Flextronics gained ownership of all the physical assets and the human resources. To some degree it also acquired the plant's old practices, but because they were so tied up with the rest of the Ericsson organization they were not readily 'accessible' to Flextronics. Rather than try to decipher and make use of these practices, Flextronics chose to build its own.

5. The Evolution of the Multinational Enterprise

This distinction between activities and practices has important implications for the multinational enterprise. As a way of cutting into this issue, let us first consider how MNEs have evolved over the last hundred years, and how practices are managed at each stage.

In the latter part of the nineteenth century and the early part of this century, the MNE was looked upon as a firm that either internally exploited a certain technology on world markets, or a firm that internally exploited global standardized, low-cost, factor markets. Focus was put on global optimization and efficiency. Most of the foreign direct investment (FDI), on which the MNE was built, was in fact oriented towards exploiting goods or services on a worldwide scale.

In order to maximize the potential for exploitation, early MNEs were forced to build local operations across national markets in order to circumvent all sorts of barriers to trade and government and customer demands. This led to a dominant type of polycentric or multidomestic MNE (Perlmutter 1969; Bartlett 1986; Dunning 1993). These MNEs were perfectly adapted to a world of fragmented national markets involving not only national trade barriers, but maybe more important differing technical standards, local distribution systems, and customers loyal to local brands (Sölvell 1987).

If we depict the MNE—and its foundation for competitive advantage—as building on a mix of activities and practices, the multidomestic or polycentric firms were run with locally confined activities (e.g. local plants, product development, brands, and distribution) as well as locally confined practices (e.g. business practices, quality issues, customer handling). A typical example was Electrolux a globally dispersed firm with locally confined activities and practices (see Figure 4.2).

Örjan Sölvell and Julian Birkinshaw

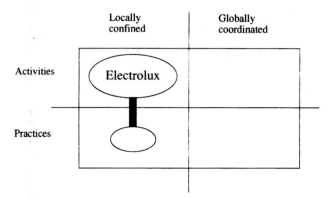

FIG. 4.2. An MNE combining locally confined activities and locally confined practices

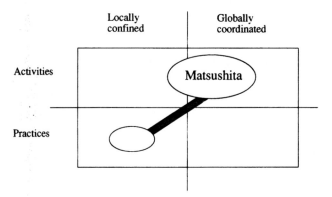

FIG. 4.3. An MNE combining globally coordinated activities with locally confined practices

As trade barriers came down in the 1960s we saw a new type of MNE emerging. Japanese MNEs in particular, and alter Korean and other Asian MNEs, now received a fresh start in an economy built on relatively free trade. Activities involving component production, assembly, and R&D could be built from a few core plants for global markets (exporting out of a dynamic home cluster), and therefore activities of these MNEs were globally coordinated from the outset. A case in point was Electrolux's competitor, Matsushita, a world leader in a wide range of appliances (see Figure 4.3).

The old MNEs were clearly disadvantages in the new world of open borders, larger and more internationally oriented distributors, and evolving global brands. Established MNEs began a process of restructuring activities across nations, beginning a process of specialization of plants and other activities (Doz 1986) in order to achieve similar economies of scale as the new MNEs. However, following

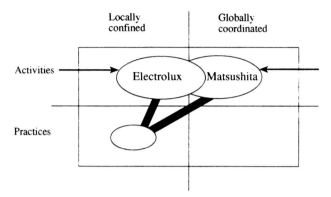

FIG. 4.4. The two types of MNEs converging

from a remarkable export success, the new MNEs were forced to disperse activities as new trade borders were erected, especially in Europe and the USA. This was witnessed in industries such as automobiles, consumer electronics, and office machinery. As research has shown this restructuring process has indeed been slow and fraught with difficulties (e.g. Bartlett and Ghoshal 1989), presented in Figure 4.4.

Important here is that the two types of MNEs were focusing on ways of configuring and coordinating their *value-adding activities* globally as a means of achieving economies of scale and scope (Porter 1986). This emphasis on activities is in fact pervasive in the MNE literature. It is evident in the major theories of the MNE (Hymer 1960/1976; Buckley and Casson 1976; Dunning 1981; Rugman 1981); it is evident in the traditional definition of the MNE (i.e. owning and controlling income-generating assets in more than one country); and it is evident in the many cases studies of successful MNEs from the 1970s and 1980s (Porter 1986).

5.1. From Activities to Practices

The emergence of the knowledge economy has caused many MNEs to rethink their competitive strategy, and in particular the benefits they achieve from a multinational presence. Central to that process of rethinking, we argue, is a shift from activities to practices as the major source of competitiveness. Of course MNEs have always had practices and they have always been valued to some degree. The shift we are arguing for is a greater recognition of the importance of leveraging practices overseas, and thus an enhanced level of competitiveness in MNEs that are effective in this. Consider the following examples:

- McKinsey, the management consultancy, has no assets beyond the raw brainpower of its consultants (who can leave any time) and the 'structural capital' of the firm as held in its routines, approaches to client management, and knowledge databases. In such a firm, the ability to identify and leverage best practices across borders is the primary source of advantage over local competitors.

- ISS, the Danish cleaning company, is operating in an industry where activities are by definition local. The only benefits ISS has from multinationality is its ability to develop a global brand and to identify and transfer new practices between countries.
- Millicom, the Luxembourg-based mobile telephone operator, has activities around the world, but each is a free-standing entity. It is successful because it is able to apply a business model developed by founder Jan Stenbeck that promotes early entry, very rapid start-up, and an entrepreneurial management style.
- Nike, the sportswear and equipment manufacturer, has no manufacturing activities of its own. Instead it focuses on marketing and product design, and applies these on a consistent basis throughout the world.

If we use the framework as presented in Figures 4.2–4.4, we can put in the two 'bottom-heavy' firms Millicom and Nike (Figures 4.5 and 4.6). In the case of Millicom, practices are globally leveraged, whereas activities (units operating the mobile system) are locally confined. Because of its economics, these types of firms have developed in many service industries such as management consulting (McKinsey, Andersen) and telecommunication services.

In the case of Nike, global practices are combined with globally coordinated flows of products (see Figure 4.6). To some extent one can also see McKinsey taking this form as project work becomes more transnational in scope.

The argument suggested by the these four examples is a simple one: as we move into a 'knowledge economy' the *benefits MNEs gain from multinationality will be far more a function of their ability to manage practices across borders than activities*. There are several reasons for this. First, practices—and the

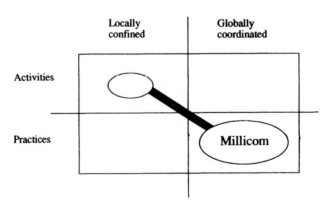

FIG. 4.5. An MNE combining globally leveraged practices with locally confined activities

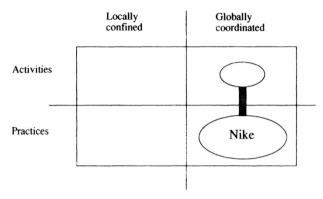

FIG. 4.6. An MNE combining globally leveraged practices with globally coordinated activities

ability to leverage them across borders—represent the main source of competitive advantage for many firms. Second, a lack of competitiveness in activities can be partly solved by outsourcing those activities to more competitive firms, whereas the same cannot be said for practices. Certainly, many firms use benchmarking as a means of identifying and using leading-edge practices from elsewhere, but the logic of this approach is fundamentally about bringing new practices into the firm, rather than getting rid of them. Finally, practices are typically causally ambiguous, which means that the process through which they were created is not well enough understood to replicate it easily. This provides the firm with a potential source of competitive advantage if it is also valuable. The same cannot be said for activities (Barney 1991).

6. Global Practices and the Theory of the MNE

We should acknowledge at this point that the shift from activities to practices has already been captured to varying degrees in the existing literature. The dominant theory of the MNE, for example, builds on the logic that the market for intangibles is imperfect and is thus internalized (Buckley and Casson 1976; Rugman 1981). While intangibles in this context frequently refers to technology, it could just as easily apply to business practices. In more recent years, Dunning (1993) has also incorporated many practices explicitly into his eclectic paradigm of international production.

Kogut and Zander's (1995) evolutionary theory of the multinational corporation represents an attempt to put forward a theoretical rationale for the existing of MNEs *without* relying on the internalization of market failures across borders. Their proposition that 'firms are social communities that specialize in the creation and internal transfer of knowledge' (1995: 625) represents an explicit focus on the practices of the firm rather than its activities. Related studies based on the so-called dynamic capabilities perspective (Nelson and Winter 1982; Madhok 1997; Teece, Pisano, and Shuen 1997) are also concerned with practices or capabilities, though not with a specific multinational perspective.

The more applied literature concerned with multinational management has also acknowledged both activities and practices, though an explicit distinction between the two is rarely made. Perlmutter's (1969) seminal article, for example, was concerned with ethnocentric, polycentric, and geocentric *mindsets* among managers, but many of his examples actually refer to firm practices. Porter's (1986) configuration–coordination framework is explicitly based around activities, but many of the mechanisms for coordinating activities worldwide are actually practices, e.g. 'transferring process technology among plants' or 'transferring market knowledge' (1986: 18). Finally, Bartlett and Ghoshal (1989) talk about the need for global integration (i.e. activities) and worldwide learning (i.e. practices), as distinct but equally important imperatives for the multinational corporation.

A related body of literature has emerged in recent years that is concerned with knowledge management in large firms. This has brought the identification and transfer of 'best practices' to the forefront as a way of making use of a firm's dispersed capabilities (e.g. Szulanski 1996; Kostova and Cummings 1997; Arvidsson and Birkinshaw 1998; Moore and Birkinshaw 1998).

The apparent trend in the literature then, is from a relative focus on activities to a relative focus on practices. The reason for this is partly novelty in that there is much less literature on practices, but it may also be because the potential benefits of effective practice management in a knowledge-based economy are substantial. In effect, this recent line of empirical research reflects the growing emphasis by leading established MNEs to put more emphasis on practices and to reap the advantages of leveraging these on a global scale (see Figure 4.7). This would involve, for example, the implementation of a corporate-wide total quality programme that had been successfully developed in one country. In the remainder of this chapter, we will examine some of the implications of this thesis.

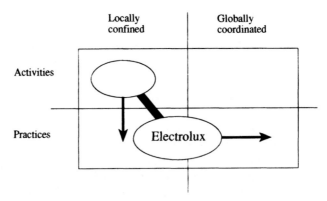

FIG. 4.7. Two movements of established MNEs

6.1. Implications: Practices and Attitudes

An important issue to consider in a discussion of practices is Perlmutter's (1969) classic argument that MNEs can have ethnocentric, polycentric, and geocentric attitudes. Perlmutter forecast in this article that MNEs would become more sophisticated in building their global market potential through the development of geocentric attitudes. But to a large degree this never happened. The well-established MNEs did of course continue to build activities throughout the world through greenfield establishment of subsidiaries and more recently through alliances and mergers and acquisitions. At first, internationalization involved more peripheral functions such as sales, service, assembly/packaging, and sometimes some local adaptation. Then in the last couple of decades internationalization has included strategic functions such as core manufacturing plants, R&D laboratories, and headquarters' functions being dispersed all around the world. So how can we argue that MNEs never really did go into the geocentric stage? As the discussion has suggested, the emphasis of these MNEs was predominantly on global activities—not global practices. Activities were dispersed—and coordinated to varying degrees—but knowledge embedded in practices was rarely leveraged on a global scale. The emerging changes discussed in this chapter suggest that maybe practices are now becoming more globally coordinated, which indicates that maybe Perlmutter's prophecy will finally come true.

Perlmutter's argument reveals one additional complication to the discussion of shared practices, namely that such practices can be ethnocentric or they can be geocentric. Ethnocentric practices are those that emanate from head office and are applied uniformly overseas in an almost imperialistic style. Geocentric practices emerge anywhere in the world, and are applied and adapted as appropriate. Geocentrism thus involves two components: (i) an openness to practices that first arise in a subsidiary company rather than in head office, and (ii) a willingness to adapt the practice *if necessary* to make it viable in the new context. This distinction makes it clear that ethnocentrism is not necessarily a bad thing. Some firms have been extremely successful in taking a standard practice that worked at home and applying it uniformly in new markets—Japanese transplant factories are examples that springs to mind (Florida and Kenney 1994). What is important, in this case, is not the source of the idea *per se*, but an awareness of the extent to which that idea should be tailored to the demands of the local context.

6.2. Implications for Foreign Direct Investment

One critical issue that emerges from the discussion of activities versus practices is *location*. The widely accepted 'eclectic' paradigm of overseas production (Dunning 1980) emphasizes the importance of location-specific advantage in the decision about where a given activity should be placed. While certain activities, such as sales and logistics, are located according to the demands of the customer, many others such as manufacturing and R&D are *potentially* mobile. As a result, they gravitate (with considerable inertia) towards the location in the world where they have some sort of comparative advantage—be it low labour costs, cheap factor inputs, preferential tariffs, or learning opportunities in a local cluster. In organizational theory terms, this represents a differentiation of the activities of the multinational corporation according to the demands of the heterogeneous task environment. Moreover, as the host country economy evolves, so too do the activities of the multinational in that country. Manufacturing that used to be cost competitive in Ireland is moved to East Europe; Nokia opens up an R&D centre in Stockholm to tap into Ericsson's cluster of expertise around GSM technology, and so on.

The same logic applies to practices, but with important differences. First, leading-edge practices can be expected to emerge as a function of the unique demands of the task environment. Customer focus programmes might be developed first in the USA; total quality initiatives might first arise in Japan; and so on. Second, what is a leading-edge practice today may not be tomorrow, so the multinational has to be continually open to the emergence of new practices, and be prepared to shift its 'centre of excellence' for that practice accordingly.

But on the question of *mobility*, there are massive and important differences between activities and practices. If we consider for a second the physical manifestations of the two, activities consist of large factories, offices, or R&D centres staffed with hundreds if not thousands of employees. Practices, by contrast, either have no physical existence (they are simply 'embedded' in the activity), or they can be traced to the ideas and influence of a small number of key people. On the face of it, activities would therefore seem less mobile than practices. Moving an activity from one place to another is expensive both in transportation costs and in loss of productivity. In contrast, if a practice can be traced back to a couple of individuals, then it would appear to be relatively straightforward to move them to another location and get them to create the same practice there.

But practices are often not as mobile as one would hope. The classic example is GM's failed attempt to take the productivity and quality standards from their NUMMI joint venture with Toyota and apply them to their other manufacturing operations. Clearly in this case something was 'lost in the translation'. What exactly that was does not matter—it is simply enough at this point to observe that there is a high level of causal ambiguity in the development of practices, and this makes their transfer far from straightforward. And even if the practice could be clearly identified, there is the additional risk that its effectiveness is context-specific, and thus that it would not work when transferred to another location.

And to complicate the story even more, there are some interesting cases of large-scale activities being moved quite long distances. To give an extreme example, in the early 1990s the Hällefors steelworks in Sweden was taken apart, shipped to China, and then put back together. And cases of light machinery, e.g. for office equipment, being shipped from West to East Europe are commonplace.

So the mobility issue is not that simple. There is enormous inertia associated with moving activities, but at least it is obvious what should be moved. Practices have less inertia and can sometimes be moved very rapidly, but at the same time they are often context-dependent and causally ambiguous, so their movement between locations is not guaranteed. One additional point should be made here that is in some ways rather obvious. When an activity moves from A to B, it is lost by A. When a practice moves from A to B, it is still retained by A. In other words, the 'cost' of transferring a practice (from A's perspective) is much lower than the cost of transferring an activity.

The implications of all the above to host country policy-makers are quite profound. On the face of it, they are concerned only with activities, because they provide the investment, the jobs, and the exports that are so essential to the host-country economy. But what gives an activity its real 'value added' to the corporation are the practices that go with it. If a manufacturing plant has the highest productivity in the corporate system, it is likely to attract additional investments and may become viewed as the centre of excellence from which other plants can learn. But if its performance is average or poor, it will become an obvious candidate for closure or downsizing if the corporation comes under pressure to cut its costs. The point, then, is that it is the practices associated with the activities that determine whether a host-country investment will move into a positive spiral of upgrading, or whether it becomes a 'branch plant' investment that is closed down as quickly as it was opened. Policy-makers should still focus on attracting activities, but this discussion suggests that they should devote a much greater amount of attention to building leading-edge practices among their indigenous and foreign-owned firms than they do at present. This can be done at the level of practice transfers between individual sites, but probably more useful is for policy-makers to focus on enhancing the innovatory systems and the organization of work in their country as the roots of superior business practices (Kogut 1993).

To summarize, the increasing importance of practices as the basis of competitiveness in multinational corporations creates some interesting dynamics for foreign direct investment. As observed earlier, there is a paradox that globalization is actually putting more emphasis on local processes of innovation and competition (Dunning 1998; Enright 2000). This chapter makes it possible to sharpen that argument by suggesting that *practices* are developed incrementally in the local context through the efforts of local management whereas *activities* are shifted in discrete steps through decisions made many miles away in the corporate headquarters.

6.3. Implications for the Management of the MNE

This chapter has focused primarily on theoretical issues, so the 'managerial implications' are not directly relevant. Nonetheless, in the interests of pushing the framework forward and understanding its potential, there is value in considering some of the ways it could influence the management of the MNE.

The first and most obvious issue that surfaces relates to the generic approaches described in Figures 4.2 to 4.5. Some firms have an implicit policy of developing their practices at headquarters and using them worldwide (Millicom); others prefer to adapt their practices to the needs of the local market (Electrolux in the 1980s). And many are attempting to move towards the right side of the figure by coordinating their activities and practices worldwide. Intuitively this appears to be the most attractive position, but of course it is unlikely to be as simple as that. For one thing, there are significant costs associated with the identification and transfer of best practices, with no guarantee of success. Secondly, there are advantages in standardization on a global basis, and this is hard to achieve if foreign subsidiaries are invited to adapt practices from wherever they choose.

But on the assumption that there are net benefits in moving in this direction, there are certain mechanisms that MNEs can use to facilitate that change. While we do not claim an exhaustive list, the following appear to be the most popular approaches:

- Knowledge management systems, for keeping track of valuable practices used in one place that could be applied elsewhere. McKinsey, for example, has a system called PDNet, on which information about recent projects, conceptual models, and clients is stored. This system is managed professionally to ensure that it represents the leading-edge ideas in McKinsey. Consultants working on a new client project can tap into this system and gain access to the collective knowledge base of the firm on a worldwide basis.
- Centres of excellence, which are 'best practices' recognized by the corporation with a view to the practice being made available to other units in the corporation. 3M Europe, for example, has centres of excellence in key account management, Internet services, customer loyalty, and business intelligence. The individuals behind these centres are based in their local offices, but frequently offer their services to other offices in Europe.
- 'Model plants' which are replicated in their entirety in new locations around the world when expansion is needed. Ericsson Mobile, for example, has model plants in Sweden and the USA that are used as models for new investments in Asia and South America.
- 'League tables' that chart the performance of R&D centres, manufacturing plants, or marketing units on key metrics such as productivity, quality, or market share. These tables are designed to highlight the differences in practices between units, and therefore to encourage the weaker performers to learn from the higher performers. Many companies use these sorts of tables, including ABB, Ericsson, and Motorola.
- Personnel management systems, such as secondments, transfers, and international training programmes. Such approaches aid in the informal transfer of practices between units, and in the development of strong personal ties between managers around the world.

- External benchmarking of practices against competitors or firms in other industries.
- Alliances between competing or complementary firms can provide access to practices that the MNE currently lacks. There is a considerable literature on the processes of learning between alliance partners, which in our terminology can be seen as the mutual transfer of practices (Dunning 1995; Inkpen 1995).

Anecdotal evidence collected about firms' experience with these mechanisms indicates that the transfer of practices is often fraught with difficulty. Any given transfer, even if it has been identified as a good idea in principle, can meet resistance from the source unit (why should I help them?), from the receiving unit (the not-invented-here syndrome), and in the course of the transfer itself across large geographical and cultural distances. As von Hippel (1998) has stated. knowledge assets of this sort are 'sticky' which makes their exploitation (inside the firm) and their imitation (outside the firm) difficult.

Not all practices are sticky though. Consider the rise of the benchmarking industry, whose primary purpose is to take practices that other firms have excelled in and apply them inside one's own firm. The success of benchmarking suggests that there are many cases of 'off-the-shelf' practices that can be identified and applied quite easily. Consulting companies play a valuable role in facilitating the movement of such practices. But at the same time, we know that there are other practices that defy replication. Firms have marvelled at 3M's innovative culture for decades, for example, but none has demonstrably been able to copy it.

The framework in Figure 4.8 puts some structure around this discussion. 'Off-the-shelf' practices are those that can be transferred easily inside the firm but that are equally easy for other firms to replicate—a new employee benefits programme, for example. 'Opaque' practices, like 3M's innovative culture, are hard

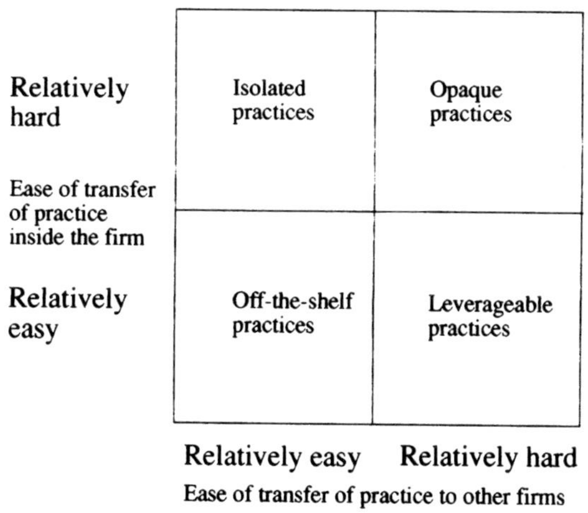

Relatively hard	Isolated practices	Opaque practices
Ease of transfer of practice inside the firm		
Relatively easy	Off-the-shelf practices	Leverageable practices

Relatively easy   Relatively hard
Ease of transfer of practice to other firms

FIG. 4.8. Transfers of practices inside and outside the MNE

for other firms to copy, but are equally hard for 3M to make sense of. But the interesting categories are the top-right and bottom-left corners. In the bottom right we have 'leverageable practices' which are those that can be readily transferred within the firm but not to outsiders. Toyota and Honda's transplant factories in the USA exemplify this category of practices. Despite the very different working environment, these transplants were quickly able to achieve similar levels of productivity to the factories back in Japan, and it then took the 'big 3' many years to build similar practices of their own in the USA. Such practices lie at the heart of Kogut and Zander's (1995) theory, and they end up becoming a key source of competitive advantage to the firm. Strategic alliances are often formed with the intention of gaining access to these sorts of practices, but as noted above the process is far from straightforward (Hamel 1995; Inkpen 1995).

Finally, the top-left corner is 'isolated' practices which are hard to transfer internally but relatively easy to transfer outside the firm. This would seem to be a strange combination, but it could easily occur in a foreign subsidiary in a distant market, because the subsidiary unit is in closer and more frequent contact with its local partner firms than with head office. Some Western firms' R&D centres in Japan, for example, are reputed to have been much better at sharing ideas with one another than with their parent firms back in the USA or Europe. Such a situation is of course very unsatisfactory for the MNE, because it represents an inability to achieve any of the benefits of multinationality.

7. Concluding Remarks

The globalization of economic activity is an ongoing process. It is driven in large part by the actions of firms seeking out new markets and new sources of competitiveness. But it is also represents a new set of challenges to which firms have to adapt.

In this chapter we have argued that the emergence of the knowledge economy adds a new dimension to the challenges firms face in addressing globalization. Early MNEs, those that emerged prior to the Second World War, developed in a polycentric manner with operations all over the world. In the post-war years declining tariffs made it possible for new MNEs to get a 'fresh start' and build a global presence from a strong centralized hub. Rather than spread activities all around the world, MNEs such as Matsushita were able to focus R&D and production in Japan and achieve far greater economies of scale than their polycentric rivals such as Philips. Now as we move into the knowledge economy, there are signs that another 'fresh start' is possible for MNEs that are building a global presence on a very limited set of activities. Firms like Nike and Dell computer are achieving such a presence by outsourcing production to independent firms. And new telecommunications firms like Millicom are building a mobile telephone business with extremely lean country operations backed up with strong centralized control.

The implication of this shift is that value-adding activities *per se* are no longer the key source of competitiveness for MNEs. Instead, we suggest that it is the practices of the MNE that represent the emerging source of competitiveness in the knowledge economy. Practices are the 'way things are done' by the MNE. They are intangible, and as a result very hard to clearly define. And more important, they are driven by very different 'economics' than activities.

Practices can be used over and over again without losing their value—indeed they often become *more* valuable with usage. They can be transferred at low cost, and can potentially be applied at a global scale from the outset. But at the same time, they are very hard to manage—the knowledge in practices is sticky, they are context-dependent or 'embedded' in their local environment, and there is often a great deal of causal ambiguity inherent in any valuable practice. Managing practices on a global scale presents both new challenges and new opportunities to MNEs.

But one of the key differences between practices and activities is their provenance, i.e. where they arise. As we discussed above in the section on regions and clusters, practices are formed in a day-to-day process where learning takes place within the firm and in connection with outside actors. Proximate actors are typically the most critical ones in this day-to-day process of accumulating new knowledge. Accordingly, MNEs are dependent upon certain home bases for their innovation process, and for the development of new practices. Foreign direct investment is then used both to create new home bases and to augment established ones. In summary, the knowledge economy and increased global competition lead to the increased importance of globally leveraged practices within MNEs, which in turn lead to the somewhat paradoxical conclusion of an increased importance of clusters or innovative regions if the MNE is to continuously upgrade its competitive advantage through improved practices.

REFERENCES

Almeida, P. (1996), 'Knowledge Sourcing by Foreign Multinationals: Patent Citation Analysis in the US Semiconductor Industry', *Strategic Management Journal* 17 (special issue): 155–65.

Amin, A., and Malmberg, A. (1992), 'Competing Structural and Institutional Influences on the Geography of Production in Europe', *Environment and Planning* A 24: 401–16.

Amit, R., and Schoemaker, P. (1993), 'Strategic Assets and Organizational Rent', *Strategic Management Journal* 14: 33–46.

Arvidsson, N., and Birkinshaw, J. (1998), 'Identifying Leading-Edge Market Knowledge in Multinational Corporations', Presented at the Academy of Management Annual Conference, San Diego.

Aydalot, P. (1986), *Milieux innovateurs en Europe* (Paris: GREMI).

Barney, J. (1991), 'Firm Resources and Sustained Competitive Advantage', *Journal of Management* 17(1): 99–120.

Bartlett, C. A. (1986), 'Building and Managing the Transnational: The New Organizational Challenge', in M. E. Porter (ed.), *Competition in Global Industries* (Cambridge, Mass.: Harvard Business School Press).

—— and Ghoshal, S. (1989), *Managing across Borders: The Transnational Solution* (Cambridge, Mass.: Harvard Business School Press).

Buckley, P. J., and Casson, M. (1976). *The Future of the Multinational Enterprise* (London: Macmillan).

Cairncross, F. (1997), *The Death of Distance* (Cambridge, Mass.: Harvard Business School Press).

Cantwell, J. (1989), *Technological Innovation and Multinational Corporations* (Oxford: Blackwell).

De Meyer, A. (1991), 'Tech Talk: How Managers are Stimulating Global R&D Communication', *Sloan Management Review*, Spring: 49–58.

—— (1992), 'Management of International R&D Operations', in K. Morgan (1995), 'Institutions, Innovation and Regional Renewal. The Development Agency as Animateur'. Paper presented at the *Regional Studies Conference* on 'Regional Futures'. Gothenburg, 6–9 May.

Doz, Y. L. (1986). *Strategic Management in Multinational Companies* (Oxford: Pergamon Press).

Dunning, J. H. (1980), 'Towards an Eclectic Theory of International Production; Some Empirical Tests', *Journal of International Business Studies* 11: 9–31.

—— (1981), *International Production and the Multinational Enterprise* (London: Allen & Unwin).

—— (1988), 'The Eclectic Paradigm of International Production: A Restatement and Some Possible Extensions', *Journal of International Business Studies* 19(1): 1–31.

—— (1993), *Multinational Enterprise and the Global Economy* (London: Addison-Wesley).

—— (1994), 'Multinational Enterprises and the Globalization of Innovatory Capacity', *Research Policy* 23: 67–88.

—— (1995), 'Reappraising the Eclectic Paradigm in an Age of Alliance Capitalism', *Journal of International Business Studies* 26(3): 461–92.

—— (1998), 'Globalization, Technological Change and the Spatial Organization of Economic Activity', in A. D. Chandler, P. Hagström, and Ö. Sölvell, *The Dynamic Firm* (Oxford: Oxford University Press), 289–314.

Enright, M. J. (1994), 'Regional Clusters and Firm Strategy', in A. D. Chandler, P. Hagström, and Ö. Sölvell. *The Dynamic Firm* (Oxford: Oxford University Press).

—— (2000), 'The Globalization of Competition and the Localization of Competitive Advantage: Policies toward Regional Clustering', in N. Hood and S. Young (eds.), *The Globalization of Multinational Enterprise Activity and Economic Development* (Basingstoke: Macmillan), 303–31.

Florida, R., and Kenney, M. (1994), 'The Globalization of Japanese R&D: The Economic Geography of Japanese R&D Investment in the Untied States', *Economic Geography* 70(4): 344–69.

Fredriksson, C., and Lindmark, L. (1979), 'From Firms to Systems of Firms: A Study of Interregional Dependence in a Dynamic Society', in F. E. I. Hamilton and G. J. R. Linge (eds.), *Spatial Analysis, Industry and Industrial Environment: Progress in Research and Applications* (Chichester: Wiley).

Freeman, C. (1982), *The Economics of Industrial Innovation*, 2nd edn. (London: Frances Pinter Publishers).

Frost, T. (1996), 'The Geographic Sources of Innovation in the Multinational Enterprise: US Subsidiaries and Host Country Spillovers, 1980–1990', Paper presented at the Academy of International Business annual meeting, Banff, Canada.

Hägerstrand, T. (1967), *Innovation Diffusion as a Spatial Process* (Chicago: University of Chicago Press).

Håkansson, H. (1989), *Corporate Technological Behavior: Co-operation and Networks* (London: Routledge).

Hamel, G. (1995), 'Competition for Competence and Inter-Partner Learning within International Strategic Alliances', *Strategic Management Journal* 12 (special issue): 83–104.

Hoover, E. M. (1948), *The Location of Economic Activity* (New York: McGraw-Hill).

Hymer, S. H. (1960/1976), *The International Operations of National Firms: A Study of Direct Investment* (Boston: MIT Press).

Inkpen, A. (1995), *The Management of International Joint Ventures: An Organizational Learning Perspective* (London: Routledge).

Kogut, B. (1993), *Country Competitiveness: Technology and Organizing of Work* (Oxford: Oxford University Press).

—— and Zander, U. (1995), 'Knowledge of the Firm and the Evolutionary Theory of the Multinational Corporation', *Journal of International Business Studies* 25(4): 625–46.

Kostova, T., and Cummings, L. L. (1997), 'Success of the Transnational Transfer of Organizational Practices within Multinational Companies', Presented at the Carnegie Bosch Institute's conference on Knowledge in International Corporations in Rome, Italy, 6–8 November.

Krugman, P. (1991), *Geography and Trade* (Cambridge, Mass.: MIT Press).

Laage-Hellman, J. (1989), 'Technological Development in Industrial Networks', *Acta Universitatis Upsaliensis*, 16, Faculty of Social Sciences, Uppsala University.

Leonard-Barton, D. (1982), *Swedish Entrepreneurs in Manufacturing and Their Sources of Information* (Boston: Center for Policy Applications, MIT).

Lindqvist, M., Sölvell, Ö., and Zander, I. (1998), 'Technological Advantage in the International Firm: Local and Global Perspectives on the Innovation Process', Working Paper, Institute of International Business, Stockholm School of Economics.

Lloyd, P. E., and Dicken, P. (1977), *Location in Space. A Theoretical Approach to Economic Geography*, 2nd edn. (London: Harper & Row).

Lundvall, B.-Å. (1988), 'Innovation as an Interactive Process: from User–Producer Interaction to the National System of Innovation', in G. Dosi *et al.* (eds.): *Technical Change and Economic Theory* (London: Pinter Publishers).

Madhok, A. (1997), 'Cost, Value and Foreign Market Entry Mode: The Transaction and the Firm', *Strategic Management Journal* 18: 39–61.

Maillat, D. (1994), 'Compotements spatiaux et milieux innovateurs', in J. P. Auray *et al.* (eds.), *Dictionnaire d'analyse spatiale* (Paris: Economica).

Malmberg, A., Sölvell, Ö., and Zander, I. (1996), 'Spatial Clustering, Local Accumulation of Knowledge and Firm Competitiveness', *Geografiska Annaler* 96: 2.

Marshall, A. (1890/1916), *Principles of Economics. An Introductory Volume*, 7th edn. (London: Macmillan).

Moore, K., and Birkinshaw, J. M. (1998), 'Managing Knowledge in Service Multinationals: Centres of Excellence', *Academy of Management Executive*, Nov.

Nelson, R. R. (ed.) (1993), *National Innovation Systems: A Comparative Analysis* (Oxford: Oxford University Press).

Nelson, R. R., and Winter, S. (1982), *An Evolutionary Theory of Economic Change* (Cambridge, Mass.: Harvard University Press).

Nohria, N., and Eccles, R. G. (1992), 'Face-to-Face: Making Network Organizations Work', in N. Nohria and R. G. Eccles (eds.), *Networks and Organizations: Structure, Form, and Action* (Boston: Harvard Business School Press).

Pavitt, K. (1984), 'Sectoral Patterns of Technical Change: towards a Taxonomy and a Theory', *Research Policy* 13: 343–73.

Perlmutter, H. (1969), 'The Tortuous Evolution of the Multinational Corporation', *Columbia Journal of World Business*, Jan.–Feb.: 9–18.

Piore, M., and Sable, C. (1984), *The Second Industrial Divide* (New York: Basic Books).

Porter, M. E. (1986), *Competition in Global Industries* (Boston: Harvard Business School Press).

—— (1990), *The Competitive Advantage of Nations* (London: Macmillan).

—— and Sölvell, Ö. (1998), 'The Role of Geography in the Process of Innovation and the Sustainable Competitive Advantage of Firms', in A. D. Chandler, P. Hagström, and Ö Sölvell, *The Dynamic Firm* (Oxford: Oxford University Press).

Pred, A. (1977), *City Systems in Advanced Economies. Past Growth, Present Processes and Future Development Options* (London: Hutchinson).

Putnam, R. D., with Leonardi, R., and Nanetti, R. Y. (1993), *Making Democracy Work. Civic Traditions in Modern Italy* (Princeton: Princeton University Press).

Rugman, A. M. (1981), *Inside the Multinationals: The Economics of Internal Markets* (London: Croom Helm).

Saxenian, A. (1994), *Regional Advantage. Culture and Competition in Silicon Valley and Route 128* (Cambridge, Mass.: Harvard University Press).

Scherer, F. M. (1984), *Innovation and Growth: Schumpeterian Perspectives* (Cambridge, Mass.: MIT Press).

Schmookler, J. (1966), *Inventions and Economic Growth* (Cambridge, Mass.: Harvard University Press).

Schonberger, R. J. (1987), 'Frugal Manufacturing', *Harvard Business Review* 65(4): 95–100.

Scott, A. J. (1983), 'Industrial Organisation and the Logic of Intra-Metropolitan Location—1: Theoretical Considerations', *Economic Geography* 59: 233–50.

—— (1988), *New Industrial Spaces: Flexible Production Organisation and Regional Development in North America and Western Europe* (London: Pion).

—— (1995), 'The Geographic Foundations of Industrial Performance', *Competition and Change* 1: 51–66.

Sölvell, Ö. (1987), *Entry Barriers and Foreign Penetration*, published Doctoral diss. (Stockholm: IIB).

—— and Zander, I. (1995), 'Organization of the Dynamic Multinational Enterprise: The Home-Based and the Heterarchical MNE', *International Studies of Management & Organization* 25(1–2): 17–38.

—— —— and Porter, M. E. (1991), *Advantage Sweden* (Stockholm: Norstedts).

Storper, M. (1995), 'The Resurgence of Regional Economies, Ten Years Later: The Region as a Nexus of Untraded Interdependencies', *European Urban and Regional Studies* 2: 191–221.

Szulanski, G. (1996), 'Exploring Internal Stickiness: Impediments to the Transfer of Best Practices within the Firm', *Strategic Management Journal* 17 (special issue): 27–44.

Teece, D., Pisano, G., and Shuen, A. (1997), 'Dynamic Capabilities and Strategic Management', *Strategic Management Journal* 18(7).

Von Hippel, E. (1988), *The Sources of Innovation* (Oxford: Oxford University Press).

—— (1998), ' "Sticky Information" and the Locus of Problem Solving: Implications for Innovation', in A. D. Chandler, P. Hagström, and Ö. Sölvell, *The Dynamic Firm* (Oxford: Oxford University Press).

Weber, A. (1909/1929), *Theory of the Location of Industries* (Chicago: University of Chicago Press).

Winter, S. G. (1987), 'Knowledge and Competence as Strategic Assets', in D. Teece (ed.): *The Competitive Challenge: Strategies for Industrial Innovation and Renewal* (Ballinger Publishing Co.).

PART TWO

MACROREGIONAL INTEGRATION AND THE KNOWLEDGE-BASED ECONOMY

5

Regional Integration and Foreign Direct Investment

Magnus Blomström, Steven Globerman, and Ari Kokko

1. Introduction

In recent years, there has been a proliferation of new regional integration agreements (RIAs) throughout the world, with acronyms such as APEC, EU, MERCOSUR, and NAFTA. These agreements are attracting increasing attention and some concern.[1] Although some RIAs have been motivated by political considerations, economic considerations are generally the driving force. Countries enter into RIAs because integration promises various economic benefits. This chapter discusses one of the potential economic benefits of RIAs: increased foreign direct investment (FDI) flows in the integrating region.

Increased FDI flows are generally seen as being economically beneficial for the region in question, because they facilitate increased production specialization, both across countries and within multinational companies (MNCs). Increased production specialization along the lines of comparative advantage directly improves allocative efficiency. Increased specialization across affiliates within MNCs can provide additional indirect efficiency gains associated with the capture of product-level economies of scale. Increased FDI flows can also promote the faster international diffusion of new technology with relatively large social benefits in the form of lower producer costs and increased consumer surplus.

Perhaps the most serious challenge facing a study of the relationship between regional integration and foreign direct investment is the multidimensional nature of the issue. In particular, there is reason to believe that the relevant linkages will vary between different integration agreements, and between countries and industries participating in any specific agreement. Section 2 therefore sets out some broad theoretical considerations surrounding the linkages between RIAs and FDI. Section 3 refines these broad considerations into a more focused framework that accounts for some indirect linkages that have, hitherto, been largely ignored in the relevant literature. Section 4 briefly examines three recent, and very distinct, cases of regional integration in the Americas with reference to the framework discussed in the preceding section. Section 5 offers a brief summary and some tentative conclusions.

2. Regional Integration Agreements and FDI: Some General Considerations

The term regional economic integration typically refers to reductions of regional trade barriers and investment restrictions. To identify the broad theoretical linkages between RIAs and FDI, it is therefore convenient to structure the discussion along these two dimensions of integration. Hence, we begin by discussing effects of *trade liberalization*, and distinguish between the impact on FDI that is mainly a response to trade barriers, and FDI that is primarily motivated by the need to internalize firm-specific intangible assets that cannot be traded efficiently in arm's-length markets. We go on to consider the impact of special *investment provisions* and other institutional changes that are sometimes connected to integration agreements. The focus in these paragraphs lies on static effects: the possible dynamic effects of regional integration on investment flows are considered separately. The discussion is summarized in a template for classifying entire countries and specific sectors according to the expected impact on investments.[2]

2.1. Effects of Trade Liberalization: Tariff-Jumping and Internalization

The impact of trade liberalization on FDI largely depends on what is assumed about investment motives. The early theoretical and empirical literature on foreign investment tended to regard trade and capital movements as substitutable modes of serving foreign markets.[3] This view of the relationship between trade and factor mobility suggested that FDI was largely a way of getting around tariff barriers, and that general tariff reductions would reduce FDI flows or even stimulate a 'repatriation' of foreign-owned assets to the home countries of MNCs. However, more recently, research has come to emphasize the exploitation of intangible assets as the major motive for foreign investment (see Caves 1996 for a review). In order to compete successfully in a foreign market—where local firms have superior knowledge of the local market, consumer preferences, and business practices—the internationally oriented firm must possess some firm-specific intangible asset, such as technological and marketing expertise, that gives it a competitive edge. The effective exploitation of these assets sometimes requires firms to 'internalize' their international operations by establishing foreign affiliates, since other modes of international business, including exports and licensing of technology to foreign firms, carry relatively high transactions costs (Buckley and Casson 1976; Dunning 1977). Some FDI of this kind can therefore be expected to occur even when there are no formal trade barriers between countries.

These two views of the motives for FDI give partly contradictory predictions regarding the effects of regional integration, particularly for intraregional investment flows. It is reasonable to expect reduced flows of tariff-jumping FDI within an integrating region because trade liberalization makes exporting from the home country relatively more attractive than FDI as a way to serve the regional market.[4] However, regional integration would not create incentives to reduce investment or repatriate capital for projects primarily undertaken to internalize the exploitation of intangible assets. In fact, the reduction of regional trade barriers could instead stimulate overall FDI flows by enabling MNCs to operate more efficiently across international borders. A predictable and liberal trade environment is particularly important for vertically integrated FDI, where the operations of the MNC's different affiliates are specialized according to the locational advantages of the host country. Hence, the static impact of trade liberalization on intraregional FDI flows is subject to partially offsetting influences, and the net impact of any specific RIA on individual member country is largely determined by the motives for pre-existing investment. A reasonable generalization, however, is that countries with low initial trade restrictions are more likely to receive increased intraregional FDI flows as trade barriers are reduced, since they are not very likely to host import-substituting FDI projects that might be withdrawn.

Turning to inter-regional FDI flows, both the tariff-jumping and internalization models suggest increased inflows of FDI. The investments by 'outsiders' could obviously go up if the average level of protection increases as a result of the RIAs, or if the establishment of a RIA raises fears about future protection (as in the debate on 'Fortress Europe'). The inflows of foreign capital would also increase if the volume of incoming FDI were initially restricted by the limited size of the individual national markets. Contrary to the national markets, the integrated 'common' market may be large enough to bear the fixed costs for the establishment of new foreign affiliates. This surge of inward FDI would probably not be evenly distributed, but rather concentrated in the geographical areas with the strongest locational advantages.[5] In addition, to the extent that the integration agreement results in trade diversion, it may also motivate strategic investment responses by outside firms who lose export markets when their former customers turn to suppliers based in the region.[6]

The potential effects of a RIA on outflows of FDI from the integrating region are rarely discussed in formal models. This is mainly related to the simplifying assumption that nothing happens with trade barriers in the rest of the world. However, some changes in outward FDI are feasible even when trade policies in the rest of the world remain unchanged. For instance, it is possible that a firm's capacity to undertake new FDI projects is restricted by its administrative capability or the availability of investment capital (Stevens and Lipsey 1992). In that case, it is likely that FDI within and outside the region are substitutes. If integration reduces intraregional FDI, it may therefore increase the scope for outflows of FDI from the integrating area to other regions. This notwithstanding, it is reasonable to expect that the net impact of trade liberalization is an increase in the inflows of FDI to the region. However, the effects on individual countries may well differ—FDI can be expected to cluster to those parts of the RIA where the investment environment is most favourable.

In summary, the net impacts of trade liberalization on both intraregional and extraregional FDI flows within an RIA are theoretically ambiguous. In particular, intraregional flows can be either net complements to or net substitutes for the underlying production relocation and rationalization decisions made by MNCs depending, in part, upon the degree to which previous FDI was largely motivated by trade barriers. The net impacts are even more difficult to predict at the level of any individual RIA member country.[7]

2.2. Explicit Investment Provisions and Other Influences

To the extent that RIAs also liberalize capital flows among member countries —e.g. by reducing or eliminating restrictions on inward FDI—an additional stimulus is provided to the investment process. Inward FDI should also be encouraged by 'national treatment' provisions ensuring that foreign investors are treated no less favourably than domestic investors. In addition, many RIAs feature explicit dispute resolution mechanisms. To the extent that such mechanisms are effective, they should reduce trade and investment disputes between the participating nations and encourage FDI. Obviously, the practical relevance of such provisions depends on the scope and magnitude of pre-existing barriers to inward FDI, as well as the extent and nature of host-government discrimination against foreign investors. Hence, the impact of the RIA on the institutional environment is an important determinant of the total effects.

Inward FDI could also be stimulated by the elimination of trade-related investment measures (TRIMs), such as requirements for foreign affiliates to satisfy specific export targets, and by the presence of strong investor property rights which reduce the risk of direct or indirect expropriation. Both types of initiatives may be institutionalized in RIAs. In this context, it is possible that a significant effect of some RIAs may be that they 'lock in' economic reforms in the participating countries. By raising reform decision from the national to the international level, the agreements may create a more predictable policy environment for foreign investors, who might otherwise fear that purely national reform efforts are temporary and that various kinds of restrictions may be reintroduced when the political regime changes. These effects are likely to be most important in North–South agreements, where the participation of developed countries adds credibility to the reforms.[8] Moreover, to the extent that 'market forces' become a stronger influence on capital investment decisions compared to political risk, international differences in factor endowments should become stronger influences on investment location decisions. This strengthens the tendency for FDI to be concentrated to the most attractive investment locations in the integrating area.

To the extent that provisions liberalizing the migration of labour are featured in the RIA enabling legislation, an indirect but potentially significant indirect impact might be exerted on FDI flows. Neoclassical trade theory views the movement of goods and the movement of factor inputs as substitutes. However, modern theories of the MNC acknowledge the potential complementarity between FDI and trade flows. Indeed, relatively high transactions costs associated with 'arm's-length'-exchange may mandate the internalization of exchange within the MNC for many types of international transactions. Hence, an increased volume of such international transactions will be accompanied by increased FDI.[9] Less well recognized is the potential complementarity between FDI and the international migration of skilled professionals and managers. The latter are frequently required to help 'transfer' the bundle of tangible and intangible assets that comprise FDI from the home country to the host country. Reductions in legal and other barriers to (particularly temporary) migration may well reduce the costs associated with FDI and/or increase the returns to FDI.

2.3. Dynamic Effects of Regional Integration

In addition to the static effects discussed above, it is possible that the establishment of RIAs also generates various dynamic effects that affect FDI flows. For instance, evaluations of the economic impact of the European Single Market have argued that this specific integration process has led to significant efficiency benefits that will raise the participating countries' growth rates over the medium or long term. The higher growth rates may be temporary, persisting until the economies adjust to the higher real income that comes about because of tougher competition and more efficient allocation of resources in the common market (see e.g. Emerson *et al.* 1989). It is also possible that there are permanent growth effects that occur as the initial gains in efficiency and output raise factor rewards and generate new savings and investments that contribute further to output growth (Baldwin 1989). These dynamic benefits should make the integrated region a more attractive location for domestic as well as foreign investment. However, the exact links between regional integration and dynamic growth effects are not well specified, and it is not uncommon that analyses and empirical estimates of dynamic benefits are considered vague or speculative (Smith 1992). It should also be remembered that some of these effects might be specific to the Single Market, since the Maastricht Treaty is a much more comprehensive agreement than most other RIAs.

Yet, FDI may actually be an essential catalyst for many of the proposed dynamic benefits. Some of the improvements in economic efficiency associated with increased specialization, exploitation of scale economies, and greater geographical concentration of individual economic activities are likely to be driven by inter- and intra-regional FDI. Increased FDI flows are also important forces behind the heavier competitive pressure that is expected to encourage local producers to adopt efficiency-enhancing strategies, such as rationalizing plant capacity or reducing slack in the production process (Smith and Venables 1988). In addition, it is likely that FDI will stimulate technology transfer and diffusion, both directly and through *spillovers* to local firms (see Blomström and Kokko 1998).

Furthermore, if regional integration creates a larger market, it is also conceivable that some dynamic effects occur because regional integration influences various firm characteristics, such as the stock of intangible firm-specific assets that facilitate FDI. A larger market may simply allow some firms to grow larger and stronger than would have been possible in individual national markets. Alternatively, integration may motivate firms to seek strategic alliances or merge with former competitors in order to manage in the more competitive environment that is created when intraregional trade barriers are removed. As firms become larger, they may be able to invest more in R&D and marketing, which may lead to the creation of new intangible assets that stimulate new FDI, within as well as outside their own region.

Including these types of dynamic considerations into the analysis creates the potential for significantly stronger linkages between RIAs and FDI than is implied by static models of trade liberalization. The main impact of the dynamic effects is to make the integrating region a more attractive investment location, which should stimulate intraregional FDI flows as well as inflows from the rest of the world. However, FDI is a powerful source of international technology spillovers (Coe and Helpman 1995). Hence, in the longer run, diminishing returns to technology transfer may set in which, *ceteris paribus*, would discourage future transfers of technology through FDI. Of course, in a dynamic technological environment, there is no necessary reason to assume that diminishing returns will be a relevant consideration constraining future FDI flows. This caveat is supported by evidence that rates-of-return to research and development activities have not diminished appreciably in the post-war period (Griliches 1998).

In summary, technological change and other 'dynamic' efficiencies should strengthen the positive linkages between RIAs and intraregional FDI flows. They should also lead to the integrating region being a more attractive location for extraregional FDI, both because rising incomes generally attract inward FDI, and because 'knowledge-seeking' FDI is likely to find the newly integrated region a source of technological knowledge. However, it is unclear whether the (positive) conditioning influence of dynamic efficiencies on the FDI–RIA linkage will offset the negative influence of the shuttering of 'tariff-factories' after tariff and other trade barriers are eliminated. The factors conditioning the nature and extent of the 'conventional' interactions between trade liberalization and FDI therefore merit closer consideration.

3. Specific Hypotheses

In the discussion above, we argued that the presence of dynamic efficiency gains from closer economic integration contribute to the presumption (although far from a certainty) that the creation of a RIA will lead to increased intra- and inter-regional FDI flows. We also noted that the effects of regional integration are likely to differ between countries and industries. Obviously, the investment environment of an individual country or industry, relative to the rest of the integrating region and the world, will determine how likely it is that the potential increases in FDI inflows will cluster there.[10] There are a multitude of factors that condition the relative attractiveness of countries to foreign investors, and an RIA can affect these factors in complex ways, as suggested by the discussion in the preceding section.[11] What is relevant for our purposes here is whether the RIA is likely to strengthen or weaken the FDI advantages enjoyed by an individual country or industry and how substantial that strengthening or weakening is likely to be.

In Figure 5.1, the determinants of FDI attractiveness have been condensed into a general summary framework relating trade and investment liberalization initiatives to country and industry characteristics. The attribute labelled environmental change summarizes the degree to which trade and investment flows are liberalized by the integration agreements in question. The attribute labelled locational advantage summarizes the degree to which it is advantageous from a profitability standpoint to locate an economic activity in a particular location. Identifying the position of a specific country or industry in Figure 5.1 will provide a starting point for developing hypotheses about the investment impact of regional integration for specific countries and industries.

Along the horizontal axis in Figure 5.1, a country or region is assumed to enjoy a strong locational advantage for a specific activity given the implementation of the RIA. The vertical axis measures the extent to which the RIA actually alters the relative prices of goods and factor inputs. As one moves down the vertical axis, it is presumed that the RIA has a progressively weaker impact on those relative prices. In effect, it is presumed that the pre-RIA market equilibria are progressively less affected by the implementation of the RIA as one moves down the vertical axis.

The most pronounced positive impact the RIA on FDI would presumably be experienced by those economic sectors falling into cell 1. The sectors in this cell enjoy a strong 'latent' locational advantage, and the presumed impact of the RIA is large. That is, the post-RIA changes in relative output and/or factor prices are relatively large and presumably create and/or strengthen the cost and/or other competitive advantages enjoyed by producers in cell 1. Hence, one would anticipate relatively strong, positive capital flows from both foreign and domestic investors to the sectors in cell 1.

In cell 2, the hypothesized impact of the RIA on investment is weaker than in cell 1, albeit likely to be still positive. Cell 2 contains those economic activities for which the country in question has a strong locational advantage, but for which the impact of the integration agreement is relatively weak. Specifically, post-RIA relative prices may not differ significantly from pre-RIA relative

	Locational advantages (positive to negative)	
Enviromental change (strong to weak)	1 2	4 3

FIG. 5.1. Classification dimensions
Source: Globerman and Schwindt (1996).

prices across a range of product and factor markets. Economic integration between OECD countries, where the formal and informal barriers to trade and investment are relatively low prior to the RIA being implemented, can be expected to provide many examples of industries falling into this category.

The hypothesized impact of integration on sectors clustered in cell 3 is similar to that for sectors clustered in cell 2. While the country or industrial sectors clustered in cell 3 suffer a locational disadvantage in terms of the activities in cell 3, the impact of the integration agreement on the overall economic environment is also presumed to be quite weak. Examples of this include sectors that are excluded from the RIA (e.g. often the case of broadcasting) or that are substantially protected from relative price changes by supply agreements (such as quotas) or by trigger-mechanisms that allow tariffs to be enacted by the importing country. Agriculture and textiles serve as possible examples of the latter. In some, though rare, cases, the sector in question may be too small to attract the attention of foreign competitors in the post-RIA environment.

Moving to cell 4, the expected impact on inward FDI is negative and the potential for actual disinvestment significant. Specifically, the sectors in cell 4 are strongly affected by the integration agreement, but the countries and/or industries in question suffer locational disadvantages in a post-RIA environment. Countries and industries where the bulk of existing FDI was established in order to avoid trade barriers would be classified in this area.

In summary, a simple generic framework of the RIA–FDI linkage focuses attention on the potential significance of the RIA in terms of its impact on relative prices of goods and factor inputs, as well as on the divergence between pre-RIA and post-RIA patterns of locational advantage. Where both are relatively large, substantial impacts on the regional distribution of FDI can be anticipated from the implementation of the RIA. Sectors that enjoy a 'natural' locational advantage can be expected to increase their share of investment from both within and outside the region, with the opposite being true for economic sectors suffering natural locational disadvantages.[12]

In the next section, we consider the robustness of this simple generic framework in terms of its ability to explain the short-run impacts of recent RIAs implemented in North and South America.

4. Three Cases of Regional Integration

In the theoretical discussion, we concluded that, while it is difficult to make precise predictions about the expected impact of RIAs on foreign direct investment decisions, identifying the positions of specific countries or industres in terms of Figure 5.1 should provide crude predictions regarding the direction and magnitude of the likely impacts. In this section, we examine the empirical evidence on the investment effects of three recent but distinctly different cases of regional integration: (i) Canada joining CUSFTA (illustrating a case of North–North integration);

(ii) Mexico's accession to NAFTA (North–South integration); and (iii) The first stage of integration in the MERCOSUR (South–South integration). In each case, we begin by identifying where in Figure 5.1 the country in question should be classified, and go on to examine whether the empirical evidence on changes in FDI flows is consistent with the hypotheses provided by Figure 5.1.

4.1. North–North Integration: Canada in the CUSFTA

The essence of the Canada–USA Free Trade Agreement (CUSFTA), which came into effect on 1 January 1989, was the phased bilateral elimination of tariffs. In addition, a number of provisions reduced discrimination against bilateral foreign direct investment, including the extension of rights-of-establishment and national treatment. Yet, it should be remembered that bilateral trade between Canada and the USA had been substantially liberalized well before the event studied here, through successive GATT rounds as well as special bilateral agreements such as the Auto Pact and the Defense-Sharing Agreement. Moreover, a range of prominent sectors, such as basic telecommunications, was effectively excluded from coverage under the investment liberalization provisions of the CUSFTA. Canada's existing foreign investment screening procedures were also left in place (Globerman and Walker 1993).

In terms of the first classification dimension of Figure 5.1 (degree of environmental change), it therefore seems reasonable to characterize the Canadian position as an intermediate one, with moderate changes resulting from the agreement.[13] Regarding the locational advantages of Canada with respect to the USA and the rest of the world, it is also reasonable to suggest an intermediate position. Hence, Canada should belong roughly at the centre of Figure 5.1, which implies relatively moderate investment effects of the CUSFTA agreement. Does the empirical evidence support this hypothesis?

Bilateral trade between the USA and Canada has become relatively more important from 1988 onward, which indicates that CUSFTA significantly liberalized the North American trade environment (see Blomström, Globerman, and Kokko 1996). It is, however, difficult to discern a consistent pattern in FDI flows between the two countries that would clearly be related to the CUSFTA. Table 5.1 presents an overview of the Canadian foreign direct investment pattern between 1986 and 1995. Bilateral (other) inward and outward direct investment refers to US (non-US) direct investment inflows to Canada and Canadian direct investment outflows to the USA (rest of the world), respectively. While there are substantial changes in FDI flows for individual years, the overall magnitude of bilateral direct investment was relatively stable over the period 1988–92. Substantial increases in the nominal value of inward direct investment from the USA emerged in 1993 and continued through 1995, while the nominal value of outward direct investment to the USA increased in 1994 and 1995—but only back to levels experienced in the mid-1980s. It is unlikely that these fluctuations in investment flows are directly related to the CUSFTA, since they emerged in 1993, well after

TABLE 5.1. Canadian inward and outward foreign direct investment
($Canadian millions)[a]

Year	Bilateral		Other	
	Inward	Outward	Inward	Outward
1983	29	1,686	2,438	1,558
1984	3,196	3,209	2,960	1,563
1985	−191	3,144	1,965	2,130
1986	−743	3,362	4,607	1,502
1987	6,028	7,278	4,632	4,044
1988	2,052	2,963	5,899	1,775
1989	2,091	3,510	3,850	1,918
1990	3,246	2,800	5,917	2,722
1991	1,961	1,925	1,187	4,553
1992	2,719	1,315	2,673	3,144
1993	5,308	968	1,117	6,522
1994	7,279	2,456	960	4,070
1995	10,229	3,570	5,122	2,996

Source: *Statistics Canada* (various issues).

[a] Net flows including reinvested earnings accruing to direct investors.

the implementation of CUSFTA, and coincided with a general boom in outward FDI flows from the USA at that time. Furthermore, it is suggestive that a substantial decline in the value of the Canadian dollar began in 1992 following five years during which the Canadian dollar strengthened against its US counterpart. This depreciation may well have constituted an important motive for the increased US investments in the country.

Inward direct investment from countries other than the USA exhibits no consistent pattern over the period studied, although the largest inflows took place between 1988 and 1990, right after the implementation of the CUSFTA. However, there is an interesting pattern in the development of Canadian outward direct investment to countries other than the USA. Until 1990, Canadian outward FDI was primarily directed to the USA, but the early 1990s saw a significant decrease in the relative importance of the USA as a destination for Canadian outward direct investment. This decrease is mirrored by an increasing share (beginning in 1991) going to EU member countries other than the UK, and an even more dramatically increasing share going to regions other than the EU, the USA and Japan. The profitable opportunities encouraging a redirection of Canadian direct investment outflows presumably had nothing to do with CUSFTA. However, CUSFTA may have played an important role in guaranteeing access to the US market, so that available FDI resources could instead be used to establish Canadian presence in other markets.

TABLE 5.2. Foreign firms' share of Canadian GDP, 1977–1993 (per cent)

Year	US Affiliates in Canada/Canadian GDP	All Foreign Firms in Canada/Canadian GDP
1977	13.8	n.a.
1982	11.3	n.a.
1983	n.a.	16.2
1988	n.a.	15.6
1989	9.5	n.a.
1990	8.8	14.8
1991	8.0	n.a.
1992	7.9	14.3
1993	8.2	15.1

Sources: Mataloni and Goldberg (1994), Mataloni (1995), and World Bank (various issues).

As a complement to the flow data on FDI, Table 5.2 presents some data on the gross product of US foreign affiliates in Canada. The second column of the Table measures the share of US majority-owned foreign affiliates in Canadian GDP. The US share fell from well over 11 per cent in the early 1980s to about 8 per cent in the early 1990s. Coupled with the observation that bilateral trade with Canada increased as a result of the CUSFTA, this suggests that regional integration has resulted in FDI becoming a relatively less important mode for US firms to serve the Canadian market. In other words, there is some indication that trade has substituted for inward FDI from the USA.

Another indication of the same development is that Canada's share of US MNCs' foreign production has fallen significantly since the implementation of the CUS-FTA. The ratio of US affiliates' production in Canada to the aggregate production of all US affiliates abroad fell from 16.3 per cent in 1989 to 12.6 per cent in 1993 (see Blomström and Kokko 1997). At the same time, it appears that Canada has become a somewhat more attractive investment location for outsiders. The last column of Table 5.2 shows that the aggregate output share of all foreign affiliates has remained roughly constant, at about 15 per cent of Canadian GDP, which indicates that other foreign investors have made up for the reduction of the US share of Canadian production. This seems to parallel the observation that the European Single Market led to an increased inflow of FDI from outsiders.

Hence, Canada offers a potentially instructive case study of the impacts of an RIA on foreign direct investment flows for a small open economy. Since the environmental change connected with the CUSFTA was not dramatic, it is hardly surprising that no significant increase in US FDI can be discerned. However, the guaranteed access to the US market may have stimulated FDI flows from the rest of the world to Canada.

4.2. North–South Integration: Mexico and NAFTA

Shortly after the establishment of the CUSFTA, Canada and the USA initiated negotiations with Mexico about a possible southern expansion of the integration agreement. In December 1992, the three countries signed the North American Free Trade Agreement (NAFTA). This agreement, which came into effect on 1 January 1994, was the first formal regional integration agreement involving both a developing and developed countries. In essence, the NAFTA is an extended version of the CUSFTA. In addition to the trade and investment liberalization measures already in the CUSFTA, the new treaty included major advances in areas such as government procurement (where coverage is extended to services and construction), intellectual property, and investor's rights, as well as more stringent rules of origin. In the present context, it is particularly notable that the agreement also introduced a clear, rules-based framework for the impartial treatment of FDI, placed strict limits on the use of performance requirements, and established dispute-settlement mechanisms specifically designed to deal with investment issues (see e.g. Hufbauer and Schott 1993 and Gestrin and Rugman 1994 for details).

The overall effects on Mexico of a free trade arrangement with Canada and the USA might be expected to be significant, for several reasons. One important determinant is Mexico's geographical location. In the 1970s, many Mexicans considered it to be a drawback to be 'so far from heaven and so close to the United States'. Today, when regional trade and investment barriers have been reduced as a result of the NAFTA, proximity has become a major advantage. The North American share of Mexican exports has increased from around 70 per cent in the late 1980s to over 86 per cent in 1995 (UN Trade Tapes). The value of Mexican exports more than quadrupled over the same period, with the largest increases occurring between 1992 and 1995. The North American share of Mexican imports has also grown over this period, but not quite as dramatically.

Another reason to anticipate substantial impacts of the NAFTA on the Mexican economy is related to the significant policy changes that have taken place in recent years. Traditionally, Mexico has been a closed economy. In the mid-1980s, however, important market-oriented reforms were introduced in several sectors, and the economy began to open up. Arguably, a substantial liberalization of the Mexican economy had already taken place prior to NAFTA; however, NAFTA could reasonably be perceived as 'locking in' those reforms, as well as reforming other sectors, such as cars, textiles and apparel, finance, telecommunications, and land transportation (see Hufbauer and Schott 1993). The coincidence of significant domestic policy reforms, distinct locational advantages in the form of relatively cheap labour, and an integration agreement that provides free access to a substantial part of the Canadian and US markets suggest that Mexico belongs in area 1 of Figure 5.1. The prior is, thus, that the effects on FDI should be significant.

TABLE 5.3. Foreign direct investment flows into Mexico, 1989–1994 ($US million)

Year	1989	1990	1991	1992	1993	1994
FDI inflows	2,785	2,549	4,742	4,393	4,389	7,978

Source: IMF (various issues).

TABLE 5.4. US direct investment position in Mexico on a historical-cost basis at year end, 1992–1995 ($US million and share of total US FDI position)

Year	1987	1992	1993	1994	1995
US FDI Stock	4,900	13,730	15,229	15,714	14,037
		(2.73)	(2.72)	(2.53)	(1.97)

Sources: *Survey of Current Business*, 75(8) Aug. 1995 and Lowe and Bargas (1996).

It is seems clear that the reforms undertaken by Mexico in the pre-NAFTA period substantially encouraged increased inward FDI. As shown in Table 5.3 above, the inflows of FDI increased significantly from less than $US 3 billion in 1989 to nearly $US 8 billion in 1994. Unfortunately, it is difficult to construct a consistent longer-run time series on inward FDI in Mexico. This is because the classification system was changed in 1995 so that intended investment is excluded from the annual total FDI inflows reported after 1995. The implication is that total FDI inflows to Mexico are biased upward prior to 1995 with the magnitude of this bias being unknown. The collapse of the Mexican economy and the value of the peso in the post-NAFTA period also undermine the relevance of simply comparing FDI flows in the pre- and post-NAFTA periods. Nevertheless, the fact that total FDI inflows were substantially larger in 1996 than in 1994 suggests that the NAFTA did have a significant positive influence on inward FDI to Mexico given that the prevailing biases are to reduce reported inward FDI in the post-NAFTA period.

Since US multinationals dominate the FDI scene in Mexico it is relevant to look specifically at their responses to the NAFTA agreement. Table 5.4 suggests that US firms have expanded their presence in Mexico, but that much of the investment increase took place before the formal NAFTA agreement was closed. The US FDI position in Mexico has not increased much since 1992, and the share of Mexico in total US investment actually declined in the immediate post-NAFTA period. This indicates that outsiders account for an increasing share of the recent inflows of FDI to Mexico. To some extent, these investments are probably directed to serving the local market, in response to the country's improving economic and institutional environment, but the investment flows are also likely to reflect the improved access to the US market.

The timing and character of the changes in the US investment position suggest that the comprehensive reforms of the country's FDI regulation that commenced prior to NAFTA were an important stimulus to inward FDI. The Mexican regulatory framework for FDI, which dates back to 1973, was very restrictive and served as a disincentive for investment from abroad (Blomström 1989). In the backwash of the Mexican debt crisis, these regulations were changed dramatically in 1989 to attract foreign investment in Mexico. It appears that US investors responded quite strongly to this first round of reforms. A few years later, the investment regime was further liberalized through the NAFTA, as noted above. The US response may have been relatively mild, because many US firms had already responded to Mexican investment liberalization. It is unclear why US firms would have responded rather than other firms to pre-NAFTA liberalization initiatives, although this appears to be the case. A possible explanation, alluded to above, is that European and Japanese MNCs may see investment in Mexico as a cost-efficient way to serve the US market in labour-intensive activities, since the US market can now be served without tariff penalties.

4.3. South–South Integration: MERCOSUR

Regional integration in the Southern Cone of the western hemisphere dates back to a 1986 bilateral agreement between Argentina and Brazil, which stipulated the elimination of all trade barriers over a ten-year period. Five years later, in 1991, this agreement was extended under the Treaty of Asunción, with the purpose of creating a Common Market in the region by the year 2006. The resulting agreement, known as MERCOSUR, also includes Paraguay and Uruguay as members.

Intraregional trade has gradually been liberalized since the early 1990s, culminating in the establishment of a Customs Union on 1 January 1995. The MERCOSUR Customs Union stipulates free trade in (most) goods among the four member countries and a common external tariff (ET) for trade with third countries (see Laird 1995). Although the implementation of the ET has proved more difficult than expected, and important sectors like automobiles, telecommunications, and computer equipment are excluded from the agreement, it is estimated that 85 per cent of all goods are now traded freely within the bloc. In addition to the trade arrangements, a partially new investment regime has also been established to promote and protect investment in the MERCOSUR region (IDB 1996).

Looking at the recent reforms of the trade and investment rules in the MERCOSUR region, it is clear that the change has been substantial, although it can be debated how much of it should be credited to the formal integration agreement. Unilateral liberalization has been important and preceded the RIA in several areas, and there are other fields where reforms are mainly related to multilateral initiatives, such as the GATT. Yet, in terms of the classification

TABLE 5.5. External Trade of MERCOSUR, 1988–1994

	1988	1989	1990	1991	1992	1993	1994
Total exports (US$ million)	44,829	46,555	46,433	45,911	50,487	54,085	62,027
Intra-MERCOSUR exports (per cent)	6.5	8.2	8.9	11.1	14.3	18.6	19.3
Total imports (US$ million)	23,076	26,061	29,302	34,264	40,649	48,509	62,422
Intra-MERCOSUR imports (per cent)	13.3	15.1	14.5	15.5	18.4	19.6	19.6

Source: Laird (1995).

dimensions of Figure 5.1, it is clear that the environmental changes coinciding with the MERCOSUR process have been strong in all of the participating countries. Regarding the investment environment, it can be argued that Argentina and Brazil possess strong locational advantages, thanks primarily to abundant natural resources, relatively well-developed industrial sectors, and large domestic markets. Hence, for these two countries, participation in the MERCOSUR should classify them in cell 1 of Figure 5.1, which suggests a significant potential for increased FDI inflows (mainly from the rest of the world). The expected impact on the two remaining members, Paraguay and Uruguay, is more uncertain due to their smaller markets and weaker locational advantages.

The initial effects of trade liberalization in the Southern Cone are evident from Table 5.5. A very rapid increase in total exports and imports during the first half of the 1990s has been matched by even faster increases in intraregional trade. Intra-MERCOSUR exports as a share of the region's total exports more than doubled, to reach nearly 20 per cent in 1994. Intraregional imports as a share of total imports increased significantly as well, from 13 per cent in 1988 to about 20 per cent in 1994. It should be remembered that these changes refer to the period immediately before the establishment of the MERCOSUR Customs Union in 1995, and that the shares of intraregional trade are likely to have increased further since then.

There is also a renewed interest in the MERCOSUR on the part of foreign investors. Inflows of foreign direct investment into the region more than tripled between 1989 and 1993, as shown in Table 5.6. As expected, Argentina and Brazil have been the favoured locations for FDI, with Argentina recording the largest investment inflows during the period. Paraguay and Uruguay have been lagging behind, although Uruguay recorded significant increases in FDI in 1993 and 1994.

Unfortunately, there are no aggregate data available to analyse FDI flows for the period after the establishment of the Customs Union in 1995. However, looking at home-country data for the major foreign investor in the region, the USA,

TABLE 5.6. Foreign direct investment flows into MERCOSUR, 1989–1994 ($US million)

	1989	1990	1991	1992	1993	1994
Argentina	1,028	1,836	2,439	4,179	6,305	n.a.
Brazil	1,131	989	1,103	2,061	1,292	3,072
Paraguay	12.8	76.3	83.1	42.0	50.0	n.a.
Uruguay	37.7	38.6	30.3	n.a.	101.5	170.0

Source: IMF (various issues).

TABLE 5.7. US direct investment position in MERCOSUR on a historical-cost basis at year end, 1992–1995 ($US million and shares of total US FDI position)

	1992	1993	1994	1995
Argentina	3,327	4,331	5,945	7,962
	(0.66)	(0.77)	(0.96)	(1.12)
Brazil	16,313	16,822	18,798	23,590
	(3.25)	(3.01)	(3.03)	(3.31)
MERCOSUR[a]	19,640	21,153	24,743	31,552
	(3.91)	(3.78)	(3.99)	(4.43)

[a] Excluding Paraguay and Uruguay, for which no data are available.

Source: *Survey of Current Business* 75(8), Aug. 1995 and Lowe and Bargas (1996).

it appears that the real boom in FDI did not occur until after this event. Table 5.7 shows that in 1995 alone, the US stock of FDI in the region increased by more than 25 per cent, which is significantly higher than the growth rate of US investment in the rest of the world. It should, therefore, be noted that we risk underestimating the investment responses to the MERCOSUR by restricting the analysis to the period for which data are available.

The aggregate data do not distinguish between intra- and inter-regional investment flows, but the significant increases in the investment position of the USA suggest that most of the inflows come from outside the MERCOSUR. It is also obvious that the increases in FDI flows occurred at different times in the individual countries, which motivates a closer look at the individual countries.

Argentina registered the largest increases in FDI inflows before 1994, and there is reason to expect that much of this was unrelated to the regional integration process. Chudnovsky, López, and Porta (1995) suggest three major explanations for the increases in foreign investment in Argentina since the early 1990s. The most important attraction for foreign investors was arguably Argentina's comprehensive privatization programme, which opened several public service industries to foreign investment. Several public companies in the telecommunications and transportation sector were sold to foreign investors. Another important determinant was the country's successful macroeconomic reforms, which managed to bring down public deficits, inflation, and interest rates, and ensured the convertibility of the currency. Unlike the present situation in Europe, where the members of the EU are obliged to fulfil certain macroeconomic 'convergence criteria', economic integration in the form of MERCOSUR was not a motive for Argentinian macroeconomic stabilization. A third factor influencing foreign investors was the new wave of protectionism in the region's car sector in the early 1990s. In 1991, Argentina introduced a system of quotas on imports of finished automobiles, which contributed to an increase in foreign investment inflows to the sector.

Foreign investment in Brazil has fluctuated widely in past years, and the inflows of FDI have fallen well short of those to Argentina, although the Brazilian market is about four times larger. One reason is that market-oriented reforms were introduced later and macroeconomic stabilization was achieved later in Brazil than in the other countries in the region. Consequently, the positive prospects associated with regional integration were tempered by an unpredictable macroeconomic environment. However, recent years have witnessed successful reforms and stabilization in Brazil as well, and inflows of FDI have increased markedly. For instance, Brazil replaced Argentina as the favoured MERCOSUR location for US direct investment in 1994 and 1995 (see Table 5.7). The strong locational advantages of Brazil—in terms of its large market and supply of labour and natural resources—suggest that we should expect substantial inflows of foreign investment in the medium run, assuming that the country's macroeconomic environment remains stable.

The experiences of the two smaller countries in the region, Paraguay and Uruguay, are mixed. While the flows of FDI to Uruguay seem to have increased, there is no clear trend for Paraguay. However, neither Uruguay nor Paraguay is likely to be influenced greatly by static investment effects. Instead, their benefits of economic integration are likely to derive from possible dynamic effects that lead to growth and increased demand for their exports in the entire MERCOSUR region. It is also possible that economic integration will have a stabilizing impact on the political and macroeconomic environment in both countries, in the sense that radical policy changes are less likely because of the commitment to the RIA.

5. Summary and Conclusions

The linkage between regional economic integration and foreign direct investment is theoretically multifaceted and ambiguous. Nevertheless, we argue in this chapter that a relatively simple generic framework is capable of summarizing the linkages in a 'reduced form' context. Specifically, two relationships are of primary relevance: (i) the stronger the environmental change connected with regional integration, the larger the impacts on FDI; (ii) the stronger the locational advantages of the individual country or industry, the more likely it is that the integration agreement will lead to inflows of FDI from the outside as well as from the rest of the integrating region.

The empirical evidence in the second part of the chapter provided some support for this rough hypothesis, although the cases also highlighted some of the cross-country differences in the investment effects of regional integration. The first case focused on the Canadian participation in the CUSFTA, and illustrated a situation where the RIA did not appear to cause any radical changes in the inflows of FDI to the country in question. The main reasons for the moderate impact of the CUSFTA are probably that the environmental change connected with the agreement was not dramatic (since trade between Canada and the USA was already relatively free to start with) and that there was already considerable cross-investment between the two countries.

The relatively modest investment response to this specific agreement might well be a general characteristic of many North–North agreements, where the trade and investment regimes are relatively open and markets are *de facto* integrated before formal integration agreement.

The second case examined the impact of the NAFTA agreement on foreign investment in Mexico, and suggested that this specific agreement has had a significant impact on the inflows of FDI. The establishment of the NAFTA coincided with and deepened other reforms that liberalized the institutional framework of the country. Hence, the agreement contributed to very significant and positive environmental changes. Nevertheless, it is difficult to identify NAFTA's impact separately from earlier reforms. In particular, NAFTA may have rendered earlier reforms more credible in the minds of foreign investors.

Thanks to its geographical proximity, and abundance of relatively cheap labour, Mexico also possesses strong natural locational advantages in labour-intensive manufacturing processes with respect to its northern neighbours. Consequently, regional integration has created new commercial opportunities for domestic and foreign investors, in the domestic Mexican market as well as in the US and Canadian markets. The response has been a significant increase in inflows of FDI, particularly from countries outside the NAFTA region. The Mexican experience may capture some general characteristics of North–South agreements, primarily related to the potential for improved policy credibility and gains from guaranteed access to large northern markets.

The third case examined the impact of regional integration in the Southern Cone, involving Argentina, Brazil, Paraguay, and Uruguay. Although the MERCOSUR Customs Union was not formally established until the beginning of 1995, a gradual liberalization of intraregional trade commenced in 1991, and most internal trade barriers were removed by 1995. The available evidence, although patchy, shows that a strong investment expansion coincided with this integration process, and it is reasonable to assume that the continuing integration process will stimulate further significant investment responses. However, the inflows of FDI have not been distributed equally to all participating countries. The two countries with the strongest locational advantages, Argentina and Brazil, have been the main beneficiaries of increased FDI inflows in the short to medium run. Hence, the early MERCOSUR experience is in broad agreement with the predictions drawn from our simple generic framework. The experience of the MERCOSUR region also suggests an important caveat that may be relevant for many other instances of South–South RIAs; namely, macroeconomic stability and related measures may be important influences on the FDI environment independently of trade and investment liberalization measures. Indeed, macroeconomic stability may have been a more important determinant of FDI inflows to both Argentina and Brazil than regional integration.

The present chapter is admittedly limited in its focus. Specifically, the analysis has focused on the impact of RIAs on FDI flows, but the more general welfare effects have not been discussed in detail, either for the integrating region or for the world at large (see Fernandez 1997 for an analysis of some related welfare aspects of RIAs). Moreover, we have concentrated on ownership issues, interpreting FDI flows as changes in the ownership of production factors. Future research should of course consider welfare effects in closer detail, and also take into account factors that determine production location rather than ownership issues alone (see Puga and Venables 1996 for a formal treatment of location and welfare issues). Regarding the empirical cases, the discussion has focused on entire countries, and individual sectors and industries have seldom been addressed. However, the conceptual framework presented suggests that the impact of RIAs is likely to differ between countries and industries, and more detailed sectoral studies are clearly desirable.

NOTES

Thanks are due to Robert Lipsey, Maurice Schiff and Alan Winters for useful discussions and comments on an earlier draft of the paper. The standard disclaimer applies.

1. Traditional concerns include the potential for trade and investment diversion. A less traditional concern relates to the loss of commitment on the part of RIA member countries to continued multilateral trade and investment liberalization.
2. It should be noted at the outset that the discussion does not explicitly address the welfare effects of changes in investment flows. As suggested above, while increased FDI flows can have beneficial impacts on growth and development in the integrating region, the overall welfare effects may, in fact, be negative if the RIA creates or exacerbates trade and/or investment distortions. For a classic reference, see Brecher and Díaz Alejandro (1977).
3. See e.g. Mundell (1957). Note, however, that Mundell and other authors writing in the Heckscher–Ohlin tradition seldom refer specifically to foreign *direct* investment: the strict distinction between FDI and foreign portfolio investment did not become

essential until it was recognized that the exploitation of firm-specific intangible assets is a major motive for FDI, whereas portfolio investment is mainly motivated by international differences in capital yields.

4. To the extent that regional integration results in trade creation, it is necessary to temper this conclusion somewhat—intraregional FDI in some member countries may increase in response to changes in the regional production structure—but the general prediction would still be a reduction of intraregional investment flows.

5. For a formal analysis of location decisions, see Puga and Venables (1996).

6. It is also possible to picture situations where RIAs could cause a reduction of FDI from outside the region. Specifically, if the initial stock of outside FDI consists of horizontally organized affiliates in several or all of the countries in the region, it is likely that this structure would not be optimal after the establishment of the RIA. A possible response to integration might be a rationalization of the network of affiliates, so that the entire region could be supplied from a smaller number of affiliates located in the member countries with the most favourable economic conditions.

7. The theoretical considerations raised in this section are also discussed in Dunning (1997a and b).

8. This was certainly a purported consideration in arguments for including Mexico in a North American RIA. See Ramirez De la O (1993).

9. The relevant literature is both substantial and well known. A comprehensive and relatively recent consideration of the internalization issue is found in Rugman (1986).

10. There are, of course, a host of other determinants as well. For instance, countries characterized by relatively unprotected and efficient domestic markets prior to regional integration are likely to enjoy the strong increases in foreign as well as domestic investment. The *ex ante* structure of trade and investment flows is another important factor. See further Blomström and Kokko (1997).

11. A review of the empirical literature on factors influencing the location decisions of foreign investors is provided in Globerman and Shapiro (1999).

12. A natural locational advantage can be thought of as a comparative advantage that has been offset by trade and/or investment restrictions. A symmetrical interpretation can be given to the notion of a natural locational disadvantage.

13. For a similar conclusion, see Bond (1996).

REFERENCES

Baldwin, R. (1989), 'The Growth Effects of 1992', *Economic Policy* 9: 247–81.

Blomström, M. (1989), *Foreign Investment and Spillovers* (London and New York: Routledge).

—— Globerman, S., and Kokko, A. (1996), 'Small Economies Joining Large Common Markets: Effects on FDI', mimeo, Vancouver: Simon Fraser University, July.

—— and Kokko, A. (1997), 'Regional Integration and Foreign Direct Investment: A Conceptual Framework and Three Cases', Policy Research Working Paper (Washington, DC: World Bank).

—— —— (1998), 'Multinational Corporations and Spillovers', *Journal of Economic Surveys* 12: 247–77.

Bond, E. W. (1996), 'The Impact of the Canada–U.S. Free Trade Agreement on Anti-dumping Filings and Decision', mimeo (Washington, DC: IECIT, World Bank).

Brecher, R. A., and Díaz Alejandro, C. F. (1977), 'Tariffs, Foreign Capital and Immis-erizing Growth', *Journal of International Economics* 7: 317–22.

Buckley, P., and Casson, M. (1976), *The Future of the Multinational Enterprise* (London: Macmillan).

Caves, R. E. (1996), *Multinational Enterprise and Economic Analysis*, 2nd edn. (Cambridge: Cambridge University Press).

Chudnovsky, D., López, A., and Porta, F. (1995), 'New Foreign Direct Investment in Argentina: Privatization, the Domestic Market, and Regional Integration', in M. R. Agosin (ed.), *Foreign Direct Investment in Latin America* (Washington: Inter-American Development Bank).

Coe, D. T., and Helpman, E. (1995), 'International R&D Spillovers', *European Economic Review* 39: 859–87.

Dunning, J. H. (1977), 'Trade, Location of Economic Activity and the MNE: A Search for An Eclectic Approach', in B. Ohlin, P-O Hesselborn, and P. M. Wijkman (eds.), *The International Allocation of Economic Activity* (London: Macmillan).

—— (1997a), 'The European Internal Market Programme and Inbound Foreign Direct Investment', *Journal of Common Market Studies* 35(1): 1–30.

—— (1997b), 'The European Internal Market Programme and Inbound Foreign Direct Investment', *Journal of Common Market Studies* 35(2): 189–223.

Emerson, M., Aujean, M., Catinat, M., Goybet, P., and Jacquemin, A. (1989), *The Economics of 1992* (Oxford: Oxford University Press).

Fernandez, R. (1997), 'Returns from Regionalism: An Evaluation of Non-Traditional Gains from RTAs', mimeo (Washington, DC: IECIT, World Bank).

Gestrin, M., and Rugman, A. M. (1994), 'The North American Free Trade Agreement and Foreign Direct Investment', *Transnational Corporations* 3: 77–95.

Globerman, S., and Schwindt, R. (1996), 'International Trade Agreements and Foreign Direct Investment in the Agri-Industrial Sector', mimeo (Vancouver: Simon Fraser University).

—— and Shapiro, D. (1999), 'The Impact of Government Policies on Foreign Direct Investment: The Canadian Experience', *Journal of International Business Studies* 30: 515–32.

—— and Walker, M. (1993), *Assessing NAFTA: A Trinational Analysis* (Vancouver: The Fraser Institute).

Griliches, Z. (1998), 'Issues in Assessing the Contribution of Research and Develop-ment to Productivity Growth', in Z. Griliches (ed.), *R&D and Productivity: The Econometric Evidence* (Chicago: University of Chicago Press): 17–45.

Hufbauer, G. C., and Schott, J. J., assisted by Dunnigan, R., and Clark, D. (1993), *NAFTA. An Assessment*, revised edn. (Washington, DC: Institute for International Economics).

IDB (1996), *Regimenes de inversion extranjera en los paises de las Americas. Estudio comparativo* (Washington, DC: Banco Interamericano de Desarrollo).

IMF (various issues), *International Financial Statistics* (Washington, DC: International Monetary Fund).

Laird, S. (1995), 'MERCOSUR Trade Policy: Towards Greater Integration', mimeo (Geneva: World Trade Organization).

Lowe, J. H., and Bargas, S. E. (1996), 'Direct Investment Positions on a Historical-Cost Basis', *Survey of Current Business* 76: 45–55.

Mataloni, R. J. Jr. (1995), 'U.S. Multinational Companies: Operations in 1993', *Survey of Current Business* 75: 31–51.

—— and Goldberg, L. (1994), 'Gross Product of U.S. Multinational Corporations, 1977–91', *Survey of Current Business* 74: 42–63.

Mundell, R. A. (1957), 'International Trade and Factor Mobility', *American Economic Review* 47: 321–35.

Puga, D., and Venables, A. (1996), 'Trading Arrangements and Industrial Development', mimeo (Washington, DC: IECIT, World Bank).

Ramirez De la O, R. (1993), 'The North American Free Trade Agreement from a Mexican Perspective', in S. Globerman and M. Walker (eds.), *Assessing NAFTA: A Trinational Analysis* (Vancouver: The Fraser Institute): 60–86.

Rugman, A. M. (1986), 'New Theories of Multinational Enterprises: An Assessment of Internalisation Theory', *Bulletin of Economic Research* 38(2): 101–18.

Smith, A. (1992), 'Measuring the Effects of "1992"', in D. Dyker (ed.), *The European Economy* (London and New York: Longman).

—— and Venables. A. (1988), 'Completing the Internal Market in the European Community: Some Industry Simulations', *European Economic Review* 32: 1501–25.

Statistics Canada (various issues), *Canada's Balance of International Payments* (Ottawa: Ministry of Industry).

Stevens, G. V. G., and Lipsey, R. E. (1992), 'Interactions between Domestic and Foreign Investment, *Journal of International Money Finance* 11: 40–62.

World Bank (various issues), *World Tables* (Baltimore and London: Johns Hopkins University Press for the World Bank).

6

The Impact of the Completion of the European Internal Market on FDI

John H. Dunning

1. Introduction

This chapter considers the impact of the completion of the European Internal Market Programme (IMP) on the geographical distribution of economic activity within the European Community (EC).[1] More particularly, it considers the empirical validity of a number of hypotheses, drawn from FDI theory, on the likely effect of the removal of tariff barriers on intra-EC and extra-EC trade and FDI flows, and the relationship between the two. The evidence strongly suggests that the twin forces of regionalization and localization, identified in Chapter 1, have been accelerated as a result of recent European integration; and that the balance between the two is strongly determined by the knowledge intensity and mobility of the economic activities involved.

2. European Integration prior to 1985

During the late 1960s and 1970s, there were several scholarly attempts to assess the impact of the European Common Market (ECM)—the first phase of macroeconomic regional integration within the European Community (EC)—on foreign direct investment (FDI).[2] Although their results were sensitive to the data and the econometric models chosen, all the studies supported the proposition that, while the removal of intra-tariffs, and the establishment of a common external tariff, increased both intra- and extra-FDI—and sometimes significantly so[3]—other determinants of FDI (e.g. market size, market growth, relative factor costs, agglomeration economies, etc.) were at least as, if not more, important, particularly once the initial (and sometimes once-for-all) effects of the ECM had worn off.[4]

Furthermore, the studies showed that the impact of European integration (hereafter called Mark 1 integration) on FDI was strongly conditional on the type of, or motives for, such investment, and on the time-frame of the analysis. Thus, while the direct, or first-order, impact of the removal of tariffs was to reduce *defensive import-substituting* FDI, and to replace it by exports from the investing country, it also led to the restructuring of existing intra-European FDI wherever its trade-creating consequences led to a geographical concentration of production in those activities in which foreign-owned firms had a competitive advantage. The indirect, or second-order, effects of integration (e.g. increased competitiveness of local firms, augmented income levels, and market growth) were shown to lead to more *rationalized* (or efficiency) seeking and *offensive* market-seeking investment. While the former was also associated with an increase in trade (particularly intra-EC trade), the effects of the latter were more ambiguous.

An examination of the FDI data for the period 1957–85[5] reveals the following main points:

1. Although, as a proportion of their total outbound FDI, that of both EC countries and of non-EC countries—particularly the USA—rose quite substantially, non-EC MNEs continued to account for the majority of FDI in the EC.[6]
2. Around 90 per cent of inbound extra- and intra-EC FDI prior to 1985 was concentrated in the 'core' countries of the EC;[7] and, much of this (a rough estimate would be about three-fifths) was within a 500-mile radius of Frankfurt. This geographical pattern of economic activity was broadly similar for both extra- and intra-EC FDI; although the latter tended to favour the UK and Germany relatively less, and Belgium and France relatively more.
3. In the early 1980s, about one-third of all FDI from EC countries was directed to *other* EC countries; this compared with 35 per cent of US FDI and 15 per cent of Japanese FDI to *all* EC countries. The total share of the inbound FDI stock in the EC originating from other EC countries (i.e. the EC's *FDI-intensity* ratio) was generally higher than its share of worldwide FDI (excluding the FDI stock of the investor country).[8] Corresponding *trade-intensity* ratios for intra- and extra-EC transactions for the same year were very similar, although a little higher for intra-EC transactions (UNCTAD 1994; EAG 1998).
4. There are few reliable data on the impact of Mark 1 integration on the sectoral distribution of FDI in the EC. The best we have relate to the sales of US manufacturing subsidiaries in the EC. Here, there is some suggestion that the growth of such sales between 1972 (the year before the UK acceded to the Community) and 1985 was most pronounced in those manufacturing sectors subject to plant economies of scale; where the US firms had the most marked competitive (or ownership-specific) advantages; where the pre-EC, intra-EC tariffs were highest; and where the post-EC barriers to USA–EC trade were the most severe.
5. There is some casual evidence that, apart from some extra-EC defensive import-substituting FDI, most intra- and extra-EC FDI was either trade-neutral or trade-enhancing. Molle and Morsink (1991) found that, over the period 1973–83, there was a direct correlation between the intensity of intra-EC trade and FDI flows, once the trade-intensity index had reached a certain level. US data suggest that the ratio between the sales of US

manufacturing affiliates in the EC and exports from the USA to the EC increased markedly in the 1960s—and much more so than in the UK, which did not join the EC until 1973. Thereafter, this ratio fell from a peak of 5.8 to 4.9 in 1977 and to 4.0 in 1985 (UN 1993*a*).

However, perhaps the most dramatic affect of Mark 1 integration was on intra-EC trade between the affiliates of US firms. In 1957, 85 per cent of all sales by such affiliates were to domestic purchasers, and 1 per cent were exported to the USA; almost all of the rest, viz. 14 per cent, went to other EC countries or the UK. By 1966, the exports to countries other than the USA had risen to 26.7 per cent, by 1977 to 38.3 per cent, and by 1982 to 45.7 per cent (UN 1993*a*); and in both 1977 and 1982, 69 per cent of these exports were between US affiliates (i.e. intra-firm exports). Other data suggest that intra-EC trade was most pronounced between the core European countries, and was particularly concentrated in sectors characterized by plant economies of scale and (relatively) low or declining transport costs.

In short, the first phase of macroregional integration in Europe was accompanied by a substantial net increase in EC-related FDI and trade flows. However, the largest increases in FDI were from countries outside the EC; and the evidence strongly suggests that US (and later Japanese) MNEs were able to take advantage of the removal of tariff barriers, and surmount the transaction costs of the remaining non-tariff barriers better than their EC equivalents.[9] Although, during the period 1958 to 1985, there was a sizeable increase in intra-EC FDI,[10] intra-EC trade grew much faster—and the great majority of this was between, rather than within firms. By contrast, US FDI in the EC increased more rapidly than US exports for the first twenty years of the ECM, after which (until 1985 at least) exports rose more rapidly.

3. European Integration: 1985 to date

3.1. Some Theoretical Insights

In 1985, the Internal Market Programme (IMP) was initiated by the European Commission in Brussels. The intention of the programme was to eliminate all remaining non-tariff barriers to trade in goods, services, and assets between the member countries of the EC by the mid-1990s. These barriers were classified into four main groups, viz. discriminatory purchasing procedures, border controls, differences in technical standards, and differences in fiscal duties. Between 1985 and the late 1990s, it was anticipated that some 319 directives, intended to remove or drastically reduce these barriers, would have been in effect by the (then) twelve member states.

Like the eradication of tariff barriers, that of the non-tariff barriers was expected to have different consequences for individual countries, industrial sectors, and firms; and for the modalities of production and servicing markets. For example, the principal consequence of Mark 1 integration was to allow member countries to better exploit their dynamic trading advantages, based both on their natural and created resource endowments and economies of scale. It also helped promote the common ownership of cross-border activities in FDI-intensive sectors (Markusen 1995). Insofar as the transaction costs of non-tariff barriers are different from those of tariff barriers[11] and differentially affect countries, sectors, and firms, it may be expected that their impact on the modalities of production and servicing markets may also be different.

However, before proceeding to consider how EC 1992 has affected, and is affecting, FDI in the EC, it might be helpful to rehearse the kind of expectations suggested by received economic analysis. As shown in the previous chapter, economists normally draw upon two sets of analytical tools to analyse the consequences of economic integration, viz. the theory of trade and the theory of FDI, or more especially the theory of international production.[12] These should be regarded as complementary, rather than competing, theories. The theory of trade in essentially concerned with the effects of economic integration on the *location* of economic activity, and the extent to which particular markets in the integrated area are serviced by exports or by local production. However, for the most part, received trade theory pays little attention either to the nationality of ownership of economic activity, or to the possibility that such activity might be part of a diversified or multinational firm.[13]

By contrast, the theory of FDI is primarily interested in the impact of macro-regional integration on FDI, either into or out of the member states. While, in so doing, it draws upon the theory of trade, it is also concerned with identifying the consequences of the *foreign* ownership of economic activity within the integrated region on the structure and location of that activity. In other words, FDI theory examines the impact of integration on the competitive advantages of firms of different nationalities, the location of activities associated with these advantages, and the way in which these advantages are organized jointly with the resource capabilities of the host countries.[14]

There is, of course, much in common between these two approaches, if for no other reason than many of the factors which influence the location of economic activity are likely to be independent of the nationality of ownership. However, in most cases, the consequences of economic integration for trade and FDI are less predictable. For example, the increased competitive pressures arising from the removal of trade barriers, together with the improved opportunities to exploit plant economies of scale, might lead to *strategic asset-augmenting* FDI. In this case, there may be a change in the *ownership* of economic activity (e.g. an investment *diversion* effect) but not its location; as a result, the consequences of trade flows—initially at least—may be quite trivial. Similarly, where integration leads MNEs to rationalize the existing value-added activities of foreign subsidiaries, this may lead to both a geographical concentration of scale-related production, and an increase in intra-EC trade, over and above that which might be expected to occur between independently owned EC firms.

To keep this chapter to manageable proportions, while attempting to address the more important economic consequences of the IMP, we shall concentrate on four generic hypotheses suggested by the trade and FDI literature.

Hypothesis 1. The first hypothesis is that the IMP will have a positive effect on *intra*-EC trade, and an ambivalent effect on *intra*-EC FDI. Depending on the form and height of existing non-tariff barriers, it is likely to have an ambivalent effect on *extra*-EC trade, but a positive effect on *extra*-FDI and on the *intra*-EC trade by the foreign affiliates of non-EC MNEs. Both trade and FDI theory suggest that intra-EC trade *creation* will arise as a result of more efficient resource allocation within the EC; and will be most pronounced in those sectors which supply products subject to *plant* economies of scale, and which cost little to transport. While, depending on the level of the external tariff, extra-EC defensive FDI will be relatively unaffected or increased, depending on the competitive-enhancing effects of integration, efficiency seeking FDI may increase.[15] The IMP is also likely to affect the value of at least some of the variables determining FDI. It might, for example, be hypothesized that demand-related variables, e.g. market size and growth, will become less important for integrated, compared with stand alone, EC affiliates, while supply-related variables, e.g. infrastructure and agglomerative economies, may become relatively more important.

Hypothesis 2. The second hypothesis is that the IMP will have an ambivalent effect on the geographical distribution of FDI *within* the EC, both by EC and non-EC MNEs. However, while the literature suggests that the locational response of foreign investors will vary according to the country of origin of the parent companies, there is no obvious reason why the site-specific factors affecting the allocation of activity between an MNE's home country and an EC country (or, in the case of intra-EC FDI, another EC country) will be very different from that as between two separately owned firms in the two countries. At the same time, Markusen and Venables (1995) have shown that, as countries become similar in size, factor endowments, and technical efficiency, cross-border activity will become increasingly dominated by MNEs, which will displace trade, provided that transport costs are not insignificant. More generally, they, and other trade economists (e.g. Helpman and Krugman 1985; Krugman 1990), suggest that macroregional integration will lead to a greater concentration of economic activity in knowledge-intensive sectors in which plant economies of scale, relative to transport costs, are important, but less concentration in sectors which are more dependent on natural resource endowments for their competitiveness. A corollary to this hypothesis is that the FDI/trade ratio among the high-income and more industrialized countries of the EC (or between them and wealthier external investors, e.g. USA, Japan, and Switzerland) is likely to be higher than that between these countries and the medium-income and/or less industrialized countries (Markusen and Venables 1995: 26).

Hypothesis 3. The third hypothesis is that depending on both country and sector-specific factors, the IMP will have an ambivalent effect on the *ownership* of production in the EC. Both the trade and FDI literature suggest that perhaps the most critical component explaining the presence of FDI between and among industrialized countries is the juxtaposition between firm-level economies of scale and scope, e.g. such as those that arise from the spreading of various headquarter activities and research and development; plant-level economies of scale; the costs of coordinating cross-border activities, and intra-national spatially related costs. MNEs are likely to dominate those sectors where the first and last ingredients are significant, relative to intrafirm coordination costs and plant-level scale economies (Markusen 1995; Caves 1996). If it could be shown that those sectors which are the most sensitive to the effects of the IMP were more FDI-intensive than the non-sensitive sectors, *and* that integration enhances the kind of ownership advantages specific to MNEs, then it may be reasonably hypothesized that the IMP will lead to an increased share of the foreign ownership of activities in the EC in those sectors.

Hypothesis 4. This hypothesis naturally follows on from Hypothesis 3. Since, as the European Commission has suggested, some sectors are likely to be affected more by the IMP than others, it follows that its consequences for trade and FDI will, at least to some extent, be sector-specific. Moreover, both the extant literature and empirical data on FDI clearly show that MNEs tend to concentrate in sectors which demonstrate one or more of the following characteristics: (i) a high level of R&D relative to sales, (ii) supply intermediate products that are either technically advanced and complex, or offer opportunities for scale economies in their production, (iii) supply end products which are highly differentiated and income-elastic in demand, (iv) are trade and/or FDI-supporting and (v) where the cross-border intrafirm coordinating costs of MNE activities are low, relative to the cross-border transport of the goods and services being produced by their foreign affiliates (Hirsch 1976). As it happens, most of the sensitive goods and services sectors identified by the European Commission possess one or other of these attributes. Therefore, it is reasonable to hypothesize that FDI in these sectors, or in countries in which these sectors tend to concentrate, will be more affected by EC 1992 than the less sensitive sectors and countries in which the FDI is less well concentrated.

3.2. Some Stylized Facts

Before proceeding to analyse the evidence for and against these hypotheses, let us first briefly outline the main trends in intra- and extra-FDI in the EC since 1985, and its distribution between member states. The experience of Mark 1 integration (the completion of which took longer to accomplish than is intended for Mark 2 integration),[16] and our knowledge about FDI trends prior to the prescribed date for market unification (viz. 1 January 1993),[17] suggests that the first five to eight years after the start of the implementation of economic integration are (for most sectors at least) the most critical.

3.2.1. *The geography of FDI*

Table 6.1 gives details of the changing share of the EC as a host region to foreign direct investors between 1980 and 1995. It shows that in 1980, the stock of FDI directed to the EC[18] was 36.7 per cent of that of all recipient economies, and 47.4 per cent of that of developed economies. Over the five years immediately *prior to* the announcement of the IMP, these shares *declined* to 29.4 and 40.0 per cent respectively. However, by the end of five years after its announcement, the EC's shares had *risen* to 40.0 per cent òf all economies and 49.8 per cent of all developed economies. Thereafter, the EC's share of FDI directed to all developed economies stabilized, and by 1996 it was 48.3 per cent (a slight *decrease* over 1993 of 51.3 per cent). At the same time, because of the increasing attractiveness of developing economies, and particularly China to foreign investors, the EC's share of the worldwide FDI stock in that year was even less than 1980, 33.5 per cent compared with 36.7 per cent (UNCTAD 1998).

Whatever else these data show, they reveal a substantial increase in the activity of foreign investors in the EC in the latter part of the 1980s. Normalizing for differences in the growth of GNP between the EC and the rest of the world does not affect this conclusion.[19] However, what *is* of interest (and we shall explore this in more detail later in the chapter) is that at least part of this increase in inbound FDI may have been at the expense of the capital formation of indigenous firms. For example, while gross fixed capital formation (GFCF) in the EC hovered around one-fifth of gross domestic product between 1981 and 1995, the contribution of FDI inflows to that capital formation rose from 2.6 per cent in the 1981–5 period to 5.9 per cent in the 1986–90 period.[20] Between 1991 and 1993 it ranged from 5.5 to 5.7 per cent, but by 1995 it had risen to 7.2 per cent (UNCTAD 1998).[21]

Table 6.2 gives some details on changes in the distribution of the FDI stock[22] within the EC between 1980 and 1995. We have chosen to divide such countries into two groups, viz. the six core countries of the EC, which are also the high-income countries, and the non-core or largely medium-income countries.[23] The Table shows that, between 1980 and 1985, the core countries accounted for 78.4 per cent of the increase in FDI stock. In the following five years (1986–90), this ratio increased marginally to 84.5 per cent; but, in the following five years (1991–6), mainly due to a fall in the dollar value of UK inbound FDI stocks, it fell back again to 78.8 per cent. Even allowing for the country-specific differences in the compilation of data, they do not point to any increases to the *overall* geographical concentration of FDI in the EC, but this point will be further investigated later in the chapter.

We now turn to consider similarities and differences between the extra- and intra-EC FDI in the EC over the past decade or so.

Table 6.3 presents data on the distribution of inbound FDI in the EC by the leading source regions and countries since the mid-1980s; and, Table 6.4 looks at the significance of the EC as a host region from the perspective of the three

TABLE 6.1. Changing share of inward foreign investment stock by host region and economy, 1980–1996 (percentages)

Host region/economy	1980	1985	1990	1993	1996
Developed economies	77.5	73.5	80.3	75.2	69.2
Western Europe	41.4	33.3	44.4	42.5	37.9
European Community (12)	36.7	29.3	40.0	38.6	34.9[a]
Core Countries	32.8	25.7	34.2	31.5	27.9
Non-Core Countries	3.9	3.6	5.8	7.1	7.0
Other Western Europe	4.7	4.0	4.4	3.9	3.0
North America	28.6	34.3	29.7	26.5	24.7
Canada	11.3	8.9	6.6	5.1	4.2
USA	17.3	25.4	23.1	21.4	20.5
Other developed economies	7.5	5.9	6.2	6.2	6.6
Australia and New Zealand	3.4	3.7	4.9	4.8	4.9
Japan	0.7	0.7	0.6	0.8	1.0
South Africa	3.4	1.5	0.7	0.6	0.4
Israel	—	—	—	—	0.3
Developing economies	22.5	26.5	19.6	24.1	29.2
Africa	4.3	3.7	2.4	2.4	2.0
Latin America and the Caribbean	10.0	10.0	6.8	8.1	10.5
Asia	7.9	12.6	10.2	13.4	16.5
Other developing economies	0.3	0.2	0.2	0.2	0.2
Central and Eastern Europe	0.0	0.0	0.1	0.7	1.5
Total inward stock	100.0	100.0	100.0	100.0	100.0
Total inward stock value (in US$ million)	480,611	727,902	1,709,299	2,079,538	2,732,649

[a] Excludes Austria, Finland, and Sweden which joined the European Union (previously called the European Community) in 1995.

Source: UNCTAD (1998). All figures obtained directly from official sources by UNCTAD have been converted into $US at the average exchange rate for the year in question.

TABLE 6.2. The geographical distribution of changes in the inward foreign direct investment stock within the EC, end of year 1980–1985 to 1991–1996[a]

	1980–5 (%)	1985–90 (%)	1990–6 (%)
(1) Core countries			
Belgium and Luxembourg	4.1	5.9	21.6
France	28.6	11.3	20.6
Germany	0.8	15.8	8.0
Italy	26.8	8.3	5.1
Netherlands	15.4	10.4	13.5
UK	2.7	32.8	10.0
TOTAL	78.4	84.5	78.8
(2) Non-core countries			
Denmark	−1.5	1.2	4.2
Greece	10.1	1.2	1.9
Ireland	2.4	0.1	2.6
Portugal	0.6	0.8	0.5
Spain	10.1	12.2	11.9
TOTAL	21.7	15.5	21.2
All EC countries	100.0	100.0	100.0

[a] Excluding Austria, Finland, and Sweden, which joined the European Union (previously the European Community) in 1995.

Source: As for Table 6.1.

TABLE 6.3. Sources of FDI flows and FDI stocks in the European Community, 1984–1987 to 1990–1993

	Flows—% of total[a]			Stocks—% of total[b]		
	1984–7	1988–90	1991–3	1985	1990	1993
1. North America	21.7	13.8	18.7	34.6	32.2	29.7
of which US	19.6	12.6	15.7	33.4	30.3	28.0
2. Western Europe	58.5	68.3	69.2	53.3	55.4	57.4
of which EC	45.0	52.9	59.4	40.4	39.2	43.5
3. Other OECD	7.3	10.2	5.7	3.0	7.6	7.3
of which Japan	5.3	7.3	2.8	2.7	4.7	4.6
4. Other countries	12.5	7.7	6.4	9.1	4.8	5.6
TOTAL	100.0	100.0	100.0	100.0	100.0	100.0
Total amount in US$ million	72,325	214,025	180,145	173,832	498,561	586,012

[a] Annual average.
[b] Included countries: France, Germany, Italy, Netherlands, and UK.

Source: OECD (1993).

TABLE 6.4. Japanese, US, and EC foreign direct investment by host regions and countries, 1985–1993 (% of world total)

Host region/economy	Japan (annual average)			USA (annual average)			European Community (annual average)		
	1985–7	1988–90	1991–3	1985–7[b]	1988–90[b]	1991–3	1985–7	1988–90	1991–3
Developed economies	68.2	77.3	71.3	64.3	68.7	61.7	88.1	89.3	82.0
European Community (12)	17.0	20.9	20.3	38.8	44.6	44.2	30.6	50.8	57.7
Core countries:	15.9	20.1	18.8	33.5	38.9	40.1	26.4	42.9	45.1
Belgium and Luxembourg	5.0	1.4	1.0	1.2	3.0	2.9	2.7	8.3	8.6
France	0.8	1.7	1.6	4.0	5.7	4.7	3.7	6.8	6.7
Germany	1.2	1.6	2.4	3.2	2.9	8.9	1.4	6.4	8.8
Italy	0.2	0.4	0.7	1.9	4.4	3.2	2.4	3.0	3.6
Netherlands	3.1	5.7	5.0	9.9	3.1	0.7	8.1	9.4	9.7
UK	5.7	9.4	8.2	13.4	19.8	19.7	8.2	9.1	7.7
Non-core countries:	1.0	0.8	1.5	5.3	5.7	4.1	4.2	7.8	12.5
Denmark	0.0	0.0	0.0	-0.7	0.2	0.3	0.1	0.3	0.5
Ireland	0.3	0.1	0.6	3.6	3.0	2.8	0.7	1.8	4.0
Southern Periphery[a]	0.7	0.7	0.9	2.4	2.5	1.0	3.4	5.7	8.0
Other Western Europe[b]	0.7	1.3	1.1	5.5	6.7	7.8	2.8	4.0	5.4
USA	44.8	47.0	41.9	0.0	0.0	0.0	48.1	27.9	15.9
Canada	1.5	1.8	1.9	14.6	9.8	4.8	3.2	2.7	0.9
Japan	0.0	0.0	0.0	3.1	2.9	1.8	0.6	0.9	-0.1
Australia and New Zealand	4.2	6.3	6.2	2.4	4.8	3.3	2.8	2.9	2.2
Developing economies	31.8	22.7	28.3	35.8	31.3	37.0	11.8	10.5	15.3
Africa	1.1	1.1	1.4	-0.1	-2.0	0.7	0.7	1.1	1.1
Latin America	17.5	8.8	8.2	33.0	26.4	23.1	5.3	4.9	3.8
Middle East	0.2	0.2	0.9	0.4	-0.3	1.7	0.7	0.6	0.6
Asia	12.8	12.2	17.1	3.6	6.9	11.1	2.3	1.8	3.5
Other developing economies[c]	0.2	0.4	0.7	-1.1	0.4	0.4	2.9	2.2	6.3
Central and Eastern Europe	0.0	0.1	0.4	0.0	0.0	1.3	0.1	0.2	2.6
Total	100.0	100.0	100.0	100.0	100.0	100.0	100.0	100.0	100.0
World total ($US million)	67,497	170,922	111,212	59,405	79,771	124,910	125,876	268,431	268,352

[a] Greece, Spain, Portugal.
[b] Austria, Finland, Norway, Sweden, Switzerland.
[c] Includes Malta and Cyprus and other countries not reporting separately.

Source: Japanese Ministry of Finance, US Dept. of Commerce (various issues), OECD (1993).

largest source countries or regions. The main conclusion to be drawn from Table 6.3 is that, the EC countries[24] have attracted a rising share of FDI since the mid-1980s; although part of the reason for this was the sharp retrenchment of MNE activity in the USA in the late 1980s and early 1990s.[25] Within the EC, the *stock* of FDI directed to the core countries decreased slightly from around 90 per cent in 1995 to nearer 85 per cent in 1993.

By contrast, Table 6.4 shows that the intra-EC share of FDI by EC countries (excluding Ireland and Greece) more than doubled between the mid-1980s and the early 1990s. These data immediately suggest that EC-specific factors—such as the IMP—may have had a considerably greater impact on intra-EC FDI than on extra-EC FDI, a conclusion quite the opposite from the one we drew about the effects of Mark 1 economic integration.

Throughout the late 1980s and early 1990s, a somewhat higher proportion of intra-EC FDI was attracted to the non-core countries, as compared with that of Japanese and US FDI; while, over the period as a whole, there is some suggestion of a decentralization of intra-EC FDI, particularly to Southern Europe.[26] However, *within* the core countries, a noticeable difference between extra- and intra-EC FDI is the considerably lower attraction of the UK as an investment outlet in the former case.[27] The closer linguistic, cultural, legal, and institutional ties between the UK and the USA, relative to that of the other core countries of the EC and the USA, might have something to do with this.

To what extent does FDI tend to cluster in particular regions or countries, and how far has such clustering, e.g. to take advantage of agglomerative economies, increased in recent years? Table 6.5 compares the FDI-intensity ratios[28] of EC countries in selected host regions in the late 1980s or early 1990s with the respective ratios in the early 1980s. Looking, first, at intra-EC FDI intensities, the Table reveals that, in all countries except the UK, these intensities were greater than 1.00 in the latter period, although, again, apart from the UK, they were even more pronounced for non-EC European countries. Second, in the five EC countries for which we have data, the intra-EC intensity ratios increased in the 1980s. Third, the FDI intensity ratios of EC countries in non-European countries were generally less than 1.00 in 1990 (an exception is the above-average UK/USA ratio); and that, except in the case of FDI in Japan, these ratios generally fell in the previous decade. Fourth, the FDI intensity ratios of both the USA and Japan in the EC rose in the 1980s, in spite of the attractions of other parts of the world (notably East Asia) for US investors and the USA for Japanese investors.

3.2.2. The sectoral distribution of FDI

Data on the changing sectoral distribution of extra- and intra-EC FDI are only available for a few countries. Perhaps the best statistics are those compiled by the US Department of Commerce. Unfortunately, such data are only published for selected years.[29] In Table 6.6, we set out the increases in the sales of US affiliates in Europe[30] between 1982 and 1989 (which embrace the years before

TABLE 6.5. FDI intensity ratios of selected foreign investing countries by host regions, early 1980s–1992

Investor country	Year	European Community	Other Western Europe	North America	USA	Canada	Japan	Rest of the world
European Community								
Belgium and Luxembourg	1980	1.65	2.18	-0.14	-0.31	0.09	0.29	1.26
	1988	n.a.	n.a.	n.a.	n.a.	n.a.	n.a.	n.a.
Denmark	1982	1.31	3.68	0.86	0.86	n.a.	0.01	0.62
	1991	1.42	5.45	0.38	0.36	0.45	0.77	0.40
France	1982	1.00	1.88	1.15	1.99	-0.21	0.11	0.79
	1991	1.37	1.63	0.62	0.72	0.30	0.16	0.49
Germany	1980	1.02	2.44	0.84	1.21	0.25	0.17	0.84
	1992	1.19	2.60	0.79	0.91	0.27	0.84	0.38
Italy	1980	n.a.	n.a.	n.a.	n.a.	n.a.	n.a.	n.a.
	1992	1.52	2.84	0.31	0.37	0.12	0.41	0.59
Netherlands	1984	0.89	1.65	1.19	1.44	0.43	0.15	0.44
	1992	1.03	2.27	0.99	n.a.	n.a.	0.48	0.52
UK	1981	0.50	0.52	1.09	1.43	0.55	0.09	1.25
	1992	0.58	0.80	1.32	1.52	0.65	0.61	0.89
Portugal	1985	1.23	0.04	0.49	0.65	0.01	—	1.27
Spain	1988	n.a.	n.a.	n.a.	n.a.	n.a.	n.a.	n.a.
	1989	1.39	1.02	0.31	0.39	0.06	0.18	1.13
Other countries								
USA	1980	0.60	1.05	0.47	—	1.14	0.26	0.63
	1990	0.73	1.34	0.41	—	1.80	1.74	0.73
Canada	1980	0.45	0.45	2.24	3.63	—	0.06	0.66
	1990	0.45	0.38	1.91	2.44	—	0.40	0.62
Japan	1980	0.30	0.26	0.98	1.44	0.24	—	2.13
	1990	0.38	0.24	1.26	1.54	0.24	—	1.28

Ratios are derived from data on stock of foreign direct investment using formula set out in note 28.

Sources: Based on UN (1993a) and a variety of national statistical sources.

TABLE 6.6. Growth of sales by US affiliates in Europe and the Rest of the World, by sectors, 1982–1993

	1982–9 (1982=100)			1989–93 (1989=100)			1982–93 (1982=100)		
	All countries	Europe	Rest of world	All countries	Europe	Rest of world	All countries	Europe	Rest of world
High impact									
Beverages	173.9	162.2	183.3	170.1	204.3	147.2	295.8	331.4	269.9
Drugs	182.0	214.8	141.3	167.3	168.6	164.7	304.5	362.2	232.7
Office/computing	324.3	296.4	400.2	116.1	101.7	145.0	376.6	301.5	581.4
Radio, TV communications	80.5	98.2	84.7	132.4	96.9	143.2	106.6	95.2	121.3
Electronic components	229.5	203.5	244.6	147.5	154.9	143.9	338.5	315.2	352.2
Instruments	195.6	181.2	247.6	125.3	125.1	125.6	245.1	226.7	311.1
Finance, except banking	247.8	555.8	164.6	159.5	206.2	98.8	372.7	1146.1	162.6
Insurance	182.4	183.0	182.1	143.7	138.8	153.0	262.1	254.0	278.6
Total high impact	219.9	255.0	187.4	138.2	145.3	131.8	289.6	370.5	247.0
Moderate impact									
Other food products	164.5	218.0	112.8	154.1	155.1	152.4	253.5	338.1	175.0
Other chemical products	145.6	193.6	100.4	115.1	114.3	116.4	167.6	221.3	114.8
Other machinery	127.9	124.2	132.3	92.5	99.8	78.6	118.3	124.0	104.0
Household appliances	321.1	311.5	328.8	119.0	151.5	94.4	382.1	472.0	310.4
Transportation equipment	200.0	218.8	185.1	115.2	186.5	114.2	230.3	253.4	211.4
Textile products and apparel	148.9	140.6	158.7	142.4	160.6	123.8	212.1	225.8	196.5
Rubber products	144.5	237.8	101.9	110.4	102.5	118.8	159.5	243.7	121.1
Glass products	187.0	180.0	200.2	95.4	115.7	61.6	178.4	208.2	123.3
Wholesale trade	179.8	174.5	192.4	120.7	112.4	138.4	217.0	196.1	266.3
Business services	158.1	152.9	171.4	194.4	201.5	178.2	307.4	308.1	305.4
Total moderate impact	177.2	185.6	165.5	120.7	119.0	123.4	213.9	220.9	204.2
Total low impact	161.9	168.0	155.8	122.8	135.1	112.7	198.8	227.0	175.6
All industries (less petroleum)	181.1	193.0	167.3	126.0	125.5	126.7	228.3	242.2	212.0

Source: US Dept. of Commerce Department Benchmark Surveys (various) since 1989.

and immediately after the announcement of the IMP), and between 1989 and 1993. The sectors are classified into three groups according to their likely sensitivity (as perceived by the European Commission) to the IMP.[31] We also present similar data for the rest of the world (ROW). The difference between the Europe and the ROW indices might be interpreted as reflecting, in part at least, the 'European' (including the IMP) effect.

The data clearly reveal two things. First, the sales of US affiliates in the highly and moderately sensitive sectors rose distinctly faster than those in other sectors between 1982 and 1989 but only marginally so between 1989 and 1993.[32] Second, the average rate of growth in sales for all sectors—but particularly for some of the most sensitive sectors between 1982 and 1989 in Europe—have consistently outstripped that of the ROW.

Other data published by Eurostat (1994) demonstrate an increasing concentration of FDI by both EC and non-EC investors in the tertiary sector, and particularly in finance, banking and insurance, telecommunications, and business services.[33] How much this is due to the IMP *per se*, and how much to the deregulation and liberalization of service-related markets in general, it is difficult to say. But, it is, perhaps, worth noting that the sectoral composition of intra-EC foreign direct investment flows, and that of non-EC countries in the EC between 1984 and 1992 is broadly similar.

This conclusion is supported by a study by Agarwal, Hiemenz, and Nunnenkamp (1995), which shows that the industrial composition of post-1985 French, German, Dutch, and UK FDI in the EC has been very similar to that in other industrialized countries. Their work also reveals that only very modest changes have occurred in the sectoral composition of intra- and extra-EC FDI by these same countries between the mid-1980s and the early 1990s;[34] while there is no real evidence that the growth of extra-EC FDI in the sectors in which intra-EC trade has expanded the most rapidly has been at the expense of extra-EC FDI in other developed countries.[35] The only exception may be in some service sectors—notably in finance, insurance, telecommunications, and data-processing services, where the gains from IMP have been higher simply because the earlier barriers to intra-EC trade or investment were so high.

3.2.3. The share of FDI in EC capital formation

While much of our previous discussion has been concerned with the *locational* competitiveness of EC, and that of its member states, it is possible that part of any increase in FDI (or sales by foreign firms) might represent an increased *share* of the total investment (or sales) of all EC located firms. Such an increase in the foreign ownership of production might occur either as a result of the improved competitiveness of established foreign affiliates, or through foreign firms acquiring or merging with domestic firms in individual European countries.[36] As an earlier section has shown, the received literature would regard such M&As as a means of sustaining or increasing the ownership advantages of the acquiring firms.

However, while in some cases the location of the acquired company may be relevant, in others it may have no significance at all.

Table 6.7 reveals that the share of foreign direct inflows to GFCF in the world economy increased in the second half of the 1980s, but that this increase was mainly confined to the EC and North America. By contrast, in the 1990s, the rise in the foreign share of GFCF was most marked in the case of developing economies and in other Western Europe economies, and particularly so in the case of Sweden, which, in 1995, along with Finland and Austria, joined the EU. The increased participation of foreign-owned firms in the EC (which is confirmed by other data)[37] is entirely consistent with our knowledge about M&As. Both intra-EC and M&As, and cross-border acquisitions of EC firms by non-EC corporations,[38] and vice versa, increased more than tenfold between 1985–86 and 1989–90, before dropping back in the early 1990s to nearer their 1986–7 levels, since when they are increased again isolating the effects of the IMP (DeLong, Smith, and Walter 1996).

4. Isolating the Effects of the IMP

So much for some stylized facts about recent FDI in the EC, which lend some support to the four hypotheses set out earlier in this chapter. We now turn to examine more rigorously the empirical evidence for these hypotheses, and also some related work of other scholars on the effect of IMP on extra- and intra-EC FDI and trade. In doing so, we are faced with a difficult, indeed almost an intractable, problem—viz. how to isolate the specific impact of the IMP from the other variables which might influence the level and pattern of extra- and intra-FDI in the EC. For, even if all the data were available (which they are not), the answer would be conditional on (a) the kind of FDI being discussed, (b) particular country- and industry-specific factors, (c) how one measures the IMP effect, and (d) what assumptions one makes about what would have happened in the absence of the IMP, viz. the *anti-monde* or *alternative* position.

Basically, there are two main ways of proceeding. One is to construct a model in which an IMP variable is added to the usual determinants of FDI hypothesized by received FDI, and/or trade theory; and then attempt to estimate the significance of that variable. In principle, such an exercise could be conducted for extra- and intra-EC FDI, and for different kinds of FDI. In practice, the data on FDI only allow us to travel this path to a limited extent. We shall, however, review the research which has recently been conducted on this issue.

The second approach is more deductive and predictive, and seeks to test a number of specific hypotheses about the likely effects of economic integration on FDI. The particular hypotheses we shall seek to test are most which have been set out earlier in this chapter.

In practice, the two approaches are quite similar, and use almost identical statistical procedures. They also confront the same analytical and measurement

TABLE 6.7. The ratio of foreign direct investment inflows to gross fixed domestic capital formation, 1981–1995 (%)

Host region/economy	1981–5[a]	1986–91[a]	1991	1992	1993	1995
All economies	2.3	3.6	3.5	3.3	4.4	5.6
Developed economies	2.2	3.5	3.3	3.0	3.0	3.9
Western Europe	2.6	5.6	5.4	5.3	6.1	7.2
European Community (12)	2.7	5.7	5.7	5.5	6.0	7.0
Belgium and Luxembourg	7.6	17.5	22.8	25.2	26.1	20.4
Denmark	0.4	3.8	7.3	4.6	8.4	15.3
France	2.0	4.5	5.9	8.2	9.0	8.6
Germany	1.2	1.1	1.2	0.6	0.5	2.6
Greece	6.0	5.9	8.7	5.5	5.2	4.8
Ireland	4.0	5.9	1.3	17.0	15.3	14.2
Italy	1.1	2.0	1.0	1.7	2.6	2.6
Netherlands	6.1	12.8	10.7	12.2	14.2	14.8
Portugal	3.0	9.9	13.7	8.3	7.9	2.7
Spain	5.3	9.6	10.0	10.5	8.6	5.4
UK	17.6	13.6	9.5	9.8	11.0	13.1
Other Western Europe	1.7	4.3	4.0	2.5	3.9	6.2
North America	2.8	6.3	2.9	2.7	8.4	14.1
Canada	1.0	5.8	2.4	2.4	5.1	11.0
USA	2.9	6.5	3.0	5.0	8.8	5.8
Other developed economies	0.7	0.9	0.7	0.9	0.5	1.2
Developing economies	3.3	3.4	4.0	4.2	6.1	7.4
Africa	2.3	3.9	4.2	5.2	6.1	7.9
Latin America and the Caribbean	4.1	5.3	5.2	7.6	6.4	9.8
Asia	3.1	2.8	3.4	3.2	6.0	6.6
Central and Eastern Europe	neg.	0.1	0.4	1.1	7.4	10.2

[a] Annual average.

Sources: UNCTAD (1995, 1996, 1998).

problems. Both, for example, need to construct a quantifiable proxy for what is essentially a non-quantifiable phenomenon, viz. the removal of non-tariff barriers to intra-EC trade. Both, too, in the design and specification of their chosen models face the difficulty that many of the other variables hypothesized to influence FDI are, themselves, likely to be affected by the IMP. Introducing leads and lags may help resolve this latter problem, but only to a limited extent.

Since, up to now, most attempts to explain recent movements in FDI into the EC have followed the first approach, we will give most of our attention to these.

5. Incorporating IMP into Traditional FDI Models

We are aware of only two attempts to do this, viz. Clegg (1995) and Pain and Lansbury (1996), although other models have identified the significance of non-IMP variables influencing FDI in the EC (or Western Europe).[39] In such cases, it *could* be argued that the value of the residual (i.e. unexplained) variables might be taken as a proxy for the IMP,[40] or, at least, a reflection of its importance, *apart* from its effects on the value of the other variables. An alternative procedure would be to estimate the impact of the IMP on the non-IMP variables, and then to credit the IMP with that impact in any explanation of FDI. Thus, for example, if it could be shown that, over the five-year period 1987–92, the IMP had raised GNP by 6 per cent (the most optimistic forecast of the Cecchini report (Cecchini *et al.* 1988); then, using the estimates of Julius (1990) and the UNCTAD (1993a), of the elasticities of FDI with respect to changes in the GNP—viz. between 3.5 and 4.5 per cent—one could then infer that between 21 and 27 per cent of any increase in FDI over those years was due to the IMP.

Of the more recently published research which has sought to evaluate the determinants of FDI in the EC, those of UNCTAD (1993a), Buigues and Jacquemin (1994), Clegg (1995), and Pain and Lansbury (1996), Srinivasan and Mody (1998) are worthy of special attention. We will now briefly summarize the results of their work in the following paragraphs.[41]

5.1. UNCTAD (1993a)

The UNCTAD study regressed the annual flows (at times 't') of FDI (both intra- and extra-EC) into the EC and other developed countries, over the period 1972–88, against five explanatory variables, viz. the level of GNP in year $t-1$, the change in GNP between $t-1$ and t, the ratio of *domestic* investment to GNP in year $t-1$, the exchange rate at year t (defined as the ratio of the domestic currency to the US dollar), and the squared deviation of the exchange rate from its mean over the period 1972–88. The authors found that, apart from the exchange rate variable, which was insignificant, the remaining four factors explained about 90 per cent of the fluctuations in FDI in *both* the EC and other developed countries, and that the coefficients of the explanatory variables always had the correct size. Of these variables, GNP was consistently found to be the most significant, with its coefficient being much larger for the EC than for the other developed countries. The share of domestic investment in GNP was also positively and significantly associated with FDI for both the EC and other developed countries. The variance in the exchange rate was seen to have a significant negative effect on FDI inflows.

The UNCTAD study also estimated the elasticity of the response of FDI to changes in the value of the independent variables. It found that an increase in both the level of GNP and the ratio of domestic investment to GNP in the EC in one year coincided with an increase in the inflow of FDI of 4 per cent in the following year, while a 1 per cent change in the variance of the exchange rate would have a relatively small negative (but statistically significant) impact on FDI inflows of $37 million.

Unfortunately, the data in the UNCTAD study do not go up beyond 1988; nor do the authors split their analysis into a pre- and post-IMP time-frame. But, some estimates for the period 1989–95, made from a variety of sources, including the IMF and World Bank—and which implicitly take account of the IMP—predicted that the annual rate of growth of FDI flows in the EC would outpace that of other developed nations, except Japan.[42] Primarily, this was because the projected growth of GNP and the ratio of domestic investment to GNP was higher in the EC[43] than in other regions of the world. Although the UNCTAD study did not specifically incorporate an IMP variable into their model, the results do suggest that the *indirect* approach to evaluating its significance, viz. by its effect on GNP, domestic investment and the exchange rate, might offer a promising line for further research.

5.2. Srinivasan and Mody (1998)

This study was confined to US and Japanese FDI for the period 1977 to 1992. It embraced thirty-five countries, including ten EC countries. One of its main purposes was to evaluate the significance of four rather different groups of factors which the literature have suggested influence FDI. These are:

(a) *Classical factors*—which the authors proxied by host-country market size, and labour and capital costs.
(b) *Agglomeration factors*—proxied by the previous level of FDI and the quality of supportive infrastructure to FDI.
(c) *Trade restricting factors*—proxied (in reverse) by the degree of openness of an economy; and a dummy for the IMP variable.
(d) *Risk factors*—proxied by information provided by various corporate data banks on country-risk assessment.

The authors compiled a number of multiregression equations, using mainly log linear estimates of the FDI function for all developed countries, and for the EC separately.[44] They found that, for each group of countries, both the size of market and cost of labour were significant explanatory variables—but not the cost of capital in the case of the EC. Agglomeration factors, measured in this instance by the production of electricity per capita, and the number of telephone lines *per capita*, were significantly related to FDI in the case of the EC, but not for developed countries as a whole.[45] As might be expected, and in contrast to the situation in developing countries, country risk was of only trivial importance, but openness (or negative trade restrictions) was positively and significantly signed in both groups. Eliminating country risk, these three groups of factors explained about 70 per cent of the variation in FDI in the EC (and rather less in the case of FDI in all developed countries).

In some additional (unpublished) calculations undertaken by the authors, Srinivasan and Mody found that, when they split their data into three time periods, viz. 1977–81, 1982–6, and 1987–92, there was no evidence that the formation of the IM significantly improved the EC's share of either US or Japanese FDI. Indeed, the case of Japanese FDI, assuming East Asia to be the benchmark group of countries, the share of FDI directed to the EC fell in the period 1987–92.

5.3. Clegg (1995)

In a long-range longitudinal study, Clegg attempted to model the determinants of US FDI in the original six member countries of the EC between 1951 (seven years before the European Common Market (ECM) came into effect) and 1990. The unique characteristics of his model were: first, an attempt to incorporate both real and financial variables into three multiple regression equations (one embracing the whole and one each for two subperiods, 1951–72 and 1973–90); and second, in the latter subperiod, the introduction of a dummy variable for the IMP.[46]

Clegg found that of the ten or eleven explanatory variables included in his equations, market size (proxied by GNP or GDP deflated to constant prices), market growth, a trade discrimination variable, the exchange rate (of the dollar against the six EC currencies), and relative interest rates were all significantly and correctly signed for one or other of the subperiods, and for the forty-year period as a whole. However, contrary to expectations, for the longer period, market size was shown to be negatively associated with FDI—and significantly so—although, for the first two decades, the two variables were positively correlated. Clegg suggested the reasons for this was that, whereas in the 1950s and early 1960s, most US FDI was defensive and was directed to the larger local markets in Europe, in the later years, particularly after the UK joined the EC, it was more of an efficiency or strategic asset-seeking kind, and geared to exploiting the EC market as a whole.[47]

Clegg's insertion of a dummy variable for the IMP (set to unity for the period 1987–90) gave inconclusive results. For the period 1951–90, the variable was positively but insignificantly associated with FDI; but for the subperiod 1973–90, it was negatively associated. Part of the reason for the apparent conflict in these findings may be that the significance of the other variables in the equation (e.g. market size) quite dramatically changed in the 1980s. At the same time, as Clegg himself recognized, the use of an *aggregate* dummy for the IMP inevitably fails to capture the industry-specific effects of the programme.

5.4. Buigues and Jacquemin (1994)

One of the distinctive features of this study was its attempt both to evaluate the relationship between extra-EC FDI in the EC and exports to the EC, and to estimate the significance of trade barriers as a determinant of FDI. Taking the share of global FDI directed to seven or nine manufacturing sectors in the EC by US and Japanese MNEs as the dependent variable, the authors regressed its value against that of four independent variables, viz. the share of total US and Japanese exports directed to the EC, intra-EC non-tariff barriers, the sectoral growth in demand in the EC divided by the growth in demand in the USA and Japan, and the Community's sectoral specialization, which they defined as the EC's exports for particular sectors as a percentage of the total EC exports of manufactured goods, divided by the same index for all OECD countries.[48]

The relevant linear regressions produced results which were generally supportive of expectations. In particular, extra-EC FDI and trade were shown seen to be significantly complementary to each other (see Hypothesis 1). Second, while non-tariff barriers to trade were a significant determinant of Japanese FDI, they played only a minor role in influencing US FDI.[49] For US sectoral demand growth and EC sectoral specialization, the results were different for US and Japanese investors. In the Japanese case, both variables were shown to have a significant positive association with FDI, while, for the USA, only the sectoral specialization variables were significantly related. Although the authors did not include an agglomeration variable in their analysis, they found that both US and Japanese firms tended to strengthen their share of FDI and exports in those sectors in which they already had a comparative advantage in 1980, while they contracted their share of FDI and exports in the sectors in which they had an initial comparative disadvantage.

5.5. Pain and Lansbury (1996)[50]

Since, as we have seen, the effects of the IMP are unlikely to be evenly distributed between industries, it is only by incorporating sector-specific variables that one can properly evaluate the impact of the IMP. Moreover, apart from our own estimates presented later in this chapter, the Pain and Lansbury study is the only one we know which has made a formal attempt to incorporate *discriminate* dummy variables to proxy the IMP.

The Pain and Lansbury study is unique in another respect, in that it examined the impact of the IMP on the *outward* intra-EC FDI[51] of two of the core EC countries, viz. the UK and Germany.[52] In doing so, it used received FDI theory to test three hypotheses. These are:

1. That intra-EC FDI by UK and German firms has risen more rapidly than it would have done in the absence of the IMP.
2. That intra-EC by UK and German firms has risen either more rapidly than that outside the EC or at the expense of such investment.
3. That the IMP has had a more marked effect on the growth of FDI by UK and German firms in the less trade-intensive sectors, notably financial services, since, in the past, non-tariff barriers have constrained both FDI and trade in these sectors relative to that in the more trade-intensive sectors.

The econometric model devised by Pain and Lansbury consisted of both location- and internalization-specific explanatory variables.[53] Of the former, they included the size of the sectoral output in the host country, relative factor costs, currency variability, the extent of trade barriers, and the corporate financial conditions in the home country.[54] Of the latter, they used data on the US registered patents of UK and German firms as proxy for their preferences for FDI, rather than cross-border licensing; the idea being that firms would be more likely to internalize the markets for their technology and organizational expertise in high-value-added sectors than in low-value-added sectors.[55] Estimates of the non-tariff barriers—ranging along an ordinal scale of 1 to 3—as they were perceived to effect particular sectors—were obtained from the Buigues, Ilzkovitz, and Lebrun (1990) and Sapir (1993).

The sample period taken for the dependent and explanatory variables apart from the IMP was 1981–92 in the UK case and 1980–92 in the German case. For each country, the authors first calculated a (log linear) multiregression equation *excluding* the IMP variable. In each case, the results were similar and broadly consistent with those of other studies. Host-country output was shown to be positively and significantly correlated with UK and German FDI in the EC, although the (sectoral) output elasticities (1.54 and 0.84) were considerably lower than that recorded for GNP by the UNCTAD study (4.34).

Both the UK and German equations recorded a positive, but insignificant, relationship between relative unit labour costs and FDI. This finding is consistent with the notion that high labour costs may reflect the availability and productivity of high-skill labour, and be associated with agglomeration economies, rather than with low (real) labour productivity. Both the corporate gearing ratios and the proxy variable used to capture the currency variability were correctly signed, but insignificant. Taking a three-year cumulative measure of patents registered by the two groups of firms in the USA, they found that in equations the coefficients were correctly signed and significant. Overall, Pain and Lansbury estimated that the coefficient between the dependent and the five explanatory variables was very high at 0.972, although, almost certainly, there was some auto-correlation between the explanatory variables.

The authors then produced two equations embodying the IMP indicator ordinally ranked according to perceived sensitivity (3 = high, 1 = low). This variable was shown to be positively and significantly related to FDI in the case of both the UK and Germany, i.e. it led directly to an increased level of FDI in the EC, although the coefficient was somewhat higher for the UK. The effect of the inclusion of this variable was to reduce the elasticities on output (in the UK case) and patents (in the UK and German cases), which confirms an earlier point made in this chapter that, in the absence of a specific IMP variable, some of its effects are captured by other variables.

The next part of the Pain and Lansbury exercise was to estimate the difference made to the *value* of FDI in the EC as a result of the IMP. The authors calculated that, by the end of 1992, the IMP may have raised the constant price stock of UK FDI by $15 billion (or 31 per cent of the capital stake at that date) and the stock of German FDI by $5 billion (or 6 per cent of the aggregate stock level). In both instances, the prime gainers were shown to be the financial and other service sectors and the electronics sector (which includes telecommunications equipment). For the UK, major gains were also recorded in the distribution, and in the food, drink, and tobacco sectors, in both of which the UK has a comparative advantage.

Because of the differences in the industrial structure of individual EC countries, the impact of the IMP on UK and German intra-EC FDI investment is likely to be country-specific—at least to some extent. Thus, according to Pain and Lansbury, the primary beneficiary of the IMP, insofar as it has affected German outward FDI, has been in the UK, in which it is estimated that the German stake in 1992 was $4.3 billion, or a third higher than it might otherwise have been. Other gainers appear to be Italy, the Netherlands, and Portugal; but France and Belgium are both shown to have lost German investment as a result of the IMP, mainly, it would seem, because of the size of German chemicals and distribution investment there. Overall, the study offers little support for the proposition that the IMP has led to a more pronounced intra-EC concentration of economic activity.

6. Formulating Specific Hypotheses about the Efficiency of the IMP

So much for an examination of a selection of studies which have sought to add an IMP dimension to the explanation of extra- or intra-FDI in the EC; or which help shed light on that dimension if its impact on other explanatory variables could be assessed. The following paragraphs return to consider more specifically the hypotheses set out earlier in this chapter, and to examine first how far the studies so far described throw light on these, and second to present some new findings of our own.

Hypothesis 1. While the Barrell and Pain study showed that Japanese FDI in the EC was significantly and positively related to non-tariff barriers, the Buigues and Jacquemin and Clegg studies supported the proposition that the IMP is leading to an increase in extra-EC FDI, as USA and Japan seek to be 'insiders' in a market favouring the production of firms located in that market.[56] At the same time, research by Agarwal, Hiemenz, and Nunnenkamp (1995) and Pain and Lansbury (1996) would appear to refute the hypothesis that intra-EC FDI will fall as a result of deeper economic integration. On the relationship between FDI and trade, the Buigues and Jacquemin research confirmed that US and Japanese exports to the EC were likely to be complementary to, rather than substitute for, US and Japanese FDI in the EC. Another study conducted by ourselves (to be considered later in the chapter) shows a positive relationship exists between these variables and intra-EC transactions, although, consistent with trade theory, the ratio between exports and FDI flows is higher in intra-, than in extra-, EC transactions.

Other evidence on the relationship between intra- and extra-trade and FDI is more casual, although none the less instructive. Data on both extra- and intra-FDI in the EC suggest that the growth in downstream services (notably wholesale trade and business services) is closely correlated with exports from the investing country. For example, the gross product (= value added) of EC-based wholesale trading affiliates of US firms rose by 102.9 per cent between 1982 and 1989, and by 9.6 per cent in the following three years; while over the same time periods, the exports of the US MNEs shipped to their European affiliates rose by 73.7 and 28.2 per cent. Over the period 1982 and 1989, the rank correlation coefficient between changes in the stock of US assets in EC wholesaling affiliates and US exports to EC countries about which data are available was +0.53, but for that of 1989–93 it was –0.08.[57]

How far do the above conclusions hold for intra-EC trade and FDI, and to what extent are they country- and industry-specific? Certainly, as shown by both Eurostat and national data, there appears to be a significantly positive correlation between the recent growth in intra-EC FDI in trade-related activities and exports from the investing countries, although the former has tended to outpace the latter.[58] Since, in their more general model, Pain and Lansbury calculated that the IMP programme raised intra-EC UK and German FDI in distributive activities by 27 and 2 per cent of the 1992 stock of FDI, so it may be concluded that, in part at least, the rise in intra-EC trade is also the result of the IMP.[59]

What next of the interface between trade and FDI in particular industrial sectors? In their analysis of the changing share of US and Japanese FDI in, and exports to, the EC, for the period 1984–90, by two-digit manufacturing sectors, Buigues and Jacquemin (1994) found a Pearson coefficient of +0.10 for the former and +0.64 for the latter. (The respective coefficients which related the share of exports and of FDI for 1990 were +0.75 and +0.28.) However, a more detailed industrial breakdown between changes in the sales of US affiliates in Europe and exports shipped by parent companies to their European affiliates between 1982 and 1989 reveals less impressive correlation coefficients of +0.15 in the case of twenty-two sensitive sectors and a +0.08 in the case of twelve 'non-sensitive sectors'.

TABLE 6.8. Comparisons between shares of intra-EC FDI and trade by broad industrial sector, 1984–1992 (%)

	1984–6[a]		1987–9		1990–2	
	FDI	Trade	FDI	Trade	FDI	Trade
More technology intensive	73.0	59.9	47.0	61.3	50.6	62.1
Chemicals	30.8	18.4	28.4	16.6	9.9	15.9
Non-electrical machinery	15.7	10.6	3.2	11.4	10.1	11.1
Electrical and electronic equipment	18.4	14.8	13.3	15.4	15.3	15.6
Transport equipment	8.1	16.1	2.1	18.0	15.3	19.5
Less technology intensive	26.9	40.1	43.0	38.7	49.5	37.9
Primary and processed food products	9.6	12.5	22.7	11.3	27.2	10.8
Metal and metal products	0.7	3.6	6.4	3.8	3.5	4.1
Other industries	16.5	23.9	23.9	23.7	18.8	23.1
All industries	100.0	100.0	100.0	100.0	100.0	100.0
ECUs (billion)	1.33	319.9	6.67	424.2	9.02	547.2

Details on the relationship between the sectoral distribution of *intra*-EC FDI and trade are hardly better! We have drawn on two sources of information. The first is that contained in a study by Davies and Lyons (1996), which examined changes in intra- and extra-EC FDI penetration ratios and the export shares of German, French, and Spanish industries, between 1987 and 1992.[60] The authors showed there was little systematic relationship between the level of foreign ownership, or changes in that ownership, and the level and change in either intra- or extra-EC trade. While, for example, trade and FDI appeared to closely parallel each other in computers, this was not so in the aerospace and the more traditional sectors, while in the Spanish telecommunications sectors and German electrical machinery sectors, a *decrease* in foreign ownership was associated with an increase in the significance of both intra- and extra-EC trade flows.

The second source of data is that of intra-EC FDI and intra-EC trade, published by Eurostat (or related agencies) for the years 1984 to 1992; these data are only available for some two-digit industrial groups. In Table 6.8 we set out a comparison between the changing share of intra-EC FDI flows and intra-EC trade; and, in Table 6.9, the changing trade/FDI ratios over this period.

Three particularly interesting features emerge from these tables. The first is the increasing share of intra-EC FDI flows directed to the less technology-intensive sectors particularly in the 1980s; this is in marked contrast to the industrial pattern of US and Japanese direct investment in the EC. However—and second—as shown by the changing share of trade flows, it would seem that the intra-EC exports of EC countries is also becoming less technology-intensive. Since the more technology-intensive sectors are also those which tend to be more integrated across national boundaries, these data suggest that, even by the early 1990s, the European MNEs had still not fully geared their European operations to meet

TABLE 6.9. Intra-EC trade/FDI ratios, 1984–1992

	1984–6	1987–9	1990–2
More technology intensive	196.4	82.9	74.4
Chemicals	142.7	37.1	97.2
Non-electrical machinery	160.8	325.5	66.5
Electrical and electronic equipment	192.9	73.8	61.9
Transport equipment	478.1	540.3	77.5
Less technology intensive	355.6	46.4	46.6
Primary and processed food products	312.2	31.5	24.1
Metal and metal products	1,047.2	37.7	69.7
Other industries	346.5	62.9	74.6
All industries	239.5	63.5	60.7

[a] Annual Average. Intra-EC FDI is defined as inward investment flows into all member states of the EC from other member states of the EC; and intra-EC trade as value of exports between members of the community. The ratio of trade to investment is multiplied by 100.

Source: Eurostat (1994).

the needs of the internal market. Third, as revealed by Table 6.9, the trade/FDI ratios have fallen substantially over the last decade, although there is no distinct sectoral pattern which emerges.

Hypothesis 2. We set out some of the changes in the geographical distribution of both extra- and intra-FDI in the EC over the past decade or so. Overall, the share of all FDI by the major EC countries directed to the EC increased in almost all manufacturing and service sectors between the mid-1980s and mid-1990s. However, there seems little to suggest that there has been any general increase in the geographical concentration or agglomeration of FDI *within* the EC, except in a few technology or information-intensive sectors thought likely to be the most responsive to the IMP programme. For example, the UK, which already had a revealed comparative FDI advantage in financial services has continued to maintain that advantage. In the pharmaceutical sector, there has been further concentration of both intra- and extra-EC FDI in the UK and France. The six core countries accounted for more than four-fifths of the EC-related cross-border M&A transactions between 1989 and 1994 (UNCTAD 1998). However, if anything, the data—fragmentary as they are—suggest that there has been a modest decrease in concentration of FDI in the electronic components, office and computing machines, industrial instruments, and business services in the four most populated EC countries.

Outside the knowledge-intensive sectors, we observe that, while the core EC countries have continued to attract the bulk of new FDI and cross-border M&A activity, in automobile components and in automobile assembling, Spain has become a major new production outlet and has attracted both Japanese car companies and joint ventures of EC and US MNEs. In chemicals, too, there has been some geographical restructuring of new FDI, particularly from Germany and the UK towards the Netherlands and Spain. At the same time, all the major EC chemical MNEs have increased their share of production elsewhere in the EC (and, outside the EC, in the USA) since the IMP programme was first announced. This pattern of localization and globalization going hand and hand is also repeated in the textile and clothing industry; but, in spite of the increased Europeanization of this sector, imports from outside the EC continued to rise at the expense of the output of indigenous firms (Agarwal, Hiemenz, and Nunnenkamp 1995).

A related hypothesis to the one stated at the beginning of this section is that the lowering or removal of non-tariff barriers will reduce the growth of *extra*-EC FDI in those sectors in which *intra*-EC FDI expands the most rapidly. But, according to Agarwal, Hiemenz, and Nunnenkamp (1995), this has not happened. By considering up to nine sectors for each of five countries, viz. France, Germany, the Netherlands, and the UK, the authors secured bivariate correlation coefficients between changes in the intra- and extra-FDI between 1985 and 1992, which were generally positive, rather than negative as might be predicted. This, in the words of the authors, suggests that the 'globalization strategies of the major EC investors were largely independent of integration in Europe' (Agarwal, Hiemenz, and Nunnenkamp 1995: 12).

Hypothesis 3. Earlier in this chapter we showed that the share of FDI inflows to the GFCF of all EC countries, except Ireland, increased markedly in the five years immediately following the announcement of the IMP, since when it has fluctuated between 5.3 and 7.2 per cent. It may be further noted that, although the share of inbound FDI flows to GFCF varies between member states (in 1995 it varied from 2.6 per cent in Germany and Italy to 20.4 per cent in Belgium), the same or similar rate of increase between the first and second half of the 1980s was experienced by most countries.

When the foreign participation ratio of the EC is compared with that of other developed countries, including the rest of Europe, it can be seen that, in the early 1990s, there was some relative retrenchment of FDI in North America, although, in 1994, the ratios for both Canada and the USA were nearer their level of the late 1980s. The buoyancy of the foreign participation ratio in the EC in the 1990s is entirely consistent with the increased share of intra-EC cross-border M&As in all cross-border M&As.

Although we only have piecemeal evidence about the *changing* share of the foreign ownership of particular sectors in EC countries, we do know that, during the 1980s, the share of foreign enterprises in the manufacturing production of five EC countries, viz. France, Germany, Ireland, Italy, and the UK, increased in all cases except for Germany where it remained the same. We also know the sectors in which MNEs or their affiliates tend to concentrate, viz. computers, motor vehicles, pharmaceuticals, electronic equipment, and industrial instruments (OECD 1993; Dunning 1993*a*). If one, then, examines the industrial composition of the sales of US affiliates in the EC manufacturing in 1993, one sees that between 70 and 75 per cent were one or the other sensitive sectors identified by the Commission; and that this percentage has hardly changed since 1982.[61] This percentage compares with a figure between 50 and 55 per cent of the value added in all manufacturing by *both* indigenous and foreign-owned firms in the Community (Buigues, Ilzkovitz, and Lebrun 1990). Since the pattern of FDI by the other major European countries in the EC is broadly similar to that of the USA, it may be reasonably concluded that, relative to locally owned firms, the affiliates of foreign MNEs are more concentrated in IMP-sensitive sectors; and, excepting for medical instruments, that their share of the output of the *most* sensitive sectors has increased—at least marginally—since the early or mid-1980s.[62]

To some extent, then, these data are further corroboration that, since the mid-1980s, quite a substantial part of FDI in both North America and Europe has been undertaken as part of a deliberate strategy of MNEs to maintain or advance their global competitive positions. Insofar, too, as economic integration increases interfirm rivalry, and reduces the transaction costs of engaging in cross-border M&As, it may lead to a change in the ownership of firms, without there being any change in the location of production or trading patterns.

Again, such fragmentary evidence as we have points to M&As being concentrated in the sectors which have been most affected by the IMP. Using data on M&As involving US and European companies[63] between 1985 and 1991 and classified by nineteen industrial sectors, it can be shown that 69 per cent of the value of the transactions, in which US firms were the buyers and 75 per cent of those in which European firms were the buyers, were in the sensitive sectors. For this chapter, we conducted an additional econometric exercise which attempted to test the proposition that changes in the sectoral distribution of US FDI in the leading EC countries would be related to the sensitivity of the sectors to the IMP programme. The proposition here, derived from the trade and FDI literature, is that the FDI directed to the EC, both absolutely and relative to trade, will be positively correlated to the removal of the trade barriers as US firms seek to become 'insiders' in a more liberalized EC market.

In testing this hypothesis, we compared (by use of pooled data for two time-periods, viz. 1982–9 and 1989–93), the change in the sales of US affiliates in Europe, in thirty-one industrial sectors between 1982 and 1993 to five explanatory variables, viz. (i) the sales of established US affiliates in 1982 and 1989 (this we took to be a proxy for agglomeration economies and a 'familiarity' index for new investors),[64] (ii) changes in market size of the EC, (iii) changes in the value added per person employed in the EC (as a measure of labour productivity), (iv) changes in exports of US MNEs to their European affiliates, and (v) a dummy variable for the IMP, which we relate to the perceived sensitivity of the sectors on a scale of 1 (little sensitivity) to 3 (high sensitivity).[65]

We calculated two equations: one with and one without an IMP variable. The results of the former are set out in Table 6.10. Only the market-size variable was statistically significant at the 5 per cent level for a one-tailed test. The perceived impact of the IMP was shown to be negatively (although not significantly) related to the sectoral increases in the sales of US subsidiaries.

TABLE 6.10. The determinants of changes in sales of US industrial affiliates in Europe, classified by industrial sector, 1982–1993

	Δ Sales[a]
Constant	.5317
	(.7407)
Actual sales[b]	−.0171
	(1.0563)
Change in market size[c]	.6500*
	(.3694)
Change in productivity[d]	.4444
	(.7065)
Change in exports[e]	−.0298
	(.0688)
Dummy[f]	−.1175
	(.1360)
Adjusted R^2	.1020
F Statistic	1.976

[a] Change in sales of US affiliates in Europe 1982–3 and 1989–93. These are treated as pooled data.
[b] Actual sales of US affiliates in Europe 1982, 1989.
[c] Change in EC market size 1982–9 and 1989–93.
[d] Change in EC labour productivity 1982–9 and 1989–93.
[e] Change in exports of US MNEs to Europe 1982–9 and 1989–93.
[f] Dummy variable on a scale of 1 to 3 to reflect perceived sensitivity of the sector to IMP.
* Significance level 5% (one-tailed test).

Sources: US Dept. of Commerce 1985, 1992, and 1995; Eurostat 1994; Buigues, Ilzkovitz, and Lebrun (1990).

Inadequate sectoral statistics preclude us from conducting such a detailed exercise for intra-EC FDI. The best we can do is to use the Eurostat data on the sectoral composition of intra-EC FDI flows for the period 1985–92, and see how far these are related to the kind of variables identified in the earlier exercise. However, we did not, in this instance, calculate an agglomeration variable, partly because there are no data on the stock of intra-EC FDI in the early 1980s; and partly because the sectoral breakdown is too broad to calculate a meaningful index. Also, in place of variable (iv) in the previous exercise, we computed an index of intra-EC trade published by DEBA (v.d.). However, because Eurostat FDI data are only available for seven industrial sectors—and there are no sectoral breakdowns by countries—we have divided the period into six three-year intervals[66] to obtain an acceptable number of observations. All FDI data are then expressed as a ratio of the three-year average flow to the average FDI flow for 1984 and 1985. For the first three explanatory variables, viz. change in market size, labour productivity, and intra-EC trade, we adopt a similar procedure. However, instead of introducing of a dummy variable for the IMP of (i)–(iii),

TABLE 6.11. The determinants of changes in intra-EC FDI flows

	Δ Intra-EC FDI[a]
Constant	−28.4742
	(8.9720)
Change in market size[b]	−2.0322
	(19.5751)
Change in productivity[c]	36.0070**
	(9.4544)
Change in intra-EC trade[d]	−.3782
	(14.8770)
Dummy[e]	1.3865**
	(.2225)
Adjusted R^2	.6521
F Statistic	15.244

[a] Intra-EC FDI flows, expressed as 3-year moving averages from 1985 to 1992, as a percentage of an average of the base years 1984 and 1985.
[b] Change in EC market size by industrial sector; 3-year moving averages (apparent consumption).
[c] Change in EC labour productivity by industrial sector; 3-year moving averages.
[d] Change in intra-EC trade by industrial sector; 3-year moving averages.
[e] Dummy variable on a scale of 1 to 7 to reflect perceived sensitivity of the sector to IMP.
** Significance level 1%.

Sources: US Dept. of Commerce 1985, 1992, and 1995; Eurostat 1994; Buigues, Ilzkovitz, and Lebrun (1990).

we ranked each of the seven sectors according to their perceived sensitivity of that to the removal of non-tariff barriers (1 = high and 7 = low).[67]

We again formulated two regression equations: one with and one without the IMP variable. The results of the former are set out in Table 6.11. Although these should be treated with even greater caution than the previous exercise, they suggest that the negative effect of IMP on defensive market-seeking FDI was outweighed by its positive effect on other forms of FDI—including strategic asset-seeking FDI; productivity was also significant at the 1 per cent level and correctly signed.

Hypothesis 3. Previous sections of this chapter have, in fact, touched upon this hypothesis indirectly inasmuch as we have shown that many of the effects of the IMP have been sector-specific. Moreover, we have indicated the types of sectors in which the foreignness or multinationality of enterprises is perceived to confer a competitive advantage. However, it is worth recalling that the main indigenous competitors to foreign firms investing in the EC are significant MNEs in their own right. Moreover, for the most part, the MNEs for Europe are from the same industrial sectors in which inbound FDI is concentrated.[68]

To test hypothesis 4, we decided to sidestep the issue of the distinctive characteristics of MNEs—and, indeed, that of the intrafirm coordination and

John H. Dunning

transaction costs—by estimating the revealed employment advantage (REA) of foreign—in this case the US—affiliates in the EC. This we did by calculating the share of *total* EC employment in the EC accounted for by US affiliates in each of some thirty industrial sectors in 1993 and then dividing that share by the share of all EC industrial employment accounted for by all US affiliates. A ratio above 1 would indicate US firms had a comparative REA in that sector; and a ratio below 1 that they had a comparative disadvantage.

The REA is the first of the explanatory variables we relate to the dependent variable, which, again, is the increase in the sales of US affiliates in Europe between 1982 and 1993. The other independent variables are export/local sales (FDI) ratios of US MNEs, which we use as a proxy for the preference of US firms to satisfy their European markets from a US as compared with a European location, and a dummy variable (on a scale of 1 to 3) which measures the perceived sensitivity of the sector to the IMP.

The results, which are also set out in Table 6.12 explain almost 30 per cent of the sales growth of US affiliates. Both the REA and export/local sales ratios

TABLE 6.12. Some determinants of change in sales of US affiliates in the EU, classified by industrial sector

	Δ Sales[a]
Constant	.9814**
	(.3258)
REA[b]	.7227*
	(.2776)
Log export/FDI intensity[c]	−.3891**
	(.1389)
DUM[d]	−.0309
	(.1182)
Adjusted R^2	.2827
F Statistic	7.174

[a] Change in the sales of US affiliates in Europe, 1989/1982 and 1993/1989. These are treated as pooled data.

[b] Revealed Employment Advantage (REA) of US affiliates in Europe (EU). The first step was to calculate individual year values for 1982, 1989, and 1993. The numerator here is the ratio of the percentage of employment in US affiliates of all employment in the EC for each industrial sector, and the denominator is the percentage of the employment in US affiliates of all employment in the EC for all industrial sectors. The second step was to use these values to calculate changes in the REA ratio between 1982 and 1989, 1989 and 1993.

[c] Export/FDI intensity is the ratio of the growth of exports of US MNEs to their European affiliates (1989/1982 to 1993/1989), the growth of sales of the EC affiliates of US firms (1989/1982 and 1993/1989).

[d] Dummy variables (on a scale of 1 to 3) perceived sensitivity of the sector to the IMP.

* Significance level 5%.

** Significance level 1%.

Sources: US Dept. of Commerce 1985, 1992, and 1995; Eurostat 1994; Buigues, Ilzkovitz, and Lebrun (1990).

are significant at the 5 per cent level; however, the IMP variable adds little explanatory value. The REA variable is positively related and the export/FDI ratio is negatively related to the increase in the sales of US subsidiaries in Europe.

7. Conclusions

The preparation of this chapter has been similar to doing a difficult jigsaw puzzle with many pieces missing! Only very faintly and imperfectly is one able to see the full picture.

We have used most of the statistical evidence at our disposal to examine changes in the extent and pattern of extra- and intra-FDI in the EC (or Western Europe) since the early 1980s. That part of the jigsaw is reasonably clear. FDI in the EC has risen faster than in most other parts of the world (save for Japanese FDI in parts of East Asia); but there is little reason to suppose that this has been at the expense of non-EC FDI.

Within the EC, there have been some discernible changes, both in the industrial structure and in the geography of economic activity. Of the former, the relative growth of FDI in knowledge-intensive activities is, perhaps, the most significant trend—although this is by no means confined to Europe. Of the latter, the access of Greece, Portugal, and Spain—and particularly Spain— has led to a modest decentralization of other than the most technology- and information-intensive activities from the six core EC countries.

Our analysis also confirms that the growth of intra-EC and Japanese FDI has outpaced that of the USA over the last decade or more. However, whereas the proportion of goods exported from US subsidiaries in the EC has remained about the same since 1982, other forms of intra-EC trade, including that of European MNEs, have risen quite rapidly.

When trying to isolate the significance of the possible explanation for these events, one is faced with the most challenging conceptual and data problems; and our conclusions must be extremely tentative. We would, however, make five observations:

1. While regionalization and globalization are distinct spatial concepts, it is difficult to perceive how globalization could have had the consequences it has in Europe if the IMP programme (or something like it) had not come about. This is particularly the case in sectors which are the most internationalized, although, it is worth recalling that even the most globally oriented MNEs tend to practise regional, rather than global R&D and production strategies (UNCTAD 1993*b*; Rugman 2000).

2. Almost all the studies examined in this chapter point to the fact that the main dynamic impact of the IMP on FDI flows has been through its effects on other variables affecting FDI—and noticeably market-size, income levels, the structure of economic activity, and agglomeration economies.

Inter alia, this makes it very difficult—and, indeed, of questionable value—to consider IMP (or a proxy for same) as an independent variable—except, perhaps, in the years immediately following 1985, when FDI was influenced more by the expectations of the programme's outcome. But, even considering the IMP as an independent variable, the few studies—including some new ones presented in this chapter—all generally agree that it has stimulated both extra- and intra-EC FDI, but the former more than the latter —but not as significantly so as have other variables.

3. It seems clear that the effects of IMP are sector-specific, and there is some evidence that, as hypothesized by trade and FDI theory, extra-EC FDI has increased more in sensitive than in non-sensitive sectors since the early 1980s—and equally important—more in these sectors than elsewhere in the developed world. The Pain and Lansbury study also reveals that, within the IMP, both UK and German FDI in either EC countries would have been less—and particularly so in some of the more sensitive sectors, e.g. finance and insurance.

4. Our chapter has examined the validity of several propositions which emerge from trade and FDI theory. First, it has shown that there is only limited evidence that the geographical concentration of economic activity has increased, even in the sectors which benefit from substantial plant economies of scale. At the same time, the fact that higher-value, e.g. innovatory, activities, have remained so highly embedded in the core countries, while the markets for the products have increased substantially, is testimony to the continuing drawing power of the economies of agglomeration in these sectors. Again, consistent with the predictions of neoclassical trade theory, the IMP may well have helped disperse resource-based and/or lower-value activities, and, in part, this is documented by the changing structure of intra-EC FDI and trade.

Second, we have found that there is a complementarity between FDI and trade in most of (but not all) industrial sectors, and that the IMP has done nothing to lessen this complementarity. However, this relationship is less strong for intra-EC than for extra-EC FDI. Third, as predicted by FDI theory, the most significant growth in the *share* of sales of foreign affiliates, has occurred in those sectors and countries in which the competitive advantages of these firms—relative to their indigenous rivals—are the most marked. Such fragmentary evidence as we have gives no support to the proposition that non-MNEs have improved their competitive positions vis-à-vis MNEs; though, in some sensitive sectors, EC based MNEs have improved their competitive position vis-à-vis US and Japanese MNEs; and it is highly likely the IMP has contributed towards this improvement.

5. A substantial proportion of the extra- and intra-EC FDI in the EC since the mid-1980s has taken the form of M&As; and part of the rationale for this has been to acquire strategic assets to advance the regional and/or global competitiveness of the acquiring firm. Although such M&As are essentially

a global phenomenon (Walter 1993), those involving EC firms as sellers have undoubtedly been facilitated by the IMP. The effect of these M&As on the intra-EC location (compared with the ownership) of economic activity is ambiguous; but, in the majority of cases, there has been some restructuring of activity of the acquired firm; and this, as well as the distinctive sourcing and exporting policies of the acquiring firms may well effect both intra- and extra-EC trade.

Our final observation is that, while for some sectors and for some foreign investors, the dynamic effects of the IMP programme have already largely materialized, for others—and especially for the service sectors and for Japanese (and possibly some European) investors—these consequences have yet to work themselves out. It is to be hoped that the next few years will help us fit some new pieces into the jigsaw portraying the effects of the IMP, although these will become increasingly difficult to isolate from the consequences of European monetary integration—Mark 3—in the ever-deepening integration of Europe.

NOTES

This chapter is a modified and condensed version of two articles which were initially published by the *Journal of Common Market Studies* 35 (March 1997): 41–56 and (June 1997): 189–220.

1. Now called the European Union (EU). However, as most of the analysis contained in this chapter predates the formation of the European Union, we shall use the expression European Community (EC) throughout.
2. For a review of these studies, see UN (1993*a*).
3. Particularly in the Irish case, where intra- and extra-EC inward investment increased dramatically in the decade after Ireland joined the EC in 1973.
4. A good example is provided by Spain and Portugal. In the five years after their accession to the EC, the average annual increase in the stock of extra- and intra-EC FDI into Portugal was 56.7 per cent and into Spain 128.3 per cent. In the period 1990–6, the corresponding increases were 5.7 and 10.2 per cent (UNCTAD 1998). Moreover, a serious deficiency of multivariate studies is that they rarely consider the second-order affects of FDI on the other variables—notably market size and GNP per head—which are usually included in the regression equations.
5. The year prior to the announcement of the Internal Market Programme (IMP).
6. Estimates by scholars vary. Yannopoulos (1992) calculated that, for the period 1980–4, extra-EC FDI *flows* were two-thirds of all inbound FDI; this compared with an estimate made by Molle and Morsink (1991) for the years 1975–83 of 75 per cent; and that by Pelkmans of the percentage of extra-FDI stocks for 1978 of total FDI in the EC of 57 per cent (Pelkmans 1984).
7. Defined both in terms of their GNP per head, and the proximity of their industrial and commercial heartlands to Central Western Europe, viz. Belgium, Luxembourg,

France, Germany, Italy, Netherlands, and UK. We accept, of course, that *parts* of industrial France, the UK and Italy are as far removed from the Ruhr Valley as is southern Denmark!

8. The ratio is a kind of revealed comparative advantage of the EC in attracting FDI from other EC countries. In 1980 the ratio for German/EC FDI was 1.06; for France 1.00; for Belgium/Luxembourg 1.65; for Denmark 1.31; for the Netherlands 0.89; and for the UK 0.50. The below-average figures for the Netherlands and the UK reflected the above average share of North American FDI attracted to these countries. By contrast, the US/EC intensity ratio was 0.60 and the Japanese/US ratio was 0.30.

9. Obviously there were exceptions to this rule. Philips of Eindhoven is one example of an EC MNE which totally restructured its European activities in the first twenty years of the ECM.

10. The most noticeable increase was, perhaps, recorded by the UK where the share of its outward stock directed to the EC rose from 7 per cent in 1960 to 15 per cent in 1971 and 21 per cent in 1985.

11. The transaction costs of tariff barriers primarily represent an addition to the transport costs of exporting or importing goods and services. Those of non-tariff barriers represent a whole range of cost-enhancing measures which affect not only the plant-specific costs for production of goods and services, but firm-specific costs of transacting and coordinating the various extra-plant activities, including the procurement of inputs and the marketing and distribution of outputs. It is only very recently that economists have paid serious attention to the effects of economic integration on these latter costs—and on how integration may help upgrade the competitive advantages of multiproduct firms whose activities spread across national boundaries.

12. The theory of international production attempts to explain the extent and pattern of the foreign-owned value activities of firms (i.e. production financed by FDI). Like trade, the unit of account is the output of firms and countries, as distinct to FDI, which is an input measure. At the same time, FDI is often taken to be a proxy for foreign production.

13. As e.g. illustrated by the contents of most articles in a special edition of the *Oxford Review of Economic Policy* 14(2) on Trade and Location. Exceptions include the work of trade theorists, such as Helpman and Krugman (1985), Markusen (1995), and Markusen and Venables (1995).

14. For a survey of the current state of FDI theory, see Dunning (1993a) and Caves (1996). For a recent examination of the impact of MNEs on the geography of international production, see Dunning (1998) and Kozul-Wright and Rowthorn (1998).

15. This it may do for two reasons. First, the IMP is likely to improve the efficiency of 'insider' relative to 'outsider' firms (this, after all, is one of its main intentions). Second, it will encourage the restructuring of activities by foreign firms inasmuch as the unified market enables a more efficient disposition of resources.

16. Although the Common Market came into being on 1 January 1958, it was not until the late 1960s that a tariff-free zone in the EC was finally accomplished.

17. Although between 1985 and 31 December 1992, the majority of directives designed to remove non-tariff barriers had already been put into effect.

18. Throughout, we consider the twelve countries. These include Spain, Portugal, and Greece which joined the EC in the early 1980s, but exclude Austria, Finland, and Sweden, which acceded to the EU in 1995.

19. There are, of course, other normalizing factors which one should consider, e.g. changes in exchange rates. Most data in this chapter are expressed in US dollars and there have been some noticeable fluctuations in the value of that currency relative to European countries over the past fifteen years—and particularly in the £/$ rate.
20. Of course, for individual sectors of the EC, the share of FDI was considerably higher. For further details see UN (1993*b*).
21. Before dipping again in 1996 to 5.9 per cent.
22. Broadly equivalent to flows, except that changes in stock are more likely to incorporate reinvested profits than the flow data.
23. For the purposes of this exercise, we have included Denmark in the non-core countries.
24. Greece joined the nine EC countries in 1981 and Portugal and Spain in 1985.
25. For further details, see the various annual surveys on foreign direct investment in the USA, published in the Survey of Current Business (US Department of Commerce).
26. These two countries alone increased their share of intra-EC FDI from 3.3 per cent in 1985–7 to 8.6 per cent in 1992–3.
27. Particularly—and rather surprisingly—in the financial services sector. While, for example, in the period 1989–94, 56.9 per cent of all extra-EC mergers and acquisitions (M&As) involved UK target firms, the corresponding UK proportion for intra-EC M&As was 15.4 per cent.
28. Defined as the ratio of the share of a recipient (host) country (or region) (b) of the total FDI from another (= home) country (or region) (a) to the share of the former country (or region) of the total FDI from all countries, excluding that of the investor country. Expressed algebraically, $qab = Iab/Ia^*/[I^* b/I^*-I^*a]$, where qab = intensity of a's investment in b, Iab = investment by a (home country) in b (host country) and * = summation of FDI across all countries (world). See Petri (1994).
29. In 1990, the European Commission identified forty industrial (e.g. goods-producing) sectors which, prior to the announcement of the IMP, were subject to high or moderate non-tariff barriers. To this list may be added some service sectors, notably finance, insurance, business services, and wholesale trade in the service sector. See Buigues, Ilzkovitz, and Lebrun (1990) and Sapir (1993).
30. Namely the years of the benchmark surveys of US foreign direct investment (1977, 1982, and 1989) and for each year from 1991 onwards.
31. Unfortunately, there are no recent separate data for the EC itself, but, since the sales of FDI in the EC in 1992 were 90 per cent of those in all Western Europe, these data serve as a good proxy for those of the EC.
32. One exception is the business services sector. Particularly impressive was an increase in sales of computer and data-processing services of US affiliates in Europe of 399.6 per cent between 1989 and 1993.
33. Which includes business services.
34. The authors note some exceptions to the rule e.g. German FDI in all developing countries and in Asia, and UK FDI in Asia.
35. Contrary to the investment diversion hypothesis, the authors found that the correlation coefficients (again for France, Germany, Netherlands, and the UK) between trade and investment were shown to be positive and significant.
36. Notably where agglomerative economies are present e.g. in some high technology sectors.

37. When expressed as a proportion of the GNP of EC countries, the stock of inbound FDI increased from 4.8 per cent in 1980 to 10.9 per cent in 1990 and 12.2 per cent in 1993, and to 13.0 per cent in 1996.
38. Mainly USA. According to Walter (1993), the value of cross-border M&As involving EC firms (but excluding extra-EC M&As, where EC were the buyers) rose from $11,526 million in 1985 to $139,033 million in 1989–90.
39. Often taken as a proxy for EC when separate data on the EC are not available.
40. And, of course, of other determinants not identified by the other variables.
41. For a more detailed specification and formal results of these models, see Dunning (1997*a, b*).
42. In fact, the growth of the FDI stock into the EC between 1990 and 1995 was almost exactly the same as that into other developed countries (excepting Japan), viz. 37.7 per cent compared with 37.9 per cent (UNCTAD 1998).
43. A prediction which seems unlikely to be borne out by the facts!
44. For US FDI only. The study also included an analysis of FDI in developing countries, but we are not concerned with these results here.
45. A recent study on Swedish FDI, covering the period 1975–90, confirmed the significance of agglomerative effects, particularly in high-technology sectors, but finds that market size and the availability of skilled labour are generally more important locational determinants (Braunerhjelm and Svensson 1995).
46. A dummy variable of 1 was included for each year from 1986 onwards and 0 for 1985 and previous years.
47. The size of which was, itself, increasing as a result of more intra-EC trade and FDI. This idea is confirmed in a study by Yamawaki (1993) on the intra-EC distribution of employment in 236 Japanese manufacturing subsidiaries in 1988. Yamawaki found that the most significant explanatory variables were relative labour costs, market size, and the quality of indigenous technological capacity. His regression analysis supports the predictions of trade theory that inbound FDI will be attracted by the advantaged factor endowments of host countries.
48. As set out by Buigues, Ilzkovitz, and Lebrun (1990).
49. This is also the conclusion of Barrell and Pain (1993), in a study of trade barriers (proxied by anti-dumping measures) to Japanese FDI in Europe.
50. The following paragraphs set out some of the results of a study by the authors, commissioned by the Economists Advisory Group (EAG). Full results appear in EAG (1998). For a more general analysis of the interaction between FDI, technological change, and economic growth in Europe, see Barrell and Pain (1997).
51. Apart from that in Ireland.
52. These two countries accounted for 45 per cent of the outward FDI stock of EC countries in 1994.
53. As identified in the FDI literature. See Dunning (1993*a*).
54. These were predicated to affect the availability of finance for foreign investment.
55. Perhaps an even more telling statistic might have been the share of US registered patents by firms of particular countries attributable to research undertaken by their foreign affiliates. See e.g. Cantwell and Hodson (1991).
56. Swedenborg and Agmon and Hirsch came to a similar conclusion in respect of Swedish and Israeli FDI in the EC (Swedenborg 1990; Agmon and Hirsch 1995).
57. Viz. share of total US exports directed to EC growth of demand in EC divided by growth of demand in the US/European market and non-tariff barriers.

58. Between 1984–6 and 1990–2 intra-EC FDI in manufacturing industry rose by 239.4 per cent, and inter-EC exports of manufactured goods by 70–9 per cent (Eurostat 1994).
59. Presumably it would be possible to test this hypothesis directly by replacing the FDI-related dependent variable by a trade-related variable.
60. For the pharmaceuticals, computers, electrical machinery, telecommunications, aerospace, medical instruments, boilers and containers, shipbuilding and rail stock sectors.
61. These and other data are derived from the periodic benchmark surveys of US foreign direct investment published by the US Dept. of Commerce. More exact estimates are not possible due to differences in the industrial classification used by the Dept. of Commerce and the European Commission.
62. In their estimates of the changing foreign ownership ratios of nine sensitive sectors in three countries, viz. France, Germany, and Spain (27 observations), Davies and Lyons (1996) found that in eighteen of these the ratio had increased or remained the same.
63. As derived by the Securities Data Corporation Merger and Corporate Transactions Database.
64. See also a discussion on the relationship between information costs and FDI, see Mariotti and Piscitello (1995).
65. Again, as derived from the European Commission.
66. These are (i) 1985, 1986, 1987, (ii) 1986, 1987, 1988, (iii) 1987, 1988, 1989, (iv) 1988, 1989, 1990, (v) 1989, 1990, 1991, (vi) 1990, 1991, 1992.
67. We did this by expressing employment in the three-digit sensitive sectors—as identified by the Commission as a proportion of the employment in the seven two-digit sectors, and ranked these latter sectors by the size of the percentages we obtained.
68. In other words, the EC is involved in a good deal of intra-industry FDI (as well as intra-industry trade).

REFERENCES

Agarwal, J. P., Hiemenz, U., and Nunnenkamp, P. (1995), *European Integration: A Threat to Foreign Investment in Developing Countries*, Discussion Paper 246 (Kiel Institute of World Economics).

Agmon, T., and Hirsch, S. (1995), 'Outsiders and Insiders: Competitive Responses to the Internal Market', *Journal of International Business Studies* 26(2): 1–18.

Barrell, R., and Pain, N. (1993), *Trade Restraints and Japanese Direct Investment Flows* (London: NIESR, mimeo).

—— —— (1997), 'Foreign Direct Investment, Technological Change and Economic Growth within Europe', *Economic Journal* 107: 1170–97.

Braunerhjelm, P., and Svensson, R. (1995), *Host Country Characteristics and Agglomeration in Foreign Direct Investment* (Stockholm: Industrial Institute for EC and Social Research, mimeo).

Buigues, P., Ilzkovitz, F., and Lebrun, J. (1990), 'The Impact of the Internal Market by Industrial Sector: The Challenge of Member States', *European Economy*, special edn., 1–114.

—— and Jacquemin, A. (1994), 'Foreign Investment and Exports to the European Community', in M. Mason and D. Encarnation (eds.), *Does Ownership Matter?* (Oxford: Clarendon Press).

Cantwell, J., and Hodson, C. (1991), 'Global R&D and UK Competitiveness' in M. C. Casson (ed.), *Global Research Strategy and International Competitiveness* (Oxford: Blackwell): 133–82.

Caves, R. (1996), *Multinational Firms and Economic Analysis* (Cambridge: Cambridge University Press).

Cecchini, P., Catinat, M., and Jacquemin, A. (1988), *The European Challenge 1992. The Benefits of a Single Market* (Aldershot, Hants: Wildwood House).

Clegg, J. (1995), 'The Determinants of United States Foreign Direct Investment in the European Community: A Critical Appraisal' (Bath: University of Bath, mimeo).

Davies, S. and Lyons, B. (1996), *Industrial Organization in the EC* (Oxford: Oxford University Press).

DeLong, G., Smith, R. C., and Walter, I. (1996), *Global Merger and Acquisition Tables 1995* (New York: Salomon Center, mimeo).

DEBA (Data for European Business Analysis) (v.d.), Various Statistics on EC Trade, Production and Employment Issues (Brussels: European Commission).

Dunning, J. H. (1993a), *Multinational Enterprises and the Global Economy* (Workingham, England and Reading, Mass.: Addison-Wesley).

—— (1993b), *The Globalization of Business* (London and New York: Routledge).

—— (1997a and b), 'The European Internal Market Program and Inbound Foreign Direct Investment', *Journal of Common Market Studies* 35(1–2): 1–30, 189–224.

—— (1998), 'Globalization and the New Geography of Foreign Direct Investment', *Oxford Development Studies* 26(1): 47–69.

Economists Advisory Group (EAG) (1998), 'The Single Market Review Sub-Series IV', *Impact on Trade and Investment, 1: Foreign Direct Investment Brussels* (European Commission).

Eurostat (1994), EU Direct Investment 1984–1992 (Luxembourg: European Commission).

Helpman, E., and Krugman, P. R. (1985), *Market Structure and Foreign Trade* (Cambridge, Mass.: MIT Press).

Hirsch, S. (1976), 'An International Trade and Investment Theory of the Firm', *Oxford Economic Papers* 28: 258–70.

Julius, Dee Anne (1990), *Global Companies and Public Policy* (London: Royal Institute of International Affairs).

Kozul-Wright, R., and Rowthorn, R. (1998), 'Spoilt for Choice? Multinational Corporations and the Geography of International Production', *Oxford Review of Economic Policy* 14: 274–92.

Krugman, P. (1990), *Rethinking International Trade* (Cambridge, Mass.: MIT Press).

Mariotti, S., and Piscitello, L. (1995), 'Information Costs and Location of FDIs within the Host Country: Empirical Evidence from Italy', *Journal of International Business Studies* 26(4): 815–41.

Markusen, J. R. (1995), 'The Boundaries of Multinational Enterprises and the Theory of International Trade', *Journal of Economic Perspectives* 9(2): 169–89.

—— and Venables, A. (1995), *Multinational Firms and the New Trade Theory*, NBER Working Paper 5036 (Cambridge, Mass.: NBER).

Molle, W. T. M., and Morsink, R. L. A. (1991), 'Intra-European Direct Investment', in B. Bürgenmeier, and J. L. Mucchielli (eds.), *Multinationals and Europe 1992* (London: Routledge).

OECD (1993), *The Contribution of FDI to the Productivity of OECD Nations* (Paris: OECD).

Pain, N., and Lansbury, M. (1996), 'The Impact of the Internal Market on the Evolution of European Direct Investment'. (London: NIESR, mimeo).

Pelkmans, J. (1984), *Market Integration in the European Community* (The Hague: Martinus Nijhoff).

Petri, P. A. (1994), 'The Regional Clustering of Foreign Direct Investment and Trade', *Transnational Corporations* 3(3): 1–24.

Rugman, A. M. (2000), *The End of Globalization* (London: Random House).

Sapir, A. (1993), 'Sectoral Dimension in Market Services and European Integration', *European Economy* 3: 23–40.

Srinivasan, K., and Mody, A. (1998), 'Japanese and US Firms as Foreign Investors. Do They March to the Same Tune?', *Canadian Journal of Economics* 31(4): 778–99.

Swedenborg, B. (1990), 'The EC and the Locational Choice of Swedish Multinational Companies', Working Paper 284 (Stockholm: Industrial Institute for Economic Social Research).

UN (1993*a*), *From the Common Market to EC* (New York: UN Transnational Corporations and Management Division, Dept. of Economic and Social Development).

—— (1993*b*), *World Investment Directory, 1992: iii. Developed Countries* (New York: UN Transnational Corporations and Management Division, Dept. of Economic and Social Development).

UNCTAD (1993*a*), *Explaining and Forecasting Regional Flows of Foreign Direct Investment* (New York: UN).

—— (1993*b*), *World Investment Report 1993, Transnational Corporations and Integrated International Production* (New York and Geneva: UN).

—— (1994), *World Investment Report 1994, Transnational Corporations, Employment and the Workplace* (New York and Geneva: UN).

—— (1995), *World Investment Report 1995, Transnational Corporations and Competitiveness* (New York and Geneva: UN).

—— (1996), *World Investment Report 1996, Investment Trade and International Policy Arrangements* (New York and Geneva: UN).

—— (1998), *World Investment Report: Trends and Determinants* (New York and Geneva: UN).

US Department of Commerce (v.d.), *US Direct Investment Abroad* (Washington, DC: Government Printing Office).

Walter, I. (1993), 'The Role of Mergers and Acquisitions on Foreign Direct Investment', in L. Oxelheim (ed.), *The Global Rule for Foreign Direct Investment* (Berlin and New York: Springer-Verlag).

Yamawaki, H. (1993), 'Location Decisions of Japanese Multinational Firms in European Manufacturing Industries', in K. Hughes (ed.), *European Competitiveness* (Cambridge: Cambridge University Press): 11–28.

Yannopoulos, G. N. (1992) 'Multinational Corporations and the Single European Market', in J. C. Cantwell (ed.), *Multinational Investment in Modern Europe: Strategic Interaction in the Integrated Community* (Aldershot Hants and Brookfield, Vermont: Edward Elgar).

7

Regional Integration:
NAFTA and the Reconfiguration of North American Industry

Lorraine Eden and Antoine Monteils

1. Introduction

Multinational enterprises (MNEs) are agents of change in the global economy: they are the largest source of technology creation, transfer, and diffusion; their activities tie countries together in terms of production, trade, and investment flows; and they dominate most industries at the national and international levels. Over the last twenty years multinationals have changed their strategies for investment and production, shifting from simple stand-alone strategies (whereby the parent firm set up miniature replicas of itself, designed to serve local markets) to simple integration strategies (shifting labour-intensive stages of production to developing countries, e.g. subcontracting, using export-processing zones). More recently, these enterprises have begun to develop complex or deep integration strategies (rationalizing production on a regional or worldwide basis, integrating MNE across locations, placing greater reliance on created assets such as workforce quality and organizational innovations) (UNCTC 1993).

An important causal factor in the development of complex integration strategies has been regional integration. When two or more countries move to set up a free trade area (FTA), eliminating trade barriers on intra-FTA trade, the change in policy rules affects the MNE's plant location choices. For example, if tariff barriers had induced earlier defensive, tariff-jumping foreign direct investment (FDI) in order to access a local market, the removal of the barriers could lead to plant closures or rationalizations. Given the type of regional integration (which barriers are eliminated and how fast, the degree of harmonization), *ceteris paribus*, we argue that the location effects will vary depending on the motivations behind the plant location decision (the value-adding activity) and the nature of the firm (insider, outsider, domestic).

Dunning (1993) has stressed that there are four major motivations to invest in foreign countries: market-seeking, resource-seeking, efficiency-seeking, and strategic asset-seeking FDI. Building on Dunning's list of FDI motivations, we develop a micro approach to plant location that focuses on the value-adding activity which the foreign plant is expected to perform within the MNE group. Using value-chain analysis, we explore the links between the firm's general motivation for setting up a plant within an FTA, the value-adding activity to be performed by the plant, and the plant location decision. We also argue that the firm's position prior to the FTA is critical for predicting its location choices post-FTA. If the firm already has investments in the other FTA partner countries, its responses are likely to be quite different from a firm with no intraregional trade or investment linkages. Thus the type of firm (insider, outsider, domestic) will be important for predicting firm responses to regional integration. The first part of the chapter develops a theoretical framework linking plant location motivation and firm characteristics to the MNE plant location strategies in a free trade area.

As an example of the impact of FTA formation on plant location, we examine regional integration in North America, where the 1989 Canada–US Free Trade Agreement (CUSFTA) and the 1994 North American Free Trade Agreement (NAFTA) have lowered trade and investment barriers, making it possible and necessary for firms to adapt to changes in government policies. The regional integration process in North America is liberalizing intraregional trade not only in goods, but also in business services and investment (Rugman and Gestrin 1993*a*, 1993*b*; Globerman and Walker 1993; Hufbauer and Schott 1993; Eden 1994*a*; Lipsey, Schwanen, and Wonnacott 1994). As these barriers fall, MNEs have begun to integrate their international production decisions at the regional level. Such deep integration strategies are most noticeable in the automotive and consumer electronics industries, but are diffusing to other industries.

We investigate the impacts of regional integration on firm location strategies post-1989 in North America using three different data sets. First, *World Investment Report* data (UNCTAD 1998) show changes in the stock of North American inward and outward FDI over the 1985–97 period. Second, two-way FDI stock data from the OECD (1997) provide a snapshot of intraregional and extraregional North American in 1989 and 1994. Third, using US inward FDI data for the 1989–94 period, we compare the investment patterns of insider firms (Canada and Mexico) with outsider firms (all others) along four dimensions: timing of FDI, mode of entry, state location, and industry choice. Since NAFTA took effect on 1 January 1994, our data should be seen as more reflective of the Canada–US Free Trade Agreement. However, we find some interesting patterns of responses to regional integration that suggest the regional integration process in North America is significantly affecting plant location decisions.

The chapter is organized as follows. First, we develop a theoretical framework for predicting MNE location responses to the formation of an FTA, in terms of the plant location motivation and firm characteristics. We apply the model to the case of North American free trade. Lastly, we provide some evidence on MNE location decisions in North America over the 1985–97 period, looking at intra-NAFTA FDI patterns and inward FDI patterns in the USA, in order to draw some conclusions about the impact of regional integration on firm location patterns.

2. Plant Location Strategies in a Free Trade Area

There are four major types of foreign direct investment, according to Dunning (1993): market-seeking, resource-seeking, efficiency-seeking, and strategic-asset seeking FDI. In this section, we expand on Dunning's explanation for FDI by developing a micro approach to the plant location decision in a free trade area (FTA). We argue that the location decision depends on: (i) the value-adding activity which the foreign plant is expected to perform within the MNE group, and (ii) the position of the firm prior to introduction of the FTA. When these are placed in the context of the locational advantages of the FTA member countries, together with the specific form of free trade area, we can hypothesize how firms will make their location decisions in response to regional integration. We conceptualize the process as one of shocks and responses: introduction of a free trade area is a policy shock (e.g. elimination of tariff and non-tariff barriers) to which firms adjust through short-run and long-run responses. Changes in locational strategies are one form of response to the shock of regional integration.

Figure 7.1 outlines our model of plant location decisions in a free trade area. The formation of an FTA is a policy shock to which businesses must adjust. The size of the shock depends upon the type (depth, breadth, rapidity of reform phase-in) of the FTA, the existing trade and investment linkages among the member and non-member countries, and the country and region-specific advantages of the FTA. Given the FTA shock, how firms respond depends upon (i) the firm's underlying motivation for investing in the region, (ii) the actual value-adding activity under consideration for location or relocation within the region, and (iii) the type of the firm making the location decision. Each firm, based on its perception of the policy shock and its own goals, value chain, and characteristics, must decide where its plants are most efficiently and effectively located within the new FTA.

The location decision is not just 'Which value-adding activity in which country?', but also involves making decisions on whether value-adding activities should be centralized or dispersed through the region, and whether certain activities should be clustered with other firms (and if so, where). Since the locational response to the FTA is expected to vary over time (e.g. FTA provisions are phased in; sector-specific investments and immobile assets are constraints in the short run), our analysis needs to include both short-run and long-run locational responses to the formation of a free trade area. We explore the model below.

2.1. Value-Adding Activity

The plant location choices of multinationals—that is, how and where the enterprise places its value-adding activities—involve developing entry and expansion strategies for engaging in foreign production, deciding where to put different stages of production (the firm's value chain), and how many plants to have at each stage.

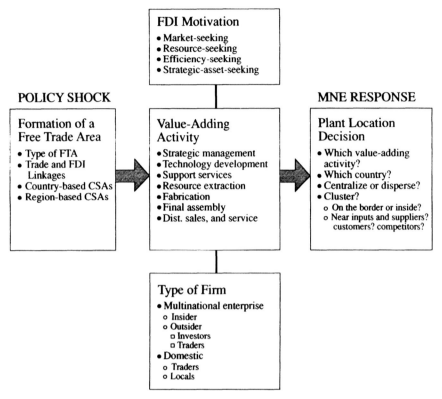

FIG. 7.1. Plant-location decision in a free trade area

The line of causation runs from the MNE's choice of the value-adding activity to its choice of plant location and then to foreign direct investment in this plant. The location selected for an affiliate therefore depends on the affiliate's role in the value chain of the firm. Plant function drives the FDI choice (Eden 1994*b*). In this section, we explore the types of value-adding activity and the general factors that influence plant location. We then hypothesize how a regional integration shock will affect the plant location decision.

2.1.1. Value-Adding Activities and Plant Location

Figure 7.2 shows the components of a typical value chain. It illustrates the *primary activities* (resource extraction and processing; the manufacture of parts, components, and sub-assemblies; final assembly; distribution, sales and service) and *support activities* (strategic management; technology development; business support services) that may make up the firm's value chain. The MNE must choose how many of the stages of production are to be internalized within the firm (i.e. the degree of vertical integration) versus carried on at arm's length with

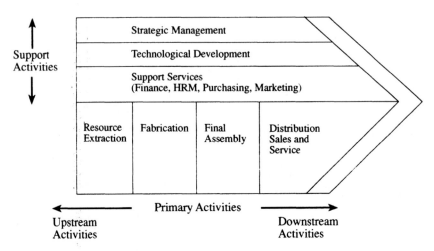

FIG. 7.2. Value-adding activities

unrelated firms. Within each of the production stages, the MNE must determine product scope (the number, type, and technological sophistication of the product lines) and geographic scope (the market served by each plant and the number and location of plants). The latter determines the degree of horizontal integration of the MNE. Both vertical and horizontal integration imply intrafirm trade flows within the MNE group.

There are four basic motivations for going abroad: resource-seeking, market-seeking, efficiency-seeking, and strategic asset-seeking FDI. The first two motivations (resource- and market-seeking) can be either first-time or sequential investments; the latter two (efficiency- and strategic asset-seeking), however, are sequential investments generally taken once the MNE is established in foreign markets. Given these four general locational motivations for FDI, we argue that multinationals construct their overall production structure by choosing among a range of locational structures for their foreign affiliates. We argue that, paralleling the value-chain analysis, we can develop a theoretical framework for analysing the MNE's plant location decision. Each stage in the value chain corresponds to a value-adding motive for establishing a foreign plant. Each MNE, depending on the length of its value chain and the nature of the industry, can therefore be seen as a set of foreign plants (or affiliates), strategically located according to their underlying value-adding function within the MNE organization. Our analysis should therefore be seen as supplementing Dunning's fourfold list of motivations for FDI, with a narrower focus on plant's value-adding function within the MNE group. We outline the basic types of value-adding foreign plants below, and summarize these in Table 7.1.[1]

Resource extraction. Resource extraction plants are set up to extract and process renewable and non-renewable natural resources; this is Dunning's resource-seeking motivation for FDI. The key factor driving location of extractor plants is a source of high-quality raw materials in abundant supply. Since processing plants turn natural resources into fabricated materials, inputs needed for processing are key to location of these plants. Where the weight/value ratio is high, economies of scale at the two stages are similar, and foreign tariffs on processed imports are not high, extracting and processing may occur in the same plant.

Fabrication. Downstream from the resource extraction stage is the production of parts and sub-assemblies. Plant location decisions are normally driven by general resource- or efficiency-seeking motivations. The simplest of these plants, offshore factories, are set up to use cheap local inputs, particularly labour, to assemble simple parts for the parent company. Export-processing zones (EPZs) generally attract such plants (e.g. Mexican *maquiladoras* along the US border). Fabrication plants, on the other hand, use low-cost labour to produce specific components and sub-assemblies for the MNE. They are globally or regionally rationalized plants in a vertical integration sense since the plant produces one segment of the value chain which is then sold for further assembly and final sale elsewhere in the MNE network. Sometimes offshore and fabricator activities are contracted out to unrelated firms rather than in-house. For example, subcontracting to OEMs (original equipment manufacturers) has been extensively used by US MNEs such as NIKE as part of a worldwide sourcing strategy.

Final assembly. The final assembly state of production can be met in a variety of forms. The motivation for establishing foreign assembly plants is generally market-seeking FDI. Once established, sequential investment often occurs, particularly in an FTA, for efficiency (rationalization) reasons. The simplest foreign plants are local assemblers, import-competing factories that assemble components for domestic sale (e.g. bottling plants, drug preparation, and packaging). Local assemblers are often set up in response to government regulations requiring a local presence, such as content legislation. Higher up the technology ladder are focused factories, globally or regionally rationalized subsidiaries that produce one or two product lines in mass production runs for final sale in both local and foreign markets, purchasing other product lines in horizontal intrafirm trade from sister affiliates. These plants can be rationalized on a region or global basis.[2] One final assembly plant that is now seen less often, but was frequent in the 1950s and 1960s, is the miniature replica (copycat) plant. When national trade barriers were high, US MNEs used tariff-jumping FDI to set up assembly plants behind the trade walls. Such plants were nationally responsive, with a high degree of local autonomy, generally assembling and selling locally a full range of products similar to their parent's production line. Such plants tend to be high cost when domestic markets are small, with excess product variety and short production lines.

Distribution, sales, and service. The stage theory of foreign direct investment hypothesizes that distribution affiliates are the first form of FDI, replacing exporting when foreign market sales are sufficiently large to support a local plant.

TABLE 7.1. Value-adding activities and motivations for going abroad

Value-adding activity	Motivations for setting up foreign plant	Examples of value-adding foreign plants
Resource extraction	• search for higher-quality, lower-cost, or more secure sources of natural resources • process natural resources (processing, refining, smelting, fabricating) • avoid government regulations that raise costs • diversify the MNE's resource base	MNEs set up foreign plants to extract natural resources (e.g. copper, bauxite, crude oil, natural gas) and/or process natural resources (e.g. alumina).
Fabrication	• access cheaper inputs in the production process (e.g. labour, energy) • avoid government regulations (e.g. taxes, tariffs, environmental regulations)	MNEs set up foreign plants or use subcontractors in export-processing zones to manufacture parts or sub-assemblies. MNEs set up fabricator plants to manufacture more sophisticated parts and sub-assemblies (e.g. engines) for use within the MNE or for sale to downstream customers.
Final assembly	• enter new or expanding markets • avoid tariff and non-tariff barriers • meet foreign government requirements for local assembly	Local bottling and packaging plants set up to fulfil domestic content regulations. In a multidomestic strategy, the MNE might use miniature replica plants to manufacture complete product lines for sale in the host country market. Under a transnational strategy, the MNE sets up globally rationalized plants that assemble final products for sale in a regional or global market, using world product mandates.

Distribution, sales, and service	• enter new markets and be close to consumers • capture economies of scale and scope in distribution • avoid tariff and non-tariff barriers • provide after-market service to customers	New MNEs often use simple distributors as a first mode of entry into foreign markets, with the distributors importing finished products for sale in host market. Retailers provide a full line of MNE products for sale to final customers in the local market. Trading companies provide a full range of trading services to the MNE's manufacturing affiliates.
Technology development	• be a window on innovations in other countries • access strategic assets (high-skilled labour and other inputs such as software programmers)	R&D centres may perform basic and applied research, clinical testing, and engineering services in the host country. R&D outposts may be established as a window on foreign science and on key competitors. Technology strategic alliances may be used to access complementary strategic assets.
Support services	• follow their downstream customers • enter new or expanding markets • avoid government regulations (e.g. taxes, financial, environmental)	Foreign affiliates may provide support services to the MNE group (e.g. advertising and marketing, accounting and financial). At least one unit may be set up in a tax haven for the purpose of minimizing global taxes.
Strategic management	• provide strategic management of the MNE's affiliates within a regional grouping	In free trade areas, the MNE may set up a regional headquarters to coordinate affiliates within the region.

Thus one would expect the size (population, income level, sophistication) of market would be a key location factor attracting distribution plants. Distributors can provide a variety of services: distribution, marketing, sales, service, and warehousing facilities.

Support services. As the MNE network grows, affiliates that can provide support services to parts or all of the MNE family (e.g. finance, centralized purchasing, accounting) can be set up to serve the MNE group as a whole, or a regional network (e.g. a Belgium international financial centre may service all the MNE affiliates within the European Union). Infrastructure, tax breaks, and skilled labour are country attributes that attract such plants. In addition, many MNEs have affiliates in tax haven or entrepôt countries that engage in tax planning and tax-avoidance activities and in channelling financial flows among affiliates at the lowest possible cost. The primary determinants affecting the location of tax haven affiliates are differences in national tax rates, tax deferral or exemption from home country taxation for foreign source income, and the existence or absence of bilateral tax treaties and information exchange agreements.

Technology development. The evidence is very strong that MNEs, particularly US ones, prefer to centralize R&D units in the home country. However, since the early 1990s, both US and foreign MNEs have been setting up R&D units in Triad markets, outside the home country. The primary reason appears to be strategic asset-seeking FDI. For example, the MNE may decentralize some of its technology development activities to an R&D outpost. These outposts can provide a window on competitors' technological activities in host countries, take advantage of differences in human capital endowments among countries (e.g. lower-cost engineers and computer scientists in India), facilitate foreign sales by adapting MNE products to local market conditions and tastes, and meet host-country regulations in the clinical testing and health areas.

Strategic management. Under a simple integration strategy, strategic management of the MNE is located in the enterprise's home-country headquarters. Decisions are top-down, with local plants implementing directives from the parent firm. However, under a complex integration strategy, the MNE may have one or more lead plants that are effectively equal partners with the parent firm, placed in strategic locations within the Triad. Lead plants are responsible for technology and product creation, and distribution of lead products in each Triad market. Lead plants may also function as a regional headquarters for the foreign affiliates in a regional trade area, with the affiliates reporting to the lead plant which reports to the MNE parent.

In summary, each MNE has a value chain of primary and support activities that is some part of the industry value chain. Each firm decides how extensive its own value chain is relative to the complete industry value chain. The motivations for establishing parts of the value chain in foreign countries are fourfold: resource-, market-, efficiency-, and strategic asset-seeking FDI. The MNE's network of affiliates is organized around the various primary and support value-adding functions that foreign affiliates perform within the MNE.

2.1.2. Plant Location in a Free Trade Area

Table 7.2 provides some hypotheses about the likely impacts of the introduction of a free trade area on plant location decisions. The table outlines each of the value-adding types of plants, the locational advantages that should attract each type of plant, and the impact of the formation of a free trade area on the location decision.

In terms of the MNE's value-adding activities, an FTA should cause rationalization of *resource extraction* plants within the region. There should be more investment in endowment-rich areas where inward FDI has been previously restricted or closed to foreign firms. In addition, one can expect general upgrading of resource-based plants from simple extraction to processing activities as downstream tariff and non-tariff barriers fall.

Reduction of trade barriers should increase the importance of economic factors such as unit labour costs as influences on the location of *fabrication* plants. MNEs with labour-intensive parts plants located outside the FTA may close those plants and shift production to the FTA, thus causing investment diversion. Tight rules of origin in the FTA should also encourage more onshore sourcing of parts and components. Rationalization of parts plants and sub-assemblies based on lowest-cost location (including subsidies) is likely as MNEs move to set up new plants in the most cost-effective location. This should lead to increased vertical integration, and the possible closure of inefficient plants both inside and outside the region.

The days of 'copycat' or miniature replica *final assembly* plants are gone; a plant has to fit into existing structure of the MNE by playing a role in its overall strategy. If the FTA brings a previously closed economy into the trading area, any miniature replica plants are likely to be either closed or rationalized for the regional market as the FTA reduces the need to be located in a specific national market. Rationalization of existing plants in terms of products and/or processes is therefore likely, increasing the degree of horizontal and vertical integration within the MNE, and thus the amount of intrafirm trade flows within the region. Where economies of scale are important, these will favour the location of production within the largest market or where costs are the lowest; in such cases, we expect closure of inefficient plants in small markets. On the other hand, where a local presence is important for local sale, as, for example, in *distribution, sales, and service*, or where consumer tastes vary widely between national markets, the activities are not footloose so that the FTA should not shift such activities.

If firm-level economies of scale favour centralizing the activity, *support activities* formerly performed in each country (local management, business services, and technology development) may be closed and their staff relocated to a regional office. The removal of local content rules and performance requirements may similarly lead to closure of R&D labs set up to meet domestic regulations. Where sectors have been closed to inward FDI prior to the FTA, there should be increased inward FDI into these sectors, particularly if strong market growth is expected. This may be particularly true in business services where non-tariff barriers tend to be high and firms are often nationalized or FDI is limited.

TABLE 7.2. Value-adding activities and plant location in a free trade area

Value-adding activity	Function of plant	Factors affecting plant location decision		Impact of formation of free trade area
		Country location advantages		
Resource extraction	Extracts and processes natural resources	Abundant, cheap natural resources (including energy and capital). Low transport costs		FTA encourages rationalization for larger market. Shift FDI and production to resource-rich countries. More FDI into endowment-rich countries that had restricted inward FDI prior to FTA. Upgrading of plants from simple extraction to processing. More interregional vertical intrafirm trade.
Fabrication	Manufactures parts and sub-assemblies	Low-cost labour and capital. Geographic proximity to downstream firms where lean production technologies important. Trade preferences that encourage offshore production (e.g. EPZs).		FTA encourages rationalization based on lowest-cost location to achieve economies of scale. New FDI in cost-effective locations. Closure of inefficient plants. Upgrading of efficient plants. More intraregional vertical intrafirm trade flows. Need to meet rules of origin requirements for intra-FTA trade. Expect EPZs to either upgrade from simple assembly or close.
Final assembly	Simple (packaging and/or bottling) or complex (automotive) assembly for final sale	Size and attractiveness of local market, access to Triad. Local content rules that require local production to access local market. Tariffs and NTBs that hinder access to local market. Good transportation network.		FTA encourages closure of tariff factories and replacement with exports from hub country where EOS important and need for national responsiveness low. Shift of remaining plants from focus on national to regional market. Possible world product mandates. Rationalization of product lines, leading to more intraregional horizontal intrafirm trade.

Distribution, sales, and service	Imports and/or distributes products in local market	Physical presence in local market important for sales.	FTA encourages downstream FDI into previously closed markets. Since local responsiveness is important at downstream stages, expect decentralization of plants to each country, but may be clustered within country borders.
Support services	Provide support to MNE group (e.g. advertising, HRM, tax), supply services to local customers	Location in Triad market. Skilled labour. Telecommunications infrastructure. Physical presence necessary for local delivery of services to consumers.	FTA encourages downstream FDI into previously closed markets. Support services provided on regional level to MNE group; may be centralized in one location. Local services (e.g. marketing) may be closed and consolidated in hub country unless local responsiveness important. May cluster where best available infrastructure and related and supporting industries.
Technology development	R&D centre, window on technology in foreign markets, local content regulations	Presence of other high-tech firms, related and supporting industries. Skilled labour. Location in Triad market. Government R&D subsidies.	FTA encourages clustering of high-tech activities where agglomeration externalities are important. If local content requirements are eliminated under the FTA, may close and centralize local R&D activities (e.g. clinical testing).
Strategic management	Strategy formulation and implementation	Location in Triad market. Access to world markets.	FTA encourages closing of national headquarters and replacement by regional HQ, unless national responsiveness important. May cluster with other regional headquarters in lead centres.

2.2. Type of Firm

A second factor affecting firm location decisions in response to a free trade area is the type of firm. We argue that the strategic responses to an FTA will be partly determined by (i) whether the firm is headquartered inside or outside the area and (ii) whether the firm has significant investments inside the region.

Following Eden and Molot (1993) and Vernon (1994), we identify three categories of firms that are likely to have different responses to regional integration: *insiders* (well-established multinationals located inside a free trade area with significant investments in the partner countries prior to the agreement), *outsiders* (foreign firms outside the area, which may have been exporting into the area or may have investments inside the area), and *domestics* (local firms inside the area that are primarily focused on their national market (or a subunit within that market) without significant investments in the other partner countries; they may or may not already be exporting to these countries). The likely responses, by type of firm, are outlined in Table 7.3.

Insiders should see benefits from lower intraregional barriers and respond by rationalizing product lines (horizontal integration) and/or production processes (vertical integration) to better exploit economies of scale and scope across the region. There is both a short-run response as MNEs engage in locational reshufflings in response to the falling trade barriers, and a long-run response where insiders locate, close and/or expand their plants with the whole regional market in mind. The result should be reduced numbers of product lines in various plants and increased horizontal trade among plants. MNEs are also likely to segment their production process among plants so that more vertical intrafirm trade takes place. Certain product lines, industry segments, and plant functions will shift among the three countries and these will cause job losses and plant closures in certain locations. Where country sizes are very different, in the short run, there may be a tendency for firms to shift their activities to the largest market. As a result, insider firms should respond by creating more cross-border vertical and horizontal intrafirm trade flows.

The formation of an FTA leaves tariff and non-tariff barriers against non-member countries unchanged while new and possibly more restrictive rules of origin are introduced. *Outsider firms* exporting into the FTA may face trade and investment diversion as the FTA gives preferential treatment to member countries in terms of products and investment locations. For defensive reasons, outsiders that are currently exporting into the FTA may shift to foreign direct investment; they are likely to locate in the largest market or where costs are the lowest, depending on whether they represent efficiency- or market-seeking FDI. The larger, regional market is also more attractive as an investment location for market-seeking FDI. Outsider firms that are unlikely to meet the rules of origin tests are more likely to cluster in the largest country, thus reducing their intra-FTA tariff duties.

TABLE 7.3. Plant location responses to the formation of a free trade area

Firm type	Definition	Responses to formation of free trade area
Insiders	MNEs in the FTA that already have FDI in the other FTA member countries.	Closure of tariff factories and inefficient plants; replacement with exports from hub country where economies of scale important and need for national responsiveness low. New FDI in cost-effective locations. Upgrading of efficient plants, and shift from focus on national to regional market. Possible regional/world product mandates for FTA subsidiaries. Rationalization of product lines for regional market and more intraregional horizontal intrafirm trade across product lines with sister affiliates. Increased interregional vertical intrafirm trade from upstream to downstream affiliates. May shift from non-FTA imports to local inputs to meet rules of origin requirements (trade diversion). May also shift investments from outside to inside the FTA (investment diversion). MNEs located in the 'hub' country may already see the FTA as their natural market; MNEs in the 'spoke' economies will need to adopt a 'double diamond' perspective on competitive advantage, seeing the FTA as one regional market.
Outsiders	Firms headquartered outside the FTA. They may be either INVESTORS (MNEs with investments in one or more FTA partner countries) or TRADERS (foreign firms that trade with unrelated firms but have no investments in FTA countries).	*Outsider investors* Similar responses as insiders except that need to meet rules of origin requirement may more strongly affect outsider firms since more inputs tend to be sourced outside FTA. *Outsider traders* Possible shift from exporting to inward FDI due to pull of larger FTA market (carrot) and push of fear of higher barriers to foreign firms (stick). May be deterred from entry due to high rules of origin; location in the hub (if sales are primarily to largest market) can minimize this impact.
Domestics	Firms inside the FTA that do not have investments in other FTA countries. These firms may be either TRADERS with other FTA members or LOCALS (firms with no international trade experience).	*Insider traders* See increased trading opportunities from larger FTA market. Shift from trade to FDI if costs warrant and regional market is attractive to firm. Entry into previously closed markets (e.g. where FDI restrictions are lifted). Setting up of new plants based on low-cost location and/or access to largest market. Market-seeking plants will most likely be located in hub market. Competitive firms in the spoke countries are likely to set up new plants in the hub country. *Locals/Nationals* Fear of new competitors (both from FDI and imports). If not protected by local barriers, may be bought up (M&A). Inefficient firms likely to close. Some firms can shift to trade/investment in other FTA country, possibly through joint ventures. Export assistance may be needed to penetrate other FTA markets, especially where complementary assets (e.g. distribution network) are important.

Outsiders that have already established transplant operations within the region, if not deterred by the FTA's rules of origin or any remaining investment barriers, are likely to also expand and rationalize their investments to take advantage of the larger market size. If rules of origin are tightened, transplants will have to upgrade production and source more inputs locally or restrict their sales to the largest market. Parts plants may be induced to follow distributors and assembly plants in order to meet these rules of origin.

For *domestics*, firms without established links to other potential FTA members, a free trade area will be seen as both an opportunity (i.e. new markets, access to lower cost inputs) and a threat (i.e. more competition). Such firms, with encouragement, may start or increase their exports within the region and possibly open up distributors or offshore plants where market size or costs warrant. They will, however, have to face the difficult task of breaking into established distribution networks of domestics and MNEs already located in the other FTA markets. The key question is whether to 'go regional' and branch outside the home country into other parts of the region, or stay at home and become less competitive.

2.3. MNE Response to the Formation of a Free Trade Area

As Figure 7.1 shows, our model argues that the formation of a free trade area is a policy shock. Firms will alter their plant location choices in response to this shock, depending on their motivation for FDI, the nature of the value-adding activity, and their own characteristics. The plant location response requires deciding, 'Which value adding activity should be located in which country?' The location decision depends initially on the country-specific advantages (CSAs) of each of the member countries and the region-specific advantages that will be available once the FTA is fully phased in (Rugman and Gestrin 1993*b*). But implicit in this question are two others: (i) Should the activity be centralized or dispersed? and (ii) Should the activity be clustered with other firms? The plant location decision involves both centralization and clustering choices.

In deciding where to locate a plant, the firm must first choose whether to centralize the activity by locating it at home (with the parent firm) or decentralize the activity to a foreign location. Economies of scale at the plant level encourage centralization of production in one location with exports being used as the mode to supply foreign markets. Transportation and communication costs, on the other hand, raise the costs of exporting and encourage decentralization. High tariffs act like transport costs, discouraging foreign firms from locating production in one central place and exporting to a variety of foreign markets. Tariff-jumping FDI is likely to occur as foreign firms set up domestic plants in order to supply the local market, particularly where the market is large and attractive.

Where firms are likely to locate is also partly dependent on agglomeration economies, or the advantages of firms clustering in one location.[3] A second component of the plant location decision is therefore whether or not to locate near other firms (upstream suppliers, downstream customers, or competitors). External economies and the benefits of information-sharing encourage clustering of firms, particularly in knowledge-intensive sectors. Access to natural resources or specialized assets and infrastructure will also encourage resource-seeking firms to cluster in one location. The benefits of labour-pooling can similarly encourage clustering, for example, where highly specialized workers are needed. Horizontal clusters, firms engaged in similar lines of activity, are likely to form in these circumstances.

The shift from mass to lean production methods can also cause clustering. New process technologies have reduced the importance of labour, transport, and communications costs; shortened the minimum efficient scale of production (thus reducing the importance of economies of scale at the plant level); and increased the need for supplier firms to locate close to their downstream customers in order to use just-in-time production and delivery methods. Lean production therefore encourages the formation of vertical clusters of suppliers and buyers. In many cases, these clusters may form around one or more flagship firms, with upstream and downstream firms as satellites around them.

Regional integration can therefore affect the location of economic activity inside countries. As tariff rates fall in a free trade area, where plant-level economies of scale are important, firms that had tariff-jumping factories may close down smaller plants and shift production to the largest, most efficient plant, relying on exports to reach the smaller markets. If the FTA is also accompanied by a decline in transportation costs (e.g. liberalization of cross-border transport routes is part of the FTA package), this also encourages centralization of production. This suggests that insider MNEs with investments throughout the FTA are more likely to rationalize production by closing inefficient plants and centralizing production, where economies of scale gains are significant and transport costs low. Alternatively, rationalization of product lines between plants and increased intraindustry horizontal trade is an alternative solution for differentiated product industries.

Outsider firms may be induced by the FTA to locate inside the region. Their locational patterns may also cluster if they are following downstream producers (particularly where lean production techniques are prevalent), choose to locate their market-seeking FDI in urban centres, or are attracted to knowledge-based clusters for their external economies and information-sharing. Such firms may be more likely to see the region as a whole and make decisions from a regionally efficient perspective, thus increasing their competitiveness relative to member firms.[4] On the other hand, outsider firms may be less well equipped to take advantage of clustering, particularly where the advantages are based on knowledge spillovers (Enright 1996: 204).

For domestics, an FTA expands the set of markets available to firms if they had not previously engaged in exports or FDI to the member countries. In order to access these new markets, these firms are likely to move to locations with good access to the other markets, such as border areas and port cities. As firms move to border locations, a self-reinforcing movement may occur due to agglomeration economies, creating new regional centres. Thus, some regions should expand as a result of an FTA while other regions will shrink.

Hanson (1998) argues that two types of border clusters may be encouraged by the formation of an FTA. Small cities along the border may develop into transportation and wholesale trade hubs, facilitating cross-border flows of goods and services liberalized under the FTA. Large cities, on the other hand, may develop into full-sized regional production-sharing networks, where firms from both countries specialize their value-adding activities along the value chain, and engage in sophisticated subcontracting strategies and crossborder alliances.

When the FTA consists of countries with very different market sizes (in terms of population and income), clustering decisions may differ for firms headquartered in the 'hub' economy (the largest market in the region) and those in the 'spoke' economies (small countries) (Eden and Molot 1993). The formation of a free trade area may lead to clustering within the largest market, as MNEs headquartered in the hub economy close tariff factories in the smaller markets, and retreat to supplying these market with exports from large-scale hub plants.

Firms located in the spoke economies with investments in the hub market prior to the FTA might be expected to open or expand their operations in the hub economy and begin to serve the region as a whole from the hub. Although they may need to change their market focus from the national to the regional market, adapting to what Rugman and D'Cruz (1991) call the 'double diamond' model of competitive advantage. On the other hand, firms located in the spoke economies that have not invested in the hub market (the domestics) are likely to respond to an FTA by moving closer to the border. The move to relocate to border areas and port cities should be more pronounced for firms in small countries owing to the relatively stronger pull of the larger market.

In summary, we have outlined a model of shocks and responses: the creation of a free trade area is a policy shock that causes firms, both inside and outside the FTA, to respond by altering their locational decisions. We have argued that the nature of the value-adding activity and the type of firm are two key determinants in predicting that response. Let us now turn to the case of North American free trade and see what light this model can shed on plant location decisions within North America.

3. Plant Location Decisions after NAFTA

3.1. The Emerging North American Trade and Investment Regime

NAFTA, which became law in Canada, the USA, and Mexico on 1 January 1994, will eliminate tariffs and reduce most non-tariff barriers within the region by the year 2003. Each country maintains its own trade barriers vis-à-vis non-member countries, but intracontinental trade barriers are falling dramatically. Thus tariffs will cease to be a major factor influencing intra-NAFTA where rules of origin tests are satisfied. Where these tests are not met, tariffs continue to apply.

NAFTA is more than a free trade agreement; it has the most extensive regulations on investment of any trade agreement.[5] The key commitments in the investment chapter are to national treatment (NAFTA partners must be treated at least as well as domestic investors) together with most-favoured-nation treatment (NAFTA investors must be treated at least as well as any foreign investor) for all North American investments and investors, including firms controlled by non-North Americans. There are some exceptions (investments in financial services are covered elsewhere in the agreement; many existing federal measures such as Canadian cultural industries are exempt; existing practices in the states and provinces are grandfathered if listed; public procurement and investment incentives are not included, nor are FDI restrictions on national security grounds). However, the protection for investors and investments is unprecedented in a trade agreement.

NAFTA extends the list of proscribed performance requirements and mandates that most existing requirements be phased out over ten years. NAFTA forbids restrictions on capital movements, including all types of payments and profit remittances, except for balance of payments reasons. Expropriation is outlawed, except for a public purpose and on a non-discriminatory basis, and full and prompt payment of fair compensation is required. Investors can also seek binding arbitration against a host government for violations of NAFTA obligations, using either the World Bank's International Centre for the Settlement of Investment Disputes or the United Nations Commission on International Trade Law.

Thus, the trade and investment rules within North America have moved far beyond shallow integration (the removal or reduction of tariff barriers on goods) into deep integration (the removal or reduction of most barriers to flows of goods, services, and investments) (Eden 1996). One can argue that an international trade and investment regime is emerging in North America. How will MNEs configure their value-adding activities in this emerging NAFTA regime?

3.2. Plant Location Strategies under NAFTA

In the year 2004, NAFTA will be fully phased in, all tariffs should have been eliminated, and most non-tariff barriers either reduced or harmonized. National treatment and MFN status, together with sophisticated dispute settlement techniques, should complete the level playing-field. What impacts will the NAFTA regime have on multinational decision-making?

We argue that the NAFTA regime means that multinationals must alter their existing configuration and coordination strategies, developed when the three countries were separated by tariffs, non-tariff barriers and tax differentials, to take advantage of a more level playing-field. Prior to the mid-1980s, MNEs in North America established their own configuration of value-adding activities in domestic and foreign plants, based on the historical 'blocks' national governments had positioned on the North American 'chessboard' (Eden 1994*b*).[6] With governments removing these blocks, the underlying economic factors will have more impact on MNE configuration and coordination strategies. Because MNEs are international oligopolists, concerned about their shares of global and regional markets, they will change the configuration of their activities so as to increase their international competitiveness. Both plant functions and locations—through decisions on new and reinvestments—can be expected to change.

Based on our model developed above, we argue that two factors are likely to be key influences on plant location strategies in response to NAFTA: The type of firm and the motivation for plant location. We discuss each in turn below.

3.2.1. The Type of MNE: Insiders, Outsiders, and Domestics

The key to investment decisions is the reduction in policy risk for firms provided by a free trade area (Eaton, Lipsey, and Safarian 1994; Eden 1994*b*; Vernon 1994). In general, security of market access should be improved by the elimination of tariffs and non-tariff barriers under NAFTA. The investment chapter guaranteeing national treatment should also reduce the risk for firms so that intra-NAFTA FDI flows should increase. Thus, FDI should increase as MNEs move to consolidate their positions on a regional basis. In addition, where sectors have been previously closed to FDI, the desire for first-mover advantages should generate inward FDI, with possible bunching as firms follow the leader MNE. The strategic responses of firms to NAFTA will be partly determined by factors such as: (i) whether the firm is headquartered inside or outside the area; (ii) whether the firm has significant investments inside the region; and (iii) the industry(ies) in which the firm competes.

Insiders. Firms inside NAFTA will see benefits from lower intraregional barriers and will rationalize product lines (horizontal integration) and/or production processes (vertical integration) to better exploit economies of scale and scope. There should be both a short-run response as MNEs engage in locational reshufflings in response to the falling trade barriers, and a long-run response. US multinationals are best placed to take advantage of the falling tariff and non-tariff barriers because the firms are already located in all three countries. The configuration of US subsidiaries in North America was historically based on the 'blocks' governments had positioned on the North American 'chessboard'. With governments now removing these blocks, the underlying economic factors will have more impact on location decisions. These veterans will locate, close, and/or expand their plants with the whole North American market in mind. This should lead to reduced numbers of product lines in various plants and increasing horizontal trade among plants. MNEs are also likely to segment their production process among plants so that more vertical intrafirm trade takes place. As a result there should be more cross-border vertical and horizontal intrafirm trade flows. In the short run, there may be a tendency for firms to shift their activities to the largest market, i.e. the USA.

Veteran multinationals that are resource-seeking are likely to use NAFTA to relocate extractor and processor affiliates where resources are relatively more abundant and capital and energy costs lower. Cost-reducing affiliates may be induced to relocate to North American countries with lower unit labour costs. Market-driven affiliates are likely to rationalize production in existing plants, creating more vertical integration through fabricator factories and more horizontal integration through focused factories. MNEs that have not yet opened up branch plants in potential NAFTA members may do so.

In terms of the support activities in the value chain (head office, R&D, support services), veteran MNEs engaged in integrated production on a North American basis are likely to centre such activities in one head office. With the reduction in tariff and non-tariff barriers, there is less need for a fully autonomous and large national head office; in fact, such an office can be non-productive in a centralized, regionalized MNE. Thus, for US multinationals, we expect headquarters functions in the Canadian and Mexican spokes to become less important over time, as their activities are centralized in their US parents.

In many ways, what we are predicting has already happened in the auto industry as a result of the 1965 Auto Pact. Production is organized on a continental basis (defined, until NAFTA, as Canada and the USA) with assembly plants responsible for individual product lines, exchanging models with each other to fill out the product range, and with a wide variety of parts and components plants supplying inputs to the assembly operations. The Canadian head offices of the Big Three are small, little R&D is done here, and key decisions are made in the USA (see Eden and Molot 1993). This process of vertical and horizontal rationalization, as a result of CUSFTA and NAFTA, will now occur in other industries.

Therefore the responses of parents and affiliates will involve relocation and expansion, taking advantage of lower trade and investment barriers to develop a more integrative regional strategy. In the short run, existing plants are unlikely to be closed but in the longer term economic efficiency will determine locational decisions within North America. The key here is rationalization of demand for the regional market as a whole, and of supply to capture specialization and economies of scale.

Outsiders. Outsiders, non-North American MNEs that have already established transplant operations within North America, if not deterred by investment barriers, are likely to also expand and rationalize their investments to take advantage of the larger market size. As rules of origin are tightened, in order to meet North American content, transplants may be forced to upgrade production and source more inputs locally. Thus parts plants may be induced to follow distributors and assembly plants. Outsiders that are currently exporting to North America may shift to foreign direct investment. They are likely to be drawn to the larger market, the US market, or the *hub*, unless cost differentials make location in the *spokes* (Canada and Mexico) more attractive and/or interregional barriers are completely eliminated.

Domestics. For domestics, firms without established links to other potential NAFTA members, a free trade area will be seen as both an opportunity (i.e. new markets, access to lower cost inputs) and a threat (i.e. more competition). Such firms, with encouragement, may start or increase their exports within North America and possibly open up distributors or offshore plants where market size or costs warrant. They will, however, have to face the difficult task of breaking into established distribution networks of domestics and MNEs in the North American markets. The key question is whether to 'go regional' and branch outside the home country into other parts of North America, or stay at home and most likely be acquired by a NAFTA multinational.

Summary. From the above, we conclude that multinational strategies in a regional trade area, such as the emerging North American trade and investment regime, are the following: (i) for the insiders, rationalizing and extending existing investments throughout the region; (ii) for the outsiders, new investments and deepening of existing investments within the region as the firms, particularly Asian and European MNEs, seek to become true regional insiders; and (iii) for the domestics, their first steps across the border, either directly or indirectly through their supplier relationships to insider and outsider MNEs. US multinationals dominate, and will continue to dominate, these trends. Thus, we predict that the hub-and-spoke nature of the economic relationships in North America will continue to strengthen, and that the pattern we see within the North American auto industry will be a bell-wether for change in other North American industries.

3.2.2. The Type of Plant: NAFTA and Plant Location Decisions

In general, security of market access for North American firms should be improved by the elimination of tariffs under the NAFTA. The NAFTA investment rules also reduce the risk for firms investing within North America so that intra-North American FDI flows should increase. Thus strategic risk-reducing FDI should increase as MNEs move to consolidate their positions on a North American basis. In addition, where sectors have been previously closed to FDI, as in the Mexican financial and telecommunications sectors, the desire for first-mover advantages should generate inward FDI, with possible bunching as firms follow the leader MNE. More FDI should occur over the longer term, particularly in sectors that had been closed to FDI.

NAFTA should cause insider MNEs to rationalize their *resource extraction* plants within North America. There should be more investment in endowment-rich areas where inward FDI has been previously restricted in Mexico. FDI should flow into the Mexican petrochemical sector, but not directly into petroleum extraction due to Mexican constitutional restrictions. In addition, one can expect general upgrading of resource-based plants from extraction to processing activities as downstream tariff and non-tariff barriers fall. Where resource-based industries are pollution-intensive, such as the mining and petrochemical industries, the NAFTA's environmental side agreement should tighten the application of these rules in Mexico, reducing its attractiveness as a haven for polluting activities (Mayer 1994).

Where agglomeration effects and economies of scale are important, these will favour location of production within the largest market, the US hub, rather than the Canadian or Mexican spokes. In such cases, we expect closure of inefficient plants in small markets and their replacement with local distributors. Related to this, where the MNE is using lean production technologies based on just-in-time delivery and production, parts plants are likely to follow downstream firms. Thus the first-round location decisions of market-driven assembly plants are likely to be followed by a second round of parts plants investments (e.g. auto parts are likely to follow assemblers). On the other hand, where a local presence is important for local sale (e.g. distribution, consumer services) or consumer tastes vary widely between national markets, the activities are not footloose so that the NAFTA should not shift such activities.

Reduction of trade barriers under the NAFTA should increase the importance of economic factors such as unit labour costs as influences on the location of *fabrication* and *final assembly* plants. MNEs with labour-intensive parts plants located in the ASEAN and Caribbean countries are closing their plants and shifting production to Mexico. Tight rules of origin, particularly in the autos and textile sectors, should also encourage more onshore sourcing of parts and components. Rationalization of parts plants and sub-assemblies based on lowest-cost location (including subsidies) is likely as MNEs move to set up new plants in the most cost-effective location. This should lead to increased vertical integration, and the possible closure of inefficient plants both inside and outside North America. For Canadian and Mexican MNEs, the opening of the US market should lead to the setting up of US *sales and distribution* affiliates.

NAFTA should encourage the rationalization of *support services* on a North American basis. Marketing services, for example, may be directed at the North American market as a whole. For US multinationals, this means closing of some business service affiliates (e.g. advertising, purchasing) and the reallocation of these functions to the US parent. Centralization of *technology development* in the parent firm is likely to continue since the NAFTA prohibits the use of non-tariff barriers such as local content rules and performance requirements that encourage location of some R&D to host countries.

3.2.3. Summary: Plant Location Strategies under NAFTA

In summary, two factors are likely to be key influences on MNE investment strategies after NAFTA: the type of firm and the motivation for setting up a foreign plant. We expect that the NAFTA will induce substantial rationalization and possibly some downsizing and closure of inefficient foreign affiliates in North America. As a result, the degree of horizontal and vertical integration of these MNEs should increase, creating more intrafirm trade and investment flows inside NAFTA, and perhaps smaller trade and investment flows between North

America and Europe and Asia. We anticipate substantial investments in Mexico because its barriers to trade and investment prior to NAFTA were the highest. This investment should occur primarily in market-seeking and resource-seeking investments in sectors where FDI has been restricted.

3.3. Literature Review: MNE Responses to NAFTA

MNE rationalization of operations within North America is not new. Spurred initially by reductions in tariffs under the Tokyo Round of the GATT and then by the 1989 Canada–US Free Trade Agreement (CUSFTA), many manufacturers have already organized themselves for production in a North American market (Litvak 1991; Blank *et al.* 1995). There have been at least two different types of empirical studies of the impact of NAFTA on MNE configuration and coordination strategies: survey research and econometric studies. We briefly review these studies below.

3.3.1. Survey Research

There have been at least four surveys of MNE responses to North American free trade. The first by Rugman (1990) focused on the anticipated responses of MNEs in Canada and the USA to the Canada–US FTA. His work showed the expected support of large firms in both countries for free trade, their anticipation of few adjustment problems, and their attention to issues of competitiveness. Soon afterwards, the Conference Board of Canada (Krajewski 1992) posed questions to its members about the likely impact of CUSFTA on plant structure in Canada. The study looked at two groups: Canadian parents with US subsidiaries and Canadian subsidiaries of US parents. CUSFTA was seen by the respondents as a primary driver, in addition to globalization of markets in general, pushing multinationals in Canada to rationalize their production and sales for the North American market. The firms had a sense of new opportunities in the US market and/or felt the necessity to compete globally to survive.

In 1993, Johnson *et al.* (1995) surveyed senior operations executives at 139 North American manufacturers. The managers were asked to assess the impact of free trade on their operations strategies and to outline the responses to free trade undertaken in the previous two years. The survey results showed that Canadian firms did not expect to meet global competition through low manufacturing costs, but through superior customer service, dependable deliveries, and high quality. Their response was to improve capacity in these areas, seek more international customers, and avoid markets where fast deliveries and product proliferation were critical. Canadian firms (like their Mexican counterparts) saw their greatest potential in the US market, but also saw their US competitors as their greatest threat.

Lastly, Blank *et al.* (1995) surveyed thirty-four US Conference Board member multinationals about their strategies after NAFTA. The survey confirmed that US MNEs were moving towards a North American strategy and structure, and that Canadian subsidiaries were being integrated more rapidly than Mexican ones into a continental production system. The drivers for change were the emerging 'architecture' of North America: a North American economic space as well as intensified global competition, the recession of the early 1990s, and techno-logical change. For Canadian subsidiaries, the impact of continental reorganiza-tion was unclear: many predicted a rise in intrafirm trade as fewer goods will be produced in Canadian plants; a decrease in subsidiary autonomy; a loss of production capacity and jobs along with the redefinition of their role within the corporate network; and growing intrafirm competition for product and market-ing mandates (Blank *et al.* 1995: 46–55).

3.3.2. Econometric Studies

While there have been several econometric studies of CUSFTA and NAFTA focus-ing on trade flows and/or economic welfare gains from regional integration, there have not been many analyses of how firms (MNEs or otherwise) are responding to regional integration.

Using a database of trade and FDI flows at the state and provincial level, Little (1996) examined the US and Canadian responses to CUSFTA. She found that US and Canadian firms tend to rely on trade rather than FDI to serve the in-tegrating market between the USA and Canada. More specifically, there are important changes in the industrial composition of trade at the regional level, which tend to be disguised when national-level data are employed. For instance, New England has maintained a favourable export base with Canada in the years studied. Inward FDI from Canada and geographic shifts in the US industry activ-ity significantly affect New England's export performance, because trade activ-ity has shifted to the South and West with the implementation of CUSFTA.

Schwanen (1997) compared the growth rates in sectors liberalized by CUS-FTA, relative to those which were already basically free from barriers, over the 1988–95 period. Canada–US bilateral trade grew more quickly in the liberalized sectors. Intraindustry specialization, as evidenced by rapid growth in two-way trade, occurred in several sectors. On the other hand, North America's share of global FDI fell over the period, as did the importance of Canada and US in each other's FDI portfolio. Schwanen concluded that external events (e.g. liberaliza-tion and privatization in South America, rapid growth in Asia) attracted FDI out-side of North America.

Hanson (1996), studying economic activity in the US–Mexico border cities, found evidence that export-manufacturing expansion in these border cities has increased manufacturing employment in the US border cities, suggesting that NAFTA can positively influence the relocation of US manufacturing production to the US–Mexico border region, especially when transport costs are an import-ant consideration for industry location. In a recent paper summarizing the results of several earlier studies, Hanson (1998) found that, parallel to US manufacturing relocation, is a similar pattern of relocation in Mexico. Manufacturing employment has increased in northern Mexico and decreased in central Mexico, suggesting relocation to the border cities with the USA. Even though NAFTA is eliminating the duty drawback programmes which gave the *maquiladoras* preferential status, the border plants continue to receive the bulk of inward FDI in Mexico, and Mexican manufacturing firms continue to be drawn north towards the US border. The author concludes that NAFTA will have more impact on Mexican industry location than on US or Canadian location decisions.

The US International Trade Commission (ITC) conducted a major three-year review of the impacts of NAFTA on the US economy and on nearly 200 industrial sectors (ITC 1997; see also the analysis in GAO (1997)). The ITC concluded that NAFTA has minimal impacts on the US economy in terms of trade, employment, or hourly earnings. *Maquiladora*-related trade expanded sharply, leading the ITC to conclude that production-sharing along the US–Mexico border would continue to expand due to the complementaries of the US and Mexican economies. Intraindustry trade, both Canada–US and Mexico–US, increased in sectors characterized by product differentiation and a high percentage of manufactured components. US–Mexico integration is perhaps proceeding fastest in the auto sector, where high Mexican trade barriers (tariffs on autos, domestic content regulations, trade-balancing requirements) are being dismantled and the potential gains from continental integration are large (USTR 1998).

What is evident from these studies is that, in response to NAFTA, multinationals are engaged in locational reshuffling, as Vernon (1994) predicted, designed to integrate Mexican industry into a regional production network—at least in the manufacturing sector. This is proceeding fastest in the automotive, electronic equipment, and textile sectors, as evidenced by the rapid growth in two-way trade in components and finished manufactured goods and the movement of Mexican and US firms to the border region.

In the next section, we provide some new evidence on multinationals and their plant location choices in North America post-1989. These statistics both confirm, and shed some new light on, these trends.

4. MNE Location Patterns in North America, 1989–94

We now turn to some evidence on how insider and outsider MNEs have been responding to the pressures for regional integration in North America. Our data are for the 1989–94 time-period only so that our evidence applies primarily to the impact of the 1989 CUSFTA. However, we argue that it is indicative of the impact that regional integration should have on plant location strategies. We use three data sets. The first is UNCTAD data from the 1998 *World Investment Report*. The second is OECD data on two-way FDI stocks in 1989 and 1994 (OECD 1997). Third, the US International Trade Administration (ITA) for several years, until the series ended in 1994, published data on US FDI entries by state location (ITA 1989–94). We analyse US inward FDI location patterns over the 1989–94 period, using the ITA data.

4.1. FDI Stocks and Crossborder M&A Purchases, 1985–97

UNCTAD (1998) provides data on FDI inward and outward stocks, by country, for the years 1985–97 (the 1997 data are preliminary). Analysis of these data in Table 7.4 shows that even though inward FDI (IFDI) in Canada increased by an average of 9.34 per cent per year over the period, its share of world IFDI fell from 8.55 per cent in 1985 to 3.97 per cent in 1997. The US share has also fallen from 24.40 per cent in 1985 to 20.86 per cent in 1997, even though US IFDI increased by an annual rate of 24.2 per cent. Only Mexico has maintained its share (approximately 2.5 per cent) of world IFDI. Because world IFDI grew at an average annual rate of 29.72 per cent, compared to 21.03 per cent for NAFTA, the region's share fell from 35.43 to 27.34 per cent over the same period. Thus, NAFTA has become a less attractive region, in a relative sense, for world FDI. This may reflect the reduced attractiveness of NAFTA as an investment location or, more likely, the increased attractiveness of other regions.

The same patterns hold for NAFTA's share—and for the individual country's shares—of outward FDI. As a percentage of world outward FDI (OFDI), in 1989 NAFTA's share was 42.78 per cent, but by 1997 it had fallen to 29.61 per cent. Even though OFDI stocks by NAFTA countries have grown at an annual average rate of 21.3 per cent, the region's share has declined steadily because foreign countries have expanded their outward stocks faster than North American investors. The one exception is Mexico: its OFDI has grown more rapidly (42.9 per cent on an annual basis) than world OFDI (34.50 per cent).

UNCTAD (1998) also provides data on cross-border mergers and acquisitions for the 1990–7 period. The pattern is very different: North America dominates other countries both as a purchaser and seller of M&As. Looking at North America as a purchaser of M&As, its share rose from 16.4 per cent in 1990 to 31.29 per cent in 1997. Both the US and Canadian shares increased significantly over the period, driving up NAFTA's share of world M&A purchases. M&A purchases grew at an annual rate of 16.23 per cent over 1990–7 for all countries, compared with 43.92 per cent for NAFTA countries. On the other hand, from the seller's perspective, NAFTA's share fell from 38.59 per cent in 1990 to 24.94 per cent in 1997; this was due primarily to a drop in US sales from 33.94 to 19.07 per cent. Again, this suggests the declining attractiveness of NAFTA as a location for investments, relative to other regions.

4.2. Cross-border Patterns in North American FDI Stocks, 1989 and 1994

The OECD collects data on inward and outward FDI flows and stocks by year, for OECD member countries. Tables 7.5 and 7.6 show the FDI stocks, by home and host country for the years 1989 and 1994. In both cases, we show the numbers and percentages for each NAFTA member country, all others, and all countries. The table allows us to see whether FDI is becoming more or less

TABLE 7.4a. FDI stocks, by country, 1985–1997 ($US millions)

Year	1985 Total	% Dist.	1990 Total	% Dist.	1995 Total	% Dist.	1997 Total	% Dist.	Avg. annual % change 1985–97
Inward FDI Stock									
Canada	64,657	8.55	113,054	6.51	122,469	4.48	137,113	3.97	9.34
Mexico	18,802	2.48	32,523	1.87	66,566	2.44	86,836	2.51	30.15
USA	184,615	24.40	394,911	22.74	560,850	20.52	720,793	20.86	24.20
NAFTA	268,074	35.43	540,488	31.13	749,885	27.44	944,742	27.34	21.03
All others	488,589	64.57	1,195,838	68.87	1,982,764	72.56	2,510,767	72.66	34.49
World	756,663	100.00	1,736,326	100.00	2,732,649	100.00	3,455,509	100.00	29.72
Outward FDI Stock									
Canada	43,143	6.26	84,807	4.98	117,576	4.21	137,715	3.89	18.27
Mexico	533	0.08	575	0.03	2,564	0.09	3,282	0.09	42.98
USA	251,034	36.44	435,219	25.53	714,631	25.58	907,497	25.63	21.79
NAFTA	294,710	42.78	520,601	30.54	834,771	29.88	1,048,494	29.61	21.31
All others	394,198	57.22	1,183,943	69.46	1,958,771	70.12	2,492,890	70.39	44.37
World	688,908	100.00	1,704,544	100.00	2,793,542	100.00	3,541,384	100.00	34.50

TABLE 7.4b. FDI cross-border M&A purchasers and sellers, by country, 1990–1997 ($US millions)

	1990		1995		1997		Avg. annual % change 1990–7
	Total	% Dist.	Total	% Dist.	Total	% Dist.	
Purchaser, All Cross-border M&As							
Canada	4,544	2.84	14,806	6.24	24,707	7.23	63.39
Mexico	—	—	169	0.07	743	0.22	169.82
USA	21,691	13.56	65,580	27.65	81,442	23.84	39.35
NAFTA	26,235	16.40	80,555	33.96	106,892	31.29	43.92
All others	133,724	83.60	156,629	66.04	234,761	68.71	10.79
World	159,959	100.00	237,184	100.00	341,653	100.00	16.23
Seller, All Cross-border M&As							
Canada	5,746	3.59	11,115	4.69	12,016	3.52	15.59
Mexico	1,681	1.05	1,435	0.61	8,034	2.35	53.99
USA	54,297	33.94	62,903	26.52	65,151	19.07	2.86
NAFTA	61,724	38.59	75,453	31.81	85,201	24.94	5.43
All others	98,235	61.41	161,731	68.19	256,452	75.06	23.01
World	159,959	100.00	237,184	100.00	341,653	100.00	16.23

Note: Average annual per cent change for Mexico's M&A calculated for 1995–7 only.

Source: Authors' calculations based on data in the appendices of UNCTAD (1998).

Table 7.5. FDI stocks by home and host country, 1989 ($US millions)

Host country	Canada		Mexico		USA		NAFTA		All others		Total home	
	Stock USD	% Dist.	Stock USD	% Dist.	Stock USD	% Dist.	Stock USD	% Dist.	Stock USD	% Dist.	Stock USD	% Dist.
Canada — Stock USD			8.00	n.a.	63,948	16.75	63,956	n.a.	12,849	n.a.	76,805	n.a.
Canada — % Dist.			0.01		83.26		83.27		16.73		100.00	
Mexico — Stock USD	300	0.63			8,264	2.16	8,564	n.a.	8,261	n.a.	16,825	n.a.
Mexico — % Dist.	1.78				49.12		50.90		49.10		100.00	
USA — Stock USD	30,370	63.72	350	n.a.			30,720	n.a.	338,204	n.a.	368,924	n.a.
USA — % Dist.	8.23		0.09				8.33		91.67		100.00	
NAFTA — Stock USD	30,670	64.34	358	n.a.	72,212	18.91	103,240	n.a.	359,314	n.a.	462,554	n.a.
NAFTA — % Dist.	6.63		0.08		15.61		22.62		77.68		100.00	
All others — Stock USD	16,995	35.66	n.a.	n.a.	309,569	81.09	n.a.	n.a.	n.a.	n.a.	n.a.	n.a.
All others — % Dist.												
Total host — Stock USD	47,665	100.00	n.a.	n.a.	381,781	100.00	n.a.	n.a.	n.a.	n.a.	n.a.	n.a.
Total host — % Dist.												

Note: Some Mexican data calculated by construction from other data in the table.

Source: Authors' calculations based on OECD International Direct Investment Statistics Yearbook (1997).

TABLE 7.6. FDI stocks by home and host country, 1994 ($US millions)

Host country		Canada Stock USD	Canada % Dist.	Mexico Stock USD	Mexico % Dist.	USA Stock USD	USA % Dist.	NAFTA Stock USD	NAFTA % Dist.	All others Stock USD	All others % Dist.	Total home Stock USD	Total home % Dist.
Canada	Stock USD	——	——	109	n.a.	74,987	12.07	75,096	n.a.	18,454	n.a.	93,550	n.a.
	% Dist.	——		0.00		80.16		80.27		19.73		100.00	
Mexico	Stock USD	692	0.86		n.a.	15,714	2.53	16,406	n.a.	18,377	n.a.	34,783	n.a.
	% Dist.	1.99				45.18		47.17		52.83		100.00	
USA	Stock USD	42,133	52.34	2,342	n.a.		n.a.	44,475	n.a.	457,935	n.a.	502,410	n.a.
	% Dist.	8.39		0.47				8.85		91.15		100.00	
NAFTA	Stock USD	42,825	53.20	2,451	n.a.	90,701	14.60	135,977	n.a.	494,766	n.a.	630,743	n.a.
	% Dist.	6.79		0.39		14.38		6.36		78.44		100.00	
All others	Stock USD	37,670	46.80	n.a.	n.a.	530,343	85.40	n.a.	n.a.	n.a.	n.a.	n.a.	n.a.
	% Dist.												
Total host	Stock USD	80,495	100.00	n.a.	n.a.	621,044	100.00	n.a.	n.a.	n.a.	n.a.	n.a.	n.a.
	% Dist.	100.00		n.a.		100.00		n.a.		n.a.		n.a.	

Note: Some Mexican data calculated by construction from other data in the table.

Source: Authors' calculations based on OECD International Direct Investment Statistics Yearbook (1997).

concentrated inside the North American region, and whether the 'spoke' economies (Canada and Mexico) are becoming more or less dependent on the 'hub' economy (the USA).

Comparing the two tables, we can see that in 1989, 83.26 per cent of inward FDI (IFDI) in Canada came from the USA. Mexico was much less dependent on US FDI at 49.12 per cent of all Mexican IFDI. By 1994, even though US FDI in both countries had increased in value terms, the percentages had fallen to 80.16 per cent for Canada and 45.18 per cent for Mexico. Looking at the same numbers but from the US perspective, US outward FDI (OFDI) to Canada fell from 16.75 per cent of all US OFDI in 1989 to 12.07 per cent in 1994; however, it rose slightly to Mexico from 2.16 per cent in 1989 to 2.53 per cent in 1994. Given the small stock of US FDI in Mexico relative to Canada, it is not surprising that the Mexican share increased; what is surprising is the small extent of the increase.

In general, North American economic integration does not appear to have increased the US FDI stock in its North American partners in relative terms. One reason could be that the underlying economies of scale and agglomeration economies favour centralization of production in the US hub with exports to Canada and Mexico. Thus, elimination of trade barriers is causing US firms to close inefficient plants in the two spoke economies, replacing that production with exports from the USA. Another explanation could be simply that investments elsewhere (e.g. Asia, the former Soviet Union, Latin America) were more attractive over this period than investments in North America.

Looking at the FDI destined for the USA, the tables show that Canadian OFDI to the USA fell significantly in relative terms from 63.72 per cent in 1989 to 52.34 per cent in 1994, as a share of all Canadian OFDI, although the stock rose in US dollar terms. From the US perspective, Canadian FDI, as a share of all inward FDI in the USA, rose slightly from 8.23 per cent in 1989 to 8.39 per cent in 1994. Canada's FDI in Mexico increased very slightly from 1.78 to 1.99 per cent of Canadian OFDI over the same period. (Unfortunately, the statistics are not available for Mexican OFDI.) Thus, both Canada and the USA diversified their outward FDI away from each other, in relative terms, over this period. On the other hand, Mexico's share of US inward FDI, while minuscule, rose from 0.09 per cent in 1989 to 0.47 per cent in 1989.

Evidence from FDI stock data within North America over 1989–94 therefore suggests decreasing integration; however, this may not be a response to the Canada–US FTA but rather the relative attractiveness of investments outside the region.

4.3. US Inward FDI Patterns, by Home Country, 1989–94

Our second data set focuses on FDI entries into the USA over the 1989–94 period. The FDI statistics are 'counts', that is, number of FDI entries. As such, they do not reflect the size or value of the FDI flow, simply that it occurred.[7] There were

4,433 individual investments made by foreign firms in the USA over the 1989–94 period; of these, 318 were made by Canadian firms and only twenty-six by Mexican investors. The small number of Mexican investments suggests the statistical pattern should be interpreted cautiously.

Tables 7.7 through 7.12 provide some evidence on FDI flows in the USA, for all industries and for manufacturing only, over the 1989–94 period.[8] The data are reported for the following home countries: Canada, Mexico, and all others. Four patterns are illustrated by these tables: timing of inward FDI (Table 7.7), the mode of entry (Table 7.8), the choice of state location (Tables 7.9, 7.10, and 7.11), and the choice of industry (Table 7.11). We can use this data set to address some of the locational questions raised by our model:

- Do FDI entries in response to the formation of a free trade area tend to cluster in time, state location, and industry choice?
- Do insiders (Canada; Mexico can be seen as a quasi-insider over this time-period) respond differently to the formation of a free trade area from outsiders in terms of their location decisions?
- Do FDI entries in manufacturing behave differently from all FDI entries?

To test whether insiders behave differently from outsiders, for each table, we calculate an Index of Revealed Comparative Advantage (RCA). This is simply Canada's percentage for the relevant variable divided by the all home country percentage. Where the RCA index is significantly above (below) one, this suggests that the patterns of FDI entries is quite different for Canada than for all home countries.

4.3.1. Timing of Entry

Table 7.7 shows that Canadian FDI entries were highest in the first year of the Canada–US FTA (eighty-eight entries) and fell steadily through 1993, rising slightly in 1994. The same pattern is observable in the manufacturing data. Our earlier tables suggest that the total dollar amount of Canadian FDI into the USA increased over this period, suggesting that perhaps larger investments were made in the later periods. The RCA index for Canada does not vary significantly from 1, suggesting that Canada's investment pattern was similar to non-member countries in terms of timing of FDI over the period.

Looking now at Mexico, although the number of entries for all industries and for manufacturing are both small, the RCA index suggests that 1993 (the year before NAFTA takes effect) was a banner year (RCA exceeds 2 in both cases) as Mexican firms geared up for NAFTA by increasing their investments in the US market.

4.3.2. Mode of entry

Table 7.8 breaks the US FDI entries into groups by mode of entry: new plants, equity increases, plant expansions, mergers and acquistions, and joint ventures.

TABLE 7.7. Timing of US inward FDI, by home country, 1989–1994

	Canada		Mexico		All others		All home countries		RCA CA-All	RCA MX-All
	No. of entries	% Dist.	No. of entries	% Dist.	No. of entries	% Dist.	No. of entries	% Dist.		
All Industries										
1989	88	27.67	7	26.92	1,008	24.65	1103	24.88	1.11	1.08
1990	46	14.47	2	7.69	970	23.72	1018	22.96	0.63	0.33
1991	50	15.72	3	11.54	672	16.43	725	16.35	0.96	0.71
1992	32	10.06	2	7.69	478	11.69	512	11.55	0.87	0.67
1993	42	13.21	6	23.08	443	10.83	491	11.08	1.19	2.08
1994	60	18.87	6	23.08	518	12.67	584	13.17	1.43	1.75
All Years	318	100.00	26	100.00	4,089	100.00	4,433	100.00	1.00	1.00
Manufacturing										
1989	35	28.46	4	26.67	488	25.89	527	26.05	1.09	1.02
1990	22	17.89	1	6.67	407	21.59	430	21.26	0.84	0.31
1991	18	14.63	2	13.33	305	16.18	325	16.07	0.91	0.83
1992	16	13.01	1	6.67	219	11.62	236	11.67	1.11	0.57
1993	12	9.76	4	26.67	189	10.03	205	10.13	0.96	2.63
1994	20	16.26	3	20	277	14.69	300	14.83	1.10	1.35
All years	123	100.00	15	100.00	1,885	100.00	2,023	100.00	1.00	1.00

Source: Authors' calculations from US Dept. of Commerce (1989–94).

TABLE 7.8. Mode of entry for US inward FDI by home country, 1989–1994

Mode of entry	No.	Canada		Mexico			All others			All home countries			RCA CA-All	RCA MX-All
		Rank	% Dist.	No.	Rank	% Dist.	No.	Rank	% Dist.	No.	Rank	% Dist.		
All Industries														
New plant	27	3	8.49	1	4	3.85	410	3	10.03	438	3	9.88	0.86	0.39
Plant expansion	8	6	2.52	1	4	3.85	333	4	8.14	342	5	7.71	0.33	0.50
Equity increase	20	4	6.29	0	6	—	190	6	4.65	210	6	4.74	1.33	0.00
Joint venture	17	5	5.35	3	3	11.54	331	5	8.09	351	4	7.92	0.68	1.46
A&M	159	1	50.00	16	1	61.54	1,685	1	41.21	1,860	1	41.96	1.19	1.47
Other FDI	87	2	27.36	5	2	19.23	1,140	2	27.88	1,232	2	27.79	0.98	0.69
Total, All Industries	318		100.00	26		100.00	4,089		100.00	4,433		100.00	1.00	1.00
Manufacturing														
New plant	26	2	21.14	1	3	6.67	362	2	19.20	389	2	19.23	1.10	0.35
Plant expansion	7	4	5.69	1	3	6.67	304	3	16.13	312	3	15.42	0.37	0.43
Equity increase	7	4	5.69	0	5	—	111	6	5.89	118	6	5.83	0.98	0.00
Joint venture	3	6	2.44	3	2	20.00	150	5	7.96	156	5	7.71	0.32	2.59
M&A	66	1	53.66	10	1	66.67	767	1	40.69	843	1	41.67	1.29	1.60
Other FDI	14	3	11.38	0	5	—	191	4	10.13	205	4	10.13	1.12	0.00
Total, Manufacturing	123		100.00	15		100.01	1,885		100.00	2,023		100.00	1.00	1.00

Source: Authors' calculations from US Dept. of Commerce (1989–94).

Equity increases and plant expansions are clearly sequential investments. New plants could be seen either as first-time investments or the building of new facilities; similarly, M&A and joint ventures could be either new or sequential investments. In the case of Mexico, probably most of the investment entries are first-time entries; this will be less true for Canada where the history of investment in the US economy is much longer.

M&As were the top-ranked mode of entry for Canada, Mexico, and all others, for both all industries and manufacturing. Half of all Canadian entries were M&As compared to two-thirds of all Mexican entries. In manufacturing, the second-ranked mode of entry was new plants for Canada and joint ventures for Mexico.

In terms of RCA indexes, the only statistic which suggests a significantly different pattern from that for all home countries is the Mexican joint-venture statistic in manufacturing, which is more than twice the percentage share for all home countries. The international business literature suggests that firms from small developing countries tend to use joint ventures because of limited resources and the need to source technology. This statistic provides some support for this hypothesis.

4.3.3. Location of Entry

Here we present three tables. Table 7.9 shows the state location of FDI entries, for all industries, over the 1989–94 period. Table 7.10 repeats the table for manufacturing entries only. Table 7.11 addresses the question of border FDI: do Canadian FDI entries tend to cluster along the US–Canada border, and Mexican entries along the US–Mexico border, as argued by Hanson (1998)?

Table 7.9 shows the percentage distribution of FDI entries, for all industries, across the fifty US states, Puerto Rico, and the District of Columbia (DC), and ranks the top ten states by number of entries. Mexican entries cluster in nine states only, while Canadian entries are spread across forty-three out of fifty-two states. Only North Dakota has no entries. The top four state location choices for Canada and Mexico are the same: New York, Texas, Florida, and California. The high RCA indexes for Canada and for Mexico are misleading, given that in each of the cases the number of actual entries is small.[9] This suggests that the overall pattern for Canada and Mexico, on a state-by-state basis, is not much different from that of all home countries.

Table 7.10 looks at state location for manufacturing FDI only. Canadian FDI entries are more concentrated for manufacturing than for all industries (twenty-nine versus forty-three states); the same is true for Mexico (seven versus nine states). Four locations have no FDI entries: Montana, North Dakota, Puerto Rico, and Wyoming. For Canada, the top five state locations are, in order: New York, Ohio and North Carolina (tied), and California and Florida (tied). For Mexico, the top locations are: Texas, California, Florida and New York (tied), and North Carolina, Missouri, and Arizona (all three tied). Canada and Mexico share five of their ten top states in common. The RCA indexes for manufacturing have

TABLE 7.9. State location of US inward FDI, all industries, by home country, 1989–1994

State	Canada			Mexico			All others			All home countries			RCA CA-All	RCA MX-All
	No.	Top 10	% Dist.	No.	Top 10	% Dist.	No.	Top 10	% Dist.	No.	Top 10	% Dist.		
AK	1		0.32	0		0	15		0.37	16		0.36	0.89	0
AL	2		0.63	0		0	23		0.56	25		0.57	1.11	0
AR	0		0	0		0	16		0.39	16		0.36	0	0
AZ	6		1.89	1	5	3.85	36		0.88	43		0.97	1.95	3.97
CA	25	4	7.89	5	2	19.23	742	1	18.2	772	1	17.46	0.45	1.10
CO	9	10	2.84	0		0	71		1.74	80		1.81	1.57	0
CT	4		1.26	1	5	3.85	56		1.37	61		1.38	0.91	2.79
DC	3		0.95	0		0	47		1.15	50		1.13	0.84	0
DE	5		1.58	0		0	10		0.25	15		0.34	4.65	0
FL	28	3	8.83	3	4	11.54	230	4	5.64	261	4	5.9	1.50	1.96
GA	5		1.58	0		0	128	7	3.14	133	10	3.01	0.52	0
HI	0		0	0		0	84		2.06	84		1.9	0	0
IA	1		0.32	0		0	21		0.51	22		0.5	0.64	0
ID	1		0.32	0		0	2		0.05	3		0.07	4.57	0
IL	11	8	3.47	1	5	3.85	125	9	3.07	137	8	3.1	1.12	1.24
IN	3		0.95	0		0	73		1.79	76		1.72	0.55	0
KS	4		1.26	0		0	19		0.47	23		0.52	2.42	0
KY	6		1.89	0		0	71		1.74	77		1.74	1.09	0
LA	5		1.58	0		0	48		1.18	53		1.2	1.32	0
MA	14	6	4.42	0		0	121		2.97	135	9	3.05	1.45	0
MD	2		0.63	0		0	67		1.64	69		1.56	0.40	0
ME	2		0.63	0		0	4		0.1	6		0.14	4.50	0
MI	15	5	4.73	0		0	108		2.65	123		2.78	1.70	0
MN	3		0.95	0		0	41		1.01	44		1.00	0.95	0
MO	5		1.58	1	5	3.85	34		0.83	40		0.9	1.76	4.28
MS	2		0.63	0		0	6		0.15	8		0.18	3.50	0

TABLE 7.9. (cont'd)

State	Canada			Mexico			All others			All home countries			RCA CA-All	RCA MX-All
	No.	Top 10	% Dist.	No.	Top 10	% Dist.	No.	Top 10	% Dist.	No.	Top 10	% Dist.		
MT	2		0.63	0		0	2		0.05	4		0.09	7.00	0
NC	13	7	4.1	1	5	3.85	126	8	3.09	140	7	3.17	1.29	1.21
ND	0		0	0		0	0		0	0		0	1.00	1.00
NE	0		0	0		0	1		0.02	1		0.02	0	0
NH	1		0.32	0		0	11		0.27	12		0.27	1.19	0
NJ	6		1.89	0		0	173	5	4.24	179	5	4.05	0.47	0
NM	1		0.32	0		0	8		0.2	9		0.2	1.60	0
NV	2		0.63	0		0	15		0.37	17		0.38	1.66	0
NY	47	1	14.83	4	3	15.38	504	2	12.36	555	2	12.55	1.18	1.23
OH	10	9	3.15	0		0	140	6	3.43	150	6	3.39	0.93	0
OK	2		0.63	0		0	19		0.47	21		0.48	1.31	0
OR	3		0.95	0		0	53		1.3	56		1.27	0.75	0
PA	8		2.52	0		0	109		2.67	117		2.65	0.95	0
PR	1		0.32	0		0	7		0.17	8		0.18	1.78	0
RI	1		0.32	0		0	9		0.22	10		0.23	1.39	0
SC	6		1.89	0		0	48		1.18	54		1.22	1.55	0
SD	0		0	0		0	1		0.02	1		0.02	0	0
TN	5	8	1.58	0		0	78		1.91	83		1.88	0.84	0
TX	34	2	10.73	9	1	34.62	305	3	7.48	348	3	7.87	1.36	4.40
UT	0		0	0		0	17		0.42	17		0.38	0	0
VA	6		1.89	0		0	125	9	3.07	131		2.96	0.64	0
VT	0		0	0		0	6		0.15	6		0.14	0.00	0
WA	6		1.89	0		0	73		1.79	79		1.79	1.06	0
WI	0		0	0		0	28		0.69	28		0.63	0	0
WV	1		0.32	0		0	14		0.34	15		0.34	0.94	0
WY	0		0	0		0	8		0.2	8		0.18	0	0
Total	317		100	26		100	4,078		100	4,421		100	1.00	1.00

Note: Some state locations not identified in the data so the total sums to less than the total number of entries.

Source: Authors' calculations from US Dept. of Commerce (1989–94).

TABLE 7.10. State location of US inward FDI in manufacturing, by home country, 1989–1994

State	Canada			Mexico			All others			All home countries			RCA CA-All	RCA MX-All
	No.	Top 10	% Dist.	No.	Top 10	% Dist.	No.	Top 10	% Dist.	No.	Top 10	% Dist.		
AK	0		0	0		0	3		0.16	3		0.15	0	0
AL	1		0.81	0		0	18		0.96	19		0.94	0.86	0
AR	0		0	0		0	11		0.59	11		0.55	0	0
AZ	0		0	1	5	6.67	12		0.64	13		0.64	0	10.34
CA	7	4	5.69	3	2	20	319	1	16.99	329	1	16.32	0.35	1.23
CO	2		1.63	0		0	28		1.49	30		1.49	1.10	0
CT	2		1.63	0		0	25		1.33	27		1.34	1.22	0
DC	0		0	0		0	8		0.43	8		0.40	0	0
DE	4		3.25	0		0	4		0.21	8		0.40	8.19	0
FL	7	4	5.69	2	3	13.33	45		2.4	54		2.68	2.12	4.98
GA	3		2.44	0		0	55		2.93	58		2.88	0.85	0
HI	0		0	0		0	2		0.11	2		0.10	0	0
IA	1		0.81	0		0	13		0.69	14		0.69	1.17	0
ID	1		0.81	0		0	0		0	1		0.05	16.33	0
IL	6	6	4.88	0		0	61	10	3.25	67	10	3.32	1.47	0
IN	2		1.63	0		0	61	10	3.25	63		3.13	0.52	0
KS	4		3.25	0		0	14		0.75	18		0.89	3.64	0
KY	6	6	4.88	0		0	57		3.04	63		3.13	1.56	0
LA	1		0.81	0		0	20		1.06	21		1.04	0.78	0
MA	5	8	4.07	0		0	69	9	3.67	74	9	3.67	1.11	0
MD	0		0	0		0	26		1.38	26		1.29	0	0
ME	0		0	0		0	2		0.11	2		0.10	0	0
MI	5	8	4.07	0		0	84	6	4.47	89	6	4.41	0.92	0
MN	2		1.63	0		0	21		1.12	23		1.14	1.43	0
MO	3		2.44	1	5	6.67	20		1.06	24		1.19	2.05	5.60
MS	1		0.81	0		0	4		0.21	5		0.25	3.27	0

TABLE 7.10. (cont'd)

State	Canada			Mexico			All others			All home countries			RCA CA-All	RCA MX-All
	No.	Top 10	% Dist.	No.	Top 10	% Dist.	No.	Top 10	% Dist.	No.	Top 10	% Dist.		
MT	0		0	0		0	0		0	0		—	1.00	1.00
NC	8	2	6.5	1	5	6.67	89	5	4.74	98	5	4.86	1.34	1.37
ND	0		0	0		0	0		0	0		—	1.00	1.00
NE	0		0	0		0	1		0.05	1		0.05	0	0
NH	0		0	0		0	2		0.11	2		0.10	0	0
NJ	0		0	0		0	84	6	4.47	84	7	4.17	0	0
NM	0		0	0		0	6		0.32	6		0.30	0	0
NV	0		0	0		0	6		0.32	6		0.30	0	0
NY	23	1	18.7	2	3	13.33	150	2	7.99	175	2	8.68	2.15	1.54
OH	8	2	6.5	0		0	107	4	5.7	115	4	5.70	1.14	0
OK	0		0	0		0	7		0.37	7		0.35	0	0
OR	1		0.81	0		0	20		1.06	21		1.04	0.78	0
PA	2		1.63	0		0	76	8	4.05	78	8	3.87	0.42	0
PR	0		0	0		0	0		0	0		—	1.00	1.00
RI	0		0	0		0	7		0.37	7		0.35	0	0
SC	3		2.44	0		0	38		2.02	41		2.03	1.20	0
SD	0		0	0		0	1		0.05	1		0.05	0	0
TN	5	8	4.07	0		0	58		3.09	63		3.13	1.30	0
TX	5	8	4.07	5	1	33.33	109	3	5.8	119	3	5.90	0.69	5.65
UT	0		0	0		0	6		0.32	6		0.30	0	0
VA	3		2.44	0		0	60		3.19	63		3.13	0.78	0
VT	0		0	0		0	1		0.05	1		0.05	0	0
WA	2		1.63	0		0	36		1.92	38		1.88	0.86	0
WI	0		0	0		0	20		1.06	20		0.99	0	0
WV	0		0	0		0	12		0.64	12		0.60	0	0
WY	0		0	0		0	0		0	0		—	1.00	1.00
Total	123		100	15		100	1,878		100	2,016		100.00	1.00	1.00

Note: Some states not identified so the total sums to less than the total number of entries.

Source: Authors' calculations from US Dept. of Commerce (1989–94).

TABLE 7.11. Border state location of US inward FDI by home country, 1989–1994

State location	Canada			Mexico		All others		All home countries		RCA CA-All	RCA MX-All
	No. of states	No. of entries	% Dist.	No. of entries	% Dist.	No. of entries	% Dist.	No. of entries	% Dist.		
All Industries											
Border Canada	16	110	34.70	5	19.23	1,241	30.43	1,356	30.67	1.13	0.63
Center States	27	103	32.49	3	11.54	1,432	35.12	1,538	34.79	0.93	0.33
Border Mexico	9	104	32.81	18	69.23	1,405	34.45	1,527	34.54	0.95	2.00
Total, All Industry	52	317	100.00	26	100.00	4,078	100.00	4,421	100.00	1.00	1.00
Manufacturing											
Border Canada	16	51	41.46	2	13.33	624	33.23	677	33.58	1.23	0.40
Center States	27	50	40.65	2	13.33	721	38.39	773	38.34	1.06	0.35
Border Mexico	9	22	17.89	11	73.33	533	28.38	566	28.08	0.64	2.61
Total, Mfg.	52	123	100.00	15	100.00	1,878	100.00	2,016	100.00	1.00	1.00

Source: Authors' calculations based on US Dept. of Commerce (1989–94).

more variation than for all industries; in particular, note the high RCA scores and number of entries for Canada in Delaware, and for Mexico in Texas. However, the small number of entries suggests that these RCAs should be discounted.

A different way to ask the question about clustering, and whether insider states like Canada and Mexico have a different pattern of entry from investors from non-member states, is to look at border states. Are Canadian investments clustered along the US–Canada border, and Mexican investments along the US–Mexico border? Has CUSFTA—and is NAFTA—pulling spoke country investments to their border with the hub? Table 7.11 provides some evidence that this, in fact, is the case. For Canada, 34.7 per cent of all investments over the 1989–94 period were made in US–Canada border states; in manufacturing, the percentage jumps to 41.48 per cent. In the case of Mexico, the pattern is even more pronounced: 69.24 per cent of all investments and 73.3 per cent of manufacturing investments were made along the US–Mexico border. Relative to all countries, Mexican investors were more than twice as likely to invest along the US–Mexico border than were all country investors (RCA =2.01 for all industries and 2.61 for manufacturing). This trend is very significant because it provides evidence in support of the theory that manufacturing FDI will tend to cluster near a country's borders, especially when transport costs are significant (Hanson 1996).

4.3.4. Industry Choice

Table 7.12 shows the allocation of FDI entries by two-digit SIC code. Both all industries and manufacturing (SIC 20 through SIC 39) are represented in the table. The top industries for Canadian FDI entries are, in order, printing and publishing (SIC 27), chemicals (SIC 28), electricity, gas, and sanitation services (SIC 49), business services (SIC 73), metal mining (SIC 10), oil and gas extraction (SIC 13), electric and electronic (SIC 36), communication (SIC 48), food (SIC 20), and real estate (SIC 65). Only four of the top ten are in manufacturing. For Mexico, the top industries are stone, clay, and glass (SIC 32), communication (SIC 48), security brokers (SIC 62), and printing and publishing (SIC 27). Looking at the RCA indexes, Canada is relatively more heavily invested in metal mining (SIC 10), railroad transport (SIC 40), and personal services (SIC 72), and Mexican investments are relatively clustered in stone, clay, and glass (SIC 32).[10] Looking at manufacturing as a whole, 27.9 per cent of Canadian and 36.6 per cent of Mexican entries went into this sector, compared with 31.3 per cent for all home countries. Thus, Mexican FDI is relatively more concentrated in manufacturing, and Canada less; which is perhaps to be expected from the complex production-sharing arrangements developing along the US–Mexico border.

5. Discussion and Conclusions

The literature on North American economic integration is voluminous, but highly focused on trade patterns, particularly for goods trade. Much less work

TABLE 7.12. Industry choice for US inward FDI, all industries by home country, 1989–1994

SIC	Industry	Canada No.	Canada Top 10	Canada % Dist.	Mexico No.	Mexico Top 10	Mexico % Dist.	All others No.	All others Top 10	All others % Dist.	All home countries No.	All home countries Top 10	All home countries % Dist.	RCA CA-All	RCA MX-All
**	Non-specified	32		7.26	1		2.44	307		5.14	340		5.27	1.38	0.46
01	Agric. prod. crops	1		0.23	0		0.00	6		0.1	7		0.11	2.09	0
02	Agric. pr. livestock	0		0.00	0		0.00	4		0.07	4		0.06	0	0
07	Agric. services	0		0.00	0		0.00	1		0.02	1		0.02	0	0
10	Metal mining	12	5	2.72	0		0.00	21		0.35	33		0.51	5.33	0
12	Coal mining	0		0.00	0		0.00	18		0.3	18		0.28	0	0
13	Oil gas extraction	12	5	2.72	0		0.00	79		1.32	91		1.41	1.93	0
14	Non-metallic minerals	0		0.00	0		0.00	14		0.23	14		0.22	0	0
15	Building construction	0		0.00	0		0.00	5		0.08	5		0.08	0	0
16	Heavy construction	0		0.00	0		0.00	7		0.12	7		0.11	0	0
17	Special trade contra.	0		0.00	0		0.00	3		0.05	3		0.05	0	0
18	n.a.	0		0.00	0		0.00	1		0.02	1		0.02	0	0
Manufacturing SIC 20–39															
20	Food	9	10	2.04	0		0.00	128	8	2.14	137	8	2.12	0.96	0
21	Tobacco	0		0.00	0		0.00	1		0.02	1		0.02	0	0
22	Textiles	4		0.91	1	6	2.44	29		0.49	34		0.53	1.72	4.60
23	Apparel	1		0.23	0		0.00	24		0.4	25		0.39	0.59	0
24	Lumber	4		0.91	0		0.00	10		0.17	14		0.22	4.14	0
25	Furniture	2		0.45	0		0.00	6		0.1	8		0.12	3.75	0
26	Paper	7		1.59	1	6	2.44	26		0.44	34		0.53	3.00	4.60
27	Printing, publishing	26	1	5.9	2	3	4.88	104		1.74	132	10	2.04	2.89	2.39
28	Chemicals	16	2	3.63	0		0.00	330	1	5.52	346	1	5.36	0.68	0
29	Petroleum, coal	1		0.23	1	6	2.44	14		0.23	16		0.25	0.92	9.76
30	Rubber, plastics	3		0.68	0		0.00	84		1.41	87		1.35	0.50	0
31	Leather	0		0.00	0		0.00	8		0.13	8		0.12	0	0
32	Stone, clay, glass	2		0.45	6	1	14.63	65		1.09	73		1.13	0.40	12.95

TABLE 7.12. (cont'd)

SIC	Industry	Canada			Mexico			All others			All home countries			RCA CA-All	RCA MX-All
		No.	Top 10	% Dist.	No.	Top 10	% Dist.	No.	Top 10	% Dist.	No.	Top 10	% Dist.		
33	Primary metal	12	5	2.72	0		0.00	118	10	1.98	130		2.01	1.35	0
34	Fabricated metal	6		1.36	0		0.00	80		1.34	86		1.33	1.02	0
35	Comput equip. mach.	6		1.36	0		0.00	298		4.99	304		4.71	0.29	0
36	Electric, electronic	10	8	2.27	1	6	2.44	290	2	4.85	301	2	4.66	0.49	0.52
37	Transportation equip.	9	10	2.04	3	2	7.32	135	3	2.26	147	3	2.28	0.89	3.21
38	Instruments	2		0.45	0		0.00	108	7	1.81	110	6	1.7	0.26	0
39	Misc. manufacturing	3		0.68	0		0.00	27		0.45	30		0.46	1.48	0
SUM	All mfg. as % of total	123		27.89	15		36.59	1885		31.55	2023		31.34	0.89	1.17
40	Railroad transport.	7		1.59	0		0.00	2		0.03	9		0.14	11.36	0
41	Passenger transit	0		0.00	0		0.00	1		0.02	1		0.02	0	0
42	Trucking warehousing	6		1.36	1	6	2.44	44		0.74	51		0.79	1.72	3.09
44	Water transportation	9	10	2.04	0		0.00	114		1.91	123		1.91	1.07	0
45	Transportation by air	3		0.68	1	6	2.44	45		0.75	49		0.76	0.89	3.21
47	Transport. services	6		1.36	0		0.00	55		0.92	61		0.94	1.45	0
48	Communication	10	8	2.27	2	3	4.88	57		0.95	69		1.07	2.12	4.56
49	Elect. gas sanit. serv.	14	3	3.17	0		0.00	27		0.45	41		0.64	4.95	0
50	Whol. tr. durable good	2		0.45	1	6	2.44	249	4	4.17	252	4	3.9	0.12	0.63
51	Whol tr. non-durable	3		0.68	0		0.00	101		1.69	104		1.61	0.42	0
52	Build mat garden sup.	1		0.23	0		0.00	4		0.07	5		0.08	2.88	0
53	Gen marchand stores	0		0.00	0		0.00	16		0.27	16		0.25	0	0
54	Food stores	1		0.23	1	6	2.44	22		0.37	24		0.37	0.62	6.59
55	Auto deal. serv. stat.	1		0.23	0		0.00	14		0.23	15		0.23	1.00	0

Code	Industry	n	rank	%	n	rank	%	n	rank	%	n	rank	%	%	%
56	Apparel access. stores	7		1.59			0.00	128	8	2.14	135	9	2.09	0.76	0
57	Furniture stores	1		0.23			0.00	28		0.47	29		0.45	0.51	0
58	Eating drinking places	5		1.13			0.00	33		0.55	38		0.59	1.92	0
59	Miscellaneous retail	3		0.68			0.00	62		1.04	65		1.01	0.67	0
60	Banking	3		0.68	1	6	2.44	41		0.69	45		0.7	0.97	3.49
61	Other credit agencies	1		0.23			0.00	16		0.27	17		0.26	0.88	0
62	Secur. com. broker	3		0.68	2	3	4.88	49		0.82	54		0.84	0.81	5.81
63	Insurance carriers	1		0.23			0.00	40		0.67	41		0.64	0.36	0
64	Ins. agent broker serv.	0		0.00			0.00	11		0.18	11		0.17	0	0
65	Real estate	9	10	2.04			0.00	22		0.37	31		0.48	4.25	0
67	Holdings other invest.	5		1.13			0.00	20		0.33	25		0.39	2.90	0
70	Hotels, lodging	3		0.68			0.00	142	6	2.38	145	7	2.25	0.30	0
72	Personal services	3		0.68			0.00	0		0.00	3		0.05	13.60	0
73	Business services	14	3	3.17			0.00	151	5	2.53	165	5	2.56	1.24	0
75	Auto repair garages	2		0.45			0.00	10		0.17	12		0.19	2.37	0
76	Misc. repair services	0		0.00			0.00	2		0.03	2		0.03	0	0
78	Motion pictures	2		0.45			0.00	45		0.75	47		0.73	0.62	0
79	Amus. recre. services	2		0.45			0.00	50		0.84	52		0.81	0.56	0
80	Health services	4		0.91			0.00	12		0.2	16		0.25	3.64	0
81	Legal services	0		0.00	1	6	2.44	2		0.03	3		0.05	0	48.80
82	Educat. services	0		0.00			0.00	16		0.27	16		0.25	0	0
86	Membership orgs.	0		0.00			0.00	1		0.02	1		0.02	0	0
87	Ing. acc. mgmt serv.	2		0.45			0.00	87		1.46	89		1.38	0.33	0
91	Exec. legisl. gvt.	0		0.00			0.00	1		0.02	1		0.02	0	0
92	n.a.	0		0.00			0.00	1		0.02	1		0.02	0	0
96	Admin. econ programme	5		1.13			0.00	17		0.28	22		0.34	3.32	0
	Total	441		100.00	41		100.00	5,974		100.00	6,456		100	1.00	1.00

Source: authors' calculations from US Dept. of Commerce (1989–94).

has been done on the impacts of regional integration on foreign direct investment, and, in particular, on the production decisions and location patterns of multinational enterprises in response to the formation of a free trade area.

One of the underlying research questions which motivates this book is: *In what ways is the spatial unit changing from the nation state to the macroregion?* We have argued in this chapter that the location strategies of multinationals are affected by the formation of an FTA because the FTA causes the appropriate spatial unit for strategic decision-making to broaden from the nation to the region as a whole. Given the degree of integration within the FTA and the location advantages of each country, *ceteris paribus*, MNE location responses to a free trade area should be influenced by two factors: (i) the value-adding activity to be undertaken in the foreign plant and (ii) the characteristics of the firms.

First, the plant location decision is related to the underlying motivations for setting up a foreign plant (market-, resource-, efficiency-, and strategic-asset-seeking FDI). Our analysis supplements these general motivations by focusing directly on the actual value-adding activity to be undertaken in the host country. We show that plant function (whether final assembly, support services, or technology development, for example) matters in terms of firm responses to regional integration pressures. Second, we argued that the type of firm (insider, outsider, domestic) should affect the nature of the firm response to regional integration. For example, insider firms with affiliates in the member countries are best placed to take advantage of the opportunities for rationalization and specialization. We have also shown that the relative sizes of country markets are important in influencing MNE location patterns, with 'spoke' firms more likely to engage in new investments in the 'hub' market.

In the case of CUSFTA and NAFTA, the answer to the question: 'In what ways is the spatial unit changing from the nation state to the macroregion?' is that the appropriate spatial unit is no longer the individual member country but the region as a whole. For firms located in the US hub, the definition of 'home base' has historically been defined by the US borders. The one exception to this rule is the auto sector where the 1965 Auto Pact has created one integrated US–Canada auto sector. The Canada–US FTA enables both US and Canadian firms to define 'home base' as including both countries. With the passage of NAFTA, Mexico is now being redefined as part of the definition of North American economic space. This is most clearly seen along the US–Mexico border where production-sharing arrangements are integrating Mexican manufacturing into the US economy.

While our empirical work provides some evidence that North America became a relatively less attractive region for foreign direct investment over the 1985–97 period, we argue that this is mostly due to the relative attractiveness of investments in other parts of the world after 1989 (e.g. in East Asia and the former Soviet Union). CUSFTA and NAFTA, on the other hand, do not appear to have resulted in significantly increased investments. Although the dollar value of the FDI stock increased among all the NAFTA partners and in both directions, relatively more investments were directed outside of North America.

Looking specifically at inward FDI entries to the USA we provided some evidence that insider firms in a spoke economy (Canadian MNEs) invested more frequently at the beginning of the Canada–US Free Trade Agreement, and engaged in relatively more new FDI entries, primarily through mergers and acquisitions. Insider FDI entries, for Canada, while more clustered in geography and industry than FDI entries from non-NAFTA countries, were overall similar in terms of the top ten destinations for inward FDI. Mexican investors, reflecting Mexico's joining the FTA only in 1994, its higher trade barriers, and developing country status, engaged in small numbers of new investments in the US market which were geographically and industrially clustered. Mexico, in particular, invested more heavily along the US–Mexico border and in manufacturing industries relative to all home-country entries.

The evidence presented here suggests that North American firms have been making their locational decisions from a macroregional perspective, but that in the 1990s this has meant primarily locational reshufflings as firms have rationalized their investments on a continental basis. Over the longer term, once NAFTA is fully phased in, we expect new investment decisions to be made treating the North American macroregion as the 'home base'.

In subsequent work on this topic, we hope to explore the location patterns of MNEs within North America in more depth. Our data do not distinguish the motivation behind each FDI entry so we are unable, for example, at present to link our theoretical framework on the value-adding motivation behind each plant decision to the US FDI entry data. Perhaps other authors will be able to explore this topic more fully.

NOTES

An earlier draft was presented at the CIBER/Carnegie Bosch Workshop on 'Regions, Globalization and the Knowledge-Based Economy', Rutgers University, 24–5 October 1998. We would like to thank Richard Eberhart of the US International Trade Administration for providing the 1989–94 US inward FDI data by state, and William Wan and Srikanth Goparaju for their assistance. Bruce Kogut, John Dunning, Michael Enright and the other seminar participants provided helpful comments. The responsibility for any remaining errors is the authors.

1. See Ferdows (1989), Eden (1994b), and Brush, Maritan, and Karnani (forthcoming) for various topologies of plant functions.
2. Somewhat similar to a focused factory is a foreign plant with a regional or world product mandate (WPM). WPMs are plants with the full responsibility for all, or at least all downstream, stages of the value chain for a single product line within the MNE. The WPM is different from the focused factory since the responsibility for technology development, and for final sale, is shifted to the subsidiary under a WPM but not in a focused factory.

3. On the theory of clustering and agglomeration economies, see Krugman (1991), Eaton, Lipsey, and Safarian (1994a), Enright (1995, 1996, 1998), Markusen (1996), Dunning (1997a), Puga and Venables (1997), Hanson (1998), and Porter (1998a, 1998b).

4. e.g. Dunning argues that US multinationals were the major beneficiaries from Mark I regional integration in the European Community because they 'were able to take advantage of the removal of tariff barriers, and surmount the transactions costs of the remaining non-tariff barriers better than their EC equivalents' (1997a: 5).

5. The recent failure of the Multilateral Agreement on Investment (MAI) talks makes NAFTA's Ch. 11 even more exceptional among trade agreements.

6. Except in the auto industry where the Canada–US auto pact enabled producers to rationalize production on a Canada–US basis.

7. The ITA data set has been used previously by Kogut and Singh (1998) and Kogut and Chang (1991). Kogut and Chang (1991: 404) found the correlation between the ITA data set and FDI balance of payments data to be 0.89. Kogut also found the ITA data highly correlated with Bureau of Economic Analysis (BEA) FDI data and unpublished plant and equipment data (unpublished correspondence with the author).

8. The 'Manufacturing Only' data exclude from the data set mainly three categories of industry: natural resources (agriculture and extraction), services (transportation, communication, retailing, banking, education, legal, health), and real estate.

9. For example, there were only three FDI entries for Idaho over the whole period, one of which was from Canada. This gives Canada an RCA of 4.57, suggesting that Canada invests almost five times as much as all countries in Idaho, but the numbers are so small the index has little meaning in this case.

10. While other RCAs are high, the number of investments are very low and so are not mentioned here (e.g. Mexico's RCA of 55.00 in legal services where one of three total investments was made by a Mexican firm).

REFERENCES

Blank, S., and Krajewski, S., with Yu, H. S. (1994), 'Responding to a New Political and Economic Architecture in North America: Corporate Structure and Strategy', *Northwest Journal of Business and Economics* (Bellingham: Western Washington University): 17–29.

———— ——— (1995), 'U.S. Firms and North America: Redefining Structure and Strategy', *North American Outlook* 5.2 (Washington, DC: National Planning Association).

Brush, T., Maritan, C. A., and Karnani, A. (forthcoming), 'The Plant Location Decision in Multinational Manufacturing Firms: An Empirical Analysis of International Business and Manufacturing Strategy Perspectives', *Production and Operations Management*.

D'Cruz, J. R., and Rugman, A. M. (1993), 'Developing International Competitiveness: The Five Partner Model', *Business Quarterly* 58: 101–7.

Dunning, J. H. (1993), *Multinational Enterprises and the Global Economy* (Reading: Addison-Wesley).

—— (1994), 'MNE Activity: Comparing the NAFTA and the European Community', in L. Eden (ed.), *Multinationals in North America* (Calgary: University of Calgary Press).

—— (1997a), 'A Business Analytic Approach to Governments and Globalization', in *Governments, Globalization and International Business* (Oxford: Oxford University Press).

—— (1997b), 'The European Internal Market Programme and Inbound Foreign Direct Investment', *Journal of Common Market Studies* 35: 1–30 and 189–223.

Eaton, C., Lipsey, R., and Safarian, A. E. (1994a), 'The Theory of Multinational Plant Location in a Regional Trading Area', in L. Eden (ed.), *Multinationals in North America* (Calgary: University of Calgary Press).

—— —— —— (1994b), 'The Theory of Multinational Plant Location: Agglomerations and Disagglomerations', in L. Eden (ed.), *Multinationals in North America* (Calgary: University of Calgary Press).

Eden, L. (1991), 'Multinational Responses to Trade and Technology Changes: Implications for Canada', in D. McFetridge (ed.), *Multinationals, Technology and Economic Growth* (Calgary: University of Calgary Press).

—— (1993), 'Thinking Globally, Acting Locally: Multinationals in the Global Political Economy', in L. Eden and E. Potter (eds.), *Multinationals in the Global Political Economy* (London: Macmillan; New York: St Martin's Press; and Toronto: McClelland & Stewart).

—— (ed.) (1994a), *Multinationals in North America* (Calgary: University of Calgary Press).

—— (1994b), 'Who Does What after NAFTA? Location Strategies of US Multinationals', in L. Eden (ed.), *Multinationals in North America* (Calgary: University of Calgary Press).

—— (1995), 'Foreign Direct Investment in Canada: Charting a New Policy Direction', *Canadian Foreign Policy* Winter 1994–5: 43–60.

—— (1996), 'The Emerging North American Investment Regime', *Transnational Corporations* 5(3): 61–98.

—— and Molot, M. A. (1993), 'Insiders and Outsiders: Defining "Who Is Us?" in the North American Auto Industry', *Transnational Corporations* 2(3): 31–64.

Enright, M. J. (1995), 'Organization and Coordination in Geographically Concentrated Industries', in N. R. Lamoreaux and D. M. G. Raff (eds.), *Coordination and Information: Historical Perspectives on the Organization of Enterprise* (Chicago and London: University of Chicago Press).

—— (1996), 'Regional Clusters and Economic Development: A Research Agenda', in U. H. Staber, N. V. Schaefer, and B. Sharma (eds.), *Business Networks: Prospects for Regional Development* (Berlin and New York: Walter de Gruyter).

—— (1998), 'Regional Clusters and Firm Strategy', in A. D. Chandler, Jr., P. Hagstrom, and O. Solvell (eds.), *The Dynamic Firm: The Role of Technology, Strategy, Organization, and Regions* (Oxford: Oxford University Press).

Ferdows, K. (1989), 'Mapping International Factory Networks', in K. Ferdows (ed.), *Managing International Manufacturing* (Amsterdam: North-Holland).

Globerman, S., and Walker, M. (1993), *Assessing NAFTA: A Trinational Analysis* (Vancouver: Fraser Institute).

Hamid, S., Mathis, R., Dandapani, K., and Prakash, A. (1997), 'The Impact of the U.S.–Canada Free Trade Agreement on the Large and Small U.S. Firms in the Textiles, Computer, Oil and Gas, and Auto Industries', *International Trade Journal*, 11 (Summer): 221–46.

Hanson, G. H. (1996), 'Economic Integration, Intraindustry Trade, and Frontier Regions', *European Economic Review*, 40: 941–9.

Hanson, G. H. (1998), 'North American Economic Integration and Industrial Location', *Oxford Review of Economic* Policy 14: 30–44.

Head, K., Ries, J., and Swenson, D. (1995), 'Agglomeration Benefits and Location Choice: Evidence from Japanese Manufacturing Investments in the United States', *Journal of International Economics* 38: 223–47.

Hufbauer, G., and Schott, J. (1993), *NAFTA: An Assessment* (Washington: Institute for International Economics).

Johnson, F., Kamauff, J., Schein, N., and Wood, A. (1995), 'Manufacturing Strategies under NAFTA.', *Business Quarterly*, 59(4): 60–6.

Kogut, B. (1994), 'An Evolutionary Perspective on the NAFTA', in L. Eden (ed.). *Multinationals in North America* (Calgary: University of Calgary Press).

—— and Chang, S. J. (1991), 'Technological Capabilities and Foreign Direct Investment in the US', *Review of Economics and Statistics* 73(3): 401–13.

Kogut, B., and Singh, H. (1988), 'The Effect of National Culture on the Choice of Entry Mode', *Journal of International Business Studies* 19(3): 411–32.

Krajewski, S. (1992), *Intrafirm Trade and the New North American Business Dynamic* (Ottawa: Conference Board of Canada).

Krugman, P. (1991), *Geography and Trade* (Cambridge, Mass.: MIT Press).

Kudrle, R. (1994), 'Regulating Multinational Enterprises in North America', in L. Eden (ed.), *Multinationals in North America* (Calgary: University of Calgary Press).

Lipsey, R., Schwanen, D., and Wonnacott, R. (1994), *The NAFTA: What's In, What's Out, What's Next* (Toronto: C. D. Howe Institute).

Little, J. S. (1996), 'U.S. Regional Trade with Canada during the Transition to Free Trade', *New England Economic Review* (Jan.–Feb.): 3–21.

Litvak, I. (1991), 'Evolving Corporate Strategies: Adjusting to the FTA', in F. O. Hampson and C. J. Maule (eds.), *After the Cold War: Canada Among Nations 1990–1* (Ottawa: Carleton University Press).

Markusen, A. (1996), 'Sticky Places in Slippery Space: A Typology of Industrial Districts', *Economic Geography* 72: 293–313.

Mayer, Frederick (1994), 'The NAFTA, Multinationals and Social Policy' in L. Eden (ed.), *Multinationals in North America* (Calgary: University of Calgary Press).

OECD (1997). *International Direct Investment Statistics Yearbook 1997* (Paris: OECD).

Porter, M. F. (1998a), 'Clusters and the New Economics of Competition', *Harvard Business Review* (Nov. 1): 77–89.

—— (1998b), 'The Adam Smith Address: Location, Clusters, and the "New" Micro-economics of Competition', *Business Economics* 33: 7–13.

Preston, L., and Windsor, D. (1992), *The Rules of the Game in the Global Economy: Policy Regimes for International Business* (Boston: Kluwer).

Puga, D., and Venables, A. J. (1997), 'Preferential Trading Arrangements and Industrial Location', *Journal of International Economics* 43: 347–68.

Rugman, A. (1990), *Multinationals and the Canada–U.S. Free Trade Agreement* (Columbia, SC: University of South Carolina Press).

—— (ed.) (1994a), *Foreign Direct Investment and NAFTA* (Columbia, SC: University of South Carolina Press).

—— (1994b), 'Strategic Management and Canadian Multinationals', in S. Globerman (ed.), *Canadian-Based Multinationals* (Calgary: University of Calgary Press).

—— and D'Cruz, J. (1991), 'The Double Diamond Model of International Competitiveness: Canada's Experience', *Management International Review* 33(2): 17–39.

—— and Gestrin, M. (1993a), 'The Investment Provisions of NAFTA', in S. Globerman and M. Walker (eds.), *Assessing NAFTA: A Trinational Analysis* (Vancouver: Fraser Institute).

—— (1993b), 'The Strategic Response of Multinational Enterprises to NAFTA'. *Columbia Journal of World Business* 28 (Winter): 318–29.

—— Kirton, J., and Soloway, J. A. (1997), 'Canadian Corporate Strategy in a North American Region', Paper presented in the *Annual Meeting of the Academy of International Business*, Monterrey, Mexico.

Schwanen, D. (1997), 'Trading Up: The Impact of Increased Continental Integration on Trade, Investment, and Jobs in Canada'. *C. D. Howe Institute Commentary*, 89 (Mar.).

United Nations Centre for Trade and Development (UNCTAD) (1998), *World Investment Report 1998: Trends and Determinants* (New York: United Nations).

United Nations Centre for Transnational Corporations (UNCTC) (1993), *World Investment Report 1993: Transnational Corporations and Integrated World Production* (New York: United Nations).

US General Accounting Office (GAO) (1997), *North American Free Trade Agreement: Impacts and Implementation*, Testimony before the Subcommittee on Trade, Committee on Ways and Means, House of Representatives, 11 September, GAO publication 97–256 (Washington, DC: USGPO).

US International Trade Administration (ITA) (1989–94), *Foreign Direct Investment in the United States* (Washington, DC: International Trade Administration).

US International Trade Commission (ITC) (1997), *The Impact of the North American Free Trade Agreement on the US Economies and Industries: A Three-Year Review*, USITC Publication 3045 (Washington, DC: US International Trade Commission).

US Trade Representative (USTR) (1998), *4th Annual Report to Congress—Impact of the NAFTA on US Automotive Exports to Mexico (and on Imports from Mexico)* (Washington, DC: US Trade Representative).

Vernon, R. (1994), 'Multinationals and Governments: Key Actors in NAFTA', in L. Eden (ed.), *Multinationals in North America* (Calgary: University of Calgary Press), 25–52.

PART THREE
COUNTRY CASE STUDIES

8

Foreign Direct Investment into the USA: *A Subnational Investigation*

Lorna H. Wallace

1. Introduction

The industrial distribution of inbound foreign direct investment (FDI) within a national economy is uneven, differing among and also within the subnational units (i.e. regions and states within regions). Contrary to the claims of some analysts about how 'the logic and dynamics of territorial development are increasingly placeless' (Castells and Henderson 1987: 7), or those who predict the end of geography (O'Brien 1992), or the end of the nation state (Ohmae 1995), the global economy seems in the works of Scott (1996: 409) 'to be entering a phase of capitalist development in which the regional concentration of production is becoming more pronounced as a mode of spatial economic organization.' By reducing the size of the more commonly used unit of analysis—the nation state—to that of the subnational segment, this chapter presents readers with an approach which provides a more micro, although still macro, perspective from which to examine the impact of the globalization of production and markets. The chosen spatial unit is the state of New Jersey (NJ) in the USA.

There are three basic issues that are identified and examined. Section 2, based on earlier research (Wallace 1998), presents a summary of quantitative statistics from secondary data sources analysing the trends, significance, concentration, and source of FDI in the state. Section 3 examines the determinants of FDI in the state of New Jersey from an academic and business literature view as well as interviews with practitioners—key executives of selected, representative agencies engaging in FDI in New Jersey. In addition, the policy implications for corporate practitioners and the role of government in the attraction, development, and retention of inbound FDI to the state are briefly addressed. Finally (Section 4), policy implications for the advancement of theory are presented.

2. Trends, Significance, Concentration, and Source of Foreign Direct Investment into the State of New Jersey

2.1. Trends of Foreign Direct Investment into the State of New Jersey

New Jersey, as a part of the tristate region (New York, New Jersey, and Connecticut) has historically been attractive to foreign companies seeking to locate

TABLE 8.1. Foreign direct investment in the state of New Jersey and the USA, 1974–1995

	New Jersey No. of employees ('000s)	USA Rate of Change (%)	USA No. of employees ('000s)	NJ % of USA
1974	79.4	—	—	—
1977	85.0	7.1	1,218.7	6.98
1978	98.0	15.3	1,429.9	6.85
1979	110.5	12.8	1,753.2	6.30
1980	120.5	9.1	2,033.9	5.93
1981	134.9	12.0	2,416.6	5.58
1982	132.1	−2.1	2,448.1	5.40
1983	136.5	3.3	2,546.5	5.36
1984	140.8	3.2	2,714.3	5.19
1985	154.8	9.9	2,862.2	5.41
1986	161.7	4.5	2,937.9	5.50
1987	173.3	7.2	3,224.3	5.38
1988	203.9	17.7	4,844.2	5.30
1989	222.8	9.3	4,511.5	4.94
1990	227.0	1.9	4,734.5	4.80
1991	229.6	1.2	4,871.9	4.71
1992	216.3	−5.8	4,715.4	4.59
1993	212.6	−1.7	4,765.6	4.46
1994	209.3	−1.6	4,840.5	4.32
1995	209.3	0.0	4,928.3	4.25

Sources: Foreign Direct Investment in the United States, 1: Report of the Secretary of Commerce to the Congress, US Dept. of Commerce, April 1976; Foreign Direct Investment in the United States. Operations of US Affiliates of Foreign Companies, 1977–80 and annual volumes 1981–95, US Dept. of Commerce, Bureau of Economic Analysis.

on the East Coast of the USA. Its harbours and direct access to rail, highways, and international airports make New Jersey an ideal site for many headquarters and distribution activities. In addition, the sheer size and concentration of the regional market, along with New Jersey's research and development activities, and skilled labour pool have influenced numerous knowledge- and technology-based firms to locate in the state.

Table 8.1 shows the fluctuating trends of the number of persons employed by US affiliates of foreign firms over the period 1974 to 1995 in NJ and the USA as a whole. In 1995, there were 1,621 affiliates with property, plant, and equipment from fifty-seven (Ziele 1997) countries in New Jersey employing approximately 209,300 persons. Between 1977 and 1995, both the number of such affiliates (increasing from 551 to 1,621) and employment in foreign-owned businesses operating value-adding activities in the state (increasing from 85,000 to 209,300) nearly tripled.

From 1977 to 1982, the average annual rate of increase in affiliate employment was approximately 12.5 per cent for the state of NJ, compared with 19.7 per cent for the USA as a whole. Following a brief decline during the 1982 recession, foreign employment in New Jersey continued to expand from 1982 through 1991, although at a decreased annual rate of approximately 6.5 per cent, approximately half the 12.6 per cent annual growth rate of change for the USA. Therefore, although FDI into New Jersey for the period 1974–91 increased, it grew at a decreasing rate.

For the period 1991 to 1995 FDI employment in New Jersey actually declined by 20,300 persons (from 229,600 to 209,300). New Jersey is now receiving a smaller share of the FDI coming into the USA as a whole (4.3 per cent in 1995 down from 7.3 per cent in 1974).

A useful way to analyse FDI in NJ is by comparison with other states in the nation. New Jersey ranked ninth nationally in employment by foreign companies in 1995, accounting for approximately 4.3 per cent of all foreign employment in the country. This ranking is lower, however, than in 1974 when New Jersey held the third-ranking position accounting for 7.3 per cent of all foreign employment in the USA, indicating that New Jersey's share of the total FDI coming into the nation has declined in absolute terms and relative to other states. In effect, New Jersey has been slowly losing position in the competition for FDI into the USA.

2.2.1. Economic Significance of Foreign Direct Investment in the State of New Jersey

Following the research of Graham and Krugman (1989, 1991, 1995) the significance of inward FDI to the economy of the state of New Jersey is measured by the percentage of foreign to total employment located in the state. Foreign direct investment employment in New Jersey, as a share of the total employment in the state, has gradually increased in significance from 3.5 per cent in 1974 to 6.6 per cent in 1995. Within the state, FDI employment grew from 79,400 employees in 1974 to 209,300 persons in 1995 a factor of over four-and-a-half times that of the rate of total domestic employment growth in the state which increased from 2,198,200 in 1974 to 2,975,200 over the same twenty-one-year period.

Comparisons between manufacturing and non-manufacturing sector industries reveal that FDI in New Jersey is more and increasingly significant to the state than the national economy in virtually every industry sector for which data are available for the years 1974 and 1995. During the period 1974–95, employment at foreign manufacturing affiliates in New Jersey almost doubled, increasing from 52,100 to 96,900 persons, while employment at domestic manufacturing operations was nearly cut in half, declining from 784,400 in 1974 to 449,500 in 1995. FDI employment in manufacturing, as a share of total employment in the state, went from 6.2 per cent in 1974 to 17.7 per cent in 1995. These percentage share figures further demonstrate the increasing significance of FDI employment to New Jersey.

2.2.2. Economic Significance of Foreign Multinational Enterprise Technological Activity in New Jersey

In the analysis of inbound FDI it is useful to distinguish not only among industries but according to the 'level' of activity. The level of activity can be taken as an indication of the sophistication of the operations—the higher the level of activity, the greater will be the ratio of highly skilled and professional employees to total employees. This enables researchers to analyse what Dunning, in the opening chapter of this volume, describes as the increasing relative significance of the knowledge-intensive competencies of firms. No economy can be competitive in all industries or at all 'levels' of activity but each economy is likely to seek to attract and retain activities which are at the 'higher end' of the value-adding chain (Gray and Wallace 1996).

The analysis of FDI-related research and development (R&D) is based on an examination of the number of professional staff employed in technologically related activities in New Jersey. Of the total 782 firms with R&D activities listed in the Bowker *Directory* (1992), 697 are indigenous firms and eighty-five are US affiliates of foreign firms indicating that the percentage of professional staff employed by US affiliates of foreign firms in R&D activities, in relation to the total number of professional staff employed by all R&D-related firms in New Jersey in 1992 was approximately 11 per cent, which is significant (Wallace 1998).

2.3. **Industrial Concentration of Foreign Direct Investment in New Jersey**

Identification of industries in which New Jersey is 'competitive' relies on an understanding of the extent of FDI concentration in the various industrial sectors. Following the industrial restructuring competitiveness model developed by Dunning (1988) in a UK case study, the concentration of inbound FDI is analysed in terms of the revealed comparative advantage (RCA), or revealed location advantage (RLA) as it is referred to in this research, of a region for attracting foreign direct investment. FDI coming into New Jersey will be attracted to areas perceived to have, or perceived likely to develop, such an advantage (Dunning 1988).

Previous research (Wallace 1998) revealed that New Jersey had an RLA in two industry categories in 1974 (total manufacturing and wholesale trade). New Jersey's RLAs increased to four industry categories in 1995 (wholesale trade, finance [except banking], insurance, and other industries). Analysis of detailed manufacturing data showed that the manufacturing industries in which FDI had the greatest economic significance in 1988 and in 1991 were chemicals and allied products, and instruments and related products. A cluster of knowledge-based activities in the chemical and allied products industry exists in New Jersey, as a result of the location, within the state, of many pharmaceutical MNEs including Merck, Johnson & Johnson, Novartis, Hoechst, Rhone-Poulenc, Schering-Plough, Hoffmann-La Roche, and others.

2.4.1. Source of Foreign Direct Investment in New Jersey

The source of foreign direct investment or ultimate beneficial owner (UBO) is relevant to analysis of the role of FDI, especially as a key piece of evidence in favour of industrial organization rather than cost-of-capital explanations of FDI (Wilkins 1979; Graham and Krugman 1989, 1991, 1995). Following the research of Graham and Krugman the sources of FDI in New Jersey, measured by the percentage distribution of inbound FDI by country of parent or ultimate beneficial owner (UBO), are shown in Table 8.2.

Table 8.2 shows the most dramatic changes in the source country FDI employment in New Jersey from 1977 to 1995, and the declining shares from Europe (except Germany) and the increases from Canada and Japan. This is not surprising given the implementation of the Canada–US Free Trade Agreement during the late 1980s (particularly given the northern physical proximity of New

TABLE 8.2. Foreign direct investment in New Jersey and the USA by ultimate beneficial owner, 1977–1995 (no. of employees)

	1977				1995			
	USA	% of USA	NJ	% of NJ	USA	% of USA	NJ	% of NJ
Canada	189.3	15.5	3.5	4.1	703.7	14.3	23.6	11.3
Total Europe	855.6	70.2	72.0	84.7	2,991.0	60.7	139.2	66.5
France	130.2	10.7	12.3	14.5	348.2	7.1	19.9	9.5
Germany	134.1	11.0	12.2	14.4	580.6	11.8	31.5	15.1
Netherlands	152.2	12.5	6.7	7.9	334.2	6.8	12.1	5.8
Switzerland	80.3	6.6	17.5	20.6	308.3	6.3	23.1	11.4
United Kingdom	286.4	23.5	16.4	19.3	986.5	20.0	36.9	17.6
Other Europe	72.4	5.9	6.9	8.0	433.2	8.7	15.7	7.1
Japan	76.2	6.3	4.8	5.7	758.2	15.4	30.7	14.7
Middle East	4.6	0.4	0.1	0.1	46.6	1.0	1.1	0.5
Latin America and Other Western Hemisphere	n.a.		n.a.		166.6	3.4	4.2	2.0
Australia	n.a.		n.a.		73.6	1.5	1.1	0.5
Africa	n.a.		n.a.		20.8	0.4	G	n.a.
Other Asia and Pacific	n.a.		n.a.		122.8	2.5	4.9	n.a.
Other	—		—		45.0	0.9	H	n.a.
All countries	1,218.7	100.0	85.0	100.0	4,928.3	100.0	209.3	100.0

Notes: 1. Employment size ranges are suppressed by the Dept. of Commerce, in some cells. The size ranges are: G-1,000 to 2,499; and H-2,500 to 4,999.
2. No state data by source country is available prior to 1977.
3. The country data not available for 1977 is due to grouping.

Sources: US Dept. of Commerce, Bureau of Economic Analysis, Foreign Direct Investment in the United States, Operations of US Affiliates, 1977–1980, US Government Washington, 1985. Preliminary 1995, published May 1997.

Jersey and Canada) and the shift of Japanese outward investment largely away from portfolio to direct investment (attributable, in part at least, to the surge in the strength of the yen against the US dollar—particularly after the Plaza Accord in 1985).

2.4.2. Source of Foreign Multinational Research and Development Activity in New Jersey

The source of foreign direct R&D investment in New Jersey, measured by the distribution of FDI research and development by country of parent or UBO, is shown in Table 8.3. The distribution used as the basis for this analysis is both the number of US affiliates with R&D activities and the number of professional staff of the affiliates with R&D-related activities in New Jersey in 1992.

From a review of the information contained in Table 8.3, we see that the countries with the most involvement in R&D-related activities in New Jersey, from the perspective of the number of foreign firms engaged in R&D efforts, are England and Germany each with approximately 27 and 26 per cent respectively for the total eighty-five firms. It is not surprising, given the original colonization of the USA, that the majority of foreign firms in the East coast state of New Jersey are from Europe. In addition, it is not surprising given the technological dominance by Germany and the historically favourable trade relations with Great Britain that these two countries make up the bulk of foreign R&D investment in the state.

TABLE 8.3. R&D foreign affiliates in New Jersey by ultimate beneficial owner, 1992

No. of affiliates Rank		%	No. of professional staff Rank		%
Europe			Europe		
1. England	23	27.1	3. England	681	14.7
2. Germany	22	25.9	1. Germany	2,087	45.2
3. France	9	10.6	5. France	175	3.8
4. Switzerland	8	9.4	2. Switzerland	956	20.7
5. Netherlands	6	7.1	4. Netherlands	537	11.6
7. Sweden	4	4.7	6. Sweden	99	2.1
9. Denmark	1	1.2	11. Denmark	3	0.1
9. Finland	1	1.2	8. Finland	24	0.5
9. Italy	1	1.2	9. Italy	7	0.2
9. Unidentified UK	1	1.2	10. Other UK	5	0.1
Total Europe	76	89.4	Total Europe	4,574	99.0
5. Japan	6	7.1	7. Japan	46	1.0
8. Canada	3	3.5	12. Canada	n.a.	n.a.
Total	85	100.0	Total	4,620	100.0

Source: Bowker Study, 1992 as compiled by Wallace (1995*b*).

The right-hand side of Table 8.3 presents a slightly different picture. Although England and Germany had a similar number of affiliates operating R&D-related activities in New Jersey in 1992, the employment of professional staff varies considerably. Germany accounted for the employment of 2,087 professional staff in R&D-related activities in 1992 or over 45 per cent of the total FDI professional staff. Whereas, from the perspective of professional staff, England now ranks third with 681 professional staff members or approximately only 15 per cent of the total, behind Switzerland who employed 956 professional staff in 1992, approximately 21 per cent of the total.

The analysis of these statistics not only reveals the significance of German, Swiss, and English FDI in New Jersey but the particular 'power' of individual MNEs such as the leaders (demonstrated by the employment of professional staff)— Siemens (1,220) and Hoechst Celanese (803). This power of individual MNEs emphasizes the need for government policy to understand international transactions from the perspective of FDI (UNCTAD 1992).

3. Determinants of Foreign Direct Investment in New Jersey

3.1. Introduction

The determinants of the location of foreign direct investment have been studied from a great many perspectives. Some scholars, for example, have analysed country-specific FDI location determinants.[1] Others have made a separation between the motivations of MNEs in manufacturing and non-manufacturing industries (for example: Swamidass 1990; Coughlin 1992; Schoenberger 1994; Doms and Jensen 1995; Shaver 1995) and research and development activities (Lall and Siddharthan 1982; Dunning and Narula 1995). In addition, analysis has been made by separating out greenfield-location determinants and differences found between location and employment choices of 'new firms' (Carlton 1983).

FDI location-determinant research, distinguished by the different types of FDI (resource-seeking, market-seeking, strategic-asset-seeking, and efficiency-seeking) has also been conducted (Dunning 1993). OECD (1994) outlines how until the middle of the 1980s, the determinants of much FDI location were viewed from the perspective of the strategic necessity of introducing cost-cutting measures or efficiency-seeking FDI. More recently, with the introduction of increased technological advances and consumer demand sophistication for higher-product quality, low labour and production costs, albeit still important, have become a less significant motive for FDI-location decision-making. Rather than being cost-minimization-driven spatial location patterns, much recent FDI is motivated by strategic-asset-seeking necessity—access to new technologies that aim to increase market share (OECD 1994). As described by Dunning, in the opening chapter of this volume, the nature, implications, and hence determinants of FDI for host regions is a changing phenomenon.

This section analyses the determinants of FDI location in New Jersey from 1974 to 1995. It comprises a review of the literature by both academics and practitioners, on the determinants of inbound FDI, combined with the information obtained in New Jersey executive interviews. In addition, it presents an empirical analysis of subnational FDI-location determinants in the USA. The argument, supported by the research of Porter (1990) and Solvell and Zander (1995), is that the location-bound resources peculiar to a geographic area play a continued or possibly increasingly important role for the global firm.

By drawing upon interdisciplinary findings related to the 'embeddedness' (Granovetter 1985, 1992) of FDI, this chapter deals not only with the attractions' determinants surrounding inbound FDI flows but also the retention of FDI stock. Agglomeration economies, as first identified by Marshall (1916) and built upon and extended to explain the evolvement of regional production systems (Scott, 1988a, 1988b; Storper 1995), industrial districts (Piore and Sabel 1984; Markusen 1994), learning regions (Saxenian 1994), innovative milieux (Aydalot 1986; Maillat 1995),[2] and industry clusters (Porter 1990) are reviewed and evaluated in light of the specific needs of New Jersey in a globalizing world economy.

3.2. The Determinants and Policy Implications of Foreign Direct Investment in NJ

The strategy and tactics of economic development have become increasingly important aspects of state and local government policy (Schmenner 1991). Industry location and growth are major determinants of the local tax base, and thus the provision of local services (Herzog and Scholttmann 1991). Industrial structuring on the part of New Jersey requires attention to the capabilities and influence of foreign-owned firms in the domestic economy (Wade 1989). A fuller knowledge and understanding of the determinants of inward FDI cannot but enable the government of New Jersey, to take action to ensure that this FDI efficiently promotes the state's economic and social goals (Dunning 1994).

US government policy towards inbound FDI is essentially (with the exception of perceived national security concerns) neutral. This 'hands-off' approach largely permits the 'free play' of market forces in MNE FDI-location decisions (Pugel 1985). In contrast, public policy at the subnational or state level is very 'hands on'. Government policy at the subnational level influences business siting decisions by creating an environment that attracts or repels firms relative to other places. It is expected that MNE managers decide to conduct value-adding activities in a particular area after comparing the potential profit to be earned and the quality-of-life available in one area with the combination of these same factors at other possible sites. But firms of different sizes and in different industries respond differently to the mix of public policies and other locational factors. No single set of policies and locational characteristics, therefore, can broadly attract firms of all different types. As a result, the government of New Jersey must determine the somewhat unique mix of multidimensional public policies consistent with its economic goals. It must be recognized that the strategy of 'doing government well' may not cause all county economies within New Jersey to boom. There may be counties that cannot attract significant levels of economic activity because of characteristics that cannot be altered by policy—for example, natural resource endowments and proximity to markets (Fox and Murray 1991).

The number of dimensions which can or do influence the locational decisions of foreign firms is high. The methodology undertaken for the initial research into the diverse motivations for the location of non-US multinational value-adding activities into NJ was open-ended field interviews with key executives of selected, representative agencies engaging in FDI in New Jersey.[3] In many ways, the results parallel or highlight the academic literature findings (see Wallace 1988). Nine motivations, as revealed by the practitioners interviewed, are summarized and listed below.

3.2.1. Market Access

The size and rate of growth for the American market is probably the most frequently cited reason for investing in the USA (Kieschnick 1981; Pugel 1985; Bartik 1989; US Dept. of Commerce 1991; Crone 1997). The strong regional consumer market based in New York (primarily greater New York City), New Jersey, Connecticut, and Pennsylvania is a critical attribute of the region. The existence of this large and growing market is an attribute which require more erosion prevention, through appropriate macroeconomic strategy, than creation efforts (Plaut and Pluta 1983; Goode 1986).

New Jersey is located in the heart of the world's richest consumer market. More than 60 million consumers with a collective purchasing power of $800 billion are within a 250-mile radius (US Dept. of Commerce). NJ also has the second-highest per capita income in the USA (ibid.). But New Jersey is part of a wider region. And the whole is greater than the sum of its parts. The area generally regarded today as the New York metro-area encompasses twenty-four counties, and 1,849 incorporated cities and towns in parts of New York, New Jersey, and Pennsylvania (Lyne 1995). It includes more than 19 million residents, 8.5 million jobs accounting for personal income of more than $490 billion, seventy-nine members of Fortune 500 companies, including twenty-five of the top 100, seventy-nine headquarters for Fortune 500 firms, more than 78 million air passengers annually, and 20 per cent of world financial assets banked in metro-area institutions (Lyne 1995). 'If you want to be a big player, you have to be in the New York market'—particularly maintaining an office presence in the area, is the view of one management consultant (ibid.).

3.2.2. Labour

In 1995, the results of a manufacturing executive questionnaire show that labour availability and quality is of greater interest to corporate manufacturing-site seekers today than it was only six years ago, a higher percentage than for any other factor rated by the respondents (Maturi 1995). Low labour costs are no longer a major draw in the site selection process—especially at the subnational level within the USA (ibid.). Labour cost minimization emphasis (see studies by Carlton 1979; Bartik 1985; and Papke 1991) has been replaced by the significance of labour availability and quality due to the increasing skill-level needed for activities, which, once rote, now often require decision-making skills and knowledge of highly computerized processes. The availability of skilled workers—which includes the importance of a network of firms in the same industry in a site as well as an undertaking to upgrade labour to suit the needs of an incoming firm— is a crucial determinant of subnational foreign MNE-location strategy, especially for Schumpeter firms (Kieschnick 1981; Hekman 1982; Stafford 1985; Calzonetti and Walker 1991). Companies are taking a closer look at critical skills and benchmark positions to make their facilities as efficient and productive as possible.

Re-engineering of manufacturing processes has created a technology-driven workforce. Within the USA, it is unusual for workers to perform a single unskilled task and the re-engineering trend is affecting operations beyond the traditional manufacturing environment as well. This shift to a higher dimension of work skill from the purely clerical function requires a workforce backed by quality education and training.

In 1995, the New Jersey had a population of approximately eight million people, a labour force of over four million, and an unemployment rate of just over 6 per cent (US Dept. of Commerce). It is not a 'right-to-work' state.[4] The regionally competitive states of New York, Pennsylvania, and Connecticut are also not 'right-to-work' states.[5] Table 8.4 addresses the issue of unionization from the perspective of right-to-work legislation for comparable states.

Table 8.4 shows that right-to-work states among the top competitive states have increased their share of the total FDI coming into the USA over the 21-year period from 12.9 to 19.0 per cent. These data have two possible interpretations: firstly, inward FDI may be consciously seeking out regions which have corporate friendly labour laws (the executive interviews indicated that Germany is such an example); secondly, the growth of inward FDI during the period has been predominantly in production activities in which the costs of labour are relatively important so that FDI strategically locates in right-to-work states. The two factors are mutually compatible with both rather than any single one contributing to the relative redistribution of FDI.

In addition, the emphasis on the availability and quality of skilled labour is affected by the existence of the North American Free Trade agreement (NAFTA) and the globalization of international trade. In recent years, footloose activities requiring less in the way of labour skills are seldom located in the USA and certainly not in the North-East. Straightforward resource endowment theories of international trade recognize that industries in which rote learning and undemanding repetitive tasks constitute the major part of the production process will be most effectively performed 'offshore' (for example, East Asia, northern

TABLE 8.4. Competitive states' right-to-work legislation

State Right-to-work	1974 and 1995		FDI employment ('000s)	
	Yes	No	1974	1995
1. New York		N	146.6	348.7
2. California		N	104.4	549.6
3. New Jersey		N	79.4	209.3
4. Illinois		N	71.4	235.6
5. Pennsylvania		N	56.5	232.9
6. Texas	Y		50.1	320.7
7. Ohio		N	44.3	218.0
8. North Carolina	Y		41.7	224.9
9. Michigan		N	31.3	164.1
10. Wisconsin		N	29.7	71.5
11. Florida	Y		25.3	209.6
12. Georgia	Y		22.2	180.3
Total No. of right-to-work comparable states	4	8		
Total FDI employment in the right-to-work comparable states			139.3	935.5
Total FDI employment in the USA			1,083.4	4,928.3
Per cent			12.9	19.0

Source: Greenwald (1994) compiled by the author.

Mexico, or the Caribbean nations). NAFTA has significantly reduced the impediments to the passage of goods and Mexico's *maquiladora* policy has made northern Mexico a low-wage economic appendage of the USA and Canada. NAFTA has also reduced the perceived level of political risk and of risk to intellectual capital so that FDI in Mexico is *pro tanto* facilitated.

There are over fifty-five colleges and universities in New Jersey and many more, such as Columbia University, New York University, the University of Pennsylvania, and Yale within commuting distance as a source for skilled professionals. It is the 'output' of the educational process, rather than its 'inputs' that attracts FDI: it is a long-term phenomenon (Moore *et al.* 1991).

The increased need for technologically sophisticated or skilled workers is part of an overall trend in industry as well as in services: this process can be seen as narrowing the skill gap between different types of activities. This trend puts even greater stress on the educational systems of different regions and will emphasize educational programmes that can be directly applicable to specific enterprise activities. The precise mix of service jobs created in NJ will depend upon the quality of the labour available in the state. Its economic progress is dependent upon the state's successful adaptation and adjustment to this change. New Jersey must take advantage of the more flexible forms of high-end manufacturing and attempt to ultimately anchor the industry to the region's skilled workforce. New Jersey must act to ensure the availability of highly skilled labour to promote FDI investments into Schumpeter industries.

Mia Gray's research (1997) also points out that although New Jersey is host to both Princeton and Rutgers Universities, MNEs in the region have relatively few links with these prestigious institutions. To retain research here and encourage new biopharmaceutical firm formation, she suggests that NJ state policy could increase its investment in our universities' bioscience departments, sponsor scientific forums of interest to private and public sector biopharmaceutical scientists, and encourage entrepreneurial effort in the universities. In addition, the state could encourage a state or regional association of drug producers. Although there is currently a statewide group for biotechnology firms, there is not a corresponding one for pharmaceutical firms or, more importantly, one for both sectors. This type of association could strengthen the regional agglomeration by encouraging an innovative milieu, local linkages between firms, and the 'embeddedness' (Granovetter 1985) of biotechnology and pharmaceutical firms (Gray 1997).

From the research of Parker and Rogers (1995) and Parker (1996), New Jersey could benefit from government policy promotion of a regional approach to workforce skills in the drug-producing industry. Mia Gray's research (1997) suggests that this initiative could be modelled after successful measures in other states such as Wisconsin's Regional Training Program, which has become a national model for training in manufacturing.[6] New Jersey's efforts could involve MNEs, major unions, and interested educational institutions in a joint training effort.

The role for the government of New Jersey is to reduce intrinsic market failure characteristics by upgrading primary and secondary education, encouraging basic research in universities, developing an innovation policy, and help in the financing of high-risk projects, by providing more information—information asymmetry (i.e. ensuring that buyers and sellers have access to the same information and reducing 'haggling' (Williamson 1985)) and by having clearly defined long-term systemic policies, all of which could lead to increased productivity and increased competitiveness.

3.2.3. Infrastructure

'If you build it, they will come.' This was true when 'it' was railroads: jobs and the people to fill them soon followed. The adequacy of a region's infrastructure is tied to future productivity and living standards (Carlino and Mills 1987; Bartik 1989; Mofidi and Stone 1990). According to the OECD (1994), a 1 per cent rise in infrastructure stock is associated with a 1 per cent increase in gross domestic product (GDP)—infrastructure capacity grows in step with economic output (Pennington 1995). It is surprising, therefore, that there are relatively few academic studies on the role of infrastructure in attracting and retaining foreign MNE investment, especially given that infrastructure requirements of investors usually occupy a significant part in FDI-location negotiations (Peck 1996).

Biehl (1991) argues that public investment in infrastructure improves both the levels of productivity of existing businesses and the attractiveness of regions for new investment. Quality, sophisticated, and advanced infrastructure is a significant determinant when firms short-list possible location sites, but by itself infrastructure is rarely viewed as the decisive factor in the final decision (Diamond and Spence 1984; Ball and Pratt 1994). This may be due to the public goods nature of infrastructure which, by definition, refers to those facilities which provide 'the collective and integrative basis of economic activity' (Spence 1992: 229).

Communities around the world are keenly aware of the importance of cutting-edge telecommunications in today's information-intensive corporate facilities (Goddard and Gillespie 1986; Gillespie 1987; Goddard 1988; Gillespie and Richardson 1992). States within the USA and the provinces of Canada are busy installing fibre-optic lines, digital switching systems, and other infrastructure to ensure their place along the much discussed 'information highway'. Successful communities must be able to offer, at competitive prices, a telecommunications infrastructure that is: (i) robust—the breadth and depth of available technology; (ii) reliable—a zero tolerance for 'down time'; and (iii) available—so that data flow is never interrupted (Venable 1995b). The telecommunications infrastructure is an increasingly important aspect of the group of support services that qualify as 'technological infrastructure'.[7]

Peck (1996) points out that potential inward investors focus in upon not only the general level and quality of such infrastructure in a geographic area, but that they are also trying to meet their own specific requirements through customized space. This concept of a tailored infrastructure, also shown in the research works of Amin *et al.* (1994), Young and Hood (1993), Young, Hood, and Peters (1994), and Wheeler and Mody (1992) in regards to FDI retention issues of clustering and embeddedness, has interesting implications for New Jersey state policymakers.

3.2.4. Regulatory Environment

The regulatory or commercial environment includes the 'hassle costs' of doing business as well as the degree of restriction on activities that the region of location imposes through government. Examples are: (i) the existence of safety laws governing workers; (ii) the freedom of action of firms with respect to pricing products and cooperative strategic alliances; (iii) environmental protection legislation; and (iv) the time required for permit-approval processing. While investment incentives, differences in labour availability, and costs, etc., may affect *de novo* FDI, ever-increasing globalization is likely to enhance the importance of other locational variables. These include the general business climate within the subregion for international investment and trade, the extent of regional integration, the efficiency of markets for intermediate products transferred across national boundaries, the international market structure in which MNEs compete, and economies of scale. Finding an optimum degree of regulation and focusing on generating a cost-efficient means of regulating, in which compliance costs are identified as a cost of doing business, are also components of macro-organizational strategy.

Several academic studies (UNCTC 1988, 1989; Contractor 1990; UNCTAD 1993, 1994) have shown that a negative correlation exists between inward FDI and imposed regulatory requirements. The research of Wint (1992) describes foreign firms as 'most interested' in the actual investment climate in which they will operate.

The executive interviews conducted suggest that there has, in the past, been a sense that the state of New Jersey was anti-business. This perception persisted for a time, when businesses, seeking to expand facilities, found themselves caught in the state's regulatory and permitting process. The vice-president of a major chemical MNE is reported (Houston 1995) as saying that he would not even try to modernize the company's large plant in New Jersey because the permitting process would take longer than the technological life-span of the new equipment the company wanted to install. Houston (ibid.) cites one study, listing states that were best for business from a regulatory standpoint, which placed New Jersey third from the bottom: only Alaska and Hawaii were worse.

The regulation and regulatory difficulties experienced by firms in New Jersey—both the antagonistic attitude of personnel and the bureaucracy that they administer—are substantial. It routinely takes six months to get a permit in New Jersey against thirty to ninety days in, for example, North Carolina. This disadvantage turns into a revenue loss for MNEs. In today's global knowledge-economy speed-to-market and first-mover advantages are becoming increasingly significant and put a premium on rapid permit approval (Dunning, Chapter 1 of this volume; Stalk and Hout 1990; Smith and Reinertsen 1991).[8] With respect to New Jersey's environmental regulations, it is not so much the concept of compliance with environmental regulations that poses a problem for business as it is the administration of the regulations (Schmenner 1982; Hake, Ploch, and Fox 1985; Stafford 1985; Bartik 1988; McConnell and Schwab, 1990; Duffy-Deno 1992; Garofalo and Malhotra 1995; Houston 1995).

These examples point out an aspect of New Jersey's policies towards business that is in need of overhaul. It is the essence of the problem of efficiency with which government operates in trying to minimize the costs for itself and its sought-after clients to enforce the values of the community.

New Jersey is generally recognized as a low-tax state. It has one of the lowest corporate income tax structures in the North-East. There is no net worth tax, no business personal property tax, no commercial rent or occupancy tax, and no retail gross-receipts tax. In addition, there exist four foreign-trade zones (Port Elizabeth in Essex County, Mount Olive in Morris County, Port Salem in Salem County, and Mercer County Airport). Within these zones, businesses may manufacture, assemble, process, and exhibit merchandise without paying customs duties until the goods are moved into the distribution system for sale in the USA. If re-exported, no duty is assessed on the merchandise.

The NJ government can help create more friendly (less imperfect) markets as indeed can firms by a voice strategy (i.e. reduce market failure) or they can intervene directly and replace markets—an exit strategy. In a market-friendly approach, the government of New Jersey must allow markets to function well by concentrating their interventions on areas in which markets prove inadequate (Dunning 1992).

3.2.5. Incentives

State governments, like firms—but on behalf of their constituents—compete with each other for resources and markets increasingly through the provision of investment incentives. Financial incentives affect the profitability of MNEs directly. They may include everything from subsidized job training programmes and moving expense reimbursement, foreign trade and enterprise zones, to tax credits and rebates, loan assistance, and reduced rates for utility consumption.[9] Such incentives are important because they can be clearly defined, their effect is easily calculated, and they can be entered directly into net-present-value computations.[10]

The corporate interviews and practitioner literature review for this dissertation reveal that incentives are increasing in significance as a FDI-location determinant at the subnational level within the USA. Other things being equal, incentives within the USA are designed to 'tilt the scales' in favour of a particular state as host for FDI. While companies definitely seek the location that works for them from an operational standpoint, many companies view a widening range of communities as virtually equal. When competing sites are essentially equal in all other key location criteria, incentives can, and do, make the difference between winning or losing.

The significance of incentives as a determinant influencing the location strategy of MNEs, at other than the subnational level, is debatable.[11] However, from UNCTAD (1996) research, incentives do appear to have an effect on investors' decisions within a country. This suggests, that incentives, as with marketing and promotion efforts (see Sect. 3.2.7 below), become more important *at the margin*, especially for projects that are cost-oriented and footloose. New Jersey should limit its concern to the incentive packages (and the efficiency of their delivery) of states which are direct competitors.

Efforts to influence the locational decisions of MNEs have led many governments to offer incentives to attract investment into their borders and often away from other geographic areas. Established firms (both indigenous and foreign) may, by threatening to leave the geographic area, be able to capture an incentive. 'Whipsawing'[12] and investment contests result when two or more states *vie* to attract the location of a specific investment (Atik 1992).

Not everyone is a fan of incentives, but the trend towards more and bigger incentive packages seems to be gaining momentum. Communities react to what the competition is doing so it ends up being a vicious cycle or downward spiral. One counterthrust within the USA is already apparent. An attorney from North Carolina has filed a lawsuit to challenge local governments' use of cash incentives to recruit and retain business. The lawsuit charges that local economic development programmes that give public moneys to private companies violate the state's constitution. Another source of opposition is public employee unions that are often opposed to the give-aways because they undercut the revenue base —public tax funds—on which their remuneration and fringe benefits rely. Similarly, urban politicians tend to oppose incentives because they facilitate development in outlying areas further draining the economic base for urban core areas (Venable 1995*a*). Voluntary guidelines aimed at calling a halt or at least a temporary cease-fire in the incentive bidding wars in the USA were passed by the National Governors' Association in 1993, but there seems to be little evidence that American state government officials are following those guidelines.[13]

Many of the incentive and promotion efforts of the New Jersey government have been unfocused in relation to source country and/or industrial sector. OECD (1994) research shows that the effectiveness of such an approach should be questioned both for the value for dollar spent and in terms of seeking long-lasting improvements in the competitiveness of the state for its inward FDI stock position.

The government of New Jersey must therefore ensure that incentives and incentive packages are negotiated realistically, implemented effectively, administered efficiently, and monitored closely. New Jersey's long-term competitive advantages do not lie in short-term advantages gained through incentives (OECD 1994). It may be advantageous for the state of NJ to lobby the federal government for acceptable curtailments on interstate incentive wars. Or, failing the will to do this, implement an unbiased review system to ensure that negotiated incentive packages work to the best advantage of both the state's MNEs and its constituents.

3.2.6. Access

In order to gain or sustain competitive advantage in today's global economy, the efficient movement of goods to market is of primary importance. This involves efficient intermodal systems linking together different transportation modes. The ability of the intermodal system to transfer cargo from one mode of transportation to another without additional packing and handling makes it efficient, cost-effective, and fast. The efficiency of this kind of infrastructure is especially important for a region that has its large consumer market as a prime attribute.

To access major markets, New Jersey offers more than 35,000 miles of highways, twelve airports, the Port of Newark/Elizabeth, and the most railroad track per square mile in the USA (US Dept. of Commerce). Competition for US distribution business from Montreal, Quebec—North America's closest major port to northern Europe—has long played a key role in handling international freight with origin or destination in the USA (Bowman 1995). According to Bowman, Montreal's port has, for years, taken substantial volumes of European cargoes away from the Port Authority of New York and New Jersey. And, although this region's costs have come down considerably since then, Montreal still commands a meaningful share of the North Atlantic trade, especially since the implementation of the Canada/USA Free Trade Agreement in the late 1980s and more recently, NAFTA.

The efficiency of the available transportation network creates the potential for efficient distribution of goods to regional hinterlands as well as overseas markets (Kieschnick 1981; Hekman 1982; Schmenner 1982; Crone 1997). The Port Newark/Port Elizabeth facility in northern NJ accounts for more than 75 per cent of the total tonnage that moves through New York harbour and is one of the largest container ports in the world. Air cargo traffic at Newark International airport is more than 650,000 tons annually. When the new air cargo facility at Newark becomes operational, cargo capacity will double (ibid.). The dredging of the port is the most important issue facing the state's economy. There are 180,000 jobs and a $20 billion economy linked to the port which, together with the financial markets, is the fulcrum of the region (Bansal 1996; Crone 1997).

New Jersey has the physical location advantage of a time zone which is relatively compatible with that of Europe. Dennis Donovan, in an interview, explained that the simple fact that supervisors are awake during the normal working hours gives this state an advantage for inbound European direct investment. But technology improvements are gradually expanding the traditional 9 to 5 'same place/same time' concept giving way to the 'anytime/anyplace' office—a fact that must be considered in the business development, retention, and attraction issue.

The issue of trade-offs between time and space is heightened with foreign as opposed to domestic direct investment. Investments in transportation and communications infrastructure aim to reduce not only the monetary costs of movement over space, but the reduction of time in circulation (Schoenberger 1997). Distance equals time because, as Marx noted, 'the important thing is not the market's distance in space but the speed with which it can be reached' (quoted in Schoenberger 1997: 22). Schoenberger points out how the upheaval in today's competitive environment and the associated time-space transformation has profound implications for the organization of production systems, the chances of MNE survival, and the life prospects of different regions in the global economy.

3.2.7. State Information Availability

Investment promotion represents efforts by the government of New Jersey (and other interested parties such as PSE&G) to transfer information to foreign investors about the nature of the state's investment climate, and to persuade and assist MNEs to invest, expand investments, and continue to maintain their investment(s) in the state (Wells and Wint 1990; Wint 1992). The annual budgets other subnational entities allocate for business retention or expansion are considerably higher than New Jersey's—just over \$0.5 million annually (New York \$3.1 million; California \$2.9 million; North Carolina \$2.4 million; Alabama and Virginia \$1.3 million each. The city of Jacksonville spends \$3 million a year. Charlotte and Kansas City spend \$20 million each).

Wint (1992) emphasizes the significance of marketing in New Jersey. His research points out that investment promotion operates 'at the margin'—most successful in situations where the MNE has identified the particular region of the world to produce (i.e. NAFTA, the USA, or the New York City area). In other words, at the subnational level.

Modelling techniques now play a part in site selection by generating a 'short list' (i.e. they are capable of eliminating obvious misfits). Some state and regional investment-promoting administrations have facilitated their inclusion in such models by having data on the state easily available from electronic sources. In South Carolina, the geographic information system provides comprehensive information about vacant parcels of land, zoning ordinances, population distribution, and projected population growth rates. It becomes a market as well as a site location aid. In New Jersey, PSE&G Company has developed a self-contained compact disc to address many of the questions that prospective site selectors may be interested in. New Jersey must focus its efforts and expenditures to create interest in markets where firms have viable strategic reasons to seek out the state as a location for their value-adding activities—to those firms, in those markets that would likely find NJ's investment climate both attractive and competitive.

Every state and hundreds of communities currently use the Web to attract companies, open new markets for business, and to promote tourism (Du Brow 1996). New Jersey, through PSE&G, shares a Web site and is presently developing a location of its own as an economic development tool for the state.

According to Bob Henningsen, Bureau Chief of Marketing and National Expansions for the Iowa Department of Economic Development in Des Moines, 'the states that succeed will be those that manage their information best and can present it to their best advantage' (Venable 1995a). This is the comparative cost of information that clarifies the MNE's potential status *vis-à-vis* its competitors (Schoenberger 1997).

This research acknowledges the general problem of uncertainty and imperfect information.[14] In addition, it points out human tendencies (such as bounded rationality and risk-aversion) and market imperfections—location specialists, state promoters, and business consultants do not convey perfect information or indeed the same information to all who inquire. Timely and low-cost access to accurate information on the realities of New Jersey are essential to foreign firms contemplating locating value-adding activities in the state. Marketing the state as a 'good place' to conduct business is important in order that MNE executives can be made aware of New Jersey as a possibility in their site selection decision-making. As information about NJ is made available to these MNE managers, awareness is increased and uncertainty and risk reduced.

Following the research of Wint (1992), FDI promotion for NJ should include: (i) image building activities, such as advertising, that seek to build a favourable image of New Jersey for inward FDI; (ii) investment-generating activities, such as presentations to specific firms, that try to generate investment directly; and (iii) investment service activities, such as providing information and assistance in obtaining permits that provide a variety of services to prospective (i.e. FDI attraction) as well existing (i.e. follow-up support—FDI retention) investors. Wint's research cautions promoters—the government of New Jersey must carefully consider the interaction and trade-off between the generation of: (i) FDI and (ii) a favourable investment climate.

Investment promotion efforts should be pursued when New Jersey is confident that it has an acceptable product to market. Potential FDI and regional promotional models (see for example the research of Brown in Chapter 17 of this volume) should be investigated. A perfect investment climate in New Jersey is not a necessary prerequisite for promoting the state as a 'good place for international business', but New Jersey should not be significantly less attractive than that of competing states. If it is, or could be eroded into such, New Jersey must further its efforts to gain an acceptable, competitive climate for international investment, then market it!

3.2.8. Quality of Life

Quality-of-life considerations can be important attributes of a site but the importance varies according to the size of the locating company; individual preferences of its top management; and the activity to be undertaken (Kolz 1995). The mix of transferees and new hires is also important. In the 1990s, two quality-of-life issues have become highly publicized—children's education and local crime. Others are the availability of affordable housing, climate, groceries for diets based on national culture, and places of worship.

New Jersey seems to be most noted for its accessibility to the cultural and sports entertainment of New York City and Philadelphia. But it has its own symphony, opera, and ballet companies. There are more than 235 golf courses, the Meadowlands Sports Complex, and vast pinelands, hills, and beaches along the 127-mile Jersey shore (Venable 1995a). Atlantic City is home to gambling casinos; there is also the Thomas H. Kean New Jersey State Aquarium, the NJ Performing Arts Center, and the Liberty Science Center offering additional activities for people of all ages.

If quality-of-life issues were the major criteria for locating a company, then the rural, relatively unpopulated, outdoor recreational-oriented areas of the country would soon be overpopulated and the cities would be empty. If, on the other hand, social and cultural factors were paramount, then the opposite would be true: everyone would be moving to the larger urban centres. But neither of course is solely the case. It depends upon individual preferences of management, their perceived preferences of employees, and upon economic and other operating costs.

George Tobjy, an executive with KPMG Peat Marwick, stated in one of the executive interviews that 'the service base for international business is in the four northern New Jersey counties—the beaches at the New Jersey shore are not the draw.'

3.2.9. Clusters of Firm Activities

'When analysing the local environment of globally competitive firms, geographic clustering of production appears as a striking feature' (OECD 1994: 4). Clusters of economic activity have been addressed and analysed by political economists, sociologists, political scientists, geographers, and international business scholars. In the fields of regional economics, development economics, and economic geography, regional growth and decline, location patterns of economic activity and regional economic structure are well-developed domains of inquiry. Economic geography theory on the potential benefit (and implicitly the attractiveness) of location in a cluster is based on agglomeration economies. The theory on the formation of 'industrial districts' is based on organizational dynamics.

Business scholars focusing on the MNE (such as Prahalad and Doz 1987; Bartlett and Ghoshal 1990; Hedlund and Rolander 1990; Ridderstrale 1997) have conveyed doubts about the local environment as having any important role to play for how global firms formulate their location strategies and build competitiveness (Malmberg, Solvell, and Zander 1996). The research of Appold (1995) argues that in order for spatial clustering to be viewed as a location determinant—having the potential for a positive effect on organizational performance—forward-thinking MNEs would have to choose locations in anticipation of improved operational advantages. Appold points out that firms may be advantaged by seeking out better-performing distant suppliers rather than being constrained to the potential suppliers available within the cluster. Location in a cluster, therefore, appears to be neither a necessary nor a sufficient explanation for enhanced performance, successful collaboration, or as a determinant. Indeed, Appold (ibid.) finds no support for the contention that location in a cluster increases establishment performance. In addition, due to advancements in communication technologies, MNEs may no longer need to be as closely huddled in order to gain agglomeration economies.

Historically, both the classical and neoclassical schools of economics have analysed determinants of the business-location decision as if atomized (Granovetter 1985, 1992) from the influence of relations with others, of these others' decisions and behaviours, and from the history of these relations. These traditional approaches fail to capture the intertwining relationships of today's global economic reality. Marshall, more than a century ago, made a point of this 'social effect' of localization when it comes to the promotion of upgrading:

When an industry has thus chosen a locality for itself, it is likely to stay there long: so great are the advantages which people following the same skilled trade get from near neighborhood to one another. The mysteries of the trade become no mysteries; but are as it were in the air, and children learn many of them unconsciously. Good work is rightly appreciated, inventions and improvements in machinery, in processes and the general organization of the business have their merits promptly discussed: if one man (or woman) starts a new idea, it is taken up by others and combined with suggestions of their own; and thus it becomes the source of new ideas. And presently subsidiary trades grow up in the neighbourhood, supplying it with implements and materials. (Marshall 1890/1916: 271)

This socioeconomic approach to the clustering of firms is also grounded in the works of Weber (1922) who presents in the famous chapter 'Sociological Categories of Economic Action' his theoretical programme for economic sociology.

Results from practitioner interviews (Gray and Wallace 1996) stress that the economy of New Jersey is part of the social world, it cannot and should not therefore be isolated from society. Information flows are commonly cited as both the reason for and result of firm clusters. But, 'information flows between people rather than between plants' (Casson and Paniccia 1995: 8).

To the extent that New Jersey may be disadvantaged due to its high costs of labour and as a relatively high cost-of-living state its attractiveness to high value-adding activity requiring highly trained and often specialized employees is a major issue. The attraction and retention of managerial and technical personnel are vital for these high value-adding, white-collar demanding facilities. 'Locations that have a demonstrable supply of these workers will have an advantage; other locations must prove that the local quality-of-life factors are such that these workers can be readily attracted to the area' (Ady 1986: 80) (see also Hoechst 1979).

Large urban regions (through quality-of-life, labour pools, and transportation accessibility) offer considerable advantages to critical corporate activities in a knowledge-based economy. The attraction of large urban areas is likely to be even stronger for dual-career couples, which have become an important component of the labour force (von Glinow 1988). Dual-career couples reinforce the effect of agglomeration, particularly for high-technology firms (Malecki 1987, 1991; Gibbs *et al.* 1985; Ady 1986; Macgregor *et al.* 1986; Breheny and McQuaid 1987; Oakey and Cooper 1989).

Worker preferences do not 'determine' the location of R&D or of high-technology MNEs generally (Storper and Scott 1989). Rather it shows that the common interests of mobile professionals and of their employers may be satisfied best in areas possessing such attributes. R&D workers, like other professionals, are mobile in the sense that their relative scarcity gives them labour market mobility, but they are in effect geographically somewhat immobile in that they are willing to live only in distinct types of places (Buswell 1983). This parallels the discussion of the MNE which although 'footloose' is constrained in its location options to those geographic areas that provide immobile attributes for its goal of increasing long-term competitiveness (see Dunning's reference to this in Chapter 1 of this volume). Clusters of firms, due to the tremendous costs of relocation, are more than just a temporary situation. A reason for their 'stickiness' (Markusen 1996) is that the economic relations are embedded in networks and enhanced by other than pure economic forces—the local milieu.

The popular notion of embeddedness (Granovetter 1985) facilitates understanding of the conceptual interconnection between the structure of clusters and the social action which influences them. Embeddedness, as used in this research to describe FDI retention, requires strong backward, forward, and horizontal linkages (Young, Hood and Peters 1994). Durkheim (1964) emphasized 'how pure economic action fails to bind people together for more than a few moments' (Swedberg and Granovetter 1992: 7).

Transaction costs are inherent in the executive recruitment and retention issue. In addition, social costs are exacerbated in this globalizing world by the issue of the 'trailing spouse'. Many MNE executives accept employment with the understanding that international relocations to subsidiary locations may be necessary. Trailing spouses, as a result of strict immigration and employment laws existing in host countries, are not allowed to work, or, at the very least, are significantly delayed in obtaining documentation to enable work in the foreign area. Social costs are therefore experienced indirectly by MNEs as the spouses of executives (often faced with cultural and language barriers) experience isolation and depression—'international wives, miserable lives'. Such social costs become naturally integrated into the transaction costs of business for the MNE.

4. Policy Implications for the Advancement of Theory

4.1. **Introduction**

This chapter has argued that the intranational distribution of inward FDI stock provides a sensitive guide to the attractiveness of a subnational units' resources, capabilities, and policies (Gray and Wallace 1996). The usual analysis of FDI at the national level is no longer sufficient, nor perhaps necessary, to gain the detailed understanding of the drivers of the international economy. FDI, it is proposed, can only be fully understood by viewing it from the subnational level. Krugman's (1995) 'new' geographical economics suggests that analysis of the process of economic development within nations can increase understanding of global trade and investment flows.

Many similarities are found between a national and subnational inbound FDI investigation. Examples fall within the broad motivation categories of inward FDI such as: (i) market-seeking FDI (i.e. market size) and (ii) strategic-asset-seeking FDI (i.e. to gain access to and/or acquire technological and/or managerial know-how). In addition, theories on issues of broad monetary and fiscal policy from, for example, Aliber's partial macrofinancial or exchange rate theory (i.e. the value of the currency and interest rates) as well as the research from Kobrin (1995) on political risk (one exception is the province of Quebec in Canada) set at the national level are as sufficient to aid understanding of inward FDI-location decision-making at the national level as at the subnational level. MNE location decisions in these areas can be dealt with accurately within the current academic literature.

The research contained in Part Three of this volume (relating to Scotland, Australia, Korea, Bangalore, Singapore, and Hong Kong) as well as the works of Graham and Krugman (1989, 1991, 1995) and Pugel (1985), on FDI into the USA, and Dunning (1985, 1988) on the UK's foreign direct investment position, provide researchers with excellent examples of national FDI studies whose methodology can be easily adapted and applied to subnational inward FDI investigations, particularly related to the significance and source of inbound FDI. Likewise, the empirical revealed comparative advantage (RCA) analysis—which facilitates understanding of the industrial concentration of inbound FDI, as seen in the research of Dunning (1985) and Pugel (1985)—along with the comparable location quotient (LQ) analysis popular with scholars in economic geography and related disciplines—serve the analysis of this subject equally well at the national or subnational level, given of course that quality industry-level data exist or can be made available to researchers.

Both governmental units, federal and state, are concerned with increasing the welfare of the people located within its political jurisdiction. Both the country and the subnational unit contained within gain competitive advantage by upgrading the quality of their indigenous resources and the competitive position of the firms located within their borders. One distinction, however, relates to the spillover effects of public policy. It is expected that both positive and negative spillover effects of public policy and their influence on productivity, competition, and human capital formation will be greater between and among subnational units than between and among national units given the simple assumption that increased overriding similarities exist within a nation than between and among nations.

Many subtle, yet distinct differences, however exist between national and subnational inward FDI investigations. Such differences among subnational geographic unit offerings to the MNE location decision-maker are due to their separate and individual control over public policy—the priority each places on created assets, in that increasingly location-specific assets have themselves become created assets—and God-given endowments. Although no new variables need to be introduced to specifically address subnational level investigations, the broad issues of firm clustering and the determinants of MNE location are more appropriately examined at the subnational rather than the national level.

Subtle yet distinct aspects of MNE subnational location-specific determinants are as follows:

1. Geography and climate, although the presence of natural assets (or traditional 'resource-seeking' FDI) is no longer of pivotal importance in deciding the location of FDI especially in those sectors and industries which are technology or capital intensive (Dunning and Narula 1995).
2. Access to port facilities.
3. Quality of infrastructure including transportation and communications infrastructure.

4. To gain geographic proximity to a spatial agglomeration of related value-added activities.
5. Quality of education.
6. Costs of living (i.e. housing costs and auto insurance rates).
7. Labour costs and 'right-to-work' legislation.
8. Labour mobility with particular emphasis here to professional and highly skilled workers who, at the subnational level of investigation, are geographically mobile without the need for relocation (i.e. an individual may have been raised in New York, educated at Yale, and be seeking employment within the pharmaceutical industry cluster located in New Jersey never once having left the 'tri-state' area or the 'permanent' residence).
9. Quality and price of natural resources.
10. Prices of internationally immobile inputs.
11. Tariffs and non-tariff barriers or 'foreign trade and enterprise zones'.
12. Economies of marketing such as the proximity to New York City.
13. Incentives 'that appear to shape the new regional pattern of FDI' (OECD 1994: 30) and impact site decision making 'at the margin'.
14. Psychic distance and quality-of-life issues impacting executive recruitment and retention.
15. Market access including the efficient movement of goods to market.
16. Market share and size or the size of the market within the New Jersey, New York, Connecticut 'tri-state' region.
17. Regulatory environment or the 'business climate', including speed to market considerations.
18. Inward FDI promotion.
19. Transaction costs of using the market.
20. Idiosyncratic high customer-tailoring requirements.
21. Tacit and non-codifiable knowledge and information.
22. Highly segmented markets leading to increased opportunities for price discrimination.
23. Trading location-specific advantages over space.

The current OLI framework for analysis of international production, stemming from the research of Dunning (1977, 1993, 1995) is an excellent and appropriate tool to aid subnational inward FDI research. The eclectic paradigm identifies three types of advantages: (O) ownership-specific advantages endogenous to firms; (I) internalization incentive advantages which recognize that without incentives to internalize the markets for and production of technology, FDI would give way to licensing agreements or the outright sale of knowledge on a contractual basis; and (L) location-specific advantages or factors that favour production either at home or abroad. The EP is, therefore, a juxtaposition of not only national but also subnational characteristics as well as industry characteristics, in the location advantages of both countries and subnational units, with the ownership-specific advantages of firms.

Partial interdisciplinary theories and Porter's (1990) national 'diamond of competitive advantage' require modification to expand their level of focus beyond that of the national level to the subnational level—the drivers of international trade and foreign direct investment.

5. Conclusions

Because of the increased mobility of foreign direct investment different blocs. countries, regions, and states compete in efforts to attract and retain the 'right kind' of businesses and their investments into their borders in order to counteract the technological forces which lead to structural unemployment. New Jersey is susceptible to an exodus of industries (and jobs) attracted elsewhere by the perception of greener pastures. It has therefore become necessary for New Jersey to understand the determinants of FDI location in order to strive to supply greater economic advantages relative to those obtainable in competing states: to be dynamically competitive (Gray and Wallace 1996).

As the research presented in this chapter has revealed, the state of New Jersey is slowly losing ground with respect to its FDI stock position relative to other states in the USA. A reversal of this 'trend' is a process requiring time, but, once began, the pattern can be self-reinforcing (Larre and Torres 1991).[15] A goal for improvement is however, insufficient. From the research of Elmslie and Milberg (1996), Portugal failed to converge (in the positive sense) not because of a lack of systemic government intervention, but as a result of its misdirection and perhaps mismanagement. Government intervention and a long-term systemic government policy are therefore necessary but insufficient conditions for conversion.

No assumption is made in this research that inward FDI is a purely beneficial phenomenon. However, in order to attract the 'right kind' of MNE activity and to increase the likelihood that beneficial effects will result, the government of New Jersey must take certain actions. The research of Wallace (1998) has shown that history and geography matter—the path-dependence nature of inward FDI. Policy-makers must therefore seek to learn from the successes and failures of New Jersey in the past as well as from the experiences of other countries and states. 'The optimum policy mix depends upon the natural and inherited attributes of the region' (Gray and Wallace 1996: 15).

The concept of a strong and positive New Jersey government does not necessarily imply more government intervention in economic affairs, but rather better focused state government involvement. What is necessary, is an ideology on behalf of the New Jersey government which is coherent and adaptable and where there is the least distance between the prevailing ideology and the actual practice of the state's institutions (Lodge and Vogle 1987). New Jersey must not be guided by the laissez-faire philosophy for government action present during the time of Adam Smith (1776) when the disbenefits of non-market intervention were perceived to be greater than the benefits (Dunning 1997).[16] It must not focus more on redistributing than creating; give in to interest groups pressures not related to enhanced competitiveness; further distort markets; create undesirable social effects; invite retaliation; discourage inbound FDI; and/or cause more problems than it solves (Dunning 1994). The government of New Jersey must try to get rid of the typical American focus on Jefferson's 'the best government is the government that governs least'. Even if this were found to be valid domestically, it fails in today's knowledge-intensive globalizing economy. The distinction must be made between government leadership and control.

The set of multidimensional policies requires selectivity on the part of the New Jersey government. The research presented in this chapter shows that some sectors and products are more important to the economy of New Jersey's future growth prospects than others (Wade 1989). A 1994 OECD study showed that regions are relatively successful at attracting FDI in their own specialty industry. Any strategy towards attracting FDI, therefore, has a greater chance to succeed when the existing regional production structure is taken into account. It is therefore suggested that the government focus its promotion and incentive policies in line with its competitive advantage, increasing its potential to attract the 'right kind of MNE', alter and enhance comparative advantage. It must identify priority areas according to its comparative advantage; the actions of competing states; its political system; stage of development; size; and industrial structure—the overall OLI configuration (Dunning 1977). Research has shown that government has a role to play in shaping the 'diamond of competitive advantage' in a country (Porter 1990; Dunning 1997).

New Jersey has a 'specialized centre of excellence' (see Dunning, Chapter 1 of this volume) in knowledge-based activities in the chemicals and pharmaceutical industry. To the extent that the accumulation and exploitation of intellectual capital in today's globalizing economy is a significant wealth creator and magnet for positive spillover effects, a priority of the government must include the nurturing of this cluster of economic activities. New Jersey's explicit, overall public policies towards the continual upgrading of indigenous innovatory activity (including R&D) are relatively competitive when weighed against competitive states within the USA. However, when analysed from a budgetary perspective, the efforts of the government of New Jersey pale in comparison.

The government of NJ must have a commitment to building up the competitiveness of the economy by its macroeconomic and industrial policies; enhancing the natural attributes of the area; and facilitating the creation of location-specific advantages in order to attract and retain inward FDI. Both macroeconomic and structural policies (such as the complex web of governmental regulations and taxes that discourage job creation and job search) need to be strengthened to improve FDI growth and its capacity to increase labour market performance.

New Jersey government strategies and policies focus not solely on static state competitiveness but to ones which revolve around the concept of long-term sustainable advantage. It suggests that the government of New Jersey should encourage an assortment of interlinked firms, diversified by sector, size, and occupational requirements—of clusters that will contribute to growth (as MNE investments spur complementary commitments by related firms) and stability (as cross-commitments reduce the mobility of firms) in New Jersey (Schoenberger 1997).

New Jersey government policy-makers may have little or no control over some of the factors relevant to the attraction and retention of FDI into the state. However, with the holistic understanding presented, priorities can be established and promising industry sectors targeted for economic development policy both in the short run and for the long haul (Gray and Wallace 1996).

NOTES

For intellectual guidance and financial support I am indebted to Dr John H. Dunning and the Center for International Business Research, Rutgers University.

1. A few examples are: Sweden (Clegg 1987; Swedenborg 1985); Spain (Benton 1989); Canada (Braithwaite 1975; Globerman 1985; Globerman *et al.* 1994; Caves, Porter and Spence 1979; Caves 1974; Saunders 1982; Gupta 1983); Portugal (Simoes 1985); Italy (Harrison 1992; Stopford 1995); France (Michalet and Chevallier 1985; Wins 1993); Belgium (Van Den Bulcke 1985); Germany (Juhl 1985); the UK (Morris 1988*a*, 1988*b*; Dicken 1987; Collis and Noon 1994; Dunning 1985, 1988; Buckley and Dunning 1976); Wales (Davies and Thomas 1976; Adams 1983); the USA (Pugel 1985, 1986); Latin America (Wallace 1990); Latin America, Asia, and Africa (Hyun and Whitmore 1989); Developing Countries generally (Brewer 1991; Root and Ahmed 1978; Schneider and Frey); India (Kumar 1990; Lall and Mohammed 1983; Lall 1985); Singapore (Lecraw 1985); Korea (Koo 1985); and Japan (Ozawa 1985; Kenney and Florida, 1994; Dunning 1996).

2. The view of local milieux in this dissertation is based on the 'innovative milieu approach' developed predominantly in the French-speaking world (Aydalot 1986; Maillat 1995). The milieu is both a result of and a precondition for learning—an asset that is constantly being produced and reproduced—rather than a passive surface (Coffey and Bailly 1996). It is an environment within which physical and human capital is created and accumulated over time, which translates into sustainable competitiveness among incumbent firms.

3. The descriptive portion of this chapter is an extension of the research of Gray and Wallace (1996) and Dunning and Wallace (1998).

4. Right-to-work refers to state right-to-work laws which mandate that neither membership nor non-membership in a labour union may be made a condition of new or continued employment. Such laws exist in the following 21 states: Alabama, Arizona, Arkansas, Florida, Georgia, Idaho, Iowa, Kansas, Louisiana, Mississippi, Nebraska, Nevada, North Carolina, North Dakota, South Carolina, South Dakota, Tennessee, Texas, Utah, Virginia, and Wyoming.

   In recent years, right-to-work laws (which have the practical effect of making illegal any closed shop, union shop, agency shop, or maintenance-of-membership clauses in union contracts) have been the subject of considerable controversy (Greenwald 1994).

Where right-to-work protection exists, no person can be required, as a condition of employment, to join, assist, or financially contribute to a labour organization.

Right-to-work legislation is per Section 14(b) of the Taft Hartley amendments (1947) to the National Industrial Recovery Act. The first state to provide explicit right-to-work protection was Florida in 1944, the most recent state was Idaho, by statute, in 1986. In only two cases has existing right-to-work protection in the private sector been removed: Indiana in 1965 and Louisiana in 1956, but reenacted in a broader form in 1976.

The research of Greenwald *et al.* (1983) explains that in practice, right-to-work laws have proven to be relatively ineffective, merely giving rise to 'bootleg' closed shops (for further detail refer to Thomas R. Haggard, *Compulsory Unionism: The NLRB and the Courts: A Legal Analysis of Union Security Agreements*, Industrial Research Unit, Wharton School, University of Pennsylvania, Philadelphia, 1977).

5. See studies by Newman (1983); Hake *et al.* (1985); Bartik (1985); Wheat (1986); and Calzonetti and Walker (1991).

6. See Parker and Rogers (1995) for an assessment of the Wisconsin programme.

7. See the research of Wymbs (1996) for a detailed investigation into the telecommunications industry in New Jersey.

8. The research of Smith and Reinertsen (1991), through empirical examples, shows that in rapidly changing markets, a new product to market delay of six months can reduce its lifetime profit yield by a full one-third.

9. Refer to studies by Carlton (1979, 1983); Kieschnick (1981); Hekman (1982); Schmenner (1982); Hake *et al.* (1985); Bartik (1989); and Papke (1991) which show that generally high energy costs are a disadvantage in attracting manufacturing firms.

10. Not all firms include incentives in their net present value computations (Gray and Walter 1983).

11. See studies such as Barlow and Wender (1955); Walker (1965); Ahroni (1966), Robinson (1961); Dunning (1979); Agarwal (1980); and Guisinger and Associates (1985); Arpan (1981) (whose research on regional incentives in the USA found that incentives did not have a significant influence on the investment location of MNEs); and Morse and Farmer (1986); Coughlin *et al.* (1991) (whose research found that differences in state taxes were an important locational determinant).

Agarwal's (1980) research, showing the general ineffectiveness of incentives, is based primarily on developing countries. In this work, he argues that incentives merely compensate for structural disincentives (p. 762). Agarwal does acknowledge that while incentives do not affect the overall FDI flows, they may influence the distribution of inbound FDI in these developing countries.

12. The term 'whipsawing', according to the research of Atik (1992), probably originated in the USA. It originally described the management practice of pitting one plant against another to gain labour concessions. Governments may also be victims of whipsawing. The research of Atik (1992) points out the following example.

In late 1991, General Motors (GM) announced that it would either close its Arlington, Texas plant or its Willow Run, Michigan plant. GM Chairman, Robert Stempel insisted that GM was not whipsawing; GM would make its selection on the basis of efficiency considerations alone. Both Texas and Michigan officials reacted, however, by offering incentives to keep its plant open (see 'Michigan Joins Texas in Bidding War to Save One of Two GM Plants Set to Close' in *Daily Lab. Rep.* (BNA) No. 11, at A10, 16 Jan. 1992).

See also Guisinger (1975) for detailed case studies on the role of incentives in the automobile, international food-processing, computer, and petro-chemical industries.

13. The Commerce Clause of the USA Constitution appears not to limit incentive wars between or among states within the USA. See Cappelletti, Mauro *et al.* (1986), *Integration Through Law: Europe and the American Federal Experience*: 131–2.
14. Supported by the well-known works of Simon (1961); Cyert and March (1963); Akerlof (1984); Williamson (1985); Perrow (1986); and Stinchcombe (1990).
15. This statement utilizes the Larre and Torres (1991) research on convergence.
16. The recent research of Dunning (1997: 8.5 citing the research of Steiner (1953)) points out that classical economists believed that laissez-faire and the 'invisible hand of government' recommendations were not so much about allowing efficient markets to work but rather about not allowing powerful governments to take control. Knowledge regarding the workings of markets and governments has expanded appreciably since then.

REFERENCES

Ady, R. M. (1986), 'Criteria Used for Facility Location Selection', in *Financing Economic Development in the 1980s*, in N. Walzer and D. Chicoine (eds.) (New York: Praeger).

Agarwal, J. P. (1980), *Determinants of Foreign Direct Investment: A Survey Welt Wirtschaftliches Archiv* 116: 739–73.

Amin, A., Bradley, D., Howells, J., Tomaney, J., and Gentle, C. (1994), 'Regional Incentives and the Quality of Mobile Investment in the Less Favoured Regions of the EC', *Progress in Planning* 41(1): 1–112.

Appold, Stephen J. (1995), 'Agglomeration, Interorganizational Networks, and Competitive Performance in the US Metalworking Sector', *Economic Geography* 71: 27–54.

Atik, Jeffery (1992), 'Investment Contests and Subsidy Limitations in the EC', *Virginia Journal of International Law* 32(4): 838–69.

Aydalot, P. (1986), *Milieux Innovateurs en Europe* (Paris: GREMI).

Ball, R., and Pratt, A. (1994), *Industrial Property: Policy and Economic Development* (London: Routledge).

Bansal, Sangeeta (1996), 'The Impact of the Ocean Transportation Industry on a Port: The Case of New York/New Jersey', CIBER Conference Presentation (New Jersey: Rutgers University).

Barlow, E. R., and Wender, I. T. (1955), *Foreign Investment and Taxation* (Englewood Cliffs, NJ: Prentice-Hall).

Bartik, Timothy J. (1985), 'Business Location Decisions in the United States: Estimates of the Effects of Unionization, Taxes, and Other Characteristics of States', *Journal of Business and Economic Statistics* 3(1): 14–23.

—— (1988), 'The Effects of Environmental Regulation on Business Location in the United States', *Growth and Change* 19: 22–44.

—— (1989), 'Small Business Start-ups in the United States: Estimates of the Effects of Characteristics of States', *Southern Economic Journal* 55: 1004–18.

Bartlett, C. A., and Ghoshal, S. (1990), 'Managing Innovation in the Transnational Corporation', in C. A. Bartlett, Y. Doz, and G. Hedlund (eds.), *Managing the Global Firm* (London: Routledge).

Biehl, D. (1991), 'The Role of Infrastructure in Regional Development', in R. W. Vickerman (ed.), *European Research in Regional Science 1. Infrastructure and Regional Development* (London: Pion).

Bowker, R. R. Inc. (1992), *Directory of American Research and Technology*, 26th edn. (New Providence, NJ: R. R. Bowker Co.).

Bowman, Robert J. (1995), 'Assessing Markets: A Global View', *Area Development* 30(Mar.): 35–8.

Breheny, M. J., and McQuaid, R. W. (1987), 'HTUK: The Development of the United Kingdom's Major Centre of High Technology Industry', in M. J. Breheny and R. W. McQuaid (eds.), *The Development of High Technology Industries: An International Survey* (London: Croom Helm).

Buswell, R. J. (1983), 'Research and Development and Regional Development', in A. Gillespie (ed.), *Technological Change and Regional Development* (London: Pion).

Calzonetti, F. J., and Walker, Robert T. (1991), 'Factors Affecting Industrial Location Decisions: A Survey Approach', in H. W. Herzog and Alan M. Scholttman (eds.), *Industry Location and Public Policy* (Knoxville: University of Tennessee Press).

Carlino, Gerald A., and Mills, Edwin S. (1987), 'The Determinants of Country Growth', *Journal of Regional Science* 27: 39–54.

Carlton, Dennis W. (1979), 'Why New Firms Locate Where They Do: An Econometric Model', in W. C. Wheaton (ed.), *Interregional Movements and Regional Growth* (Washington, DC: Urban Institute).

—— (1983), 'The Location of Employment Choices of New Firms: An Econometric Model with Discrete and Continuous Endogenous Variables', *Review of Economics and Statistics* 65: 440–9.

Casson, Mark, and Paniccia, Ivana (1995), 'Business Networks and Industrial Districts: A Comparison of Northern Italy and South Wales', Working Paper 301, Series A, Vol. VII, Dept. of Economics, University of Reading.

Castells, M., and Henderson, J. (1987), 'Techno-economic Restructuring, Socio-political Processes and Spatial Transformation: A global perspective', in J. Henderson and M. Castells (eds.), *Global Restructuring and Territorial Development* (London: Sage).

Coffey, William, and Bailly, Antoine (1996), 'Economic Restructuring: A Conceptual Framework', in W. Lever and A. Bailly (eds.), *The Spatial Impact of Economic Changes in Europe* (Aldershot, UK: Ashgate): 13–39.

Contractor, Farok J. (1990), 'Ownership Patterns of US Joint Ventures Abroad and the Liberalization of Foreign Government Regulations in the 1980s: Evidence from Benchmark Surveys', *Journal of International Business Studies* 1(1): 55–73.

Coughlin, Cletus C. (1992), 'Foreign-owned Companies in the United States: Malign or Benign?' *Federal Reserve Bank of St Louis Review* 74(3): 17–31.

Crone, Theodore M. (1997), 'Where Have All the Factory Jobs Gone—and Why?' *Business Review* (May/June): 3–18.

Diamond, D., and Spence, N. (1984), 'Infrastructure and Regional Development: Theories', *Built Environment* 10: 262–9.

Doms, Mark, and Jensen, J. Bradford (1995), 'A Comparison Between the Operating Characteristics of Domestic and Foreign Owned Manufacturing Establishments in the United States', Working Paper prepared for the Conference on Research in Income and

Wealth conference on Geography and Ownership as Bases for Economic Accounting, May (paper dated July).

Du Brow, M. L. (1996), 'Surveying the Web', *Area Development* 31 (Mar.): 34–8.

Duffy-Deno, Kevin T. (1992), 'Pollution Abatement Expenditures and Regional Manufacturing Activity', *Journal of Regional Science* 32: 419–36.

Dunning, John H. (1977), 'Trade, Location of Economic Activity and the Multinational Enterprise: A Search for an Eclectic Approach', in B. Ohlin, P. O. Hesselborn, and P. J. Wijkman (eds.), *The International Allocation of Economic Activity* (London: Macmillan).

—— (1985), The United Kingdom, in John H. Dunning (ed.), *Multinational Enterprises, Economic Structure and International Competitiveness* (Chichester, England: Wiley).

—— (1988), *Multinationals, Technology and Competitiveness* (London: Allen & Unwin).

—— (1992), 'The Competitive Advantage of Countries and the Activities of Transnational Corporations', *Transnational Corporations* February: 135–69.

—— (1993), *Multinational Enterprises and the Global Economy* (Wokingham, Berks.: Addison-Wesley).

—— (1994), 'Reevaluating the Benefits of Foreign Direct Investment', *Transnational Corporations* 3(1): 23–51.

—— (1995), 'Think again Professor Krugman: Competitiveness Does Matter', *International Executive* 37(4): 315–24.

—— (1997), 'Government and the Macro-organization of Economic Activity: A Historical and Spatial Perspective', in John H. Dunning (ed.), *Governments, Globalization. and International Business* (Oxford: Oxford University Press).

—— and Narula, R. (1995), 'The R&D Activities of Foreign Firms in the US', *International Studies of Management and Organization* 25(1–2): 39–75.

—— and Wallace, Lorna H. (1998), 'New Jersey in a Globalizing Economy', in N. Phelps (ed.), *FDI and the Global Economy: Corporate and Institutional Dynamics of Globalisation* (Kingsley: University of Wales).

Durkheim, E. (1964), *The Division of Labor in Society* (New York: Free Press; repr. from original monograph in 1893).

Elmslie, Bruce, and Milberg, William (1996), 'The Productivity Convergence Debate: A Theoretical and Methodological Reconsideration', *Cambridge Journal of Economics* 20(2): 153–82.

Fox, William F., and Murray, Matthew (1991), 'The Effects of Local Governments Public Policies on the Location of Business Activity', in Henry W. Herzog and Alan M. Scholttman (eds.), *Industry Location and Public Policy* (Knoxville: University of Tennessee Press).

Garofalo, Gasper A., and Malhotra, Devinder, M. (1995), 'Effect of Environmental Regulations on State-level Manufacturing Capital Formation', *Journal of Regional Science* 35: 201–16.

Gibbs, D. C., Alerman, N., Oakey, R. P., and Thwaites, A. T. (1985), 'The Location of Research and Development in Great Britain', Working Paper of the University of Newcastle (Newcastle upon Tyne: Center for Urban and Regional Development Studies).

Gillespie, A. (1987), 'Telecommunications and the Development of Europe's Less-favoured Regions', *Geoforum* 18(2): 229–36.

—— and Richardson, R. (1992), 'The Effects of Recent Changes in Telecommunications Regulation on North-east Businesses', *Business Review North* 4(3): 16–22.

Goddard, J. (1988), 'New Technology and the Local Economy: The Need for an Information Policy', *Northern Economic Review* 16: 2–8.

—— and Gillespie, A. (1986), 'Advanced Telecommunications and Regional Economic Development', *Geographical Journal* 152: 383–97.

Goode, Franke M. (1986), 'The Efficacy of More Refined Demand Variables in Industrial Location Models: Note', *Growth and Change* 17: 66–75.

Graham, Edward M., and Krugman, Paul R. (1989, 1991, and 1995), *Foreign Direct Investment in the United States* (Washington, DC: Institute for International Economics).

Granovetter, Mark (1985), 'Economic Action and Social Structure: The Problem of Embeddedness', *American Journal of Sociology* 91: 481–510.

—— (1992), 'The Sociological and Economic Approaches to Labor Market Analysis: A Social Structural View', in M. Granovetter and R. Swedberg (eds.), *The Sociology of Economic Life* (Boulder: Westview Press).

Gray, H. Peter, and Walter, Ingo (1983), 'Investment-Related Trade Distortions in Petrochemicals', *Journal of World Trade Law* 17 (July–Aug.): 283–307.

—— and Wallace, Lorna H. (1996), 'New Jersey in a Globalizing Economy', CIBER Working Paper Series 96.003 (Newark: Rutgers University).

Gray, Mia (1997), 'New Jersey Prospects: The Pharmaceutical Industry in a New Age', CIBER Working Paper Series 97.002 (Newark: Rutgers University).

Greenwald, Douglas, Arnold, Henry C. F., Blitzer, David M., Brown, William J., Kaflowitz, Lewis I., Mattersdorff, G. H., Myers, Edward G. (1983), *The McGraw-Hill Encyclopedia of Economics* (New York: McGraw-Hill).

—— (ed.) (1994), *The McGraw-Hill Encyclopedia of Economics*, 2nd edn. (New York: McGraw-Hill).

Guisinger, Stephen E. (1983), *Investment Incentives and Performance Requirements: A Comparative Analysis of Country Foreign Investment Strategies* (Washington, DC: International Finance Corporation).

Hake, David A., Ploch, Donald R., and Fox, William F. (1985), 'Business Location Determinants in Tennessee', Working Paper (Knoxville: University of Tennessee).

Hedlund, G., and Rolander, D. (1990), 'Action in Heterarchies: New Approaches to Managing the MNC', in C. A. Bartlett, Y. Doz, and G. Hedlund (eds.), *Managing the Global Firm* (London: Routledge).

Hekman, John S. (1982), 'Survey of Location Decisions in the South', Federal Reserve Bank of Atlanta *Economic Review* (June): 6–19.

Herzog, Henry W., and Scholttmann, Alan M. (1991), 'Introduction', in H. W. Herzog and A. W. Scholttman (eds.), *Industry Location and Public Policy* (Knoxville: University of Tennessee Press).

Hoechst (1979), *Hoechst Pronounced Success: America and Hoechst 1953–1978* (American Hoechst Corporation: K.A.S. Graphics).

Houston, David T. Jr. (1995), 'Is New Jersey a Good Place to Do Business?' *Profiles* 7–8.

Kieschnick, Michael (1981), 'Taxes and Growth: Business Incentives and Economic Development', *Studies in Development Policy* (Washington, DC: Council of State Planning Agencies).

Kobrin, Stephen J. (1995), 'Regional Integration in a Globally Networked Economy', *Transnational Corporations* 4(2): 15–33.

Kolz, Alan C. (1995), 'Quality of Life: Is it Essential to Consider in the Site Selection Process', *Area Development* 30(July): 27–28.

Krugman, Paul (1995), *Development, Geography and Economic Theory* (Cambridge, Mass.: MIT Press).

Lall, S., and Siddharthan, N. S. (1982), 'Monopolistic Advantages of Multinationals: Lessons from Foreign Investment in the US', *Economic Journal* 92(Sept.): 668–83.

Larre, Benedicte, and Torres, Raymond (1991), 'Is Convergence a Spontaneous Process: The Experience of Spain, Portugal and Greece', *OECD Economic Studies* 16(Spring): 169–98.

Lodge, G. C., and Vogle, E. F. (1987), *Ideology and National Competitiveness: An Analysis of Nine Countries* (Boston: Harvard Business School Press).

Lyne, Jack (1995), 'IDRC's New York-New Jersey Chapters Add Billion-dollar Bite to the "Bigger Apple" ', *Site Selection* 40(Aug.): 644–6.

McConnell, Virginia D., and Schwab, Robert M. (1990), 'The Impact of Environmental Regulation on Industry Location Decisions: The Motor Vehicle Industry', *Land Economies* 66: 67–81.

Macgregor, B. D., Langridge, R. J., Adley, J., and Chapman, J. (1986), 'The Development of High-Technology Industry in Newbury District', *Regional Studies* 20: 433–47.

Maillat, D. (1995), 'Territorial Dynamic, Innovative Milieus and Regional Policy', *Entrepreneurship and Regional Development* 7: 157–65.

Malecki, E. J. (1987), 'The R&D Location Decision of the Firm and "Creative Regions" ', *Technovation* 6: 205–22.

—— (1991), *Technology and Economic Development: The Dynamics of Local, Regional and National Change* (New York: Longman Scientific and Technical).

Malmberg, Anders, Sölvell, Örjan, and Zander, Ivo (1996), 'Spatial Clustering, Local Accumulation of Knowledge and Firm Competitiveness', *Geografiska Annaler* 78(B): 85–97.

Markusen, Ann R. (1994), 'Studying Regions by Studying Firms', *Professional Geographer* 46(4): 477–90.

—— (1996), 'Sticky Places in Slippery Space: A Typology of Industrial Districts', *Economic Geography* 72(3): 293–313.

Marshall, A. (1890/1916), *Principles of Economics. An Introductory Volume* (London: Macmillan).

Maturi, Richard J. (1995), 'The Skilled Labor Imperative', *Area Development* 30(Nov.): 89–90.

Mofidi, Alaeddin, and Stone, Joe A. (1990), 'Do State and Local Taxes Affect Economic Growth?' *Review of Economics and Statistics* 72: 686–91.

Moore, John R., Neel, C. Warren, Herzog, Henry W., and Schlottmann, Alan M. (1991), 'The Efficacy of Public Policy', in H. W. Herzog and A. M. Schlottmann (eds.), *Industry Location and Public Policy* (Knoxville: University of Tennessee Press).

Newman, Robert J. (1983), 'Industry Migration and Growth in the South', *Review of Economics and Statistics* 65(1): 76–86.

Oakey, R. P., and Cooper, S. Y. (1989), 'High-Technology Industry, Agglomeration and the Potential for Peripherally Sited Small Firms', *Regional Studies* 23: 347–60.

O'Brien, R. (1992), *Global Financial Integration: The End of Geography* (London: Pinter).

OECD (1994), 'Globalization and Local and Regional Competitiveness', OECD Working Paper (Paris: OECD).

Ohmae, K. (1995), *The End of the Nation State: The Rise of Regional Economies* (London: HarperCollins).

256   *Lorna H. Wallace*

Papke, Leslie E. (1991), 'Interstate Business Tax Differentials and New Firm Location: Evidence from Panel Data', *Journal of Public Economics* 45: 47–68.

Parker, Eric (1996), 'Regional Industrial Revitalization: Implications for Workforce Development Policy', CIBER conference (Newark, NJ: Rutgers University).

—— and Rogers, Joel (1995), 'The Wisconsin Regional Training Partnership: Lessons for National Policy', Unpublished report to the National Center on the Workforce.

Peck, F. W. (1996), 'Regional Development and the Production of Space: The Role of Infrastructure in the Attraction of New Inward Investment', *Environment and Planning A* 28: 327–39.

Pennington, Audrey (1995), 'Project Pioneers Fund: Global Infrastructure', *Site Selection* 40(Aug.): 572–9.

Piore, M., and Sabel, C. (1984), *The Second Industrial Divide* (New York: Basic Books).

Plaut, Thomas R., and Pluta, Joseph E. (1983), 'Business Climate, Taxes and Expenditures, and State Industrial Growth in the United States', *Southern Economic Journal* 50: 99–119.

Porter, Michael E. (1990), *The Competitive Advantage of Nations* (New York: Free Press).

Prahalad, C. K., and Doz, Y. (1987), *The Multinational Mission: Balancing Local Demands and Global Vision* (New York: Free Press).

Pugel, Thomas A. (1985), 'The United States', in J. H. Dunning (ed.), *Multinational Enterprises, Economic Structure and International Competitiveness* (London: Allen & Unwin).

Ridderstrale, J. (1997), 'Global Innovation: Managing International Innovation Projects. ABB and Electrolux', Doctoral diss., Institute of International Business, Stockholm: Stockholm School of Economics.

Saxenian, Anna Lee (1994), *Regional Advantage: Culture and Competition in Silicon Valley and Route 128* (Cambridge, Mass: Harvard University Press).

Schmenner, Roger W. (1982), *Making Business Location Decisions* (New Jersey: Prentice-Hall).

—— (1991), 'Geography and the Character and Performance of Factories', in H. W. Herzog and A. M. Schlottmann (eds.), *Industry Location and Public Policy* (Knoxville: University of Tennessee Press).

Schoenberger, Erica (1994), 'Foreign Manufacturing Investments in the United States: Competitive Strategies and International Location', *Economic Geography* 61(3): 241–59.

—— (1997), *The Cultural Crisis of the Firm* (Cambridge, Mass.: Blackwell).

Scott, Allen J. (1988a), *New Industrial Spaces: Flexible Production Organisation and Regional Development in North America and Western Europe* (London: Pion).

—— (1988b), *Metropolis: From the Division of Labor to Urban Form* (Berkeley and Los Angeles: University of California Press).

—— (1996), 'Regional Motors of the Global Economy', *Futures* 28(5): 391–411.

Shaver, Myles J. (1995), 'Do Foreign-owned and US-owned Establishments Exhibit the Same Location Pattern in American Manufacturing Industries?' Working Paper Series No. IB-95-6 (New York: Stern School of Business Administration).

Smith, Adam (1776), *An Inquiry Into the Nature and Causes of the Wealth of Nations* (London; reprinted in 1976 by W. Strahan and T. Cadwell, Oxford: Clarendon Press).

Smith, P., and Reinertsen, D. (1991), *Developing Products in Half the Time* (New York: Van Nostrand).

Solvell, O., and Zander, I. (1995), 'Organization of the Dynamic Multinational Enterprise: the Home-based and the Heterarchical MNE', *International Studies of Management and Organization* 25: 17–38.

Spence, N. (1992), 'Impact of Infrastructure Investment Policy', in P. Townroi and
R. Martin (eds.), *Regional Development in the 1990s: the British Isles in Transition*
(London: Jessica Kingsley).

Stafford, Howard A. (1985), 'Environmental Protection and Industrial Location', *Annals
of the Association of American Geographers* 75: 227–40.

Stalk, G., and Hout, T. (1990), *Competing against Time* (New York: Free Press).

Storper, Michael (1995), 'The Resurgence of Regional Economies, Ten Years Later: The
Region as a Nexus of Untraded Dependencies', *European Urban and Regional Studies*
2(3): 191–221.

—— and Scott, A. J. (1989), 'The Geographical Foundations and Social Regulation
of Flexible Production Complexes', in J. Wolch and M. Dear (eds.), *The Power of
Geography: How Territory Shapes Social Life* (Boston: Unwin Hyman).

Swamidass, Paul M. (1990), 'A Comparison of the Plant Location Strategies of Foreign
and Domestic Manufacturers in the US', *Journal of International Business Studies* 21(2):
301–17.

Swedberg, Richard, and Granovetter, Mark (1992), 'Introduction', in *The Sociology of
Economic Life* (Boulder: Westview Press).

UNCTAD (1992–1996), *World Investment Report, Transnational Corporations and
Competitiveness*, Annual volumes (New York: United Nations).

—— (1996), *Incentives and Foreign Direct Investment*, UNCTAD/DTCI/28, Current
Studies, Series A., 30 (New York: United Nations).

UNCTC (1988), *Transnational Corporations in World Development: Trends and
Prospects*, 4th Survey, UN Sales No. E.88.11A7 (New York: United Nations).

—— (1989), *Foreign Direct Investment and Transnational Corporations in Services*, UN
Sales No. E.89A1 (New York: United Nations).

US Department of Commerce (1974–1995), *Foreign Direct Investment Operations of US
Affiliates of Foreign Companies*, various annual volumes (Washington, DC: Bureau of
Economic Analysis, Govt. Printing Office).

—— (various annual years data), *State Level Export Locator Series*, International Trade
Administration, State and National Export Data (Washington, DC: US Government Printing Office). Internet address: http:www.ita.doc.gov/industry/otea/state/state&re.html

Venable, Tim (1995a), 'Incentive Lures: Firmly Embedded in the Location Equation',
Site Selection 40(Apr.): 254–71.

—— (1995b), 'Worldwide Information Infrastructure Explosion Paves the High-tech
Highway for Business', *Site Selection* 40(June): 3–12.

Von Glinow, M. A. (1988), *The New Professionals: Managing Today's High-Tech
Employees* (Cambridge, Mass.: Ballinger).

Wade, R. (1989), 'The Role of Government in Overcoming Market Failure: Taiwan, Republic
of Korea and Japan', in H. Hughes (ed.), *Achieving Industrialization in East Asia* (Sydney:
Cambridge University Press).

Wallace, Lorna H. (1995a), 'Foreign Direct Investment into the State of New Jersey',
Baruch College Conference (29 Sept.), City University of New York.

—— (1995b), 'Foreign Direct R&D Investment into the State of New Jersey', (Newark,
NJ: Rutgers University), mimeo.

Wallace, Lorna H. (1998), 'Foreign Direct Investment into the State of New Jersey', Ph.D.
diss., Rutgers University, New Jersey.

Weber, Max 1922[1978], *Economy and Society: An Outline of Interpretive Sociology*
(Berkeley and Los Angeles: University of California Press).

Wells, L. T. Jr., and Wint, A. G. (1990), Marketing a Country: Promotion as a Tool for Attracting Foreign Investment, in *Foreign Investment Advisory Service*, Occasional Paper 1, (Washington, DC: International Finance Corporation Multilateral Guarantee Agency, US Govt. Printing Office).

Wheeler, D., and Mody, A. (1992), 'International Investment Locational Decisions: The case of US firms', *Journal of International Economics* 33: 57–76.

Wilkins, Mira (1979), *Foreign Enterprise in Florida: The Impact of Non-US Direct Investment* (Miami: University Presses of Florida).

Williamson, Oliver E. (1985), *The Economic Institutions of Capitalism* (New York: Free Press).

Wint, Alvin G. (1992), 'Public Marketing of Foreign Investment: Successful International Offices Stand Alone', *International Journal of Public Sector Management* 5(5): 27–39.

Wymbs, Cliff (1996), 'Spatial Determinants of Sector Investment in an Emerging Information Economy: A Case Study of New Jersey's Telecommunications Industry', CIBER Working Paper Series, 96.005 (Newark, NJ: Rutgers University).

Young, Stephen, and Hood, Neil (1993), 'Inward Investment Policy in the European Community in the 1990s', *Transnational Corporations* 12(2): 35–62.

—— —— and Peters, Ewen (1994), 'Multinational Enterprises and Regional Development', *Regional Studies* 28(7): 657–77.

Ziele, Dr (1997), is a senior research analyst with the US Dept. of Commerce. Dr Ziele provided me with non-published secondary data during our 1997 telephone conversations.

9

Policy Partnership in the Development of Knowledge Industries in Scotland

Ewen Peters, Neil Hood, and Stephen Young

1. Introduction

This chapter explores the ways in which policy partnerships between the public and private sectors in economic development have devolved within one region of the United Kingdom (UK) over an extended period of time. It concentrates on two elements of the knowledge industries, namely software and semiconductors in a context where the majority of leading actors are multinational enterprises (MNEs) which are being progressively shaped by the globalization process. The chapter highlights both processes and challenges facing partnerships which are essentially designed to stimulate economic development within a particular part of the economy, yet where most of the businesses involved are pursuing strategies for Europe and beyond.

The academic influences on the chapter are twofold. Firstly, it recognizes the existence of 'alliance capitalism' as a useful way of characterizing the policy environment of the late 1990s. Secondly, the specific initiatives illustrated owe much to traditions of agglomeration theory, and especially to its most recent manifestations in the identification and categorization of industry clusters. In the latter context, it recognizes the ubiquitous nature of such concepts in economic development practice in recent years, without wishing to view it as an all-embracing paradigm. The healthy scepticism reflected in some recent work on this topic (Enright 1999) is shared by the authors.

The chapter takes the following shape. Section 2 briefly sets the academic context within which this subject is being considered. Section 3 concerns the evolution of policy partnership as an economic development catalyst in the Scottish case, having set this into its broader UK context. This traces a background of collaboration over a fifty-year period and illuminates the foundations of the current structures and policies. Section 4 provides a more fine-grained consideration of the current approach to two subsectors of the Scottish information industry, namely software and semiconductors. The final section both draws conclusions and points to policy implications.

2. Conceptual Background

In recent years there has been a growing level of debate about the appropriate role of government in a world largely dominated by the thinking of liberal economics and the process of globalization. Dunning is correct in Chapter 1 of this volume to claim that globalization is a process leading to the structural transformation of firms and nations. It is evident that governments continue to play a decisive role in influencing the competitiveness of economic activities located within their borders, whether of indigenous firms or of MNEs. Dunning (1997*a*: 114) has captured this well in his observation that:

[Governments] do so both by providing the appropriate incentives for domestic firms to upgrade the quality of their ownership-specific assets; and by ensuring that the location-bound general purpose inputs (including educational facilities and communications infrastructure) necessary for these assets to be fully and effectively utilized, are available.

While he contends that globalization as such does not materially alter this relationship, it is recognized that this process does require a reappraisal by both firms and governments, especially with regard to the creation, development, and location of core competencies. In his terms the macro-organizational policies of government concerning issues such as trade, industry, and education, have to be deployed in a competitive manner in order to obtain and retain mobile assets, recognizing that it will require a wide-ranging and flexible mix of arrangements to achieve these ends.

The exact nature of these arrangements are, as Dunning cites in Chapter 1, shaped by several key trends of the past two decades. Of particular relevance in this context is the relative growth of the knowledge economy and the related growth of alliance capitalism inasmuch as they are evidenced in the forces working in either direction between globalization and regionalization (Markusen 1996). At the country level this raises the critical question as to what types of wealth-creating activity will be more concentrated in subnational clusters of whatever type. It already appears unlikely that globalization will render the demise of the region as a meaningful unit of economic analysis (Audretsch 1998), not least because innovation based on tacit knowledge cannot easily be transferred across distance.

This chapter directs attention to these issues and applies them to the UK environment. As a whole the UK has been consistently supportive of inward investment and has fostered a variety of cluster-related initiatives at regional level over a long period of time (Hood and Young 1997). In that sense it has been an environment in which alliance capitalism could prosper recognizing as it does the need for partnership between different organizational modes of resource allocation. In the economic development context, there is a long history of regional development agencies within the UK with an extensive track record in innovation in development projects (Hughes 1998). There is little doubt that this has at least been an enabler for the types of partnership considered here.

While the above discussion establishes the principle of alliance capitalism, it leaves open many questions about appropriate policy directions, partnership forms, and so on. It will be evident from the next section that in Scotland, as elsewhere in the UK, these have evolved through several stages. As globalization has accelerated, interest in localized groups of firms in the same or related industries (or 'regional clusters') has also increased (Porter 1990; Storper 1992; Enright 1998). The clustering of industries and leading firms within them is evidenced in many countries, both developed and developing (Humphrey and Schmitz 1996). What is clear, however, is that not every local economy can hope to participate in the localization process brought about by the globalization of MNCs (Dicken 1994). A number of studies have suggested the globalization/localization process makes 'competitive place' (and in particular the attributes which determine whether a given place will benefit or suffer from this process) more rather than less important to a region's economic well-being (Scott 1998; Enright 1999). Whether for these or other reasons including the tendency to encourage local economic initiatives in several countries, governments with very different political philosophies have instituted cluster promotion strategies.

The contemporary examples from Scotland cited in this chapter follow that broad direction, although the software sector does not display the characteristics of a cluster and is not being formally treated as such. Nevertheless, the principles of business environment improvement, fostering networking and interfirm collaboration, community building, and so on are at the core of both examples of partnership.

3. The Evolution of Policy Partnership as an Economic Development Catalyst

3.1. The UK Context

Prior to launching into an assessment of policy partnerships in Scotland, it is important to understand the wider UK economic development and policy context within which these initiatives must be placed. In so doing it is appropriate to sound a note of caution as to what realistically can be expected. As a region within the UK, the broad policy framework is set by national government. Since 1979 the improvement of competitiveness has been a continuing theme, with governments' role being that of creating the right kind of enabling environment. The latter has included the provision of a stable macroeconomic framework to enable business to plan ahead with confidence; policies to make markets work more efficiently; the pursuit of tax policies to encourage enterprise; and improved value for money in the services provided by the public sector (Hood and Young 1997).

Thus key dimensions of policy, including macroeconomic policy, technology and R&D policy, employment and labour market policy, FDI policy and regional policy, and the funding associated with them, are determined at UK level. There is a close relationship between the latter two areas of policy. As a less favoured region within the UK historically, Scotland has benefited from the ability to offer Regional Selective Assistance (and other incentive packages in earlier periods). The result has been that the assisted areas, which include parts of Scotland along with northern England and Wales, have attracted shares of new foreign manufacturing investment well in excess of their relative size. Therefore even Scotland's FDI strategy, rightly acclaimed as a success story in the regeneration of industry, is strongly rooted in UK policy measures.

The Scottish dimension of economic development policy, operated primarily through Scottish Enterprise and Highlands & Islands Enterprise as noted above, is 'second tier'; and it represents a very small proportion of total identifiable public expenditure in Scotland (Hood and Young 1984). The economic development challenges for the Scottish economy moreover continue to be formidable, including low levels of business start-up activity; low levels of business investment in research and innovation (there is a strong polarization of innovative activities in the south-east of England—see Cantwell and Iammarino 1998); relatively few high-value-added tradable services; and on average poor performance in manufacturing other than electronics (Scottish Enterprise Network 1999). As against this, there are significant strengths in the economy, such as some world-class scientific research in universities and other institutions: a high proportion of graduates: a strong reputation in markets in financial services, food, and cultural industries; and, of relevance to the present chapter, a powerful position in areas of international trade, including oil and gas, electronics and related industries, whisky, and tourism. The Scottish Enterprise strategy for 1999 and the early years of the new millennium, which focuses on cluster strategies, is rightly ambitious but also requires a strong dose of realism.

The next section of the chapter briefly traces the roots of policy partnership in Scotland, suggesting that it can be evaluated in four broad phases.

3.2. Laissez-Faire: Scotland's First Wave of Development

The importance of a strong knowledge base as a stimulus to regional growth has been evident from the early stages of Scotland's industrial development. Scotland has a heritage of excellence in scientific discovery and invention stretching back over two hundred years (Wills 1983). Combining this know-how with local venture-capital enabled indigenous entrepreneurs in the nineteenth century to build a cluster of heavy industries. Local resources combined with traditional economies of agglomeration accounted for the initial location and subsequent concentration of this cluster of activity in Scotland's Central Belt. Links to the British Commonwealth and Empire (in the context of rapidly expanding world trade) acted as the main market drivers. The resultant cluster was large, well integrated, and self-sustaining. At its zenith it comprised hundreds of firms linked by purchasing and trading networks, and often by ties of kinship (Saville 1985). Such development was largely the product of the invisible hand of the market (Smith 1776) and, in the post-war period, the more visible hand of government (under nationalization) and managerial capitalism (Chandler 1966) as shipbuilding, steel, and coal were returned to the private sector.

3.3. Tripartite Corporatism: Scotland's Second Wave of Development

Scotland's high dependence on heavy industry was still very apparent in the interwar years as revealed[1] in the Census of Production for 1935. Its development seriously lagged behind other regions of the UK such as the Midlands and south-east of England in relation to the new, lighter manufacturing industries which supplied emerging fast-growth and mass markets (e.g. cars, aircraft, and domestic appliances). Thus, with around 10 per cent of the UK's population, Scotland's share of UK output in the new lighter industries in 1935 was less than 5 per cent.

Furthermore, in Scotland unemployment at the time was over 20 per cent of the total insured workforce; real incomes were growing more slowly than elsewhere in the UK (as was the size of the insured workforce); and migration had reached 111 per cent of the natural increase. In short, Scotland's economic performance was in decline relative to the UK as a whole and a growing North–South divide was apparent. Scotland's heavy industries were seen to offer little, if any, growth potential and continued to attract too many of Scotland's best people and ideas[2] while development of the newer industries was neglected (Buxton 1980). A growing consensus of opinion saw the solution to Scotland's economic under-performance in industrial restructuring (especially rapid diversification), and rationalization and reorganization at the level of the enterprise.

This call for a more micro-approach contrasted with the prevailing national consensus on economic management espoused by the Treasury and the Board of Trade which emphasized the importance of rectifying general economic failure, boosting aggregate demand, and increasing the state's involvement in economic life (Saville 1985). The difference in policy climate from that prevailing in the rest of the UK can be attributed in part to the partnership approach adopted to industrial development in Scotland by industry, government, and the trade unions. This tripartite approach was perhaps best exemplified in the establishment of the Scottish Council (Development and Industry) (SCDI) in 1931 and its offshoot the Scottish Economic Committee (SEC) in 1936 which together as voluntary bodies played an important role in informing and shaping the policy debate in Scotland.

In its evidence in 1939 to the Royal Commission on the Distribution of Industrial Production, the SEC was perhaps the first organization to promote the idea of the need for a parastatal body whose sole concern was the development of industry in Scotland. Its primary duty was seen as the formulation of national plans and strategies for industrial development including the question of industrial location. Though these ideas began to influence the direction of policy in Scotland more or less immediately, development efforts on the ground often remained fragmented and poorly coordinated due to institutional factors and lack of appropriate funding. In short, the implementation mechanisms lagged behind this type of thinking by some twenty-five years, although the earliest institutional arrangements to attract foreign investment date from this period, led by SCDI.

3.4. Government-led Collaborative Action: Scotland's Third Wave of Development

Some of the second-wave policy prescriptions were taken up and developed in later post-war analysis.[3] However, these found their fullest expression under Labour Governments which established the Highlands and Islands Development Board (now Highlands and Islands Enterprise) in 1965 and the Scottish Development Agency (now Scottish Enterprise) in 1975—the latter covering the area containing the vast majority of the industrial and commercial base of the country. The factors which contributed to the establishment of the latter were a complex mix of the economic (unemployment rose sharply in Scotland in the early 1970s and again in 1974–5 and economic development was uneven: the Central Belt continued to suffer as the decline in heavy industry proved irreversible while the north-east was benefiting from the oil boom); the practical (key development activities continued to function in an unco-ordinated and fragmented manner and a more integrated approach was deemed desirable);[4] and the political (the establishment of the SDA was one element in the expansion of the Secretary of State for Scotland's economic role in response to the re-emergence of nationalism prompted by the contentious matter of the use of North Sea oil revenue).[5] In the pursuit of its statutory objectives, the SDA attached particular importance to high-technology sectors which offered good prospects for long-term growth such as electronics, healthcare, offshore engineering, and advanced engineering.

In this era private-sector partners were rarely involved in the formal design and development of sectoral studies and had limited access to the baseline information and detailed rationale which influenced subsequent strategy formulation and implementation. At least three factors help to account for this: first, the primary purpose of any sectoral study was to assist the SDA with the strategic planning of its own operations (Cunningham 1977); second, much of the information collected by consultants was company-specific and commercially sensitive and therefore subject to strict rules on confidentiality; thirdly, appropriate industry or trade bodies had yet to be established in a number of key sectors. In this sense, the partnerships that emerged between the public and private sectors were formed *de facto* and tended to have a narrow operational, rather than policy, focus. These partnerships were only concerned with the question of know 'why' insofar as it affected the know 'what' and know 'how' of project/programme implementation.

Though the main findings were often published by the SDA, the intellectual property vested in a sectoral study was not commonly owned. The SDA's early work on the electronics sector is a prime example of this approach (Firn and Roberts 1984). This phase was thus one of a rather weak set of partnership relations at the sectoral level, where the focus was on vision and direction for the economy, highlighting opportunities and elements which corporate actors were encouraged to take into account in their planning. In many senses this reflected the spirit of the age in UK economic management at that time.

3.5. Industry-led Policy Partnership: Scotland's Fourth Wave of Development

Change proceeded at an unprecedented rate in the 1990s and the global business environment altered fundamentally from that of a decade earlier. Regions such as Scotland thus face a new type of economic challenge. Keeping abreast of change, never mind anticipating its direction, speed, and possible impact, has proved daunting even for the most sophisticated of policy-makers. Furthermore, the resources available to parastatal economic development bodies in the UK have become significantly scarcer over this period as successive Chancellors have pursued policies which seek to bridle associated public expenditures.

A new approach was required if Scotland was to maintain its international reputation as a leader in economic development in general and as a home for inward investment in particular. To meet these challenges, development strategies have had to become more holistic, organizational structures flatter and more flexible, development activities better integrated, public-sector attitudes more entrepreneurial, and the actions of key players better aligned with commonly agreed and owned priorities. Furthermore, new ways had to be found to continuously upgrade corporate development effort and achieve more rapid gains in productivity and better value for the taxpayer. Unlike the 1980s, the early buy-in of key partners and stakeholders in strategic industries is now held to be a prerequisite for development success in the Scottish context.

In 1991, after a two-year consultation process, the Conservative Government established Scottish Enterprise (Hood 1991). This new body subsumed the powers of the SDA and Training Agency in Scotland and, for the first time, adopted a fully integrated approach to enterprise development and training which were in large part delivered by a local network of enterprise companies.

SE explored the advantages of formally adopting a cluster approach to economic development in Scotland (Porter 1990) as a new means of stimulating early engagement with key external partners and stakeholders and stimulating stronger industry-leadership of the strategy development process. Following the application of the Porter methodology to the Scottish economy (Monitor 1993), around thirty existing/emerging industry and service clusters with long-term development potential were identified. This analysis informed the cluster priorities set out in SE's published strategies. However, SE Board approval for the formal adoption of the cluster approach was only secured in 1996[6] in a paper which highlighted: the difficulty of trying to advance on all industry fronts simultaneously at a time when the resources available to the SE network were being reduced; the need to reprioritize clusters at least in the short run; and the need for the rapid adoption of a more fully integrated and outward-looking approach by SE if broad-based progress were to be achieved in the long-run. In 1997, four priority clusters were selected to pilot the cluster approach and £25m. was ring-fenced by SE to incentivize the development of cluster-enhancing projects by the network. This was designed to encourage strong commitment to action. These clusters were: semiconductors (from within the broader grouping of Scotland's information industries), energy, food, and biotechnology. Furthermore, a communications strategy was undertaken in 1998 to formally introduce key partners and stakeholders to the principles of the cluster development as conceived by Scottish Enterprise Operations, the main operating division of SE (Scottish Enterprise 1998).

3.6. Summary

This section has set out the evolution of policy partnerships in economic development in Scotland. It will be evident that the phases differ substantially in several regards. For example, phases two and three were more to do with the provision of factories and subsidies by the public sector to address chronic market failures and stimulate private-sector investment. The phase of the 1990s presumed some elements of market imperfection, but in areas such as coordination and integration of effort (as in clusters), knowledge development, dissemination, and so on. With these changes have come different expectations on the part of both sets of actors. For example, public-sector bodies are more conscious of the global competitive demands placed on business and the fact that many different locations can achieve the same ends when a company chooses where to place its business. Greater emphasis is placed on the milieux in which public and private bodies jointly evaluate their contributions to economic and corporate development.

The two cases chosen in the next section are reflective of the fourth phase of this development in Scotland. They both concern the vitally important information-industries sector which has a substantial impact on the Scottish economy (Peters 1994). They reflect the more collaborative and more iterative nature of contemporary partnerships, one with high dependence on indigenous business (software), the other in semiconductors where all the major determinants of MNE subsidiary strategy are critical to the expected outcome of any partnership interaction in a given location (Birkinshaw and Hood 1998). In both cases they constitute 'work-in-progress' reports, and are current manifestations of partnership arrangements which have previously existed in different forms.

4. Strategy Partnership in Action

4.1. Software

4.1.1. Context

Based on scanning (Ernst & Young 1998) of Scottish software's international business environment, the following section summarizes the key trends and issues judged most likely to influence Scotland's future development prospects in software.

With global sales estimated to be worth nearly $500bn. in 1997, software products and services are currently the world's largest knowledge industry. Running at around 8–10 per cent per annum, global growth has been strong and this is set to continue for the foreseeable future. Accounting for around 50 per cent of the global sales, the USA dominates the world market for software products and services and is expected to maintain its leadership. Though certain countries in Europe and Asia have at times experienced greater sales growth than the USA, this dynamism has yet to be sustained over time. Growth in the European market is forecast to lie somewhere in the range of 9–11 per cent over the next three to five years. The market in the UK is expected to grow slightly ahead of the rest of Europe.

The shift to open and pseudo-open systems is recognized as the key strategic issue in software which could empower new entrants and smaller independents. The rise of the Internet could also be the critical factor that will enable more rapid progress in this direction. This view is supported by the growing importance of web browsers compared to operating systems or hardware platforms, and the way in which web browsers have become the focal point for the increasingly heated debate in the USA about the alleged anti-competitive practices of Microsoft. Certainly, a significant business development opportunity would result if small, innovative software companies could easily enter new markets for JAVA tools and applications and provide new services via the Internet.

The move to more open systems is also making operating systems the critical interface between application software and a variety of hardware. Thus partnership between major operating systems developers and hardware manufactures is becoming more important and standard-forming alliances are widely expected to play a key role in setting future business parameters. Collaboration is increasingly mission-critical for software independents as hardware manufacturers (especially for platforms such as PCs and workstations) seek first-mover advantage and reductions in time-to-market as central planks of their competitive strategy. However, shorter product life cycles, especially in packaged software, are raising development costs. In turn, these costs need increasingly to be shared and then amortized by achieving high sales volumes, usually through exporting. Greater collaboration is also necessary if software independents intend to develop more applications which are stand-alone and self-supporting, thus requiring less service content in the product bundle and being less expensive to support, and which can be more readily standardized, packaged, and distributed. Collaborative ties of the sort referred to above are more noticeable by their absence in Scotland.

4.1.2. Software in Scotland

Latest estimates indicate that there are 19,600 people currently employed in Scotland's software community which has a turnover of around $2.5bn. per annum. The make-up of employment is as follows: 7,400 people employed in 220 indigenous software firms; 250 sole traders and around 3,000 individual contractors; and 8,950 employees in the software development departments of large Scottish-based users and the software divisions and subsidiaries of non-Scottish firms. Averaging 15 per cent per annum since 1995, growth in turnover has been strong, and this is expected to continue in the immediate future.

The community is characterized by a large number of small and micro businesses, though there is evidence of a growing number of star performers who have developed successful products and services across a variety of market applications (see Table 9.1). However, these activities are broad-based with no obvious focus or key strength and have little linkage to the market segments offering the highest growth. As a whole the community lacks a strong export orientation and is largely focused on meeting the demands of the Scottish and UK market place. Furthermore, relative to other similarly peripheral locations such as Ireland and Israel, software inward investment has been low and no major internationally recognized software producer currently develops products in Scotland. Thus, Scotland's international linkages and profile generally remain underdeveloped.

Though survival rates of new start-ups in software in Scotland do not deviate from the UK average, the number of new starts may be constrained by lack of access to the advanced and specialist advice and resources available in more successful software regions. Critically, the current bias within Scotland's software activity towards local-for-local service provision represents an important mismatch with the market trends outlined above. Furthermore, increased commoditization within services combined with the growing dominance of large international service providers will reduce the service market currently available to Scottish firms.

4.1.3. Strategy Partnership in Action

Against the backdrop of the above, concern grew within the software community that Scotland, unlike Ireland, lacked strategic direction in a key growth area of the local economy. In 1994 this concern was expressed directly to the Industry Minister at the Scottish Office by the Scottish Software Federation (SSF)[8] Scottish Enterprise was then asked to support the industry in its attempt to develop a national strategy. A strategy steering group was established by SSF

TABLE 9.1. Star firms in Scottish software

ASCADA Ltd.	Provides new generation distribution network systems for management systems in the utilities sector About 28 employees
DMA	World-class consumer games developers with almost all output exported to the USA About 27 employees
Graham Technology Ltd.	Top-level benchmarkable product in call centre platforms market About 80 employees
Kingston-SCL Ltd.	Took off with an excellent product in mobile communications billing systems Now has about 370 employees
Newell & Budge Ltd.	Specialist services in IT consultancy, training and applications, bespoke systems building and support services About 150 employees
Quadstone Ltd.	High-tech/high-risk technology in the area of decision support; emerged from the Edinburgh parallel computing centre About 60 employees
Real-Time Engineering Ltd.	Advanced manufacturing for the oil and gas, petrochemical, aviation, and power generation industries About 85 employees
Scottish Computer Services Ltd.	Technology-based solution provider for financial services industry About 23 employees
Valstar Systems Ltd.	Provides software consulting and products for business performance improvement and manufacturing systems About 60 employees
Weir Systems Ltd.	Main product is state-of-the-art using Powerhouse 4GL and structured-using relation theory About 200 employees

Source: Ernst & Young.

which brought together leading companies, academics, and key public-sector bodies (i.e. Scottish Office, Locate in Scotland, and Scottish Enterprise). Together, this group designed and directed the strategy development process, while day-to-day project management was led by SSF with support from Scottish Enterprise. The main knowledge-building was undertaken by consultants. The strategy was formally launched in summer 1998 by the Industry Minister with SSF and SE. The intellectual property vested in the strategy is jointly owned by SSF and SE who are now actively engaged in promoting the findings amongst key partners and stakeholders.

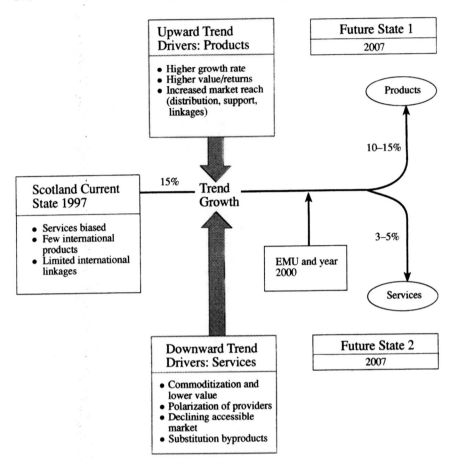

FIG. 9.1. Strategic options for Scottish software

The National Software Strategy (Ernst & Young 1998) identifies three over-arching development objectives for Scotland. These are: the need to build a greater scale of activity; the need to achieve more rapid structural adjustment; and the need to secure better access to key specialized resources of risk capital, risk appraisal, and commercial expertise. A 'do nothing' scenario was judged untenable beyond three to five years as jobs in Scotland would then be put at serious risk (see Figure 9.1). The vision of realignment which the National Strategy offers is one moving from local-for-local service provision to local-for-global product provision based on new products, developed independently or in collaboration with other leading international players. This will help Scotland to achieve a greater critical mass of software activity and enhance its innovative capabilities.

The thrusts of the strategy (see Figure 9.2) are: increased *productization* which will help to increase the geographic reach of Scottish software companies, increase value-added, and move the community away from a risky future

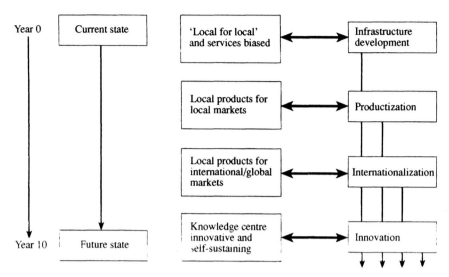

FIG. 9.2. A development routemap for Scottish software

in commoditized services; increased *internationalization* which is essential if Scottish companies are to begin to engage more effectively with global market opportunities, maximize business potential, and better align with industry trends; developing *innovation*, the dominant feature of software, in order to increase the number of new starts and improve their chances of survival and to help the activity profile of existing companies become more product-based; and improving *infrastructure* where the focus in on nurturing entrepreneurship and new firm formation by improving access to specialized skills and expertise and developing more of this locally.

Furthermore, to help 'kick start' a process of wider consultation amongst key partners and stakeholders, the consultants, based on their research, proposed a programme of eleven related initiatives (see Figure 9.3). If such a programme is successfully implemented, the consultants conservatively estimate that the Scottish software community is capable of doubling its size in employment terms within a ten-year period. Thus, the current challenge to SSF and SE is to develop a joint action plan which sets out agreed priorities (i.e. agreed both within the Scottish software community and between the Scottish software community and SE) along with resource implications and lead responsibility for implementation.

It is clearly too early to draw any conclusions on the value of this strategy in terms of deliverables on the ground. However, industry leadership has succeeded in producing a broad-based development strategy which has won equally broad-based support among key partners and stakeholders. In terms of Scotland's economic development, this is a first for the software community and a first for Scotland. Furthermore, the strategy currently under discussion contains a number of initiatives which, if successfully implemented, will help to enlarge

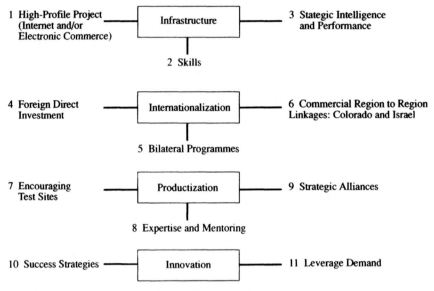

FIG. 9.3. Component of strategies for Scottish software

and embed software activities in Scotland while simultaneously integrating these more fully with global software community and market place. Thus, if these aspirations for software are fulfilled, Scotland in this instance may well become a more sticky place in an inherently dynamic and slippy global economic space.

4.2. Semiconductors

4.2.1. Context

As a direct result of inward investment from the USA and Japan, Scotland has a strong presence in the design, fabrication, assembly, and testing of semiconductors. The six facilities located in the country include NEC and Motorola, respectively the world's second and third largest fabricators, after Intel which has some 15 per cent of the global market. In 1997 the global market for semiconductors was some $40bn. In the European context, the Scottish sector represents about 13 per cent of European and some 50 per cent of UK capacity. In spite of being located within an information-industries cluster in Scotland, almost all of the $2–3bn. semiconductor output is exported. Conversely, most of the $5–6bn. value of semiconductors built into the electronics goods produced in Scotland is imported from other parts of the world. Clearly the scope for enhanced economic impact through a closer matching of supply and demand would appear substantial, although this sector already directly constitutes 1 per cent of Scottish GDP, with its supply chain adding an additional 1 per cent.

There are a number of critical market and technology trends working to reshape this industry—all of which pose policy challenges for Scotland and similar locations. Firstly, as regards markets, they continue to grow rapidly at a 15 per cent CAGR but display highly volatile growth cycles. Thus semiconductors make up a significant proportion of the cost of electronics goods (some 15–20 per cent); but while rising sharply as a percentage of world GDP, they have displayed sharp slowdowns or declines eight times in the past thirty-five years. The cycles could not, however, be readily described as conventional business cycles, but are more to do with specific technologies, markets, and investment patterns since the latter tend to follow sales after a two-year lag. Overall the market is still mainly driven by the personal computer business which uses memory chips and microprocessors. A shift is occurring from technology-driven to both application- and consumer-driven products, with the resultant expected faster growth in application specific integrated circuits (ASICs) and analog products. The second series of issues are technological where dramatic advances in both solid state physics and engineering have led to the convergence and acceleration of computer and communications technologies. Technological change has enabled the number of transistors on a chip to double every eighteen months, with consequential enhancement of performance. The miniaturization of transistors]remains fundamental to the continuing advances in semiconductor performance.

In addition to these market and technology trends, there are a number of other factors contributing to corporate reorganization within this industry. Such changes affect internal structures, relationships with suppliers and customers, as well as relationships between the major semiconductor producers themselves. These factors include the size of annual investment required by the industry—a single fabrication plant costing some $2bn in 1998. Secondly, more complex devices are required by customers. In particular, system-level integration (SLI) which combines memory, microprocessors, and logic on a chip involves application-oriented intellectual property and skill sets which are not located in a single production company. This in turn may lead to both market power and profitability moving downstream to original equipment manufacturers (OEMs) and system integrators, away from component manufacturers. In short, some basic products will become even more commoditized, the market for them ever more competitive, and the value added in the industry will move away the commodity end of the value chain. One possible structural outcome of these trends is a change from the historical pattern where semiconductor vendors designed and sold chips to OEMs of electronic equipment. New relationships are likely to include OEM semiconductor producers in partnership focusing on design, while large high-volume and flexible fabrication plants emerge, either owned by consortia or operating independently under contract. An important consequence of this is that there may be fewer semiconductor vendors who are able to invest in new fabrication plants as the OEMs claw both more of the value and profitability of the end equipment.

The preceding paragraphs set out some of the context within which specific public–private partnerships for the development of the semiconductor clusters in

Scotland have taken place. This section of the chapter concentrates upon policy initiatives related to semiconductors, but it should be borne in mind that this is only a part of a well-established electronics industry in the country which has developed over the past five decades and which directly employs some 45,000 in and around 550 electronics companies (Hood 1998), a high proportion of which have been attracted by a concerted inward-investment strategy over that period. Electronics now represents over half of Scottish exports and some 5 per cent of Scottish GDP.

4.2.2. Policy Partnership in Action: Strategy and Structures

Following extensive analysis of the competitiveness of the Scottish economy by the Monitor Group, a series of priorities were established in collaboration between public and private bodies and covering a number of industry groups. Chief among these were those relating to the information industries where it was clear that there were a number of deficiencies within the cluster structure in the early 1990s (Peters 1994). These included the concentration on manufacturing with relatively little R&D, the gaps in the supply base, and the need to focus on emerging skill needs as the sector developed. Supported by Scottish Enterprise, the establishment of the Scottish Supplier Base Forum (SSBF) in 1991 and the Scottish Electronics Forum (SEF) in 1993 provided the electronics industry with a new means of articulating its collective view on future policy direction. In particular, Monitor worked closely with leading OEMs during the establishment phase to develop a strategy for SEF that drew directly from the Monitor analysis and secured the early buy-in of leading manufacturers. While there had already been extensive collaboration between these bodies, a broader consensus was reached that collaboration efforts needed to be redoubled if a Scottish electronics industry was to be built which was robust, sustainable, and internationally competitive. Accordingly, a strategy was established to address both longer- and short-term issues. It was recognized that in the long term Scotland should aspire to evolve from predominantly a least-cost cluster of manufacturing excellence to a more knowledge-intensive information hub.

Applying this philosophy to semiconductors, there is a strategic aim to increase the quality and quantity of Scotland's involvement in this sector. Figure 9.4 shows the vision that was set out for the partnership by Monitor in 1993, within which the critical linkages and the vital areas of value-added activity were identified. The figure also highlights the key structural weaknesses in the sector in Scotland. For example, there has been a specific focus on improving the supply infrastructure over the past decade, and the fabrication plants find many of their inputs from local operations. There has been growth and development on the left side of Figure 9.5 in areas such as cleanroom construction and gas systems; equipment maintenance and applications support; and raw materials, such as silicon, quartzware, photomasks, and chemicals. However, many of these come through local service delivery by major international companies whose strategic base is

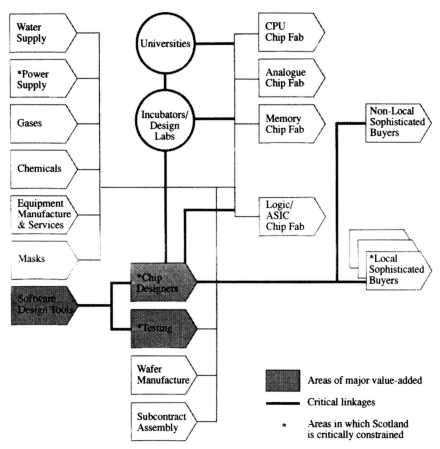

FIG. 9.4. A vision for the Scottish semiconductor sub-cluster
Source: Monitor Co.

elsewhere, although the Scottish supply base does service other UK and European fabricators. Another area to which attention has been directed concerns the need to strengthen internal linkages in supply and demand—not least by encouraging investment in leading-edge technologies generated from local universities. At the market end the aim has been to establish chip manufacture for electronic devices made or assembled in Scotland, and to capture a wide range of non-production activities. Critical to both of these are joint skill development initiatives at both the production and design level, forging linkages between related and supporting firms, stimulating exporting from service and supply companies, and so on. The two examples considered below directly derive from planned action flowing from the vision in Figure 9.5. Both are examples of upgrading the scope of the cluster.

It will be evident that these are ambitious aims which can only be pursued over the medium to longer term. Moreover, while appropriate partnership structures are a necessary condition to achieve them, they are not in themselves sufficient and the jury is out as to whether some of the MNEs concerned will be nudged in a policy direction beneficial to Scotland. Having said that, there is ample evidence of strategic collaborative activity. These include the National Micro-electronics Institute (NMI), a collaborative UK-wide R&D facility established in Edinburgh in 1996 and owned by major US and European semiconductor companies; the Scottish Advanced Manufacturing Centre (SAMC), capable of training 5,000 employees per annum; Edutronic, a specialist industry-led surface mount training facility; and the Microelectronics Imaging and Analysis Centre (MIAC) in Edinburgh University, whose focused ion beam system enables the modification of prototype chips to assess the effects of small design changes.

4.2.3. Projects

In order to give a closer and more in-depth appreciation of the outworkings of the strategy partnership in semiconductors in Scotland, this subsection provides two examples of cluster upgrade. The first concerns local plant initiatives regarding the co-location of design and development, the second a major national-level initiative.

Smart Card R&D at Motorola. Motorola established a wafer fabrication plant in Scotland in 1969 as the second of its European manufacturing investments, the first being set up in Toulouse, France, in 1967. European headquarters and design facilities were established in Geneva. Over the years there has been little direct linkage between the UK and French plants, not least because they are in different technologies—the UK being MOS and Toulouse, bipolar. The fundamental role of the Scottish plant has not changed since it was established as a global supply source for MOS products, but with particular reference to the EC. In recent years its activities have been focused upon demands from Motorola's own cellular communications products, for PCs and for the automotive industry. It has become progressively more specialized and its employment mix (of close to 2,000) has contained more design/customer application engineers and marketing staff in line with these changes. Motorola has some twenty-two wafer fabrication facilities worldwide. In performance terms, two of the leading three in their world rankings are within the Scottish plant. The senior management of the local Motorola plant played a leading role in the formation and development of SEF and in the energizing of sectoral collaboration in general.

This operation had a substantial development role for some time, even before it was granted a worldwide mission for semiconductors for Smart Cards in 1995. For example, it had roles in wafer fabrication and assorted technologies working with two group R&D units in the United States; in designing products for customer applications in Europe; and in process development. It did not, however, have a truly global design role and there was widespread recognition at the local plant level that this was desirable and possible, given the support of the relevant public partnerships with Scottish Enterprise and the Scottish Office.

The Smart Card franchise established at East Kilbride in Scotland in 1995 stemmed from European research initiatives undertaken in Geneva. The market for these cards first developed in Europe, initially in the French banking system. Thus the developers of the early systems were primarily in Europe. Moreover, all the original Motorola chips for Smart Cards were designed in Europe. The second important set of variables leading to this development was that European managers were pushing to have more recognition of the size and characteristics of the market outside the USA and were keen to have worldwide units based in Europe. In consequence the Scottish plant gained the Smart Card franchise while that in Toulouse was granted the mission for chemical sensors. In the former case, this has resulted in a completely integrated operation being established for this product, with R&D, product design, manufacturing, worldwide operations and world-wide marketing, customer support, and engineering all being at East Kilbride.

This case is a classic example of corporate opportunity (arising from internal competence and performance levels, together with managerial pressure) being facilitated by close working with government and its agencies in a measure of start-up financial and skill development support, reinforced by the nature of the milieux in Scottish electronics. It has resulted in a fundamental change in the standing of the Motorola plant within the worldwide corporation over the past ten years or so, and has produced a much more embedded operation in economic development terms.

Project Alba. Arising from the industry trends identified above, it becomes evident that semiconductor companies are at a vital stage in system design. This is driven by three main factors, namely the pace of semiconductor technology, shortening product cycles which require much reduced time to market in order to meet consumer demands, and the nature of contract law, within which it can take much longer periods to contract for the usage of blocks of intellectual property than can be tolerated in terms of market pressures. Scottish Enterprise and its partners recognized the significance of this trend and in 1996–7 set out to find a way of creating a unique environment in which companies could better exploit the opportunities offered by systems level integration (SLI) and system on chip (SOC) design. Leadership in this came from the chief executive of SE who was formerly a senior executive in several leading electronics companies in the USA. These fundamental business and technical changes also required new thinking on educational priorities, legal and contracting practice, and methods of organizing business. The outcome was the launch in 1997 of the Alba Centre, in collaboration with Cadence Design Systems, one of the world's leading US suppliers of semiconductor design technology and services in a 100-acre site near Edinburgh.

The concept centres round the creation of an open design community with three core elements. The first is the SLI Institute, acting as the focus for leading think-ing in SOC implementation. Its activities involve a distinctive collaboration with the four Scottish universities (and other leading universities worldwide) within which the relevant technology resides in research and graduate training. The second is the Virtual Component Exchange (VCE) which will source intellectual property and provide a mechanism to trade and contract in it in short order under the helpful provisions of the Scottish legal system. The third is a Central Services unit. In effect Cadence is the first of (hopefully) many firms which will recognize the benefit of undertaking SOC semiconductor design from a Scottish base. Cadence already has a worldwide network of centres and this one is planned to be its largest, employing 2,000 people.

The Alba project is regarded as a vital and innovative element of the electronics strategy in Scotland. It clearly offers the prospect of upgrading the added-value activity, should assist in attracting RD&D, capitalize on research and training excellence in Scottish universities, and strengthen the whole electronics cluster as internationally competitive companies are fostered. As yet it is, of course, too early to make any assessment of this initiative. It has attracted much favourable comment throughout the industry and it has the potential to move the semiconductor industry in Scotland on to a new plane provided the anticipated milieux of actors responds to what is being created. The latter could include other design centre companies, intellectual property providers or brokers, fabless semiconductor companies, system houses, and so on. It constitutes a serious and novel attempt to mobilize the relevant resources to respond to market and technology trends, and as such is in the mainstream of economic development strategy requiring enduring and broadly based partnerships.

It will be evident from trends in the global environment that semiconductors is currently a troubled segment of the electronics industry. This merely serves to emphasize in the Scottish context that this is a challenging area in which to pilot a cluster-based partnership strategy. Scotland has not been immune from the global effects as evidenced by recent announcements of redundancies at National Semiconductors and by Seagate's declared intention to progressively close its plant. Most spectacularly a major fabrication plant which was under construction for Hyundai was mothballed early in 1998 as a consequence of the Asian crisis. Taken together, these pressures point up the need for the strategy outlined to be pursued with increasing pace. However, there are many imponderables in such exercises and these are readily acknowledged, especially in semiconductors where there is limited scope for any geographical area or partnership arrangement to influence the course of events in MNE board rooms. All these issues are compounded by the fact that many other areas in the world have evaluated their clusters and arrived at similar conclusions and are adopting similar strategies. Alliance capitalism takes many forms and operates in a highly competitive environment.

5. Conclusions and Policy Implications

5.1. The Scottish Roots of Alliance Capitalism

Alliance capitalism is the relatively recent term that has been used to describe the 'deep structural interdependence' between the key stakeholders in the wealth-creating of activity in society (Dunning 1997*b*). In this context, alliance capitalism in Scotland today may be understood as a product of both the economic forces at work in the contemporary global economy and institutional history. In particular, the origins of present-day partnership structures and approaches in Scotland can be traced to the policy debate of the interwar years when business, government, and the trade unions came together to determine appropriate responses to the problem of abnormally high levels of structural unemployment and chronic under investment in new industry.

The following paragraphs focus on some of the specific lessons for other regions. At the more general level, these are broader lessons. Scotland has benefited from having a cultural context in which public and private collaboration in economic development is broadly welcomed. Moreover, it has had powerful economic development institutions with broad enough remits and sufficient funding to make flexible approaches to policy partnership possible. Part of that flexibility has included being open to examining best practice on a global basis for many years and the willingness to adapt it to local conditions. Even within the UK, there are some distinctive elements of the Scottish approach, but most of them can be adopted by others since economic development is an area where good ideas spread with considerable rapidity.

5.2. Evolving Forms of Partnership

The form of public–private sector partnership in Scotland's economic development has also evolved. The chapter broadly characterizes this progression as a four-phase movement from an early *laissez-faire* through the *corporatism* of the interwar period and beyond, to the *collaborative action* (on public-sector strategy implementation) of the 1960s, 1970s and 1980s, and the private-sector-led *policy partnership* approach now promoted by Scottish Enterprise. The latter has been promoted by government in its attempt to encourage better-designed policy which is more capable of rapidly harnessing and deploying resources from both the public and private sectors in better alignment with the long-term competitive needs of business. As such it is a classic illustration of a structured response to the need to upgrade indigenous resources and capabilities in the hope that some will become world-class players.

5.3. The Changing Rationale for Intervention

The evolution of the partnership approach in Scotland has been accompanied by a related change in the rationale for public-sector intervention. While still in evidence (Hood 1998), the use of financial subsidies, public-sector provision of factories in advance of need, directive planning controls, and so on under UK regional policy and Scottish industrial policy (Hood and Young 1984) is now less prevalent and powerful than was once the case. The distorting effects on market behaviour, especially with respect to the operation of key factor markets, is commensurately lower. Where intervention occurs to address chronic market failure, this is now seen as a measure of last resort and exit routes are designed from the outset as part of current best practice in the public sector.

The main change, however, that this chapter highlights is the emergence of development bodies as key influencers and shapers of the local institutional landscape and as expert brokers, facilitators, and network managers. This change is also evident elsewhere in the UK where other commentators have described the emerging role of the Welsh Development Agency, for example, as a network 'animateur' (Cooke and Morgan 1998). Rather than chronic failure, such intervention seeks to address market imperfections associated, inter alia, with coordination and information deficiencies due to bounded rationality, information asymmetries, and high information search costs and so on.

5.4. Recognizing Private-Sector Leadership

The findings of the chapter are consistent with Porter's view (1990) that it is firms, not governments, which have a lead role to play in the rapid formation and upgrade of advanced and specialized factor inputs that are key to innovation and the long-run growth in output-based productivity, the main economic indicator of international competitiveness.

Albeit at the margin, public-sector intervention of the type highlighted in the chapter remains strategically important, especially for less favoured, entrepreneurially constrained regions that have to compete for high-quality inward investment and reinvestment which is becoming increasingly mobile. From the perspective of multinational enterprise, such intervention can both stimulate and complement the asset-augmenting activity of local subsidiaries and enhance the location-specific advantages of a region. In turn, a richer local operating environment may assist strategically able subsidiary plant managers as they seek to champion their bid for additional higher-level functions from their corporate parents.

5.5. Partnership and Learning Communities

Learning has clearly a fundamental role in promoting more rapid technical progress embodied conventionally in more innovative products and processes. The institutional and regional setting within which innovation occurs may be characterized by more or less rapid approaches to learning. Hence, the recent interest with concepts such as lifelong learning for individuals, the learning organization, the intelligent island (Singapore), innovative regions, and the intelligent state and so on. The policy partnership approach adopted by SE seeks to promote greater learning amongst communities of industrial partners and stakeholders by promoting wider ownership of strategy and action based on deeper, future-led exchanges of industry-specific knowledge and information.

In the case of software, the engagement in the strategy development phase was protracted as key players climbed a difficult learning curve together. However, this process gave project partners a better appreciation of each other's strengths and weaknesses. The public sector grew in its understanding of the software community and its long-term development aspirations and needs, and industry was encouraged to adopt a broader policy perspective. The main benefit of this process has been the opportunity created for early implementation, especially of key initiatives, on the basis of the broad ownership that has been established. However, leadership is still needed to maintain the development momentum or the integrated approach proposed to implementation may be weakened as (a) individual interest groups begin to 'cherry pick' the findings of the strategy and/or (b) dominant interests 'hijack' the strategy for their own purposes.

In the case of semiconductors, the cluster strategy is currently being revisited. Scottish Enterprise is leading this process and has established a cross-divisional cluster term charged with the development of a new strategy. The danger in the current process is the apparent absence of any formal industry-leadership. This may damage credibility with key stakeholders (both internally and externally) and perhaps hinder subsequent implementation.

5.6. Partnership and Industry Cluster Development

The evidence of the case studies suggests that intervention may also help strengthen technological spillovers by catalysing new forms of partnership which promote the freer exchange of ideas and information between key partners and stakeholders involved in industry-specific innovation processes. In turn, this may also reinforce proximity benefits and thereby enhance cluster formation, especially among industries which are particularly knowledge-intensive and innovative. Accordingly, the chapter would suggest that the existence of externalities such as technological spillovers continues to provide a complementary explanation to that offered by transaction cost analysis as to why such clusters exist (Dunning 1997b).

Borrowing from Enright (1998), the chapter highlights how the unprecedented severity of the present global downturn in semiconductor activity has exposed the 'narrowness' and 'shallowness' of Scotland's semiconductor cluster. This reinforces the need for more rapid plant-upgrading and the importance of fast delivery of more activity-rich, high-value initiative such as Project Alba if Scotland is to nurture a larger, more deeply embedded semiconductor cluster that is capable of sustaining competitive advantage through continuous innovation and upgrade.

5.7. Partnership and Software

In terms of job creation, the position in semiconductors also adds new urgency to the implementation of the recently launched National Software Strategy. However, it is presently difficult to conceive of this group of activities as a cluster, whether existing or embryonic. For example, while some independent Scottish software firms have important forward links to key local customers in financial services, North Sea oil activity, utilities, and advanced manufacturing (including electronics), the software supply chain is generally quite truncated and, as a whole, the software community lacks critical mass. Product innovation can be successfully undertaken in a 'virtual network'. Moreover, the research of Ernst & Young (1998) also suggests that the tendency for software activities to agglomerate in more peripheral regions is strongly related to the availability of suitable skills, rather than the proximity benefits associated with more mature and successful clusters.

Accordingly, it is unclear how software will fit with the cluster approach now promoted by Scottish Enterprise. However, the present initiative has succeeded in securing industry leadership of the strategy development process (an industry first in Scotland) and there has been early buy-in from Scottish Enterprise and key Local Enterprise Companies. In short, the software initiative has already achieved a number of the more important aims of the cluster approach adopted by SE. Whether within the context of a cluster approach or not, software is likely to remain a high priority for existing policy partners because of its growth potential, its importance as a key specialized factor input to so many strategic industries in Scotland, and its potential importance of becoming Scotland's most valuable tradable service.

5.8. Summary

It will be evident that the Scottish case touches on many of the issues central to this volume. It illustrates for example the efforts of one microregion within a developed economy to apply various types of agglomeration analysis to economic development over a long time-period, of which cluster analysis is the most recent manifestation. The two specific cases considered demonstrate many of the tensions between the globalization of business and microlevel economic development needs. Inward and outward investment have been shown to have a role in both of these and are regarded as pro-active stimulants to such development. The sectors considered are both knowledge-intensive and place high demands on continued upgrade of the support infrastructure in the country. However, the jury is still out in the Scottish case and while it will be evident that there are many lessons, there are also many uncertainties about the efficacy of the particular policy partnerships.

NOTES

1. This indicated that in a range of heavy engineering industries the percentage of UK output accounted for by Scottish production was respectively: 65 per cent of sewing

machines (mainly based on the production of the large Singer plant at Clydebank, regarded as Scotland's first inward investment from the USA), 54 per cent of non-ship boilers, 42 per cent of marine engines, 30 per cent of ships. 25 per cent of mining and hydraulic equipment, and 21 per cent of power pumps.

2. See e.g. the Board of Trade (1932), *Industrial Survey of the South West of Scotland*.
3. See e.g. *Inquiry into the Scottish Economy 1960–61*, Report of a Committee of the SCDI under the Chairmanship of J. N. Toothill, Edinburgh 1962; and the *West of Scotland Plan*, 1974.
4. The statutory purposes set out in the 1975 Scottish Development Agency Act were furthering economic development, promoting industrial efficiency and international competitiveness, and furthering the improvement of the environment. The functions attached to these purposes were previously undertaken by a variety of bodies: the responsibility for environmental improvement and land renewal lay with local authorities; the provision of industrial premises lay with the Scottish Industrial Estates Corporation; small business development in rural areas beyond the Highlands and Islands was the responsibility of the Small Industries Council for Rural Scotland, formerly a subsidiary of the Scottish Development Council; and the Scottish Council (Development and Industry) played a lead role, especially through the 1960s, in trade promotion and the attraction of inward investment.
5. See e.g. Industry Department for Scotland (1987), *The 1986 Review of the Scottish Development Agency*: 17–18.
6. Scottish Enterprise (1996). *Cluster Development: Taking the Network Strategy Forward*, Scottish Enterprise Board Paper.
7. Packaged software is the single most important market for software globally and is currently estimated to be worth in excess of $150bn.
8. The Scottish Software Federation was formed in 1985 by a number of leading software companies and support from the Scottish Development Agency. Its aim is to promote Scotland as a centre of excellence in the design, development, and marketing of quality software. It now has over 250 members and represents Scotland at UK and European levels through its association with CSSA and EISA. Though now more self-standing, it continues to be supported in its aims by Scottish Enterprise.

REFERENCES

Audretsch, D. (1998), 'Agglomeration and the Location of Interactive Activity', *Oxford Review of Economic Policy*, 14(2): 18–29.
Birkinshaw, J., and Hood, N. (eds.) (1998), *Multinational Corporate Evolution and Subsidiary Development* (London: Macmillan).
Buxton, N. (1980), 'Economic Growth between the Wars: The Role of Production Structure and Rationalisation', *Economic History Review* (2nd series) 33(4): 538–55.
Cantwell, J., and Iammarino, S. (1998), *Multinational Corporations and the Location of Technological Innovation in the UK Regions*. Discussion Papers in International Investment and Management, 262, Dec. (Dept. of Economics, University of Reading).
Chandler, A. D. (1966), *The Visible Hand: The Managerial Revolution in American Business* (Cambridge, Mass.: Harvard University Press).

Cooke, P., and Morgan, K. (1998), *The Associational Economy* (Oxford: Oxford University Press).

Cunningham, E. (1977), *The Functional Role of the Scottish Development Agency*, Address to the Annual Residential Conference of the Regional Studies Association, Bristol.

Dicken, P. (1994), 'Global-Local Tensions: Firms and States in the Global Space Economy', *Economic Geography* 70: 101–28.

Dunning, J. H. (1997a), 'A Business Analytic Approach to Governments and Globalization', ch. 3, in J. H. Dunning (ed.), *Governments, Globalization, and International Business* (Oxford: Oxford University Press): 114–31.

——— (1997b), *Alliance Capitalism and Global Business* (London: Routledge).

Enright, M. J. (1998), 'Regional Clusters and Firm Strategy', in A. D. Chandler, Jr., Ö. Sölvell, and P. Hagstrom (eds.), *The Dynamic Firm: The Role of Technology, Strategy, Organization and Regions* (Oxford: Oxford University Press).

——— (1999), 'The Globalization of Competition and the Localization of Competitive Advantage: Policies towards Regional Clustering', in N. Hood and S. Young (eds.), *The Globalization of Multinational Enterprise Activity and Economic Development* (London: Macmillan): 303–31.

Ernst & Young (1998), *A National Software Strategy for Scotland* (Confidential Report for Scottish Enterprise and the Scottish Software Federation).

Firn, J., and Roberts, D. (1984), 'High Technology Industries', in N. Hood, and S. Young (eds.), *Industry, Policy and the Scottish Economy* (Edinburgh: Edinburgh University Press): 288–325.

Hood, N. (1991), 'The Scottish Development Agency in Retrospect', *Royal Bank of Scotland Review* 171: 3–21.

——— (1998), 'Inward Investment Attraction and Development: Lessons from the Scottish Case', in J.-L. Mucchielli (ed.), *Multinational Locational Strategy: Economic Management and Policy* (Greenwich, Conn.: JAI Press): 211–31.

——— and S. Young (eds.) (1984), *Industry, Policy and the Scottish Economy* (Edinburgh: Edinburgh University Press).

——— ——— (1997), 'The United Kingdom', in J. H. Dunning (ed.), *Governments, Globalization, and International Business* (Oxford: Oxford University Press): 244–82.

Hughes, J. T. (1998), 'The Role of Development Agencies in Regional Policy: An Academic and Practitioner Approach', *Urban Studies* 35(4): 615–26.

Humphrey, J., and Schmitz, H. (1996), 'The Triple C Approach to Local Industrial Policy', *World Development* 24: 1859–77.

Markusen, A. (1996), 'Sticky Places in Slippery Space: A Typology of Industrial District', *Economic Geography*, 72(3): 293–313.

Monitor Company (1993), *The Competitive Advantage of Scotland* (Confidential Report for Scottish Enterprise).

Peters, E. (1994), 'Restructuring of Scotland's Information Technology Industries: Strategic Issues and Responses', in A. Amin and J. Tomaney (eds.), *Behind the Myth of European Union* (London: Routledge): 263–81.

Porter, M. (1990), *The Competitive Advantage of Nations* (New York: Free Press).

Saville, R. (1985), 'The Industrial Background to the Post-War Scottish Economy', in R. Saville (ed.), *The Economic Development of Modern Scotland 1950–1980* (Edinburgh: John Donald Publishers).

Scott, A. J. (1998), 'The Globalization and Foundations of Industrial Performance', in A. D. Chandler, Jr., Ö. Sölvell, and P. Hagstrom (eds.), *The Dynamic Firm: The*

Role of Technology, Strategy, Organization, and Regions (Oxford: Oxford University Press).

Scottish Enterprise (1998), *The Cluster Approach: Powering Scotland's Economy into the 21st Century* (Glasgow).

Scottish Enterprise Network (1999), *The Network Strategy*, Jan. (Glasgow).

Smith, A. (1776), *An Inquiry into the Nature and Causes of the Wealth of Nations* (London: Strahan & Cadell).

Storper, M. (1992), 'Regional "Worlds of Production": Learning and Innovation in the Technology Districts of France, Italy, and the USA', *Regional Studies* 275: 433–55.

Wills, E. (1983), *Scottish Inventors and Innovators* (Scottish Development Agency).

10

Large Firms and Industrial Districts in Europe:
Deregionalization, Re-regionalization, and the Transformation of Manufacturing Flexibility

Gary Herrigel

1. Introduction

Despite a common interest in regional competitiveness, the literature on industrial districts that emerged in the late 1980s and early 1990s differs in significant
particulars from the contemporary discussions of the relationship between
regional clusters, globalization, and competitiveness—including those that animate this volume. While the latter, regional cluster literature is very concerned
with identifying the factors contributing to regionally concentrated increasing
economies, however constituted, and specifying the broader conditions for
regional competitiveness in general (see Porter 1990; Enright 1993, 1996; Scott
1998 and Dunning's introduction to this volume), the industrial district literature
is concerned with the relative competitiveness in world markets of a very particular form of regional industrial order, i.e. decentralized and cooperative industrial practices among small, medium, and quite often large firms (Sabel 1989;
Zeitlin 1992). To the extent that the decentralized regional structures of production
that interest those who study industrial districts are competitive in world markets and attractive to multinational investment, they are also of interest to the
students of regional clusters. But as Enright (1993, 1996) and others have extensively demonstrated, there are many regions in which there is competitiveness,
but little decentralization. And, as this chapter will attempt to elaborate, it is also
possible for there to be regions with considerable industrial decentralization, but
in which the competitiveness of the decentralized practices is suspect. This latter possibility is likely to fall through the cracks in the regional cluster literature
because it does not make the organization of the firm and production the focus
of its concern. Such problems are, however, at the centre of analysis of those
studying industrial districts.

To be sure, the literature on industrial districts has until now focused primarily on successful cases of adaptation. This is in large part a result of the fact

that the literature first emerged in the context of critiques of large-scale mass production and the vertically integrated, so called Fordist enterprise (Piore and Sabel 1984). At a time when the latter organizational forms were experiencing serious crisis throughout the industrial world, the smaller scale, flexible, specialized, decentralized, inter- and extra-firm forms of collaboration and strategy that governed entire regions of producers in south-west Germany, the third Italy, Jutland in Denmark, and elsewhere were constructed in debate as attractive alternatives out of the crisis. They were successful on world markets while the large vertically integrated mass producers were not, and their success seemed to stem from their flexibility in production and their capacity to engage in seemingly permanent innovation. Both of these capacities were traced back to the non-traditional organization of markets and production in the districts. The attractiveness of industrial districts as a flexible alternative was reinforced at the time by the contemporaneous success of Japanese producers who also, by most accounts, rejected the hierarchical rigidity of Fordist governance and organized production in more decentralized, collaborative, and flexible ways. The crisis of Fordism was a crisis both of mass production and of the vertically integrated firm. Flexibility and inter- and extra-firm mechanisms of governance seemed to be in the ascendant (Friedman 1987; Sabel 1989; Pyke, Becattini, and Sengenberger 1990; Pyke and Sengenberger 1992; Saxenian 1992; Cooke and Morgan 1998).

That was the argument at the time and after a decade it is plain that there was much that was true in it. Indeed, viewed with today's sensibility the early articles on industrial districts are almost quaint in the excitement and self-conscious boldness that couches their suggestion that hierarchy and the vertically integrated firm could not compete with the more collaborative and specialized systems. People take the possibility for the success of this form of competitive organization in the world economy for granted today. Far from being an endorsement of the contemporary and continuing relevance of the industrial district example, however, I want to argue that the passage of time and the diffusion and evolution of flexible organization in the world economy has actually revealed both the peculiarity of the forms of flexibility that characterize industrial practice in industrial districts and, more importantly, the weakness and vulnerability of at least some of those forms of practice relative to alternative forms of flexible industrial production (particularly those currently being developed by large manufacturing multinationals). What the old debate overlooked in its attention to the superiority of flexibility and decentralization over rigidity and vertical integration, was that not all ways of combining flexibility and collaboration were alike and that some ways were better than others.

Ironically, today it is large, very often multinational firms, vastly reconstituted from their earlier vertically integrated incarnations that pose the largest potential challenge to the industrial districts. These MNC's are increasingly learning how to organize flexibility in ways that utilize collaboration and collective self-monitoring to foster continuous learning, innovation, and, crucially, permanent organizational redefinition. These new forms (better: principles) of flexible organization are far more flexible and competitive than the essentially craft-based forms of flexibility that formed the foundation for the organization of production in industrial districts. Moreover, in contrast to many of the forms of flexible practice in industrial districts which emerged over long periods of time and which have a distinctly embedded and taken-for-granted quality among the actors, the new principles seem to be portable and can be introduced into contexts in which previously there had been little cooperation or flexibility in industry (Kaplinsky 1994; Dorf and Sabel 1998).

My claim below will be that this process of transfer, initiated by MNC's, involves both deregionalization and re-regionalization of production relations. By this I mean that in the process of implementing the new flexible production principles with suppliers in a region, large producers insist that producers play by new rules and refuse to tolerate producers who will not or cannot do so. In this way the production of a good is figuratively but systematically shifted or removed from one mode of regional industrial organization and inserted in a different, but equally as regionally concentrated one. In the terms of this volume, large-firm or MNC productive investment in industrial districts is currently undergoing a shift from asset-exploiting investments to asset-augmenting investments. My point is that in so doing, they must utterly redefine forms of practice in the region: deregionalization and re-regionalization are two sides of the same strategy.

At the moment, not all European industrial districts are confronted by this kind of challenge because many hold very strong monopoly or niche positions in world markets for high-quality products that have been ignored by multinational players. Moreover, there is no immanent reason in the contemporary global competitive environment for this insulation to give way or break down. I do not want to claim that there is a general crisis of the industrial district model of decentralized craft production. I do want to claim that important districts are very vulnerable in the current environment—especially those with a large regional presence of multinational manufacturers such as Baden-Württemberg in south-west Germany. Many producers there have become much less insulated from global competition than they used to be, and as a result have been experiencing significant adjustment pressure from the alternative form of flexible production. Indeed, so serious is the challenge in Baden-Württemberg in particular that it actually threatens to throw traditional craft-based decentralized production into decline and undermine the high-wage character of the regional economy. This chapter will attempt to outline the nature of this threat and present a range of possible scenarios for how that particular industrial district can (or cannot) cope with it.

2. Varieties of Industrial Flexibility

All systems of flexible production differ from the old Fordist mass production system by attempting to integrate conception and execution in production. Fordism was based on the systematic separation of conception and execution throughout all parts of production and management. The canonical Fordist firm was hierarchical and rigid because it divided labour and production in the extreme: unskilled workers or workers with extremely specialized skills populated the factory floor and did not have the capacity and certainly lacked the authority to alter their activity relative to changes in the quality and quantity of demand. Plant managers and foremen were the ones with overviews of the production process and who had the authority to change the organization of production. But in most cases they did not even participate in the design or development of the product—this activity was allocated to yet another part of the firm—so they were themselves constrained in the degree to which they could intervene in the organization of production. The same separation of design and production applied to large firm relations with subcontractors: firms tried to control all aspects of design in-house and utilized outsiders only as producers and even then most often on an arm's-length, lowest-bid basis.

Hierarchy, vertical integration, and the rigid fragmentation of knowledge worked for large firms when there was little competition in markets and when the rate of product and technological change was relatively slow. When markets became competitive and product and technological change more rapid, as they did beginning in the 1970s, this form of organization proved to be very uncompetitive. Change was a giant bureaucratic procedure that took a long time.

The flexible forms of organization that captured attention as alternatives to Fordism in the 1980s, including the industrial districts, gained their advantage by integrating conception and execution in production and management. Firms employed skilled workers with knowledge about products and production that exceeded the specific manufacturing arrangements and product designs that existed at any given time. Indeed, most reports on all varieties of flexible production systems indicate that skilled workers are often systematically included in discussions with management about the organization of work and production and how to transform product designs into the practical details of manufacturing. The organizational structures that produced such workers and such discussions with management made change in product or in the organization of production comparatively easy to accomplish. Not a bureaucratic procedure, it was simply the natural outcome of the interaction of habitual interlocutors about what was working and not working in production and on the market.

In most systems, this same kind of continuous discussion about conception and execution applied to relations between firms and their suppliers as well. In truly horizontal systems such as the Italian industrial districts, the difference between a supplier and an end-user (OEM) was a temporal artefact of who was able to get a contract first: the winner subcontracted the loser, but winners and losers continually traded places. Producers collaborated on the development of the product and the organization of production. The boundaries of the firm approached disintegration (Pyke, Becattini, and Sengenberger 1990; Cooke and Morgan 1998). In less completely horizontal systems such as those which existed in the German district of Baden-Württemberg, the identity of OEMs tended to remain constant, but they also tended to cultivate long-term relations with important suppliers. Informal collaboration on the development of the subcontracted parts and on the continued development of the OEM's product was constitutive of these relations. The tendency towards collaboration was intensified through common associational affiliations, common utilization of local educational institutions for consulting and applied research, and through the circulation of skilled workers in local labour markets. In both the extreme horizontal cases and in the more hierarchical German ones, product change (if only in the form of accommodation of particular customer wishes in a standard type) was a taken-for-granted aspect of the system that all parties continually negotiated (Herrigel 1996; Cooke and Morgan 1998; Heidenreich and Krauss 1998).

Flexible systems differ amongst themselves in the degree to which they integrate conception and execution in their organizations. As it turns out, the industrial district model integrates conception and execution less well than others do because it continues to rely on the permanent fragmentation and division of knowledge and capacity in production. By this I mean that craft-production-based firms tend to be reliant on skilled workers with very particular self-understandings of the boundaries of their skill: they are trained as tool-makers or milling machine operators and have the expectation that their role in production will always be to make tools or operate milling machines. Likewise, individual firms specialize on specific aspects of a production chain and make their reputations on their capability in that specific area. This kind of fragmentation of knowledge in production, following an observation that Adam Smith made many years ago, produces hierarchy in that managers (or OEMs) are forced to step in and coordinate the activities of specialized actors to ensure the stable and optimal flow of production. Thus, the existence of fixed identity positions in the division of labour creates a logic of fragmentation and hierarchy that systematically blocks the integration of conception and execution—or reproduces their organizational separation, whichever you prefer.

The extent to which this is a problem varies within industrial districts. In the hierarchical German systems, in which all shop-floor groupings of worker skill identity are created within the pillarized vocational training system, and in which the relations between OEM and subcontractor remain stable over time, the problem of fragmentation as described above is considerable. In the horizontal Italian systems, in which the boundaries of skill categories are not defined by a public educational system and in which the identity of OEM and supplier are interchangeable over time, the problem is less severe—though even here, Italian commitment to the independence of producers can inhibit tactical integration (Varaldo and Ferrucci 1996). In both cases, institutionalized identities of fixed role positions tend to endure and perpetuate specialization that ultimately helps reproduce hierarchy and separation between conception and execution.

Many of the other non-industrial district forms of flexible organization out there in the global economy these days explicitly attempt to break from the notion of fixed role positions and break down all forms of organizational separation between conception and execution. These alternative flexible arrangements have their inspiration—or at least their initial coherently articulated historical origins—in Japanese industry, though the principles have long since been transformed, extended, and made better by others. Essential to this alternative form of flexibility is the group or work team into which managerial, developmental, and production capabilities and responsibilities are allocated, but in which no fixed roles or identities are allowed. Teams are created with the understanding that all members can be expected to undertake a broad array of possible tasks and fulfil a variety of different functions. There are no fixed specialities; there are only contextually specific tasks to perform and problems to solve by the group. Because problems are solved and new ones emerge, tasks continually change and are reallocated. No one is expected or expects to do the same general thing all the time. In fact, the more experience group members have at performing different roles, the more flexible and capable of problem-solving the group is likely to be. Group self-coordination and re-coordination is a collective learning process. The expertise of groups does not involve specific functions or skills; rather it involves the ability to collectively solve problems in production under conditions of rapid technological and product change (Sabel 1996a).

This same logic extends itself into relations between groups within a firm and to subcontracting relations between producers as well. Problem-solving-oriented groups communicate with one another about their common tasks and coordinate their interactions in ways that allow for rapid absorption of new technology and production arrangements as well as continuous monitoring of the quality of common process throughput. Similarly, as suppliers follow (or are pushed by) OEMs to increasingly constitute themselves in cross-functional groups, those groups then engage in collaborative development and implementation work with counterpart groups in the OEM as well as with other collaborating suppliers (Helper, MacDuffie, and Sabel 1998).

This is a very flexible form of organization in the division of labour: it utilizes the principle of specialization, but detaches it from specific persons, roles, or even firms, while constructing the Smithian coordinator through cooperative self-monitoring rather than bureaucratic hierarchy. In this way, conception and execution at work are completely unified over time and never have fixed or permanent locations in the organization (and at the limit, across organizations) —indeed, crucially, the whole idea of a permanent organizational form is inconsistent with the new principles of flexibility. Modern flexible production arrangements are increasingly congeries of these self-coordinating groups, where cooperation across group boundaries in solving common problems complements cooperation within groups. The firm is increasingly becoming an abstraction, a moving target of permanently shifting boundaries: groups within it cooperate with groups outside it, both of whom in time invariably turn to others when new problems arise (Helper, MacDuffie, and Sabel 1998).

This is not to say, however, that the firm is irrelevant or without power. On the contrary, increasingly in modern flexible production complexes, firms—as units of strategic interest and capital—are the creators of clusters of groups. They make flexible agglomerations. In the terms of this volume, firms, primarily large MNC firms, create flexible congeries of productive groups as a way of creating asset-augmenting dynamics in a region. We will see presently that this can involve a fundamental change in the character of a region.

But before we go there, it is important to see that the alternative principles of flexible organization—what Sabel (1996a) has called 'Learning by Monitoring' —are superior to the craft-based industrial district form of industrial flexibility on a number of counts. First, the great liability of the industrial district model, especially in its more Teutonic hierarchical incarnations, is that it incorporates an extra conversation into problem-solving deliberations that is not necessary in the learning-by-monitoring group-based model of flexibility. Not only do managers and workers have to figure out how to solve the problems in production and in the product that they confront, they also have to figure out how to come up with a solution that will preserve (reproduce) all of the roles and fixed functions of the participants in the conversation. Elegance of design and optimality in solutions are sacrificed for the internal politics of the craft-production world. Quality and rapid product change give way to plodding over-engineering. The alternative group-based flexible production principles present no such constraints (Herrigel 1997).

A further decisive difference between the two forms of flexibility is in the relative transferability of the two models. Transferability in the case of industrial districts is relatively low. As most of the literature on these systems shows, the accumulation of skill, collaborative practices, institutional supports, and trust among actors that makes the flexible system work as it does seems to be the result of a very long historical and regionally specific process of conflict and struggle for survival during the process of industrialization. It is difficult to imitate the craft-based flexibility of industrial districts because the systems seem to depend for their survival so significantly on the intangible shared forms of knowledge that makes for a common socioeconomic culture (Storper, 1998; Storper and Salais 1997). Introducing a German-style dual-training system into a region, for example, without also creating an array of supporting institutions for workers and firms as well as a specific set of competition policy rules and associational governance practices is not likely to create manufacturing flexibility in the region. Transferring the whole complex system is not only unrealistic, but it is also not likely to work unless those working within the system understand the tacit ways that action in the system is self-limited—as most Germans somehow actually do.

The alternative form of flexibility apparently does not have this kind of embedded limit on its transferability—at least if one judges by the degree to which the alternative form of flexibility has spread across the industrial economies of the world in the last ten years. Flexible systems of group-based collaboration and self-monitoring learning processes have been created in a broad array of cultural and regional contexts: the American midwest, Mexico, Taiwan, Hungary, Poland, Spain, the Czech Republic, Ireland, Scotland—the list is very long

(Elger and Smith 1994; Kaplinsky 1994; Humphrey 1995; Boyer *et al.* 1998; Kochan, Lansbury, and Macduffie 1997; Liker, Fruin, and Adler 1999; Haipeter 1999). This system seems to be more transferable than the industrial district craft system because it does not rely on trust or common culture or other forms of intangibles or tacit knowledge for its operation. Indeed, according to Charles Sabel, a central feature of the learning-by-monitoring system is that by constantly bringing people and groups together into monitoring discussions, they are forced to make explicit the tacit dimensions of their more local interactions. When something works in a team, the members have to be able to explain why to others outside the team. Goals for groups of teams are formulated through common monitoring discussions regarding how and why previous decisions and strategies succeeded or not and how collective endeavours can be made even better (Sabel 1996*a*; Dorf and Sabel 1998).

This form of interaction does not presuppose a common heritage and history or even extensive sets of extra-firm supporting institutions. Rather it requires a congery of non-hierarchically organized multifunctional groups staffed by human beings with a capacity to learn and an openness to change. There is no specific, delimited range of skill or technical know-how that is required for this alternative system of learning by monitoring to work. What is required is that people have the capacity to participate in collaborative team environments and that those teams develop the capacity to solve problems. This turns out to be a pretty plentiful raw material and is compatible with a very broad array of substantially disparate institutional, cultural, and market arrangements and practices (Enright 2000). The diffusion of these practices does not involve and should not be confused with organizational, institutional, cultural, or any other kind of convergence: Producers and regions are not embracing particular organizational forms; they are adopting common sets of principles that by their nature involve organizational variety and which are compatible with a broad array of local circumstances. Those who embrace new principles never do so from within unitary, unreformable systems. They selectively adapt the new principles to the possibilities of their own situation (Zeitlin 2000).

3. Deregionalization and Re-regionalization of Production Led by Large Firms

The irony in this observation about the relative transferability of alternative forms of flexibility is that in many cases, worldwide, where the group-based learning by monitoring system has flourished, it has been created by large, frequently multinational firms. Over the last decade, large firms in major manufacturing sectors such as automobiles, electronics, machinery, along with their major suppliers, *as sectoral communities*, decided to restructure their internal organizations and their mutual interactions along group-based learning-by-monitoring lines in order to enhance their manufacturing flexibility and maintain their competitiveness.

A crucial aspect of this movement towards the new principles has been the creation of regional agglomerations or clusters of similarly oriented, learning-by-monitoring-oriented firms. For the large firm and the broader sectoral community, in the terms of this volume, the process involved the creation of regionally concentrated asset-augmenting practices.

Crucially, this movement towards the creation of a particular form of regional industrial practices has nearly always involved the destruction of old regional realities, both within and among local firms. The American automobile makers Chrysler and Ford, for example, revamped much of their product development and production organization during the late 1980s and 1990s, introducing multifunctional teams at various levels of their organizations, constructing collaborative development and production relations among them with significant injunctions for continuous self-monitoring, and insisted that their suppliers do the same. If the suppliers resisted, they were cut out of the system. If they agreed to participate, they were incorporated into the self-monitoring collaboration of teams at all relevant levels of the auto producer (Helper 1992, 1995). Loyalty in this process was not important to those trying to construct the new alternative form of flexible production; the capacity to cooperate and solve problems was. If old trusted suppliers could not adjust, new supplier firms who could demonstrate their problem-solving capacity were employed. This shift on the part of large producers has transformed major manufacturing regions across the globe, in both the developed and the developing world.

This process of destroying the old and constructing the new involves both processes of deregionalization and re-regionalization. The deregionalization comes with the decision by the large producer and its major suppliers to abandon the old way in which they engaged in production and by extension were embedded in the region. All ties are cut in the sense that all are put under pressure to shift to the alternative system. The instigators are not under obligation to take any relations that they had under the old system into the new system, and in any case only those who are willing to produce in the new way, old friend or new, will be incorporated into the collaborative design and production process. The old production system and the old regional division of labour between producers and suppliers are in this way (and in a manner of speaking) killed and a new system with a new, and perhaps even more dense and extensive regional division of labour is put in its place. If anyone has followed the history of automobile regions in the USA, France, or Germany over the last ten years, it should be plain that this process of deregionalization and re-regionalization is a very traumatic and brutal process.

But the success of these efforts to move towards collaborative, team-based flexibility cannot be denied. And, that it does not depend on a pre-existing tradition of flexibility or craft knowledge or skill is proven by the fact that some of the most successful cases are regions in which there had long been a tradition of rigid mass production (the American midwest, Czech Republic, Hungary), or regions in which there had been relatively little industrialization at all (Ireland; Scotland;

Austin, Texas; Singapore) (Sabel 1996*b*; Hall 1997; Wong 1997; Wittke and Kurz 1998). The role of the sectoral communities around large firms in accomplishing this de-regionalization/re-regionalization is also most clear in those regions, such as Hungary and the Czech Republic, where the new flexible system was imported by multinationals. In Hungary and the Czech Republic, German and American automobile producers, along with their core new-style suppliers, went in, closed down most of the existing automobile capacity in each place and next to the old factories and with only those of the old workers that were needed and who could demonstrate a willingness to work in the new way, constructed new production facilities and in the end a collaborative team-based learning-by-monitoring automobile production cluster. Automobile production is very regionally clustered and collaborative. But it has very little to do with the traditional structures and practices that previously organized automobile production in the region (Mickler *et al.* 1996; Van Tulder and Ruigrok 1998; Wittke and Kurz 1998).[1]

4. Whither Industrial Districts?

This scenario of the emergence and diffusion of the alternative mode of industrial flexibility raises significant questions for the long-term viability of industrial districts—or at least for those, such as Baden-Württemberg in Germany, which have extensive integration with multinational actors who are actively engaged in trying to adopt the new principles of flexible practice. Before I enumerate what my concerns are and why I have them, I want to first indicate at least one way in which I think that many European industrial districts may not be directly affected by these developments.

There is no reason to think that there will be any movement away from the traditional craft-production-based forms of flexibility that characterizes industrial production in industrial districts if firms in the districts compete in markets in which the alternative form of flexibility is not present. That is, if firms in districts operate in niches that they dominate and experience very little challenge to this domination, then they are not likely to feel pressure to change from the alternative mode of flexibility. For example, it is very unlikely that certain kinds of circular knitting machinery producers in south-west Germany, who together control 98 per cent of the world market for the product, will be pressured to change any time in the near future. Likewise, many of the highly specialized Italian districts making designer plastics and textiles or speciality machinery, in similarly insulated niches, are likely to be spared pressure to confront the alternative mode of flexibility. Finegold and Wagner (1999) have done a very extensive study of the pump sector in south-west Germany and have found, for example, that the kind of pressures facing these on the whole fairly insulated producers have not resulted in significant departures from the craft system of flexibility.

There is, however, a relatively short list of lines of business that are insulated from modern trends in the nature of global competition in this way. Indeed, in an industrial district such as Baden-Württemberg, insulation from the pressures of the global economy is very far from the case. There are very large automobile and electronics producers located in the region who have felt the competitive pressures and the ideological furore of their major colleagues and competitors in their respective global sectoral communities. Such producers have become acutely aware of the advantages of the new forms of flexibility and of the disadvantages of their own traditional craft-production forms of flexibility. Loss of market share to the Japanese and other global competitors using the alternative production methods, declining profits, bad productivity numbers, and declining quality as managers pressure the craft system to change models and technologies faster than it is capable of changing have underscored the superiority of the alternative system. Similarly, machine tool producers in Baden-Württemberg have been pressured to change by the growing competitiveness of American machine tool producers on world markets and the continuing excellence of Japanese producers —both of whom deploy the alternative system (Herrigel 1999; Griffin 1996). Most of the producers in the industrial district known as Baden-Württemberg have had an extremely hard time of it on the world market during the 1990s and have been under enormous pressure to make themselves more competitive. That has given rise to very serious regional debates about the viability and desirability of the alternative flexible team-based production arrangements in the local economy (Herrigel 1997; Cooke 1997; Cooke and Morgan 1998; Heidenreich and Krauss 1998).

From my point of view, it is very easy to see how movement towards the alternative form of flexibility will be bad for the local industrial district in Baden-Württemberg. The key reason for my pessimism is that I don't see how the deregionalization process will be followed by a re-regionalization process inside the old regional boundaries of Baden-Württemberg, or if it will, that this will involve many of the older and numerous producers that characterized small and medium-sized firm production in the old industrial district. As noted above, albeit figuratively, the deregionalization that has accompanied efforts on the part of large producers in other regions to adopt the alternative form of flexibility has involved killing the old regional system: removing the firm from traditional ties, submitting all of those ties to rigorous re-evaluation, rejecting all claims to loyalty, hiring strangers able to demonstrate their ability to work in a team-based learning by monitoring system.

Daimler-Benz, Audi, Robert Bosch, IBM, Hewlett Packard, SONY—all large MNC's based in Baden-Württemberg—have in fact begun engaging in this process of killing off the old regional division of labour that they were embedded in. This has involved a sharp winnowing of the number of suppliers that firms engage with not simply in general, but also within the region itself. Collaborative production in autos or electronics blurs the boundaries between firms, but it also involves significantly fewer firm boundaries: multiple sourcing has been replaced with long-term contracting with smaller numbers of intimate firms. These firms can be local firms, *but they need not be*. Consistent with the general process of deregionalization, the large firms have shown a willingness to invite in foreign expert collaborative suppliers, such as the Canadian firm Magna, to set up Greenfield operations in the region. Such firms already know how to produce in the alternative way and are experts at setting up the alternative system of continuous problem-solving that the producers desire. More ominously for the region, expert collaborator firms can be accessed from their locations elsewhere in Germany and even elsewhere in Europe (including Eastern Europe) without requiring relocation into the old industrial district. Re-regionalization occurs, but it does not have to occur within the old geographic boundaries of the traditional district.

This process of deregionalization and re-regionalization is in the end good for the long-term health of the sectoral communities that initiate them.[2] And it is not horrible for many firms and workers in the old region who are able to survive the killing that goes on in the transition from old to new. But it is indisputably bad for many firms and workers who become victims of the deregionalization process. It is not at all clear what will happen to those regional actors (and there are many many of them in the automobile and electronics branches in Baden-Württemberg). Not many will be able to turn to the production of circular knitting machines or pumps.

One major hope is realistic, but it carries with it a very serious probability that the standard of living in the region will decline. The hope is that the firms who are shut out of the re-regionalization process initiated by the sectoral community of large producers, will be able to learn from their mistakes, move in the direction of the new problem-solving forms of production, and solicit work from producers elsewhere in Europe. Like the auto workers and managers in Hungary and the Czech Republic before multinational investment, those in Baden-Württemberg left behind by the re-regionalization process initiated by Daimler-Benz and Robert Bosch could be attractive raw material for other multinationals in other sectoral communities looking to set up flexible clusters of collaborative production. They can learn too. This is absolutely true. But in order to compete for that kind of asset-augmenting investment, producers in Baden-Württemberg will have to be willing to offer their capacity to learn at the level of wages that their colleagues in Hungary and the Czech Republic currently receive. And this is not attractive.

5. What Can Regional Governments Do?

The process described above is an emergent one and it involves considerable complexity for policy-makers. On the one hand, plainly policy-makers in regional governments want to do everything they can to assist large producers and their sectoral communities reconstitute themselves on a competitive basis within their regions. Successful re-regionalization carries with it inward investment, high-quality jobs, and significant secondary and tertiary development effects. I am not suggesting, and there is certainly no local evidence in Baden-Württemberg to the effect, that regional policy-makers should attempt to block the deregionalization/re-regionalization dynamic described above. Indeed, policy-makers in Baden-Württemberg are doing all they can to encourage the success of this dynamic by accommodating the large land-intensive and Greenfield construction projects of Daimler-Benz and others large MNCs in the region which seek to create a new spatial location for the newer production practices. There is in any case much about the current infrastructure of the region that is attractive to high-quality manufactures: the many universities and research institutes (in particular the Frauenhof Institute) are extremely valuable resources for producers, as are the more practical production oriented and vocational institutions in the region which provide services to those on the shop floor. These traditional objects of regional industrial strategy retain their value to producers within the new production systems. The problem is that they do not address the difficulties of those cut out of the new system.

These difficulties are of two kinds, only one of which, in my view, can be addressed at the regional level and even then with considerable difficulty. The first difficulty those cut out of the new system experience is that they have to learn how to produce according to the new principles of flexible production (or find a niche in which their strengths in the craft system continue to have value). Regional policy in Baden-Württemberg can be helpful here by encouraging the institutional agents who have continuous contact with producers—such as agents of the para-public Steinbeis Stiftung and the various community colleges (*Fachhochschulen*)—to provide their clients with necessary information and knowledge of the principles as they are being implemented by other producers elsewhere in the region. This was a classic mechanism for the transfer of knowledge and know-how in the old craft-production-based system. But in order for it to function properly in the new context reforms have to be introduced into the service institutions. Most particularly, within the educational institutions, specialized divisions of knowledge tend to reflect the pillarized structure of the old craft system. In order for educational institutions to play a role in the diffusion of knowledge about group work and cross-functionality, specialists in the universities need to recognize the rigidity of their own institutional identities. Regional educational policy can instigate this kind of change in the core supporting institutions around the economy (Herrigel 1997). Trade associations in Baden-Württemberg—but also throughout the German economy—have been encouraging regional governments and educational institutions in this direction. They have also been lobbying hard for regional and federal subsidy for firms to receive ISO 9000 certification—a crucial, if perhaps superficial, indicator of familiarity with the new principles of production organization (Hancké and Casper 1996; Alig 2000).

Such are the kind of local policies that regions and regional actors in Baden-Württemberg can and have been following in an effort to cultivate the capacity of local producers to participate in the re-regionalization process being initiated by large firms. None of these policies, however, addresses the second difficulty that the dynamic of deregionalization and re-regionalization of production as described above poses to the region. Local producers excluded from the new production networks established by local multinationals will be forced to look elsewhere in Europe to sell their production capacity, and in so doing will have to do so at a level of wages that is being established, at least for now, by the low-wage, high-quality flexible producers in Central Europe. Here regional actors are inadequate by themselves to address regional problems. National and even European Union-level actors will have to address problems of regional deregionalization or lowering of living standards as a result of investment and wage patterns elsewhere in the community. To date this problem of uneven wage levels and MNC cross-border production has been posed more or less exclusively as a trade union and social issue that exists within globalizing multinationals (Simons and Westermann 1997; Haipeter 1999). But this example suggests that many workers within small and medium-sized specialists in (formerly) high-wage areas could be affected. Whether or not the social actors in Europe will have the capacity to act concertedly on this matter is a notoriously open question. The example of the consequences of the adoption of new principles of flexible production in the industrial district of Baden-Württemberg, however, suggests that social actors could conceivably find allies in unexpected quarters of subnational government.

NOTES

In addition to John Dunning and the participants of the conference that produced this book, I would like to thank Helmut Voelzkow, Volker Wittke, Henry Farrell, Ulrich Glassmann, Dieter Rehfeld, and Hans Joachim Braczyk for interesting discussions that led to the arguments in this chapter. The usual disclaimers apply.

1. Its important to at least point out that this crass abandonment of the old practices is not the case generally in Eastern Europe. It is simply, at least according to the cases that I have read, true of automobile restructuring driven by Western multinationals. For the continued salience of the old in the new in sectors not assaulted by MNC's see the great book by David Stark and Llazlo Bruszt, *Post Socialist Pathways* (1998).

2. And this could account for the discrepancy between the pessimistic tone of my argument compared to the relatively optimistic perspective represented by Cooke and Morgan in their excellent *Associational Economy* (1998). In their view, the problems in B-W are essentially cyclical and health will return with the return of better economic times. I have no argument with this, though my claim is that the recovery (when it comes) will be on the basis of a very different small and medium-sized firm industrial structure from that which has traditionally dominated the region.

REFERENCES

Alig, Julie (2000), 'The Adoption of ISO 9000 Manufacturing Standards in the German Machinery Industry', PH.D. diss. in progress, Department of Political Science, University of Chicago.

Boyer, Robert *et al.* (1998), *Between Imitation and Innovation* (Oxford: Oxford University Press).

Cooke, Philip (1997), 'Regions in a global market: the experiences of Wales and Baden Württemberg', in *Review of International Political Economy* 4(2): 349–81.

—— and Morgan, Kevin (1998), *The Associational Economy* (Oxford: Oxford University Press).

Dorf, Michael, and Sabel, Charles (1998), 'A Constitution of Democratic Experimentalism', in *Columbia Law Review* 98(2): 267–473.

Elger, Tony, and Smith, Chris (eds.) (1994), *Global Japanization? The Transnational Transformation of the Labour Process* (London: Routledge).

Enright, Michael (1993), 'The Geographic Scope of Competitive Advantage', in Elke Dirven, Joost Groenewegen, and Sjef van Hoof (eds.), *Stuck in the Region? Changing Scales for Regional Identity*, Nederlands Geografische Studies 155: 81–102.

—— (1996), 'Regional Clusters and Economic Development: A Research Agenda', in Udo Staber, Norbert Schaefer, and Basu Sharma (eds.), *Business Networks. Prospects for Regional Development* (Berlin: Walter de Gruyter): 191–233.

—— (1998), 'Regional Clusters and Firm Strategy', in Alfred Chandler, Peter Hagström, and Örjan Sölvell (eds.), *The Dynamic Firm. The Role of Technology, Strategy, Organization and Regions* (Oxford: Oxford University Press), 315–42.

—— (2000), 'The Globalization of Competition and the Localization of Competitive Advantage: Policies toward Regional Clustering', in N. Hood and S. Young (eds.), *The Globalization of Multinational Enterprise Activity and Economic Development* (Basingstoke: Macmillan), 303–31.

Finegold, David, and Wagner, Karin (1999), 'Can German Manufacturers Retain Their Competive Edge? Restructuring in the Pump Industry', in David Finegold and Pepper Culpepper (eds.), *The German Skills Machine* (Providence: Berghahn Books), forthcoming.

Friedman, David (1987), *The Misunderstood Miracle* (Ithaca: Cornell University Press).

Griffin, John (1996), 'The Politics of Ownership and the Transformation of Corporate Governance in Germany, 1973–(1995)', Ph.D diss., Dept. of Political Science, Massachusetts, Institution Technology.

Haipeter, Thomas (1999), 'Zum Formwandel der Internationaliserung bei VW in den 80er und 90er Jahren', in PROKLA 29(1): 145–171.

Hall, Christopher (1997), *Steel Phoenix: The Fall and Rise of the US Steel Industry* (London: Macmillan).

Hancké, Bob, and Casper, Steven (1996) 'ISO 9000 in the French and German Car Industry. How international quality standards support varieties of capitalism', Working Paper, FS I 96-313, Science Centre, Berlin.

Heidenreich, Martin, and Krauss, Gerhard (1998), 'The Baden Württemberg production and innovation regime: Past successes and new challenges', in Hans-Joachim Braczyk, Philip Cooke, and Martin Heidenreich (eds.), *Regional Innovation Systems* (London: UCL Press): 214–44.

Helper, Susan (1991), 'An Exit-Voice Analysis of Supplier Relations', in Richard M. Coughlin (ed.), *Morality, Rationality and Efficiency: New Perspectives on Socioeconomics.*
—— (1994), 'Three Steps Forward, Two Steps Back in Automotive Supplier Relations', *Technovation* 14.
—— and Levine, David (1992), 'Long-Term Supplier Relations and Product Market Structure', *Journal of Law, Economics, and Organization* 8(3).
—— MacDuffie, John Paul, and Sabel, Charles (1998), 'Boundaries of the Firm as a Design Problem', unpublished manuscript, Columbia University Law School.
—— and Sako, Mari (1995), 'Supplier Relations in Japan and the United States: Are They Converging?' *Sloan Management Review* 36(3).
Herrigel, Gary (1996), *Industrial Constructions. The Sources of German Industrial Power* (New York: Cambridge University Press).
—— (1997), 'The Limits of German Manufacturing Flexibility', in Lowell Turner (ed.), *The Political Economy of Unified Germany: Reform and Resurgence or Another Model in Decline?* (Ithaca: ILR-Cornell University Press).
—— (1999), 'Governance of Small and Medium-Sized Firm Manufacturing in Germany: Transformation of the Machine Tool industry in the 20th Century', in *Economie et Historie.*
Humphrey, John (ed.) (1995), 'Special Issue: Industrial Organization and Manufacturing Competitiveness in Developing Countries', *World Development* 23(1).
Kaplinsky, Raphael (1994), *Easternization: The Spread of Japanese Management Techniques to Developing Countries* (Ilford, Essex: Frank Cass).
Kochan, Thomas A., Lansbury, Russell D., and Macduffie, John Paul (ed.) (1997), *After Lean Production: Evolving Employment Practices in the World Auto Industry* (Ithaca: ILR Press).
Liker, Jeffrey, Fruin, Mark, and Adler, Paul (eds.) (1999), *Remade in America: Transplanting and Transforming Japanese Production Systems* (Oxford: Oxford University Press).
Mickler, Otfried, Englehard, Norbert, Lungwitz, Ralph, and Walker, Bettina (1996), *Nach der Trabi-Era: Arbeiten in schlanken Fabriken. Modernisierung der ostdeutschen Automobilindustrie* (Berlin: Sigma).
Piore, Michael, and Sabel, Charles (1984), *The Second Industrial Divide* (New York: Basic Books).
Porter, Michael (1990), *The Competitive Advantage of Nations* (New York: Free Press).
Pyke, F., Becattini, G., and Sengenberger, W. (eds.) (1990), *Industrial Districts and InterFirm Co-operation in Italy* (Geneva: International Institute for Labour Studies).
—— and Sengenberger, W. (eds.) (1992), *Industrial Districts and Local Economic Regeneration* (Geneva: International Institute for Labour Studies).
Saxenian, AnnaLee (1992), *Regional Advantage* (Cambridge, Mass.: Harvard University Press).
Sabel, Charles (1989), 'Flexible Specialization and the Re-emergence of Regional Economies', in Paul Hirst and Jonathan Zeitlin (eds.), *Reversing Industrial Decline? Industrial Structure and Policy in Britain and Her Competitors* (London: Routledge): 17–70.
—— (1996a), 'Learning by Monitoring', in Richard Swedberg and Neil Smelser (eds.), *The Handbook on Economic Sociology* (Princeton: Russell Sage/Princeton University Press).
—— (1996b), *Ireland: Local Partnerships and Social Innovation* (Paris: OECD).

Scott, Allen (1998), 'The Geographic Foundations of Industrial Performance', in A. Chandler, P. Hagström, and Ö. Sölvell (eds.), *The Dynamic Firm* (New York: Oxford University Press): 384–401.

Simons, Rolf, and Westermann, Klaus (eds.) (1997), *Standortdebatte und Globalisierung der Wirtschaft* (Marburg).

Stark, David, and Bruszt, Llazlo (1998), *Post Socialist Pathways* (New York: Cambridge University Press).

Storper, Michael (1998), *Regional Worlds* (New York: Guilford Press).

—— and Salais, Robert (1997), *World of Production: The Action Frameworks of the Economy* (Cambridge, Mass.: Harvard University Press).

Van Tulder, Ron, and Ruigrok, Winfried (1998), 'European Cross-National Production Neworks in the Auto Industry: Eastern Europe as the Low End of the European Car Complex', Working Paper 121 (May), Berkeley Roundtable of International Economics (http://socrates.berkeley.edu/~briewww/pubs/wp/wp121.htm).

Varaldo, R., and Ferrucci, L. (1996), 'The evolutionary nature of the firm within industrial districts', *European Planning Studies* 4: 16–23.

Wittke, Volker, and Kurz, Constanze (1998), 'Using Industrial Capacities as a Way of Integrating Central-East European Economics', Working Paper 123 (May), Berkeley Roundtable on International Economics (http://socrates.berkeley.edu/~briewww/pubs/wp/wp123.html).

Wong, Poh-Kam (1997), 'Creation of a Regional Hub for Flexible Production. The Case of the Hard Disk Drive Industry in Singapore', *Industry and Innovation* 4(2): 183–205.

Zeitlin, Jonathan (1992), 'Industrial districts and local economic regeneration: Overview and comment', in F. Pyke and W. Sengenberger (eds.), *Industrial Districts and Local Economic Regeneration* (Geneva: International Institute for Labour Studies): 279–94.

—— (2000), 'Introduction: Americanization and Its Limits: Reworking US Technology and Management in Postwar Europe and Japan', in Jonathan Zeitlin and Gary Herrigel (eds.), *Americanization and Its Limits: Reworking US Technology and Management in Postwar Europe and Japan* (Oxford: Oxford University Press).

11

Firms, Regions, and Strategy in a Diverging World:
The Australian Case

Peter Sheehan and Bhajan Grewal

1. Introduction

This volume is concerned with the implications of the knowledge economy for the spatial distribution of economic activity, and with the role played by foreign direct investment (FDI) and multinational enterprises (MNEs) in influencing that distribution. In Chapter 1, Dunning draws attention to two antithetical sets of forces in play globally: those working towards greater geographical *dispersion* of economic activities and those working towards increased geographical *concentration* of those activities. Indeed, he argues that 'globalization and localization are opposite sides of the same coin' (Sect. 5.2). That is, at the same time as economic activities, and perhaps particularly those of MNEs, are becoming dispersed around the world they are also being increasingly concentrated in particular regions or 'sticky places'. An important part of this process, he suggests, is the emergence of clusters of asset-augmenting activities, whereby MNEs and local firms concentrate many of their activities in small regional areas, *inter alia* to take advantage of the dynamic externalities associated with the use of intellectual capital.

For countries removed from the mainstream of knowledge-based wealth creation—whether by the 'tyranny of distance', by the fact of underdevelopment, or by immersion in processes of transition to a market economy—these are issues of fundamental importance. The concentration of economic activity in particular regional clusters may well lead to a process of divergence between nations, and between regions within nations. For example, if these growing clusters are heavily concentrated in the Triad countries, per capita income levels in countries outside the Triad may well fall relative to those of the leading nations, rather than converging towards common levels in line with standard economic theory and national aspirations. On the other hand, if individual 'distant' countries can capture MNE activity in dynamic regional clusters, this is likely to contribute strongly to accelerated economic growth. Further, where the activities of national firms and MNEs do develop some vigorous regional clusters in individual nations, the disparities between regions within those nations may be greatly exacerbated.

This clustering may promote overall growth, but if adjustment is slow between regions it may also lead to real hardship and to underutilization of resources in slower-growing regions.

Thus many countries distant from the mainstream of knowledge-based wealth creation have a number of related concerns:

- whether it can be ensured that, as nations, they will participate fully in emerging global growth processes;
- what policies, in respect of both MNEs and local firms, will best secure this participation; and
- whether this participation, if it is achieved, will generate growing divergence on a regional basis within the nation.

The objective of this chapter is to explore the reality of these phenomena, and the diversity of policy responses to them, for the case of one small, open economy far removed from the main sources of knowledge generation—Australia. After briefly reviewing some recent relevant developments in economic theory, our analysis focuses particularly on the role of foreign direct investment and of both local firms and MNEs within Australia, and on some of the regional aspects of this involvement.

There are three main themes in the argument. Firstly, two recent developments in economic theory (new growth theory and the new economic geography) both explore, in different ways, the impact of the forces of dispersion and concentration in the growth process referred to above. They imply that in certain circumstances these forces can lead to increased divergence in growth outcomes between nations or regions, as activity is concentrated in certain 'sticky places' at the expense of other regions. In both cases this concentration may become more pronounced in the knowledge-based economy, as access to relevant knowledge becomes a central determinant of competitiveness.

Secondly, the particular outcome for a given nation or region will depend heavily on the activity of MNEs and local firms within that nation. In Australia, MNEs tend to be dominant, especially in the higher-tech manufacturing industries, but often lack substantial export or innovation focus. That is, many of the activities of MNEs are directed at making use of Australian assets or producing for the domestic market, rather than at creating new assets for global markets. Australian-owned firms, while in many cases more active in such matters, are generally very small and find it difficult to compete globally. The past pattern of activities of MNEs has contributed to the pronounced concentration of manufacturing in particular areas in Australia, and changes in the regional distribution of manufacturing have reflected changes in the global positioning of MNEs and the difficulties of local firms. But Australia has not as yet captured many substantial asset-generating activities of MNEs, which may have created knowledge-based developments of world scale. There is little sustained evidence yet for Australia of the emergence of dynamic clusters of asset-augmenting activities, whereby MNEs and local firms concentrate many of their activities in small regional areas, to create and produce products for global markets. But there are some hopeful signs.

Our third theme relates to the policy issues raised by these facts. In Australia the policy debate on such matters has turned upon a central choice: that between pure market forces and measures to enhance the operation of markets, on the one hand, and more interventionist policies in the pursuit of MNE activity and of the development of local firms on the other. We note certain examples of national and state policies and conclude that, after two decades of active experimentation and in spite of a range of successful initiatives, neither the Australian government nor regional authorities have settled on adequate responses to the forces of the knowledge economy. While the reasons for this relate partly to failures in Australian institutions and policy processes, the underlying issues may be of more general interest. Certainly, the future prosperity of Australia—whether it continues to keep pace with leading nations such as the USA in growth in GDP per capita or falls behind—largely depends on effective national strategies to develop dynamic clusters of asset-augmenting activities.

2. Divergence in the Knowledge Economy

The presumption among many economists for some time has been that, given a growing reliance on market mechanisms and an open world economy, a steady process of convergence among nations towards common income levels could be expected. The IMF expressed this consensus when it said that 'there are many reasons to expect a converging pattern, especially in a more open and integrated world economy' (IMF 1997: 78). The reasons cited included large technology gaps between countries, providing much scope for technological catch-up, and big differences across countries in capital/output ratios, implying that in a world with free capital movements funds should flow to countries in which capital is relatively scarce and the rate of return higher. Similar arguments should apply to regions within countries, for which the barriers to factor mobility are even lower.

This confidence was in part based on a particular interpretation of standard neoclassical growth theory. This theory, drawing on the seminal models of Solow and Swan, predicts that economies subject to market forces will converge in terms of per capita GDP levels, either absolutely (if the factors determining the steady state such as technology and preferences are assumed to be common among countries), or conditionally, that is relative to individual country steady-state levels, if these and other factors assumed to determine the steady state vary across countries. A substantial body of literature (such as Mankiw, Romer, and Weil 1992 and Sala-i-Martin 1996) argues that the neoclassical model with conditional convergence is consistent with the time-series evidence for a wide range of countries, and parallel studies have suggested convergence within regions of major countries. But, if the determinants of individual country steady-state

levels differ significantly across countries, conditional convergence may involve
'convergence' to very different per capita GDP levels, and hence be consistent
with marked divergence rather than with convergence in per capita income levels,
as these terms are commonly understood.

Recent developments have thrown doubt on this general consensus from two
directions. On the empirical side, recent work (e.g. Durlauf and Johnson 1995;
Quah 1996*a*, 1996*b*; Durlauf and Quah 1998) as well as recent global trends
have called into question whether there is any sense in which the world's nations
or regions can be realistically said to be converging to common income levels.
On the theoretical side, there has been over the past decade or so an explosion
of new theoretical literature bearing on these issues, initially in terms of new
growth theories and more recently in terms of 'the new economic geography'.
Neither the theoretical nor empirical issues can be pursued extensively here (for
a detailed discussion see Sheehan and Grewal 1999), but some further comments
on the theoretical literature may serve to place the subsequent discussion about
Australia in a richer context.

There are many similarities in both the problems addressed and the techniques
used in the new growth theory and in the new economic geography literature.
The new growth models abstract from transport costs and study the endogenous
factors influencing long-term growth rates, while the new economic geography
explores the implications of transport costs and related factors for the distribution of economic activity. Both address the impact of increasing returns, and make
extensive use of the framework of monopolistic competition to model increasing returns in an otherwise competitive framework. But while the new growth
theory literature considers a wide range of mechanisms generating increasing returns,
the new geography literature focuses primarily on pecuniary externalities, whose
value may be influenced by transport costs.

2.1. New Economic Geography Models

The new economic geography models explore the implications of transport costs
in a situation in which there are no differences in history or in technical capability between regions or countries, and regional outcomes emerge from the
interaction of transport costs and particular characteristics of production and
consumption. Typically, these models have two sectors—agriculture which is
dispersed in fixed locations and shows constant returns, and manufacturing
which is mobile and shows increasing returns. They generate a tension between
centrifugal forces working towards regional dispersion of economic activity
and *centripetal* forces favouring concentration. These are the equivalents of
Dunning's forces of dispersion and concentration referred to earlier. Some ver-
sions (e.g. Krugman 1991, 1995) have mobility of manufacturing labour as
well of capital, and can be thought of as modelling the distribution of activity
within a country; others (e.g. Krugman and Venables 1995) do not permit labour

mobility, and can be thought of as addressing the distribution of activity *across countries.*

In the Krugman (1991) model, for example, the centrifugal force opposing concentration is the economies to be achieved by dispersed production in serving a widely spread market, so that if manufacturing is small relative to agriculture its plants will be highly dispersed to meet the needs of the farmers. The centripetal forces arise from the forward and backward linkages between manufacturing and the market: manufacturing both supplies goods to workers and creates locations with higher income than other locations, so that there are incentives for manufacturing firms to cluster in specific locations. In Krugman and Venables (1995) there are two types of manufactured goods (intermediate goods and final goods) and specialization in the production of intermediate goods with increasing returns generates external economies, the counterpart of the linkages between firms in the earlier model.

Taking these two models together and abstracting from differences in their production structure, the broad message is reasonably clear. When transport costs are very high each nation or region has to be self-sufficient. When transport costs fall below a critical value exchange between areas becomes a possibility. In this stage differences between areas (including real wage differences between countries in the international case) will set in train forces to bring about a concentration of activity, as the strength of the centripetal forces (firm linkages or external economies) begins to offset the declining advantages of diversification. But as transport costs continue to fall to very low levels, the strength of these centripetal forces will also begin to erode. The value of being close to suppliers and markets will fall relative to real wage differences, peripheral nations will gain, and a new stage of convergence emerges. In the extreme, at zero transport costs, there are no proximity benefits in firm linkages nor any reason for intermediate goods production to cluster in particular countries.

So both models generate a three-stage process, related to transport costs: at very high transport costs activity is widely dispersed; as transport costs fall concentration begins to take place, as the centripetal forces related to backward and forward linkages prevail; as transport costs become very low activity again becomes dispersed, as the value of those linkages is eroded by the continued fall in transport costs.

2.2. The New Growth Models

The new growth models abstract from transport costs, effectively assuming them to be zero, and generally exclude labour mobility. They can be used, however, to study two main types of situation closely related to the topic of the regional implications of the global knowledge economy. One type is that in which nations differ in history, typically in the starting stocks of human or physical capital or of technology. The other consists of situations in which, because of endogenous changes in the range of products available on the market, imperfect competition and incomplete markets prevail and lead to multiple equilibrium growth paths for countries similar in economic conditions and history. Using a range of other assumptions and the standard techniques of neoclassical economics the new growth models study the properties of the steady-state optimum growth path(s). For a review of this literature see Romer (1994*a*) and Aghion and Howitt (1998).

In such models differences in history or initial technical capability can generate sustained and even growing divergence in economic outcomes in the absence of transport costs, and such divergence can also emerge from cumulative processes in a context of imperfect competition and endogenous products. The resulting position of countries which are locked into low-income levels is often referred to as a poverty trap. Azariadis (1996) has valuably surveyed the emergence of poverty traps, and of divergence more generally, in new growth theory models with complete markets and a given set of products. In this analysis three important types of case which generate divergent outcomes in appropriate growth models are:

- external increasing returns, arising from technology and/or human capital;
- industrialization under increasing returns; and
- internal increasing returns and complementarities between industries.

While the details of individual models differ widely, in broad terms the country relatively strong in the factor generating increasing returns and driving growth (say R&D, human capital, increasing-returns manufacturing, or linkages in the form of complementarities between industries) will enter a sustained growth path, while the country relatively weak in the relevant factor will enter a low or indeed even zero growth path. Similar results can be obtained in models introducing the endogenous development of new goods into the economic system (e.g. Romer 1990, 1994*b*; Grossman and Helpman 1991).

2.3. Impact of the Knowledge Economy

It is beyond the scope of this chapter to elaborate either of these sets of models further, or to explore the impact of the rise of the knowledge economy on them in a systematic way. Our central conjecture is simple, namely that the knowledge economy intensifies, for both sets of models, the strength of the centripetal forces generating concentration relative to that of the centrifugal forces driving dispersion. Rising knowledge intensity is likely, in the context of these models, to generate increased concentration of economic activity.

The knowledge economy is envisaged as a world in which goods and services are becoming much more complex and knowledge-intensive, both in terms of broad product capability and in terms of being tailored to the specific requirements of particular users. Frequently cited characteristics[1] of such an economy include the following:

- increasing R&D intensity, with much shorter lead times for the development of new products and shorter product lives;
- heavy sunk costs related to the creation, production, and distribution of goods, giving rise to increasing returns to scale;
- increasing externalities and indeed complementarities between firms and industry, and within the firm increasing economies of scope, as products and the product chain become more complex:
- the increasing importance, as products become more closely targeted to customer needs, of backward and forward linkages to suppliers and customers, with these linkages often geographically driven in spite of lower-cost communications; and
- the vital role of human capital, and of the substantial external benefits available to firms from a high general level of human capital.

In the new economic geography models, the centripetal forces arise either from backward or forward linkages between firms or from external economies deriving from the production of intermediate goods. But because, in a standard neoclassical framework, these benefits are mediated only by transport costs, their benefits reduce as transport costs become very low. In a knowledge-intensive economy, these linkages will be driven, for example, by shared tacit knowledge and human capital, and by learning by doing. Thus although transport costs will continue to fall as the economy becomes more knowledge-intensive, reducing the centrifugal forces related to the costs of supplying remote regions, the value of linkages or external economies driven by knowledge factors will increase.

A similar argument applies to the new growth models. The rise of the knowledge-based economy seems likely to intensify precisely those features (e.g. externalities associated with R&D and human capital, increasing returns internal to firms, complementarities between industries and between firms, factors associated with the creation of new goods) which generate geographic concentration and divergent outcomes between economies in new growth models.

Thus on either approach there seem to be general theoretical reasons for anticipating an increasing divergence in levels of economic activity between countries as the knowledge economy develops. Countries which possess strong capabilities for the generation and application of knowledge, or which can develop those capabilities through the attraction of MNEs or the development of their own firms, are likely to prosper. Furthermore, the development of the relevant capabilities is likely to involve the growth of geographical clusters of innovative, knowledge-based firms and related institutions. As Audretsch argues in Chapter 3 of this volume, the increased importance of new ideas based on tacit knowledge has 'triggered a resurgence in the importance of local regions as a key source of comparative advantage'. Countries which do not meet these conditions are in danger of falling further behind the leading nations.

3. Multinational Enterprises, Local Firms, and Policy Challenges

In the face of such renewed pressures for economic polarization, the outcome for individual countries in the knowledge economy will depend on many factors. Of these factors, three—the activities of MNEs, the performance of local firms, and the development of clusters of asset-augmenting activities—are likely to be of special importance. Economic outcomes are being increasingly driven by flows of capital, technology, and management expertise across borders and by the activities of MNEs which lie behind these flows, as they pursue their desired global allocation of activities. Central also will be the character and dynamism of local firms and the interplay of MNEs with these local firms. For example, do the resource and knowledge flows from abroad enhance rather than destroy local firms and local structures for the generation and application of knowledge? Finally, the emergence of geographical clusters of firms and knowledge-based institutions facilitating the innovation process will also be critical. Indeed Audretsch argues (Chapter 3 above) that innovative regional clusters are becoming in some ways more important than footloose MNEs in the production and application of new knowledge. These three factors, together with their regional impact and the policy challenges to which they give rise, are addressed in relation to Australia in the remainder of this chapter.

3.1. Foreign Direct Investment in Australia's Development

Since the arrival of the First Fleet in 1788 and the displacement of the aboriginal occupants of the continent, foreign direct investment has played a central role in the development of a Western society and economy in Australia. This was true not only for the colonies in the nineteenth century, when the focus of such investment was primarily on agriculture, property, and mining, but has continued to be true since Federation in 1901, with an increasing emphasis on manufacturing and more recently on service industries. The nature of the Australian economy and the structure of firms cannot be understood without close attention to foreign investment and to the resulting ownership patterns.

The two decades after the Second World War saw substantial net foreign investment flows into Australia, even though this post-Bretton Woods period was one of only modest capital flows internationally. This is evident from Figure 11.1 which shows net direct foreign direct investment into Australia as a share of GDP (using a three-year moving average to smooth out annual fluctuations) since 1948–51. As the figure shows, net investment averaged 1.8 per cent of GDP between 1951 and 1973 inclusive, but fell substantially after 1973, to average only 0.8 per cent between 1974 and 1997. Thus the net flows of direct investment into Australia were much lower in the later period.

It is important to note, however, that since the mid-1980s, that is since the opening up of the Australian economy to global markets, the low level of *net*

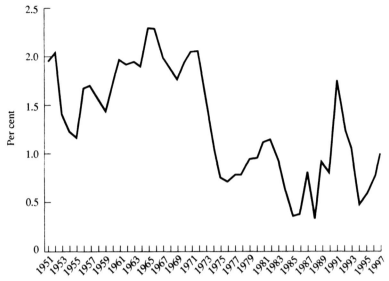

FIG. 11.1. Foreign direct investment, net inflow per cent of GDP, 1951–1997
Source: Australian Bureau of Statistics, Balance of Payments, Cat. No. 53020.

inflows relative to the pre-1974 period is due to increased *outflow* rather than to lower *inflows*. From the mid-1980s outward foreign investment from Australia, traditionally quite low, has increased sharply, exceeding 2 per cent of GDP in the early 1990s and remaining over 1 per cent of GDP in 1994–6. Thus the reduction in net inflows shown in Figure 11.1 is consistent with a continuing gross inflow of about 2 per cent of GDP after 1985 and a much higher net outflow than in the earlier period.

Since the Plaza Accord of 1984, foreign direct investment has increased rapidly on a global basis. For example, gross outflows of direct investment from OECD countries (the sum of gross outflows from each country rather than the gross outflow from the region as a whole) averaged 1 per cent of OECD GDP over 1982–4, but by 1995 reached 3 per cent of GDP. Australia has not been a major beneficiary of this upsurge, with gross inflows of foreign direct investment after 1985 being at about the same level (as a share of GDP) as in the pre-1974 period. The major change has been the growth in Australian investment abroad, in large part driven by the emergence of Australian MNEs. In spite of this recent change, Australia's domestic industrial structure needs to be seen as resulting in good part from continuing waves of foreign investment, but with continuing interplay between local and international investors.

In his discussion of MNEs in Chapter 1, Dunning distinguishes between the multidomestic MNE and the globally integrated MNE, and for the latter between three types of specialization: horizontal, vertical, and asset-augmenting specialization. Australia has covered both types of governance structure and each form of specialization, together with some further variants, particularly related to resource-based activities. For our purposes it is useful to simplify this somewhat and simply distinguish between three types of *motive* lying behind foreign direct investment and the activities of MNEs:

- asset-utilizing activity, which seeks to make use of existing assets in Australia (particularly resource assets) as the basis for national or international businesses;
- market-utilizing activity, which aims to develop businesses (perhaps based on existing MNE products or technology) to serve the Australian market; and
- asset-generating activity, which aims to create in Australia or to harness new assets recently created in Australia (often of a knowledge-intensive kind) for the development of global businesses.

Asset-utilizing investment, particularly based on the agriculture and mining industries, was central to the development of the Australian economy, and remains important today. During much of the twentieth century, and particularly in the two decades of rapid growth after the Second World War, much foreign direct investment in the manufacturing industry has been market-utilizing, designed to develop businesses to serve the Australian market behind tariff walls rather than to compete globally. Thus two among the many challenges facing policy-makers since the mid-1970s were to reorient inward-looking manufacturing to a global vision and to encourage asset-generating activity. The reality of these challenges can be more clearly understood by examining the structure of Australian industry and its ownership composition.

3.2. Foreign Ownership and the Structure of Australian Industry

Viewed from the perspective of international competitiveness, one of the key deficiencies of the Australian economy, especially in the manufacturing sector, lies in its firm structure. This has two principal aspects: the small scale by international standards of many firms, especially Australian-owned firms, and the relatively dormant state of many of the foreign-owned firms operating in Australia. Given the limited scale of the overall economy, the dominance of foreign-owned firms in many industries and other factors such as a weak venture-capital industry and the distance from larger markets, most Australian-owned firms are small by international standards. Many multinational companies have established subsidiaries in Australia as either representative sales offices or as production units to serve the local market, with little mandate for innovation, product development, or exporting. The end result has been a firm structure not well suited to the requirements of the global economy.

A significant proportion of *large* firms operating in Australia are foreign owned, and many have limited commitment to innovation, R&D, and export activity in Australia. Whereas only 1.9 per cent of all firms operating in Australia had any foreign ownership as at 30 June 1995, 34.5 per cent of firms with 200–499 employees and 46.7 per cent of firms with 500 or more employees are at least partly foreign owned (IC and DIST 1997). Indeed, 29.3 per cent of these larger firms are at least 50 per cent foreign owned. Thus foreign ownership is of very substantial dimensions in the ranks of larger firms operating in Australia. This increases the economic importance of their limited business mandate and goals within Australia and the global economy.

One important feature of the two Innovation Surveys conducted by the Australian Bureau of Statistics (in relation to 1993–4 and 1996–7) is that they provide us with a rare glimpse of the firm size and ownership structure of Australian manufacturing industry. While these detailed data are confined only to manufacturing industry, the surveys do provide information on performance by ownership for disaggregated manufacturing industries. Using these data, Tables 11.1 and 11.2 provide information for 1993–4 on a more restricted set of firms than the full set of manufacturing firms covered by the Innovation Survey, namely all manufacturing firms undertaking R&D over the three-year period to June 1994. Subsequent comments here refer only to such firms, unless otherwise stated. The technology classification used is that of OECD (1994).

The estimated number of firms operating in each of the four R&D-intensity categories in Australian manufacturing, and undertaking R&D over the three-year period to June 1994, is shown in Table 11.1, classified by Australian and foreign ownership. A firm is defined at the management unit level, which in most cases corresponds to the legal company unit, but in large diversified companies may correspond to business units. It is classified as foreign owned if more than 50 per cent of its shareholding is held by overseas interests although, as we will see below, a slightly broader classification is available for 1996–7. Tables 11.1 and 11.2 provide the total value of sales, exports, and R&D for those firms by ownership, and a range of analytical ratios.

For manufacturing firms undertaking R&D, the ABS estimates that foreign firms accounted for $46.6 billion or 36.7 per cent of total sales in 1993–4. The foreign share of sales was particularly pronounced in higher-technology industries—being 53.0 per cent in the high R&D-intensity category and 65.4 per cent in the medium-high category—but was less pronounced in the medium-low and low R&D-intensity categories (26.3 and 25.6 per cent respectively). In other words, foreign firms have a truly dominant position in Australian high-tech and medium-high-tech manufacturing industry, but are much less dominant in lower-tech industries. These facts are, of course, explicable in terms of the historical development of Australian industry, but nevertheless define the context in which industry and technology policy must operate.

A quite clear picture about the performance in 1993–4 of manufacturing firms which undertake some R&D emerges from the tables, particularly in relation to the higher R&D-intensity industries. In these industries a small number of foreign firms, which are large in scale by comparison with their Australian counterparts, controlled a high proportion of sales, but had a lower R&D/sales ratio

TABLE 11.1. Number and size of firms: Australian manufacturing, by ownership and technology intensity, 1993–1994

R&D intensity	No. of firms		Average sales			Total sales (all firms)
	Australian	Foreign	Australian ($m.)	Foreign ($m.)	Ratio: Foreign/ Australian (%)	Share Foreign/ Total (%)
High	377	43	8.9	87.8	8.9	56.0
Medium High	1,415	167	7.4	119.3	16.1	65.4
Medium Low	2,745	213	7.4	34.0	4.6	26.3
Low	3,779	225	12.0	69.6	5.8	25.6

Source: ABS Innovation Survey 1993–4, unpublished data. Refers only to firms undertaking some R&D over the 3-year period to June 1994, except when stated.

TABLE 11.2. Sales, exports, and R&D: Australian manufacturing by ownership and technology intensity, 1993–1994

R&D intensity	Foreign share of sales	Exports/Sales		R&D/Sales	
		Australian	Foreign	Australian	Foreign
High	53.0	24.4	11.6	6.2	4.9
Medium High	65.4	12.6	12.7	2.5	1.6
Medium Low	26.3	26.0	20.8	1.7	0.9
Low	25.6	16.4	14.0	1.0	0.6
Total Manufacturing	36.7	18.7	14.3	1.6	1.4

Source: ABS Innovation Survey 1993–4, unpublished data. Refers only to firms undertaking some R&D over the 3-year period to June 1994.

and a lower propensity to export in 1993–4 than the Australian firms. In the high-tech category, the forty-three such foreign firms had average sales of $87.8 million, by comparison with average sales of $8.9 million for 377 Australian firms, exports as a share of sales of 11.6 per cent (Australian firms 24.4 per cent), and an R&D/sales ratio of 4.9 per cent (Australian firms 6.2 per cent). Thus both the size and the performance differences between Australian and foreign high-tech firms are dramatic.

Given the importance of high-tech firms in the knowledge economy, this fact clearly has given rise to some important policy issues. One is the vital importance of developing improved R&D and export performance by high-tech foreign firms operating in Australia. The other is the importance of fostering small, high export, and relatively high R&D Australian companies in the high-tech sector. The interplay between these two themes is something to which we will return in the final section of this chapter.

The picture is similar in the medium-high-tech group, with one exception. Relative to Australian firms, foreign firms were even larger (average sales of $119.3 million as against $7.4 million for local firms) but Australian firms had a 50 per cent higher R&D/sales ratio (2.5 per cent as against 1.6 per cent). The difference is that neither group has a high export/sales ratio, the figure in both cases being less than 13 per cent. In the medium-low and low R&D-intensity industries, the dominance of foreign firms is much reduced, as is their size relative to Australian firms, but for both groups Australian firms have substantially higher export propensities and R&D/sales ratios.

These data thus bring out several central facts about Australian manufacturing of immediate relevance to Australia's response to the global knowledge economy, including:

- the dominance of foreign firms in the higher-tech industries, but their relatively poor performance in terms of R&D and exports;
- the small scale of Australian firms generally but their relatively strong export and R&D performance, particularly in the high R&D-intensity group; and
- the problematic character of the medium-high-tech industries, of which motor vehicles and chemicals are the largest elements, which have low export and R&D performance and two-thirds of the sales of which is controlled by foreign firms.

While it is beyond the scope of this study to seek comparable international data, it is clear that these three facts are distinctive features of the Australian industrial structure, and have been central facts determining the policy challenge facing Australian and regional governments.

4. Industrial Activity by Ownership and State

It has been argued above that the nature of Australian industry has been heavily shaped by the activity of foreign MNEs, and that the character of their involvement in the economy and their interplay with local firms remain of critical importance. These issues inevitably have strong regional dimensions, and these dimensions also constrain the available policy responses. Thus before examining the policy issues we explore the geographical aspects of the role of MNEs and local firms in industry development in Australia. In this section consideration is given to the pattern of ownership of industry by state, and to some trends in that pattern over a limited time span, while in Section 5 we examine the geographical concentration of Australian industry by microregion. Both analyses are heavily constrained by data limitations, arising from the paucity of data on foreign ownership and the limitations imposed by confidentiality requirements when information is sought by ownership, industry, and region. In this section the source of data is again the ABS Innovation Survey, and we again limit the coverage to firms undertaking some R&D.

4.1. Industrial Activity by Ownership and State

Australian manufacturing is heavily concentrated in the two largest states, New South Wales and Victoria, and within those states in Melbourne and Sydney. In 1993–4, 39.2 per cent of total manufacturing sales originated from NSW and 38.5 per cent from Victoria, with the other major contributors being Queensland (10.3 per cent) and South Australia (6.8 per cent). A similar position is evident for exports in 1993–4, although the position of the smaller states is stronger in exports than in sales, reflecting the reduced importance of the domestic market as a reason for manufacturing activity outside the two largest states (see Table 11.3). Taking account of the different sizes of the states, the greatest concentration of manufacturing activity, in terms of sales per capita, in 1993–4 was in Victoria and South Australia.

Even in the period of only three years separating the two data sets, substantial change has taken place in terms of the location of activity. The main trends have been the decline of NSW (especially in terms of sales), of Queensland and Tasmania as locations of manufacturing, with some increase in Victoria and more substantial relative increases in South Australia and Western Australia. The growth of the share of sales in these last two states, and of the export share in Western Australia, has been very striking. As this has been a period of slow growth in total manufacturing sales overall—an increase of only 4 per cent in value over the three-year period—these quite sharp changes reflect both specific industry developments and the activity of MNEs in consolidating, reducing, or expanding production in particular locations. These influences become clearer in the more detailed data considered below.

TABLE 11.3. States' share of total manufacturing sales and exports, 1993–1994 and 1996–1997

	Sales (%)		Exports (%)	
	1993–4	1996–7	1993–4	1996–7
New South Wales	39.2	34.3	31.8	30.7
Victoria	38.5	40.5	35.0	36.6
Queensland	10.3	9.6	12.5	8.2
South Australia	6.8	8.8	10.3	10.3
Western Australia	3.1	5.6	4.2	12.2
Tasmania	1.8	0.9	4.7	1.9
Australia	100	100	100	100

Source: ABS Innovation Surveys 1993–4 and 1996–7, unpublished data. Refers only to firms undertaking some R&D over the 3-year period to June 1994.

TABLE 11.4. Sales and R&D intensity, by ownership and state, Australian high-tech industries, 1993–1994

State	Share of total Australian sales (%)			Ratio of R&D to sales (%)		
	Foreign	Australian	Total	Foreign	Australian	Total
1993–4						
NSW	36.2	26.3	62.5	5.9	2.6	4.6
Victoria	15.7	14.9	30.5	2.6	10.4	6.4
Other States	1.1	5.8	6.9	2.9	11.1	9.7
Australia	53.0	47.0	100	4.9	6.2	5.5
1996–7						
NSW	32.4	11.1	43.5	6.3	8.3	6.8
Victoria	21.0	17.5	38.5	2.1	10.0	5.7
Other States	9.3	8.7	18.0	9.9	7.4	8.7
Australia	62.7	37.3	100	5.4	8.9	6.7

Source: ABS Innovation Surveys 1993–4 and 1996–7, unpublished data. Refers only to firms undertaking some R&D over the 3-year period to June 1994. Ownership categories refer to majority foreign ownership and majority Australian ownership respectively.

4.1.1. The High-Tech Industries

These factors are particularly evident in the high-tech industries (Table 11.4), which show both pronounced regional patterns and sharp changes in those patterns. In 1993–4 the high-tech industries were heavily foreign owned and heavily concentrated in NSW. In this year, 53 per cent of sales originated from foreign-owned firms, and 62.5 per cent of sales (and 60 per cent of exports) originated from NSW, with only 30.5 per cent of sales (and 27.6 per cent of exports) originating in Victoria. There were, however, quite substantial differences between the foreign and Australian-owned components of these industries in the two states.

In NSW foreign companies had a modest R&D intensity (but a very low export propensity of only 9.4 per cent) whereas locally owned firms had a very low R&D intensity but a high export propensity, exporting 27 per cent of sales. This presumably reflects the concentration of foreign firms in computing, telecommunications, and pharmaceutical activities directed primarily at the local market, with local firms concentrated in office machinery and equipment and telecommunications equipment manufacture with a low development capability but a genuine export focus. In Victoria, the reverse is true—local firms had a high R&D intensity (10.4 per cent) while foreign firms a low one (2.6 per cent), while both types of firm had export propensities in the 16–17 per cent region—and this is also broadly the case for the other states taken as a whole.

The three-year period has seen quite dramatic change. Overall sales of high-tech firms operating in Australia fell by 8.7 per cent over this three-year period, and the nation's reliance on imports of high-tech products increased further. Sales of Australian-owned high-tech firms fell by 27.5 per cent. High-tech sales in NSW fell by 36.4 per cent over this time, while rising by 24.9 per cent in Victoria and more than doubling in the other states combined, albeit from a low base. Relevant factors in these trends were the collapse of the office and computing equipment industry, sales of which fell by 78.6 per cent, the activity of MNEs in acquiring small Australian companies, perhaps particularly in the telecommunications equipment industry, and the continuing involvement of multinationals in a small way in response to Federal and State Government programmes.

One result of these trends has been a sharp increase in the role of MNEs in Australian high-tech industries—MNE sales rose by 8.1 per cent by contrast with the fall in local-firm sales of 27.5 per cent over the three-year period, while MNE exports rose 95.1 per cent and local-firm exports fell 32.2 per cent. By any standard these must be regarded as disturbing trends, with only a few bright spots. Many small, low R&D local firms have not been able to survive, and have collapsed or been taken over by MNEs. MNE activity has increased slightly, and their exports have increased substantially, but this has been in part by taking over local firms, and the average scale of MNE activity in Australia has fallen. *Far from signalling the emergence of dynamic, knowledge-intensive clusters, these data suggest that the expansion of large-scale high-tech manufacturing is bypassing Australia.* The main bright spot is the growth of a significant amount of locally owned, R&D-intensive activity in Victoria.

4.1.2. The Medium-High-Tech Industries

The picture for medium-high-tech industries, of which the dominant items are motor vehicles and chemicals excluding pharmaceuticals, is in some respects the mirror image of that for the high-tech industries (Table 11.5). The industries are heavily concentrated in Victoria rather than in NSW and are highly dominated by MNEs, with a very low R&D intensity and a low export propensity, both of which are uniform over MNEs and locally owned firms. They are thus the classic case of industries established by foreign investment in an era of protection, with a focus on the domestic rather than world market. For some time now an emphasis in policy has been to shift these industries to a more outward-looking, innovative focus. Total sales have increased slowly over the period, but exports have increased by 25 per cent, implying a significant rise in export intensity from a low base. The main dynamic within the industry has been a regional one, as large MNEs have consolidated their activities in a smaller number of locations in search of globally more competitive plants.

5. Concentration of Activity by Microregion

Given the history and ownership patterns of Australian industry, sketched above, it is to be expected that there has been substantial concentration of manufacturing

TABLE 11.5. Sales and R&D intensity, by ownership and state, Australian medium-high-tech industries, 1993–1994

State	Share of total Australian sales (%)			Ratio of R&D to sales (%)		
	Foreign	Australian	Total	Foreign	Australian	Total
1993–4						
NSW	13.5	11.2	24.7	1.5	3.5	2.4
Victoria	39.5	15.9	55.4	1.7	1.5	1.6
Other States	12.4	7.4	19.8	1.2	3.2	2.0
Australia	65.4	34.6	100	1.6	2.5	1.9
1997–6						
NSW	8.7	11.9	20.6	2.1	2.0	2.1
Victoria	36.7	13.4	50.1	1.8	1.8	1.8
Other States	19.0	10.2	29.2	1.8	1.9	1.8
Australia	64.4	35.6	100	1.8	1.9	1.8

Source: ABS Innovation Surveys 1993–4 and 1996–7, unpublished data. Refers only to firms undertaking some R&D over the 3-year period to June 1994. Ownership categories refer to majority foreign ownership and majority Australian ownership respectively.

activity at a small-scale regional level in Australia. As will be outlined below, the data suggest that this is indeed the case. Such geographical concentrations of activity could prove to be a base for dynamic clusters of asset-augmenting activity, of the type suggested by Dunning in Chapter 1, and should certainly reflect the diverse dynamics associated with the rise and decline of both MNEs and local firms. The data set used to analyse these issues is the ABS Manufacturing Census for 1993–4 and 1996–7, which provides information on manufacturing performance by industry and region, although the level of cross-classified detail is restricted by confidentiality requirements. More specifically, we study the pattern of manufacturing turnover for these two years for nine manufacturing industries and 183 statistical subdivisions throughout the country.

Table 11.6 provides information on two main measures of concentration for 1993–4, in this case applied to the concentration of industry turnover in specific regions across the 183 subdivisions. The first three columns of figures show the shares of industry turnover held by the top five, ten and twenty regions or subdivisions, and the next column shows the Herfindahl index of concentration (the sum across the full 183 subdivisions of the squares of individual shares). It is clear that Australian manufacturing is highly concentrated regionally. For manufacturing as a whole, 36.6 per cent of turnover is located in the top ten regions, and for four of the nine industries over half of turnover is in the top ten regions. Levels of concentration are particularly high in three industries—printing and publishing; petroleum, coal, and chemicals; and machinery and equipment. In each of these cases more than 70 per cent of turnover is located in the top twenty regions, and for the first two industries over 40 per cent is in the top five regions.

TABLE 11.6. Measures of the geographical concentration of Australian industry, 1993–1994

Industry	Share of total manufacturing turnover (%)			Herfindahl index of concentration	Foreign ownership share (%)
	Top 5 regions	Top 10 regions	Top 20 regions		
Food, beverages, and tobacco	21.8	31.5	46.3	1.7	40.5
Textiles, clothing, and footwear	37.5	52.3	66.5	4.0	27.3
Wood and paper	20.9	33.7	52.6	1.8	n.a.
Printing and publishing	47.0	60.9	75.6	6.4	n.a.
Petroleum, coal, and chemicals	40.7	57.9	72.7	4.4	60.0
Non-metallic minerals	29.7	44.4	62.2	3.0	13.9
Metal products	34.5	45.8	57.9	3.5	11.4
Machinery and equipment	32.5	52.3	74.4	3.6	61.6
Other manufacturing	25.3	40.0	61.5	2.6	34.7
Total manufacturing	23.7	36.6	56.2	2.1	36.9

Source: For columns 1–4, ABS Manufacturing Census, 1993–4, unpublished data. The Herfindahl index of concentration is measured over the 183 subdivisions, and is equal to the sum of the squares of the market shares of each subdivision, multiplied by 100. Thus if each of the 183 subdivisions had an equal share of turnover the index value would be 0.55; if only ten regions had an equal share of all the turnover the value would be 10. For column 5, ABS Innovation Surveys 1993–4, unpublished data. Refers only to firms undertaking some R&D over the 3-year period to June 1994. The ownership category refers to majority foreign ownership.

In each of these three industries high concentration levels seem to be linked to the activities of MNEs, although not necessarily only foreign-owned MNEs. In printing and publishing the concentration of activity is particularly focused on the inner-Sydney region, and is clustered around the centres of activity of the big Australian media empires of Fairfax, Packer, and Murdoch. In the other two industries much of the concentration seems to be linked to the activities of large foreign-owned MNEs in particular locations, notably the petroleum refiners, the major chemical companies, and the motor vehicle manufacturers. Two other areas with relatively high concentration levels in spite of low levels of foreign ownership are textiles, clothing and footwear, and metal products. The former has traditionally been concentrated in the inner-city areas of Melbourne and Sydney, and is heavily dependent on migrant workers, while the latter has been dominated by the activities of one company (BHP), and by the specific locations of those activities. As one would expect, concentration levels are a good deal lower in the resource-related industries of food, beverages, and tobacco, wood and paper products, and non-metallic minerals, given the need for many types of plant to be located close to the source of the input materials.

TABLE 11.7. Regional concentration, growth, and decline in the machinery and equipment industry, 1993–1994 and 1996–1997: activity of the top 30 regions

Region	Turnover ($m.)		Share of national turnover (%)		Growth in turnover (%)
	1993–4	1996–7	1993–4	1996–7	1993–4 to 1996–7
South-Eastern and Eastern Inner Melbourne (2 regions)	1,739	2,895	4.9	7.1	71.7
Western and Northern Melbourne (4 regions)	5,717	8,457	16.1	20.6	47.9
Perth (4 regions)	1,339	1,948	3.8	4.8	45.4
Darling Downs	197	257	0.6	0.6	30.7
Newcastle	699	849	2.0	2.1	21.5
Geelong	508	587	1.4	1.4	15.6
Brisbane City	1,465	1,640	4.1	4.0	11.9
Adelaide (3 regions)	6,087	6,547	17.2	16.0	7.6
Sydney (10 regions)	7,700	8,011	21.7	19.5	4.0
Central Melbourne	1,954	1,189	5.5	2.9	−39.1
South-Eastern and Eastern Outer Melbourne (2 regions)	1,868	1,063	5.3	2.6	−43.1
Total: 30 top regions	29,272	33,443	82.6	81.6	14.2

Source: ABS Manufacturing Census, 1993–4 and 1996–7, unpublished data.

Thus manufacturing industry in highly concentrated on a regional basis in Australia, in patterns which reflect the activities of foreign and Australian-owned MNEs and the specific characteristics of the industries. How is this pattern of concentration responding to the new pressures on both MNEs and small local firms arising from the global knowledge economy? Indeed, does it provide a base for the emergence of dynamic clusters of asset-generating activities, involving both MNEs and local firms, which are the special focus of this book?

It is not possible to provide a general answer to these vital questions here, but some indications can be gleaned by looking in more detail at one of the nine industries covered in Table 11.6—machinery and equipment. As we are dealing at a high level of industry aggregation to maximize the amount of regional detail available, this is a broadly defined industry, covering motor vehicles and other transport equipment, electronics equipment and appliances, scientific instruments, and industrial machinery. In Table 11.7 we analyse the characteristics of the top thirty regions in Australia in terms of turnover in this industry, grouping them by contiguous regional clusters where these exist. Some interesting dynamics are apparent.

While total turnover for the machinery and equipment industry grew by only 14.2 per cent between 1993–4 and 1996–7, in three areas a much more rapid growth rate was experienced. In the inner areas of south-eastern and eastern Melbourne, turnover grew by 71.7 per cent and the regional share of industry turnover rose from 4.9 to 7.1 per cent. While activity is still small in absolute terms, this is a region of rapid growth in knowledge-based instruments and equipment, drawing on the strong knowledge resources of Melbourne. It is indeed one of Australia's best prospects for a dynamic, asset-generating cluster.

In the northern and western parts of Melbourne there is a larger concentration of activity, with turnover in four contiguous regions growing by 47.9 per cent over the period and these regions accounting for 20.6 per cent of national turnover in this industry in 1996–7. This is particularly driven by the motor vehicle industry. As the MNEs dominating this industry have moved from a multidomestic form of organization to integrated global production in search of greater competitive efficiency, the Australian industry has become leaner, more efficient, and more concentrated in areas such as northern and western Melbourne. With increased specialization, a more competitive range of local suppliers to the MNEs has also arisen, and these tend to be clustered around the major plants. Again, this region shows signs of further expansion. based on specific local application skills and cost advantages rather than major R&D activities.

Finally, turnover in the machinery and equipment industry in Perth has grown strongly between 1993–4 and 1996–7. amounting to nearly 5 per cent of total national turnover in the latter year. Of particular importance here is the expansion of these industries to serve the growth of the mining industries in Western Australia and the remarkable cluster of shipbuilding activities in this region.

6. Cross Currents in Australian Policy

The policy issues confronting contemporary governments are daunting, to say the least, as they seek to find the best path to advance national prosperity in a period of fundamental change. In Australia the policy debate on such matters has turned upon a central choice: that between pure market forces and measures to enhance the operation of markets on the one hand, and more interventionist policies in the pursuit of MNE activity and of the development of local firms on the other. While there have been important achievements in both these areas, the overall coherence of policy settings and their long-run effectiveness have been undermined by continued dispute on this central issue. Two examples are used here to briefly illustrate some of the successes and the failures, and their relevance to the matters documented above.

6.1. **Australian Economic Policy, 1983–1990**

Economic policy in Australia at the federal level has traditionally been dominated by the Australian Treasury, which has been a high-quality institution pursuing the common agenda of most Treasuries around the world, namely market-based efficiency, government frugality, fiscal balance, and low inflation. The Hawke

Labor Government was elected in March 1983, while the Australian economy was still in the midst of the 1982–3 recession. Its election policy emphasized recovery from recession and job creation in a context of contained inflation, the proposed policy initiatives being primarily expansionary and mildly interventionist in nature.

Under the influence of a range of diverse forces, from Treasury to Australian Council of Trade Unions, the structure of economic policy which emerged in Australia over the period 1983–93 was quite distinctive. On the one hand, free market principles were pursued aggressively in some areas, as evidenced in the deregulation of the financial system, the virtual abolition of tariffs, the introduction of competition into many hitherto monopoly sectors, and the extensive programme of microeconomic reform which was put in train. Yet the linchpin of policy over the decade remained the Prices and Incomes Accord, a centralized agreement to contain wages in the context of other policies to spur growth. A complex series of industry-specific policies were put in place, in areas ranging from motor vehicles and footwear, clothing and textiles to information technology products and pharmaceuticals. Major new science and technology policies were put in place, which have contributed to a fundamental change in the innovative activities of much of Australian industry. However, these 'interventionist' policies were directed not at protecting inefficient or unproductive activities but at assisting firms and individuals to prepare for and then to engage in internationally competitive activities. Australia indeed developed its own unique blend of 'plan and market'. (For further documentation see Sheehan, Pappas, and Cheng 1994; Sheehan *et al.* 1995; and Sheehan 1997.)

For example, there is little doubt that, taken as a whole, the science and technology policies amounted to the most powerful set of measures for the development and commercialization of science and technology that Australia has yet seen. And the impact was equally striking. Business spending on R&D as a share of GDP increased fourfold between 1981–2 and 1995–6; the R&D intensity of manufacturing (the ratio of R&D to value added) also trebled, from 1.0 per cent in 1983 to 3.2 per cent in 1993, and many industries approached or exceeded OECD average levels; high-tech exports grew by 26 per cent per annum (in current $US) between 1986 and 1993, albeit from a low base.

In many respects the results of the broader mix of policies were impressive too, at least up until 1990. The orientation of Australian business changed dramatically over this time, there was a flowering of new technology-based businesses, employment grew strongly, and inflation was relatively well contained, even in the late 1980s boom. But many of these benefits were swept away in the serious mismanagement of monetary policy over the period 1988–92, and the resulting deep recession of 1990–2. However, even from a broader perspective, the distinctive set of policies was deeply flawed. In particular:

• they arose from the fortuitous outcome of strong, contending forces rather than from a shared vision of optimum economic policies;

- individual elements were always at risk, as the balance of power between contending forces changed;
- as a consequence, there were no structures put in place for overall coordination of the policy set, or for assessing outcomes and planning future developments; and
- individual policies were often introduced in a crisis situation, when a particular development provided a political opportunity, and hence without proper planning or foresight.

In short there was no national or even government consensus about this set of policies, but rather competing views about free markets and intervention, and hence no systematic coordination mechanisms but rather intense institutional competition.

In the 1990s views of successive governments shifted away from the view that both open, free market policies and judicious, market-conforming interventions form an inevitable part of the optimum mix in the knowledge economy. The emphasis has been on opening markets and removing impediments to competition; incentives for local firms and for the commercialization of technology have been scaled back, as have systematic policies to change the character of existing MNE activity, to encourage other multinational firms to undertake asset-generating activities in Australia and to influence the regional pattern of economic activities. While in some respects the results of these policies have been impressive, the continued erosion of high-tech manufacturing activity in Australia remains a matter of serious concern.

6.2. The Victorian Economic Strategy, 1983–1990

In April 1982 the Cain Labor Government was elected in Victoria, a state which contains about 25 per cent of Australia's population but accounts for about 35 per cent of national manufacturing output and R&D. Perceptions about Victoria's long-term future were depressed in the early 1980s, because of its dependence on manufacturing at a time when growth prospects in Australia were seen as being largely concentrated on resources and tourism. One element of this government's election policy was that it would introduce systematic, strategic initiatives to address Victoria's long-term economic growth and competitiveness. In April 1984 the first strategy statement *Victoria: The Next Step* was published, and for the next six years this strategy was the overriding focus of government policy.

Its basic objective was to promote long-term growth in income and employment by strengthening the international competitiveness of the economy. This was to be achieved by action on two fronts. Firstly, diverse reforms impinging on both the public and the private sector would be pursued (e.g. increased efficiency in public instrumentalities, reform of taxes and charges, improved regulatory processes), to make the general environment more competitive. Secondly, nine areas of competitive strength were identified—areas where Victoria was seen as having the foundations of continuing international competitiveness—and plans of action were developed to enhance those strengths and to encourage greater economic development on the basis of them.

Another important feature of the Economic Strategy was action driven by the view that, especially in the knowledge-intensive sectors, Victoria lacked the competitive firms and other institutions to take full advantage of its competitive strengths. This led to a systematic attempt to create, in partnership with the private sector, firms and other institutions which were of a scale to compete effectively themselves or which would assist firms to become more competitive. Many but not all of these institutions were effective, and companies spawned lie at the heart of the relatively strong level of high-tech activity in Victoria noted in Section 4.1.1 above. While not all initiatives were equally successful, this aspect of the experiment did suggest that carefully planned initiatives involving public–private cooperation can indeed augment the nation's competitive base.

It is difficult to separate the impact of the Economic Strategy from the turmoil of 1990 and the controversy to which it gave rise. On the one hand, the attempt to provide a coherent long-term vision was strongly supported by business and other economic agents; Victoria's performance relative to other states on the major economic indicators was much stronger over the 1983–90 period than either before or since; many institutions and structures were created which are central to the state's economy today. On the other hand, the experiment in coordination was abandoned in 1990 in an environment of great hostility and controversy, with accusations of uncontrolled debt levels and with an intense focus on initiatives which proved unsuccessful. Reflecting a collapse of confidence and other factors, the economic performance of Victoria in the early 1990s was weaker than that of the rest of Australia taken as a whole, although recovering in recent years.

6.3. Conclusion

As the twentieth century drew to a close, economic policy in Australia as in many other countries remained uncertain about the proper balance between policies to facilitate and policies to govern the market. The opening of the Australian economy over the past decade and a half has brought both benefits and costs. But the lack of any major Australian capability in rapidly growing high-tech industries is a matter for serious concern, as is the lack of major concentrations of knowledge-intensive activity. Certainly, the future prosperity of Australia —whether it continues to keep pace with leading nations such as the USA in growth in GDP per capita or falls behind—largely depends on effective national strategies to develop dynamic clusters of asset-augmenting activities. While the debate is growing, the strategies are not yet in place.

NOTE

The authors are much indebted to Galina Tikhomirova, Fiona Sun, and Margarita Kumnick for advice and assistance in relation to this chapter.

1. See e.g. OECD (1996) and Sheehan and Tegart (1998).

REFERENCES

Aghion, P., and Howitt, P. (1998), *Endogenous Growth Theory* (Cambridge, Mass.: MIT Press).

Australian Bureau of Statistics (ABS), *Balance of Payments*, Cat. No. 5302.0 (Canberra: ABS).

Azariadis, C. (1996), 'The Economics of Poverty Traps: Part One: Complete Markets', *Journal of Economic Growth* 1(4): 449–96.

Durlauf, S., and Johnson, P. (1995), 'Multiple Regimes and Cross-Country Growth Behaviour', *Journal of Applied Econometrics* 10(4): 365–84.

—— and Quah, D. (1998), 'The New Empirics of Economic Growth', NBER Working Paper 6422 (Cambridge, Mass.: National Bureau of Economic Research).

Grossman, G., and Helpman, E. (1991), *Innovation and Growth in the Global Economy* (Cambridge, Mass.: MIT Press).

Industry Commission (IC) and Department of Industry, Science and Tourism (DIST) (1997), *A Portrait of Australian Business: Results of the 1995 Business Longitudinal Survey* (Canberra: Small Business Research Program).

International Monetary Fund (IMF) (1997), *World Economic Outlook, May 1997* (Washington, DC: International Monetary Fund).

Krugman, P. (1991), 'Increasing Returns and Economic Geography', *Journal of Political Economy* 99(3): 483–99.

—— (1995), *Development, Geography and Economic Theory* (Cambridge, Mass.: MIT Press).

—— and Venables, A. J. (1995), 'Globalisation and the Inequality of Nations', *Quarterly Journal of Economics* 110: 857–80.

Mankiw, N., Romer, D., and Weil, D. (1992), 'A Contribution to the Empirics of Economic Growth', *Quarterly Journal of Economics* 107: 407–37.

OECD (Organization for Economic Cooperation and Development) (1994), *Science and Technology Policy: Review and Outlook 1994* (Paris: OECD).

—— (1996), *Technology, Productivity and Job Creation* (Paris: OECD).

Quah, D. (1996a), 'Convergence Empirics with (some) Capital Mobility', *Journal of Economic Growth* 1(1): 95–125.

—— (1996b), 'Empirics for Growth and Convergence', *European Economic Review* 40(6): 1353–75.

Romer, P. (1990), 'Endogenous Technological Change', *Journal of Political Economy* 98(5): S71–102.

—— (1994a), 'The Origins of Endogenous Growth', *Journal of Economic Perspectives* 8(1): 3–22.

—— (1994*b*), 'New Goods, Old Theory and the Welfare Costs of Trade Restrictions', *Journal of Development Economics* 43(1): 5–39.

Sala-i-Martin, X. (1996), 'The Classical Approach to Convergence Analysis', *Economic Journal* 106: 1019–36.

Sheehan, P. (1997), 'Learning to Govern in the Knowledge Economy: Policy Coordination or Institutional Competition?', in *Industrial Competitiveness in the Knowledge-Based Economy: The New Role of Governments* (Paris: OECD).

—— and Grewal, B. (1999) 'Convergence and Divergence in the Knowledge Economy' (Melbourne: Centre for Strategic Economic Studies, Victoria University), Mimeo.

—— Pappas, N., and Cheng, E. (1994), *The Rebirth of Australian Industry: Australian Trade in Elaborately Transformed Manufactures 1979–1993* (Melbourne: Centre for Strategic Economic Studies, Victoria University).

—— Pappas, N., Tikhomirova, G., and Sinclair, P. (1995), *Australia and the Knowledge Economy: An Assessment of Enhanced Economic Growth Through Science and Technology* (Melbourne: Centre for Strategic Economic Studies, Victoria University).

—— and Tegart, G. (1998), *Working for the Future: Technology and Employment in the Global Knowledge Economy* (Melbourne: Victoria University Press).

12

Innovation Systems, Networks, and the Knowledge-Based Economy in Korea

Sam Ock Park

1. Introduction

During the last decade, Korean industry has undergone a considerable restructuring in order to maintain or regain international competitiveness with the promotion of high technology and high value-added industries. The Korean economy is now, however, in tremendous difficulties owing to the problems resulting from the national financial crisis. A rapid and strong process of economic restructuring is now being implemented with the financial support of the IMF. Breaking up the *chaebol* (large conglomeration) system, downsizing existing firms, mergers, and acquisitions, closing inefficient firms, and privatization of public firms are progressing as processes of economic restructuring. Along with the macroeconomic process of economic restructuring, the government also promotes the strengthening of regional competitive advantages and the development of a knowledge-based economy.

Because of the changes in the government's industry and technology policies and dynamics of industrial structure, regional networks and innovation systems have been significantly changed during the last three decades in Korea. Since the rapid industrialization period of the 1970s, *chaebols* emerged in Korea as a leading actor in industrial development at the expense of SMEs. During the rapid industrial growth of the 1960s and 1970s, technological developments and innovations were not the key issues for the large firms. Rather, the introduction of production technology in a mass production system was the key issue for the government and large enterprises. Since the 1980s, however, firms have gradually put emphasis on the development of technology and R&D activities. Along with this emphasis of technological development, the significant role of SMEs in job generation and innovations has been recognized in the 1990s. In recent years, local innovation systems for SMEs are also recognized as an important mechanism for the regional economic development with the improvement of regional innovation potentials and fostering venture businesses. That is, the role of region and SMEs are rediscovered for economic development and regional competitiveness (Morgan 1997).

This chapter aims to examine innovation systems in Korea and local global networks of high-technology industry with regard to the evolution of the knowledge-based economy. Major data for the study are derived from the questionnaire survey for SMEs, which was conducted at the beginning of the financial support of the IMF last November and December, and from an interview survey conducted in 1995 for the high-tech industries in Korea.

2. Regions, Networks, and Innovation Systems

Regions are dynamic over time through the industrial development and evolution of regional innovation systems. Evolution of agglomeration economies, dynamic characteristics of industrial districts, development of high-technology industrial clusters over time represent the dynamic aspects of regions. The dynamic pattern of a region can be examined through the development of networks and innovation systems of firms.

Firms in an industrial district have interfirm or intrafirm relations in input and output materials, technology and market information, financing, and labour. These relations are important for making suppliers and customer networks. Firms in a region have also relations with trade associations, local and state governments, and other institutions sharing information, financing, labour training, and education. Firms have networks even with competitors through strategic alliances. The firms' networks in a region with suppliers, customers, competitors, and trade associations have spatial dimensions such as local, regional, or national, and global networks. Based on these network patterns, Park (1996) identified six types of new industrial districts, which can be characterized by spatial dimension of networks, production systems, firm size, and division of labour. The six types are three basic types of Marshallian, hub-and-spoke, and satellite industrial districts, and three hybrid types of advanced hub-and-spoke, mature satellite, and pioneering high-tech industrial districts. Park emphasized not only the types of industrial district but also the dynamic evolution of these districts through the development of local and non-local networks and competitive advantages (Park 1996). The dynamic pattern of the industrial districts can be applied to the dynamic evolution of a region. In application to the region, however, innovation systems should be considered beyond the network pattern.

Two major distinctive types of innovation system can be identified. One is the system which takes a specific sector or a specific technology as a point of departure; the other is one which builds on a geographical dimension—either a local, regional, national, international, or even global system of innovation (Gregersen and Johnson 1997). Since the innovation systems are affected by national industrial and innovation policies, geographical proximity of interactions, and local institutional factors, territorially based innovation systems can be identified. In the territorially based innovation systems, firms, organizations, and government interact with each other and become the actors of an innovation system. National innovation systems are important when the economic development and innovation are mainly directed by government policies. However, local innovation systems become more important than before with increasing globalization of economic processes, accordingly losing the importance of national boundaries as a barrier to economic activities and the significant role of local authorities and local milieu.

In the territorially based innovation systems, there are several important notions for contributing to innovation of firms. Regions, networks, and the knowledge-based economy are interrelated in the territorially based innovation systems. Firstly, collaboration and interfirm networks are important for innovation of firms. Especially for SMEs, collaboration with other firms and organizations makes it possible to gain access to a diverse specialist expertise in meeting customer needs and to share risk and costs (Keeble 1997). Because of the significant impact of networks, the design of technology networks has been regarded as an important policy issue at a local and national level in countries like Denmark. The main strength of networks of SMEs is derived from the ability that small firms have shown to learn from each other and from an intermediary system which has acted as a successful catalyst for cooperation (Huggins 1996). In the interfirm networks, relationships between large and small firms as well as those between small and small firms are also important for innovation (Young, Francis, and Young 1994; Park 1996).

Secondly, innovation is an interactive process and shaped by a variety of institutional routines and social conventions. Innovation is an interactive process between different functions within firms, between suppliers and customers at the interfirm level, and between firms and the wider institutional milieu (Morgan 1997). Routines and conventions may help to regulate economic life by reducing uncertainty and facilitating coordination and cooperation for mutual benefit. The interactive process can be regarded as a process of interactive learning in which institutional routines and conventions can play a role (OECD 1992).

Thirdly, regional clustering and specialization are important for innovation. In recent years, the region has been rediscovered as an important source of competitive advantages and organization of global space economy (Scott 1995). Clustering and specialization in a region are regarded as some of the key elements of growth and competitiveness, due to the reduction of transaction costs, agglomeration economies, and technological and skill advantages (Porter 1994; Krugman 1995). Beyond this regional competitiveness based on the economies of clustering, geographical studies of recent years suggest the importance of locally embedded social, cultural, and institutional arrangements as a source of knowledge and learning (Amin and Thrift 1995; Storper 1996). Informally constituted knowledge and information environments, derived from local tacit knowledge and face-to-face exchange, the quality of local institutions, long-standing social habits, and local conventions of communication and interaction, contribute to a firm's learning-based competitiveness. In this institutional perspective, Silicon Valley and Italian industrial districts are regarded as 'learning regions', which display intensive interfirm interaction, shared know-how, spillover expertise, and strong firm-support systems (Amin 1998).

In the local innovation systems, accordingly, organization in terms of interfirm networks and collaboration, learning dynamics with interactive processes, and territorial dimension with regional clustering are regarded as three important dimensions. Since the Korean economy has been restructuring since the late 1980s and the government has promoted the development of high-tech industries, it is expected that regional or local innovation networks have been emerging in the 1990s. In the following section, innovation performance and R&D intensity will be compared between the core region (Capital Region) and peripheral regions in Korea.

3. Regional Variation of Innovation Performance in Korea

3.1. Government's Industrial Policy

The Korean national government has taken a leading role in the promotion of sectoral and spatial industrial policies, working with dominant *chaebols*. Export-oriented industrialization has been the major strategy since the early 1960s, and it was fashioned to promote the most promising industries at an appropriate period. Labour-intensive industries such as textiles and apparel were the key sector for the expansion of industrial exports before the mid-1970s, while heavy and chemical industries such as petrochemicals, shipbuilding, automobiles, and consumer electronics were the leading industries for export expansion in the late 1970s and early 1980s. The government's heavy and chemical industrial policy contributed to the evolution of the *chaebol* system in Korean economy, due to the borrowing of foreign capital being permitted and several incentives for investment in the heavy industrial sector. Since the mid-1980s, high-technology industries such as semiconductors have been increasingly favoured (Park and Markusen 1995). Since the mid-1990s, especially following the foreign exchange crisis in November 1997, the Korean government has made great efforts to open the country fully to trade and capital movements, restructure the financial sector, break up the *chaebol* system, and make the labour market flexible.

Along with the sectoral policies, the national government established several large industrial estates especially in the south-eastern part of the country in order to decentralize industries from the Capital Region, which comprises Seoul and its surrounding areas of Kyonggi province and Inchon city. The major new industrial cities of Ulsan, Changwon, Pohang, Kumi, and Ansan are the result of industrial policies in the 1970s. Free export zones in Masan and Iri were constructed to attract foreign direct investment. However, the role of inbound FDIs was relatively insignificant in the 1970s and 1980s, compared to imported technology and foreign capital borrowing. Rather, *chaebols* contributed to the development and growth of the industrial cities by establishing large branch plants with imported technology and borrowed foreign capital. At first, the industrial estates in the industrial cities had only limited local interfirm linkages, but considerable local industrial networks have formed in recent years.

The government industrial decentralization policy has contributed to the spatial division of labour, concentrating headquarters of *chaebols* in Seoul and decentralizing production functions to the non-Capital Region (Park 1993). The high-technology industrial policy since the mid-1980s has resulted in the reconcentration of industry in the Capital Region, due to its locational advantages. The concentration of high-technology industries and advanced services, including R&D activities, in the Capital Region has intensified the spatial division of labour in the Korean economy (Park 1993). The establishment of science and high-tech parks in the non-Capital Region seems to have contributed to the dispersion of knowledge-based industries from the Capital Region. Taeduck Science Park is now developing as a government-anchored industrial district. Several local governments have made significant efforts to attract knowledge-based industries through the development of local autonomy since the mid-1990s. However, knowledge-based industries are still overwhelmingly concentrated in the Capital Region due to its favourable location factors such as availability of high-quality and skilled labour, advanced information infrastructure, easy access to financial centres, other advanced producer services, and so on. That is, even though new industrial districts have developed in the non-Capital Region by the government's industrial policy, regional variation in the development of knowledge-based industries persists.

3.2. Regional Variation of Innovation Performances

There has been a considerable variation in industrial growth and innovation performance among regions in Korea. Seoul was the centre of manufacturing growth in the early industrialization phase of the 1960s. Since the 1970s, however, the rate of manufacturing growth in Seoul has been continually lower than the national average due to a decentralization to its suburbs in the Capital Region and a dispersion to the non-Capital Region. The Capital Region is about 11.8 per cent of the total area of Korea and increased its share of the national population from 28 per cent in 1970 to 45 per cent in 1995 (KRIHS 1997).

The spatial division of labour in Korea is between Seoul and provincial areas, and even within the Capital Region with the concentration of control and management functions and producer services in Seoul and with decentralization and dispersion of production functions of large firms which mainly belong to *chaebols* (Park 1987). In addition to the decentralization to suburban areas and dispersion to peripheral areas of manufacturing plants, many firms in Seoul have also invested in industrial plants in China and South-East Asia since the late 1980s in order to reduce production costs, while corporate headquarters, engineering services, software industries, design and advertising, and other producer services have concentrated in Seoul (Park and Nahm 1998).

In the early 1970s, Seoul was the centre of the electronics industry in Korea, but now its suburbs have supplanted its function with decentralization of manufacturing plants, and it is now no more the centre of manufacturing, even for the technology-intensive manufacturing. Instead, it has been transformed into the centre of producer or advanced services in Korea.

During the restructuring period since the late 1980s, the Capital Region has intensified its role as innovation centre in Korea. The share of the Capital Region in the total number of patents registered it Korea increased from 69 per cent in 1985 to 80 per cent in 1995 (Korea Industry Property Office 1986, 1996). The overwhelming concentration of the number of patents may not be directly related to the innovation potential since the patents of large firms will be registered at the location of the headquarters or main plant of the firms, and there has been a trend of decentralization of patents registration. However, Seoul is continuing to take the leading role as innovation centre in Korea. The share of Seoul in the national total number of patents registered has decreased since 1985, but it still shares about 44 per cent of patents registration in Korea. The relative decentralization of the patents registration from Seoul to Kyonggi is consistent with the decentralization of high-tech industries from Seoul and the relative concentration of the high-tech industries in Kyonggi.

The Capital Region shares about 54 per cent of the total number of innovative SMEs and about 68 per cent of the total number of new products developed in Korea, revealing a considerable concentration in the Capital Region (Kwon 1998). Inchon and Kyonggi of the region show the greater share of the number of new products developed, compared to the share of innovative SMEs. The average number of new products developed by innovative SMEs in these areas is therefore greater than that of other areas in Korea. Even though the number of new products developed may not represent the exact innovation performance of regions, it is obvious that the Capital Region has considerable competitive advantages in Korea.

4. Local Innovation Networks of SMEs in Korea

4.1. National Systems of Innovation in Korea

National system of innovation can be regarded as 'a system of actors (firms, organizations, and government agencies) who interact each other in ways which influence the innovation performance of a national economy' (Gregersen and Johnson 1997: 484). In Korea, the national system of innovation has been significantly changed owing to industrial development and severe competition in the international markets. The early 1980s was a turning point for the changes in national systems of innovation. Since the early 1980s, firms have emphasized technology development, and private firms' share of national total R&D expenditure was 56 per cent in 1981, which was the point where private firms' share was greater than that of the government. Since then the share of private firms has increased rapidly and reached 81 per cent in 1985 (MOST 1991). Because of these changes in the environment of technological development since the early 1980s, two distinctive national systems of innovation can be identified (Kim 1997).

In the 1960s and 1970s, the government took the initiative in innovation systems. Government-sponsored research institutes took a significant role in the improvement of industrial technologies in this period. Most of the firms were interested in technology transfer from the industrialized countries rather than the promotion of their own R&D activities. Firms tried to digest and learn the imported technology. They improved their technology level by learning processes of imported technology. The major role of the universities in the innovation system was the supply of human resources for technological development. Therefore, the national systems of innovation in the 1960s and 1970s were mainly directed by government policy, which supported technology transfer to firms and learning processes of imported technology (Kim 1997). The impact of inbound FDIs on the development of innovation systems was not significant in this period. Rather, imported technology was critical for technological development in the 1970s. Major actors and networks of the system are summarized in Figure 12.1.

National systems of innovation have been considerably changed since the 1980s. The major role of innovation shifted from the government to private firms. Since the 1980s, many firms have established their own R&D centres and significantly increased R&D expenditure. In 1980, only fifty-four firms, which mostly belong to *chaebols*, had their own R&D centres, but the figure had increased to 2,226 by 1995 (KITA 1995, 1996). In the early 1980s, *chaebols* aggressively established R&D centres. For example, Daewoo Group (*chaebol*) established eleven R&D centres in the early 1980s (Park 1990). In the late 1980s, even the SMEs began to establish R&D centres. At present more than two-thirds of the total R&D centres have been established by SMEs. Even though the number of R&D centres of SMEs is much greater than that of large firms, the large-scale in-house technology development projects have been mostly conducted by large firms included in *chaebols*.

The distinctive characteristics of R&D activities of firms in the national systems of innovation in recent years are as follows (Kim 1997). First, large firms of *chaebols* have established strategic alliances with worldwide high-tech firms. Types of strategic alliances established are joint venture, joint R&D activities, technology exchanges, shared technology, joint production, licensing, and so on. Inbound FDIs began to become more significant in the 1980s than before, but their role was relatively minor compared to the role of *chaebols*. Second, large firms, which mostly belong to *chaebols*, have been aggressive in establishing foreign R&D centres and labs. In 1994, there were twenty R&D centres and thirty labs in foreign countries, mostly in the USA, Japan, and the EU. Third, due to the difficulties of licensing leading-edge complex technology, large firms have been actively involved in mergers or acquisition of high-tech firms in the developed countries in order to secure original technology.

Since the financial crises, even the SMEs are attempting to establish a focal point of network in Silicon Valley. Such active behaviour of firms for technological development is completely different from the passive behaviour on

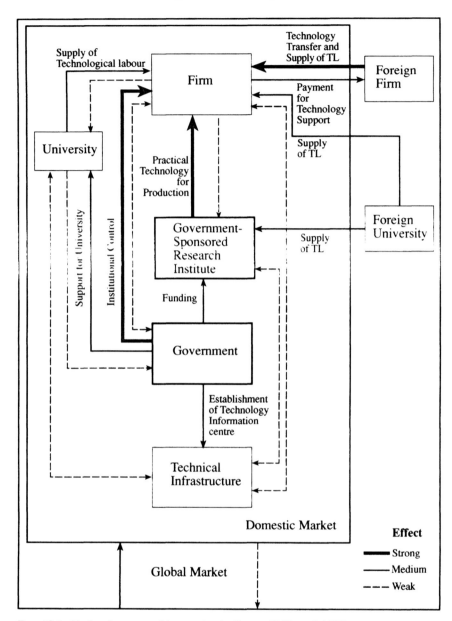

FIG. 12.1. National system of innovation in Korea, 1960s and 1970s

technological development in the 1960s and 1970s. Universities have contributed to the growth of technological manpower in terms of both quantity and quality. Distinctive characteristics and networks of actors in the national system of innovation are shown in Figure 12.2.

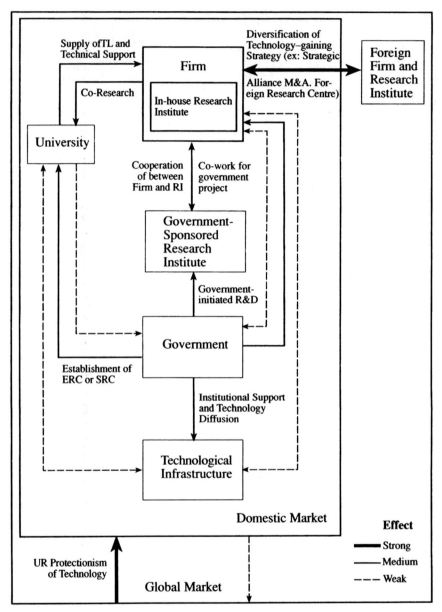

FIG. 12.2. National system of innovation in Korea, 1980s and 1990s

4.2. Local Innovation Networks of SMEs

In the 1990s, beyond the national innovation systems based on the dominant role of the large firms which belong to *chaebols*, evolution of local innovation networks is likely due to the development of regional clusters of SMEs in technology-intensive sectors. In order to examine the local innovation networks, questionnaire surveys for SMEs were conducted from 22 November to 22 December 1997, when Korea began to have financial support from the IMF. The survey was supported by the Korea Chamber of Commerce and Industry. Three thousand SMEs were selected for the questionnaire survey with random sampling by region, employment size, and type of industry. Out of 3,000 selected SMEs, 825 firms replied to the questionnaires, representing a responding rate of 27.5 per cent. In this study, some part of the survey data are analysed related to the innovation networks of SMEs.

As stated before, SMEs in Korea have been interested in technological development since the 1980s with the establishment of their own R&D centres. However, SMEs have been more involved in R&D activities during the 1990s, especially as one strategy of industrial restructuring. There was a significant increase in the proportion of SMEs that conducted research and development (R&D) activities during the 1990s. Out of the 825 firms that replied to the questionnaire, 20 per cent conducted R&D activities in 1993. The ratio of firms which conducted R&D activities increased to 34 per cent in 1996 (Table 12.1). Overall, the larger SMEs are participating in R&D activities more than the smaller SMEs. However, among the firms which conduct R&D activities, the smaller SMEs show a higher ratio of R&D expenditure to total sales than the larger SMEs, revealing that a considerable proportion of smaller SMEs which conduct R&D activities can be regarded as venture businesses. Despite the recent vulnerable financial situation of the SMEs, more than 5 per cent of the surveyed firms are planning to invest to new product innovation and process technology development.

There are several actors who contributed to the technological development and innovation of SMEs. Contract firms (customer), business associations of the same industry, and local cooperative firms are most significant actors for innovation of SMEs. About 28, 20, and 18 per cent of the surveyed firms respectively replied that contract firms, trade associations of the same industry, and local cooperative firms are major contributors to the technological development and innovation. Relationships between *chaebols* and SME suppliers are important for innovation networks of SMEs because the contract firms are mostly large firms included in *chaebols*. For example, Samsung Electronics supports cooperative SMEs for technological development, labour training, supply of qualified engineers, technical services, and so on (Samsung Electronics 1998). Government-sponsored research institutes and foreign firms were also regarded as major contributors to innovation by 7 per cent of the firms who replied. Only a few firms regarded universities, local or national governments as significant contributors to innovation.

TABLE 12.1. Ratios of R&D expenditures to total sales and of the firms participating in R&D activity (by firm size) (%)

No. of employees		% of R&D Expenditure				Total (no. of firms)	% of firms participating in R&D[a]
		below 3%	3–5%	6–9%	10% and above		
1993	5–19	20.0	37.1	10.0	32.9	100.0(70)	18.2
	20–49	42.9	32.7	16.3	8.2	100.0(49)	17.5
	50–99	24.0	48.0	4.0	24.0	100.0(25)	25.0
	100–299	50.0	35.0	0.0	15.0	100.0(20)	33.3
	Total	31.1	37.2	9.8	22.0	100.0(164)	19.9
1996	5–19	21.6	35.1	7.2	36.0	100.0(111)	28.8
	20–49	31.4	44.1	11.8	12.7	100.0(102)	36.4
	50–99	34.1	31.7	9.8	24.4	100.0(41)	41.0
	100–299	35.7	35.7	10.7	17.9	100.0(28)	46.7
	Total	28.4	37.9	9.6	24.1	100.0(282)	34.2

[a] Ratio of the number of firms participating in R&D to the total number of surveyed SMEs by sizes (%).

Source: Results of survey.

In general, smaller SMEs are more dependent on contract firms and local cooperative firms for their technological development. SMEs in the Capital Region and South-west Region are more related to the contract firms. Large parent firms of *chaebols* as contract firms take an important role for SMEs' innovation in the Capital Region, while large branch plants as contract firms seem to have a significant role for SMEs' innovation in the South-west Region. In the South-east region, local cooperative firms are regarded as important contributors for their innovation by about 29 per cent of firms. It is also noticeable that the relatively higher percentage of firms in the Middle Region regard the government-sponsored research institutes as significant contributors for their innovation. This fact reveals that government-sponsored research institutes in Taeduck Science Park are now having closer relations with local SMEs. This relation is consistent with the recent findings that the number of spin-offs from the research institutes of Taeduck Science Park has increased in recent years, and that they have close networks with parent research institutes (Jeong and Park 1999).

A considerable number of SMEs believe that interfirm networks are important for their innovation networks. About half of the firms which regard interfirm networks as related to their innovation, confirm that local firms are important for joint development of products, technological support, and acquirement of business information. Local interfirm networks are also important for technical services. About 40 per cent of the 476 SMEs, which have external linkages for technical services, have networks with local technical service firms. The interfirm networks of innovation-related services consider that local networks are regarded as important by a large proportion of the SMEs.

Less than 7 per cent of the SMEs have innovation networks with universities. Only about 5 per cent of the surveyed firms have innovation networks with public institutes such as research departments of the government and government-sponsored research institutes. Government support for SMEs is mainly financial aid for operation. Only about 7 per cent of the surveyed firms have had support from the government for technological development. The survey results support that universities and government are important for some of the SMEs, but they are not major agents for innovation networks of SMEs.

Learning at workplace is the most important source for skill formation for SMEs. About 87 per cent of the firms who replied suggested that skill development through learning at workplace is the way of labour training (Table 12.2). Smaller SMEs are more dependent on learning at the workplace for their skill formation, while about one-third of the medium-sized firms depend on irregular outside-firm training. There are, however, no significant differences in the method of skill formation and labour training by region.

The proportion of firms which conduct R&D activities and the ratio of R&D expenditure to total sales of firms is considerably different by region. In general, surrounding areas of Seoul in the Capital Region showed that a high ratio of firms participated in R&D activities (Table 12.3). In 1996, the Middle Region also showed that a high ratio of firms participated in R&D activities, which is due to the development of Taeduck Science Park and spin-offs from it. The high ratio of Kangwon and Cheju in 1996 may have exaggerated the local innovation potential owing to the small number of samples. The ratio of Seoul was relatively low, but it should be noticed that Seoul shares almost half of the SMEs which conduct R&D activities. In Seoul, new firms and new industries have been continuously developed and Seoul shows the highest performance of new-firm generation rate in the country. The data of Table 12.3 suggest that the Capital Region is the centre of innovation in Korea, since about two-thirds of SMEs which conduct R&D activities are located in the Capital Region; however, some of the SMEs in peripheral regions have actively participated in R&D activities in recent years.

Interfirm networks between large contract firms and suppliers of SMEs within local areas and collaboration with other firms and trade associations of the same industry are an important mechanism for innovation of SMEs in Korea. Large firms belonging to *chaebols* have a critical role in forming interfirm networks through establishing cooperative suppliers of SMEs. For some SMEs, collaboration with universities, government-sponsored research institutes, and other public institutes are also important contributors for their technological development and innovation. It is not clear yet at the local level, based on the questionnaire surveys, whether or not institutional factors are significant for the differences of innovation performances and local innovation systems. In order to clarify the impact of institutional factors, in-depth interview surveys and more detailed analysis of the data are required.

TABLE 12.2. Methods of job training (%, no. of firms)

		Learning by doing	Irregular training within the firm	Regular training within the firm	Irregular training outside the firm	Regular training outside the firm	Others	No. of respondents
No. of employees	5–19	91.5	7.6	5.8	17.1	3.0	2.1	(328)
	20–49	86.3	10.4	4.1	27.0	5.4	3.7	(241)
	50–99	82.1	15.5	6.0	31.0	8.3	2.4	(84)
	over 100	69.4	14.3	18.4	32.7	10.2	4.1	(49)
Present plant location	Seoul	85.0	11.9	5.7	23.2	5.4	4.5	(353)
	Inchon, Kyonggi	89.5	9.5	4.2	28.4	5.3	0.0	(95)
	Central region	82.2	15.6	11.1	20.0	6.7	0.0	(45)
	South-east region	89.1	3.4	6.1	21.8	4.1	2.0	(147)
	South-west region	92.6	13.0	9.3	22.2	3.7	1.9	(54)
	Kangwon, Cheju	100.0	0.0	0.0	12.5	0.0	0.0	(8)
Total		87.0	10.0	6.1	23.2	5.0	2.8	(702)

Note: Percentage in each cell represents a ratio of firms experienced in job-training to the number of respondents in each row.

Source: Results of survey.

TABLE 12.3. Ratios of R&D expenditure to total sales and of the firms participating in R&D activity (by plant locations) (%, no. of firms)

Present plant location		% of R&D Expenditure				Total (no. of firms)	% of firms participating in R&D[a]
		below 3%	3–5%	6–9 %	10% and above		
1993	Seoul	43.2	28.4	5.4	23.0	100.0(74)	17.7
	Inchon, Kyonggi	26.5	32.4	23.5	17.6	100.0(34)	30.9
	Central region	9.1	63.6	0.0	27.3	100.0(11)	21.2
	South-east region	20.7	44.8	6.9	27.6	100.0(29)	16.7
	South-west region	18.2	63.6	0.0	18.2	100.0(11)	17.7
	Kangwon, Cheju	50.0	50.0	0.0	0.0	100.0(2)	20.0
	Total	31.7	37.3	22.4	22.4	100.0(161)	19.5
1996	Seoul	33.6	34.4	6.1	26.0	100.0(131)	31.4
	Inchon, Kyonggi	25.5	34.0	19.1	21.3	100.0(47)	42.7
	Central region	36.4	36.4	13.6	13.6	100.0(22)	42.3
	South-east region	15.7	49.0	2.0	33.3	100.0(51)	29.3
	South-west region	15.8	57.9	21.1	5.3	100.0(19)	30.6
	Kangwon, Cheju	60.0	0.0	20.0	20.0	100.0(5)	50.0
	Total	28.4	38.2	9.5	24.0	100.0(275)	33.3

[a] Percentage of firms participating in R&D among the total of surveyed firms.
Source: Results of survey.

5. Local and Global Networks of High-Tech Clusters in Kyonggi and Kumi

Local and global networks of high-tech industries in Korea can be identified from the result of an interview survey conducted in major high-tech industrial clusters in Korea in 1995 (Park 1998). Industrial networks of thirty firms in Kyonggi and eighteen firms in Kumi were analysed and compared. The survey was conducted from the randomly selected samples located in Kyonggi area of the Capital Region and in the Kumi area of the South-eastern Region.

The importance of local linkages in production and business services can be easily found in spatial supply linkages. Local linkages are considerably important in most of supply activities (Table 12.4). Especially, local linkages of parts and components as well as business services are most significant. Overall, local-supply linkages are more important than non-local-supply linkages and the intensity of local linkages in Kumi is lower than that of Kyonggi. The intensity of local-supply linkages in Kumi, however, has significantly increased since the mid-1980s. The intensity of local linkages is related to the development of local networks through cooperation between large firms and their supply firms, spinoffs, and cooperation and competition among small and medium-sized firms in local areas.

TABLE 12.4. Spatial supply linkages of firms

Type of supply	Percentage of firms which were supplied more than 30% from			Average % of supply of firms from		
	Local	National	Foreign	Local	National	Foreign
Kyonggi						
Raw materials	68.3	46.2	38.5	37.4	36.0	26.6
Parts and components	67.1	42.9	21.4	47.8	32.5	19.7
Business services	72.7	36.4	9.1	65.5	29.5	5.0
Machinery and equipment	38.5	38.5	38.5	32.4	36.4	31.2
Overall amount of supply	66.7	46.7	40.0	38.7	35.2	26.1
Kumi						
Raw materials	50.0	62.5	37.5	34.6	45.2	20.2
Parts and components	85.7	47.6	23.8	55.5	32.1	12.4
Business services	64.7	58.8	23.5	45.9	42.4	11.7
Machinery and equipment	36.4	77.3	31.8	22.7	50.7	26.6
Overall amount of supply	54.2	79.2	33.3	36.6	46.1	18.3

Note: 'Local' radius of 30 km. from a firm.

Source: Data derived from interviews and questionnaire surveys, Park (1998).

During the restructuring period, there has been an increasing trend of intensifying linkages and cooperation between large firms, which mostly belong to *chaebol*, and small firms. The increasing trend of local linkages and of cooperation between large firms and SMEs has been promoted both by the government's policies and large firms' restructuring strategy in the 1990s. From the viewpoint of large firms, subcontracting activities contribute to savings in production costs, reducing a militant labor movement, and decentralizing uncertainties. Many large firms included in *chaebol* have organized a cooperative group of small and medium-sized supply firms in order to save production and transaction costs and to guarantee the constant supply of materials from the cooperative group of firms. Large firms of *chaebols* try to provide clusters of the cooperative supply firms around their branch plants. The large firms have increased their cooperative supply firms and have intensified localization of cooperative firms in the high-tech industrial districts. In addition, the large parent firms offer financial support; guidance on quality control, management, and manufacturing processes; and various educational and training services to the cooperative small and medium supply firms. Accordingly, collaboration and cooperation between large parent firms and small and medium-sized cooperative supply firms have significantly contributed to the formation of local networks in the hub-and-spoke-type and satellite-type new industrial districts and the dynamic development of the new industrial districts in Korea.

Spinoffs from the large firms are also an important source of increasing local networks and embeddedness in the new industrial districts. A considerable number of spinoffs from the large firms and new start-ups have appeared and have close relations with large firms in the new industrial districts. Formerly, local networks were insignificant in Kumi because there were only large branch plants of *chaebols*, but the local networks have been developed with the formation of spinoffs. In Kyonggi, the potential for innovation and entrepreneurs is significant and new start-ups are important for the strengthening of local networks.

Cooperation among the local firms is also a significant factor for the increase in local networks. A considerable number of the responding firms regarded cooperation with local suppliers (within 30 km) in training, shared equipment, technical assistance, shared personnel, joint-process development, financial cooperation, joint-marketing, and joint-product development as 'important' (Table 12.5). Cooperation with local customer firms in most of the activities in the Table 12.5 were regarded as 'important' by more than 40 per cent of the responding firms. Cooperation with local competitors was also regarded as important by a large percentage of responding firms. Cooperation with local trade associations were seen as 'important' by more than 50 per cent of the responding firms in Kyonggi. This cooperation with suppliers, customers, competitors, and trade associations located in the local area (within 30 km) are important for the evolution of local networks in the high-tech industrial districts in Korea.

There has been an increasing trend of global networks in production, research and development, and marketing in Korea in the 1990s. Strategic alliances, direct foreign investments, and subcontracting out production beyond the national boundary are the major sources for the increase in global networks and embeddedness. Large firms in the high-technology sector have initiated strategic alliances in order to gain competitive advantages. Based on the interview survey, 50 and 40 per cent of the responding firms in Kyonggi and Kumi respectively, established strategic alliances for certain activities. In general, technology transfer, direct investments, and joint R&D are relatively important types of strategic alliance. Strategic alliances are important for the formation of global networks. About 39 and 17 per cent of the responding firms in Kyonggi and Kumi respectively, maintained certain types of strategic alliance with foreign firms in 1995 (Park 1998).

An increase in FDIs is a significant factor for global networks with cross-border movement of both natural and created assets (Dunning 1993, 1998). FDIs of larger firms are strategies for reduction of production costs in developing countries or penetration of markets in developed countries. The number of FDIs from Korean firms significantly increased in the 1990s. Foreign direct investments from large companies usually accompany direct investments of supply SMEs. In addition, large firms tend to localize production linkages in host countries. Formation of intensive local networks of Korean large firms in Silicon Valley through direct foreign investments contributes to strengthening the global networks in information, technology, and R&D. Foreign direct investment from

TABLE 12.5. Importance of interfirm cooperation

Type of cooperation	Cooperation with suppliers located in		Cooperation with customers located in		Cooperation with competitors located in		Cooperation with trade associations located in	
	Local	Foreign	Local	Foreign	Local	Foreign	Local	Foreign
Kyonggi								
Training	53.3	26.7	50.0	12.5	35.3	17.6	85.7	14.3
Shared personnel	46.7	13.3	43.8	12.5	29.4	11.8	71.4	14.3
Joint product dev.	33.3	26.7	43.8	31.3	29.4	17.6	57.1	14.3
Joint process dev.	40.0	13.3	31.3	18.8	17.6	11.8	57.1	14.3
Other joint R&D	33.3	26.7	43.8	12.5	29.4	5.9	71.4	14.3
Shared equipment	53.3	20.0	31.3	12.5	23.5	5.9	57.1	14.3
Financial coop.	33.3	13.3	31.3	12.5	17.6	5.9	57.1	14.3
Joint marketing	33.3	13.3	43.8	18.8	17.6	5.9	71.4	14.3
Technical assistance	46.7	26.7	50.0	18.8	29.4	5.9	71.4	14.3
Kumi								
Training	45.8	20.8	42.3	19.2	29.6	22.2	50.0	14.3
Shared personnel	33.3	16.7	30.8	19.2	25.9	18.5	35.7	21.4
Joint product dev.	41.7	12.5	42.3	15.4	25.9	14.8	35.7	14.3
Joint process dev.	41.7	12.5	34.6	19.2	22.2	11.1	35.7	7.1
Other joint R&D	29.2	8.3	30.8	15.4	18.5	11.1	42.9	7.1
Shared equipment	20.8	8.3	30.8	15.4	18.5	11.1	28.6	7.1
Financial coop.	37.5	12.5	34.6	15.4	14.8	11.1	28.6	7.1
Joint marketing	16.7	8.3	26.9	15.4	22.2	14.8	28.6	7.1
Technical assistance	41.7	12.5	46.2	26.9	25.9	11.1	42.9	7.1

Notes: 1. 'Local' represents radius of 30 km. from a firm.
2. Values are the ratio (%) of the number of firms which regard each type of cooperation as 'important'.

Source: Data derived from interviews and questionnaire surveys, Park (1998).

the SMEs in Korea are not uncommon in recent years. Many cooperative supply firms have direct investments in foreign countries: they are either firms which have their own technology advantages or those which utilize cheap labour and other cost-reduction factors in the host country. In general the direct investments from the SMEs also contribute to the increase of global networks in information, services, and production.

Outsourcing from foreign countries and inbound FDIs are the other important factor for the increase of global networks. The overall degree of foreign supply linkages is much lower than that of local linkages, but it is considerable as seen in Table 12.4. Cooperative relationships with foreign firms are also significant for the formation of global networks. About one-quarter of responding firms regarded most of cooperative activities with foreign customers and some with foreign competitors as 'important' (Table 12.5). This value is, of course, relatively low compared to that of local firms. However, it is important to note the fact that a considerable number of Korean firms consider cooperation with foreign customers or competitors significant. Inbound FDIs in Korea have played only a minor role in total investments. However, the inbound FDIs have been significantly increased in recent years, especially since the financial crisis. Inbound FDIs in recent years have changed from resource-seeking investments to market-seeking investments (KOTRA 1998). The outsourcing activities, cooperation with foreign competitive firms, and inbound FDIs contribute to technology transfer, the increase of global networks, and gaining competitive advantages for firms in the industrial clusters in Korea. That is, local innovation systems are not closed systems, but are evolving with formation of local and global networks. The local systems can be regarded as the segment of a global circuit of learning and production systems.

6. Conclusion

The purpose of this chapter is to examine the innovation systems of Korea and local-global networks of high-technology industry with regard to the evolution of the knowledge-based economy. Major data for the study are derived from the questionnaire and interview surveys.

National system of innovation in Korea has considerably changed since the 1980s. The major role of innovation shifted from the government to private firms. In the 1960s and 1970s, the government took the initiative in innovation and government-sponsored research institutes took a relatively significant role in the improvement of industrial technologies in this period. Firms tried to digest and learn the imported technology and improve their technology level by learning processes of the imported technology. Since the early 1980s, however, many firms have become active for technological development and innovation and have established their own R&D centres. Large firms which belong to *chaebols* have been aggressive for strategic alliances with advanced foreign firms in the developed countries, in establishing R&D centres in foreign countries, and in promoting

mergers and acquisitions of high-tech firms in the developed countries in order
to secure original technology. Behaviour of such firms for technological development and innovation since the 1980s is completely different from the passive
behaviour on technological development in the 1960s and 1970s.

There has been a significant increase in the proportion of SMEs that conducted
research and development (R&D) activities during the 1990s. Generally speaking, the larger SMEs participated more in R&D activities than the smaller SMEs.
However, among the firms which conduct R&D activities, the smaller SMEs show
a higher ratio of R&D expenditure to total sales than the larger SMEs, suggesting that the considerable proportion of smaller SMEs that conduct R&D activities can be regarded as venture businesses.

Overall, networks with contract firms, the business association in the same industry, and cooperative firms within the local area are regarded as important contributors to technology development and the innovation of SMEs. The role of
the *chaebols* for the formation of interfirm networks was significant in the
1990s. Especially, support of large contract firms of *chaebols* to SME suppliers
have had a significant impact for the innovation networks of SMEs. Collaboration with universities, government-sponsored research institutes, and other public
institutes have also been important contributors for some SMEs in their technological development, but their impact was limited to only a low proportion
of SMEs.

Local innovation networks seemed to be evolving in the 1990s since local networks have been strengthened in the 1990s and there are considerable differences
in the innovation performances by region. Even though the peripheral regions
show relatively low performance of innovation compared to the Capital Region,
there is a trend towards an increasing proportion of SMEs conducting R&D
activities on the periphery and some of the SMEs in the peripheral regions are
quite active in technological development and innovation. Inbound FDIs took
only a minor role in networking and technological development before 1980s,
but during the 1990s they have significantly increased their impact on innovation systems through strategic alliances and joint R&Ds, though their share and
role are still not strong compared with those of South-East Asian countries.

The increasing degree of local networks and the evolution of global networks in the 1990s suggest that local innovation systems have been evolving in
the same period. With the increase of local networks and innovation systems,
the satellite-type and hub-and-spoke-type industrial districts, initiated by government
policy, are producing dynamic types of industrial districts. The local innovation
systems are not closed systems, but are interrelated with global networks and
circuits of learning and the production of new knowledge, and become more
important with the promotion of the knowledge-based economy as a consequence
of the major economic reforms which are currently being carried out.

However, it is not clear yet, based on the questionnaire surveys, whether
or not institutional factors are significant for the differences of innovation
performance at the local level and local innovation systems. In order to clarify

the impact of institutional factors and the learning process in detail, in-depth interview surveys and more detailed analysis of the data seems to be necessary. However, it is true that the local institutional factors are becoming important in the development of the knowledge-based economy due to the increased role of the local governments in regional industrial development. Promotion of local and global networks based on cooperation and partnerships between a broader set of actors such as multinational enterprises, large firms, SMEs, local and state governments, and other institutions seems to be critical for the improvement of local innovation potential and the development of the knowledge-based economy in Korea in the future.

REFERENCES

Amin, A. (1998), 'An Institutionalist Perspective on Regional Economic Development'. Paper presented at the Economic Geography Research Group Seminar, 'Institutions and Governance', 3 July 1998, Dept. of Geography, UCL, London.

—— and Thrift, N. (1995), 'Institutional Issues for the European Regions: from Market and Plans to Socioeconomics and Powers of Association', *Economy and Society* 21(1): 41–66.

Dunning, John H. (1993), *Multinational Enterprises and Global Economy* (Wokingham: Addison-Wesley).

—— (1998), 'Globalization, Technological Change and the Spatial Organization of Economic Activity', in A. D. Chandler, Peter Hagstrom, and Orjan Sölvell (eds.), *The Dynamic Firm* (Oxford: Oxford University Press): 289–314.

Gregersen, B., and Johnson, B. (1997), 'Learning Economics, Innovation Systems and European Integration', *Regional Studies* 31(5): 479–90.

Huggins, R. (1996), 'Technology Policy, Networks and Small Firms in Denmark'. *Regional Studies* 30(5): 523–6.

Jeong, J. Ho., and Park, S. O. (1999), 'Taeduck Science Park', Markusen, *et al.* (eds.). *Second Tier Cities*, University of Minnesota Press.

Keeble, D. (1997), 'Small Firms, Innovation and Regional Development in Britain in the 1990s', *Regional Studies* 31(3): 281–94.

Kim, H. S. (1997), 'Innovation Systems and Science and Technology Policy in Korea', in Keun Lee *et al.* (eds.), *Technology Capacity and Competitiveness of Korean Industry* (Seoul: Kyungmoonsa): 123–66.

KITA (Korea Industrial Technology Association) (1995), *Statistics of Industrial Technology* (Seoul: KITA).

—— (1996), *Directory of Korea Technology Institutes, 95/96* (Seoul: KITA).

Korea Industry Property Office (1986, 1996), *Year Book of Korean Industrial Property Office*, Seoul, Korea.

KRIHS (Korea Research Institute for Human Settlements) (1997), *The Second Consolidation Plan of Capital Region (1997–2011)* (Anyang: KRIHS).

KOTRA (1998), *Foreign Direct Investments* (Seoul: Korea Trade Association).

Krugman, P. (1995), *Development, Geography and Economic Theory* (Cambridge, Mass.: MIT Press).

Kwon, Y. S. (1998), 'An Analysis of Factors Determining the Regional Innovativeness of Korea Manufacturing Industry', unpublished Ph. D. diss., University of Seoul.

Morgan, K. (1997), 'The Learning Region: Institutions, Innovation and Regional Renewal', *Regional Studies* 31(5): 491–504.

MOST (Ministry of Science and Technology) (1991), *Science and Technology Annual, 1990* (Seoul: Sin Jin Business Affairs).

OECD (1992), *Technology and Economy: The Key Relations* (OECD).

Park, S. O. (1987), 'Recent Development and Linkages of High Technology Industries in the Seoul Metropolitan Area', *Korean Journal of Regional Science* 3: 21–35.

—— (1990), 'Daewoo: Corporate Growth and Spatial Organization', in Marc De Smidt and Egbert Wever (eds.), *The Corporate Firm in a Changing World Economy* (London: Routledge): 207–33.

—— (1993), 'Industrial Restructuring and the Spatial Division of Labor. The Case of the Seoul Metropolitan Region, the Republic of Korea', *Environment and Planning A* 25(1): 81–93.

—— (1996), 'Network and Embeddedness in the Dynamic Types of New Industrial Districts', *Progress in Human Geography* 20(4): 476–93.

—— (1998), 'Local-Global Networks of High-technology Industrial Districts in Korea', in Leo van Grunsven (ed.), *Regional Change in Industrializing Asia*, (Aldershot: Ashgate): 158–72.

—— and Markusen, Ann (1995), 'Generalizing New Industrial Districts: A Theoretical Agenda and an Application from a Non-Western Economy', *Environment and Planning A* 27: 81–104.

—— and Nahm, K. B. (1998), 'Spatial Structure and Inter-Firm Networks of Technical and Information Producer Services in Seoul, Korea', *Asia Pacific Viewpoints* 39(2): 209–19.

Porter, M. (1994), 'The Role of Location in Competition', *Journal of Economics of Business* 1(1): 35–9.

Samsung Electronics (1998), *Supports to SMEs by Samsung Electronics*, Suwon, Korea.

Scott, A. J. (1995), 'The Geographic Foundations of Industrial Performance', *Competition and Change* 1(1): 51–66.

Storper, M. (1995), *The Regional World: Territorial Development in a Global Economy* (New York: Guilford Press).

—— (1996), 'Institution of the Knowledge-Based Economy', in *Employment and Growth in the Knowledge-Based Economy* (Paris: OECD): 255–83.

Young, R. C., Francis, J. D., and Young, C. H. (1994), 'Flexibility in Small Manufacturing Firms and Regional Industrial Formations', *Regional Studies* 28(1): 27–38.

13

The Software Cluster in Bangalore

V. N. Balasubramanyam and Ahalya Balasubramanyam

1. Introduction

The developments associated with globalization are many and varied. One such development which has attracted geographers and economists alike is the clustering of specific types of economic activity in selected regions of the world. Dunning cites an impressive list of such clusters including the watch industry in Geneva, the cork and port wine industry in Portugal, the film industry in Hollywood, the tomato-canning industry of Campania in Southern Italy, and the more recent clusters centring on textiles, leather goods, and consumer electronics in ubiquitous export-processing zones in developing countries. At the end of Dunning's long list of clusters, there are the computer software clusters found in several countries including the Republic of Ireland, Israel, and the Philippines. The software cluster in the South Indian city of Bangalore though has attracted much attention in the media—it is frequently discussed on the BBC radio and television programmes and has merited special supplements in the *Financial Times* and *The Economist*. Its appeal to the British media is easily explained. The industry is located in the most anglicized city of India which retains much of its colonial grandeur in its architecture and landscape. And it is headline news when a knowledge-oriented industry in an economy which was hitherto known for its insularity from the global economy makes a breakthrough in international markets.

For the economist and the geographer however, the software cluster in Bangalore is of interest for a variety of other reasons. It represents in a microcosm several of the developments associated with globalization identified by Dunning in Chapter 1. It is a knowledge-oriented or human-capital-intensive industry that has attracted multinational firms to Bangalore both as producers and consumers of software, turning the city into an international gateway for trained labour. The state has actively assisted the growth of the industry.

But why Bangalore? Why software? Do the received explanations of clusters from geographers and regional economists fit the case of the cluster in Bangalore? How is the Bangalore cluster related to developments associated with globalization? This chapter addresses these issues. Section 2 provides a brief description of the size and structure of the software cluster in Bangalore. Section 3 discusses the Bangalore cluster in the light of received explanations of clusters. Section 4 analyses the cluster in the context of the economics of agglomeration and the developments associated with globalization identified by Dunning. Section 5 discusses policy implications. Section 6 brings together the main conclusions.

2. Size and Structure of the Software Cluster in Bangalore

It is estimated that about a quarter of the Indian software industry is located in Bangalore, earning it the sobriquet, the Silicon Valley of India. In 1995, *Dataquest* magazine reported that seventy out of 274 major software companies in India had their headquarters in Bangalore. The Software Technology Park (STP) in Bangalore started with a handful of companies in 1991, growing to 183 registered units in 1998, bringing the estimated total number of firms in the city to over 200. This cluster consists of small, medium, and large companies including wholly foreign-owned firms such as Motorola, Texas Instruments, Hewlett-Packard, and Indian-owned ones such as Infosys, WIPRO, and joint ventures such as PSI Data Systems. During the late 1980s and early 1990s, there has been an increase in the number of collaborations between Indian and foreign software companies involving informal subcontracting, semi-formal contracting, and distribution agreements (Heeks 1996).

Software firms in India are involved in a variety of activities in the domestic and export markets. The mainstay of the domestic industry is 'turnkey' or fixed-price contracts, whereas the export industry's main activity is classed as professional services. Other activities include products and packages, consultancy and training, and data processing. In the past, most of the work undertaken by Indian companies was done on-site in the locale of the customer, but in recent years, there has been a gradual shift towards more offshore work increasing from 5 to 45 per cent of the total export earnings of the industry, estimated at around $1.6 billion. This trend is attributed to increased skill and experience acquired by Indian software professionals in project management. Interviews with managers of companies in Bangalore suggested that they were using on-site work as stepping stones to project work wherein the company would execute entire projects in India with engineers travelling to the locale of the customer for short visits. Other companies such as WIPRO have begun to develop their own packages. mainly in the financial sector. Several managers were of the opinion that Bangalore was in the process of moving into the next stage in the development of the industry.

Although there is no reliable data, the National Association of Software and Service Companies (NASSCOM) estimated that the Indian software industry, which employs 140,000 people, was worth a total of $1.4 billion in 1996 and the growth rate was over 50 per cent. The STP in Bangalore reports that the city is now responsible for 53 per cent of exports from all parks in India, making it a major player in the Indian software scenario.

3. Bangalore and the Received Explanations on Clusters

Economic geographers and regional economists have provided a variety of explanations for the existence of high-tech clusters such as the Silicon Valley in California (Saxenian 1983), Silicon Glen in Scotland (Haug 1986), Silicon Fen, near Cambridge, England (Keeble and Kelly 1986; Keeble 1988) and the cluster on the borders of route 128, near Boston (Dorfman 1983). The high-tech clusters discussed by these studies include not only software, but also firms manufacturing a variety of high-tech engineering and electronic products.

The principal factors promoting clusters identified in these studies include the presence of educational institutions which produce a stream of engineers, technicians and scientists, state support in the form of tax incentives and subsidies, salubrious living conditions which enhance the quality of life, especially in university towns, availability of venture capital, and generation of forward and backward linkages.

Some of these explanations fit the case of Bangalore. The renowned Indian Institute of Science, which dates back to the days of the British Raj and pioneers research in engineering and the physical sciences is located in the city. It is also the home of the Bangalore University with its fourteen engineering colleges, which train software and computer engineers. Several large state-owned defence and communications industries including the Indian Telephone Industry, Hindustan Machine Tools, Hindustan Aeronautics, Bharath Electronics, and Bharath Earthmovers were established in the city during the 1950s. Bangalore was the chosen location for these technology-intensive industries because of its educational and scientific resources, and its strategic location away from the borders of India. These education and science establishments are a legacy from the early part of this century which the city owes to the efforts of pioneers in engineering and science education such as Sir M. Visvesvaraya and Sir Mirza Ismail. The state-owned enterprises and education and research institutions in the city have facilitated the growth of the software cluster mostly because their presence has promoted a research and learning culture in the city. Studies on clusters in the USA suggest that high-tech industries are attracted to locations with a diverse range of industries, although their subsequent growth is dependent on the presence of similar types of firms and industries (Henderson, Kuncuro, and Turner 1995). In a survey of fifty-two software firms in Bangalore, almost 50 per cent cited the availability of high-technology professionals and the presence of research institutes as the most important reason for their decision to locate in Bangalore (Srinivas 1997).

State support too is a factor in the growth of the Bangalore cluster. Besides establishing the Software Technology Park, where a number though not all of the software firms are located, the Government of India has facilitated the growth of the industry through the provision of duty-free imports of hardware, abolition of income taxes, installation of satellite facilities, and exemption from tedious customs and export clearance procedures. The survey referred to earlier reports that more than 90 per cent of the fifty-two firms included government support as one of the important reasons for their decision to locate in Bangalore.

Yet another factor cited in the literature for the presence of clusters in specific locations is their social and physical environment which promotes quality of life. Bangalore ranks high on this score. Situated at some 3,000 feet above sea level, it is well known for its salubrious climate, its greenery and gardens, which in the recent past attracted retired civil servants and army officers to this 'pensioners' paradise'. The large-scale influx of industries, including the software industry in recent years, has robbed the city of some of its famed ambience and escalated real estate prices, but compared with other megacities in India such as Bombay and Calcutta, it continues to be a desirable destination for those in search of high-quality life. The city offers excellent schooling, and sports and recreation facilities including clubs and golf courses, some of which to this day retain the architecture and traditions of the days of the Raj. It is also frequently remarked that the presence of London-style pubs and restaurants in the city are of allure to the highly paid young software engineers, but it is an untested proposition.

Most of the factors identified in the literature on clusters have contributed to the existence of the software cluster in Bangalore. But they are not adequate explanations; they fall short of painting the entire picture. Government support for the industry is available in other regions of the country too. Technology parks are to be found in Hyderabad in Andhra Pradesh, in Trivandrum in Kerala, and in five other locations. Fiscal incentives are also not location-specific to the firms. The education institutions in Bangalore do provide a rich source of supply of engineers and technicians, but the industry is not solely dependent on local talent. It draws its labour force not only from neighbouring Tamil Nadu and Andhra Pradesh but also from as afar as Rajasthan in the north. Indeed, the famed Indian Institutes of Technology which produce the *crème de la crème* of Indian engineers are located not in Bangalore but in Delhi, Madras, Kanpur, Bombay, and Calcutta. Graduates from these institutes and other regional engineering colleges located elsewhere in India are much sought after by firms located in Bangalore. Arguably, the city does not enjoy a monopoly in the production and supply of manpower for the software industry, but it does score over most others on the criterion of quality of life.

Transport costs also figure in the explanations of clusters (Krugman 1992; McCann 1995). The transport cost explanation of clusters is fairly obvious. If there are specific location advantages to be gained and if transport costs for their products are low, firms tend to flock together in one location and trade products across markets. In the presence of heavy transport costs, however, firms may be compelled to service different markets through segmented production. This may not be of relevance to the software cluster in Bangalore. Software is an intangible, it is an input used for processing information. Data and information, the raw materials for the industry, are easily transmitted to the software firms via satellite and the processed information is transmitted back via the same channel at relatively low cost to the customer or the firm. In fact, the producer and the consumer can engage in a dialogue on the screen as it were. In some cases, though, such long-distance delivery of software services may not be efficient. Customers may wish to purchase bespoke software, they may wish to train their in-house employees in the use of software, new entrants to the industry may not have the expertise required for managing a project and delivering software long distances. In some cases, the software producer sets up shop temporarily in the locale of the consumer—a form of production known as bodyshop software in the trade. Here it is not transport costs which dictate the mode of delivery but efficiency considerations. Bodyshop software is gradually decreasing as a proportion of the total value of sales of India's software firms.

4. Economics of Agglomeration, Globalization, and the Bangalore Cluster

Krugman's reformulation of Marshall's explanation of clusters emphasizes the contribution of scale economies which are external to the firm. In the words of Marshall (1901), 'such economies arise from general development of an industry and especially from the concentration of many businesses of a similar character in particular localities; or, as is commonly said, from the localisation of industry.'

The Marshallian-type scale economies or externalities are of profound significance for an explanation of the Bangalore cluster. Both the nature of the business of software and the socioeconomic and historical characteristics of the city serve to promote the sort of externalities identified by Marshall. In addition, developments such as growth in cross-border labour flows, growth in asset-augmenting type of foreign direct investment (FDI), and the growth of knowledge-oriented production of goods and services associated with the phenomenon of globalization also help explain the formation and growth of the Bangalore cluster.

The Marshallian-type scale economies evolve over time as an industry takes shape from small beginnings, with a handful of firms, and gradually mushrooms into a cluster. Who are the pioneers and what are the factors which attract the followers? The cluster in Bangalore consists of both locally owned and foreign-owned firms. The origins and growth of the cluster are to be traced to both FDI and the growth in cross-border flows of labour, a development associated with globalization.

The specific type of cross-border labour flows which has contributed to the birth and growth of the software cluster has it origins in the brain drain from India during the 1960s and the 1970s, to be attributed to both push and pull factors (Bhagwati and Hamada 1974). The push factors included excess supply of highly trained professionals and discriminatory labour market policies which compelled trained labour to seek employment in developed countries. Attractive working conditions, superior career prospects and increased wage levels were the pull factors, generated by the entry of the USA into the international market for brains to meet its vastly increased demand for skilled people for space research and defence. India supplied around 12–15 per cent of the annual inflow of around 40,000 skilled people into the USA during the late 1960s and the 1970s (Balasubramanyam 1993).

The software industry in India, which took shape during the latter half of the 1980s, owes much to the skilled professionals who emigrated to the USA during the 1960s and the 1970s. Many of them have returned home or have opted to divide their time between India and the USA, a phenomenon referred to as the to-and-fro brain drain. For several reasons, the software industry offers an attractive investment and employment outlet for both groups. A large number of these expatriates are trained engineers with higher degrees from US universities and their work experience is mostly in science and engineering-related industries. They also possess informal business contacts in the USA, they are trained in modern methods of business organization, and they are familiar with the type of information related to requirements of business in the USA. The software industry with its low fixed costs provides an ideal outlet for their talents and savings. It is estimated that per capita investment in the industry ranges from $2,000 for a bodyshopping firm with a small office to $10,000 for firms engaged in offshore development, the average being around $5,000 (Heeks 1996). There is also some evidence to suggest that more often than not, return migrants prefer to be self-employed rather than work for others. In the case of India in general and Bangalore in particular, the freedom from bureaucratic regulations and petty officialdom that self-employment offers would also be an attraction to return migrants. In addition, the programme of economic liberalization initiated by India in recent years has assisted the business initiatives of expatriates and return migrants.

Whilst software suits the talents and expertise of the expatriates and return migrants, Bangalore has added attractions as a location. Apart from the quality-of-life-enhancing characteristics of the city referred to earlier, it was also the region which contributed sizeable numbers of emigrants to the brain drain, principally because of the number of science and engineering institutions in the city. It is therefore an obvious choice for the location of software firms for return emigrants and expatriates. Their familiarity with the institutions and cultural mores of the city assists them in forging and developing essential business networks. They are also of appeal to the young software engineers who work for them, they provide a fertile training ground, they are able to impart the knowledge and skills they possess, and fire the imagination and aspirations of the locally trained young engineers. In other words, they facilitate transfer of human skills including engineering skills and methods of organization. They are also able to empathize with the aspirations of young professionals for recognition, international travel, and the desire of many to pursue career opportunities abroad. As Sunil Khilnani puts it: 'to the young MBA or software expert in Bangalore, India is merely one stopping place in a global employment market.' Bangalore attracts talented young professionals because it provides them with opportunities to seek their fortunes in the international employment market, and the software cluster more than any other industry links them with the outside world. In the process, it contributes to the growth in cross-border labour flows and as Khilnani observes. Bangalore may indeed be the non-resident capital of India.

Foreign direct investment too has aided the formation of the software cluster in Bangalore. As stated earlier sixty-six MNEs including well-known names in the information technology industry such as IBM, Hewlett Packard, Motorola, and Texas Instruments have established production facilities in Bangalore. Texas Instruments was the first foreign firm to establish a subsidiary with a stellite link in Bangalore in 1986. Hewlett-Packard, Oracle, Siemens, and Motorola followed soon after in the early 1990s. These investments are not to be equated with FDI in the export zones in East Asia which belongs to the asset-exploitation variety of FDI, designed to exploit the rents from the standardized technologies foreign firms possess in conjunction with cheap labour in these locations. Bangalore too is a source of cheap labour, wage rates for software professionals at all levels are appreciably lower than that for comparable labour in the USA and the UK. Average earnings for a software engineer in the UK in the year 1994 was around £26,000; in India earnings were £1,000 to £2,000 a year. Foreign firms stand to save substantial amounts of money from shifting their data-processing activities to Bangalore and other locations in India. For instance, British Airways is reported to pay just £4,000 a year to the 200 accounting staff in India—a fifth of the £20,000 average paid to its British counterpart.

Quite often the cluster in Bangalore is dismissed as a bit player in the world markets for software which has made it good because of cheap labour. As stated earlier, India's share in world exports of software is less than 1 per cent at the present. But it is a relatively new entrant and one which is remarkable is its phenomenal growth. But for its endowments of cheap but skilled labour, the industry would not have figured in international markets. Also, Bangalore labour is cheap relative to wage rates for software experts in developed countries, but the software professionals in India are paid substantially higher wages than professionals in India's manufacturing sector and academia, especially so because software engineers, of average age of around 25, are very young. In any case, to argue that cheap-labour-based comparative advantage is in some sense inferior to such advantage grounded in endowments of physical capital or natural resources is to argue against the grain of the celebrated theorem of comparative advantage which does not distinguish between sources of advantage and is a statement in positive as opposed to normative economics. Indeed, the Ricardian statement of the theorem identifies only labour productivity differences between trading nations and has little to say about sources of such differences. In the case of India's software, low wage rates amplify the innate productivity advantage based on labour skills it enjoys. It is a combination of low wages by international standards and professional skills of India's software engineers which has attracted foreign firms to Bangalore.

The industry owes its cheap but high-quality labour to India's education policies which emphasized tertiary or higher education, the age composition of its population, and the innate abilities of its educated population. Both the spokesmen for the software industry and the media have often noted the aptitude of Indians for abstract thinking and mathematics. The boast of Indians is that it was India which contributed the numeral zero (*shunya* in Sanskrit) to world civilization.

Software is an input which transforms information and enhances the value-added component of final goods. It is this contribution of software which augments the assets possessed by the foreign firms. The talent and skills possessed by India's software engineers is the target of the asset-augmenting variety of FDI in the software sector. The geophysical attractions of Bangalore along with its educational institutions are also an attraction to foreign firms. Employment in foreign firms is highly sought after by Indian software engineers because of the relatively high salaries and attractive working conditions they provide.

It is often remarked that the software cluster in Bangalore and others elsewhere in India are no more than export enclaves with a negligible impact on the local economy, save for the pockets of highly paid jobs they create (Pani 1998). And the visible presence of FDI in the sector suggests they may be a modern-day version of the nineteenth-century type of enclaves in plantations and minerals discussed by Hans Singer (1950, 1971). There are parallels between the two types of activities and the concerns of the critics merit discussion (Balasubramanyam and Balasubramanyam 1997). Both activities are export-oriented, FDI is a feature in both types of activities, and software is also an input rather than a final good.

But these parallels can be overdrawn, ignoring the distinctive characteristics of software. Unlike the minerals and plantation type of enclaves of the past, software is a human-capital-intensive activity, the basis for its existence is intellectual capital and not natural resource endowments. The objectives of foreign firms in software is not exploitation of natural resources, but the utilization of the skills of indigenous labour for problem-solving and creation of new knowledge. In this respect, foreign investment in the industry could be of the efficiency-seeking variety. But do the foreign firms engage in R&D in India, do they generate spillovers of technology and know-how? There are no easy answers to these questions because of the nature of software. If foreign firms do no more than utilize cheap labour in India to process information with the aid of software packages they have perfected abroad, there is no R&D. Admittedly such mundane work does form a part of the industry in India, but then again, as said earlier, foreign firms do rely on Indian expertise to perfect made-to-measure software to suit their needs. Such activity which requires Indian engineers to seek new methods of processing information is R&D. It may not be too far-fetched to say that software is quintessentially an R&D activity with problem-solving being its focus. There are considerable spillovers too as a result of movement of labour and interaction between the professionals in the industry, as discussed later in the chapter.

Typically, most Indian software professionals work on specific projects such as designing software for banks and financial institutions, for airline reservation systems, and the management of accounts of large companies. Although young Indian software engineers frequently complain that India is yet to produce a major software product such as Microsoft Word, project work stretches their abilities and provides for learning, a process in which foreign firms actively participate. Unlike the case of the export enclaves of the past or the East-Asian-type export zones, software firms do not work to order, utilizing standard technologies and designs provided by foreign firms. Foreign firms provide data and information and specify the problem to be solved and work in conjunction with Indian software engineers to arrive at a solution. The so-called Y2K problem which several Indian software firms have addressed is one such example of problem-solving.

There are also several other projects which are distinctive for their creativity. Dewang Mehta, the ebullient President of NASSCOM, citing the example of Formula 1 cars and other sports cars, captures the knowledge and learning-intensive nature of software, in his presentation to India Vision 2000 conference at Washington in 1996:

Hundreds of stages are involved in converting the initial concept or idea to a vision, to a design, to a manufactured product and to its ultimate delivery—a process that can be any business manager's nightmare. And the driving force—quality software—for many of these autos comes from software houses in India. The creation of a masterpiece requires a unique blend of intellectual capabilities of the highest degree and extraordinary skills acquired through years of experience. Today, the Indian software industry is regarded as a powerhouse of master craftsmen.

These master craftsmen of India are sought after by several foreign firms including General Electric, AT&T, IBM, Reebok, Levis, Caterpillar, Citibank, and Fujitsu who have all entered into alliances with Indian software firms, many though not all of them located in Bangalore. FDI in software is thus distinctly different from the FDI of the past. It is a knowledge-intensive activity and because of the creativity and learning involved, it is a cooperative activity. Such cooperation is sought by multinationals wherever skilled labour exists. It so happens that Bangalore provides a reservoir of such skills besides providing an attractive geophysical environment. Although the software industry originated in Bombay in the state of Maharashtra by the late 1980s, several well-known software firms soon moved to Bangalore. As Rauch (1993) notes, as one moves away from ports to inland locations, wage rates and rentals decline and wages fall in terms of importables. Several software firms relocated to Bangalore and new ones chose Bangalore because of the escalating prices for real estate in Bombay and, much more importantly, because of the presence of the large number of education and science establishments in Bangalore, because of the pool of skilled labour in the city, and also because of the physical attractions of the city. Once pioneers such as Texas Instruments were established, other firms moved into Bangalore.

And labour from other regions in India followed the firms. As writers on new growth theory have observed, human capital flows to where human capital is. The presence of pioneers in a specific location attracts others, the expectation that proximity to the great and the good is in itself beneficial attracts others.

The Bangalore cluster is to be traced to a number of factors including cross-border labour flows, foreign investment, and alliances between foreign and locally owned firms identified in Section 2. The cluster, once initiated, also grows because of the sort of externalities, technology, and knowledge spillovers external to the firm but internal to the industry it generates, identified by Marshall. Arguably, such spillover effects are the result of the existence of clusters; they do not explain the coming into being of clusters. Externalities are generated once a whole spate of firms engaged in the production of similar products locate in a specific region. It is, however, worth noting that clusters evolve over time and in many cases the potential for the generation of externalities promotes clusters.

In some respects, software is unique in the sort of Marshallian type of externalities it generates. Most young software engineers who have gravitated to Bangalore say that they chose to work in Bangalore because that is where the action is. The action they refer to is not just employment opportunities, it is also the opportunity to commune with other software engineers located in the city. Obviously, each firm would guard its expertise and intellectual property. There is though opportunity to discuss and debate the latest developments in the industry, identify general principles, and learn from each other. As Glaeser and co-authors, commenting on the Silicon Valley note 'in Silicon Valley microchip manufacturers learn from each other because people talk and gossip. Products can be re-engineered and employees move between firms' (Glaeser *et al.* 1992). In Bangalore, young software engineers do gossip and move between firms though re-engineering may not be an option in software. The nature of software business in Bangalore as elsewhere aids such learning and dissemination of information. In this respect, the software cluster in Bangalore more nearly resembles a university than a commercial centre, with each firm resembling a constituent department of a university.

In the literature, there is some dispute on the type of market structures which is conducive to the generation of externalities. According to Porter (1990), local competition accelerates innovation, firms which fail to innovate or imitate the innovators go bankrupt. Others such as Romer (1990) argue that in a competitive environment, firms will hesitate to invest in extensive R&D because of fears of imitation, but in the presence of few imitators, firms would have an incentive to innovate, a degree of monopoly would permit them to internalize the externalities their research would generate. The firms in the software cluster are mostly in the nature of non-competing groups; each firm has its own niche and dedicated group of customers; each firm is known for specific varieties of software such as software for the reservation systems of airlines, software for financial services. It is likely that cross-price elasticities for the various products produced by firms is low because of the specialized nature of the work they do. The mathematical and engineering skills of the software engineers though is pliable; the generic nature of software permits the practitioners of the trade to communicate with each other to their mutual benefit without compromising their allegiance to their employers.

In this setting, competition between firms within the cluster is not based on products they produce, although each of the firms in the cluster may be exposed to such competition in the export markets where they compete with their rivals from other countries. The competition for firms within the cluster is for skilled labour trained in the general principles of the language of software grounded in mathematics and industrial engineering. Once employed, young professionals are easily trained on the job in the production of products specific to each firm. Most firms in the cluster in Bangalore compete for skilled labour with a variety of incentives including profit-sharing and performance-related bonus schemes, attractive work environment, and opportunities for travel abroad. Such schemes promote labour training and skill formation. Even so, the turnover rate of employees in the sector is high, some firms reporting rates as high as 30 per cent. Many young engineers keen on a spell of work in the USA or a longer-term sojourn there seek employment in the reputable firms including the foreign firms. The network of fellow professionals provides information on employment opportunities and also acts as a conduit for exchange of information on technology and know-how. The high rate of turnover of employees also promotes knowledge spillovers from one group of firms to another. Here again such spillovers may not relate to specific types of software, but general principles and methods of organization. In this context, spillovers generated by foreign firms are of significance, they are externalities in the strict sense of the term; foreign firms pay wage rates above the average for the industry, impart training in modern methods of management and production of software, and provide opportunities for training abroad. All of this accrues to the local economy at little cost when professionals trained in foreign firms set up shop on their own or work for locally owned firms. For these reasons, the software cluster promotes both types of externalities, identified by Romer and Porter. Firms innovate to preserve their monopoly over specific types of software in external markets and compete with each other for skilled labour at home. The monopoly over specific types of software produced by each of the firms or small groups of firms encourages innovation, and competition for skilled labour between each of the firms in the cluster promotes labour training and skill formation.

The Bangalore cluster provides the infrastructure for flow of ideas, knowledge, and learning, not only because of the characteristics of software, a learning-oriented activity, but also because of the unique nature of the city of Bangalore. The tradition of education and learning the city enjoys and the presence of a number of state-owned enterprises in defence and communication have not only attracted skilled workers from other parts of the country, but also created a sizeable cohort of people with above-average levels of income and wealth in the city. In the year 1982, according to a survey conducted by the Indian Institute of Management in Bangalore, 28 per cent of the households in Bangalore earned an income between Rs 750 and Rs 1250, and 11 per cent of the population had an income in the range of Rs 1,250 and Rs 2,000 per month. These figures compare with an average income per head per month of around Rs 474 in the City at the end of the year 1989. As Khilnani remarks, the wealth of this class of people is not based on the traditional sources of wealth in India—control of land, bureaucratic office, or industry, but on professional and technical skills. Again, available statistics show that by the beginning of the 1980s, nearly 40 per cent of the workforce in the city was in services with another 25 per cent in manufacturing, and between 1971 and 1981 the percentage of workers in trade and commerce almost doubled, and those in transport and communications tripled. The city has thus a tradition of enterprise, learning, and creation of wealth based on skills. Young software engineers are the latest incarnation of such skill-based fortune seekers, and because of its traditions, the city not only tolerates the influx of the young engineers, but takes pride in their presence. The modern and cosmopolitan outlook of the city promotes an atmosphere for learning and innovation which are the hallmarks of the software industry. Neither the foreign-owned software firms in the city nor the well-paid young software engineers, with their yen for a Western life style and ambition to migrate to the USA, are regarded as a threat to nationalistic ideals. Instead, the software cluster is looked upon as an industry which interlinks Bangalore with the global economy.

5. Prospects and Policy Implications

What of the future? Is the software industry likely to sustain the momentum of growth? India's software sector appears to be well placed to prosper in the global market estimated to be in excess of $100 billion per annum. Her endowments of human capital and the entrepreneurial drive of leading Indian firms such as Infosys should enable the industry to identify and establish a foothold in specific segments of the industry. The future though may depend not so much upon the cost advantage the industry possesses but on its ability to advance up the value chain and compete on the basis of quality. With wage rates increasing at around 25 per cent per annum, India may find it difficult to sustain her position as a low-cost offshore centre. Also other developing countries such as China pose a threat to India's cost-based competitiveness in export markets. Indian companies are aware of the need to move up the value chain and leading Indian companies are increasingly engaged in specialist consultancy and customized software production. Infosys, a Bangalore-based firm, is planning on setting up software development centres around the world in all the time zones. It is also the first Indian software firm to go global with stock issue in the USA.

The industry owes its acknowledged success to many factors including state assistance in the form of infrastructure facilities. It has, though, fortunately escaped stifling regulations of the sort other industries have suffered, maybe because, as *The Economist* (30 May 1998) suggests, the government does not understand it well enough to regulate it. If only this happy state of affairs could continue, the industry would be blessed.

There are, however, well-meaning policy suggestions which may backfire if implemented. Dissatisfaction with the slow growth of the domestic software market, for instance, has inspired the suggestion that exports of software should be taxed. Economists have for long preached the folly of interference in trade when the objective of policy is the removal of a domestic distortion. The distortion here, if it could be called a distortion, is lack of education in information technology and woefully inadequate supplies of hardware for domestic industries and services. The first-best policy in this case is provision of facilities for training in the use of software and subsidized hardware for domestic users. A tax on exports would impair the competitiveness of profit-making firms in export markets; it is hardly likely to provide an incentive for the firms to develop domestic markets.

Equally fallacious is the suggestion that in the interests of developing the domestic hardware industry inputs required for the manufacture of hardware should be imported free of all tariffs while imports of final goods should be subject to a tariff. In other words, the hardware industry should be afforded a high rate of effective protection. This hardly makes sense at a time when world prices of hardware are rapidly declining. In any case, a highly protected domestic industry is unlikely to be efficient and cost-effective—India's long history of import substitution policies suggests as much. The only government policy which is well worth pursuing in the context of the software industry is benign neglect! It has served the industry well thus far and there is no reason to doubt that it won't do so in the future.

6. Conclusions

In the introductory chapter 'Regions, Globalization, and the Knowledge Economy', Dunning identifies three types of cross-border specialization promoted by integrated MNEs-horizontal specialization, vertical specialization, and asset-augmenting specialization. The third type of specialization is designed, as Dunning explains, not so much to promote the static efficiency of the MNE, but to enhance its future wealth-creating abilities in a learning-effective and cost-efficient way. The software cluster in Bangalore provides an example of this type of asset-augmenting specialization and seems to be an exception to the observed pattern of such division of labour which is usually between advanced industrial countries. This chapter has discussed the variety of factors which have promoted the existence and growth of an asset-augmenting type of specialization in Bangalore. Software is an input which enhances the value added of final goods production and in this sense augments the assets possessed by MNEs. It is also a knowledge-based and knowledge-creating activity. The cluster in Bangalore though is not solely a creation of MNEs, although a number of foreign-owned firms have a visible presence in the sector and several others are regular customers of software produced by locally owned firms. It also owes its origins and growth to increased cross-border flows of labour, a development associated with globalization, consisting mostly of migrants returning to India and the so-called to-and-fro type of brain drain. Both the foreign-owned producers of software in Bangalore and MNEs which are customers of the locally owned firms in Bangalore are actively engaged in a collaborative learning and knowledge-producing effort. The existence and growth of the cluster in Bangalore are explained by a variety of factors including state support, endowments of skilled labour, foreign investment, and the economics of agglomeration. The arresting feature of the cluster in Bangalore, though, is the match between the knowledge and learning-intensive nature of software and the unique attributes of the city of Bangalore, many of which, including its tradition of education and learning, appear to have been made to measure for the birth and growth of the cluster in the age of globalization.

REFERENCES

Balasubramanyam, V. N. (1993), 'Economics of the Brain Drain: The Case for Tax on Brains', in V. N. Balasubramanyam and J. M. Bates (eds.), *Topics in Policy Appraisal* (London: Macmillan): 105–19.

—— and Balasubramanyam, A. (1997), 'Singer, Software and Services', *World Development* 25(1): 1857–61.

Bhagwati, J. N., and Hamada, K. (1974), 'The Brain Drain, International Integration of Markets Professionals and Unemployment', *Journal of Development Economics* 1: 19–42.

Dorfman, N. (1983), 'Route 128: The Development of a Regional High Technology Economy', *Res. Policy* 12(6): 299–316.

Glaeser, E. L., Kallal, H. D., Scheinkman, J. A., and Shleifer, A. (1992), 'Growth in Cities', *Journal of Political Economy* 100(6): 1126–51.

Haug, P. (1986), 'US High Technology Multinationals and the Silicon Glen', *Regional Studies* 20(6): 103–16.

Heeks, R. (1996), *India's Software Industry* (New Delhi: Sage Publications).

Henderson, Kuncuro, and Turner (1995), 'Industrial Development in Cities', *Journal of Political Economy* 103(5): 1067–90.

Keeble, D. (1988), 'High Technology Industry and Regional Development in Britain: The Case of the Cambridge Phenomenon', *Environment and Planning* C7: 153–72.

—— and Kelly, T. (1986), 'New Firms and High Technology Industry in the United Kingdom', in D. Keeble and E. Weaver (eds.), *New Firms and Regional Development in Europe* (London: Croom Helm).

Khilnani, S. (1998), *The Idea of India* (London: Hamish Hamilton).

Krugman, P. (1992), *Geography and Trade* (Belgium, Leuven University Press, and Cambridge, Mass.: MIT Press).

McCann, P. (1995), 'Rethinking the Economics of Location and Agglomeration', *Urban Studies* 32(3): 563–77.

Marshall, A. (1901), *Elements of Economics of Industry*, 3rd edn. (New York: Macmillan).

Pani, N. (1998), 'The Software Dream: Anchoring Cities to an Illusion', *Sunday Times of India*, March.

Porter, M. (1990), 'The Competitive Advantage of Nations' (New York: Free Press).

Rauch (1993), 'Productivity Gains from Geographical Concentration of Human Capital: Evidence from the Cities', *Journal of Urban Economics* 34: 380–400.

Romer, P. M. (1990), 'Endogenous Technological Change', *Journal of Political Economy* 98(5): S71–S102.

Saxenian, A. (1983), 'The Genesis of Silicon Valley', *Built Environ* 9: 7–17.

Singer, H. W. (1950), 'The Distribution of Gains between Investing and Borrowing Countries', *American Economic Review*, Papers and Proceedings 12(2): 473–85.

—— (1971), 'The Distribution of Gains Revisited', in *The Strategy of International Development*, ed. A. Cairncross and M. Puri (London: Macmillan).

Srinivas, S. (1997), 'The Information Technology Industry in Bangalore: A Case of Urban Competitiveness in India?', Paper presented at the Fifth Asian Urbanization Conference, London.

14

Singapore:
Destination for Multinationals

Chia Siow Yue

1. Introduction

Singapore is a small city state in South-East Asia without natural resources. When it attained political independence in August 1965, there was deep concern over its economic viability. The new government was confronted by severe problems of a stagnating entrepot trade, withdrawal of the British military base, population explosion, high unemployment, confrontational industrial relations, and limited industrial and technological capability. Within a decade, Singapore had demonstrated its economic resilience and competitiveness and soon afterwards emerged as a newly industrialized economy (NIE) and a model of economic development. By 1997 Singapore has attained a per capita GNP of $US26,475, among the highest in the world. The World Development Report found that, adjusted for purchasing power parity, Singapore's per capita GNP is the highest in the world.

Singapore is an economic success by integrating into the global economy to overcome its small-size constraint. Total merchandise and service trade are more than triple its GNP and inward FDI stock ranks among the largest in the non-OECD world. The high trade orientation reflects a small resource base and market as well as Singapore's entrepot role and free trade policy. The high FDI penetration reflects Singapore's role as a manufacturing base for foreign MNCs and as a financial, transportation, logistics, and trading hub. In the past decade, Singapore has also been embarking on a regionalization drive to overcome its domestic land and labour constraints. The city state has made the region and the world its economic hinterland and is a favoured destination of multinational corporations.

2. Singapore as Manufacturing Base and Services Hub

In the Singapore city state, manufacturing accounted for 24.3 per cent and services (commerce, transport and communications, financial, business, and other services) for 71.5 per cent of GDP in 1997. Of the latter, financial and business services led with 30.9 per cent of GDP, followed by commerce (18.8 per cent), transport and communications (11.1 per cent), and other services (10.5 per cent).

2.1. Competitiveness Factors

In 1997 the World Economic Forum's (WEF) *Global Competitiveness Report* ranked Singapore the most competitive economy among its sample of fifty-three economies (including all OECD countries), while the Institute of Management Development's (IMD) *World Competitiveness Yearbook* ranked Singapore second to the USA among its sample of forty-six economies. Some key determinants of Singapore's competitiveness are highlighted below.

(a) Strategic location: Among the factor resources which have enabled Singapore to develop competitive advantages in several areas of manufacturing and services, only its strategic location is an inherited factor. Its location astride major sea and air routes and in the heart of a rich natural resource and economically dynamic region gives it a locational advantage in regional trade and investment. Its time-zone advantage, straddling East Asia and Western Europe, enables its financial markets and institutions to carry on transactions with Japan, Europe, and the USA within official working hours.

(b) Physical and financial infrastructures: Singapore has exploited its strategic geographical location, through investments in physical infrastructure. An efficient domestic land transportation network links the sea and airports and business and financial districts. Comprehensive air and sea transport and telecommunications networks link the city state with major cities and ports in the region and around the world, a particularly advantageous factor for time-sensitive shipments and business travellers in a hurry. Large investments in advanced telecommunications facilitates efficient business transactions with the rest of the world; Singapore has achieved world-class status in information technology. Advanced planning and careful implementation have ensured the ready availability of power, water, and telephone lines. Industrial estates, business parks, and science parks provide ready access to land and factory/office space and industrial, commercial, and research facilities and amenities; there are also specialist parks to meet the needs of chemical and electronics industries. The provision of these estates contributes to optimal use of land in land-scarce Singapore, reduces the capital investment requirements of investors, allows quick start-ups, and exploits external economies of industrial clustering. The well-developed financial markets, inflow of foreign capital, and abundance of national savings have contributed to the ready availability and low cost of capital in Singapore.

(c) Human resources: Singapore has a very small population base (3.5 million in 1997) and government policy focuses on improving its quality through education and training and augmenting its numbers through selective immigration. For the latter, more than 20 per cent of Singapore's workforce is foreign. While government policy tries to dampen the demand for foreign unskilled and semi-skilled workers, through a payroll levy on employers, there is a policy of active recruitment of foreign talent for both public service and private industry. For the former, since the 1960s, the educational system has been continually restructured —with emphasis on technical and vocational education below tertiary level to

provide a growing pool of skilled workers and technicians; and rapid expansion of engineering, business, and computer education at tertiary level. Forty per cent of the graduates from polytechnics and universities are trained in engineering and technical areas. The proportion of an age cohort enrolled in polytechnics and universities is targeted to reach 60 per cent by year 2000. Formal education is supplemented by training in specialized industrial training institutes to produce qualified craftsmen and technicians. The establishment of the Skills Development Fund provides upgrading training for those already employed. English is the primary working language.

(d) Political and social stability and good governance: Political stability and an honest and efficient political leadership and bureaucracy are important elements in Singapore's positive business environment and low transaction costs. Both the WEF and IMD have ranked Singapore top for the role the government plays in promoting the country's competitiveness. Social cohesion and consensus is seen as central to the effective implementation of major policies and programmes and the creation of a stable environment for investment and business. Social equity has been maintained with rapid economic growth, as evident in the rapid disappearance of poverty, upward social mobility, and stable income distribution. A social safety net is provided by full employment, the compulsory savings scheme under the Central Provident Fund, subsidized public housing which resulted in 85 per cent of the population living in owner-occupied housing, and subsidized education and healthcare. Singapore has enjoyed industrial peace since the 1970s. A tripartite National Wages Council, with representatives from workers, employers, and government, provides annual guidelines for orderly wage increases in an economy increasingly characterized by labour shortages.

2.2. Manufacturing Base for Export

Singapore embarked on industrialization in 1960 confronted with several difficulties, particularly a small resource base with a land area of only 581 sq. km. and lacking even water and energy, and a small domestic market with a population of 1.6 million. However, Singapore was not without advantages—a strategic geographical location and an excellent natural harbour; well-established entrepôt with developed transportation, communication, and commercial and financial infrastructure; trading and financial expertise; and a relatively literate and skilled labour force.

The key elements of Singapore's industrial strategy are the following—strong government policy intervention, initially to jump-start the industrialization process and increasingly to encourage specific types of investments and activities; reliance on an open-trade regime, with free imports and promotion of exports; reliance on foreign direct investment, particularly MNCs from industrialized countries, to spearhead the industrialization drive in the early years and for technology transfer and market channels in later years; investment in human capital and infrastructure to ease the supply constraints; maintenance of good industrial relations; maintenance of a stable macroeconomic environment; and lowering the burden of taxation over time.

In the initial years of industrialization, import substitution was pursued. Following political secession from Malaysia and independence in August 1965, Singapore moved rapidly into export manufacturing. Political, economic, and social measures were undertaken in 1967–8 to improve the investment climate—institutions were reorganized, tax incentives expanded, development of industrial estates accelerated, labour legislation introduced to improve industrial relations, the educational system restructured to emphasize technical education, and industrial training schemes expanded. The upshot of the various measures was a surge in FDI inflows during 1968–73, resulting in the rapid growth of industrial production, employment, and exports, and double-digit GDP growth.

With full employment by the early 1970s, the industrial strategy shifted from labour-intensive manufacturing towards promotion of industries with higher-skill and technology content and high-value-added services. Restructuring was pursued in earnest by the late 1970s and early 1980s and the policy instruments included accelerated wage increases to induce labour saving; encouragement of automation, mechanization, and computerization; stronger emphasis on human resource development; more selective investment promotion to focus on high-value-added, skill-intensive, and technology-intensive investments; and emphasis on research and development. Restructuring was interrupted by the 1985–6 recession and resumed in the late 1980s. The new economic strategy then focused on developing Singapore beyond a manufacturing base into a total business centre and a services hub. While continuing to promote inward FDI aggressively, the new strategy also encourages outward investment to overcome domestic land and labour constraints and to directly access overseas markets.

The 1991 Strategic Economic Plan (SEP) calls for the promotion and development of Singapore as a total business centre and the development of high-tech and high-value-added manufacturing and services as twin engines of growth. The SEP adopts Michael Porter's cluster framework to achieve competitiveness. Singapore aims to achieve competitiveness by developing a cluster strategy for industry and business services, as business enterprises need access to various suppliers, right type of qualified manpower, competence centres in relevant technologies, and efficient infrastructure and other services. Strategies for the manufacturing and service sectors were grouped under Manufacturing 2000 and International Hub 2000 respectively.

The Manufacturing 2000 programme aims at sustaining manufacturing in Singapore at not less than 25 per cent of GDP. There will be no substantial industrial hollowing-out, as the official view is that there is a close linkage between manufacturing and services, industrial manufacturing capability represents an essential component of any advanced economy, and a strong manufacturing base provides the anchor upon which other advanced capabilities in science and technology, logistics and operations management can be built. The key element of Manufacturing 2000 is the development of industry clusters, that is, the complex of vertically and horizontally linked supporting industries and resources that collectively make the end products or services competitive. The strategy is to upgrade capabilities across the entire value chain in each industry cluster, including product and process development, production, engineering, and strategic marketing. The cluster approach has been adopted for major sectors including electronics.

The Cluster Development Fund and Co-Investment Programme are key components of the cluster development plan. The $S1 billion Cluster Development Fund enables the government to provide equity participation in joint ventures and for strategic projects in Singapore and the region. The Co-Investment Programme involves government equity participation in joint ventures and supports the cluster development plan in three areas—to address critical gaps in industry clusters with the Economic Development Board (EDB) co-investing with partners in new capabilities and critical supporting industries; to accelerate the development of local enterprises; and government equity partnerships for strategic investments with local companies and MNCs going regional. Government co-investment partnerships with foreign MNCs is in recognition that the traditional tax incentive may be inadequate for capital- and technology-intensive projects, and government equity participation may be necessary to share the capital requirements and risks. Thus, to promote the semiconductor wafer fabrication industry, the EDB co-invested in SemiTech together with Texas Instruments, Hewlett Packard, and Canon to fabricate 16M-bit DRAMS.

Data from the annual census of industrial production show that by 1997 the composition of manufacturing output was as follows—electronic products and components (50.5 per cent share), followed by refined petroleum products (11.6 per cent), chemicals and chemical products (7.3 per cent), machinery and equipment (5.4 per cent), fabricated metal products (5.0 per cent), and transport equipment (4.0 per cent). Two industry clusters are discussed below, while the electronics industry cluster is discussed in a separate section.

An early industry cluster centres on petroleum-refining and petrochemicals. Singapore's role as a major bunkering centre led major international companies, including Shell, Esso, and Mobil, to establish petroleum refineries to supply bunkers to ships and aircraft calling at Singapore and petroleum products to the Asia-Pacific region. The crude was initially imported from the Middle East and later from neighbouring countries. By the 1970s, Singapore had became a major petroleum-refining centre. With the emergence of new refineries in the Middle East and in neighbouring countries in the 1980s, Singapore refineries upgraded operations to improve efficiency and flexibility and undertook contract-processing for Asian-crude suppliers; Singapore also embarked on a petrochemical complex and developed oil trading, distribution, and storage facilities.

Transport equipment, mainly marine rather than automobile, formed a second major industry cluster in the 1970s. Unlike most developing countries, there is no automobile assembly in Singapore, although there are automotive components firms linked to the electronics industry. Singapore's role as a major shipping node and port, and engineering skills from the former British naval base provided the competitive advantage. Unlike other industry clusters dominated by multinationals, the major shipyards engaged in ship-repairing and boat-building are local enterprises which grew from the conversion of British naval dockyards to commercial use in the early 1970s. The industry expanded into oil-rig construction in response to the South-East Asian oil exploration boom. In the 1980s Singapore also emerged as an aviation repair and overhaul centre and a manufacturing base for aircraft engine parts and components.

2.3. Services Hub

Singapore is a regional trading, financial, transport and telecommunications, and tourism hub. Competitive advantage arises from its strategic geographical location astride the major east–west shipping route as well as time-zone advantage straddling East Asia and Western Europe; its well-developed physical infrastructure; and its human resources. Alongside of commercial expertise, Singapore has developed skills in urban planning, port and airport management, hotel management, engineering consultancy, and business support services. Trade and investment policies also impose minimal regulations on the movement of goods, services, persons, and funds, and minimal restrictions on the right of establishment of foreign firms and, together with the widespread use of English, contribute to lower transaction costs. Political, social, and economic stability also contribute to a conducive business and living environment.

The International Business Hub 2000 programme focuses on the development of Singapore as a hub for business and finance, logistics and distribution, and communications and information. The hub strategy is based on the notion that, with globalization, these key economic activities are increasingly concentrated in a few strategic centres around the world, each one acting as a hub to service its extended hinterland and link it with the rest of the world.

Singapore is a major trading and transportation hub. It has been the entrepôt of South-East Asia since the nineteenth century, providing the functions of trading, financing, transhipment, storage, grading, and processing. The initial advantages of a strategic geographic location and natural harbour were reinforced by a free trade policy and developed infrastructure and expertise. The entrepôt function has survived despite the growth of competing ports and airports and policies of direct trading by neighbouring countries, although the trade has shifted significantly from vertical exchange of primary products of South-East Asia for Western manufactures to two-way trade in manufactures. Singapore's seaport is the second busiest in the world (after Hong Kong), while its airport deals with some of the largest passenger volumes in Asia.

Singapore is the third largest financial centre in Asia, after Tokyo and Hong Kong. Financial institutions enjoy time-zone advantage, developed infrastructure and manpower, minimal financial regulations, and attractive investment incentives, and political, social, and economic stability. In the late 1960s the Asean

Dollar Market (ADM) was established to collect offshore funds for offshore lending; by 1997 ADM assets reached $US375 billion. Also, over the years, the strategy has been to establish Singapore as a risk-management centre with active foreign exchange trading, money market operations, and trading in capital market instruments, equities, and futures, and attracting a wide variety of foreign financial institutions.

The promotion of regional headquarters (RHQ) is part of the Singapore hub strategy. Singapore plays host to over 4,000 multinational corporations and many of them have divisions performing various regional headquarters functions. Many international companies are seeking to establish regional operational headquarters to better serve the rapidly growing East Asian market, and to coordinate the activities of their regional subsidiaries and affiliates. Such headquarters provide a wide range of services to subsidiaries in the region, including business planning and coordination, treasury and risk management, sourcing of raw materials and components, marketing and sales promotion, personnel management and human resource development, technical support, and R&D. Singapore, like Hongkong, enjoys a number of advantages in hosting regional operational and business headquarters—a strategic location in the heart of South-East Asia which functions as free trade area; one of the world's busiest ports, and transportation, telecommunications, and information hub; a conducive business environment with political and social stability and harmonious industrial relations; a pro-business and efficient government; a regulatory framework which is not too intrusive for business; well-established Western legal and accounting systems; English as the language of administration and business; a favourable tax regime with corporate income tax rate of 26 per cent and liberal tax incentives which reduce the effective tax rate; and a financial centre with no controls on capital flows and foreign exchange transactions.

The hub strategy also requires building good relations with regional countries through political diplomacy as well as outward investment and joint ventures to combine the competitive strengths of Singapore and its partners to attract international investors. This view has led to Singapore-government initiatives to establish growth triangles and overseas industrial parks. The Indonesia–Malaysia–Singapore (IMS) growth triangle is discussed later. As part of this regionalization strategy, Singapore has also established industrial parks in Suzhou and Wuxi (China), Bangalore (India), and Vietnam, utilizing Singapore's capital resources and expertise in industrial infrastructure development and management.

3. Role of FDI and MNCs

3.1. FDI Penetration

FDI has played a critical role in Singapore's economic development over the past thirty or so years, in particular in the pursuit of export manufacturing and the development of the financial centre. In the early years the capital inflow from FDI helped to close the gap between investment and domestic savings, finance the net imports of goods and services, and cover the current account deficit. By the mid-1980s, however, the national savings rate exceeded 40 per cent of GNP and Singapore had become a net capital exporter. Singapore continues to rely on FDI, but for entrepreneurship, management, technology, and markets to maintain its competitive edge. Local private industrial enterprises remain weak, particularly in terms of processes and products that are internationally competitive in design and quality when compared to foreign enterprises.

By 1995, the stock of inward foreign direct equity investment reached $US59.5 billion, with $US27.0 billion or 45.5 per cent in financial and business services and $US21.6 billion or 36.3 per cent in manufacturing. Foreign penetration is highest in the manufacturing sector, where foreign investors owned around two-thirds of the total equity capital, with FDI mainly targeted at high capital-intensive industries such as electronics, chemicals, and petroleum-refining. The extent of foreign participation in the services sector was much lower than in manufacturing.

Data from the industrial census for 1992 show that 60 per cent of the equity capital was of foreign origin. Of the thirty-one industries at ISIC three-digit level, only three had foreign equity of less than 10 per cent. In the two largest industries (electronics and petroleum refineries), the foreign equity ratios were 88 and 93 per cent respectively.

3.2. FDI Policy

Attracting FDI has been a policy priority of Singapore since the early 1960s, at a time when the conventional wisdom in most developing countries was strongly influenced by the Dependency School.

FDI has played a critical role in Singapore's industrial take-off and in its widening and deepening. To attract MNCs to spearhead the industrialization drive, wide-ranging measures have been introduced to improve the investment climate. These included maintenance of political stability, measures to foster industrial peace and labour discipline, revamping of the educational system and manpower training programmes to emphasize engineering and technical education and industrial training, development of industrial infrastructure, active investment promotion, and provision of fiscal incentives (Chia 1997).

Industrialization in Singapore had to be export-oriented because of the small domestic market. Export orientation is more difficult than import substitution as export industries have to be internationally competitive right from infancy. Regional markets were heavily protected under programmes of import substitution, and the establishment of ASEAN in 1967 had not led to significant market-opening measures. For an infant industrial economy anxious to leapfrog into international markets, Singapore needed FDI and MNCs. The government felt it would be too slow and uncertain to depend on traditional local commercial capital and commercial entrepreneurship, with no experience or expertise in manufacturing. Singapore had no sizeable domestic market to absorb the learning costs of infant industries and infant industrial enterprises. FDI would enable Singapore to industrialize quickly and efficiently, since foreign investors were perceived to have the capital resources, entrepreneurial spirit and experience, technological and managerial know-how, and marketing ability and networks which would enable Singapore to have access to these resources in a convenient package and on a continuing basis.

Singapore chose FDI as a means of securing foreign resources as it did not have the bargaining leverage of a large domestic market and its bureaucrats and trading entrepreneurs did not have the wherewithal to separately secure the capital, technology, and expertise in the international market. FDI has advantage over foreign borrowing in that the risk-taking function is borne by the foreigner and profitability and outward remittances move in close tandem with the general performance of the economy and the health of the balance of payments; time and again this policy has cushioned Singapore from the balance of payments and debt crises that characterize many developing economies. Also, FDI is packaged and provides for continuing access to non-standardized and rapidly changing proprietary technologies. The main disadvantages of FDI are possible loss of national sovereignty associated with large-scale foreign ownership and control of the nation's resources and productive assets, possible crowding out of domestic enterprise, and vulnerability to trends in international investment flows. Singapore has sought to overcome these disadvantages by building a strong, efficient, and honest government and economy. Where it has not quite succeeded is in developing a robust domestic enterprise sector to countervail the MNCs.

Singapore's foreign investment policy had to be more liberal than that of most host countries so as to attract the export-oriented MNCs who are more footloose than resource-based and import substitution-based MNCs. The government adopted a holistic approach to make Singapore an attractive investment location. Attractive investment incentives were necessary to compensate for the locational disadvantages of lack of land and natural resources to attract resource-based investments and heavy industries, lack of a sizeable domestic market to attract market-based investments, and lack of abundant low-wage labour to attract labour-intensive export industries. Generous investment incentives coupled with minimal regulations and performance requirements led to maximization of net incentives. Policies contribute to minimize investor risk and assure reasonable investor returns, through improving factor supplies and infrastructure and reducing administrative, production, and distribution costs.

3.3. FDI in Manufacturing

From the outset, Singapore's export-oriented industrialization strategy hinged on attracting FDI. In the early 1960s the government rationalized that it would be too slow and uncertain to depend on traditional local capital and entrepreneurship, not only because the latter was limited, but also because local entrepreneurs were steeped in the traditions of the entrepôt and retail trade and had no expertise in manufacturing for the world market. It was believed that foreign investors, who possessed the capital resources, entrepreneurial spirit, technological and managerial know-how, and marketing networks, would enable Singapore to industrialize quickly and efficiently.

FDI for export markets became increasingly important from the late 1960s. There was a surge of Japanese and American investments in shipyards and American investments in the electronics industry. The rapid development of shipbuilding, ship-repairing, and oil-rig construction facilities was in response to the world boom in shipping and the regional boom in oil-prospecting. And American MNCs increasingly sought offshore production locations for electrical and electronic products and components to offset rising labour costs at home. The American move was soon followed by European and Japanese MNCs.

Foreign investors are mainly from the Triad. 1995 data shows that, in terms of numbers, the Japanese have the largest number, with 312 out of 858 with majority foreign capital, followed by the USA and EU. However, US firms led in their contributions, accounting for 49.7 per cent of foreign output, 51.7 per cent of foreign value added, 57.7 per cent of foreign direct exports; the Japanese ranked second and the EU third.

The distribution of FDI largely determines the composition of industries in the manufacturing sector. In turn, the distribution of FDI among the various industries has been strongly influenced by the investment promotion strategy of the EDB. In the 1960s, foreign investors in manufacturing were attracted by the ready access to South-East Asian raw materials, the protected domestic market, and the non-application at that time of quota restrictions by OECD countries on Singapore's exports of textiles and garments. Major investments flowed into basic metals, fabricated metal products, food manufacture, and textiles and garments industries. However, in value terms the bulk of FDI in manufacturing was in the highly capital-intensive petroleum refineries. From late 1970s, however, the petroleum-refining industry entered a difficult period and the annual investments in the industry declined, even though there were still sizeable investments to upgrade and rationalize operations.

FDI inflows have shifted progressively from labour-intensive activities to projects with higher-value added and higher technological content, due to growing number of foreign MNCs establishing world-class plants with highly automated operations. By 1989 the manufacturing FDI stock showed a heavy concentration in electronics (36 per cent), followed by chemical products (21 per cent), petroleum products (11 per cent), machinery (11 per cent), and transport equipment (8 per cent). Data on investment commitments show FDI flowing increasingly into the electrical, electronics, and chemical industries in the past decade.

Singapore has harnessed the technological, managerial, and marketing resources of foreign MNCs not only to spearhead export manufacturing but also to move

Singapore up the product-, process-, and functional-value chain, that is progressing from products in which technology is mature to more advanced products at earlier phases of the product cycle, adopting capital-intensive and automated production processes, and moving beyond manufacturing into both upstream and downstream activities of design, research, product development, procurement, marketing, and regional coordination.

Whether the overwhelming presence of FDI in manufacturing has crowded out local firms is a moot question. One could argue that the FDI dominance has stunted the growth of local enterprise in various ways—policy neglect of local enterprise by the government; competition for factor resources; and some degree of competition for markets, although this has not been serious except in some specific niches, because FDI in Singapore has been mainly export-oriented. However, FDI presence has also positive spillovers—foreign investors have provided a catalyst in attracting local capital and enterprise into joint ventures; foreign firms also provide business opportunities for the local firms in the supporting industries; and FDI provides role models for the upgrading of technology, management, and marketing.

3.4. FDI and the Electronics Cluster

Singapore is a major manufacturing and trading centre in the region for electronic products, components and parts, and supporting services.

Singapore's largest industry cluster is centred on electronics, a footloose industry which grew to account for over half of manufacturing production in the 1990s. An investment mission to the USA in 1967 to promote Singapore as an offshore manufacturing platform resulted in an influx of American MNCs in electronics assembly and the production of low-end components for export. European and Japanese MNCs soon followed the American lead. The Singapore electronics industry has been continuously upgrading and restructuring and by the mid-1980s had shifted away from labour-intensive products and processes towards the production of computers, computer peripherals, and components. Low-value-added goods and processes were phased out, in part transferred to neighbouring countries with abundant and low-wage labour. A large local and supporting industry emerged, facilitated by a growing pool of engineering expertise, making computer components, parts, and supplies. Many MNCs have established international purchasing offices (IPOs) to source local and regional products for their worldwide requirements. Singapore's well-developed infrastructure provides efficient, timely, and low-cost delivery to purchasers.

Data from the annual census of industrial production for 1997 show that the electronic products and components industry is the largest in the manufacturing sector, with $S63.4 billion in output and $S13.20 billion in value added in 1997, accounting for 50.5 per cent of total manufacturing output and 44.7 per cent of total manufacturing value added. The industry had a workforce of 127 thousand in 1997, or 35.3 per cent of the manufacturing workforce. In 1995, the direct exports/sales ratio was 78.1 per cent, much higher than the manufacturing average of 60.1 per cent.

The electronics industry can be divided into three sectors, namely consumer electronics, industrial electronics (including communications equipment), and electronic components. In output and sales, industrial electronics is the largest sector and consumer electronics the smallest. The large share of industrial electronics and electronic components reflects the restructuring and upgrading of production to higher-tech and higher-value-added products and the improvement in Singapore's technical and technological capabilities.

The electronics industry in Singapore began modestly in the mid-1960s with two local firms assembling black-and-white TV sets for the domestic market under licence from a Japanese electronics firm. The first influx of foreign MNCs was after the mid-1960s, following the policy shift from import substitution to export manufacturing and FDI promotion. Texas Instruments, an American MNC set up a semiconductor assembly plant in Singapore in 1967, spearheading an influx of American investments in electronics, led by semiconductor MNCs engaged in assembly and testing of simple integrated circuits (ICs) for re-export to the USA. FDI by European and Japanese electronics MNCs followed. Investments in semiconductor assemblies were followed by investments in consumer electronics.

The industry in Singapore has undergone rapid structural change and upgrading in response to rapid technological change and shortening product cycles at the global level, intensified international competition, and labour shortages. Corporate responses have been in two directions—new investments in process and product upgrading of Singapore operations (into automated manufacturing, higher-end products, product design, and R&D), and/or relocation of labour-intensive operations and mature and lower-priced product lines to neighbouring countries. Singapore shifted rapidly out of consumer electronics—MNCs have been rationalizing their production to remain competitive, by moving labour-intensive operations to other locations in the region and upgrading their Singapore operations through concentration on higher-end equipment and components, introduction of automated manufacturing, and emphasis on product design and development. The share of industrial electronics rose with production of computers and data-processing equipment, computer peripherals and disk drives, and telecommunications equipment.

The government has been actively developing the semiconductor business to reduce dependence on the disk-drive industry. The Fab I and Fab II semiconductor fabrication plants are two projects that started to give Singapore the technological edge in the production of semiconductors. Long-term, the local industry plans to reduce its dependence on Japanese suppliers for disk-drive components. The telecommunications industry has also grown rapidly with two telecoms giants AT&T and Motorola using Singapore as a primary base for the manufacture and global distribution of cellular products and communications equipment.

FDI and MNCs dominate Singapore's electronics industry. The foreign equity share in 1992 amounted to 88 per cent. FDI penetration was highest in consumer electronics and industrial electronics and lowest in electronic components. In consumer and industrial electronics, well-established international brand names and the technological superiority of foreign MNCs were strong barriers to entry of local firms. Foreign ownership was almost 100 per cent in consumer electronics and in the industrial electronics subsectors of computers and data-processing equipment, disk drives, office machinery, and equipment. Foreign dominance in communications equipment was less strong due to the presence of a large state-owned enterprise. In electronic components, foreign equity was dominant in semiconductors and capacitors, but in resistors and printed circuit boards (PCBs) with electronic parts, local ownership was dominant, with a proliferation of local firms undertaking contract manufacturing and acting as suppliers to the foreign MNCs.

Foreign MNCs dominate the computer industry in Singapore. The major companies include ALR International, Compaq, Digital Equipment, Apple, Hewlett Packard, and Siemens Nixdorf. Singapore's locational advantages are its adaptable, flexible, and well-trained workforce which make it easy for MNCs to produce high-volume products quickly. Also the strategic location allows for many PC manufacturers to establish linkages in the surrounding region to source for electronic components at reasonable prices. Besides sourcing from neighbours, Singapore has its own supporting industries which are growing in number and technological competence to support computer-manufacturing operations; their services range from PCBA houses with SMT capabilities to marketing, product development, and distribution. Although disk drives and PCs still dominate Singapore's electronics exports, the importance of production of computer peripherals and electronic components is on the rise.

Foreign electronics firms were mainly from the Triad. Of the 49 establishments with dominant Japanese equity, 15 were in consumer electronics, 14 in electronic components, and 6 in industrial electronics; Japanese firms dominate consumer electronics. Of the 48 establishments with dominant US equity, 24 were in electronic components and 21 in industrial electronics; American firms dominate the disk-drive and semiconductor industries, but were completely absent from the consumer electronics sector. Of the 21 establishments with dominant European equity, 11 were in electronic components, 4 in consumer electronics, and 3 in industrial electronics. Japanese and US firms dominate different sectors of the industry, with the Japanese in consumer electronics and the Americans in industrial electronics; this mirrors the strengths of Japanese and American electronic giants in different niches at the global level. By contrast, local firms are concentrated in the less scale-, capital-, and technology-intensive PCB sector.

The large presence of foreign MNCs in Singapore generated strong demand for materials, parts, and components, and a wide range of support services. Increasing use of JIT manufacturing also increased dependence on local suppliers. However, it took well over a decade before a significant base of local supporting industries emerged to complement the large base of foreign MNCs operating in the Singapore electronics industry. Gradually with government support and active technical and financial assistance provided by EDB, technical and financial capabilities improved. Now local SMEs and suppliers have emerged to supply components and service to support the manufacture of disk drives, computers, TVs, video-cassette recorders, and precision engineering products.

The value chain in Singapore's electronics industry extends beyond manufacturing to regional coordination and procurement activities. With the rapid growth of the electronics industry in the region, Singapore has become an important international trading hub for electronics. Increasingly, foreign MNCs are establishing affiliates in Singapore to function as international procurement offices (IPOs) to source components and parts from the region for their worldwide manufacturing needs and to establish regional headquarters (RHQs) to coordinate their various activities in the Asia-Pacific region and provide support services.

4. Regionalization and the IMS Growth Triangle

Singapore's direct investment abroad has expanded rapidly in recent years, with the stock reaching $US32.6 billion by 1995. Investments were concentrated in finance (50.1 per cent), manufacturing (24.6 per cent), commerce (9.8 per cent), and real estate and construction (8.4). The outward investment drive is spearheaded by firms with foreign-equity capital, with foreign-controlled firms (wholly and majority foreign owned) accounting for 47.5 per cent, majority local-owned firms for 28.4 per cent, and wholly Singaporean firms for only 24.0 per cent.

The outward investment, particularly in manufacturing, reflects the maturing of the city state economy after only three decades of sustained economic growth. Apart from industrial upgrading and productivity improvement, outward investment helps overcome domestic resource constraints and maintain international competitiveness. The outward push has also responded to the strong Singapore dollar and improvements in the investment climate in South-East Asia and in China. Outward investments generally move to neighbouring Malaysia (dominated by manufacturing, finance, and commerce), Hong Kong (dominated by finance), and Indonesia (dominated by manufacturing). The ASEAN region absorbed $US11.4 billion or 34.8 per cent of Singapore's global direct investments. Manufacturing dominates investments in ASEAN, unlike investments in other regions, accounting for half of the investments in ASEAN and 70.4 per cent, of total manufacturing investments abroad.

The Singapore government launched the regionalization strategy in early 1993, actively encouraging the Singapore private sector to invest in Asia. Several factors motivated the regional emphasis. First, on the supply side, a maturing Singapore economy needs to develop 'an external wing' to sustain its high-growth performance, particularly as it faces severe land and labour constraints and rising costs. Singapore has to look increasingly on the growth of GNP rather than on GDP. Second, on the demand side, to take advantage of the economic boom in East Asia and invest in manufacturing, services, and infrastructure in countries with abundant natural resources, low-cost labour, and rapidly expanding markets. While benefiting Singapore investors, such investments would also enable Singapore to share with the regional economies its expertise in economic management, development and management of infrastructure, and technology adaptation. Third, domestic enterprises with limited outward investment experience will find it easier to regionalize than go global because the geographical proximity helps reduce information and transaction costs. Fourth, for foreign MNCs, Singapore could provide them with an efficient and competitive base of operations and a strategic location to expand into the dynamic Asian region, facilitating their allocation of value-chain segments among countries according to their comparative advantage or enter into joint ventures to co-invest in other countries.

The Indonesia–Malaysia–Singapore (IMS) Growth Triangle was first proposed by Singapore in 1989 as a form of subregional economic cooperation in ASEAN, to overcome the difficulty posed by existing trade liberalization and industrial cooperation schemes. IMS-GT is formed by the contiguous areas of Singapore, Johor (south Malaysia), and Riau province (West Indonesia). It is a partnership arrangement that combines the competitive strengths of the three areas to make the subregion more attractive to regional and international investors.

The most important factor in the emergence and growth of IMS-GT has been the political commitment of the participating governments. This led to the joint development of Batam (in Riau)—Indonesia liberalized its foreign investment policy on Batam, making it more favourable than those found in the rest of Indonesia; and Singapore's public agencies became actively involved in developing the industrial infrastructure and promoting Batam as an investment location among Singaporean companies and foreign MNCs based in Singapore.

The liberalized foreign investment regulations, the assurance of the two governments that investment and operational problems in Batam would receive priority attention, provision of basic infrastructure, improved transportation facilities, and simplified customs and immigration procedures led to a surge of investments from Singapore companies and foreign MNCs in Singapore needing to relocate labour-intensive operations. The IMS-GT has also led to the relocation of Singapore industries to Johor, accelerating a trend that had been in place for some years. Traditional official and private links between Johor and Singapore have been very strong and customs and immigration facilities have been simplified.

The rationale for IMS-GT is economic complementarity and geographical proximity. Singapore, Johor, and Riau are at different levels of development and have different factor endowments, comparative advantages, and cost structures. Economic cooperation results in improved resource allocation, economies of scale, agglomeration, and clustering. Singapore's comparative advantage lies in its well-developed, financial, commercial, transportation, and telecommunications infrastructure, its relative abundance of managerial, professional, and technical expertise, and a trained labour force. Riau and Johor offer land, natural resources, and labour at lower cost than in Singapore. Ready access to Singapore's world-class infrastructure and expertise improves efficiency and competitiveness in production and distribution; Singapore provides Batam and Johor with a world-class airport and seaport for movement of goods and people, a modern and sophisticated telecommunications network for instant communication with the world, and world-class financial and commercial infrastructures to support their business operations. Singapore is closer (in both geographical and commuting distance) to Batam and Johor than the national capitals of Indonesia and Malaysia, providing a more cost-efficient and time-saving link to the world. Singaporean and foreign investors in Batam and Johor can be based in Singapore and commute daily or periodically to supervise operations and production, and maintenance engineers are close at hand to attend to problems on the factory floor. IMS-GT has led to accelerated investment (foreign and domestic) for the development of infrastructure, natural resources, industries, commerce, and tourism.

The gains differ between participating areas and over time. For Singapore, IMS-GT facilitates Singapore's industrial restructuring and outward investment strategies. Relocation of labour-intensive industries and processes to Johor and Batam help relieve Singapore's land and labour constraints and reduce the dependence on inflow of foreign workers. The GT enables Singapore to retain foreign MNCs in higher-value-added manufacturing and service activities, such as design and testing, management, financing, and marketing. Outward investments by Singaporean small and medium enterprises in Johor and Batam help reduce information and transaction costs and prepare these enterprises for eventual globalization.

5. Conclusions

Singapore has turned its major disadvantage of small physical size into an economic advantage, enabling the city state to achieve the highest PP-adjusted per capita GNP in the world. A crucial feature in Singapore's economic success is to plug into the global and regional economies so as to gain access to resources for consumption and production and markets for its goods and services. The role of foreign MNCs has been crucial in the development of Singapore as a manufacturing base and a services hub. To secure the assistance of these foreign MNCs, Singapore ensured their minimal risk and maximum profit objectives by providing an attractive investment environment with political, economic, and social stability, efficient infrastructure, skilled workforce, generous investment incentives, and minimal restrictions and performance requirements. In the process, Singapore has also gained much, as reflected in the high per capita incomes and rising standards of living, full employment, and an increasingly educated and skilled workforce, government budget surpluses, and large foreign reserves.

REFERENCES

Chia, Siow Yue (1994), 'The SIJORI Growth Triangle: Challenges, Opportunities and Strategic Response', Paper presented at the *Fourth Southeast Asia Roundtable on Economic Development: Growth Triangles in Southeast Asia: Strategy for Development*, organized by the Institute of Strategic and International Studies, Kuala Lumpur, 27–8 June.

—— (1997), 'Singapore: Advanced Production Base and Smart Hub of the Electronics Industry', in Wendy Dobson and Chia Siow Yue (eds.), *Multinationals and East Asian Integration* (Canada and Singapore: IDRC and ISEAS).

Institute of Management Development (1997), *The World Competitiveness Yearbook*.

Singapore, Dept. of Statistics (1997), *Yearbook of Statistics Singapore 1997*.

Singapore, Economic Development Board (1995), *Report on the Census of Industrial Production 1995*.

World Economic Forum (1997), *The World Competitiveness Report 1997*.

15

Globalization, Regionalization, and the Knowledge-Based Economy in Hong Kong

Michael J. Enright

1. Introduction

Among the more important features of the modern world economy have been mutually reinforcing trends towards globalization, regionalization, and knowledge-based business (Dunning 2000*b*). This chapter focuses on the impact of these trends on one place, Hong Kong. Forces of globalization and regionalization have allowed, and in fact forced, Hong Kong to move down the path to knowledge-based economy farther and faster than virtually any other economy in the world. As a result, Hong Kong has developed into a regional management, coordination, finance, and information centre for both local companies and foreign multinational firms. Whereas Hong Kong has benefited tremendously from this process, the recent Asian crisis has shown that Hong Kong has suffered somewhat in the last two years from its extensive linkages with other economies.

Examination of the Hong Kong economy yields several lessons. One concerns what is meant by a knowledge economy. The knowledge-intensity of an economy is determined as much, if not more, by the economic activities than by the specific industries that are found in a location. The key corporate management, strategy-setting, coordination, and financial activities are as, or in many cases more, knowledge-intensive than research and development. Another lesson is that a tightly clustered, knowledge-intensive economy can develop in the absence of distinct governmental policies to foster such development. Another lesson is that multinational firms can play an important part in the development of a knowledge-based economy. Many of Hong Kong's clusters, and Hong Kong's economy as a whole, have developed in an interdependent fashion with foreign multinational firms. The multinationals have made important contributions to the local economy as Hong Kong has made important contributions to the global strategies of the multinationals.

2. Globalization, Regionalization, and the Knowledge-Based Economy

A variety of forces have contributed to the globalization of economic activity. These forces have included the development of global finance and financial markets, the spread of knowledge facilitated by improved communication, the widespread availability and use of technology, the active expansion of multinational firms, the decoupling and decentralization of economic activities within and between firms, the blurring of nationality of multinationals, the development of global oligopolies, reductions in barriers to trade and investment, the increased importance and power of supranational organizations such as the European Union, and the emergence of regions and regional identities that transcend borders (see Amin and Thrift 1994*a*, *b*; Dicken 1994; Dunning 2000*b*; and Storper 1998, for example). Added to this list today would be the rise of electronic communities over the Internet and the fact that nations comprising nearly one-half of the world's population have either entered the world economy or have dramatically changed their relationship to it in the last two decades (Enright 1997).

At the same time, interest in localized groups of firms in the same or related industries, or 'regional clusters' has accelerated as well. Porter (1990), Enright (1991, 1996, 1998*a*, *c*), Storper (1992), Audretsch (1998), and Scott (1998) point out that in many industries, the leading firms are located in the same nation, region, or even city. Regional clustering is found in virtually every advanced economy and increasingly in developing nations as well (Humphrey and Schmitz 1996). Globalization can result in a geographic spread of economic activities over space, but it also can allow firms and locations with specific sources of competitive advantage to exploit their advantages over ever-wider geographic areas, often, though not always, at the expense of other areas (Enright 1993). Globalization-localization trends make specific characteristics of regional economies more important, not less important, in determining economic prosperity (Enright 1998*a*; Scott 1998; and Audretsch 1998).

Much has been written in recent years about the evolution of knowledge-based business (see e.g. Nonaka and Takeuchi 1998; Spender 1998; and Dunning 2000*b*) in which firm-specific or location-specific knowledge are distinct sources of competitive advantage. Although some researchers on the knowledge-based economy focus on high technology or research and development dependent businesses (see Audretsch 1998; Park 1998; and Balasubramanyam and Balasubramanyam 1998, for example), others focus on knowledge-intensive professional and producer services (Hansen 1994; Roberts 1994; Grosse 1996; and Bagchi-Sen and Sen 1997, for example). Knowledge-based advantages also can come from ideas, organizational forms, and management knowledge (see Enright 1995; Sölvell and Birkinshaw 1998; and Storper 1998, for example), or from the knowledge of optimal organization of production processes within a region (Herrigel 1996, 1998).

While globalization has spread some industries or activities over wider and wider space, it also has reinforced the specialization of some microregional economies. Thus the globalization of competition is completely consistent with the localization of competitive advantage. As successful regions seek to further penetrate world markets, less successful regions fight to retain a place in global production systems. The globalization of particular economic activities, particularly the expansion of markets and the commoditization of manufacturing, has forced more advanced economies to move to more knowledge-intensive activities. Thus, we would expect to see strong linkages between globalization, regionalization, and the emergence of knowledge-based business.

3. Hong Kong's Economy

The Hong Kong economy has been influenced by globalization, regionalization, and the emergence of the knowledge-based economy perhaps more than any other. Hong Kong is unique in terms of its geographic location, its position in global production and service networks, its openness to market forces, and its history. As a result, it has been able to take advantage of globalization to develop a regional economy that is among the world's most knowledge-intensive. This development has created one of the world's most prosperous economies, but it also has left Hong Kong vulnerable to external shocks such as the economic crisis that began to grip Asia in the middle of 1997.

Hong Kong's economic performance in the years up to 1997 was quite strong. Real GDP grew at an average of 8.5 per cent year from 1975 to 1985 and 6.5 per cent per year from 1985 to 1995. Between 1975 and 1995, Hong Kong's real GDP quadrupled and its real per capita GDP tripled (HKGIS 1996). Despite the uncertainty surrounding the reversion of sovereignty to China on 1 July 1997 and predictions of 'The Death of Hong Kong' (Kraar 1995), Hong Kong's economy still grew at a real rate of 4.6 per cent in 1996 and 5.3 per cent in 1997. In 1997, Hong Kong's per capita GDP reached $US26,415. According to the World Bank, Hong Kong's per capita purchasing power was exceeded by only four nations (Luxembourg, Singapore, the USA, and Switzerland) (World Bank 1998). Unemployment, which reached 3.2 per cent in 1995, fell to 2.8 per cent in 1996 and to 2.2 per cent in 1997 (HKCSD 1998*d*).

Hong Kong is one of the most externally oriented economies in the world. Hong Kong's total trade to GDP ratio in 1997 was 231.4, second only to Singapore's 260.2 among major economies (Asian Development Bank 1998). As of 1997, Hong Kong, with a population of only 6.7 million, was the world's eighth leading trading economy and the world's ninth leading exporter of services (WTO 1998). Hong Kong has been by far the leader in intra-Asian trade and investment. Hong Kong's trade with the Asia-Pacific region grew at an average annual rate of 19 per cent from 1980 to reach $US262 billion in 1997. Hong Kong accounted for 14.8 per cent of the intra-Asia-Pacific trade in 1996, despite a population that is only 0.2 per cent of that of the region (HKTDC 1998*d*). In addition, Hong Kong has been the world's fourth leading source of foreign direct investment each year since 1993 (UNCTAD various years).

The external orientation of Hong Kong's economy means that international competitiveness is critical to its prosperity. In aggregate terms, Hong Kong has been the second most competitive economy in the world according to the World

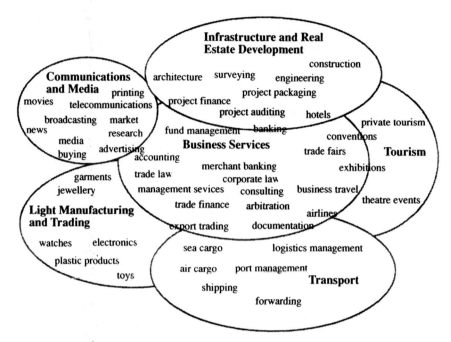

FIG. 15.1. Hong Kong's competitive clusters
Source: Enright *et al*. (1997).

Economic Forum's World Competitiveness Report and the third most competitive economy according to the IMD International Competitiveness Yearbook (World Economic Forum various years and IMD various years). Hong Kong has succeeded in a tight set of industry clusters in which Hong Kong is a leader on a regional or global basis and which account for between 70 and 75 per cent of GDP (see Figure 15.1). These clusters include light manufacturing and trading, transportation, tourism, financial and business services, infrastructure and development, and communication and media (Enright *et al*. 1997).

In light manufacturing and trading, Hong Kong was the world's largest exporter of clocks, toys and games, calculators, radios, electric hair-dressing/hand-drying apparatus, imitation jewellery, travel goods and handbags, umbrellas and sunshades, artificial flowers, fur clothing, textiles, telephone sets, electric food-grinders, and mixers and juicers in 1996. It was the world's second leading exporter of watches, footwear, and clothing (UN 1998 and HKTDC 1998*d*). In transportation, as of 1997, Hong Kong had the world's busiest container port, the world's busiest airport in terms of international cargoes, and the world's third busiest airport in terms of international passengers, and that was before the opening of its new state-of-the-art international airport in July 1998 (HKTDC 1998*d*). In international tourism, Hong Kong generates more revenue each year than any country in Asia. In business services. Hong Kong is arguably the world's fourth leading international financial centre (Enright 1998*d*; Jao 1997) and is a major regional hub for legal services, accounting services, consulting services, and others. In infrastructure and development, Hong Kong is a major market itself as well as the leading centre for putting together private-sector funded infrastructure and development projects for China and the Asian region. In communications and media, Hong Kong has more international telephone capacity than all of Japan or all of Australia and is the world's leader in terms of international calls per capita. Hong Kong also is a major Asian centre for many of the world's leading news and broadcasting companies as well as a prime communications hub for overseas multinational companies (Enright *et al.* 1997).

4. Hong Kong's Economic Transformation, 1979–1997

Hong Kong's economy has undergone a rapid transformation since the Chinese mainland began to open to trade and investment in 1979. In Hong Kong, it often is described as a transformation from manufacturing to services. While this is true as far as it goes, in reality, the transformation is better described as a shift from an enclave economy to a metropolitan economy and from a manual economy to a knowledge-based economy (Enright *et al.* 1997).

4.1. Manufacturing to Services

In terms of its overall economic structure, Hong Kong has seen a substantial shift from manufacturing to services over the last two decades. In 1980, manufacturing represented 24 per cent of Hong Kong's output and 42 per cent of its employment. By 1996, manufacturing accounted for 7 per cent of output and 13 per cent of employment. Hong Kong's service sector boomed during the period, averaging real growth of 8.6 per cent per year from 1980 to 1990 and 6.9 per cent per year from 1990 to 1996, figures that were among the highest registered by a major economy (HKCSD 1998*b* and World Bank 1998). By 1996, services accounted for 84.4 per cent of output (compared to 7.3 per cent in manufacturing, 8.3 per cent in other secondary activities, and zero per cent in primary activities), making Hong Kong more service-oriented than any national economy in the world. As of June 1998, the service sector accounted for 83.6 per cent of private-sector employment in Hong Kong (HKCSD 1998*d*).

The service sector also has dominated inbound foreign direct investment in Hong Kong. As of 1996, 92 per cent of the stock of inbound foreign direct investment in Hong Kong was in the service sector, only 8 per cent was in manufacturing. Some 87 per cent of regional headquarters of foreign multinationals in Hong Kong in 1997 came from the services sector, only 13 per cent from the manufacturing sector (see Tables 15.1 and 15.2).

TABLE 15.1. Stock of inward foreign investment in Hong Kong by sector

Sector	% share
Banking	36
Holding companies	21
Wholesale/retail/import-export	16
Other financial services, insurance	8
Communications	5
Real estate, other business services	3
Construction	2
Transportation and related services	1
Manufacturing	8

Source: HKID (1998*b*).

TABLE 15.2. Major lines of business of regional headquarters in Hong Kong, 1997

Line of business	No. of companies	% share
Wholesale/retail, import/export	448	49
Other business services	169	18
Manufacturing	120	13
Finance and banking	105	11
Transport and related services	90	10
Construction, architectural, and civil engineering	43	5
Real estate	35	4
Insurance	13	1
Telecommunication services	12	1
Restaurants and hotels	9	1
Diversified	12	1
Others	11	1

Source: HKID (1997).

4.2. Enclave Economy to Metropolitan Economy

Though aggregate statistics show a transformation from manufacturing to services, other aspects of the transformation actually have been more important. One such aspect has been Hong Kong's transformation from an enclave economy to a metropolitan economy. Because of the 'one country, two systems' framework under which Hong Kong was returned to Chinese administration, Hong Kong has inherited characteristics usually found only in nations. Hong Kong has its own currency, its own customs authority, its own tax system, and its own legal system. Hong Kong is a full member of several organizations, such as the World Trade Organization (WTO) and the Asia-Pacific Economic Cooperation forum (APEC), where membership is normally only given to nations. Hong Kong is

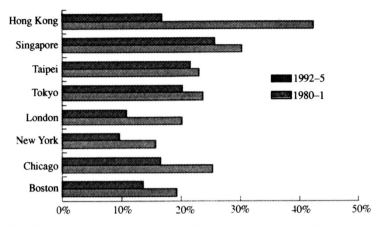

FIG. 15.2. Manufacturing as a percentage of employment (selected cities)
Source: Enright *et al.* (1997).

recognized as a 'country of origin' for international trade. However, despite these nation-like trappings, Hong Kong is in reality a city. The total land area of Hong Kong is only 1,078 square kilometres. By comparison, New York City's area is 831 square kilometres, London's is 1,610 square kilometres, and Tokyo's is 2,049 square kilometres. Hong Kong's population of 6.7 million is nearly one million less than London or New York and five million less than Tokyo. Its population density—5,780 people per square kilometre—is 34 per cent higher than that of London and almost identical to that of Tokyo (HKTDC 1998*b*).

By 1997, Hong Kong's economic size and structure were those of a major metropolitan economy. Hong Kong's 1997 GDP of $US170.1 billion exceeded that of greater London, but was substantially lower than that of either New York City or Tokyo. By the mid-1990s, the overall sectoral breakdown of Hong Kong's employment (see Figure 15.2) and GDP had become similar to those of other major cities as well. For London, New York, Tokyo, and Hong Kong, the vast preponderance of economic activity occurs in the service sectors (84.4 per cent of GDP for Hong Kong in 1996, 84.0 per cent of GDP for New York City in 1994, 82.1 per cent of GDP in London in 1995, and 74.2 per cent of GDP in Greater Tokyo in 1996). Hong Kong's focus on producer services, which is very different from advanced national economies where consumer services dominate, is quite similar to that of the New York City Region. In both cities, producer services exceed 40 per cent of GDP (Enright *et al.* 1999).

In Hong Kong, as in New York, London, and Tokyo, higher-value-added service jobs and activities have 'crowded out' lower-value-added activities, such as the physical production stages of manufacturing. In each case, the 'loss' of manufacturing represents a gain for the city. In Hong Kong, the ratio of output per employee in the service sector to output per employee in the manufacturing sector remained nearly constant at 172 per cent from 1981 to 1996 (calculated from

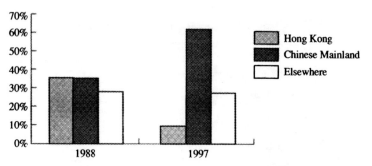

FIG. 15.3. Location of manufacturing of exports of Hong Kong firms
Source: Calculated from HKTDC (1998*c*).

data in HKCSD 1998*a*), despite the huge shift in employment.[1] Meanwhile, Hong Kong's manufacturing did not disappear, it relocated and expanded dramatically.[2] In 1980, nearly all of the exports of Hong Kong-based firms were manufactured in Hong Kong itself. By 1988 this figure had fallen to 36 per cent, and by 1997 to around 10 per cent. Production had moved to the Chinese mainland (63 per cent) and to third economies, mostly in East Asia (26 per cent) (see Figure 15.3). Total employment of Hong Kong-headquartered manufacturing firms was roughly 870,000 in 1980, nearly all in Hong Kong. By 1996, it was estimated to include roughly 300,000 in Hong Kong, more than six million in the Chinese mainland, and between 500,000 and one million elsewhere (Enright *et al.* 1997).

All major advanced metropolitan economies have experienced shifts from manufacturing to services. In Hong Kong, a transformation that took New York roughly forty years to undergo was completed in ten. During Hong Kong's transformation, real wages in the local manufacturing and service sectors more than doubled and unemployment generally stayed below 3 per cent. In other major metropolitan economies cost differentials of 20 to 30 per cent with the immediate hinterland can be expected. In Hong Kong, the differentials can be 80 to 85 per cent. Thus, while it might be more difficult for Hong Kong firms to decentralize their activities than firms from other major metropolitan economies (due to the border with the Chinese mainland), the economic rationale for doing so in Hong Kong is far greater than that found elsewhere. Since the economy of the Chinese mainland began to open, Hong Kong has moved from an enclave economy, artificially cut off from its natural hinterland on the Chinese mainland, to a metropolitan economy, closely linked to its Chinese hinterland as well as the rest of the region.

4.3. Manual Economy to Knowledge-Based Economy

Perhaps the most important aspect of Hong Kong's economic transformation, however, has been the transformation from a manual economy to a knowledge-based economy (Enright *et al.* 1997 and Enright 1999). Hong Kong's economy in the 1970s and early 1980s was based largely on manual labour and the physical production stages of manufacturing. By the mid-1990s, Hong Kong had become one of the most knowledge-intensive economies in the world. From 1981 to 1996, the knowledge-worker portion of Hong Kong's total employment (represented by the categories 'managers and administrators', 'professionals and related', and 'clerical') increased from 21 to 46 per cent. The portion of 'managers and administrators' increased from 3 to 12 per cent, while those in 'professional and related' and 'clerical' increased from 6 to 17 per cent and 11 to 17 per cent respectively. Meanwhile, the entire workforce grew from 2.4 million to some 3.2 million, indicating that the number of knowledge-based workers in Hong Kong had nearly tripled in this time (calculated from data in HKCSD 1998*a*, *d*).[3] The knowledge-intensity of Hong Kong-based production also increased. Value added per manufacturing worker in Hong Kong increased from $US10,291 in 1987 to $US32,554 in 1996 (HKID 1998*a*).

The trends in Hong Kong's service and manufacturing sectors indicate that Hong Kong is increasingly acting as a knowledge-intensive coordination and management centre for international business. In fact, as some activities have been decentralized from Hong Kong, Hong Kong firms have greatly expanded the geographic scope of their business. Hong Kong today functions very much as a coordination centre, interacting with enormous investments in its vast economic hinterland and linked closely to economies in the rest of the region and the world. Hong Kong headquartered manufacturing and trading firms, for example, have decentralized their least knowledge-intensive activities, while concentrating the most knowledge-intensive functions in Hong Kong. As a result, the Hong Kong companies have expanded their manufacturing and trading business beyond domestic production constraints and geographical boundaries (see Table 15.3).

An overwhelming 95 per cent of the Hong Kong manufacturing and trading companies surveyed by the Hong Kong Trade Development Council in 1997 indicated their intention to maintain their controlling headquarters in Hong Kong. Over 90 per cent revealed their intention to increase or maintain their activities in trade finance, business negotiation, market research, insurance, marketing, trade documentation, and arbitration in Hong Kong. This is almost precisely the opposite of their plans for the Chinese mainland, where the manufacturing is to be located. Hong Kong firms also are building up substantial activities outside both Hong Kong and the Chinese mainland, though again, not the most knowledge-intensive activities (HKTDC 1998*c*).

Overseas multinationals perform knowledge-intensive activities in Hong Kong as well. Hong Kong is the leading centre for the regional headquarters and regional offices of multinational firms in the Asia-Pacific region. Of the 4,275 multinational firms that responded to a Hong Kong Industry Department survey, 924 had a regional headquarters in Hong Kong and another 1,606 had a regional office as of June 1997.[4] Another recent survey of the managers of multinational

TABLE 15.3. Locations where Hong Kong companies are likely to perform or acquire trade/trade-supporting activities or services in the future

Activity or service	Hong Kong (%)	Chinese Mainland (%)	Third Economies (%)
Trade documentation	96.0	15.1	5.8
Trade financing	95.5	8.4	5.3
Regional headquarters/offices	94.8	12.5	4.1
Insurance	92.2	17.0	7.9
Business negotiation	90.4	32.3	18.0
Market research	82.6	26.3	18.7
Arbitration	81.3	26.5	10.2
Marketing and promotion	81.1	28.6	21.0
Freight forwarding and consolidation	79.6	42.1	12.0
Merchandizing	69.7	40.8	20.6
Material sourcing	68.2	51.5	24.0
Product development	63.9	47.9	17.9
Testing and certification	56.6	54.0	14.6
Warehousing/inventory control	50.3	66.9	8.9
Sample making/prototyping	41.2	69.1	14.4
Quality control ·	35.8	74.6	15.4
Packaging	23.6	81.2	15.5
Manufacturing	18.6	84.1	16.9

Note: The numbers add to more than 100 per cent since many companies perform a given activity in more than one place.

Source: HKTDC (1998c).

companies in Hong Kong (Enright and Thompson 1998) indicates that the most important activities multinationals perform in Hong Kong have to do with coordination and management functions for Hong Kong, China, and the Asia-Pacific. For most of these firms, Hong Kong is their most important centre for coordination and central management activities in the region (see Table 15.4).

Such regional headquarters and regional office activities are of particular value to a local economy since they bring in many of the firm's most knowledge-intensive activities, such as senior management, regional coordination, finance, strategy formulation, product development, advanced marketing, and the generation of vital information. The headquarters often represents a locus of innovation and productivity growth. At the same time, a regional headquarters or regional office embeds the host economy in the international business network of the multinational company and creates strong linkages between the host economy and the outside world. Headquarters investment also creates demand for advanced managerial skills and sophisticated support services, thus providing highly beneficial stimulus and spillover to the local economy. It results in an 'importing' of advanced managerial practice, the prompting of sophisticated demand, and the eventual spillover of hard and soft firm capabilities.

TABLE 15.4. The importance of Hong Kong as a centre for a variety of activities and functions of firms (1 = Very unimportant, 2 = Slightly unimportant, 3 = Neutral, 4 = Slightly important, 5 = Very important)

Activity or function	Mean response
Corporate coordination	
Coordination of other operations within region	4.3
Supporting regional operations	4.2
Monitoring of other regional operations	3.9
Reporting regional activities to parent company	4.1
Regional liaison centre for parent company	3.9
Central management functions	
Competitor intelligence	3.9
Regional strategy formulation	4.0
Product/service development and design	3.2
Business process development	3.5
Senior personnel management	3.5
Regional information technology management	3.3
Non-raw materials procurement	2.5
Finance and accounting	
Trade finance	3.0
Capital-investment finance	2.8
Insurance	2.7
Accounting/auditing	3.5
Sales, marketing, and customer service	
Marketing planning and execution	4.0
Sales planning and execution	4.0
Sales and marketing-related procurement	3.6
Market research	3.7
Customer servicing and support	4.0
Distributional activities	
Warehousing finished goods	2.6
Packaging	2.4
Order processing	3.0
Trade documentation	3.0
Coordinating regional distribution	2.9
Coordinating global distribution	2.4
Land distribution	2.3
Air distribution	2.5
Sea distribution	2.6
Production activities	
Manufacturing	2.2
Assembly/processing	2.2
Quality control	2.6
Testing/certification	2.4
Raw materials sourcing	2.3
Research and development	
Basic research	2.4
Applied research	2.3
New product development	2.6
Process technology development	2.2

Note: Responses of 266 Hong Kong-based managers of foreign multinational firms.
Source: Enright and Thompson (1998).

5. Hong Kong's Economic Development

Several forces have influenced the emergence of Hong Kong's knowledge-based economy, including the emergence of the economies of China and East Asia, as well as the strategies of multinational firms. These forces have allowed and forced Hong Kong to take on a series of knowledge-based roles for the Chinese, regional, and global economies (see Enright *et al.* 1997).

5.1. Hong Kong's Links with the Economy of the Chinese Mainland

The emergence of the economy of the Chinese mainland has been one of the major economic events of the last twenty years. China is not only the world's most populous nation, it also has had one of the world's fastest-growing economies. Its real GDP grew at a rate of 10.2 per cent per year from 1980 to 1990 and 12.3 per cent per year from 1990 to 1996 (World Bank 1998). By World Bank estimates, the Chinese economy is already larger than that of Japan on a purchasing power parity basis.

The Chinese mainland has become the tenth leading trading economy in the world. Its exports grew from 5 per cent of GDP in 1970 to 40 per cent of GDP in 1996. China's exports (merchandise plus services) grew at a rate of 14.2 per cent per year from 1980 to 1996 in US dollar terms, while imports grew at a rate of 13.5 per cent per year (World Bank 1998). Both growth rates were more than twice the world average. Growth in output and trade from Hong Kong's Guangdong hinterland has been roughly twice that of the mainland economy as a whole. The mainland economy also has attracted an enormous amount of foreign investment. In recent years, China, which received $US45.3 billion in foreign direct investment in 1997 has been by far the leading recipient of foreign direct investment among developing nations and has been the second leading recipient, after the USA, worldwide (UNCTAD 1997, 1998; HKTDC 1998a).

Hong Kong is often called a gateway to China, or the mainland's window on the world. Hong Kong has been these things and a great deal more. Hong Kong and its firms have served as drivers of the modernization of the mainland economy and orchestrators of its emergence into international markets. Hong Kong has provided not just capital, logistical support, and access to world markets, it also has provided management know-how, technology, equipment, design and research, marketing skills, procurement services, and quality assurance. As the mainland's export economy has boomed, so it has boomed on the basis of mainland labour, land, and natural resources allied with management and support services from Hong Kong. It is this combination that has allowed China, which was largely cut off from the international economy for forty years, to emerge as a major trading nation in a little more than a decade.

Hong Kong has long been China's interface with the rest of the world. Hong Kong is the gateway for roughly 80 per cent of international visitor arrivals into China. Hong Kong handles 50 per cent of China's exports—and 80 per cent of the international trade of neighbouring Guangdong province. Not counting re-exports to and from China, Hong Kong is China's second largest trading partner. Hong Kong is the largest source of overseas direct investment in the Chinese mainland. As of the end of July 1998, among the 314,533 overseas-funded projects registered in the Chinese mainland, 174,880 (55.6 per cent) were tied to Hong Kong investors. The stock of contracted and utilized foreign investment from Hong Kong into the Chinese Mainland was $US288.7 billion and $US135.0 billion, accounting for 52.5 per cent and 54.0 per cent of the respective totals (HKTDC 1998a). Hong Kong, in fact, is by far the leading foreign investor is almost every province and city in China.

In addition, Hong Kong is a complete business service centre for the mainland and the logistics centre for much of South China. No community has deeper practical knowledge of how to do business in the world's most populous market. Hong Kong-based professional service providers in law, accountancy, and consulting firms manage extensive office networks across China from Hong Kong. One leading accounting firm alone employs more than 200 people based in Hong Kong to perform due diligence on mainland Chinese companies. Hong Kong professional expertise is also helping China develop its own business services sector as Hong Kong-based professionals help write or rewrite the professional standards and rules in law, accounting, insurance, and other areas.

The Chinese mainland also has had an enormous influence on Hong Kong's economy. Hong Kong's shifts from an entrepôt, to a manufacturing enclave, to a sophisticated provider of services and manufacturing activities have been triggered by the closing and opening of mainland China's economy to the rest of the world. The mainland has had a crucial direct role in the Hong Kong economy as well. It has long been a source of food, water, and staples for Hong Kong (Overholt 1993). The economic opening that began in the late 1970s triggered a transformation of the Hong Kong economy that has left it more prosperous and more interdependent with the mainland.

At the same time, mainland Chinese companies also have become major players in the Hong Kong economy in their own right. With a total stock of investment of $US14.0 billion, the Chinese mainland was Hong Kong's second largest source of external investment after the UK at the end of 1996. Over 1,856 mainland-backed enterprises employed over 53,000 people in Hong Kong at the end of 1997. The market shares of mainland-backed companies in the territory were estimated at 22 per cent in foreign trade; 22 to 25 per cent in banking (in terms of deposits), insurance (in terms of insurance premiums), and cargo transportation (in terms of freight volume); 25 per cent in tourism (in terms of tourist revenue); 12 per cent in construction (in terms of completed projects); and 16 per cent of the notes issuance of Hong Kong dollars. Some seventy-two mainland-backed enterprises registered in Hong Kong were listed on the Hong Kong Stock Exchange at the end of 1997 (HKTDC 1998a).

The economies of Hong Kong and mainland China have developed increasingly close links in recent years, creating a division of labour and symbiosis in which both have benefited. The mainland has developed its economy far faster than would have been possible otherwise and Hong Kong has had the advantage of operating as a business centre for China. In almost every area of business activity, Hong Kong has favourably positioned itself to intermediate between international business and the Chinese mainland. In the process, Hong Kong has aggregated a huge critical mass of knowledge and experience about doing business in China (for foreign companies) and in the global markets (for mainland companies). This knowledge has been key to Hong Kong's economic success.

5.2. Hong Kong's Links with the Rest of Asia

A second driver of the Hong Kong economy has been the development of the economies of East Asia. Between 1980 and 1996, Asia's economic growth was nearly twice that of the rest of the world and its share of world output increased from 17 to 29 per cent (or 34.1 per cent in a purchasing power parity basis in 1996) (World Bank 1996, 1998 and WTO 1998). Today, Japan, Hong Kong, and Singapore are among the wealthiest economies in the world on a per capita basis. After more than twenty years of growth averaging 7 to 8 per cent, standards of living in South Korea and Taiwan are equal to those for many in Europe. Until the Asian economic crisis hit the region, countries like Malaysia, Thailand, and Indonesia had begun to boast substantial middle-income populations with significant purchasing power. Even China, long one of the world's poorest countries, now has tens of millions in urban centres and in the country's coastal provinces who are part of an emerging consumer economy.

Asia's trade and investment flows also have increased. Trade flows between Asia and North America have exceeded those between North America and the European Union throughout the 1980s and 1990s. Trade to and from Asia and intra-Asian trade grew significantly faster than trade elsewhere from 1980 to the mid-1990s, despite the North American Free Trade Agreement and the European Union's 1992 Programme. In 1980, intra-EU trade was 3.7 times that of intra-Asian trade; by 1994, it was 1.5 times intra-Asian trade. In 1980, intra-Asian trade was 1.9 times that of intra-North American trade; by 1994, the figure was 3.2 times (IMF various years). By 1996, Asia accounted for 25.6 per cent of world trade and 26.1 per cent of world foreign direct investment (WTO 1998). The growth of trade and investment in the Asian region has greatly benefited Hong Kong, by far the leading centre for intra-Asian trade and investment.

Hong Kong also has become *de facto* business capital of the overseas Chinese communities that account for a very large share of the entrepreneurial wealth of the Asia-Pacific. The total assets of the largest 500 public companies in Asia controlled by ethnic Chinese were estimated in 1994 to exceed $US500 billion (Wu and Duk 1995). While ethnic Chinese account for less than 10 per cent of South-East Asia's population, they control up to two-thirds of the region's retail trade and are leading players in land and property development, banking, hotels, engineering, and construction.

Hong Kong occupies a central place in this network for a number of reasons. Hong Kong is a common reference point for the millions of Chinese emigrants who have passed through it on their way to other places. Hong Kong's favourable location, excellent transportation and communication links, world-class infrastructure, advanced capital markets, sound legal system, transparent administration, low taxes, and liberal rules on movement of individuals, goods, and capital, have made it the ideal place for overseas Chinese companies to do business with each other and with the rest of the world. Hong Kong has served as a cornerstone for the overseas expansion of many of the largest and most powerful of the overseas Chinese conglomerates, including the Kuok Group of Malaysia, the Lippo Group of Indonesia, the Salim Group of Indonesia, the Sophonpanich Group of Thailand, the Pokphand Group of Thailand, and others. For these firms, Hong Kong typically is their first international location, their primary locus for tapping the international capital markets, their springboard for managing investment onto the Chinese mainland, and their primary base for foreign direct investment elsewhere.

5.3. Hong Kong in the International Networks of Foreign Multinationals

Hong Kong also plays an important part in the global strategies of foreign multinational firms. Hong Kong's international business community, originally largely British, became more diverse after the Second World War with the arrival of firms from the USA, Europe, Japan, and South-East Asia (Vogel 1989). Since the late 1970s, the opening of China to foreign investment and trade has attracted many more overseas firms to Hong Kong. By the mid-1990s, Hong Kong was home to the largest community of multinational firms in Asia outside of Japan. As of the end of 1997, over 200 of the Fortune 500 companies had a presence in Hong Kong. By 1997, the American Chamber of Commerce in Hong Kong was the largest American Chamber outside of the USA; the Canadian Chamber was the largest outside of North America; and the Japanese Chamber in Hong Kong reported that more than 2,000 Japanese companies operated from Hong Kong.

Hong Kong's overseas firm 'sector' is so large and diverse that no one knows precisely how many there are.[5] A 1997 attempt by the Hong Kong Government Industry Department to identify all overseas companies operation in Hong Kong yielded 11,819 overseas firms known to be operating in Hong Kong and 4,275 survey responses (HKID 1997). Nearly a quarter of the foreign multinationals in Hong Kong that responded to another survey (Enright and Thompson 1998) said their companies had been established in Hong Kong for over twenty-five years, while slightly over a quarter had been established in Hong Kong for five years or less. Nearly half of the multinationals indicated that their Hong Kong office would be more important in the future; 30 per cent indicated that it would stay the same; and less than one-quarter indicated that their Hong Kong office would become less important in the future (mostly due to the movement of some activities into the Chinese mainland). The overall sense was one of a healthy pattern of established and newly arriving firms.

Foreign multinational firms have played important roles in Hong Kong's economic development and are key contributors to Hong Kong's most vibrant clusters (Enright 1998*d*). In financial services, Hong Kong's three note-issuing banks (Hongkong Bank, Bank of China, and Standard & Chartered) all are headquartered outside of Hong Kong. The leading managers of investment funds in Hong Kong are major Western firms. In business services, the 'Big Six' (now 'Big Five') dominate the accounting field. All the major international management consultancy firms have a strong presence in the HKSAR as do many of the world's leading international law firms. The communication and media sector is home to a number of multinational firms, with the dominant local player, Hong Kong Telecommunications, majority owned by Cable & Wireless from the UK. Numerous foreign news and media companies have made Hong Kong a centre for their regional activities, as well.

Many of Hong Kong's leading engineering firms are actually the Hong Kong offices of foreign firms. In several cases, the Hong Kong offices have actually grown to be larger than the 'head office'. Most of the leading Hong Kong-based professionals that put together infrastructure projects for the Asian region (putting together the financial, engineering, design, architecture, legal, and other required expertise) are employed by foreign headquartered financial institutions. Hong Kong attracts wholesalers, retailers, and traders of light manufactured goods from the rest of the world, which use Hong Kong as a logistics, procurement, sales, and finance base. Hong Kong's dense air and sea route networks have allowed its transportation and logistics cluster to attract numerous foreign air carriers, shipping companies, freight forwarders, and logistics firms that use Hong Kong as a hub for their Asian operations.

Several of Hong Kong's clusters have developed, not independent of foreign firms and not dependent on foreign firms, but interdependent with foreign firms (see Enright 1998*d*). In addition to resource-seeking, market-seeking, asset-exploiting, and asset-augmenting investments (see Dunning 1998*a*, *b*, 2000*a*), many multinational firms have made investments in Hong Kong's clusters that could be termed 'market-place-seeking' (those designed, not to access markets *per se*, but to access market places, where goods, services, and assets can be traded) or 'information-seeking' (often representing the multinational firms' desire to use Hong Kong as a centre for obtaining, processing, and disseminating information for the whole Asia-Pacific region) (Enright 1998*d*).

5.4. **Hong Kong as Packager and Integrator of Economic Activity**

A common thread which runs through Hong Kong's clusters is that Hong Kong and its firms have become 'packagers and integrators' of economic activity, identifying, developing, or creating demand and identifying, developing, or creating sources of supply to meet that demand. Hong Kong firms have performed these roles on a local, macroregional, and global basis, allowing Hong Kong to benefit from economic activity that takes place well beyond its borders (Enright *et al.* 1997).

In light manufacturing, Hong Kong firms match demand, largely in the West, with sources of supply, largely in the East. In industries, such as garments, toys, plastic products, watches, and others, Hong Kong firms have developed sources of cost-sensitive mass production and assembly activities on the Chinese mainland and elsewhere in Asia. They specialize in a set of complex, knowledge-intensive activities along the length of the manufacturing value-chain, providing complete headquarters, management, financing, technology, design, prototyping, quality control, marketing, and distribution services between dispersed assembly plants on the one hand and retail buyers on the other. Rather than a 'middleman', the Hong Kong firm becomes a complete business partner for the customer, coordinating and putting together, 'packaging and integrating', a range of activities often beyond the capabilities of the customer. The Hong Kong firms add value through their knowledge of source and destination markets, their familiarity with production capabilities of literally thousands of factories scattered throughout Asia, their advanced capabilities in logistics, and their expertise in managing subcontractors.

In business services, Hong Kong firms and professionals match demand in the East with expertise and knowledge developed in Hong Kong or imported from the West. Hong Kong is a regional hub for management consulting, accounting, market research, and other business services. In financial services, Hong Kong firms match demand for investment options from the West with investments in the East and match demand for capital and funds from the East with supplies from the West. Hong Kong is the leading centre where fund managers and private bankers put together Asian investment funds, portfolios, and financial vehicles. Hong Kong professionals are prominent in initial public offerings, joint venture finance, and venture capital all over the region.

In infrastructure and development, Hong Kong-based professionals match demand in the East with capital and expertise from Japan and the West. Local Hong Kong firms have structured projects to build ports, airports, roads, power plants, mass transit systems, and low-cost housing in mainland China, the Philippines, Indonesia, Thailand, and India. In addition, the Hong Kong offices of foreign financial service firms have put together the financing for infrastructure projects all over Asia. Hong Kong-based firms and professionals bring together design, construction, engineering, legal, and financial expertise to build infrastructure in Hong Kong, on the mainland, and elsewhere in East Asia. With its long history of private-sector financed infrastructure, Hong Kong is the leading location for integrating these skills. Hong Kong, in fact, was the pioneer within Asia of the BOT (build-operate-transfer) system in which private investors build an infrastructure project, operate it under a concession arrangement for a period of time within which they try to earn back their investment plus a return, and then transfer the project to the control of a government agency.

In light manufacturing, business services, infrastructure and development, and other areas, Hong Kong is the place where the appropriate components, capabilities, and/or activities are packaged and integrated so that supply meets demand. The packaging and integrating role requires knowledge of sources of demand and sources of supply around the world and the capacity to put together new combinations to take advantage of rapid shifts in demand and in the relative capabilities and attractiveness of sources of supply. It requires expertise in all aspects of the particular business, the ability to bridge cultures into the developed and developing worlds, and the ability to assess rapidly emerging commercial opportunities. These abilities and features are present to an unusual if not unique extent in Hong Kong. In turn, they allow Hong Kong firms to capture value from economic activities that take place well beyond its borders. Although these activities do not fall neatly into categories of 'knowledge-intensive industries' or 'research and development', they represent activities that are as knowledge-intensive as those performed by firms in any industry.

6. Hong Kong's Policies

Hong Kong's economy has developed with relatively little overt direction from the public sector, a marked difference from most of the economies of East Asia (see Enright *et al.* 1997; Park 1998; and Chia 1998, for example). Hong Kong's government policies often are conspicuous by their absence or small scale. A philosophy of providing a good business environment and not showing favouritism or picking winners has resulted in Hong Kong repeatedly being named as the world's freest economy by the US-based Heritage Foundation and Canada's Fraser Institute (Heritage Foundation/ *Wall Street Journal* 1998 and Gwartney 1998).[6]

The Hong Kong economy has evolved largely free of policies to create a particular economic structure. Up until 1996, for example, Hong Kong had virtually no policies to promote its service sector. The Hong Kong Industry Department, the agency most involved in economy policy towards the economy, did not have service industries within its mandate until 1996. Similarly, the Hong Kong Trade Development Council, the primary government-related organization involved in trade promotion, did not even have service industries within its promotion mandate until 1996. It should be noted that by 1996, the service sector already accounted for 84.4 per cent of GDP. Since 1996, the policies towards the service sector have involved promoting the image of Hong Kong as a place to do business, rather than concessions, subsidies, or tax breaks.

Hong Kong has had only limited policies to promote itself as a location for foreign multinational firms. This stands in sharp contrast to Singapore and many places in Europe (see Chia 1998 and Brown 1998). For many years, Hong Kong's Industry Department had promotion of Hong Kong as a site for foreign manufacturers as part of its remit. Promotion mostly consisted of providing information on Hong Kong and the provision of land for industrial projects, not the financial incentives or tax holidays used by other governments in the region and elsewhere. As was noted earlier, manufacturing's share of foreign direct investment stock as of 1996 was only 8 per cent, indicative of the low priority placed on promotion to multinationals in general, the lack of government incentives, and the economic irrationality of locating manufacturing investment in Hong Kong.

Many national and local governments have instituted policies to promote regional clustering in recent years (Rosenfeld 1995; Chia 1998; and Enright 1998*a*). Hong Kong has developed a tightly clustered economy without having any government policies to promote clustering. The Hong Kong government has had policies to support trade promotion and tourism and has from time to time enacted measures beneficial to Hong Kong's attractiveness as a financial services hub, but essentially has had no policies equivalent to those evolving in other places to promote clusters. In fact, the term 'cluster' was only introduced into the Hong Kong parlance in 1997 (in Enright *et al.* 1997).

The transformation and development of Hong Kong's knowledge-based economy has resulted from private-sector response to the economic and market conditions. Government has made investments in infrastructure, education, training, and limited promotional activities, but has not tried to direct economic development.[7]

7. Hong Kong in the Asian Economic Crisis

Viewing Hong Kong as a metropolitan economy, dependent on economic activities that go on outside of the Hong Kong Special Administrative Region, helps us understand its current economic structure and the prosperity that Hong Kong has achieved in the last twenty years. It also helps us understand the impact of the Asian economic crisis on Hong Kong. Hong Kong managed to avoid the effects of the crisis through most of 1997. However, by October of 1998, unemployment reached 5.3 per cent, a figure not seen in more than a decade, and analysts projected that GDP would contract 5 to 6 per cent for 1998 as a whole.[8]

In the midst of the crisis, many economic activities in Asia have dried up. Asian demand for manufactured exports has fallen, affecting trade and logistics through Hong Kong. Tourism is down throughout the region as Asians adjust to diminished incomes and wealth, and long-haul tourists, who have seen a steady stream of reports of economic collapse and social unrest in some parts of Asia, have avoided the region. Hong Kong's financial sector has suffered as Western equity investors and Japanese banks pulled funds out of Asia, hurting Hong Kong's own markets as well as the equity analysts, project financiers, and financial intermediaries that dealt with the rest of Asia from Hong Kong. Furthermore, the value of Hong Kong's role as the *de facto* capital of the overseas Chinese business network, and their preferred location from which to make and manage investments in the region, has diminished given the huge losses that overseas Chinese companies have experienced in South-East Asia and the resulting curtailment of intra-Asian trade and investment.

These external features, when combined with the bursting of Hong Kong's own asset price bubble in the property and stock markets, help explain why Hong Kong could not escape from the Asian economic crisis. Hong Kong's economy is too dependent on economic activity in the region to have emerged unscathed. Hong Kong's links with the other economies of the region have been, and will be, of tremendous benefit, but in the short-run, such linkages can create pressure in a small, open economy (Enright 1998*b*).

8. Conclusions

Hong Kong's economy has been transformed from an enclave economy to a metropolitan economy and from a manual economy to a knowledge-based economy, focused on knowledge-intensive producer services and the knowledge-intensive portions of the manufacturing value-added chain. Foreign firms and local firms use Hong Kong as a centre for their knowledge-intensive activities, including management, coordination, information related activities, and finance.

The forces that have driven this transformation are consistent with the framework presented by Dunning (2000*b*). Hong Kong has benefited greatly from the emergence of new economic actors, particularly the Chinese mainland and other economies of East Asia. Economic liberalization and the globalization of competition have allowed and forced Hong Kong to move away from low-value-added activities to higher-value-added, knowledge-intensive activities. The same forces have fostered the localization of particular businesses and industries in Hong Kong, resulting in strong clusters in light manufacturing and trading, business and financial services, transportation and logistics, tourism, communications and media, and infrastructure and development. The strategies of foreign multinational firms, many of which have made Hong Kong their Asia-Pacific regional headquarters or regional office location, also have contributed to Hong Kong's development.

There are further lessons that can be drawn from an examination of the Hong Kong economy. Many discussions of the 'knowledge economy' focus on particular sets of so-called 'high-technology' industries. Examination of Hong Kong's knowledge economy suggests that knowledge-intensity is more properly framed, not as a function of industry, but as a function of activity. The knowledge economy if not based solely on 'high-technology' industries or research and development. In fact, the highest-value-added activities of firms, the truly knowledge-intensive activities, often are those involving firm management, coordination, finance, market research, and design. The 'packaging and integrating' functions of Hong Kong-based firms and professionals, the activities that require intimate familiarity with rapidly changing markets and business practices all over the world, create value almost exclusively through their acquisition and use of knowledge.

Such knowledge need not entail massive investments, but does require distinct skills and capabilities as well as a favourable business environment.

Hong Kong's economic transformation and the development of a series of competitive clusters have occurred without overt direction by the Hong Kong government. Hong Kong's policy regime has ensured that the market forces unleashed by globalization have played the dominant role in shaping the economy. Hong Kong's prosperity has been due to its unique ability to take advantage of the globalization process that has characterized the world economy over the last three decades. Hong Kong's economic difficulties in the middle of the Asian crisis show that tight linkages with other economies can leave a small, open economy vulnerable to external forces, perhaps a cost associated with globalization. It should be noted, however, that Hong Kong's policy regime has kept it from the disasters that have occurred in some other Asian economies, where the failure of government development policies has been little short of spectacular.

Foreign multinational companies have become integral parts of Hong Kong's competitive clusters. The appropriate characterization of the relationship between multinationals and Hong Kong's clusters is one of interdependence. Several of the clusters would be far less important without the presence of the multinational firms. At the same time, the presence of the clusters has been a substantial advantage to the activities of multinational firms in Hong Kong, the Chinese mainland, and the Asia-Pacific region. The interdependence leads to types of foreign investment distinct from those generally recognized in the literature. In particular, foreign investment into Hong Kong's clusters also shows what might be called 'market-place-seeking' and 'information-seeking' behaviour.

Hong Kong's 'packaging and integrating' role requires alliances, not just between firms, but between multiple economies. In many instances, Hong Kong-based firms and professionals put together new combinations involving players from three or more different economies. This involves exploiting and augmenting assets, or even creating assets, across geographies and different types of economies. In developing this ability, Hong Kong firms and professionals have moved from being intermediaries to being instigators and initiators of economic activity. For advanced economies, they might well provide insights into the globalized, regionalized, knowledge-based economy of the future.

NOTES

This work was partially funded by a competitive grant from the University Grants Committee of Hong Kong and an internal grant from the University of Hong Kong. It is based in part on research carried out jointly with Edith Scott, David Dodwell, and Edmund Thompson. I wish to thank these colleagues as well as John Dunning and the attendees of the Workshop on Regions, Globalization, and the Knowledge-Based Economy, Rutgers University, 24–5 October 1998 for their comments and suggestions.

1. The ratio of value added per worker in the service sector to that in the manufacturing sector has been far higher.
2. Some of the shift from manufacturing to services has been overstated in that establishments that have moved their production out of Hong Kong have been reclassified from manufacturing to services (see Enright *et al.* 1997). The overall picture of a shift from manufacturing to services, however, is accurate.
3. Other categories include sales workers, service workers, agricultural workers and fishermen, production and related workers, transport equipment operators, labourers, miscellaneous, and others.
4. A *regional headquarters* was defined as an organization which has control over the operation of one or more other offices or subsidiaries in other countries or economies in the region and which does not need to make frequent referrals to, or consultations with, the overseas parent headquarters. Note that Hong Kong and mainland China were considered as two different economies. A *regional office* was defined as an office responsible for general business activities in its own and other countries or economies in the region, but which is less autonomous than a regional headquarters.
5. Since there is no requirement for foreign-owned companies to register as such in Hong Kong, there are no comprehensive statistics on foreign firms in Hong Kong.
6. Government intervention in the stock market in August of 1998 and nascent efforts toward supporting so-called 'high-technology' industries have led some to question whether such policies will continue. This debate is beyond the scope of the present chapter.
7. It is ironic that a series of Scottish Financial Secretaries largely are credited with the non-interventionist policy, given the fact that Scotland itself has long engaged in fairly aggressive government-led development programmes (see Peters *et al.* 1998).
8. The unemployment figures must be viewed carefully. From 1 July 1997 to 1 October 1998, the number of people in Hong Kong's workforce increased by 6.3 per cent (from 3,172,800 to 3,381,000) due to an unexpected return of Hong Kong people who had emigrated in prior years. The number of jobs in Hong Kong actually increased by 3.4 per cent, but since the workforce grew much faster, unemployment went from 2.4 to 5.3 per cent (data from HKCSD, 1998*c, d*).

REFERENCES

Amin, A., and Thrift, N. (1994*a*), 'Holding Down the Global', in A. Amin and N. Thrift (eds.), *Globalization, Institutions, and Regional Development in Europe* (Oxford: Oxford University Press): 257–61.

—— (1994*b*), 'Living in the Global', in A. Amin and N. Thrift (eds.), *Globalization, Institutions, and Regional Development in Europe* (Oxford: Oxford University Press): 1–22.

Asian Development Bank (1998), *Foreign Trade Indicators, 1998* (Manila: Asian Development Bank).

Audretsch, D. (1998), 'Knowledge, Globalization and Regions', Paper presented at the Workshop on Regions, Globalization, and the Knowledge-Based Economy, Rutgers University, 24–5 Oct. 1998.

Bagchi-Sen, S., and Sen, J. (1997), 'The Current State of Knowledge in International Business in Producer Services', *Environment and Planning A 29*: 1153–74.

Balasubramanyam, V. N., and Balasubramanyam, A. (1998), 'The Software Cluster in Bangalore', Paper presented at the Workshop on Regions, Globalization, and the Knowledge-Based Economy, Rutgers University, 24–5 Oct. 1998.

Brown, R. (1998), 'Foreign Direct Investment and Regional Promotional Policies in Europe', Paper presented at the Workshop on Regions, Globalization, and the Knowledge-Based Economy, Rutgers University, 24–5 Oct. 1998.

Chia, S. Y. (1998), 'Singapore: Destination for Multinationals', Paper presented at the Workshop on Regions, Globalization, and the Knowledge-Based Economy, Rutgers University, 24–5 Oct. 1998.

Dicken, P. (1994), 'Global-Local Tensions: Firms and States in the Global Space-Economy', *Economic Geography 70*: 101–28.

Dunning, J. H. (1998a), 'Globalization, Technological Change and the Spatial Organization of Economic Activity', in A. D. Chandler, Ö. Sölvell, and P. Hagstrom (eds.), *The Dynamic Firm: The Role of Technology, Strategy, Organization, and Regions* (Oxford: Oxford University Press): 289–314.

—— (1998b), 'Location and the Multinational Enterprise: A Neglected Factor?', *Journal of International Business Studies 29*: 45–66.

—— (2000a), 'Globalization and the Theory of MNE Activity', in N. Hood and S. Young (eds.), *The Globalization of Multinational Enterprise Activity and Economic Development* (Basingstoke: Macmillan), 21–54.

—— (2000b), 'Regions, Globalization and the Knowledge Economy: The Issues Stated', Chapter 1, this volume.

Enright, M. J. (1991), 'Geographic Concentration and Industrial Organization', Ph.D. diss., Harvard University.

—— (1993), 'The Geographic Scope of Competitive Advantage', in E. Dirven, J. Groenewegen, and S. van Hoof (eds.), *Stuck in the Region? Changing Scales of Regional Identity* (Utrecht: Netherlands Geographical Studies, 155): 87–102.

—— (1995), 'Organization and Coordination in Geographically Concentrated Industries', in D. Raff and N. Lamoreux (eds.), *Coordination and Information: Historical Perspectives on the Organization of Enterprise* (Chicago: University of Chicago Press): 103–42.

—— (1996), 'Regional Clusters and Economic Development: A Research Agenda', in U. H. Staber, N. V. Schaefer, and B. Sharma (eds.), *Business Networks: Prospects for Regional Development* (Berlin: De Gruyter): 190–213.

—— (1997), 'Hong Kong: The Interconnected Economy', Working Paper, University of Hong Kong.

—— (1998a), 'The Globalization of Competition and the Localization of Competitive Advantage: Policies Toward Regional Clustering', Paper presented at the Workshop on Globalization of Multinational Enterprise Activity and Economic Development, University of Strathclyde, 15–16 May 1998.

—— (1998b), 'Hong Kong's Regional Roles and Competitiveness', in *Hong Kong Update* (Washington, DC: CSIS): 7–8.

—— (1998c), 'Regional Clusters and Firm Strategy', in A. D. Chandler, Jr, Ö. Sölvell, and P. Hagström (eds.), *The Dynamic Firm: The Role of Technology, Strategy, Organization, and Regions* (Oxford: Oxford University Press): 315–42.

Enright, M. J. (1998*d*), 'Regional Clusters and Multinational Enterprises: Independence, Dependence, or Interdependence?', Working Paper, University of Hong Kong.

—— (1999), 'Hong Kong's Future Competitiveness, or Do We Still Have the Hong Kong Advantage?', *HKCER Letters*, Jan. 1999: 1–4.

——, Scott, E. E., and Dodwell, D. (1997), *The Hong Kong Advantage* (Hong Kong: Oxford University Press).

——, and Thompson, E. R. (1998), 'Multinational Firms in Hong Kong', Working Paper, University of Hong Kong.

——, Leung, E., and Scott, E. E. (1999), *Overview: Hong Kong's Competitiveness—Beyond the Asian Crisis* (Hong Kong: Hong Kong Trade Development Council).

Grosse, R. (1996), 'International Technology Transfer in Services', *Journal of International Business Studies* 27: 781–800.

Gwartney, J. D. (1998), *Economic Freedom of the World* (Vancouver, BC: Fraser Institute).

Hansen, N. (1994), 'The Strategic Role of Producer Services in Regional Development'. *International Regional Science Review* 16: 187–95.

Heritage Foundation/*Wall Street Journal* (1998), *1998 Index of Economic Freedom* (Washington, DC: Heritage Foundation/*Wall Street Journal*).

Herrigel, G. (1996), 'Crisis in German Decentralized Production: Unexpected Rigidity and the Challenge of an Alternative Form of Flexible Organization in Baden Württemberg', *European Urban and Regional Studies* 3: 33–52.

—— (1998), 'De-Regionalization, Re-Regionalization and the Uncertain Future of European Industrial Districts: Thoughts Mostly on Baden-Württemberg in the Late 1990s', Paper presented at the Workshop on Regions, Globalization, and the Knowledge-Based Economy, Rutgers University, 24–5 Oct. 1998.

HKCSD (Hong Kong Census and Statistics Department) (1998*a*), *A Graphic Guide to Hong Kong's Development (1967–97)*, June 1998.

—— (1998*b*), *Estimates of Gross Domestic Product, 1961–1997*, Feb. 1998.

—— (1998*c*), *Monthly Statistical Report*, Oct. 1998.

—— (1998*d*), *Quarterly Report of Employment, Vacancies and Payroll Statistics*, Oct. 1998.

HKGIS (Hong Kong Government Information Services) (1996), *Hong Kong 1996* (Hong Kong: Government Information Services).

HKID (Hong Kong Industry Department) (1997), *Report on Regional Representation of Overseas Companies in Hong Kong*, Oct. 1997.

—— (1998*a*), *Economic Statistics*, July 1998.

—— (1998*b*), *Investment Statistics*, Mar. 1998.

HKTDC (Hong Kong Trade Development Council) (1998*a*), *Hong Kong and China Economies: Market Profile on Mainland China*, Dec. 1998.

—— (1998*b*), *Hong Kong's Manufacturing Industries: Current Status and Future Prospects*, Sept. 1998.

—— (1998*c*), *The Rise in Offshore Trade and Offshore Investment*, Mar. 1998.

—— (1998*d*), *Scoreboard for Economic Success of Hong Kong*, Nov. 1998.

Humphrey, J., and Schmitz, H. (1996), 'The Triple "C" Approach to Local Industrial Policy', *World Development* 24: 1859–77.

IMD (Institute for Management Development) (various years), *World Competitiveness Yearbook* (Geneva: IMD).

IMF (International Monetary Fund) (various years), *Direction of Trade Statistics Yearbook* (Washington, DC: International Monetary Fund).

Jao, Y. C. (1997), *Hong Kong as an International Financial Center: Evolution, Prospects and Policies* (Hong Kong: City University of Hong Kong Press).

Kraar, L. (1995), 'The Death of Hong Kong', *Fortune* 131, 26 June 1995: 40–52.

Nonaka, I., and Takeuchi, H. (1998), 'A Theory of the Firm's Knowledge-Creation Dynamics', in A. D. Chandler, Jr, Ö. Sölvell, and P. Hagström (eds.), *The Dynamic Firm: The Role of Technology, Strategy, Organization, and Regions* (Oxford: Oxford University Press): 214–41.

Overholt, W. H. (1993), *China: The Next Economic Superpower* (London: Weidenfeld & Nicolson).

Park, S. O. (1998), 'Innovation Systems, Networks and the Knowledge-Based Economy in Korea', Paper presented at the Workshop on Regions, Globalization, and the Knowledge-Based Economy, Rutgers, University, 24–5 Oct. 1998.

Peters, E., Hood, N., and Young, S. (1998), 'The Evolution of Policy Partnership in the Knowledge Industries in Scotland', Paper presented at the Workshop on Regions, Globalization and the Knowledge-Based Economy, Rutgers University, 24–5 Oct. 1998.

Porter, M. E. (1990), *The Competitive Advantage of Nations* (New York: Free Press).

Roberts, R. (ed.) (1994), *International Financial Centres* (Hants, UK: Edward Elgar).

Rosenfeld, S. A. (1995), *Industrial Strength Strategies: Regional Clusters and Public Policy* (Washington, DC: The Aspen Institute).

Scott, A. J. (1992), 'The Collective Order of Flexible Production Agglomerations: Lessons for Local Economic Development Policy and Strategic Choice', *Economic Geography* 68: 219–33.

—— (1998), 'The Geographic Foundations of Industrial Performance', in A. D. Chandler, Jr, Ö. Sölvell, and P. Hagström (eds.), *The Dynamic Firm: The Role of Technology, Strategy, Organization, and Regions* (Oxford: Oxford University Press): 384–401.

Sölvell, Ö., and Birkinshaw, J. (1998), 'Multinational Enterprises in the Knowledge Economy: Leveraging Global Practices', Paper presented at the Workshop on Regions, Globalization, and the Knowledge-Based Economy, Rutgers, University, 24–5 Oct. 1998.

Spender, J. C. (1998), 'The Geographies of Strategic Competence: Borrowing from Social and Educational Psychology to Sketch an Activities and Knowledge-Based Theory of the Firm', in A. D. Chandler, Jr., Ö. Sölvell, and P. Hagström (eds.), *The Dynamic Firm: The Role of Technology, Strategy, Organization, and Regions* (Oxford: Oxford University Press): 417–39.

Storper, M. (1992), 'The Limits to Globalization: Technology Districts and International Trade', *Economic Geography* 68: 60–96.

—— (1998), 'Rethinking the Economics of Globalization: The Role of Ideas and Conventions', Paper presented at the Workshop on Regions, Globalization, and the Knowledge-Based Economy, Rutgers University, 24–5 Oct. 1998.

UN (1998), *Yearbook of International Trade Statistics, 1998* (New York: United Nations).

UNCTAD (various years), *World Investment Report* (Geneva: UNCTAD).

Vogel, E. (1989), *One Step Ahead in China: Guangdong Under Reform* (Cambridge, Mass.: Harvard University Press).

World Bank (1996), *World Development Report, 1996* (Washington, DC: World Bank).

World Bank (1998), *World Development Indicators CD-ROM* (Washington, DC: World Bank).

World Economic Forum (various years), *World Competitiveness Report* (Geneva: World Economic Forum).

WTO (World Trade Organization) (1998), 'World Trade Growth Accelerated in 1997, Despite Turmoil in Some Asian Financial Markets', press release, 19 Mar. 1998.

Wu, F., and Duk, S. Y. (1995), '(Overseas) China, Inc', *The International Economy*, Jan./Feb. 1995: 33–5.

PART FOUR
POLICY IMPLICATIONS

16

Towards a Theory of Regional Policy

H. Peter Gray and John H. Dunning

1. Introduction

Created assets are proprietary assets whose existence is the result of firms' past investments. In the last three decades or so, these assets have become increasingly knowledge-based and mobile across national boundaries. They now form the basis for much international direct investment and cross-border strategic alliances. The newly found mobility has improved, in high-cost economic regions, the terms of trade of intangible assets at the expense of those which are location-bound. As a rising proportion of world economic output relies on knowledge-intensive inputs and as the knowledge-intensity of these inputs itself increases as a result of technological advances, established economic regions face adjustment costs as spatially mobile assets seek their most profitable locations elsewhere.

The mobility of created assets is enhanced by improvements in management skills and communications, and by greater liberalization of markets both for inputs and products. The mobility also increases as firms shift their strategic perspective from a stand-alone posture to one which acknowledges that to compete effectively in their final product markets they need to cooperate with other firms in the intermediate product market. Policy-makers in established regions must both recognize the need for, and implement policies to ease, the adjustment process to the new conditions, so as to retain or improve their prosperity.

At the same time, the mobility of knowledge-intensive assets has potentially improved the demand for immobile factors in low-cost countries/regions *if created assets can be attracted to the region*. Economic policy in high-cost industrialized regions can be seen as recognizing and reacting to the shift in the terms of intellectual and financial assets. The new spatial mobility of created assets comes at the same time as the breakdown of the old mass production (Fordist) system of management, so that there will be geographic reallocation of resources within countries as well as internationally.[1]

The reallocation of value-adding activities within countries and between subnational regions can be expected to lead the mobile assets to move to microregions in which cooperating in immobile assets are, on balance, more economical. This has important implications for the distribution of incomes within a macroregion subjected to an exodus of created assets (Wood 1995). The same will apply among countries and their constituent regions. Very important in this process of spatial reallocation are regional clusters of activity which are able to generate Marshallian and neo-Marshallian external economies.[2] The lack of such externalities in other regions can offset any appeal of low-cost immobile inputs.[3] There is little expectation that abstract analysis will yield some indication of how activities will ultimately be distributed. Such a distribution will depend upon the rate of deepening of knowledge-intensity, the increasing ease of spatial mobility of created assets, and the ability of subnational regions relatively well endowed with immobile assets to upgrade these to the requisite quality, and, at the same time, to develop complementary attributes.

Section 2 sets out some necessary building blocks, i.e. the definitions and behavioural assumptions needed, for the construction of a (targets/instruments) model of economic policy for a microregion, which is developed in Sections 3 and 4.[4] Section 5 will address the complications that arise from recognizing the possibilities that a simple target of increasing per-capita regional product may be inadequate, and that questions of income distribution and quality of life are also relevant. This section will also introduce the possibility of the existence of a vicious circle and the prospect of self-defeating competition among regional governments to attract mobile resources. Section 6 addresses the hypothesis that the power of regional policy diminishes with the degree to which a potential investment requires the presence of project-specific attributes to be present in the host region. This lays the basis for a secondary hypothesis that the more knowledge-intensive the project is, the less likely are general regional policy initiatives and inducements to affect its location. This secondary hypothesis is assessed in terms of a system of knowledge-capitalism and the increasing propensity of major corporations to engage in strategic alliances, with their competitors, suppliers, or customers.[5] Section 7 briefly addresses the dynamics of regional economies and the viability of existing clusters inherited from a time when knowledge-intensive-created assets were both less important and less easily spatially mobile. The conclusion summarizes the argument of the chapter.

2. Building Blocks

In any analysis involving layers of political authority, nomenclature must be precise. This chapter adds depth to its analysis by reference to policy issues in the context of the European Union (EU) and the federal system of the USA: these are macroregions—the most inclusive level.[6] The microregion, which is the focus of our attention, is seen as 'subnational' implying a state or a smaller region in the USA and something smaller than a member nation of the EU.[7] This layering has a necessary contextual feature: the EU recognizes the existence of an intermediate layer between a macroregion and a microregion. In general terms, the intermediate layer is likely to be less important in any consideration of regional policies in the USA.[8]

Economic policy can only be formulated by units which have the ability to tax (i.e. to generate revenues) to fund financial incentives, and the legal authority to initiate and implement a variety of measures affecting the creation, utilization, and geographical distribution of resources. As defined, macroregions have such political authority, the nature and extent of which may differ between one region and another. It is also necessary to identify microregions as having the requisite ability and authority to implement policy—albeit constrained by the actions and institutions of nation states and macroregional authorities.[9] It is also possible to conceive of submicroregions comprising cities and narrowly defined regions. Such 'regions' may have resources and capabilities with which to implement macroorganizational policies (and fund incentives—possibly deriving from grants from the national or macroregional government—but their freedom of manœuvre is considerably less than that of a microregion and is almost necessarily confined to project-specific inducements.

For our immediate purposes, we shall take the objective of regional economic policy to be the increase in gross regional product (GRP) per capita at some time in the future.[10] Such a policy has two dimensions. The first is the enhancement of the competitiveness and profitability of spatially mobile and spatially immobile activities already located within the region. The second is actively to try to attract (or retain) mobile investments which, together with the spatially fixed assets within the region, will promote the long-term comparative advantage of the region in activities with a high knowledge-intensive content. The two goals overlap in that steps which make the 'commercial environment' of the region more 'business-friendly' will accomplish both goals (Gray 1995). However, this duality immediately raises the important question as to whether policy measures should be general (across-the-board) and non-discriminatory, or be applied on a project-specific, firm-specific, or industry-specific basis.[11] Given the duality of sources of possible increases in per-capita GRP, it is not surprising that both types of policy are necessary under certain conditions (implying the possible need for a joint policy emanating from both the macro- and micro-regional authorities).

The main focus of regional policy in an innovation-driven economy is on spatially mobile knowledge-intensive activities, which, when combined with the location-bound resources of the region, are capable of generating quasi-rents for that region. This they may do by raising the technological capacity and skill levels of the region and by ploughing some of the quasi-rents back into its economy.[12]

For the most part, the creators and owners of knowledge-intensive assets operate in a world of potentially severe competition and significant uncertainty (Aharoni 1993). The severity of competition derives from the interdependence between the value of one firm's portfolios of proprietary technology and created assets, and its portfolio of locational assets; and also from the value and rate of improvement of these same portfolios possessed by competitors located in other regions (Gray 1996). It is this greater dimensionality of competition with its emphasis on the efficiency at which managers may create and allocate different genera of assets that increases the importance of the Schumpeterian entrepreneur (Gray 1999). The globalization of markets has honed competition among many large MNEs to the point that no single MNE can afford to allow its competitors to gain an advantage by improving the relative quality of either its proprietary or locational assets (Gray 1996). Little or no scope remains for leaving value-adding assets in an inefficient 'home-country' location.[13]

In previous writings, one of the authors of this chapter (Dunning 1992, 1993) has argued that if national or regional governments are to attract spatially mobile investment to their borders, they must first recognize the need to create a package of non-imitable immobile resources and capabilities which is at least as supportive of the needs of such enterprises as other regions seeking the same investment. The model of regional policy to be developed in Section 3 will be couched in terms of a host region seeking to increase the present value of per-capita GRP by attracting and/or retaining the right kind of mobile, intangible assets.[14] Thus, inducements (general or project-specific) are seen as earning a positive net rate of return for the economy on the (collective) expenditures involved (though, in the short run, the rate of return to the government sector may not be positive).[15] In a region working at full capacity, a new investment with a higher reliance on proprietary technology may require that another productive unit be sloughed off and transferred to a less well-developed region.[16] However, the recognition that governments may need to offer financial and other inducements to attract new activity or retain existing activity in a microregion opens up the very real possibility of competition among governments, both at a national and subnational level. Inducements can be financial or non-financial (e.g. immunity from certain behavioural requirements imposed in the host economy, and those relating to the quality of life) and can, in principle, include 'negative inducements' such as performance requirements (Gray and Walter 1983; UNCTAD 1996).[17]

The boundaries of a *political* microregion allow the corresponding concept of an economic microregion to be confronted. The political microregion has a degree of sovereignty and can be identified clearly as a spatial area which is under the jurisdiction of a macroregional government or as a culturally distinct, partially autonomous region of a nation (e.g. Scotland or Northern Ireland in the UK or the Commonwealth of Puerto Rico in the USA).

The concept of an economic microregion has been well described and analysed by several economic geographers, notably Storper and Scott (1995) and Scott (1998). They argue that the boundaries of economic space are defined by the need for transactional propinquity. To quote directly from Storper and Scott (ibid. 506): 'In very general terms, the greater the substantive complexity, irregularity, uncertainty, predictability and uncodifiability of transactions, the greater [is] their sensitivity to geographical distance.' These qualities lead to some activities—and particularly knowledge-intensive activities—being the beneficiary of spatial clustering, or agglomerative economies the nature and content of which is examined in some detail by several authors in this volume.

A political microregion may contain several submicroeconomic microregions. Some of these latter spatial entities, e.g. business districts, science parks, will generate clusters of related activities, which offer external economies to the firms participating in them, such as the exchange of knowledge and learning experiences, and the availability of cluster-specific infrastructures. A cluster of related activities can form the basis for the existence of an economic region and can form an important attribute of a political microregion. An economic microregion can also be identified by certain commonality of resource endowments.[18]

3. A Model of (Subnational) Regional Policy

At time *t*, a microregion possesses attributes which it has inherited from the time before created assets were as important as they now are, and were as spatially mobile. These attributes include resources, capabilities, institutions, and a set of policies, as well as a population of enterprises whose competitiveness rests on the possession of a portfolio of proprietary intangible assets which, in the main, are usable in different locations. The attractiveness of any region, and the competitiveness of activities located in it, will depend upon the degree to which its attributes match the needs of the investing enterprises in both general and industry-specific terms, relative to those of other possible locations.[19] Policy, then, depends on the ability of the relevant authority, or authorities, be they supranational, national, or subnational, to change the sum of the attributes of the region to make them sufficiently attractive to induce value-adding activities of a specific investment to locate (or not to leave) the region.

A microregion's attributes can be usefully classified into five categories.[20] These are: the resource base of the (regional) economy; the innate benefits deriving from the presence of upstream and downstream industries and parallel firms; the characteristics of demand including the size and affluence of the market that can be competitively served from the region; the contribution of the local conditions to managerial efficiency; and the 'business-friendliness' of the commercial environment (Gray 1995). These five dimensions can now be described in greater detail and the responsiveness of each category to government policy identified.[21]

1. *The resource base* of the regional economy must be broadened from the neo-classical approach, which focuses on the distribution of natural resources to include all forms of created assets which are locked into that economy. These latter assets include actions taken by governments, e.g. with respect to taxes and incentives,[22] the quality of local institutions, and the availability of physical and commercial infrastructure. This dimension is an extension of the idea of a resource base used in factor-promotions models of international trade[23] that are used in resource-based theories of the firm (Barney 1991). The resource base is largely inherited from the past and reflects the accumulation of both natural and created assets.[24] In the case of the upgrading of certain kinds of resources, e.g. skilled labour, institutional and infrastructure, this can only be accomplished over a long period of time.

2. *The efficiency of upstream and downstream industries* and of 'parallel' firms can add to the efficiency of any activity because of the ease with which

information can be transferred and intermediate goods and services can be traded within the region. Parallel firms supply core goods which are at the same stage of production as the core activity. They will have similar attributes and may be direct competitors in that they offer an alternative process for the same end use as the focus activity. They produce goods which use similar inputs and have similar infrastructural needs. The proximity of a number of parallel firms is likely to derive from, and possibly generate new, agglomerative economies. It is to be expected that the external benefits that derive from a cluster will be positively correlated with the presence of efficient upstream and downstream firms; *inter alia*, this underscores the importance of vertical integration in modern production methods.

The presence of all three kinds of firms can contribute to reductions in production costs and to the design quality and reliability of new and existing end products. Alliances in research and development (R&D) are also likely to truncate the innovatory period, and to upgrade the quality of new innovations which require complementary technologies. These industry-specific attributes are largely inherited and would be difficult, if not impossible, for government to create within the time-horizon of an individual investment project. Such clusters are likely to be more valuable, the greater the knowledge-intensity of the industry, and the higher the spatial transaction costs of knowledge transference or learning. This observation receives support from the tendency of headquarters and R&D activities to cluster.

3. The *characteristics of demand* include Porter's (1990) concept of the 'demandingness of consumers'. Within the industrialized world, this distinction between Japanese, European, and North American consumers has lost much of its force because of the success of Japanese MNEs in raising consumers' levels of expectation with respect to product reliability and after-sales servicing. However, the demandingness of customers is likely to vary between countries according to their business and consumer cultures, and levels of industralization.

The characteristics of the market are important: they include the number affluence, and tastes of potential customers that can be served from a production unit in a specified region. Thus, a subnational region which is a part of, or has easy access to, a large prosperous market by means of good transportation and communication networks, will have an advantage over a competitor region which lacks these facilities.[25] This determinant also requires identification of the important role of marketing-and-distribution (M&D) affiliates in some individual countries which do not possess a market which is large enough to warrant a local production unit. Government influence here must be considered very small.

4. *The contribution of the region to managerial efficiency* has two roots. First, the degree to which the rivalry among the competing firms in the region— including that induced by foreign-owned subsidiaries, and by the macro-organizational policies pursued by the regional authorities—promotes the

region's competitive advantage. Second, the role of the features of the society, including both culture (Casson 1993; Casson, Loveridge, and Singh 1997) and the availability of institutional infrastructure such as educational and innovatory systems, laws protecting property rights, and a good communications network, and a sophisticated financial system.[26] Some aspects of this dimension can be improved in the medium term by a business-friendly government ethos—particularly with respect to technical education, innovation, and entrepreneurship.[27]

5. Finally, the '*commercial environment*' describes the setting in which business operates within a region.[28] Internationally, differences in political stability would be included in the commercial environment, together with the ethical underpinnings of institutions and setting. In more mundane terms, the commercial environment may be seen as reflecting the degree to which the society relies—or does not rely—on the business sector to provide the revenues and resources needed for the implementation of economic programmes, e.g. those to do with the ecological environment, health, defence, etc. In other words, as articulated by Gray (1995), the commercial environment incorporates the degree to which national or subnational governments may limit the freedom of action on the part of corporations, and hold them to behavioural and other standards which are more rigorous and costly than those demanded by markets. At the same time, it supports the notion that governments, by a variety of actions, may help facilitate the efficient operation of markets by the provision of public goods, by the promotion of flexible labour markets, and by a vigorously pursued competition policy.

The commercial environment, so conceived, can be conceptualized in terms of the net tax burden (NTB) (see Box 16.1). The NTB is defined as the revenues raised from a particular sector of business activity plus any additional costs (such as compliance costs of regulations and mandatory payments for workers' benefits) imposed upon it, less the value of the public goods supplied to its benefit.[29] The net tax burden is likely to be greater in countries/regions in which society seeks to establish a welfare state. The net tax burden is likely to be activity-specific, depending upon the supply of infrastructure and other benefits to that activity, by any activity-specific fiscal incentives or reduction in the degree of regulatory severity, and by any protection given from foreign competition.[30] Given the importance of R&D for the development of subnational clusters, one strategy is to attract a lead-corporation in a particular line of activity or, alternatively, to establish a basic R&D operation as a magnet, and a source of benefits spin-off to related activities.[31] The net tax burden may be seen as the main means by which a regional authority can affect the competitiveness of a firm or an industry and make its immobile assets attractive to mobile investment.[32]

The five categories of attributes include one—the commercial environment—that can respond quickly to changes in government policy, and two—the resource

Box 16.1. Net tax burden[a]

> The *'Net Tax Burden'* for an incorporated firm (including a foreign affiliate estab-
> lished in the microregion) is defined as the ratio of the *net* costs of government (as
> defined below) to value added within a region (clearly, it is the joint macroregional
> and microregional net burden which applies):
>   The *net costs of government* of the unit are equal to:
>   Total taxes paid to national and microregional governments
>   *Plus*
>   Out-of-pocket costs of compliance with government requirements and
>   regulations
>   *Less*
>   The value of benefits received from the provision of collective goods by
>   government including (non-exhaustively) is equal to:[b]
>   1. revenues from subsidies
>   2. value of an educated labour force
>   3. value of physical infrastructure
>   4. value of government-supplied (or any subsidy element paid for) techno-
>   logical infrastructure
>   5. export support and facilitation
>   6. benefits to business of social programmes

  [a] The concept of the net tax burden applies equally well to competition among macroregions.
  [b] Each microregion will have some influence over the net tax burden borne by firms located within
its boundaries so that two competing microregions may not impose the same net tax burden. Of course,
given the greater mobility of factors of production within a macroregion (nation state or bloc), it is
possible for certain types of skilled labour to be attracted from neighbouring microregions so that
the definition of net tax burden does not hinge uniquely upon the expenditures of the government
of the host microregion.

base and the contribution of the region to managerial efficiency—that can be made
to respond only slowly. The remaining two categories cannot be influenced by
government policy within the time-frame of a single investment. Given that
the slow response of businesses to changes in the commercial environment, the
short-term effectiveness of general instruments at the disposal of government is
strictly limited. Certain aspects of all five attributes are likely to be activity- or
product-specific: of these project-specific tax incentives and the benefits to be
derived from (inherited) clusters are particularly important. The lags will be shorter
for project-specific measures than for across-the-board measures.

4. Operationalizing the Model

In considering the intent and geographical distribution of locational assets, a firm
will usually have a variety of options at its disposal.[33] Each investment project
will have its own set of requirements, and the attractiveness of a particular location
essentially rests on the degree to which the needs of the project are compatible

with the attributes of a region. A firm may be seen as identifying a short list of possible sites, and then to give each an absolute score or numerical value for each of the five dimensions. The scores will be weighted and then added to determine the attractiveness of individual regions.[34] When two or more regions score approximately equally, the location decision may be made by the individual preferences of the chief executive officer (or the board of directors) (Dunning 1998), but close scores may also prompt a decision to attempt to extract (additional) concessions from governments to improve the economic prospects of the new unit. Only then will the location decision be sensitive to regional inducements.

Regional economic policy must, therefore, confront the basic attractiveness of the region in terms of its ability to make the 'short list'—general policy—and, having made the 'short list', the extent to which project-specific policy can generate a bundle of inducements which will attract (or retain) the value-adding activity. General policy will be identified largely with the business friendliness of the commercial environment (UNCTAD 1998). It can be industry- or activity- or even firm-specific when a mix of governmental incentives is tailor-made to cater to the needs of particular investors as, for example, in the case of the Nissan investment in north-east England in the late 1980s, or when emphasis is placed on a particular form of infrastructure. Project-specific policy is likely to be limited to activities by governments in microregions (and lower layers).[35] Donahue (1997: 171–82) reviews empirical studies on the US experience of the sensitivity of site selection to microregional financial incentives. Empirical studies seem to indicate that the relative (gross) burden of taxation is not important, and that much greater emphasis should be placed on the fundamental attributes of the region, and especially the existence of infrastructure and the assured availability of an appropriately skilled workforce: the latter two are incorporated in the concept of net tax burden.[36]

The attractiveness of a region with given attributes will depend predominantly upon the characteristics of the incoming investment. An investment, the purpose of which is to gain access to a large local market, will be little influenced by factors other than the locational attributes of the microregion.[37] When the project depends heavily on the availability of the attributes of a particular industrial cluster, policy will not affect the outcome. It is reasonable, then, to surmise that the more specific the requirements of the project, the less is the scope for regional policy.[38] Policy measures will come into play when the project has no dominant specific features, and its requirements depend primarily upon the indigenous resources and capabilities of the region, and the costs of generic and some specific factors of production. Only under these conditions can governmental policies be expected to be decisive. In microregions in which the commercial environment has been determined by the macroregion, or has reached its limit of business friendliness, the remaining policies must be project-specific.

From this simple model, four inferences may be drawn: (i) product-and activity-specific attributes are important determinants of that part of a region's prosperity which is derived from spatially mobile activities; (ii) a subnational government's ability to enhance the relative attractiveness of the resources and capabilities within its jurisdiction is constrained—and possibly severely so—by the overarching structure of policies and regulations instituted by national or macroregional (e.g. the EU) governments; (iii) the degree to which a regional government can hope to change the relative attractiveness of its economy in the short run except by project-specific inducements is limited; (iv) given the potential importance of project-specific measures, the operational efficiency of the policy-making divisions of the regional government can be vital.[39] These inferences are assessed sequentially.

1. The absolute attractiveness of any region derives from the (relative) *goodness of fit* between the region's attributes, as described above, and the requirements of the investing firm. The most blatant examples of a good fit will probably derive from the existence of any agglomerative economies or a large market offered by the region. The cluster will make the region very attractive to firms in one industry (the cluster-industry) and reduce its attractiveness to firms in other industries.[40] From the latter's perspective, the region will lack the advantages of a suitable cluster, while the investments of the cluster-attracting industry will make general resources more costly, reduce the government's need to attract new industry, and probably dominate the mix of infrastructure supplied. In the same way, the presence of a large market betokens higher costs for generic resources.

2. The ability of a subnational government will inevitably be limited by the economic measures and the social environment created by the national government and/or macroregion.[41] This is, essentially, the 'commercial environment' and is, in most microregions, overwhelmingly determined by factors outside its control. Since people are freely mobile within a country or macroregion, a microregion, unless endowed with a distinctive culture and language, can have no important general effect on the quality of labour supplied (although the existence of a cluster is likely to contribute to the supply of highly skilled industry-specific labour). Although subnational governments have some authority to raise revenues, e.g. via property and sales taxes, and to devote those revenues to measures designed to promote local economic prosperity, the scope of these measures is limited: they cannot contravene the rules laid down by the national or macroregional government. Rates of national tax levied on corporations, the quantity and quality of infrastructure, the scope of regulatory oversight for both ecological and competition policy, the protection of property rights and intellectual capital are all determined at the national or macroregional level and constitute constraints for microregional policies.

   In essence then, microregional policies are best considered as permissible deviations from the national or macroregional set of policies. This does not limit the effectiveness of regional policies when the competing microregion is within the same nation, and there may exist some scope for variation in the microregional NTB at the project-specific level.[42] When a subnational region in a large country is in competition with a small nation, the latter may have the advantage insofar as it is not so closely constrained by economy-wide regulations—although, it may still be bound by international agreements on, for example, ecological practices. There is, then, a substantial difference between competition within a major regional bloc or between a large federal nation, and that between nations. The important aspect here is the degree of independence enjoyed by the subnational region. This can vary substantially depending on, for example, whether the macroregion is the European Union or a federated nation state, e.g. the USA, the North American Free Trade Agreement, or the Asia-Pacific Economic Community.

The welfare of a microregion is likely to benefit from the macro-organizational policies of the nation state or macroregion of which it is part insofar as they help promote its own. However, within a large macroregion, there are likely to exist pockets of disadvantaged areas which enjoy a below-average GDP per capita. Frequently, these microregions are not well endowed with resources, and therefore, in the absence of some political power, the mobile resources, particularly skilled labour, are likely to be attracted away to more prosperous regions: when the microregion is politically powerful or important, any policies which are designed to improve its welfare will normally depend heavily on subvention from the central government.[43]

3. A subnational government, faced with the task of drawing in or retaining mobile assets, can either improve business friendliness of the commercial environment of the spatial domain for which it is responsible—particularly in respect of the quality of life it offers—and/or focus its attention more narrowly on making its indigenous resources and capabilities more effective for a particular kind of investment or, more probably, an individual project. Several factors suggest that it is unlikely that a subnational region will adopt a general policy: as this would not distinguish between spatially mobile and spatially immobile activities. Given limited resources with which to promote the attraction and retention of economic activities, administrators will believe that they can compete better at a project level by applying the resources to any project whose needs closely fit the microregion's attributes.[44]

Policy-makers tend to argue in favour of a bureaucratic approach whereby civil servants (possibly with the support of elected officials) will set policy at the individual project level within a given budget constraint, and with delegated limits to their authority. The task of the policy-makers, then, is to identify projects which have a good 'fit' with local attributes, and to provide the investing firms with incentives which apply to their particular needs and which make the location as, or more, attractive as any alternative location (subject always to the proviso that the investment is expected to generate net positive effects for the microregion).

4. Given the potential importance of project-specific measures, the operational efficiency of the policy-making division of the regional government can be vital. This presents severe challenges: the first is the possibility that the government of the microregion will hamstring the task of those entrusted with policy; the second is the inherent difficulty of the task of picking a winning project; and the third is the possibility that the microregions will compete against each other to the ultimate benefit of the investing firm and, within a single country, to the possible detriment of the national interests.[45]

Moreover, the quintessential bureaucratic form of organization usually produced by political wrangling is unlikely to take into account the need of firms for quick and authoritative information and decisions. For firms contemplating an investment, the costs of delay in gathering information can be important and can result in the elimination of a microregion from the feasible set of locations (Gray and Wallace 1999).

5. Extending the Model

The preceding section used only a single dimension for the region's objective function (increasing future per-capita GRP); this, while defensible, may be less than ideal. Significant concern with some less desirable effects of pro-growth policies, e.g. on the environment or on income distribution and the plight of marginalized workers, will require, at a minimum, a two-target objective function (Wood 1995). A further complication may exist when the political microregion embraces more than a single economic microregion, and intraregional inequalities or structural distortions constrain the freedom of action of policy-makers to cater to mobile projects.[46]

The model used by Dunning *et al.* (1998: 24) to identify the relations between measures available to the national governments and/or macroregional authorities, and those available to microregional governments in the creation and sustenance of regional or competitiveness[47] visualizes the possibility of a ' "virtuous circle" of growth'. Good general policies project specific policies at the microregion level, reinforced by good macroeconomic and macro-organizational policies, at the national or macro- and regional level, generate a virtuous cycle, with feedback mechanisms which will steadily increase competitiveness. By contrast, if a microregion becomes locked into a 'vicious cycle', it steadily loses competitiveness; and as it does so unemployment increases and the GRP per capita falls. Moreover, a vicious cycle will be exacerbated by the repercussions of poor economic performance on crime rates, health indicators, and other 'social pathological indices' which have been empirically shown to be sensitive to macroeconomic performance (Brenner 1976; Merva and Fowles 1992). To the extent that to reduce these disbenefits more resources need to be allocated to health services, crime prevention, and incarceration of criminals, the resources available for improvements in the commercial environment and for financial inducements to mobile assets will be reduced.

The problem of an ever-growing gap between rich and poor (political) micro-regions has been analysed by Tannenwald (1998). Tannenwald addresses the ability of states in the USA to fund general competitiveness-enhancing measures, such as education and infrastructure and to offer monetary and other inducements to mobile-created assets. Using measures of 'fiscal capacity' and 'fiscal need', he identifies 'fiscal comfort' (the difference between the two). Based on comparisons of performance in 1987 and 1994, Tannenwald (ibid.) reveals that there was a wide disparity of fiscal comfort among US states varying from 152 in Nevada to sixty-eight in Mississippi (national average equals 100). What is crucial is that the effort by fiscally uncomfortable states do not show evidence of increasing their 'tax effort'.[48]

The degree of fiscal discomfort must handicap a microregion if only because the investment is made up front and the benefits comes later; and also because, for a microregion in an industrialized nation, the states with the highest levels of fiscal discomfort are likely to be the ones subjected to the most intensive rivalry from foreign developing countries competing to attract mobile created assets. Unless the host microregion can encourage its surplus resources to migrate to other states, the issue of inequality can hardly be omitted from its objective welfare function.[49]

This problem of inequality raises serious questions about the legitimacy of decentralization of national or macroregional governmental responsibilities in a world in which assets with above-average productivity are mobile and sought after while below-average productivity assets are repulsed and neglected. In an international context, regions seeking to attract created assets will have total demand for them greater than their available supply. Some regions are destined to find breaking a 'vicious cycle' progressively more difficult (Gray 1998*a*).

The possibility of different degrees of fiscal discomfort and severe inter-microregional competition for mobile assets conjures up the possibility of a 'race to the bottom' in welfare-enhancing policies. In addition, attempts to attract quasi-rent-producing investments may turn the terms of trade between mobile and immobile assets more sharply in favour of the former than would be absolutely necessary and will, in this way, aggravate the inequality of income distribution within and among microregions.

6. Regional Policy in a System of Knowledge Capitalism

To this point the argument has not explicitly distinguished among mobile investments by the *degree* of their knowledge-intensity. Undertakings with very heavy reliance upon human and physical intellectual capital create special interest in a world of global capitalism, and in the accompanying tendency of large firms to form alliances with entities that, in other activities, are competitors.[50] This section addresses the following hypothesis: because the requirements of more knowledge-intensive investment are likely to be more demanding in the attributes required for an acceptable location, the more knowledge-intensive the mobile investment, the less likely are regional policy initiatives and inducements to affect its location.[51] While, in principle, it would be possible for a subnational region to focus on customized attributes (infrastructure of varying kinds) to entice a knowledge-intensive investment, such attributes are likely to require a long lead-time and, therefore, to have, in the eyes of the investing corporation, a high degree of uncertainty.[52] Moreover, such expenditures would be likely to strain the financial resources of a subnational region although such expenditures could be, and quite frequently are, financed with a national government or macroregional authority.

Highly technology-reliant investments are likely to be drawn to areas in which a suitable cluster of related firms exists and in which industry-specific infrastructure (physical and technological) is in ample supply.[53] The establishment of strategic-asset- or capability-seeking affiliates is likely to consider an agglomeration of innovating activities, a critical attribute of any location. An R&D cluster is a special type of cluster because, once established, the firms present are likely to contribute much of the additional attributes needed to make the cluster self-sustaining. The influence of general microregional policy measures will be negligible. This assessment is likely to apply equally to knowledge-intensive strategic alliances.

Marketing-and-distribution (M&D) affiliates without any supportive manufacturing facilities will necessarily be located near a major market. It is possible that, in some countries or regions in which there is no dominating favoured location, the location of an M&D affiliates could be influenced by microregional inducements.[54]

By contrast, efficiency-seeking mobile investment is likely to be especially susceptible to actions taken by microregional authorities. The location of such units is likely to rest heavily on the cost and availability of generic assets such as skilled and unskilled labour, land and natural resources, and those that make up the commercial and institutional environment. The more microregional governments are able to influence the supply of these assets, e.g. by land grants, rent rebates, and labour subsidies, the more significant will be their role in influencing the ultimate site-selection of efficiency-seeking FDI.

The greater the importance of proprietary knowledge and complementary assets, the more will an investment be likely to prerequire certain attributes from its location. In such circumstances, general microregional policies are unlikely to be of major importance, while specific policies will be much more difficult to implement.

7. Dynamic Aspects of Competition among Microregions

The time dimension of a model of regional competitiveness policy is important because the relative attractiveness of a microregion may be subject to frequent change, for example, as a result of technological advances as well as of changes in policies by rival governments. To use the neoclassical concept of *maximizing future per-capita product* may imply more accuracy and less awareness of the uncertainties of reality than is appropriate for any analysis of a knowledge-based economy. In addition, a comparative-static general equilibrium framework has its weaknesses in an age of spatially mobile created assets. Thus, policy measures can be seen as being formulated in time t, implemented in $t+1$, and becoming effective with varying lags in $t+n$,[55] and policy-makers rely essentially on a capital-budgeting-under-uncertainty approach.

Although spatial mobility has increased over time, many existing foreign production units were put in place before executives and boards of directors were fully cognizant with (i) the concept and implications of inter-regional mobility, (ii) coordinating value-adding activities located in different macro- and microregions, and (iii) the role of microregional authorities in influencing the availability and quality of region-specific resources and capabilities.[56] There may exist substantial amounts of existing capacity which could profitably be relocated from high-cost (industrialized) to low-cost (developing) regions: the actual relocation cannot be expected to adjust quickly to the increase in the ease of mobility of value-adding activities (Gray 1998b). There is, therefore, an adjustment process under way as existing resources and capabilities adapt to the new, more liberal conditions with a lag as well as responding to ongoing evolution.

All of these events are taking place in a world economy that is growing and becoming increasingly reliant on created knowledge-intensive assets. During the adjustment period, inter-microregional competition may become particularly severe. Gray (1998b) recognizes several phenomena which have delayed the full impact of the relocation of spatially mobile activities on labour markets in industrialized countries being reached.[57] The factors impeding a quick response through relocation of capacity to differences in attributes among microregions include:

1. the larger the amount of existing assets which are no longer location-bound and which can, ultimately, be profitably relocated;[58]
2. the low availability of workers in low-cost regions with the necessary levels of education to absorb the necessary skill upgrading and the absence of the necessary complementary and supportive infrastructure;
3. the rate of growth of the total output of knowledge-based products in the region, e.g. this attribute reflects the possibility that an increase in total output of these goods could utilize much of the growth of capacity to receive relocated activities in developing microregions; clearly, most of the FDI considered here is efficiency-seeking;
4. the existence of adequate rates of return realized on older units in high-cost regions in a buoyant world economy;
5. the existence of uncertainties about the benefits of relocation—especially in countries prone to financial stress;[59] and
6. the existence or regulations which require indemnification or compensation of displaced workers.

The match between the needs of an investment project and the attributes of the microregion can vary through time 'on both sides of the equation'. Micro-regional clusters can lose their strength in the face of technological evolution in the industry and competing clusters can come into being elsewhere. It is necessary, then, to consider this 'dynamic' aspect of policies as competing microregions seek to establish the characteristics that lead to the creation of both static and dynamic externalities.

Clusters (microregions) will lose their appeal as and when the (relative) strength of the external economies which they generate wane. Such a loss might derive from: (i) the existence of a revolutionary new technology which does not benefit from the external economies available in the microregion;[60] (ii) the erosion of the net benefits provided by the existing cluster, because of its failure to maintain the quantity and quality of public goods (physical and socioeconomic infrastructure); (iii) the creation elsewhere of a more attractive cluster; and (iv) the pursuance of more aggressive competitor microregional authorities. Each of these possibilities can lead to an exodus of value-adding capacity, as well as a reduction of inward investment. Each also underlines the need for a proactive macroorganizational policy.

The possibility of a major technological advance leading to the creation of a new cluster located in another microregion is a very real one. Major changes in industry technologies do come about but, given the attachment of an industry to an existing locale, a large-scale exodus for this reason is unlikely to happen without being accompanied by a failure in microregional policy to sustain its competitive advantages on the scale needed by the incumbent firms (example (ii) above). Such a failure is considered to be a real possibility in Bangalore (Balasubramanyam and Balasubramanyam, Chapter 13).

The creation of a new cluster by deliberate plan is an important undertaking and requires commitable support by the government of the microregion. Peters, Young, and Hood (Chapter 9) identify a serious commitment on the part of Scotland to create a microregion with tremendous externalities for software and related industries. Enright (Chapter 15) describes the evolvement of the financial services sector in Hong Kong in similar terms. The success of such endeavours will most certainly have major repercussions for other microregions in which these two sectors may equally flourish; and the greater the geographic proximity, the more likely they will respond vigorously to the challenge. One might expect that the success of Scottish (or Hong Kong) regional policy will have adverse repercussions on inward FDI in adjacent regions: *per contra*, the more effective the policy response in these regions capable of supporting software and related industries, the less is the probability that the Scots will be able to create a viable and, ultimately, self-supporting microregion.

It is important that any such effort to create a viable cluster should place substantial stress on the development of R&D activities. Strength in R&D activities is, as noted in the preceding section, likely to make the cluster self-sustaining with only small marginal contributions from public authorities. The problem with the policy of creating such a cluster is the need to select a critical mass of technology which has great potential for future development, and this involves introducing a crystal ball into the policy decision.

Finally, there is the possibility that a cluster will decompose as a result of a major change in political risk in a country in which general attributes outweigh the benefits of external economies. The danger of decline in Baden-Württemberg (Chapter 10 above) is an obvious example of such an event: this change was a direct outcome of the breakdown of the U.S.S.R. in 1991, and the ability of the Czech Republic to pursue market-driven economic policies. In addition to differences in real wage-levels, the rigidity of the German social contract has not allowed either the national economy or its component microregions to adapt to the new conditions of spatially mobile investments. The exodus of the wooden furniture industry from Michigan to the southern USA in the late 1940s and early 1950s provides a similar example.[61]

8. Conclusions

Because general (across-the-board) measures have longer lags, there will be a tendency for these measures to constitute the major component of the set of policies of the nation state and/or the macroregion of which it is part. Project-specific measures which can generate more immediate effects (within the lifespan of site-selection for a single investment) are more likely to be instituted at the microregional level.

This general statement receives some support from the data set out in Tables 16.1 and 16.2, which summarize the authors' judgement about the way in which the impact of individual dimensions of policy devolve on different levels of authority. Table 16.1 addresses the major dimensions of policy and Table 16.2 the subcomponents of macro-organizational policy. The dimensions in which microregions have substantial powers, tend to be those which can be focused on a sector or an individual project. Just as the attractiveness of a microregion depends upon the match between its own attributes and those which are important to the investing from, there is also a potential, but possibly serendipitous, relationship between the attributes of the microregion and the industries which benefit more from the composition of macro-organizational policy.[62]

The dimensions of macro-organizational policies are largely laid down at the nation state or macroregional level. However, depending upon the political structure of the macroregion, microregions can be afforded some freedom of manœuvre and, of course, have the option of enforcing macroregional fiats less conscientiously.[63] The model and such evidence as it has been possible to adduce, suggest that proactive general regional policies can play a long-term role in attracting knowledge-intensive investments by making the commercial environment friendly to such investments. This constitutes, in essence, the creation of an industry- or sector-specific cluster. Macroregional, general policies may

TABLE 16.1. The relative importance of levels of policy dimensions in attracting investment[a]

Function or practice	Level of governance	
	Macroregional (Supranational or national)[b]	Microregional (Subnational)
General investment climate[c]	XXX	X
Regulatory/enabling mechanisms[c]	XXX	X
Efficiency of macroeconomic policies[c]	XXX	0
Macroorganizational policies[c]	XXX	0→X
Institutional infrastructure	XXX	X
Quality of immobile public assets[d]	XX	XXX
Firm- or industry-specific incentives	X	XXX
Importance of promotion/marketing	X	XXX

[a] Importance ranges from 0 through XXX.

[b] The net benefit deriving to a microregion from a macroregion can, as noted above, pass through an intermediate level of government (a nation in the European Union). The benefit will depend on the division of responsibility between the macroregion and the intermediate region.

[c] These four components constitute the main elements determining the business friendliness of the macroregional commercial environment.

[d] Immobile public assets are those assets (external benefits) which characterize clusters: they can be deliberately created (Peters, Young, and Hood, Ch. 9) and usually have a bias towards certain industries, or they can be inherited. It would be possible to include the 'net tax burden' in this category.

TABLE 16.2. The relative importance of levels of macro-organizational components in attracting investment

Component	Level of governance	
	Macroregion	Microregion
Innovation systems	XXX	X→XX
Intellectual property rights	XXX	0
Competition policy	XXX	0
Transport policy	XX→XXX	0
Communications policy	XXX	0
Ecological policy	XXX	X→XX[a]
International trade policy	XXX	0
FDI policy	XXX	X[a]
Education policy	XX	XX
Industrial policy	XXX	X
Regional policy	XXX	X→XX
Social contract[b]	XX	X
Safety regulations[c]	XX	0→X

[a] Ecological policy is ordinarily set at the macroregional level but it is frequently capable to discriminate among regions so that poorer regions are given licence to weaken macroregional constraints in order to attract polluting industries (Gray and Walter 1983).

[b] The social contract refers to the provision of government-financed benefits and has implications for the net tax burden.

[c] Safety regulations can vary among regions but the general pattern is set at the macroregional level and the freedom of action at the microregional level can be quite small.

contribute to increases in per-capita GRP by creating a commercial environment that is 'business friendly' and by legislating and enforcing measures repelling and neglecting the welfare of 'undesirable' constituents.

However, much more important for better economic performance are the existence of a good resource base of immobile assets,[64] the existence of clusters of technology-related activities, and a degree of fiscal comfort which allows microregional government to supply the necessary support services for continued growth. This presents a model in which virtue is 'rewarded' and vice is 'punished'. At the same time, this outcome suggests that there can be serious political problems for macroregions, particularly federal systems, which do not confront the inequality of incomes among regions, and which begin to investigate the best way in which a central government can temper the inequality while ensuring the continued growth of successful regions.[65]

Per contra, efficiency-seeking investments which prerequire little in the way of specific factors which cannot be supplied either by the investing corporation or within the macroregion, are likely to be sensitive to inducements. Subnational regions engage in these policies at the serious risk of engaging in 'a race to the bottom' or of striving to be the lowest bidder in terms of self-interest.

NOTES

1. The major difference will be the greater intranational mobility of some factors of production which are likely to be immobile among countries or macroregions.
2. As e.g. have been identified in several earlier chapters in this volume.
3. Section 7 briefly raises the issue of the permanence of the advantages of a cluster's external economies and therefore of its viability.
4. Tinbergen (1970) sets out a theory of policy: policy instruments whose values government can control or affect are manipulated in order to approach a specified set of targets (the objective function).
5. As used in this chapter, the concept of an alliance excludes alliances connected with franchising, licensing, and other forms of organization which serve as a substitute for direct investment by a dominant MNE with a small host-country unit.
6. The North American Free Trade Area (NAFTA) could constitute the ultimate macroregion in North America and could ultimately be overtaken by the proposed Free Trade Area of the Americas.
7. The EU distinguishes three levels of *nomenclature des unites territoriales statistiques*; level 1 is the nation and level 3 is equivalent to a French *département* or an English county. In addition, it distinguishes two kinds of region: a least favoured region and a development area (EPRC 1997: 86–7).
8. This presents a potential inconsistency when different parts of the world are considered: for example, a state or microregion in the USA could find itself in competition with a Caribbean *nation* or macroregion in seeking to attract an investment. It

is possible that the macroregion has greater flexibility in policy-making than a micro-region. Within a national macroregion, competition among microregions will be 'horizontal' but, internationally, competition need not be horizontal.

9. 'Institutions' here is used in North's (1990) meaning a nation's inherited code of behaviour and taboos, its body of laws and statutes, and the way in which these constraints operate to control human interaction.

   In the EU, nations surrendered much of their policy discretion to Brussels at Maastricht in 1992 and by subscribing to the introduction of the euro in 1998. By the time this book is published, there may be very little contextual difference between the EU and its component nation states.

10. This is a very simple objective function or target and is capable of elaboration. However, elaboration could add significantly to the complexity of the theory and, particularly so, if the region's objective function includes certain aspects of the social contract which may be at odds with growth-maximization, e.g. a more equal distribution of income may be sacrificed by a successful policy of encouraging growth since many technology-reliant firms will utilize higher skills and demand for low-skilled workers will decrease (Gray 1984; Wood 1995). This problem is considered in Section 3.

11. These latter measures generally aim to identify those activities whose operations are sensitive to inducements (financial and/or non-financial), and use such inducements to attract or retain desirable mobile investment (or remain) within the region. However, this may be seen as a questionable form of industrial policy for governments to attempt to 'pick the [future] winners' (Schultze 1983). This concern remains when one possible policy for disadvantaged regions is to identify a potential growth node and to establish a centre for excellence in that speciality within the region (Dunning, Bannerman, and Lundan 1998).

12. The quasi-rents may be earned from activities in a different (lower-cost) region as well as in the home microregion. These (after-tax) quasi-rents can, in principle, be 'repatriated' to the home microregion. The most obvious example would be the funding of research and development in the home microregion from profits and management fees generated from out-of-region activities. However, the quasi-rents could be 'repatriated' to a different microregion in the home country (macroregion).

13. Herrigel (ch. 10) shows how taking advantage of the cost advantages of producing in the Czech Republic was deemed essential by BMW.

14. While the text identifies the attraction and retention of investments in technology-reliant value-adding capacity as the focus of policy, it must be recognized that sub-national regions face competition for complementary inputs from other regions in the same macroeconomy. Engineers and other professional workers must be retained in or attracted to the region just as much as investment projects.

15. Non-financial inducements can be seen as involving non-pecuniary expenditures.

16. This aspect of policy is not covered in this chapter and is reminiscent of Ozawa's wild-geese flying theory in which deliberate sloughing off of an activity was recognized as necessary in a fully employed economy in which the importance of knowledge-intensive activities was growing (Ozawa 1992).

17. The purpose of a mix of incentives and requirements is to ensure that the enterprise's activities contributes to regional goals: this possibility implies a multidimensional objective function.

18. Identification of the boundaries of an economic microregion will be difficult and the boundaries may vary through time.

19. There is no suggestion that the existence of a headquarters unit in one region implies the existence of less technology-reliant activities in the same region.

20. The idea of using composite categories of attributes obviously derives from Porter (1990). Porter tried to explain the competitiveness of national industries producing technology-reliant (modern) goods rather than site-attractiveness (location) but since site-attractiveness is an important determinant of market share, the benefit of emending Porter's apparatus to fit the present problem is quite natural.

21. There is an inevitable degree of overlap with Porter (1990).

22. Individuals possess interregional mobility within a macroregion—particularly highly skilled workers who are valuable complementary assets to created assets owned by technology-reliant firms.

23. It is possible to argue that Porter's diamond was really a statement of the much broader set of determinants of net exports than was dreamt of either in the factor-proportions model or in the new theory of international trade (Helpman and Krugman 1985).

24. As e.g. identified at a microeconomic level by Nelson and Winter (1982) in their evolutionary theory of the firm.

25. Storper and Scott (1995) define a region (within a country) in economic terms: it will have better transportation and communications linkages within the region than with other regions as well as a history of developing areas of specialization in activities which are conducted better among units in close geographical proximity.

26. Differences in political risk would enter into this dimension in international comparisons.

27. These issues clearly assume major importance when an attempt is made to create a cluster by providing all of the necessary attributes for a cluster and then attracting some lead investments which will attract others.

28. This concept is what the Institute for Management Development (1997) attempts to measure for individual nations (macroregions): of course, any such measure must be a general concept and subject to significant industry-specific variability.

29. This dimension will be virtually impossible to quantify although the Institute for Management Development (1997) identifies roughly 250 variables which it uses to compute a country's competitiveness coefficient.

30. This kind of discrimination can be instituted at the firm level. Tax laws which allow expenditures on R&D to be expensed distinguish between physical- and knowledge-capital subsidies in that the former provides a tax offset as its value is decreased while the latter is expensed at once. This may be an important contributor to the success of a technology-reliant industry in comparison with older industries which rely heavily on physical capital.

31. For an assessment of the importance of trying to foster the development of a cluster see Dunning, Bannerman, and Lundan (1998). Note that the idea of establishing an academic or public research centre as a growth node is likely to be very expensive and require luck in the ability to pick a winning area of research.

32. In general, the non-pecuniary benefits supplied by government receive inadequate recognition by regional authorities, e.g. the EU, even though their importance is acknowledged in studies of the determinants of site location. This may result from the decision to treat general measures used to promote location attractiveness as 'non-incentives' (EPRC 1997: 153).

33. Note that the process of location decision is not cost-free and the ease with which information can be gathered from the subnational government is important. For a more detailed analysis, see Gray and Wallace (1999).

34. By introducing the relative appeal of different regions at this stage, it is possible to consider the assessment of individual regions as being absolute rather than relative.

35. For a somewhat dated analysis of the sensitivity of MNC international locational decisions to government influence see Gray and Walter (1983). For a review of empirical studies on US experience of the sensitivity of site selection to subnational financial incentives, see Donahue (1997: 171–82). Empirical studies seem to indicate that the (gross) burden of taxation is not important, and that more emphasis should be placed on the attributes of the region—usually the attributes which are inherited—and the existence of infrastructure (the latter being incorporated in the concept of 'net tax burden'). It follows that the greater the weights accorded to those dimensions which are immune to governmental policy, the less the locational decision is subject to policy inducements.

36. This reported insensitivity of location to policy inducements is considered in greater depth in Section 6.

37. If the market exceeds the (political) boundaries of the microregion, then there is room for competition among a group of microregions: the huge tri-state market of southern New York State, south-western Connecticut, and northern New Jersey is a clear case in point. The competition among microregions within a single economic region is damaging to the individual political jurisdictions.

38. The more general the requirements e.g. a manufacturing plant relying largely on transferred technologies and (immobile) labour can be fiercely competed for.

    In the UK, Nissan specified the requirement for locating an assembly plant that the region had no previous auto production. Clearly, this was a specific requirement which dominated any policy variable available to Sunderland.

39. The efficiency of the Irish national government policy has long been recognized: a single agency is able to provide a firm with a complete list of options available in the country and to identify any inducements which may be applicable.

40. Vertically integrated firms need not have all of their activities in a single region: for example, a region with a strong support for R&D and headquarters activities will be able to conduct its activities which are less skill-intensive in other regions.

41. This is illustrated in Dunning, Bannerman, and Lundan (1998: 23–9). The apparatus developed there distinguishes between macro-organizational policy and fiscal and monetary policies both of which are beyond the scope of the microregion. The options left available for the microregional government include meso-initiatives targeted at developing or enhancing a cluster and project-specific inducements.

42. Direct subsidies are likely to be capital subsidies rather than operating subsidies, if only because the firm will respond more sensitively to upfront support and will have reservations about the willingness or ability of governments to continue support in the future when the facility has been established.

43. Dunning, Bannerman, and Lundan (1998) analyse the problem of enhancing the GDP per capita and the competitiveness of Northern Island as a microregion within the UK which is, in turn, a member of the European Union.

44. There would be no point in New York or New Jersey seeking to attract a project which uses blue-collar labour intensively to manufacture technology-reliant differentiated goods. The state of Alabama competed heavily and won, at great expense, the competition to host the North American Mercedes-Benz plant.

45. Donahue (1997: ch. 7) sees this as a major danger within the USA especially when the investment is designed to serve the host-country market.
46. The regional government is then faced with the problem of pursuing balanced or unbalanced geographic (submicroregional) growth.
47. Strangely enough, the model seems to attribute the possibility of a 'virtuous cycle' exclusively to policy and, in the process, ignores what many would consider to be the vital factors of inherited resources and inherited industries. The ability of successful enterprises to perpetuate both themselves and the growing prosperity of the microregion derive in part from any external economies which they may create but, probably more importantly, the high net cash flow they generate. A high free cash flow can fund investment in R&D in the host region as well as allowing freedom of manoeuvre for firms' competitive policies (Milberg and Gray 1992).
48. This cannot be explained by any fiscally equalizing pattern of aid given by the federal government.
49. Donahue (1997: 132–43) identifies the pattern of behaviour within the USA towards undesirable constituents: those which are mobile are repelled while those which are immobile are neglected.
50. As used in this chapter, the concept of an alliance excludes alliances connected with franchising, licensing, and other forms of organization which serve as a substitute for direct investment by a dominant firm.
51. Thereby supporting the conclusions of many studies of the unimportant role of relative gross tax burdens on location (Donahue 1997: 171–82).
52. The likelihood that a subnational region could supply such attributes *ex ante* in the expectation of attracting knowledge-intensive activities at some future time seems remote.
53. But see Section 7.
54. If an M&D unit is located together with a headquarters unit, the importance of proximity to a major market may be reduced.
55. This suggests that competition between governments could be as time-sensitive as competition among technology-reliant firms because there is an inevitable lag between action and result: a policy measure with a pronounced lag incorporated in, say, microregion A must be matched by microregion B before the policy has become effective if microregion A is not to gain an advantage.
56. Donahue (1997: 75) reports that a single microregion in the USA offers over twenty different kinds of financial support for incoming projects together with four kinds of export-assistance programmes, technical help from nine programmes, and several sorts of workforce assistance.
57. On the implications of the increase in locational mobility of value-adding activities and the transfer of activities to developing economies on labour markets in the industrialized world, see Gray (1984) and Wood (1995).
58. The higher the level of skills and sophistication of the activities to which the microregion is best suited, the greater is the volume of such activities likely to be.
59. This is an extremely important issue as this chapter is being written. A history of financial crisis can increase the level of uncertainty allowed for in the net present value estimates substantially.
60. For an account of the way in which traditional British automobile centres lost out when Japanese auto-makers became the centre of automotive production in Britain,

see UNCTAD (1995: 234–6). Here the main cause was the existence of negative (labour) attributes in the clusters outweighing the benefits.

61. The southern USA is well known for its opposition to labour unions and its so-called 'right-to-work laws' (see Wallace, ch. 8).

62. The relationship may not be wholly serendipitous since different microregions will have different degrees of political influence at the policy-making centre of the macroregion.

63. This could allow the regional effects of the Single Market legislation in 1992 in the EU to be countered.

64. Skilled labour and intelligent, industrious labour that can be upgraded are both spatially mobile within the macroregion.

65. See the very detailed analysis of the EU's regulations which discriminate among regions in terms of the inward investment incentives which individual regions are permitted to offer (EPRC 1997: ch. 5).

REFERENCES

Aharoni, Y. (1993), 'From Adam Smith to Schumpeterian Global Firms', in A. M. Rugman and A. Verbeke (eds.), *Global Competition: Beyond the Three Generics* (Greenwich, Conn.: JAI Press): 17–39.

Barney, J. (1991), 'Firm Resources and Sustained Competitive Advantage', *Journal of Management* 17: 99–120.

Brenner, Harvey (1976), 'Estimating the Social Costs of National Economic Policy: Implications for Mental and Physical Health, and Criminal Aggression', Joint Economic Committee, 94th US Congress, 2nd Session, Oct.

Casson, Mark (1993), 'Cultural Determinants of Economic Performance', *Journal of Comparative Economics* 17 (Dec.): 418–42.

—— Loveridge, Ray, and Singh, Satwander (1997), 'Corporate Culture in Europe, Asia and North America', in Gavin Boyd and Alan M. Rugman (eds.), *Euro-Pacific Investment and Trade: Strategies and Structural Interdependencies* (Cheltenham: Edward Elgar): 96–129.

Donahue, John D. (1997), *Disunited States* (New York: Basic Books).

Dunning, John H. (1992), 'The Global Economy, Domestic Governance, Strategies and Transnational Corporations: Interactions and Policy Implications', *Transnational Corporations* 1 (Dec.): 7–46.

—— (1993), 'Globalization: The Challenge for National Economic Regimes', *Twenty-fourth Geary Lecture* (Dublin: Economic and Social Research Institute).

—— (1998), 'Location and Multinational Enterprise: A Neglected Factor', *Journal of International Business Studies* 29(1): 45–66.

—— Bannerman, Edward, and Lundan, Sarianna M. (1998), *Competitiveness and Industrial Policy in Northern Ireland* (Belfast: Northern Ireland Research Council Monograph Series, 5).

European Policies Research Centre (EPRC) (1997), *Policy Competition and Foreign Direct Investment in Europe* (Strathclyde: EPRC).

Gray, H. Peter (1984), 'Employment Arguments for Protection and the Vita Theory', *Eastern Economic Journal* 10 (Jan.–Mar.): 1–13.

—— (1995), 'The Modern Structure of International Economic Policies', *Transnational Corporations* 4 (Dec.): 49–66.

—— (1996), 'The Eclectic Paradigm: The Next Generation', *Transnational Corporations* 5 (Aug.): 51–65.

—— (1998*a*), 'Globalization: A Discriminating Force for Economic Development', in John H. Dunning (ed.), *Globalization: A Two-Edged Sword* (Newark: CIBER Occasional Studies in International Business, 3).

—— (1998*b*), 'Globalization and the Relocation of S-good Activities', Paper presented at the 1997 Annual Meetings of the International Trade and Finance Association, Atlantic City, 27–30 May.

—— (1999), *Global Economic Involvement* (Copenhagen: Copenhagen Business School Press).

—— and Wallace, Lorna H. (1999), 'The Implications of Globalization for Foreign Direct Investment in New Jersey', in John H. Dunning (ed.), *New Jersey in a Globalizing Economy* (Newark: Rutgers University, Center for International Business Education and Research).

—— and Walter, Ingo (1983), 'Investment-Related Trade Distortions in Petrochemicals', *Journal of World Trade Law* 17 (July–Aug.): 283–307.

Helpman, Elhanan, and Krugman, Paul R. (1985), *Market Structure and Foreign Trade* (Cambridge, Mass.: MIT Press).

Institute for Management Development (1997), *World Competitiveness Report 1997* (Lausanne: Institute for Management Development).

Merva, Mary, and Fowles, Richard (1992), 'The Effects of Diminished Economic Opportunity on Social Stress, Heart Attacks, Strokes and Crime', Briefing Paper, (Washington, DC: Economic Policy Institute).

Milberg, William S., and Gray, H. Peter (1992), 'International Competitiveness and Policy in Dynamic Industries', *Banca Nazionale del Lavoro Quarterly Review* (Mar.): 59–80.

Nelson, R. R., and Winter, S. G. (1982), *An Evolutionary Theory of Economic Change* (Cambridge, Mass.: Harvard University Press).

North, Douglass C. (1990), *Institutions, Institutional Change and Economic Performance* (New York: Cambridge University Press).

Ozawa, Terutomo (1992), 'Foreign Direct Investment and Economic Development', *Transnational Corporations* 1 (Feb.): 27–54.

Porter, Michael (1990), *The Competitive Advantage of Nations* (New York: Free Press).

Schultze, Charles L. (1983), 'Industrial Policy: A Solution in Search of a Problem', *California Management Review* 25: 5–15.

Scott, A. J. (1998), *Regions and the World Economy* (Oxford: Oxford University Press).

Storper, Michael, and Scott, Allen J. (1995), 'The Wealth of Regions: Market Forces and Policy Imperatives in Local and Global Context', *Futures* 27(5): 505–26.

Tannenwald, Robert (1998), 'Come the Devolution, Will States Be Able to Respond?', *New England Economic Review* (3): 53–73.

Tinbergen, Jan (1970), *On the Theory of Economic Policy* (Amsterdam, North-Holland).

UNCTAD (1995), *World Investment Report, 1995: Transnational Corporations and Competitiveness* (New York and Geneva: United Nations).

UNCTAD (1996), *Incentives and Foreign Direct Investment*, UNCTAD Current Studies Series A, 30 (New York and Geneva: United Nations).

—— (1998), *World Investment Report 1998: Trends and Determinants* (New York and Geneva: United Nations).

Wood, Adrian (1995), 'How Trade Hurts Unskilled Workers', *Journal of Economic Perspectives* 9 (Summer): 57–80.

17

The Changing Nature of Foreign Investment Policy in Europe:
From Promotion to Management

Ross Brown and Philip Raines

1. Introduction

In over two decades of active foreign direct investment (FDI) promotion, Western European approaches to attracting foreign investment have been characterized by increasing activity and sophistication in both policy design and delivery. While largely responding to the impact of greater competition between governments at a time of larger FDI flows, the scale and variety of policy responses reflect a realization that investment promotion requires both the designation of clear administrative responsibilities within government and a more adept use of both incentive and rules-based approaches to attracting FDI (see Raines and Brown 1999). Hence, at the same time as European countries have defined comprehensive national policies on foreign investment, they have developed institutional mechanisms for delivering different aspects of FDI policy. Hardly anywhere in Western Europe is the attraction of FDI projects currently regarded as an *ad hoc* policy activity: virtually every European country has considered FDI sufficiently important to warrant a set of specific policies and organizations (although with widely varying degrees of priority).

Against a background of rising FDI in Western Europe, national attitudes to the attraction of investment have become more positive. As in other parts of the world, the regulatory regimes operating in Western Europe's economies play a large role in determining the overall locational attractiveness of different countries. Policy stances designed to control and limit foreign ownership in Europe's national economies have gradually given way to more positive attitudes towards FDI, which has undoubtedly contributed to the expansion of FDI in Western Europe (UNCTAD 1995, 1997). At the same time, FDI-promotion policies have been given greater priority at regional level of policy-making as well. The number of regional agencies has increased in recent years, while foreign investment has become a more significant aspect of regional economic development strategies.

This chapter reviews these trends in Western European investment promotion policy with a view to understanding why the attraction of mobile investment has become more important in recent years and how this growth has influenced the development of policy towards FDI. In particular, it analyses the increasing region-alization of FDI promotion and the consequent shift in policy from strategies to attract investment to those designed to retain and deepen its impact on the local economy. In doing this, the chapter draws on case-study research of investment promotion undertaken by the authors.

The chapter begins with an overview of foreign investment promotion in Western Europe by examining the importance of attracting investment as a goal from a national-level perspective, emphasizing the change in attitudes that has taken place over the last decade. The section also includes a brief overview of the role of the European Commission in controlling competition between EU member states. Following this, we examine the motives and policy instruments under-pinning subnational actors in promoting FDI in Western Europe. To show these processes at work, case studies are used to compare the promotional policies of two European regions with very different approaches to attracting investment: Scotland and Nordrhein-Westfalen. The final section addresses the future of FDI-promotion policy.

2. National Attitudes to Foreign Investment Attraction in Europe

Although Western Europe in general presents a favourable and proactive FDI environment—as evidenced by the high volume of inward and outward flows —countries view the attraction of foreign investment with differing degrees of priority, both with respect to the impact on the national economy and as a contribution to solving regional economic problems. Moreover, it is clear that throughout Western Europe, the trend has been towards more positive and re-ceptive attitudes towards the attraction of FDI.

Nevertheless, key differences between countries exist in terms of the national regulations towards foreign investment, the importance attached to FDI as an indus-trial policy objective, and the level of resources devoted to promotional activit-ies. Broadly speaking, there is a division into three categories:

- countries that have long-standing policies to maximize the benefits of FDI in their regional and national economies;
- countries that traditionally either distrust losing control of domestic economic activity to foreign enterprises, fear the risk of increased competition with local businesses, or do not regard the benefits of FDI projects as justifying the costs of their promotion; and
- formerly hostile countries which have begun to pursue more positive policies.

2.1. Active Promotion

Over the past decade, the most active countries in encouraging FDI have been Belgium, Ireland, the Netherlands, Spain, and the UK. They have all been characterized by relatively deregulated approaches to foreign ownership within their national economies and a range of policy instruments for attracting foreign investment projects. In many ways, the UK and Ireland are the best examples of European countries with highly developed and sophisticated FDI-promotion strategies.

The *United Kingdom* has traditionally had the most systematic approach to targeting and attracting foreign investment projects of all European countries. The attraction of FDI has been an explicit objective of regional and industrial policies for nearly two decades, contributing to the UK having the largest share of all direct investment in Western Europe. US and Japanese investment has been particularly welcomed, allowing the UK to benefit from the surge of FDI into Western Europe catalysed by the Single Market programme. Foreign investment has been critical in the economic regeneration of certain regions, such as Scotland and Wales, where foreign investment has led to the emergence of clusters of high-technology firms in sectors such as electronics. Moreover, the UK has maintained one of the most liberal and active markets for corporate takeovers in Western Europe, so that a large share of the country's investment flows is accounted for by mergers and acquisitions.

A key measure in the UK's approach to FDI was the early liberalization of foreign ownership regulations relative to other Western European countries. During the early 1980s, the UK actively sought to eliminate all its controls and regulations governing foreign investment in order to further encourage FDI. It was one of the first European countries to abolish foreign exchange controls. In addition, sectoral restrictions have been at a minimum and pre-authorization procedures are absent. Another factor has been the UK's ambitious privatization programme—particularly in traditional state-controlled activities, such as public utilities (telecommunications, rail transport, electricity, water). As a result of this deregulation and demonopolization process, the UK has received FDI in sectors which were previously the domain of nationalized industries (e.g. water, power supply, and transport). The advanced nature of this process in the UK has been accelerated by deregulation of its financial markets, notably with the 'Big Bang' in 1986 in which UK capital markets were opened up to foreign competition. Financial deregulation made it easier for foreign investors to purchase stakes in UK firms.

Similar to the UK, *Ireland's* industrial policy places great emphasis on the attraction of foreign investment. Given the problems of high unemployment and the limited capabilities of domestic firms to expand, Ireland has looked to inward investment as the main source of employment creation for several decades (Tomaney 1995). Foreign investment has consequently had a significant impact on the levels of exports, innovation, productivity, and diversification within Irish industry, not just directly but through the knock-on effects on domestic supplier firms. The country's success in attracting projects—especially in the electronics and financial services sectors—can be attributed to a mix of its incentive advantages (e.g. Ireland has special dispensation from European Commission rules regarding its corporation tax), location factors such as a well-educated, compliant, and relatively low-cost workforce and the operation of its inward investment organization, the Irish Development Authority (IDA). Unlike the UK, however, Ireland continues to operate some policies which curtail FDI. For example, Ireland imposes some reciprocity considerations on investors from non-EU countries in certain sectors (e.g. banking, finance, and insurance). Another feature of the Irish economy which may limit FDI is the existence of state monopolies in certain sectors such as telecommunications, air transport, and energy. This structural feature of the Irish economy is, however, in the process of change with privatizations recently taking place in the insurance and food sectors.

2.2. Passive Promotion

In contrast to this first category of policy attitudes, other countries have been either disinterested, or occasionally negative towards foreign investment. In particular, Germany and Italy have undertaken relatively little promotional activity; in some cases, there have even been expressions of antipathy towards the attraction of foreign firms.

There has been much discussion in recent years of the threat to *Germany* as an industrial location for investment (the so-called *Standort Deutschland* debate). A number of barriers to investment in Germany have been identified, including excessive bureaucratic regulation; planning and building regulations and formalities; high unit labour costs; and the need for reform of the corporate and personal taxation system (Parnell 1998). Indeed, some measures have already been undertaken to address some of the issues: for example, sickness, unemployment, and benefit systems have been reformed and unit labour costs have started to come down. The most important motive for outward investment by German firms has generally been to gain new markets, but more recently firms have also been placing more importance on exploiting cost advantages abroad, especially in neighbouring Central and Eastern European countries.

Another factor preventing foreign investment is the lack of mergers and acquisition activity in Germany. This is mainly due to the country's industrial structure which is dominated by small and medium-sized enterprises and firms whose controlling ownership remains relatively stable as a result of bank or family ownership. At the end of 1995, only 678 domestic firms in Germany were publicly listed, compared with 1,971 enterprises in the UK (Bundesbank 1997). The lack of publicly quoted German companies prevents the acquisition of a major shareholding by foreign companies and clearly constitutes a major barrier to incoming FDI.

Italy has also been sceptical of the value of FDI in the past, and as a result, there are few policies to support its attraction. Structural differences between Italy and other European economies have reinforced this policy approach, as investors have been dissuaded by the mix of a large public sector and a private sector offering few acquisition opportunities because of the number of small companies and the underdeveloped stock market. Consequently, Italian industrial and regional policies have generally relied on national economic growth and the redistribution of domestic investment (especially to the *Mezzogiorno*), though the recent programme of privatization and the introduction of new legislation for the promotion of FDI suggests that the attitudes of Italian authorities will change in future. For example, a number of the restrictions applied to foreign investment have been relaxed in sectors such as banking, transport, radio, and television.

Nevertheless, both countries have recently shown greater interest in investment promotion with the creation of new agencies at national level with the aim of attracting investment. These agencies do not have powers to attract investment as wide-ranging as comparable agencies in more active countries, but they do represent the early signs of a significant attitudinal change.

2.3. Promotion in Transition

The last category of countries is the largest: there are several countries which have been wary of foreign investment in the past, but are increasingly active in encouraging its attraction, of which France, Scandinavia, and Mediterranean countries are especially prominent.

Chief among these is *France*, which until the mid-1980s, displayed little enthusiasm for foreign enterprises. Indeed, the former socialist government in the early 1980s was relatively inhospitable towards foreign investors, particularly those acquiring French businesses (Bailey, Harte, and Sugden 1991). However, over the past ten years, French government policy appears to have experienced a 'sea change', in large part a response to the persistence of unemployment. Government agencies have been more energetic in bringing in FDI and the regulatory environment for foreign companies has been considerably relaxed. With the exception of defence, air and maritime transport, there are no longer widespread sectoral restrictions limiting foreign investment in France. Prior authorization procedures have also been considerably relaxed and are now only necessary for investments that pose a threat to law and order and public safety. That said, France continues to impose reciprocity requirements in certain sectors (e.g. telecommunications, audio-visual industries, publishing, and hydrocarbons), especially on investors from outside the EEA. In particular, a degree of wariness remains in allowing large domestic companies to pass into foreign ownership, as demonstrated by the government's recent blocking of a bid for part of the Thomson electronics group by Daewoo.

Other factors are also increasing the scope for foreign investment in the French economy. In this respect, financial deregulation and the government's vast privatization programme are important. Although the process of privatization has been slow and uneven, there could be significant opportunities for foreign investment in the telecommunications sector following the process of deregulation currently underway. In addition, France is gradually amending its corporate laws to allow greater scope for foreign companies to acquire domestic concerns (UNCTAD 1995). In February 1996, for example, the French repealed a law that required prior authorization for the acquisition of French enterprises by non-EEA investors.

A more recent redirection of policy has taken place in some Scandinavian countries. In *Sweden*, long-standing inactivity with regard to FDI has ended as foreign investment is increasingly regarded as a potential means of reducing the country's rising unemployment. Until the early 1990s, Sweden had one of the most restrictive frameworks towards FDI in Western Europe but has now instigated wide-ranging liberalization. For example, in 1992, Sweden abolished the law on the foreign acquisition of Swedish firms and also overturned the need for foreigners to get permission to transact business in the country. The country's recent accession to the EU has been a major factor in this process—similar to the surge in foreign investment into Portugal and Spain in the mid-to-late 1980s after these countries joined the Community (Dunning 1997). Other important factors in Sweden include a well-skilled workforce, favourable exchange rate, and low corporation tax compared with the rest of the OECD (Blomstrom and Kokko 1995). Likewise, the recent deep recession in *Finland* has prompted a reappraisal of the benefits of foreign investment, just as its recent membership of the EU and trade opportunities in Russia have given the country a new attractiveness to foreign investors. Both Sweden and Finland have established inward investment promotion agencies for the first time in the 1990s.

Changes in FDI policy in many West European countries are illustrated by parts of the *Mediterranean* area with formerly protective approaches to foreign ownership. For example, *Portugal* is undertaking an intensive programme of liberalization to open up the country to foreign acquisitions, while the government is beginning to develop marketing tools, incentive policies, and promotion agencies to attract FDI projects. As with Ireland and Spain, foreign investment is increasingly seen as a means of introducing modernization into the country's industrial sectors through technology transfer and higher levels of productivity. The country is currently dismantling many of its sectoral restrictions on FDI (in areas such as water distribution, banks and travel agencies, and basic sanitation services). Similarly, *Greece* is gradually undergoing a similar transformation—again in large part, a response to greater integration within the EU.

2.4. EU Regulatory Control and FDI Competition

Having outlined national attitudes towards FDI promotion in Europe, it is worth highlighting the role of the European Commission in regulating competition for foreign investment. While such international monitoring is not the direct aim of the Commission's authority, it has had some influence in limiting the degree of competitive outbidding between countries and regions for major investment projects through the powers vested in Directorate General IV to regulate regional incentives, the main financial incentives awarded to foreign investors (Wishlade 1999). The European Commission has considerable influence over incentive policies operating in the EU, unlike the situation in the USA, where considerable interstate competition for FDI occurs without any federal-level regulation (Donahue 1998). The basis for Commission action lies in Articles 92 to 94 of the EC Treaty. Although member states are free to administer regional aid schemes, the Commission has to authorize all national regional aid schemes. In addition, the Commission also plays a major role in determining the ultimate shape and scope of assisted areas of the member states. Its influence over the type of assistance offered has also been decisive in a number of cases and has contributed to the growing homogeneity in regional aid design in the EU (Wishlade 1998).

Recent Commission proposals controlling regional aids will also potentially play a major role in shaping the levels of assistance which are given to large-scale mobile investment projects. In particular, the Commission's new Multisectoral Framework on Regional Aid for Large Investment Projects (LIPS) which began in September 1998 and runs for a trial period of four years, is another strong regulatory control mechanism over member states' activities in the field of regional aid. The LIPS Framework requires member states to notify the Commission if any proposal to offer regional aid under an approved aid scheme (or in the form of an *ad hoc* award) exceeds a certain size threshold. The assessment undertaken by the Commission of those cases notified are then assessed according to three main criteria: the extent of surplus capacity in the sector, the capital/labour ratio of the project and the regional impact of the project. The Commission estimates that the LIPS Framework will capture around twenty projects a year. Although this is quite limited in comparison to the number of large FDI projects in the EU, the LIPS Framework clearly has the indirect effect of transferring decision-making responsibility on major investment projects away from national authorities and into the hands of the Commission. Some observers claim that the time-consuming and inherent complexity of the LIPS Framework could potentially undermine the EU's attractiveness as an investment location for internationally mobile FDI (Wishlade 1998).

3. Regional Framework for Foreign Investment Promotion in Europe

Not only has FDI promotion become more active at national level, it has increasingly become a regionalized sphere of policy, in terms of implementation if not necessarily design. Investment promotion and development is a highly complex and resource-intensive activity, requiring numerous actors networking at various spatial and policy levels (as shown more fully in the case-study sections below). Owing to this complexity, European subnational bodies are playing an increasingly important role in this process. The following section highlights the reasons behind this trend and the policy measures used by regional bodies to attract FDI.

3.1. **Foreign Investment and Regional Development Strategies**

The shift in FDI promotional activity away from a principally national activity to an increasingly regional one does not represent so much a top-down transfer of organizational responsibilities from the centre as greater recognition by regional authorities of the links between foreign investment attraction and economic development strategies. This reflects increasing awareness by policy-makers of the long-term benefits which investment projects can bring to regional economies. The employment and income impacts of mobile investment projects have long been understood, both in terms of direct as well as multiplier effects: what has perhaps been appreciated more fully in recent years is the more *qualitative* effects of foreign investment, such as the transfer of new technologies, skills, business practices, and production approaches to local companies which might not otherwise have access to these resources (for a review of the effects, see Young, Hood, and Peters 1994).

Foreign investment attraction can become a central strut in a development strategy, especially where industrial clusters are anticipated to emerge around foreign-owned companies and act as sources of regional growth. In the context of foreign investment, large foreign-owned plants can become a source of innovation in the local economy—through new firm formation, skills upgrading, and technology transfer—via the conduits of linkages to local firms, research organizations (notably universities), and labour markets. Over time, such strategies aim for the strength of the cluster to shift from the large plant alone to a wider web of local and foreign firms in which the 'knowledge assets' of a region are formally, informally, and, above all, indivisibly encoded—by which point the region may no longer be dependent on its initial FDI catalyst. Variations of this strategy are evident throughout the world, but a strong example of the approach is in Scotland: the recent strategy of its economic development agency—Scottish Enterprise—refers to it explicitly, and its analysis of sources of regional economic competitiveness identified the role of foreign-owned large firms can have in generating industrial clusters (Scottish Enterprise 1998).

This integration of foreign investment attraction into regional development strategies provides another explanation for the emergence of promotion as a regional activity. It is not just because there is a strong incentive for regions to attract investment projects in terms of their economic benefits, but if the value of new foreign investment projects are to be maximized, they need to be linked to development strategies at regional level. Regions are often better able to identify which regional factors should be promoted to attract companies and what type of projects would best complement the region's development. Indeed, developing such clusters requires an understanding of the region's 'gaps' in the existing concentrations—whether parts of the production value chain or certain sets of skills and technologies—and action to fill those gaps so that the concentrations can reach a critical mass and produce self-sustaining growth. In fact, FDI can play a key role in many clusters where branch plants make up the bulk of the firms (Birkinshaw and Hood 1997).

This has implications for the scope of FDI policy as well as its increasing operation at regional level, as regional authorities can apply a wide range of policies to facilitate linkages between plants and the asset-generating parts of the economy (such as local suppliers and universities). Moreover, it widens the policy-maker interest in foreign investment from simply its attraction to its long-term role in the economy. This more holistic view of the value of FDI to the local economy recognizes that the scale and nature of the benefits of foreign investment to a local economy are to a large extent dependent on policy actions undertaken at a regional level.

3.2. Regional Incentives and Foreign Investment

To understand how FDI promotion at regional level can be effective in attracting companies (and thereby understand why FDI promotion has been increasingly regionalized in recent years), it is useful to review both the process of investment decision-making by companies as well as the main instruments employed by inward investment agencies to influence the process. Companies rarely make comprehensive and detailed examinations of their location requirements and options, but partially resort to 'satisficing', in which the process of finding the optimal location is set against the desire to find the first location to satisfy a set of key criteria. Where satisficing is an important if not dominant feature of the decision process, investment agencies not only have scope for influencing consideration of their region but can often be welcomed by providing a service to companies in simplifying the acquisition of the location information necessary for a decision.

The ability of agencies to affect location decisions can be summarized in three stages, though in most cases, the different stages tend to operate in parallel. Agencies can raise *regional visibility* through promotional literature and directed campaigns targeting specific companies, in which the objective is to put their region in contention for an investment project. Where serious interest is being shown in the region as a location, agencies can then supply an element of *regional certainty* by providing the company with the information it requires for the decision and addressing any questions or uncertainties. At the last stage, particularly where a large investment project is considering a few potential locations, competing investment agencies can target their promotional activities at individuals within the company—often by employing psychological factors such as hospitality— to demonstrate *regional commitment* to the project.

In the last stage of promotion, agencies often employ a variety of financial instruments to secure investment decisions (or coordinate their use by other agencies). The one most closely associated with the attraction of foreign investment in Europe has been financial incentives. These can include a range of policy instruments—including tax concessions and employment subsidies—but by far the most common form is capital grants to industry to influence location in specially designated areas. While some parts of Europe rely on other types of incentive—notably Ireland with its highly effective low rate of corporation tax

—nearly all other European countries have incentive schemes which are integral to their investment promotion activities. Indeed, the reliance on grants in Western Europe distinguishes it from other parts of the world, such as the USA, where fiscal incentives and loans are more common (UNCTAD 1995; Donahue 1998).

Such regional incentives are used by governments to compensate for a region's relative absence of certain locational advantages, as translated into the perceived additional costs to a company of locating there. Foreign investment decisions are often made through comparing a series of short- and long-term costs among several locations. These costs differ depending on the nature of the activity being placed—production, distribution or administrative facilities, in manufacturing or service sectors—but can be considered in terms of the following categories:

- *establishment costs*: those involved in the initial setting up or expansion of a facility—including the availability of an appropriate site and the costs of its development and construction—and any costs incurred in bringing the facility up to its anticipated operational strength;
- *operating costs*: those associated with the normal running of the facility, including the relative costs of labour at different skill levels and capital equipment purchase and maintenance, as well as the costs of acquiring local external inputs and services, ensuring local suppliers can provide at adequate quality levels or importing the necessary inputs and services from outside the region;
- *market costs*: those arising from accessing target markets, such as distribution and market development; and
- *development costs*: those determining the scope allowed by the investment for expanding production, entering new geographical markets, and developing new products.

In theory, regional financial incentives should directly affect establishment costs (in the case of greenfield investments) and development costs (in the case of re-investments), but the evidence for their effectiveness in attracting foreign investment is mixed. Individual company data on the importance of regional incentives tend to be lacking, owing to the widespread confidentiality of investment decisions and incentive transactions. In most cases, official information is not even available on the value of awards offered to specific companies. Nevertheless, numerous business surveys have shown that incentives tend not to be the key location factor—at least in terms of the *country* of location—and remain subsidiary to other determinants (e.g. CEC 1993).

The relatively low ranking accorded to financial incentives in surveys needs to be interpreted carefully. Financial incentives may be crucial in determining where within a country a firm invests, either regionally or at site level. Econometric research analysing FDI patterns in the UK shows that along with other cost-related factors, financial incentives are an important factor in securing projects at the regional level (Hill and Munday 1992). Owing to the fact that the location criteria for any given project will vary depending on the qualitative nature of the investment project, the importance of financial incentives in determining FDI locational patterns is clearly not constant. Christodoulou (1996) claimed that financial incentives can assume critical significance for both projects where two or three locations are identified as meeting the key criteria.

The process of determining a location can produce a range of suitable sites, especially where several locations satisfy the key decision criteria (such as market access and labour skills). While these factors may be the most important locational factors (as identified by investors in surveys), they are not necessarily *determining* factors in practice. Hence, the final selection of site has often depended on the financial package offered by the region or country. Incentives are used to bolster rather than compensate for existing location determinants, but that does not diminish their importance in competition with sites possessing the same location advantages. Although companies tend to play down the role of incentives in investment decisions—which may be in their interests in order to affirm that their commitment to a certain location will extend beyond the period of grant payments—they can be effective when a 'shortlist' of potential sites has been formed (Bachtler and Clement 1991).

Although incentive policies have a clear regional focus, in Europe they are usually operated at national level—where regional-level organizations employ such incentives, they do so within national guidelines. However, incentives tend to be supplemented by other policy measures employed at the discretion of regional agencies. These include labour training subsidies and property support. Labour grants are used to ease the training costs of incoming companies, particularly where local labour markets are unable to supply the skills needs of new investment projects without public-sector intervention. With property support, regional authorities can acquire sites on behalf of investors and undertake site preparation to suit plant needs. This often requires site-specific improvements in transport, water, and sewage infrastructure, and in some cases, commitments to attracting suppliers and other supporting businesses for the investor. The cost of these additional measures should not be underestimated. For example, in Scotland, in the 1994–6 period, £21.3 million was spent by the Scottish Enterprise network in property support and £27.7 million in training assistance for inward investment projects (however, this compares with £214.7 million offered in financial incentives) (Scottish Affairs Committee 1998).

3.3. **Aftercare and Foreign Investment**

With competition for foreign investment rising in Western Europe at a time when new investments may be levelling out or even declining, greater emphasis is being placed on securing additional investments from existing investors—for example, through site expansions. A crucial aspect of FDI promotion, therefore, is the need for flexibility in view of the dynamic nature of international production (Dicken 1998). As greenfield FDI diminishes, new investment is increasingly taking the shape of plant expansions, or in the case of some manufacturing activities, new product ranges or individual models. In addition, FDI can also change the qualitative nature of any given operation. For example, sales offices can be developed into technical design centres or manufacturing locations. Service-sector investment is also being transformed with the advent of call centres and shared technical service centres.

Thus, investment agencies are now allocating more of their resources to existing foreign-owned firms through aftercare initiatives (Young, Hood, and Wilson 1994). In brief, aftercare covers a range of services that are offered to current investors to maintain their commitment to their current location. Aftercare also embodies a wider strategic goal of enhancing the development of the regional or local economy where investors are located. Investment promotion is no longer simply concerned with the attraction of projects, but also at encouraging investors to deepen their links with the local economy. Inward investment agencies realize that higher-value investments, especially R&D, will generate stronger spillover effects in the local economy: 'not only does local research, development and design activity help to anchor companies in their locations, and generate high value-added employment, but it also allows locally produced components to be incorporated more easily into products at the design stage' (LIS 1997: 23).

The objective is to increase the value of an investment to the local economy over time, so that the investor not only contributes jobs and income to the region, but—through increasing their levels of local sourcing and links with local companies and research institutions—new skills and technologies as well: in other words upgrading 'asset-exploiting' activities into 'asset-augmenting' activities, as described by John Dunning in Chapter 1.

Some observers have highlighted the risks of aftercare policies resulting in a form of 'institutional capture', whereby development agencies become dominated —especially in terms of resources—by large FDI projects such as LG in South Wales (see Phelps *et al.* 1998). The focus on upgrading the quality of foreign investment through aftercare initiatives may also clash with the desire of MNEs to safeguard their own strategic and technological objectives (Kozul-Wright and Rowthorn 1998); nevertheless, many regions throughout Europe are actively seeking to attract more knowledge-intensive investments, in the anticipation that they will become embedded within the local economy.

4. Promotional Activities of Regional Foreign Investment Agencies

As is clear from the previous section, regions throughout Europe have faced similar pressures in adapting more FDI-focused development strategies and policies. There remains though significant variations between regions in their approaches towards FDI promotion. Some Western European countries adopt a highly centralized approach to attracting investment, with central government handling all matters to do with incoming FDI. This can lead to a 'one-stop shop' approach with one agency dealing with all matters relating to foreign investment. For example, Greece has recently established Elke, a national inward investment agency intended to market the entire country abroad and coordinate foreign investor enquiries. On the other hand, some countries, such as Germany, operate a highly decentralized approach which allows various actors (including subnational agencies) to be involved in marketing locations and determining financial assistance (e.g. each Länder has its own inward investment agency).

Although there are a common set of investment promotion techniques adopted by regional promotional agencies, substantive differences between European inward investment agencies remain. In order to explore these issues in greater depth, we shall now focus on two regions with very different approaches to FDI promotion and development: Scotland in the UK and Nordrhein-Westfalen in Germany. These two regions provide strong comparative case studies. Scotland is a small economy within the highly centralized UK, whereas Nordrhein-Westfalen is a large powerful Land within the Federal German state. While these regions form the main focus of this comparative analysis, examples will be used to illustrate FDI promotion in other European regions.

4.1. Promotion Agencies

In recent years, there has been a proliferation of regional inward investment agencies in Europe. Although nearly every region in Europe now undertakes some form of promotional activity, agencies vary considerably in size and the scope of their activities. As we shall see, FDI promotion in Scotland is undertaken by a dedicated inward investment agency while in Nordrhein-Westfalen FDI promotion is only one aspect carried out by its regional development agency.

In Scotland, the main body responsible for FDI attraction is Locate in Scotland (LIS).[1] Established in 1981, LIS is one of the oldest dedicated regional promotional agencies in Europe. LIS is directly responsible to the First Minister, the government minister who is head of the Scottish Executive. LIS has a central Glasgow-based headquarters and a network of eleven foreign missions located in the USA, Western Europe, and Asia as well as a London office (for inward investment from other parts of the UK). In its main headquarters, the agency is structured as teams along geographical lines (e.g. North America, Asia) as well as thematically (e.g. financial assistance, aftercare). LIS regards its mission to consist of:

- marketing Scotland as a location for inward investment;
- giving advice and assistance to potential investors;
- delivering development packages tailored to investors' needs; and
- providing aftercare to inward investors.

LIS employs approximately 100 people worldwide (about seventy within Scotland itself). Administrative costs attributable to LIS activities amounted to £6.6 million in 1996. These figures indicate the costs of inward investment marketing and staffing, but to this should be added the value of financial assistance to foreign investors in Scotland. For 1995–6, RSA grants to the value of £160 million were awarded to 119 foreign investment projects, creating and safeguarding estimated employment of 22,600.

It is important to emphasize that LIS works within a national framework for investment promotion. This is apparent in two areas. First, overall responsibility for marketing the UK as a whole to foreign investors lies with the Invest in Britain Bureau (IBB), a division of the UK Department of Trade and Industry (DTI) in London. The IBB's main function is to coordinate the different activities of locally based agencies and to be chiefly responsible for promoting England to foreign investors. While LIS maintains a large degree of autonomy in its promotion strategy and operations, IBB provides a strong element of monitoring, as LIS reports to IBB on a regular basis throughout the year. Second, LIS's actions are closely defined at a national level with respect to the use of financial assistance to attract inward investment projects to Scotland, particularly Regional Selective Assistance (RSA), the main incentive available to investors. A detailed set of guidelines on area designation, project eligibility, award rates, and decision-making procedures have been laid down for RSA by the DTI.

The main state body responsible for inward investment promotion in Nordrhein-Westfalen is the Economic Development Corporation for Nordrhein-Westfalen (Gesellschaft für Wirtschaftsförderung Nordrhein-Westfalen mbH (GfW)). The GfW has a very wide-ranging remit. Until the mid-1980s the work of the GfW concentrated on promoting the state as a location for business and industry. By the end of 1980s, the GfW widened its activities to include assisting local companies with internationalization and exporting. The GfW now provides information, consultancy and management services to firms in Nordrhein-Westfalen as well as investors who express an interest in locating in the Land. Based in Düsseldorf, the GfW employs fifty people, split evenly between assistance for local companies and efforts to attract incoming firms. GfW also has seven representative overseas branches, in the Far East, South-East Asia, the USA, South Africa, and the Middle East.

The GfW's activities include:

- assistance to German and foreign companies in the implementation of investment projects;
- support for Nordrhein-Westfalen companies in the development of important markets abroad;
- communication for Nordrhein-Westfalen as a business location at home and abroad;
- advising public administration and government agencies in Germany and other countries on setting up economic development structures;

• support for the establishment of European and international joint venture networks for small and medium-sized enterprises; and
• information and advice for local and regional economic development agencies.

The need for an easily identifiable national contact point for potential investors is being increasingly recognized in Germany. In February 1998, the Economic Committee of the lower house of parliament (*Bundestag*) recommended the establishment of an 'Invest in Germany' agency which would take responsibility for marketing the whole country, with the cooperation of federal and Land authorities. The Economic Committee, in making this proposal, recognizes that the barriers to inward investment need to be addressed, but feels at the same time that Germany's advantages as an industrial location are not being adequately presented, and that contacts with potential foreign investors are not being sufficiently coordinated and targeted.

4.2. Promotional Activities

The type of promotional activities undertaken by investment agencies varies considerably, often depending on resourcing issues. With the increasing competition for FDI projects among regions as well as countries, some agencies believe that it has become necessary for agencies to separate out the different parts of the marketing process and develop specific techniques for each part. These parts can be considered under the categories of general, sectoral, and company marketing. *General marketing* involves the selling of the region as a whole. These activities are not directed at specific projects, but merely aim to raise the profile of the country/region generally. *Sectoral marketing* requires the agency to have developed a clear picture of the types of sectors that it intends to target for FDI promotion. A sectoral focus is essential for promotion, in that it helps to target limited promotion resources as well as to maximize the benefits of FDI by concentrating it in certain sectors. This type of marketing normally proceeds through an analysis of the target sector in the specific geographical market, including information-gathering on new start-ups, expanding companies, and forthcoming investment projects.

Company marketing is the last stage of the promotional process. Where individual companies are known to be considering investment decisions, it is important for agencies to approach the key decision-makers. Some agencies maintain close and regular links between geographical teams located in their headquarters and the various mission offices. This enables agencies to co-ordinate effectively their domestic and foreign promotional efforts with potential investors—for example, the foreign offices of LIS can rapidly obtain specific detailed information on different aspects of Scotland from the domestic headquarters for potential investors. The final stages of company marketing may require arranging hospitality visits to the region by the company, meetings between senior government officials and company executives, and the offer of financial incentives (as described in more detail in the next section). Underlining these different activities is the ability of LIS to make use of a well-functioning network of government agencies to use for specific tasks in the promotional process. This is possible in Scotland because of the high priority that has been placed on inward investment attraction across the public sector, leading to a level of commitment that has repeatedly impressed (and influenced) investors.

Although marketing activities are quite standardized across many of the well-resourced inward investment agencies in the UK and Ireland, smaller European agencies concentrate mostly on general and sectoral marketing. Whereas LIS appears to have a highly systematic and well-developed promotional strategy, the GfW in Nordrhein-Westfalen undertakes less comprehensive promotional activities. For example, in Nordrhein-Westfalen company marketing is not given as much attention as general and sectoral marketing. Given that company marketing is the most advanced stage of the marketing process, smaller European agencies such as the GfW, without the resources needed to undertake this type of activity, may be at a disadvantage when competing for new FDI projects.

Another crucial aspect of promotional activities is the development of overseas offices. Most investors use a series of indicators to determine a 'shortlist' of potential locations before undertaking more intensive analysis to select a single site. The task of FDI agencies is to ensure that they are included on the shortlist. To achieve this, it is essential to have a local presence in the target investor market. LIS currently has overseas offices in eleven countries across Europe, Asia, and North America. This includes representative offices in different global regions—such as North America and Asia—but also in different parts of that region—such as the east and west coasts of the USA and national offices in Japan, South Korea, and Taiwan. Such offices are crucial for gathering market intelligence about future investment projects and the activities of rival agencies as well as in directly marketing the region to potential investors.

In Nordrhein-Westfalen, the GfW has less overseas representation that LIS. At present, the GfW has two overseas subsidiaries and eight representative offices. Although this is quite extensive, the geographical location of these offices seems somewhat out of step with the main sources of incoming investment. Part of the reason for this relates to the dual purpose of the GfW which simultaneously tries to attract inward investment and promote export development of indigenous firms. The main agency charged with regional promotion in Rhône-Alpes (Enterprise Rhône-Alpes International) also has this dual role. This situation can lead to offices being located in strong export markets, but with little FDI potential. For example, the GfW has two representatives in China, one in Vietnam, and one in Israel, yet virtually no foreign investment comes from these countries. In fact, there are worries that these offices may actually promote *outward* investment. Although providing the majority of foreign investment in Nordrhein-Westfalen, the GfW has no overseas offices in Europe.

4.3. Coordination between Local Actors

The importance of a network of public-sector agencies working in close cooperation to secure foreign investment cannot be underestimated. A clear division of responsibilities needs to be made between different agencies in the region—e.g. with regards to site preparation and provision and training support as well as in aftercare and monitoring the status of existing investors—with the understanding that overall coordination of investment enquiries and promotion should remain with the single agency. As well as supporting promotion activities, links between different development agencies in the region are necessary to enable more strategic activities to take place, such as decisions on which sectors (or companies) to target.

Again, close public-sector networking and partnerships, appear to be better developed in relatively small cohesive regions, such as Scotland, Ireland, Wales, and Northern Ireland. In Scotland, for example, the development of its investment strategy is a continuous process in which LIS operates closely with other public agencies, particularly Scottish Enterprise. As a crucial element in the success of investment promotion in Scotland, networking between different public-sector organizations is particularly important in identifying future directions for strategic development. Such networking involves links with other parts of Scottish Enterprise, especially the units dedicated to supporting businesses in the key sectors of the Scottish economy. In addition, close strategic coordination takes place with the Local Enterprise Companies (LECs), non-governmental organizations such as the Higher Education Institutes, major companies in the Scottish economy, and the utilities.

In Nordrhein-Westfalen, on the other hand, coordination between different actors is less coherent because Nordrhein-Westfalen does not have a single organization dedicated to the promotion of foreign direct investment. The existence of various local, Land, and federal level agencies is fragmented and non-transparent for the potential inward investor. The involvement of additional subregional actors in foreign investment promotion means that coordination between agencies in Nordrhein-Westfalen is currently poor. Certain regions and local authorities, especially the large cities in Nordrhein-Westfalen, are wary of falling behind in terms of new foreign investment and therefore want to undertake promotional activities themselves. The areas within the region which have been most successful at attracting FDI are localities with strong proactive development agencies (e.g. Aachen).

A single agency cannot act alone in investment promotion. It will be essential for it to act as a centralized coordinator of investment promotion activities, both with national level promotion (in the same way that LIS liaises with IBB in Scotland and indeed with government ministers) as well as local development organizations (such as the local authorities and the LECs in Scotland). Regions which have a weak central coordinating body may be at risk of squandering investment opportunities owing to intraregional competition for FDI. This is one of the factors behind Germany's desire to establish a national-level authority to oversee inter-Länder competition. Even in the UK, the government is examining ways of reducing inter-regional competition by monitoring the powers of agencies such as the LIS, the Welsh Development Agency (WDA), and the Northern Development Company (NDC).

4.4. Financial Support

As already noted, the use of financial assistance has increasingly become a key tool in investment attraction. The importance of incentives in influencing investment decisions is greatest when a shortlist of location sites has already been prepared. In this regard, it is not so much the size and value of incentives that matters most as the scope that the agency has for providing a variety of different types of assistance (often not directly financial, such as support with site preparation). In this respect, European agencies display a wide range of powers in this area.

The ability to combine marketing and financial award powers in a single institution has been a notable element in LIS's success. Although LIS does not directly have the authority to award or administer RSA, the main financial grant available in Scotland, the close links between LIS and the finance section of the Scottish Executive enable LIS to use incentive offers in its promotional efforts. A finance team within LIS, composed of employees working directly for the Scottish Executive Industry Department, is authorized to assess quickly what level of financial assistance can be offered to potential investors. At the same time, LIS has regular meetings with other regional inward investment agencies in the UK to prevent companies 'shopping around' for higher incentive offers, as intelligence about individual investors is quickly distributed through the IBB network.

In Nordrhein-Westfalen regional incentives are administered and controlled by the Ministry for Economics, SMEs, and Technology and Transport. As in Scotland, the Ministry has close links with the main promotional body, the GfW. However, they do not have any formal method of linking up when negotiating with new investors. As with many other regional promotion agencies, the GfW cannot make indicative offers of incentive packages to potential investors. This has often been viewed as one of the reasons why Scotland has been so successful in competing with other agencies in the UK which do not have the same power in making indicative offers of financial assistance rapidly (Raines 1998).

4.5. FDI Aftercare

Aftercare has become a central feature of FDI policy in many regions as a way of embedding foreign investors and attracting higher-value-added investment. For example, the WDA is committing considerable amount of resources to developing Wales into a so-called 'learning region' (Morgan 1997). As part of this initiative, the WDA is now seeking to harness foreign investment through various aftercare initiatives. This is in recognition of the fact that in the seven years to 1991, expansion investments accounted for 45.6 per cent of all inward investment projects in Wales. In order to develop and upgrade existing MNEs, the WDA recognized that no single agency could satisfy all these requirements. As a consequence, the WDA established a network of public-sector actors into a body called 'Team Wales'. This initiative encompasses a wide range of activities, such as technology support, skills development, and supplier development. For example, a key element of Team Wales is to encourage foreign investors to work more closely with local suppliers through the Welsh Development Agency's 'Source Wales' programme.

Although many newer investment agencies, such as those in Scandinavia, do not undertake aftercare policies to any great extent, well-established development agencies are now paying increasing attention to this issue. In Scotland, aftercare has become an increasingly important aspect of its promotion strategy and special teams within LIS work on aftercare issues. Several years ago, the tasks used to be divided between the different geographical teams, but as aftercare became a more complex activity, it was decided to have staff dedicated to it. Currently, LIS divides the responsibilities for aftercare with the Local Enterprise Companies. Major investors—or 'accounts'—are handled by LIS directly, while smaller investors are covered by LEC officials in the individual subregions of Scotland. Each LIS official on the aftercare team can be working with up to ten accounts at any one time, usually grouped together by the investor's country/region of origin. This can involve meeting with the company as often as once every two weeks.

In this context, LIS's main function is to facilitate the company with its plans. After a company has made an investment, the LIS official will meet with the company on a regular basis to ensure that it is not experiencing any problems and to find out what its future plans may be. If an opportunity to expand the investment arises, the LIS official will liase with different government agencies to assist the company with regards to acquiring new property, planning regulations, receiving training support, and possible public-sector finance. If the foreign subsidiary is aiming to secure a decision by its parent to site a new investment in Scotland, LIS will work closely with the subsidiary to persuade the parent to make a decision in favour of Scotland. LIS can draw upon ministerial support from the Scottish Executive to help persuade the company to invest in Scotland. Other public-sector officials—such as local authorities—can be brought in as required.

Like many smaller promotion agencies in Europe, very little strategic aftercare is undertaken by the GfW in Nordrhein-Westfalen. Once foreign investors locate in the region, the responsibility for aftercare passes from the GfW to local development agencies and local authorities. Although some local development agencies work on an ongoing basis with investors, many local agencies interact with investors infrequently. Some firms complain that they are concerned about the availability of skilled labour in the region and want to make this point known to local and regional policy-makers. Therefore, the decentralized system for aftercare in the region could be neglecting some investors, reducing the scope for influencing expansion projects in the future.

4.6. Cluster Development Policies

As noted above, foreign investment promotion is increasingly being integrated within overall regional development strategies. Targeting FDI in specific clusters demands very close coordination between regional development actors and promotional agencies. In Scotland, LIS now plays a key role in augmenting the country's cluster-based development strategy (Scottish Enterprise 1998). LIS has already had some success with their new strategy following a major investment within Scotland's semiconductor cluster by Cadence Design Systems (CDS). In December 1997, LIS announced plans for a major collaborative project between public-sector organizations, CDS, and the academic community in Scotland. One of the world's leading suppliers of semiconductor design technology and services, CDS is to establish a facility in Livingston to undertake design work on their next generation 'system on a chip' semiconductor devices. The project envisages the eventual creation of up to 1,900 highly skilled design jobs with CDS in Scotland. It will eventually be the largest design centre in CDS's worldwide network. The firm's motivation for establishing the design centre was influenced by the simplicity and transparency of intellectual property rights in Europe compared to the USA.

As part of the CDS operation, Scottish Enterprise is establishing a design complex in Livingston specifically to attract other such companies working in the field of system-level integration (SLI). It is hoped that other firms will form a cluster in Livingston around CDS. The complex will be assisted by advanced networking infrastructure which is being provided by IBM. In addition to the new design complex, other related initiatives are now underway. For example, in cooperation with four of Scotland's leading universities, Scottish Enterprise is creating the world's first Institute in Livingston to carry out leading edge research on SLI. In partnership with SLI companies and leading experts from around the world, the universities are offering a joint degree in SLI. The Institute will also act as a think-tank for SLI research.

In order to attract CDS, LIS had to work very closely and intensively with other economic development bodies, the academic community, and businesses for five months during the summer of 1997. The importance attached to this initiative—called Project Alba—is due to to the fact that this type of design-related investment is qualitatively different from the bulk of Scotland's assembly-oriented foreign-owned companies (Brown 1996). Furthermore, some existing foreign-owned companies use CDS for their products, which further strengthens linkages within Scotland's electronics cluster. According to Scottish Enterprise and others involved in Scottish economic development, the Cadence project redefines Scotland's position in the world of electronics. The First Minister, Donald Dewar, claimed that the project 'marks a sea-change in the nature of FDI in

Scotland. The creation of such a large number of research, development and design jobs is unprecedented.`

This type of interactive cluster-focused FDI promotion is being undertaken by several promotional bodies (e.g. the IDA in Ireland and the WDA in Wales). However, many European promotional agencies merely target certain sectors, especially electronics, automotive, and biotechnology. For example a number of geographically based sectoral clusters have been identified in Nordrhein-Westfalen as targets for FDI (e.g. chemicals in Emscher Lippe, telecommunications in Düsseldorf, logistics in Duisburg, and media-related industries in Cologne). However, the type of strategic cluster development work involved in Project Alba is not yet undertaken in Nordrhein-Westfalen.

5. Conclusions

Over the past decade, Western Europe has experienced a steady increase in FDI, reinforcing its position as the primary global recipient of foreign investment. The overall attitudes to the attraction of FDI can be seen in the increasing openness of European economies to foreign ownership. Greater liberalization has taken place through a combination of widespread deregulation of restrictions on foreign investment and the privatization of previously state-controlled parts of the economy (such as public utilities). Again, the UK has had a prominent part in this process, though the trends are pan-European. Furthermore, the trend has been towards creating more favourable environments for foreign investors and becoming more active in capturing mobile investment projects. While countries such as the UK and Ireland have long taken the lead in FDI promotion, most European countries and regions have developed policies and institutions dedicated to attracting FDI. Even countries which have traditionally eschewed FDI are beginning to develop new promotional strategies (e.g. Sweden and Germany).

Increasing interest in FDI policy is also apparent in the creation of specific regional agencies for promoting FDI. As we saw when comparing Scotland and Nordrhein-Westfalen, considerable variations exist in the organizational structure and scope of FDI promotion in Western Europe—especially the extent to which regions have policy responsibilities. Part of the reason for this is the varying level of political emphasis (and resources) which different regions place on FDI as an economic development mechanism. Hence, in Scotland, for example, FDI attraction is seen as an integral part of industrial policy whereas in the vast Nordrhein-Westfalen economy such investment is viewed as useful auxiliary to the region's large stock of strong indigenous companies.

Nonetheless, there is a degree of convergence in the types of policies operated by agencies and the increasing scope of their activities. The promotional activities of regional inward investment agencies have widened from traditional regional marketing to include more sophisticated targeting of specific sectors and clusters (and indeed, companies) as well as providing aftercare services to existing investors in order to secure future, expansion investments. As a result, the environment for FDI promotion is more difficult now than when UK regions such as Scotland, Ireland, and Wales first began actively attracting investment in the 1960s and 1970s. Many manufacturing companies have been attracted to locations such as Scotland that have already shown a track record for attracting investment. This produces a valuable 'first-mover-advantage'. This aside, regions such as Scotland still have some way to go to reach the level of interinstitutional synergy prevalent within the more dynamic regions—e.g. industrial districts such as the Rhône-Alpes—of mainland Europe which often attract high-quality, knowledge-based investment without the help of financial incentives (Amin and Tomaney 1995).

Owing to the changing nature of FDI, promotional activities in many European regions are currently reviewing their activities. European regional investment strategies were largely developed during a period when the volume and sources of greenfield investment were rapidly growing. More recently, there appears to have been a shift towards *in situ* expansion investments, as the stream of non-European companies aiming to set up within Europe has been tailing off. New sources of greenfield investment were anticipated from the Asian Tiger economies such as South Korea, but the recent economic crisis of the region has led to widespread retrenchment in Asian FDI. Consequently, investment promotion is beginning to pay more attention to measures in order to secure and deepen the presence of existing investors through aftercare policies. It also places greater emphasis on identifying the host-region's location advantages and targeting specific companies within key clusters and technologies. In order to develop regional clusters, FDI agencies will have to make changes to the ways they work by undertaking a much stronger project management role in order to put together bespoke 'packages' to offer foreign investors, as we saw from Project Alba in Scotland.

Clearly then, a stronger focus on knowledge-based production will have a knock-on effect on FDI promotional strategies. First, agencies will have to spend more time and resources working with other regional actors, putting together complex packages of assistance for incoming firms, particularly in developing the skills required by foreign investors. This will probably involve a high degree of networking with other regional actors—e.g. universities, research institutes, suppliers, and existing foreign investors—whilst actively managing new investors on a project-by-project basis. Second, policy-makers may have to examine the nature of financial incentives on offer, especially in peripheral European regions dominated by basic manufacturing facilities. R&D incentives on offer in countries such as Singapore have played a key role in upgrading the quality of production among foreign investors (Brown 1998). Such R&D-related incentives are better instruments for attracting, and encouraging, higher value-added activities within foreign investors than the capital-related grants (e.g. RSA in the UK) offered in many parts of Europe (Amin *et al.* 1994).

Finally, attracting and developing knowledge-based, asset-augmenting FDI will require much broader-based promotional approaches than in the past. Regions hoping to adapt and succeed within this new environment will have to modify their FDI institutions and policy instruments accordingly. This will be particularly difficult for countries and regions in Europe that view FDI in limited terms—as a source of new employment creation, for example—and not as a something which has to be actively developed and managed.

NOTE

1. It is important to note that LIS is also responsible for attracting inward investment to Scotland from other parts of the UK.

REFERENCES

Amin, A., Bradley, D., Howells, J., Tomaney, J., and Gentle, C. (1994), 'Regional Incentives and the Quality of Mobile Investment in the Less Favoured Regions of the EC', *Progress in Planning* 41: 1–112.
—— and Tomaney, J. (1995), 'The Regional Development Potential of Inward Investment in the Less Favoured Regions of the European Community', in A. Amin and J. Tomaney (eds.), *Behind the Myth of European Union* (London: Routledge).
Bachtler, J., and Clement, K. (1991), 'Inward Investment in the UK and the Single European Market', *Regional Studies* 24: 173–180.
Bailey, D., Harte, G., and Sugden, R. (1991), 'Dirigisme at the Core of the French Approach to Inward Investment', *Multinational Business* 2: 34–43.
Birkinshaw, J., and Hood, N. (1997), *Foreign Investment and Industry Cluster Development: The Characteristics of Subsidiary Companies in Different Types of National Industry Clusters* (Stockholm School of Economics and Strathclyde University, mimeo).
Blomstrom, M., and Kokko, A. (1995), *Foreign Direct Investment and Politics: The Swedish Model*, Discussion Paper, 1266 (London: Centre for Economic Policy Research).
Brown, R. (1996), *Foreign Direct Investment and Regional Economic Development: Backward Electronics Linkages in Scotland and Singapore*, unpublished Ph.D. thesis, University of Strathclyde, Glasgow.
—— (1998), 'Electronics Foreign Direct Investment in Singapore: A Study of Local Linkages in "Winchester City"', *European Business Review* 98: 196–210.
Bundesbank (1997), *Deutsche Bundesbank Monthly Report*, Aug.
CEC (1993), *New Location Factors for Mobile Investment in Europe*, Regional Development Studies, 6 (Brussels: Commission of the European Communities).
Christodoulou, P. (1996), *Inward Investment: An Overview and Guide to the Literature* (London: British Library).
Dicken, P. (1998), *Global Shift: Transforming the World Economy*, 3rd end. (London: Paul Chapman Publishing).
Donahue, J. D. (1998), *Disunited States* (New York: Basic Books).

Dunning, J. (1997), 'The European Internal Market Programme and Inbound Foreign Direct Investment', *Journal of Common Market Studies* 35: 189–223.

Hill, S., and Munday, M. (1992), 'The UK Regional Distribution of Foreign Direct Investment: Analysis and Determinants', *Regional Studies* 26: 535–44.

Kozul-Wright, R., and Rowthorn, R. (1988), 'Spoilt for Choice? Multinational Corporations and the Geography of International Production', *Oxford Review of Economic Policy* 14: 74–92.

LIS (1997), *Annual Review 1996–1997* (Glasgow: Locate in Scotland).

Macleod, G. (1997), '"Institutional Thickness" and Industrial Governance in Lowland Scotland', *Area* 29: 299–311.

Morgan, K. (1997), 'The Learning Region: Institutions, Innovation and Regional Renewal', *Regional Studies* 31: 491–504.

OECD (1997), *Financial Market Trends*, 67 (Paris: OECD).

Parnell, M. (1998), 'Globalisation, "Organised Capitalism" and German Labour', *European Business Review* 98: 80–6.

Phelps, N., Lovering, J., and Morgan, K. (1998), 'Tying the Firm to the Region or Tying the Region to the Firm? Early observations on the case of LG in South Wales', *European Urban and Regional Studies* 5: 119–37.

Porter, M. (1990), *The Competitive Advantage of Nations* (New York: Free Press).

Raines, P. (1998), *Regions in Competition: Inward Investment, Institutional Autonomy and Regional Variation in the Use of Financial Incentives*, Paper delivered to the IRSAI Conference, York, Sept. 1998.

—— and Brown, R. (ed.) (1999), *Policy Competition and Foreign Direct Investment in Europe* (Aldershot: Ashgate).

Scottish Affairs Committee (1998), *Inward and Outward Investment in Scotland* (London: HMSO).

Scottish Enterprise (1998), *The Clusters Approach: Powering Scotland's Economy into the 21st Century* (Glasgow: Scottish Enterprise).

Tomaney, J. (1995), 'Recent Developments in Irish Industrial Policy', *European Planning Studies* 3: 99–113.

UNCTAD (1995), *World Investment Report 1995* (Geneva: UN Conference on Trade and Development).

—— (1996), *World Investment Report 1996* (Geneva: UN Conference on Trade and Development).

—— (1997), *World Investment Report 1997* (Geneva: UN Conference on Trade and Development).

Young, S., Hood, N., and Peters, E. (1994), 'Multinational Enterprises and Regional Economic Development', *Regional Studies* 28: 657–77.

—— —— and Wilson, A. (1994), 'Targeting Policy as a Competitive Strategy for European Inward Investment Agencies', *European Urban and Regional Studies* 1: 143–59.

Wishlade, F. (1998), *RAGS and LIPS: New Weapons in the Commission's Regional Aid Control Armoury*, Regional and Industrial Research Paper Series, 31 (Glasgow: European Policies Research Centre, University of Strathclyde).

—— (1999), 'Incentives Regulation', in P. Raines and R. Brown (eds.), *Policy Competition and Foreign Direct Investment in Europe* (Aldershot: Ashgate).

18

Silicon Valley and the Resurgence of Route 128: *Systems Integration and Regional Innovation*

Michael H. Best

1. Massachusetts: A Long History of New Industry Creation

Massachusetts has a rich industrial history. Two regions within Massachusetts can lay claim to being the birthplace of American industry: one surrounds the Springfield Armory where the principle of interchangeability was first applied and which, in turn, fostered the development of the world's first machine tool industry; the other is Lowell where the Boston Associates built a canal and water-power infrastructure for America's first textile district. The machine tool industry fostered the growth of a range of industrial districts in Massachusetts such as watches in Waltham, footwear in Haverhill, furniture in Gardner, jewellery-making in Attleboro, and metal-working and specialist machine-making in Worcester. The proliferation of industrial sectors, in turn, supported hundreds of small, highly specialized tool-and-die shops and foundries engaged in the production of fixtures, tooling, gauges, and made-to-order components in Massachusetts. Just as the consumer goods industries created a market for machine tool makers, the machine makers diffused innovations across the industrial spectrum (Best and Forrant 1996*a*).

In the twentieth century, Massachusetts has been on a roller coaster caught between the decline of industries with their origins in the last century and the emergence of new industries derived from a regional competitive advantage in research and development, and technological innovation. The machine tool industry was the source of new technologies and a skill pool that fostered the emergence and sustained the growth of new industries in nineteenth-century Massachusetts. An engineering and scientific skill base linked to and diffused by technologically oriented, research-intensive universities, became its functional equivalent for the twentieth century. MIT, of course, is the exemplar. The Boston area has the highest concentration of colleges and universities, research institutes, and hospitals of any place in the world. The plethora of graduate research pro-grammes suggested that the industrial future of Massachusetts was secure in the emerging knowledge economy of the late twentieth century.

However, the research intensity of the region has not insulated the state from the vicissitudes of the business cycle. For example, after enjoying a ninety-month expansion labelled the 'Massachusetts Miracle', the Commonwealth lost one-third of its manufacturing jobs between 1985 and 1992. The country's first high-tech region had seemingly lost industrial leadership much more quickly in the new industries of the late twentieth century than in industries first established in Massachusetts in the nineteenth century.

Symbolic of the decline was the sale of the Wang Towers in Lowell Massachusetts for $500,000 in 1992, a building complex that had cost $23 million to construct during the Massachusetts Miracle. The old textile mill buildings, many of which had been refurbished and converted, were no longer the symbol of regional decline; this role had shifted to the high-tech edifices built in the 1970s and 1980s. The simultaneous collapse of the minicomputer and defence industry, with the end of the Cold War, touched off a downturn which, added to the long-term decline in traditional industries, suggested that industry in Massachusetts was in terminal decline. Combined with the decline of these major markets was the emergence of Silicon Valley based on a different business model. The new model in which horizontal integration, institutions of cooperation, and collective learning figured prominently, was fostering and commercializing innovations much faster than Route 128 (Saxenian 1994; Grove 1996). Clearly, few were willing to bet on the resurgence of Route 128.

Nevertheless, the predictions of industrial gloom turned out to be wrong, or at least premature. The Wang Towers, a new home to thirty-five companies, was sold in April 1998 for $120 million. A return to growth beginning in 1992 has lasted as long as the Massachusetts Miracle. The downturn between the two expansions can be explained in terms of the decline of the minicomputer and defence industries plus the institutional account of AnnaLee Saxenian, but why the upturn? It was not predicted and it has not been explained. Nothing in Saxenian's widely accepted account of regional decline in Massachusetts suggested a return to growth.

Any explanation should account equally for the decline and the resurgence. An account of the rise based solely on the plethora of research capability does not explain the severe downturn; an account of the decline in terms of horizontal integration, institutions of cooperation, and collective learning, such as Saxenian's, does not account for the resurgence.

2. The New Competitive Advantage

Both the decline and the resurgence of Route 128 can be explained in terms of the emergence of a new competitive advantage based upon the principle of systems integration which was both fostered and been driven by a comprehensive reorganization of the business system.[1] The old business model of vertical integration has been transcended by an open system of specialist firms; open systems, working at both the technological and organizational levels, entail decentralized, diffused, and complementary design capabilities across a wide range of business enterprises. The result has been a regional capability to rapidly reinvent products, diversify technologically, create new market niches, and invent new industrial subsectors. These processes are part of a new regional model of innovation which gives the region a competitive advantage in the capability to rapidly create, develop, and commercialize new product and technology concepts and proliferate new industrial subsectors. An understanding of these processes holds the key to understanding the resurgence of growth in Massachusetts.

The new competitive advantage did not originate with Route 128 but with Silicon Valley. It was here that the open-systems model or horizontal integration model of industrial organization was first developed in a high-tech region. And it was in Silicon Valley that a 'virtuous circle of regional dynamics' combined with the principle of systems integration to foster a regional innovation dynamic and established the contours of a New Competition which revitalized American competitiveness when it looked most vulnerable.

The severity of the decline of Route 128 following the Massachusetts Miracle is linked to the earlier development of the open-systems model of industrial organization and 'virtuous circle of regional dynamics' in Silicon Valley. What is remarkable about Route 128 has been the pace and extent of organizational change from the old, closed system to a new, open-systems model of technology management and business organization. The speed of change and the vitality of the resurgence can be explained in terms of development and diffusion of the new principle of systems integration within a unique 'virtuous circle of regional dynamics'. Massachusetts has once again become a region in which new industrial subsectors are being formed and driving growth.

In both Silicon Valley and Route 128, the new regional competitive advantage derives from the application and diffusion of the principle of systems integration at the enterprise level which, in turn, has fostered a regional innovation dynamics. The role of universities has been critical to sustaining the growth dynamic but not because of technology transfer from science laboratories. This growth dynamic has depended upon a uniquely broad, deep, responsive, and flexible skill-formation system in the region which acts as a support infrastructure for advances in technology sparked by the internal growth dynamics of entrepreneurial firms.

Systems integration, like all principles of production, is expressed both technologically and organizationally. The links between principles of production and models of technology management are elaborated elsewhere (Best 1998; Best forthcoming). Here the starting point is organizational; in the following section a model of the virtuous circle of regional dynamics is derived and its roots in the history of economic thought are indicated.[2] Next, implications are drawn for regional innovation dynamics. The model is then applied to Silicon Valley, drawing heavily from Intel's role as a diffusion agent of the principle of systems integration. We then turn to Route 128 and distinguish between two growth periods, one driven by vertically integrated enterprises and the second in which 'open systems' prevailed. The resurgence of Route 128 features a regional dynamics without an Intel as a driver; nevertheless, the same design diffusion, techno-diversification, and industrial 'speciation' processes were triggered.

3. The Virtuous Circle of Regional Dynamics

Growth involves some combination of an expanding population of firms and growing firms. New and rapidly growing firms, however, do not grow in isolation but emerge from and develop within an industrial infrastructure constituted by a larger population of specialist and affiliated enterprises. Edith Penrose's internal dynamics of the firm, complemented by George Richardson's extension to inter-firm relations, provide the micro-underpinnings to a virtuous circle of regional economic growth particularly relevant to the 'knowledge-driven' economy.

The box at the top of the Figure 18.1 signifies the degree of specialization within a regional population of affiliated industrial enterprises. Greater industrial specialization is associated with the sources of productivity gain first identified by Adam Smith and applied to a region by Alfred Marshall. *Greater special-ization among firms is part of a process by which the region, as a whole, gains unique capabilities and regional competitive advantage.* The starting point is Smith's famous theorem that the division of labour, the source of productivity gain, depends upon the extent of the market. Marshall extended the concept of the division of labour beyond Smith's primary concern with the dividing up of occupations and development of specialized crafts to enterprise specialization within an 'indus-trial district'. For Allyn Young, the 'division of labour among industries is a vehicle of increasing returns' (Young 1928: 538). Young's concept of increasing

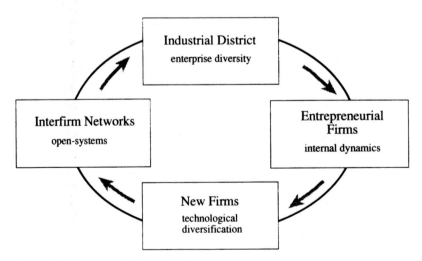

FIG. 18.1. A model of regional dynamics

returns is a process of progressive industrial differentiation independent of the size of an individual firm or a particular industry: 'industrial differentiation, has been and remains the type of change characteristically associated with the growth of production' (ibid. 537).

The process of differentiation and integration is the key to understanding 'open systems' of industrial organization. Young adds a variation to Smith's famous theorem:

[T]he division of labour depends upon the extent of the market, but the extent of the market also depends upon the division of labour. In this circumstance lies the possibility of economic progress, apart from the progress which comes as a result of the new knowledge which men are able to gain. (ibid. 540–1)

Advances in the productivity of industrial districts comes, in part, from 'an increasingly intricate nexus of specialized undertakings . . . inserted between the producer of raw materials and the consumer of the final product' (ibid. 538). Young referred to the process as one of using labour in indirect ways. But missing in the Smith, Marshall, and Young perspective on economic progress is the idea of the internal dynamics of the entrepreneurial firm. For this we need Penrose.

A dynamic industrial district is characterized by a series of feedback effects which add to the technological diversity of enterprises in the region. The driving force is the internal capability/opportunity dynamic of entrepreneurial firms. This dynamic is the outcome of an interaction between the expansion (the creation and release cycle) of productive capabilities emanating from the successful completion of projects, on the one hand, and emerging productive opportunities identified and exploited by the entrepreneur or entrepreneurial team, on the other hand.[3] The internal dynamic of entrepreneurial firms is a major source of productivity gain hidden in the technological residual or the term total factor productivity of economic growth theories.[4] It is a technologically and organizationally derived productivity gain and source of growth that does not rely on expansion in the factors of production (capital and labour) but on the development of productive capabilities and their interaction with emerging market opportunities.[5] The development of new products which reshape and multiply the number of markets is one manifestation of the internal capability/opportunity dynamic.

Richardson extended the internal growth dynamic of the Penrosian firm to account for interfirm relations and, in the process, undermined the market or hierarchy, buy or make dichotomy which is the starting point for conventional perspectives on the firm. Firms specialize on activities that utilize a similar *capability* and affiliate with other enterprises that specialize on complementary activities. Hence economic activities are no longer coordinated either by hierarchy within the vertically integrated enterprise or by price spontaneously in the market; economic activities can be coordinated by affiliated or networked groups of cooperating firms. Instead of firms as islands in a sea, Richardson's image is of industry as a 'dense network of co-operation and affiliation by which firms are inter-related' (Richardson 1972: 883).

The entrepreneurial firm is represented by the box at the right of Figure 18.1. The entrepreneurial firm generates unique productive capabilities, seeks technological advance in pursuit of new product development opportunities, and fosters opportunities for other firms, some of which will be new enterprises in the 'interstices' (see below) as represented by the bottom box.

The link between the boxes at the right and the bottom represents the dynamic between entrepreneurial firms and both 'spin-offs' and new firms which expand regional technological diversity, adds to the regional dynamic, and sustains growth. An entrepreneurial firm generates new productive capabilities in the form of new technological possibilities only some of which it can pursue; the bottom box represents the emergence of new firms to exploit the new productive opportunities. In the process they create opportunities for specialization by other enterprises. These are taken up in greater number by 'open systems' of specialized and affiliated enterprises which, together, have greater potential for forming new combinations of resources (the left-hand box in the figure), or new specialist enterprises some of which will become new entrepreneurial firms.

Furthermore, spin-offs of a technical variety can lead to new industry subsectors which also will be facilitated by an industrial district of specialist firms; a new firm can specialize in developing an innovative idea and partner with other specialists for the requisite complementary activities. While the entrepreneurial firm is the fundamental driver of economic progress, at the same time a firm's opportunity to specialize and develop its core capabilities depends upon an 'open system' of mutually adjusting firms. The box at the left of Figure 18.1 signifies 'horizontal integration', multi-enterprise integration, 'open systems', networked, or affiliated groups of specialist enterprises. Thus, horizontal integration is itself an enabler of *technological diversity*; it forms a diverse pool of collective knowledge or an 'invisible college'. It is an institutional support for the collective learning noted by Saxenian (1994) as a source of Silicon Valley's regional advantage.

The internal dynamics of the entrepreneurial firm do not depend solely upon industrial districts or regional dynamics but are equally associated with vertically integrated enterprises or the *keiretsu* model of industrial organization. However, the sustained vitality of 'open-system' industrial districts, whether in the light industries of the 'third Italy' or the high-tech regions of Silicon Valley and Route 128, illustrate that the dynamic internal to the entrepreneurial enterprise combined with techno-diversification and horizontal integration generates additional regional or district dynamics with powerful effects on growth.

This is the underlying force within the horizontal integration identified by both AnnaLee Saxenian and Andrew Grove as a major source of organizational advantage of Silicon Valley. It is the model of industrial organization most appropriate for product-led competition. Open-system networking is precluded by presupposition in conventional economic theory: economic activities are coordinated either by prices in the market or by managerial hierarchy in the vertically integrated enterprise.[6]

4. Regional Innovation Dynamics

High-income regions in the 'third Italy' have a competitive advantage in design capabilities which have fostered industrial leadership in a range of design-led or 'fashion industries'. Recently, high-tech regions have developed similar capabilities for rapid design changes and industrial innovation. In fact, regions such as Silicon Valley and Route 128 have developed regional innovation capabilities embedded in virtual laboratories in the form of broad and deep networks of operational, technological, and scientific researchers which cut across companies and universities. Silicon Valley project teams are continuously combining and recombining across a population of 6,000 high-tech firms making it an unparalleled information and communication technology industrial district.[7] While the high-tech districts are unique in terms of specific technologies and research intensity they exhibit regional innovation characteristics in an exaggerated form that are common to the virtuous circle of regional growth.[8] Five examples follow.

First, the 'Silicon Valley effect' drives a new firm creation-process. Intel's R&D strategy is based on 'the acknowledged role of the spin-off or start-up' not in creating but in exploiting new ideas. Gordon Moore, co-founder of Intel, explains:

[I]ntegrated circuits, MOS transistors, and the like proved too rich a vein for a company the size of Fairchild to mine, resulting in what came to be known as the 'Silicon Valley effect'. At least one new company coalesced around and tried to exploit each new invention or discovery that came out of the lab. (1996: 167)

Second, the high-tech industrial district is, as well, a collective experimental laboratory. Networked groups of firms are, in effect, engaged in continuous experimentation as the networks form, disband, and reform. Both the ease of entry of new firms and the infrastructure for networking facilitate the formation of technology integration teams in real time. However successful the industrial district as a mode of economic coordination has been in international competition, it has been considered appropriate to 'light' industry such as the design-led, fashion industries of the 'third Italy' and the machine tool and metal-working regions of Baden-Würtemberg in Germany.

Third, a district expands the number of simultaneous experiments that are conducted. A vertically integrated company may carry out several experiments at each stage in the production chain but a district can well exploit dozens simultaneously. In this way a district counters the barriers to introducing new ideas in firms that already have well-developed capabilities around competing technologies.

Fourth, a district fosters design modularization and, with it, the decentralization and diffusion of design capabilities. In computers, IBM got the process underway with the modularization of the 360-computer which created an open system. This was greatly enhanced when the design modules for the operating system and the microprocessor were developed by Microsoft and Intel.[9] The resulting standards have created enormous market opportunities for specific-applications software. But in addition the concept of design modularization combines common interface design rules with decentralization of component design. This diffusion of design capability has greatly strengthened the district model of industrial organization. In fact, modularization has decentralized and diffused design capability for new product development much as TQM decentralized and diffused experiments for continuous improvement.

Fifth, a district counters the inherent uncertainty of technological change with the potential for new technological combinations (Rosenberg 1992: 221). This feature of the regional-networking model of innovation is captured by a recent review of retrospective surveys of the critical conditions for successful innovation. A survey by Ronald Kostoff finds that the first and most important factor is a *broad pool of advanced knowledge*. Kostoff's review indicates that 'an advanced pool of knowledge must be developed in many fields before synthesis leading to innovation can occur.' This advanced pool of knowledge is the critical factor, not the entrepreneur. In the words of Kostoff:

> The entrepreneur can be viewed as an individual or group with the ability to assimilate this diverse information and exploit it for further development. However, once this pool of knowledge exists, there are many persons or groups with capability to exploit the information, and thus the real critical path to innovation is more likely to be the knowledge pool than any particular entrepreneur.   (1994: 61)

The knowledge pool is developed through non-mission-oriented research in a range of fields 'by many different organizations'. Successful innovations tend to be preceded by '*unplanned confluences* of technology from different fields' (ibid.). In fact, the unplanned is combined with the planned: 'mission-oriented research or development stimulates non-mission research to *fill gaps* preceding the innovation'.

The second critical condition is *recognition of technical opportunity and need*. 'In many cases, knowledge of the systems applications inspires the sciences and technology that lead to advanced systems.' The second factor suggests a feedback between the problems of application engineers and scientific investigators. Radar, for example, was 'invented' in response to a clear need.

The third, fourth and fifth critical factors are a technical entrepreneur who champions the innovation, financial, and management support. The final, sixth factor is *continuing innovation and development over many fields*. In the words of Kostoff: 'additional supporting inventions are required during the development phase preceding the innovation.'

Three of the six critical factors for success point to networking capabilities. From this perspective, an industrial district, unlike any single firm, offers the potential of a technological full-house with a variety and range of research and production-related activities which can foster creativity, fill gaps, replenish the knowledge pool, link needs to research, and incite unplanned confluences of technology.[10]

The core of the innovation process in this model is the fillip given to new product development (NPD) by the differentiation and integration process (see Figure 18.2). Firms under strong competitive pressure and in demanding markets

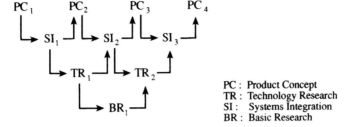

FIG. 18.2. Dip-down model of innovation

are seeking to push ahead with product improvements and new products as fast as possible. In doing so they encounter technical problems that they do not know how to solve and search for solutions, dipping down into the specialist technological and scientific bodies of knowledge that are available in other firms, universities, and elsewhere. The companies best at effective and fast NPD have developed the capability to integrate technologies, starting with software and hardware. They know where particular kinds of knowledge and expertise can be located and how to dip down into the pool of technological and scientific knowledge and expertise to solve particular problems.

5. Systems Integration: From VI to SI at Intel

America's semiconductor industry was suffering in 1990. Scientific research in the great industrial laboratories of AT&T, DuPont, General Electric, IBM, and Xerox was not being converted into a stream of commercially successful products.[11] Many warned of a 'hollowing out' of American industry given the capability of its Japanese counterpart to engage in rapid new product development, absorb technologies, diffuse innovations, and achieve new comprehensive production performance standards. Manufacturing firms that had built American industry such as General Electric and Westinghouse were downsizing and outsourcing manufacturing and diversifying into financial services and the media. In 1987, America's Defense Science Board, a governmental advisory board of distinguished scientists, claimed that the USA was in the lead in only three of more than a dozen critical semiconductor technologies (*Economist* 1995: 4).

But, by 1996, the USA had established dominant position in microprocessor chips (the most technologically complex semiconductor) and a strong leadership position in personal computers, telecommunications including Internet-related activities, and software. Sales in information and communication technology (ICT)-related industries grew from $340 billion in 1990 to $570 billion in 1995, a period during which Japanese ICT-related industries grew less than one-quarter as much, from $450 billion to $500 billion (*Economist* 1997). Not only Silicon Valley but Route 128 was booming again. What explains this turnaround in industrial leadership?

5.1. Open-Systems Business Model and IT diffusion

The economic resurgence of Silicon Valley and Route 128 is not confined to new firms in information and communication technologies. Information technology has permeated widely into non high-tech sectors, reinventing many. Electronics has, in effect, migrated from a separate industrial sector to a constitutive feature of industry of its own. A new 'open-systems' model of technology management is being diffused from applications in semiconductor fabrication and weapons systems to industry in general.[12] 'Open systems' in product architecture, in turn, has fostered a transition from vertically integrated enterprises and closed supplier networks to multi-enterprise integration.

Information technology has played a double role: enabler of systems integration and open systems in both technology design and industrial organization. In fact, the microprocessor is to the knowledge-driven economy what the machine tool industry was to the diffusion of the principle of interchangeability and unit-drive electricity was to the diffusion of the principle of flow which ushered in the age of mass production (Best 1998).[13] In each case a new principle of production was associated with the development of a new business model capable of achieving a breakthrough in performance standards which redefined the basis of industrial leadership. Like the emergence of the machine tool industry and fractionated electric power, information technology has fostered an entirely new approach to product architecture and production organization which in turn has redefined industry boundaries.

In an era of competitive strategies based on rapid new product development, these enterprises have had to reinvent themselves. Systems integration, in the form of integrating information technology and traditional production capabilities, or software and hardware, has been a key element in this resurgence. Computer-aided design is an example. The organizational initiatives required to make this transition were driven down the supply chain by entrepreneurial firms which, themselves, were restructuring to become flexible producers capable of integrating design and production. The management philosophy of total quality management and self-directed work teams provided a methodology for organizational change.[14]

In short, the old American 'Big Business' model of technological change driven by stand-alone industrial laboratories came up short against the Japanese competition. But instead of ossifying, American industry was revitalized by a 'focus and network' business model which extends the system-integration capabilities of the Japanese production system in two ways: first, by incorporating fundamental research, not as much as a driver of new product development but as an integral element in the production organization; and second, by fostering dynamic, networked groups of firms linked by design modularization. In fact, the diffusion of systems integration has fostered new regional-based industrial dynamics with the widely diffused design capabilities celebrated in internationally competitive light industries of the 'third Italy'.

5.2. Integration of Manufacturing and R&D

Intel is the symbol of America's manufacturing recovery. The microprocessor is the symbolic-artefact driver of American industrial growth in the information age of the turn of the century like the machine tool was in the era of the 'American System', the steam engine in the railroad age, the dynamo during electrification, and the car in the era of mass production (Freeman 1998).

Chip-fabrication plants are among the most complex manufacturing plants in one of the most internationally competitive industries. The historic productivity curve for chip production has followed Moore's Law of a 30 per cent reduction in cost per function per year.[15] This involves combining fast-changing technologies with high-performance manufacturing. Thirty per cent annual increases in product performance depend upon simultaneous advances in integrated circuit design tools, production technologies, and miniaturization capabilities.

Strikingly, Intel has never owned a stand-along R&D laboratory. Does this mean that Intel does not engage in R&D? Quite the contrary. Intel's R&D budget exceeds $1 billion annually. Emphasizing the D in R&D, Intel opted for the co-location of development research and manufacturing: 'development would be conducted in the manufacturing facility' (Moore 1996: 168).

Intel's integrated-manufacturing focus requires the construction of full-scale experimentation plants.[16] For Intel, new product development is simultaneously new process development. Experimentation is carried out under full-scale manufacturing facilities under actual, not simulated, operating conditions. In the words of Moore:[17]

With a product as complex as semiconductors, it is a tremendous advantage to have a production line that can be used as a base for perturbation, introducing bypasses, adding steps, and so forth. Locating development and manufacturing together allows Intel to explore variations of its existing technologies very efficiently. (1996: 168)

The experimentation activities address the challenge of integrating ever-advancing technologies into full-scale manufacturing plants as distinct from innovating in individual technologies.[18]

This is not simple, as many of the activities are rooted in distinctive science-technology domains with unique science lineage and physical characteristics.[19] Intel's concept of integrated manufacturing in which research experimentation and manufacturing are co-located is a response to the challenge of (complex) systems integration: changes in individual components will have system-altering effects some of which cannot be identified or measured except in actual operating conditions.

Basic research is pulled into the production system as a support to technological advance. Intel divides research into two types: research that 'require[s] integrated manufacturing capability to examine' and 'chunks' that do not require state-of-the-art semiconductor technology. Intel focuses on the former and networks with universities to get the latter. Moore (1996: 172) notes that a number of processes in semiconductor manufacturing are 'more of an art than a science': the plasma-etching process, for example, is not well understood. Universities have supplied invaluable research in, for example, parallel processing as well as design automation software.

Thus the integration of manufacturing and R&D, for Intel, is reinforced by partnering with universities to anchor a regional model of technology management particularly appropriate to 'knowledge-intensive' industries. It would not work without ties to a strong and growing knowledge base in fundamental research and the associated human resource development of research universities.

The research networks in regions like Silicon Valley extend beyond the firm enabling project teams to participate in a highly innovative milieu for technology management. Long gone is the day when the linear, science-push model was the driver of product development and technological advance.

5.3. Design Diffusion and Decentralization

The system integration challenge is not unique to the new model of technology management. In this Intel does not break with earlier production systems. Henry Ford and his chief engineer, Charles Sorensen, would have understood the challenge, and rewards, of system integration.[20] Applying the principle of system entails redesigning the product from inside-out and outside-in to enhance flow. Popularly known as concurrent engineering, new products (inside) are designed simultaneously with production (outside).[21]

But system integration alone does not captures Intel's uniqueness. System integration is a static concept with respect to *component design rules*; it does not imply openness to innovation or technological change. In fact, the challenge of system integration exerts pressure to freeze technological change. Kaizen, or continuous improvement management, pursues experimentation and technological improvement but *holds basic technology design rules constant*.

The organizational challenge is to manage manufacturing processes along a technology trajectory in which productivity is advancing 50 per cent every eighteen months. This involves integrating and reintegrating technologies themselves being independently redefined. Systems integration is the response. It is about building the organizational capability to incorporate rapid technological change in components into complex products. Design modularization is an enabling methodology which integrates two sets of design rules: those at the level of individual technologies or subsystems and those that integrate subsystems into a single system. The process of integrating subsystems is not an additive one, particularly when subsystems have independent design and development dynamics. Interactions amongst subsystems have dynamic feedback effects.

An advantage of design modularization is the potential to mobilize resources from outside the company for component design and to meet the challenge of rapid technological change. Unlike Ford's system, Intel depends upon, and reinforces, a network of affiliated companies constituted by multiple design nodes. Intel not only partners with a vast array of specialist producers and research institutions; Intel draws upon an extended industrial high-tech region with an extraordinary capacity to conduct experiments, carry out innovations, and conduct research.

The semiconductor manufacturing industry in the USA has more than 1,000 firms, most with sales between $1 million and $10 million per year. Turning to sales, distributors in America service a customer base of over 150,000 firms 'which are generally small and medium-sized companies in the computer, telecommunications, aerospace, instrumentation, and defense industries' (Dahmen 1993: 35). Intel partners with distribution firms which have differentiated themselves by establishing design centres.

In contrast, Japan's semiconductor manufacturing industry is highly concentrated with twelve companies accounting for 75 per cent of sales (ibid. 34–5). Most of the Japanese semiconductor manufacturing companies are members of *keiretsu* supplier arrangements. The five largest semiconductor producers in Japan (NEC, Toshiba, Hitachi, Fujitsu, and Mitsubishi Electric) have built-in customers in the form of consumer electronics, computer, and communication divisions. This business model was designed for purposes of just-in-time or 'lean' production; it lacks the decentralized and diffused design capabilities associated with systems integration.

Intel built a business model based on the concept of design modularization. Leading Japanese companies have substantial systems-integration capabilities. They, like Intel, integrate new product development with process reorganization. But the Japanese leading electronics companies have not redesigned their business systems to capture the innovation potential offered by the principle of systems integration. To do so would mean moving from a closed to an open-systems model of supplier relations and industrial organization. The new regional model, based on systems integration and reintegration, involves not only new product and new firm development but, in the process, the reinvention of the region as new patterns of multi-enterprise integration are established based on new combinations of technologies. The redefinition of the relationship between industrial innovation and basic research may not have been planned, but it has proven a powerful driver of technological change.

6. Route 128: Systems Integration and Techno-diversification

Ironically, just as the relative lack of cooperation amongst firms around Boston's Route 128 was being blamed for the area's poor performance relative to Silicon Valley, the region's capability for systems integration was laying the foundation for revitalizing its industry around a new principle highly conducive to interfirm networking. The two expansions (the 'miracle', from 1978 to 1986, and the 'resurgence', from 1992 to present) are marked by two different models of industrial organization: vertical integration versus horizontal integration or closed system versus open system. Systems integration played a role in both, but only in the 'resurgence' did it lead to widespread technological diversification, a proliferation of new industries and subsectors in a process by which the establishment of new industrial niches leads to yet new niches. Only during the resurgence have the technological and interfirm organizational aspects of open systems become mutually reinforcing and, thereby, the basis for a regional competitive advantage in industrial innovation.

CorpTech, a data-processing company, categorizes America's small and medium-sized (under 1,000 employees) 'technology manufacturers' (most of which are privately held) into seventeen industries as shown in Table 18.1. The dispersion is indicative of the diversity of industries associated with Route 128. The mix of high-technology manufacturing in Massachusetts, with approximately 2 per cent of the nation's population, is remarkably similar to the nation as a whole. CorpTech estimates that over 8 per cent of America's small and medium-sized high-tech companies are based in Massachusetts with a total of over 200,000 employees.

TABLE 18.1. Corporate technology directory of high-tech manufacturers (January 1999)

Companies	Mass.	(%)	USA (%)
Factory automation	337	10.5	12.1
Biotechnology	151	4.7	3.5
Chemicals	95	3.0	4.1
Computer hardware	435	13.6	13.8
Defence	56	1.7	2.1
Energy	105	3.3	4.5
Environmental eqpt.	203	6.3	7.1
High-tech mnfg. eqpt.	421	13.1	12.6
Advanced materials	159	5.0	6.6
Medical	248	7.7	6.3
Pharmaceuticals	95	3.0	2.5
Photonics	240	7.5	5.0
Computer software	993	30.9	24.8
Sub-assemblies/comp.	530	16.5	17.2
Test and measurement	378	11.8	11.2
Telecom and Internet	415	12.9	15.5
Transportation	92	2.9	3.6
US holding companies	245	7.6	8.4

Note: Corp Tech tracks America's 45,000-plus technology manufacturers with under 1,000 employees (90 per cent are 'hidden' private companies and the operating units of larger corporations). Of 42,342 US entities, 3,242 or 7.7 per cent are located in Massachusetts. These are independent companies, subsidiaries of major US corporations, and American operating units of foreign companies. Data extracted from Corp Tech/Web (www.corptech.com).

These data support the theme that a process of techno-diversification, not cluster-ization, has driven the 'resurgence' of the Massachusetts economy. Technology management in the 'Massachusetts Miracle' growth industries of minicomputers and defence was locked up in vertically integrated enterprises. The downturn was critical to the upturn, as the demise of these enterprises facilitated the transition to an open-system, multi-enterprise model of industrial organization. The accom-panying decentralization and diffusion of design combined with a heritage of technological skills and capabilities to fuel the internal growth dynamic of entrepre-neurial firms which, in turn, fostered techno-diversification and regional innovation dynamics.

The techno-diversification of Route 128 then can be explained in terms of the conversion of systems integration from a technological capability into a business and industrial organizational capability and thereby a basis for regional competitive advantage. The conversion can be understood in terms of the diffusion of the new model of technology management, the establishment of a complementary business model capable of driving the new principle, and an advanced, diverse, and flexible skill base. Industrial policy also played a key role, if inadvertently.

In the 'resurgence', Massachusetts, once again, is playing its historic role of creating new industries by introducing, developing, and diffusing new technologies. But this time around, the open-systems model of industrial organization provides a regional infrastructure which fosters techno-diversification and drives down the cycle time for new product development. It is as if the technological manage-ment of the region has been re-engineered; technologically integrated manufactur-ing is a core process in which the requisite elements are themselves redesigned and recombined to foster experimentation and innovation, eliminate unnecessary steps, and enhance the flow of technological knowledge.

From this perspective, the key to the resurgence of Route 128 is not the trans-fer of institutions of cooperation and collective learning; these are manifestations of the application of the principle of systems integration to production and organ-ization. The resurgence of Route 128 can best be understood as a transition in industrial organization in which a region's business model was transformed to take advantage of a new principle of production and establish and diffuse a new model of technology management. As we shall see, Route 128 had a huge advant-age over other regions in applying the new principle: systems integration had a long history in the region as a technological capability before it emerged as a production and organizational principle. Behind the technological capability lies an impressive skill base in technology-related skills which facilitated the transi-tion to the new model of technology management.

6.1. Industrial Heritage: Precision Equipment and Machine Tools

To properly understand the specific competitive advantage of Massachusetts and the resurgence of its growth in the 1990s it is necessary to look at its past and present industrial structure. The Commonwealth enjoys a world-class precision instruments and precision equipment capability made up of hundreds of firms making a range of products from jet engines to telecommunication-switching equipment to semiconductor-making equipment. Massachusetts has never been strong in high-volume manufacturing and the associated economies of scale. Precision equipment itself demands skills in systems engineering and interfirm networking to combine the complementary capabilities required to design and make complex systems. The largest manufacturing sectors in Greater Boston in the mid-1990s in employment are instruments (35,000), industrial machinery (23,000), printing and publishing (22,000), electrical equipment (21,000), and fabricated metals (11,000) (Terkla 1998: 15).

A second, closely related feature of Massachusetts's technology and science advantage, critical to the application of systems integration, is the heritage of specialist machine shops, tooling companies, instrument makers, equipment manufacturers, and injection moulders which, collectively, constitute a flexible, open-system supplier base. Emerging entrepreneurial firms can develop new products, integrate technologies, and enter or open markets by partnering with companies for complementary technical and machining capabilities.

The resulting incorporation of new product development into the multi-enterprise production process, in turn, created new opportunities for 'job shops' with design capabilities. The historic role of the machine and tooling industry was repeated and expanded. As always, it is a component of a supplier base or vendor for the whole range of down-stream producers; increasingly it has become part of an ongoing technology management process in combination with companies engaged in technology integration, modification, and diversification.

The precision equipment and machine and tooling industry has been critical to the resurgence of Route 128. It has meant that emerging enterprises have not been forced into head-to-head competition with regions that have developed unique capabilities in volume production required, for example, in consumer electronics. New England manufacturers cannot access local capabilities in high-volume, complex production activities. Furthermore, unlike Silicon Valley, Massachusetts has no Intel, Apple, Hewlett Packard, or other standard-setting companies with household names. In the resurgence only EMC, a data-software storage system company, has made the Fortune 500 list.

6.2. Integration of Hardware and Software: The Advantage of Industrial Electronics

This heritage, however, was not enough; systems integration as a driver of growth depended upon the transition of a critical mass of industrial firms from subcontractors to problem-solving enterprises with independent design and development capabilities. At the core of the new technology management model has been the integration of hardware and software. The enabler has been information technology.

The integration of hardware and software in product design has passed through three stages. First, software is embedded in hardware as a component: product design requires product designers but not software engineers. Second, proprietary software is embedded in hardware; product design requires software engineering. Third, software is unbundled in open systems and hardware is standardized; product design requires systems engineering.

Historically, much of the consumer electronics industry has historically been located in the first and second domain; success has required world-class, high-volume manufacturing capabilities and adjustments to chip *specification*, not necessarily chip *design*. The latter two domains are those of industrial electronics such as telecommunications equipment, instrument engineering, and medical devices—industries in which Massachusetts has historical strengths. The problem with minicomputers was not technological; the engineering skills are the same in both the Massachusetts Miracle and the Resurgence. The marriage of technological knowledge in these industries with information technology and the transition to an open-systems business model are the keys to the diffusion of systems integration, techno-diversification, industrial speciation, and the resurgence of the fortunes of Route 128.

The concentration of Massachusetts in industrial electronics was turned from a disadvantage to an advantage as a result of the open-systems stage of the integration of software and hardware. The old industry boundaries within electronics which separated consumer, industrial, telecommunications, computers, and semiconductors were eroding with the spread of systems-integration capabilities. But the flexibility and technology-integration capabilities required in low-volume, industrial electronics were increasingly an asset in comparison to the complex production capabilities required in high-volume, consumer electronics production. The hardware-related capabilities were increasingly commodity-like and suffered lower profit margins as a result.

6.3. Techno-Diversification and Industrial Speciation

The driver of regional growth is the virtuous circle of entrepreneurial firms driven by an internal technology and market dynamic generating both growth and new technological opportunities which, in turn, fosters firm creation in emerging subsectors followed by new patterns of interfirm networking. In the process regional innovations dynamics are fostered as the techno-diversity of the region increases and with it the probability of new technological combinations and the emergence of yet new entrepreneurial firms.

Examples of the repetition of the virtuous circle of regional dynamics leading to enterprises specializing in new technological 'species' in different technological domains are commonplace in Massachusetts of the 1990s. One example is that of data-storage systems, the 'file cabinets of the electronics age'.[22]

EMC is an entrepreneurial firm that has simultaneously developed a unique capability and spawned a new industrial subsector. The company began as a supplier of add-on memory boards for the minicomputer market in 1979, moved into mainframe storage a decade later, and 'added software to help manage its boxes as it made the switch to open systems in the middle of this decade' (Degman 1998: 1). EMC has achieved the leading edge in storage technology with an engineering staff which, in 1998, totalled 1,200 and an annual research budget of $1/3 billion. In the same year the company opened a 682,000-square foot facility in central Massachusetts to test, qualify, and assemble computer storage systems.

EMC has 'spawned a new generation of software and service companies providing ways for corporations to monitor and manage data, back up and protect it, find and fix disk-storage bottlenecks, and warn desktop computer users to clean out their hard drives before they run out of space' (Rosenberg 1999). For example, a co-founder of EMC and a ten-year employee have formed StorageNetworks, a company that offers businesses data-storage services on the networking model of telephone switches or electric power generators. Other nearby companies that are driving and redefining the data-storage business, each with a unique speciality are Astrum Software (monitor disk storage usage at each PC and server within a department), HighGround Systems (storage research management), Connected Corp. and Network Integrity Inc. (back-up systems) (Rosenberg 1999).

6.4. Skill Formation

The growth process in knowledge-intensive industries is largely conditioned by the availability of engineering and scientific personnel required to staff rapidly growing firms. The role that machinists and product engineers played in the diffusion of the principle of flow in nineteenth century American industry is taken by systems and software engineers in the diffusion of the principle of systems integration. In addition, universities, colleges, and junior colleges play a critical knowledge-providing and diffusion role in twentieth-century industry; this is particularly the case in high-tech regions.

Another strength of Massachusetts emanates from the interactive relationship between emerging enterprises and specialist curriculum in responsive technology-oriented universities. The development of industries in Massachusetts throughout the twentieth century has involved the simultaneous development of university departments, research institutes, and curricula, on the one hand, and rapidly growing entrepreneurial enterprises, on the other.

Any individual firm can attract from the existing pool by offering superior pay and conditions, but the success of the region depends upon growing the pool. William Foster of Stratus Computer Inc. uses the metaphor of a food chain to explain the process:

The most critical thing in starting a computer company is being in an area where there are a lot of big computer companies so you can draw experienced people away from them. And the big computer companies need to locate in an area where there are a lot of schools so that as they lose people to the start-ups, they can replace them with people fresh out of school. I see that as the key to the whole food chain for the Route 128 area. If the big companies weren't here, we wouldn't be here, and if the schools weren't here, the big companies wouldn't be here. (Rosegrant and Lampe 1992: 158–9)

Massachusetts is rich in technological knowledge, formal and informal. Nearly two centuries of precision machine and equipment-making has bequeathed a skill base which is critical to the emergence of new industries. This less visible skill base is easily obscured from public view in a high-tech region.

Collectively, these skills and institutional arrangements are an extraordinarily rich seedbed for new product development, new technological combinations, techno-entrepreneurs, and emerging enterprises. But the severe downturn following the 'Massachusetts Miracle' played a critical role in fostering organizational change and, in the process, converted these skills from potential into kinetic energy.

6.5. (Inadvertent) Industrial Policy and Transformational Growth

The return to economic growth in Massachusetts has also depended upon the transition to the open-systems model of technology management. This institutional transformation was not planned; nevertheless, industrial policy played a double role, if inadvertent, in the process.

The first role was a passive one in that the economic downturn did the work. While Massachusetts has a long history of creating new industrial sectors, it has done so in sequential form. The business cycle has played the Schumpeterian role of creative destruction as one major driver of industry replaced another. The downturn following the Massachusetts Miracle engendered creative destruction of an entire business model; the new model was a consequence of the emergence of new firms which took the specialized and network model for granted.

In this case, the business cycle provided a catalyst for the transition from a vertically integrated business model that drove the minicomputer and defence industries to an open-systems model which has fostered techno-diversity and the new, protean character of industry which has enabled the development and diffusion of information and communication-related technologies. The loss of one-third of manufacturing jobs was a heavy price to pay for regional organizational change and it was not a sufficient condition for fostering a new expansion. Neither may it have been necessary; the point is that if the causes of a decline in growth are the loss in competitiveness of a region's business model, then the industrial policy challenge becomes one of organizational transformation. Functional equivalents to economic downturns as a means of organizational change are imaginable, but as in the case of companies facing technology platform shifts, the barriers to change are considerable. In this case, the hesitancy of government to save firms can be considered a case of successful industrial policy, in the sense that the market itself created the condition for industrial transformation. Hugely successful enterprises during the Massachusetts Miracle, such as DEC, became, like fallen trees in the rain forest, the seedbed for (techno-) diversity and a new source of growth.[23]

But this is not the whole story. The inadvertent industrial policy of institutional transformation had a second, equally important component. Here technology policy was masquerading as industrial policy. Defence expenditure in Massachusetts played a key role in the development, application, and diffusion of the new principle of production. Parallels can be drawn between the early nineteenth-century industrial district along the Connecticut River Valley in Western Massachusetts which spawned the American System of Manufacturers and the Route 128 high-tech 'industrial district'.

In the post-Second World War era, Hanscom Air Force Base played a regional industrial development role akin to that of the Springfield Armory. Government sponsorship via defence contracts was crucial in introducing, applying, and refining the defining concept of each regional production system: *interchangeability* in the American System and *systems integration* in Route 128. The extensive material testing and measuring capabilities built up at the Armory were replicated over a century later in government-funded research facilities such as those at MIT and the associated Lincoln Labs and Mitre Corporation. Just as the Armory spawned new machine tool companies and skilled machinists which, in turn, became a vehicle for the diffusion of interchangeability to new firms, products, and industries, government-funded labs, most famously at MIT, trained and sponsored techno-entrepreneurs who became the founders of new companies and, equally important, advanced the skill base required to develop and implement system-integration capabilities across a broad range of companies.[24]

Business enterprises, however, are the agents of investment and the drivers of growth. And, as in the case of the Armory and the American System of Manufacturers, the role of the government as an inadvertent promoter of technological change and as a midwife to a new model of technology management planted the seeds for a rich harvest in new company formation. The catalyst for growth shifted from government as techno-entrepreneurial agency and midwife of technological change to the development of business enterprises which grew as a consequence of their own internal productive capability and productive opportunity dynamics. The pursuit of productive opportunities associated with new product concepts became the motivation for developing new productive capabilities and the deepening and widening of technological knowledge.

7. Conclusion: Systems Integration and the Resurgence of American Industry

Suddenly, and unexpectedly, American industry has been undergoing a resurgence. By 1995, the USA had regained the lead not only in growth segments within semiconductors such as microprocessors and digital signal processors, but in personal computers and telecommunications, software and internet-related technologies. The transformation has been most pronounced in the traditional electronics industrial centres of Silicon Valley and Route 128 and in a range of new electronics districts including Southern California, which had previously concentrated in aircraft and defence, and around Austin and Richardson in Texas.

Why, then, the resurgence of American industry? The simple answer is that the American economy has a proliferation of firms which have anticipated and seized opportunities in the rapidly developing information-technology-related areas and grown rapidly. But the phenomenon of fast-growing firms, big and small, is an expression of deeper changes which, together, represent a new industry dynamics as deep and broad as that of the American System in the nineteenth century or Big Business in the early decades of the twentieth century.[25]

The high-tech districts are 'innovative milieu' which have spawned new generations of companies, attracted many of America's most innovative big companies, proliferated new product concepts, obliterated old industry boundaries, and, in turn, been reconstituted by the emergence of new subsectors. But the resurgence has not been limited to such high-technology districts. Increasingly, electronics is migrating into previously non-electronics sectors, enabled by information technology. The integration of hardware and software, including the development of the Internet, has fostered applications in numerous and diverse industries, virtually reinventing many. Electronics has, as noted, been transformed from a separate industrial sector to a constitutive, multidimensional feature of industry itself. A new 'open-systems' model of technology management and in product architecture has, in turn, fostered a transition from vertically integrated enterprises and closed supplier networks to multi-enterprise integration.

The opportunities for innovation have also made Silicon Valley and Route 128 a magnet for high-tech firms and entrepreneurs from other parts of the world as well as to each other; investment in these regions is a way to gain entry to the unfolding opportunities of a diverse technology pool and skill base.[26] Given the inherent uncertainty of technological developments and the pace of technological change participation in the region is at least an early warning system of emerging technologies and platform shifts.

The conventional explanation of the resurgence of Route 128 focuses on spatial clusters, and on the cooperation among industry leaders, and research-intensive universities fostering techno-entrepreneurs. These factors are critical to the high-income levels of the region. Nevertheless, they do not explain either the downturn or the resurgence.[27] The regional growth dynamics model developed in this chapter suggests that the conventional explanation obscures the underlying sources of decline and resurgence.

Because of the range and depth of research universities, many have perceived the source of growth in terms of the traditional linear model of innovation. Nevertheless, as important as universities are to Massachusetts and to the innovation process, focus on them alone fails to capture the underlying processes of growth anchored in the internal dynamics of entrepreneurial firms themselves organized in terms of the new principle of systems integration, the virtuous circle of regional innovation dynamics, and heritage of technical enterprises and skills.

The resurgence of Route 128 has not been in the high-volume, consumer electronics industry in which East Asian nations have remained world leaders. Instead, the competitive advantage of Route 128 is in industrial electronics and a unique capability to marry precision equipment and instruments to information technology. Systems integration is a common feature and covers a broad range of applications but not in industries in which scale economies figure prominently in determining competitive advantage. Route 128 has the regional capability to integrate activities and technologies required for rapid new product development in industrial electronics. The regional competitive advantage is sustained by a virtuous innovation circle which converts ideas into products and, in the process, develops new technological and new scientific knowledge.

NOTES

For assistance, comments, and related conversations I wish to thank John Dunning, Giovanna Ceglie, Urska Cvek, Michael Enright, Robert Forrant, Aidan Gough, Arthur Francis, Brian Loasby, Christos Pitelis, Frederic Richard, and Sukant Tripathy. I am also thankful to participants of seminars at City University Business School, Birkbeck College, the University of Manchester Institute of Science and Technology, the University of Glasgow, INSEAD, the Judge Institute of Management Studies, and the Department of Urban Studies and Planning of MIT.

1. The concept of New Competition as industrial leadership based on the establishment of new principles of production and organization is developed in Best (1990). Application of the principle of systems integration to Silicon Valley as an example of a New Competition can be found in Best (1998).
2. The links among production principles, models of technology management, and business organization are elaborated in Best (1998; forthcoming). In the former paper the starting point is technology management capabilities. Here the focus is on regional growth dynamics.
3. The original source is (Penrose 1959; 3rd edn., 1995). For a recent survey of Penrose see Best and Garnsey (1999).
4. See Abramovitz (1956; 1993) and Solow (1957).
5. Productive capabilities are attributes of individual firms (Penrose 1959). They are to be distinguished from production capabilities which are generic attributes defined in terms of principles of production. The concept of a production capabilities spectrum is in Best (forthcoming).
6. The market or plan dichotomy is a logical consequence of the assumption of perfect competition; every effort to give integrity to concepts required for a substantive theory of the firm undermine the assumptions required for the neoclassical theory of allocative efficiency (Best 1990: 107–10).

7. The 6,000 high-tech firms of Silicon Valley have sales of approximately $200 billion (*Economist* 1997: 5). Intel is not the only driver of new products. One in five of the Silicon Valley public companies are gazelles which means they have grown at least 20% in each of the last four years (the number for the USA is one in thirty-five).

8. 'the jobs in Silicon Valley are better, paying on average close to $50,000 a year—one-and-a-half times the national average. Adding around 3,500 new companies annually, Silicon Valley's entrepreneurial activity creates huge extra demand for goods and services' (*Economist* 1999: 25).

9. See Katz (1996: 15). Katz also describes network economies and increasing returns.

10. The regional model of innovation offers a decentralized, self-organizing explanation of the success of high-tech regions but of industrial districts in general as an alternative to the linear, science-push model of innovation. In the latter, technology is thought of as applied science; in the regional model, technology is part of the industrial process. It is built into the process by which firms establish unique capabilities and network with other firms. The science-push model, in contrast, fails to capture the extent to which research is woven into the production, technology, and networking fabric of a region's industrial system as distinct from being an external, autonomous sphere of activity.

11. Eleven Nobel Prizes were awarded for science breakthroughs at Bell labs (*Economist* 1999: 1). Most of the major labs were associated with breakthrough innovations that had redefined whole industries such as the transistor at Bell labs or nylon at DuPont. Nevertheless all have suffered loss of support.

12. Systems integration was developed first in the defence industry. Hanscom Air Force base, nearly co-located with MIT's Lincoln and Mitre Labs played a key role in its development (Best forthcoming).

13. Paul David develops the concept of the 'general purpose technology' to explain surges in total factor productivity (David 1990).

14. A whole range of non-profit, quasi-governmental agencies emerged in Massachusetts to facilitate this process (Best and Forrant 1996a, 1996b).

15. E.g. in 1960, the average selling price for a transistor was $5.00; by 1985 an integrated circuit containing 500,000 transistors sold for $5.00 (Dahman 1993: 32).

16. For details on Intel's approach to technological development see Iansiti and West (1997).

17. Intel's experiment plants are enormously expensive. Iansiti and West point out that instead of a 'lean' production team driving high through-put, the experiment plants are operated by technology-integration teams (1997: 70). The teams do not conduct fundamental research but collectively team members are familiar with a whole range of technology domains each with deep roots in fundamental science. The experiments may involve an entirely new chip in which case many of the technologies will be novel applications, some of which will have never been used before. Or a team may be developing a new version of an existing chip. Intel e.g. produces some thirty different kinds of the 486 chip (*Economist* 1996: 21). Here, too, experiments will be conducted on novel applications and combinations.

18. Iansiti and West point out that a number of the technology-integration team members will be recent graduates who have done dissertations on fundamental science.

19. In this conception of technology, Intel's application is closer to the Japanese tendency to conflate science and technology into the single term science-technology. Kline (1985), Rosenberg (1992) and others offer many examples of technology assisting in the

development of science. Astronomy, for example, depended upon advances in optical instruments.

20. Ford was acutely aware of the opportunities offered by redesigning a whole system to fit the requirements of a seemingly independent technological innovation. Ford redesigned the production system to take advantage of new electric power technologies, particularly distributed or fractionated power designed into each machine (Best 1997). Technology management for both Henry Ford and Intel involves a double redesign challenge: redesign of technologies to fit production and redesign of production to fit the new technologies and technology combinations. Ford's engineers revamped machines to fit the cycle time standard by adjusting, for example, tooling, material, and machine speeds. Ford and Intel do not simply add new technologies to the existing system, the idea is to redesign the system to take full advantage of the new technology to make a leap in production performance.

21. For details see Best (1998).

22. Another example is the dozens of firms that have emerged in the Internet switching equipment sector around what the *Boston Globe* calls the 'epicenter' of Westford, Mass. While the region included ex-AT&T's Lucent Technology manufacturing site in nearby North Andover, many of the new firms can be traced to the skill base created at Cascade Communications. The emerging firms specialize in a range of products and services unified by the integration of hardware and software required to move a combination of data, voice, and video over the same line.

23. The metaphor of a tree in the rain forest, fostering new growth, can be contrasted to that of the upas tree, a species which, according to legend, kills all surrounding species (Best forthcoming). As an employer of tens of thousands of technical staff and engineers, DEC was a major developer of systems-integration-related skills in the Route 128 regions, skills which were critical to sustaining innovation and recharging regional growth after DEC had gone into decline.

24. Digital Equipment Corporation, founded by Kenneth Olsen, is the most famous example. See Rosegrant and Lampe (1992).

25. The role of information technology as an enabler of systems integration and open systems in both technology and industrial organization is developed in Best (forthcoming). The argument is made that information technology is to the knowledge-driven economy what the machine tool industry was to the diffusion of the principle of interchangeability, and fractionated electricity was to the diffusion of the principle of flow which ushered in the age of mass production. In each case a new principle of production was associated with the development of a new business model capable of achieving a breakthrough in performance standards which redefined the basis of industrial leadership. Like the emergence of the machine tool industry and fractionated electric power, information technology has fostered an entirely new approach to product architecture and production organization which in turn has redefined industry boundaries.

26. The innovation potential which attracts firms from around the world into Massachusetts is based on the skill base, the diversity of technologies which are potential inputs to systems integrators, and the time compression facilitated by the wide and deep supply base for doing new product development. For example, Michel Habib, Israel's economic consul in Boston, estimates that the number of Israeli technology firms in the Boston area grew from thirty in 1997 to at least sixty-five in early 1999. The companies span a range of technologies including optical inspection machines,

medical lasers, digital printing equipment, scanning technology, and bio-tech. In the words of one Israeli manager 'There are a lot of technological resources and know-ledge in the area we can take advantage of' (Bray 1999).

27. According to a study by the BankBoston Economics Department, MIT graduates have started 4,000 companies nationwide. The study claims that in Massachusetts, the 1,065 MIT-related companies account for 25 per cent of sales of all manufacturing firms and 33 per cent of all software sales in the state. See MIT: The Impact of Innovation, web page at <http://web.mit.edu/newsoffice/founders>

REFERENCES

Abramovitz, M. (1956), 'Resource and Output Trends in the United States Since 1870', *American Economic Review* 46(2).

—— (1993), 'The Search for Sources of Growth: Areas of Ignorance, Old and New', *Journal of Economic History* 53 (June).

Best, M. (1990), *The New Competition* (Cambridge, Mass.: Harvard University Press).

—— (1997), *Power to Compete: A Study of the Electric Power Industry and Industrial Competitiveness in America and New England*, Center for Industrial Competitiveness (Lowell: University of Massachusetts).

—— (1998), 'Production Principles, Organizational Capabilities and Technology Management', in J. Michie, and J. Grieve-Smith (eds.), *Globalization, Growth, and Governance* (Oxford: Oxford University Press).

—— (forthcoming), *The New Competitive Advantage* (Oxford: Oxford University Press).

—— and Forrant, R. (1996a), 'Community-based Careers and Economic Virtue: Arming, Disarming, and Rearming the Springfield Armory', in M. Arthur and D. Rousseau (eds.), *The Boundaryless Career* (Oxford: Oxford University Press).

—— (1996b), 'Creating Industrial Capacity: Pentagon-led versus Production-led Industrial Policies', in J. Michie and J. Grieve Smith (eds.), *Restoring Full Employment* (Oxford: Oxford University Press).

—— and Garnsey, E. (1999), 'Edith Penrose, 1914–1996', *Economic Journal* 109 (Feb.).

Bray, H. (1999), 'Hub's High-Tech Allure Drawing Israeli Firms', *Boston Globe* 7 Apr.

Dahmen, D. (1993), 'Semiconductors', in B. Wellenius, A. Miller, and C. Dahlman (eds.), *Developing the Electronics Industry* (Washington, DC: World Bank).

David, P. (1990), 'The Dynamo and the Computer: A Historical Perspective on the Productivity Paradox', *American Economic Review* 80(2).

Degman, C. (1998), 'EMC Breaks a Billion', *Mass High Tech*, 9–15 Nov.

Economist, The (1995), Survey, 16 Sept.

—— (1996), 23 Mar.

—— (1997), 'Silicon Valley: The Valley of Money's Delight', 29 Mar.

—— (1999), 'Innovation in Industry', 20 Feb.

Freeman, C. (1998), 'The Economics of Technical Change', in D. Archibugi and J. Michie (eds.), *Trade, Growth and Technical Change* (Cambridge: Cambridge University Press).

Grove, A. (1996), *Only the Paranoid Survive* (New York: Doubleday).

484   *Michael H. Best*

Iansiti, M., and West, J. (1997), 'Technology Integration: Turning Great Research into Great Products', *Harvard Business Review* May–June: 69–79.

Katz, J. (1996), 'To Market, to Market: Strategy in High-Tech Business', *Regional Review* (Federal Reserve Bank of Boston) 6(4): 12–17.

Kline, S. (1985), 'Innovation is not a Linear Process', *Research Management* 28 (July–Aug.).

Kostoff, R. N. (1994), 'Successful Innovation: Lessons from the Literature', *Research Technology Management* Mar.–Apr.: 60–1.

Moore, G. (1996), 'Some Personal Perspectives on Research in the Semiconductor Industry', in R. Rosenbloom and W. Spencer (eds.), *Engines of Innovation* (Boston: Harvard Business School Press).

Penrose, E. (1959), *The Theory of the Growth of the Firm*, 1st edn. (Oxford: Blackwell and New York: John Wiley & Sons); 2nd edn., 1995 (Oxford: Oxford University Press).

Richardson, G. B. (1972), 'The Organization of Industry', *Economic Journal* 82 (Sept.).

Rosegrant, S., and Lampe, D. (1992), *Route 128: Lessons from Boston's High-tech Community* (New York: Basic Books).

Rosenberg, N. (1992), 'Science and Technology in the Twentieth Century', in G. Dosi, R. Giannetti, and P. A. Toninelli (eds.), *Technology and Enterprise in a Historical Perspective* (Oxford: Clarendon Press).

Rosenberg, R. (1999), 'Growing with the Flow: Endless Stream of Data Spawns Computer-Storage Firms', *Boston Globe*, 14 Apr.

Solow, R. (1957), 'Technical Change and the Aggregate Production Function', *Review of Economic Statistics* 47 (Aug.).

Saxenian, A. (1994), *Regional Advantage: Culture and Competition in Silicon Valley and Route 128* (Cambridge, Mass.: Harvard University Press).

Terkla, D. (1998), 'Greater Boston: Hub of the Commonwealth's Economy', *Massachusetts Benchmarks* 1(4): 9–11.

Young, A. (1928), 'Increasing Returns and Economic Progress', *Economic Journal* 38 (Dec.).

INDEX

Lightning Source UK Ltd.
Milton Keynes UK

171414UK00002B/4/A